S. von Keitz und W. von Keitz

Dictionary of
Library and Information Science

Wörterbuch
Bibliotheks- und Informationswissenschaft

© VCH Verlagsgesellschaft mbH, D-6940 Weinheim (Federal Republic of Germany), 1991

Distribution:

VCH, P.O. Box 10 11 61, D-6940 Weinheim (Federal Republic of Germany)

Switzerland: VCH, P.O. Box, CH-4020 Basel (Switzerland)

United Kingdom and Ireland: VCH (UK) Ltd., 8 Wellington Court, Cambridge CB1 1HZ (England)

USA and Canada: VCH, Suite 909, 220 East 23rd Street, New York, NY 10010-4606 (USA)

ISBN 3-527-28385-4 (VCH, Weinheim)   ISSN 0930-6882
ISBN 1-56081-199-4 (VCH, New York)

Saiedeh von Keitz
und Wolfgang von Keitz

Dictionary of
Library and Information Science

English/German
German/English

2nd, revised Edition

Wörterbuch
Bibliotheks- und Informations-
wissenschaft

Englisch/Deutsch
Deutsch/Englisch

2. überarbeitete Auflage

VCH

Weinheim · New York · Basel · Cambridge

Autoren:
Dr. Saiedeh von Keitz
Prof. Dr. Wolfgang von Keitz
Nachtigallenweg 14
D-5463 Unkel

Published jontyl by
VCH Verlagsgesellschaft mbH, Weinheim (Federal Republic of Germany)
VCH Publishers, Inc., New York, NY (USA)

Editorial Director: Dr. Hans-Dieter Junge
Production Manager: Dipl.-Wirt.-Ing. (FH) Bernd Riedel

Library of Congress Card No. applied for

A catalogue record for this book is available from the British Library

Die Deutsche Bibliothek – CIP-Einheitsaufnahme
Keitz, Saiedeh von:
Dictionary of library and information science :
English/German, German/English = Wörterbuch Bibliotheks-
und Informationswissenschaft / Saiedeh von Keitz und
Wolfgang von Keitz. – 2nd rev. ed. – Weinheim ; New York ;
Basel ; Cambridge : VCH, 1992
  (Parat)
  ISBN 3-527-28385-4 (Weinheim)
  ISBN 1-56081-199-4 (New York)
NE: Keitz, Wolfgang von:; HST

© VCH Verlagsgesellschaft mbH, D-6940 Weinheim (Federal Republic of Germany), 1992

Printed on acid-free paper/Gedruckt auf säurefreiem Papier

Printing: betz-druck gmbh, D-6100 Darmstadt 12
Bookbinding: Verlagsbuchbinderei Kränkl, D-6148 Heppenheim
Printed in the Federal Republic of Germany

Instructions

This dictionary consists of two parts, i.e. German to English and English to German, each arranged alphabetically. Combinations of words, uniting more basic expressions, are also included, so that the user is able to identify the linguistic rules of word combinations. Boldface text is used for the source language notes. Parenthetical remarks relate the entries to special uses or fields. American spelling is given preferences.

m masculinum; f femininum; n neutrum

Benutzungshinweise

Das parat-Taschenwörterbuch besteht aus zwei Teilen entsprechend den beiden Sprachrichtungen.

Innerhalb der beiden Teile sind die Eintragungen in alphabetisch geordneten Wortnestern zusammengestellt, wobei darauf Wert gelegt ist, möglichst unterschiedliche Kombinationen des Nestwortes aufzunehmen, um die Bildungsgesetze der Wortkombinationen sichtbar werden zu lassen.

Innerhalb der Wortstellen sind die Eintragungen in der Quellsprache hervorgehoben. Eintragungen in Klammern helfen bei der Zuordnung des Begriffes zu einem speziellen Anwendungsfall oder zu einem bestimmten technischen Bereich. Es sei noch darauf hingewiesen, daß es im amerikanischen Englisch zahlreiche Abweichungen gegenüber dem „klassischen" Englisch gibt. Wie in der technisch-wissenschaftlichen Literatur üblich, wird im Zweifelsfall der amerikanischen Schreibweise der Vorzug gegeben.

Preface

Technical terminology forms the basis of each branch of science. The development of the terminology mirrors the progress of the science itself.

Today, library and information science is widely determined by technical developments in the anglo-american area. Due to problems encountered when translating scientific publications and due to the lack of suitable scientific dictionaries we decided to compile terms covering librarianship, information and documentation and to publish a dictionary of these terms.

As a result of dynamic developments in information technology and due to the growing use of computers in libraries there arose a need for a dictionary which unites these various scientific and technical areas.

This dictionary consists of two parts: English/German and German/English. The total number of entries is approximately 20000. When choosing the terms we concentrated on two main criteria. Firstly, American, British and German scientific developments and ways of looking at things were taken into consideration. Secondly, we decided to include terms from peripheral sciences only when they have general and interdisciplinary interest.

The authors would be pleased if this dictionary enjoyed intensive usage. We would also be grateful for proposals for new entries and linguistic improvements.

Saiedeh von Keitz
Wolfgang von Keitz

Preface 2. Edition

The authors intend to update each new edition of this dictionary to ensure topicality of the book. By including the constantly changing vocabulary they were continuously bringing the content up-to-date. Thus the authors now present the second edition of this Dictionary in its revised and most topical form.

5000 new and important entries were incorporated. In many cases existing words were supplied with additional meanings.

The proven structure of the Dictionary, however, remained unchanged as it showed to be one main reason for the book's widespread acceptance. Professional users especially praise the clarity of interpretation provided by the dictionary's structure.

Our warm thanks belong to our students Holger Droß, Elmar Dwarazik, Barbara Michels, Heidi Peltzer and Daniela Brommer for their enganged assistance in fulfilling the difficult task of collecting and incorporating new material for the work.

The autors

Vorwort

Grundlage jeder Wissenschaft sind fachwissenschaftliche Begriffe. Die Entwicklung der Begriffe einer Wissenschaft spiegelt die Entwicklung der Wissenschaft selbst wider.

Die Bibliotheks- und Informationswissenschaft wird heute in hohem Maße von informationstechnischen Entwicklungen aus dem anglo-amerikanischen Raum geprägt. Begriffliche Probleme bei der Übersetzung wissenschaftlicher Publikationen und der Mangel an entsprechenden Fachwörterbüchern haben uns angeregt, Begriffe aus dem Informations-, Dokumentations- und Bibliotheksbereich zu sammeln und in einem Wörterbuch zu publizieren.

Die dynamische Entwicklung der Informationstechnik und die vermehrte Benutzung von Computern im Bibliothekswesen ließ das Bedürfnis nach einem Wörterbuch entstehen, das die verschiedenen informationswissenschaftlichen und informationstechnischen Fachgebiete vereint.

Dieses Wörterbuch hat zwei Abteilungen, Englisch/Deutsch und Deutsch/Englisch. Insgesamt enthält das Wörterbuch rund 20.000 Einträge. Bei der Auswahl der Begriffe wurde darauf geachtet, daß die amerikanischen, britischen und deutschen wissenschaftlichen Entwicklungen berücksichtigt wurden und Fachbegriffe informationswissenschaftlicher Nachbardisziplinen nur aufgenommen wurden, wenn sie von fachgebietsübergreifendem Interesse sind.

Es würde uns freuen, wenn das Wörterbuch intensiv genutzt wird. Ergänzungen und Vorschläge für Neueinträge und sprachliche Verbesserungen sind uns jederzeit willkommen.

Saiedeh von Keitz
Wolfgang von Keitz

Vorwort zur 2. Auflage

Dem Wörterbuch der Bibliotheks- und Informationswissenschaft liegt die Absicht zugrunde, ein stets aktuelles Nachschlagewerk zu sein. Um die Aktualität des Wörterbuches trotz fortwährender Veränderung des Wortschatzes zu erhalten, ist es erforderlich, das Werk ständig neu zu überarbeiten. Aus diesem Grunde legen die Autoren eine überarbeitete Neuausgabe des Wörterbuches vor. Wir danken an dieser Stelle unseren Studenten Holger Droß, Elmar Dwarazik, Barbara Michels, Heidi Peltzer und Daniela Brommer, die uns bei der Überarbeitung tatkräftig unterstützt haben.

Die Überarbeitung umfaßt im wesentlichen die Aufnahme neuer Wörter, wodurch das Wörterverzeichnis um mehr als 5.000 wichtige neue Begriffe erweitert werden konnte. Vorhandene Stichwörter wurden durch Einfügen zusätzlicher Wortbedeutungen aktualisiert.

Das bewährte Prinzip des Wörterbuchaufbaus wurde jedoch nicht verändert. Gerade das System des formalen Aufbaus sowie die Aktualität und Übersichtlichkeit des Wörterbuchs der Bibliotheks- und Informationswissenschaft sind wichtige Gründe für seine große Verbreitung und Popularität.

Saiedeh von Keitz
Wolfgang von Keitz

Mai 1991

English/ German

A

abandon call erfolglose Anwahl
f.
abbreviate/to abkürzen *vrb.*,
kürzen *vrb.*
abbreviated abgekürzt *adj.*
abbreviated addressing Kurzadressierung *f.*
abbreviated catalog Kurztitelkatalog *m.*
abbreviated catalog card Kurztitelkatalogkarte *f.*
abbreviated entry Kurztitelaufnahme *f.*, verkürzter Eintrag *f.*
abbreviated term Kurzbenennung *f.*, Kurzwort *n.*
abbreviation Abkürzung *f.*
abbreviation expansion Erweiterung *f.* von Abkürzungen
abnormal condition abnormale
Bedingung *f.*
abnormal end abnormales Ende
n., Unterbrechung *f.*
abnormal end code Abbruchscode *m.*
abnormal ending abnormales
Ende *n.*, Unterbrechung *f.*
abnormal termination Pro-
grammabbruch *m.*
abnormal termination exit Ausgang *m.* bei Programmabbruch
abort/to abbrechen *vrb.*, unterbrechen *vrb.*
about to be published erscheint
in Kürze

abridge/to abkürzen *vrb.*, zusammenfassen *vrb.*
abridged code Kurzschlüssel *m.*
abridged document verkürztes
Dokument *n.*
abridged edition Kurzausgabe
f., verkürzte Ausgabe *f.*
abridged translation Kurzübersetzung *f.*
abridgment Abkürzung *f.*, Kurzfassung *f.*
absolute address absolute
Adresse *f.*
absolute addressing absolute
Adressierung *f.*
absolute coordinate absolute
Koordinate *f.*
absolute delay absolute Verzögerung *f.*
absolute dimension Bezugsmaß
n.
absolute error absoluter Fehler
m.
absolute expression absoluter
Ausdruck *m.*
absolute instruction endgültiger
Maschinenbefehl *m.*
absolute location feste Aufstellung *f.*, ortsfeste Aufstellung *f.*
absolute point absoluter Punkt
m.
absolute programming Maschinencodeprogrammierung *f.*
absolute symbol absolutes Sym-

bol *n*.

absolute term absoluter Ausdruck *m*.

absorbed by aufgegangen in *präp*.

abstract Referat *n*., Abstract *n*.

abstract/to zusammenfassen *vrb*., referieren *vrb*.

abstract bulletin Referatedienst *m*.

abstract card Referatekarte *f*.

abstract descriptor group Deskriptorengruppe *f*. für Referate

abstract journal Referatezeitschrift *f*.

abstract periodical Referatezeitschrift *f*.

abstract symbol abstraktes Symbol *n*.

abstracting Referaterstellung *f*., Referieren *n*., Erstellen *n*. von Referaten

abstracting rules Regeln *pl*. zur Referateerstellung

abstracting service Referatedienst *m*.

abstraction Abstraktion *f*., Verallgemeinerung *f*.

abstraction relation Abstraktionsrelation *f*.

abstractor Referent *m*.

academic akademisch *adj*.

academic dissertation Dissertation *f*., Doktorarbeit *f*.

academic expertise wissenschaftliche Fachqualifikation *f*.

academic librarian wissenschaftlicher Bibliothekar *m*.

academic librarianship wissenschaftliches Bibliothekswesen *n*.

academic library wissenschaftliche Bibliothek *f*.

academic publication wissenschaftliche Veröffentlichung *f*.

academic staff wissenschaftliche Mitarbeiter *pl*.

academic year Studienjahr *n*.

academy Akademie *f*.

academy of sciences library Bibliothek *f*. der Akademie der Wissenschaften

acceleration limiter Beschleunigungsbegrenzer *m*.

acceleration time Beschleunigungszeit *f*.

accelerator Beschleuniger *m*.

accept/to anerkennen *vrb*., annehmen *vrb*., akzeptieren *vrb*.

accept/to with error Fehler akzeptieren *vrb*.

acceptance Annahme *f*., Akzeptanz *f*.

acceptance rate Benutzerrelevanzquote *f*.

accepting station annehmende Datenstation *f*.

access Zugang *m*., Zugriff *m*.

access/to zugreifen *vrb*.

access authority Zugriffsberechtigung *f*.

access charge Zugriffsgebühr *f*.

access code Zugriffscode *m*.

access control Zugriffssteuerung *f*.

access control field Zugriffskontrollfeld *n*.

access cycle Zugriffszyklus *m*.

access environment Zugriffsumgebung *f*.

access exception Zugriffsausnahme *f*.

access fee Zugriffsgebühr *f*.

access forward operation Vorwärtszugriffsoperation *f.*
access group Zugriffsgruppe *f.*
access guide Codieranleitung *f.*,
Verschlüsselungsvorschrift *f.*
access inoperable kein Zugriff
access key Zugriffsschlüssel *m.*
access length Zugriffslänge *f.*
access level Zugriffsebene *f.*
access mechanism Zugriffsmechanismus *m.*
access method Zugriffsmethode
f.
access mode Zugriffsmodus *m.*
access motion time Suchzeit *f.*
access network Anschaltnetz *n.*
access path Zugriffspfad *m.*
access point Einordnungsstelle
f., Zugriffspunkt *m.*, Sucheinstieg *m.*
access right Zugriffsrecht *n.*
access safety Zugriffssicherheit
f.
access state Zugriffszustand *m.*
access time Zugriffszeit *f.*
accessibility Zugriffsmöglichkeit
f.
accessibility field Verfügbarkeitsfeld *n.*
accessible registers zugängliche
Register *pl.*
accession Neuerwerbung *f.*, Zugang *m.*, Zuwachs *m.*
accession/to inventarisieren
vrb.
accession book Akzessionsjournal *n.*, Zugangsverzeichnis *n.*
accession date Zugangsdatum
n.
accession department Zugangsabteilung *f.*, Erwerbungsabteilung *f.*

accession file Zugangsdatei *f.*
accession number Akzessionsnummer *f.*, Eingangsnummer
f., Inventarnummer *f.*, Zugangsnummer *f.*
accession order Akzessionsordnung *f.*, Zugangsordnung *f.*
accession register Akzessionsjournal *n.*, Zugangsverzeichnis
n.
accessioner Mitarbeiter *m.* der
Erwerbungsabteilung
accessioning Inventarisierung
f., Akzessionierung *f.*, Eintragung *f.* ins Zugangsverzeichnis
accessions catalog nach Num-
mern geordneter Zugangskatalog *m.*
accessions list laufendes Zugangsverzeichnis *n.*, Liste *f.*
der Neuerwerbungen
accessor Zugriffsmechanismus
m., Zugriffsberechtigter *m.*
accessor control Zugriffssteuerung *f.*
accessory Zubehör *n.*
accommodation factor Akkommodationswahrscheinlichkeit
f.
accompanying material Be-
gleitmaterial *n.*
accordion fold Harmonikafalz
m., Leporellofalz *m.*, Zickzackfalz *m.*
accordion pleat Harmonikafalz
m., Leporellofalz *m.*, Zickzackfalz *m.*
account Konto *n.*
accounting Kostenrechnung *f.*,
Rechnungswesen *n.*
accounting office Rechnungsstelle *f.*

accounting year Rechnungsjahr
n.
accredited akkreditiert *adj.*
accumulate/to akkumulieren
vrb., summieren *vrb.*
accumulated error akkumulierter Fehler *m.*
accumulator Akkumulator *m.*,
Summenfeld *n.*, Zähler *m.*,
Summenspeicher *m.*, Saldierwerk *n.*
accuracy Genauigkeit *f.*, Fehlerfreiheit *f.*, Treffsicherheit *f.*
accuracy check Genauigkeitsprüfung *f.*
achievement rate Leistungsrate
f., Erfüllungsrate *f.*
acknowledgement Danksagung
f., Bestätigung *f.*
acknowledgement procedure
Rückmeldeprozedur *f.*
acoustic coupler Akustikkoppler
m.
acoustic storage akustischer
Speicher *m.*
acquire/to erwerben *vrb.*, anschaffen *vrb.*, reservieren *vrb.*
acquiring Anbindung *f.*
acquisition Beschaffung *f.*, Anschaffung *f.*, Erwerbung *f.*
acquisition budget Anschaffungsetat *m.*, Erwerbungsetat *m.*
acquisition catalog Neuerwerbungskatalog *m.*
acquisition committee Erwerbungskommission *f.*
acquisition department Zugangsabteilung *f.*, Erwerbungsabteilung *f.*
acquisition list Neuerwerbungsliste *f.*
acquisition policy Erwerbungs-

politik *f.*
acquisition policy statement Erwerbungsrichtlinien *pl.*
acquisition record Zugangsnachweis *m.*
acquisition unit Zugangsstelle
f., Akzession *f.*
acronym Akronym *n.*, Kurzwort
n.
action Aktion *f.*, Wirkung *f.*
action chart Funktionsdiagramm *n.*
action indicator Aktionsanzeige
f.
action line Funktionslinie *f.*
action message Aktionsnachricht *f.*
action module Ausführungsroutine *f.*
action period Funktionszeit *f.*
activate/to aktivieren *vrb.*
activate button Startknopf *m.*
activated file aktivierte Datei *f.*
activation Aktivierung *f.*
active aktiv *adj.*, aktiviert *adj.*,
wirksam *adj.*
active computer arbeitende Rechenanlage *f.*
active data set aktive Datei *f.*
active dissemination weite Verbreitung *f.*
active fault aktiver Fehler *m.*
active file aktive Datei *f.*
active format aktives Format *n.*
active line aktive Leitung *f.*
active link aktive Verbindungsstrecke *f.*
active message members aktive
Nachrichtendatei *f.*
active page aktive Seite *f.*
active page frame aktiver Seitenrahmen *m.*

active page queue Warte-
schlange *f.* aktiver Seiten
active partition aktiver Bereich
m.
active repair time Instandsetzungsdauer *f.*
active sequence number aktive
Folgenummer *f.*
active state aktiver Status *m.*
active station aktive Datenstation *f.*
active user library aktive Benutzerbibliothek *f.*
activity Aktivität *f.*, Tätigkeit *f.*
activity level Auslastungsgrad
m., Aktivitätsstufe *f.*
activity rate Bewegungshäufigkeit *f.*
activity ratio Aktivitätsverhältnis *n.*
actual address tatsächliche
Adresse *f.*
actuality Aktualität *f.*
acutance Konturschärfe *f.*
adaptability Anpaßbarkeit *f.*,
Anpassungsfähigkeit *f.*
adaptable anpaßbar *adj.*
adaptation Bearbeitung *f.*, Umarbeitung *f.*
adapter Anschluß *m.*, Adapter
m., Bearbeiter *m.*
adapter memory Speicher-
adapter *m.*
adaptive control system adaptives System *n.*
adaptive device adaptives
Speicherelement *n.*
adaptive system sich anpassendes System *n.*
adaptiveness Anpassungsfähigkeit *f.*
adaptor Bearbeiter *m.*

add/to addieren *vrb.*, hinzufügen *vrb.*
add/to paper Papier nachlegen
vrb.
add carry Additionsübertrag *m.*
add key Additionstaste *f.*
add time Additionszeit *f.*
added copy Duplikat *n.*, Mehrexemplar *n.*
added edition Neuausgabe *f.*
added entry Nebeneintrag *m.*
added entry card Nebeneintragskarte *f.*
added title page zusätzliche
Titelseite *f.*
addend Summand *m.*
addend register Summandenregister *n.*
addendum Nachtrag *m.*, Zusatz
m.
adder Addierwerk *n.*
adding operator Summationsoperator *m.*
addition Anbau *m.*, Addition *f.*,
Neuzugang *m.*, Beiordnung *f.*
additional capacity Mehrleistung *f.*
additional control store Registererweiterung *f.*
additional copy Mehrstück *n.*,
Wiederholungsstück *n.*
additional device Zusatzeinrichtung *f.*
additional examination Zusatzprüfung *f.*
additional instruction storage
Instruktionsspeichermodul *n.*
additional storage Hauptspeichererweiterung *f.*
additional storage feature zusätzlicher Speicher *m.*
additional vocabulary word Zu-

satzwort *n.*
additive attribute additives Attribut *n.*
address Adresse *f.*
address adjustment Adreßrechnung *f.*
address character Adreßzeichen *n.*
address comparison Adreßvergleich *m.*
address computation Adreßrechnung *f.*
address constant Adreßkonstante *f.*
address conversion Adreßumwandlung *f.*
address directory Anschriftenverzeichnis *n.*
address enable Adreßanhängung *f.*
address field Adreßfeld *n.*, Anschriftfeld *n.*
address file Adreßdatei *f.*
address generation Adressenbildung *f.*, Adreßgenerierung *f.*
address index Adreßindex *m.*
address instruction Befehlsadresse *f.*
address key register Adreßschlüsselregister *n.*
address label Adreßaufkleber *m.*
address limit Begrenzungsadresse *f.*
address line Adreßleitung *f.*, Adreßzeile *f.*
address list Adressenliste *f.*
address management Adressierungstechnik *f.*
address marker Adreßmarke *f.*
address modification Adreßmodifikation *f.*

address out Adreßausgabe *f.*
address part Adressenteil *m.*
address plug Adreßstecker *m.*
address position Adreßposition *f.*
address printer Adreßdrucker *m.*
address printing Adressenschreibung *f.*
address range Adreßbereich *m.*
address record Adreßsatz *m.*
address reference number Adreßschlüssel *m.*
address register Adreßregister *m.*
address space Adreßraum *m.*, Adreßbereich *m.*
address stop Adreßstopp *m.*
address storage Adreßspeicher *m.*
address switch Adreßschalter *m.*
address table Adreßtabelle *f.*
address track Adreßspur *f.*
address translation Adreßumsetzung *f.*
address value Adreßwert *m.*
addressability Adressierbarkeit *f.*
addressable storage adressierbarer Speicher *m.*
addressed direct access Direktzugriff *m.* mit Adresse
addressed sequential access sequentieller Zugriff *m.* mit Adresse
addressee Adressat *m.*
addressing Adressierung *f.*
addressing character Empfangsaufrufzeichen *n.*
addressing exception Adressierungsfehler *m.*

addressing format Adreß-
format *n.*
addressing main storage
Hauptspeicheradressierung *f.*
addressing mode Adressie-
rungsart *f.*
addressing module Adreßblock
m.
addressing signal Adressierungssignal *n.*
addressing system Addressier-
system *n.*
addressing tag Kennfeld *n.*
addressing technique Adressierungstechnik *f.*
addressless instruction adressenlose Instruktion *f.*
adhere/to kleben *vrb.*, haften
vrb.
adhesive binding Klebebindung
f.
adhesive label Aufkleber *m.*
adhesive tape Klebeband *n.*
adjacency operator Abstandsoperator *m.*
adjacent channel benachbarter
Kanal *m.*
adjacent link station benachbarte Verbindungsstation *f.*
adjacent node Nachbarknoten
m.
adjacent subarea Nachbarunterbereich *m.*
adjacent term benachbarter Begriff *m.*
adjourn/to vertagen *vrb.*, aufschieben *vrb.*
adjunct professor Lehrbeauftragter *m.*
adjunct register Zusatzregister
n.
adjunct register set Zusatzre-

gistersatz *m.*
adjust/to einstellen *vrb.*, justieren *vrb.*, ausrichten *vrb.*
adjust mode Formatiermodus
m.
adjustable einstellbar *adj.*
adjustable dimension veränderbare Dimension *f.*
adjustable extent einstellbare
Ausdehnung *f.*
adjustable margin feature verstellbarer Randanschlag *m.*
adjustable shelves verstellbare
Regalbretter *pl.*
adjuster Einsteller *m.*
adjustment Justierung *f.*, Einstellung *f.*, Randausgleich *m.*
adjustment program Abstimmungsprogramm *n.*
administer/to durchführen *vrb.*
administration Verwaltung *f.*
administrative center Verwaltungszentrum *n.*
administrative data processing
behördliche Datenverarbeitung *f.*
administrative law Verwaltungsrecht *n.*
administrative library Behördenbibliothek *f.*
administrative regulation Verwaltungsvorschrift *f.*
administrative unit Verwaltungseinheit *f.*
admissibility Zulässigkeit *f.*
admission Anerkennung *f.*, Zulassung *f.*
admission card Benutzerkarte
f., Leserkarte *f.*
admission of readers Benutzungserlaubnis *f.* für Leser
admission record Aufnahme-

vermerk *m.*, Eingangsvermerk
m.
admission requirement Zulassungsvoraussetzung *f.*
adolescent library Jugendbibliothek *f.*
adopting user profil Übernahme *f.* des Benutzerprofils
ADP EDV *f.*
adult education Erwachsenenbildung *f.*
adult evening classes Volkshochschule *f.*
advance copy Vorauflage *f.*, Vorausexemplar *n.*
advance development Vorentwicklung *f.*
advance list Vorankündigungsliste *f.*
advance order Vorbestellung *f.*
advance payment Vorauszahlung *f.*
advanced computer concept fortschrittliches Computerkonzept *n.*
advanced technology fortgeschrittene Technologie *f.*
advances Projektbericht *m.*, Fortschrittsbericht *m.*
advertise/to propagieren *vrb.*
advertising Werbung *f.*
advertising budget Werbemittel *pl.*
advertising copy Belegexemplar *n.*, Belegnummer *f.*
advertising journal Anzeigenblatt *n.*
advertising leaflet Prospekt *m.*
advice to users Benutzerberatung *f.*
advisory board Beratungsausschuß *m.*

advisory center Beratungsstelle *f.*
advisory character ratgebendes Zeichen *n.*
advisory council Beirat *m.*
advisory panel beratendes Gremium *n.*
advisory service Beratung *f.*
advisory work Beratungstätigkeit *f.*
affective relation Beeinflussungsbeziehung *f.*
affiliation Aufnahme *f.*, Mitgliedschaft *f.*
affix Affix *n.*
afterword Nachwort *n.*
age Zeitalter *n.*
agenda Arbeitsprogramm *n.*, Tagesordnung *f.*
agent Grossist *m.*
aggregate Dokument *n.* mit verwandten Sujets
aggregate operations zusammenfassende Operationen *pl.*
aging Alterung *f.*
agreement Vereinbarung *f.*, Abkommen *n.*
agricultural science Agrarwissenschaft *f.*
agriculture Landwirtschaft *f.*
agronomy Agrarwissenschaft *f.*
air mail Luftpost *f.*
aisle Gang *m.*, Flügel *m.*
album Album *n.*
alerting service Schnelldienst *m.*, Schnellinformation *f.*
algebra Algebra *f.*
algebraic linguistics algebraische Linguistik *f.*
algorithm Algorithmus *m.*
algorithmic language algorithmische Sprache *f.*

alignment Ausrichtung *f.*
alignment area Ausrichtbereich *n.*
alignment consideration Zeilenausrichtung *f.*
alignment function character Hauptsatzzeichen *n.*
alignment mark Vorschubzeichen *n.*
all rights reserved alle Rechte vorbehalten, Nachdruck verboten
all that has appeared mehr ist nicht erschienen
all that has been published mehr ist nicht erschienen
all through einheitliche Wortordnung *f.*
allocate/to zuordnen *vrb.*, Speicher zuordnen *vrb.*
allocate/to numbers beziffern *vrb.*, numerieren *vrb.*
allocated storage zugeordneter Speicher *m.*
allocated variable zugeordnete Variable *f.*
allocation Zuordnung *f.*, Bereitstellung *f.*
allocation class Zuordnungsklasse *f.*
allocation of data sets Zuordnung *f.* von Dateien
allocation of funds Mittelzuweisung *f.*
allocation program Zuordnungsprogramm *n.*
allocation unit Zuordnungseinheit *f.*
allot/to zuordnen *vrb.*
allot/to the call number Signaturen vergeben *vrb.*, signieren *vrb.*

allot/to the shelf-mark Standort bezeichnen *vrb.*, signieren *vrb.*
allotment Zuordnung *f.*
allowance Wertberichtigung *f.*, Erlaubnis *f.*, Zuschuß *m.*
allowance for expansion of stock Zuwachsspielraum *m.*, Zustellraum *m.* im Magazin
allowing command keys Freigabe *f.* der Steuertasten
allusion Anführung *f.*, Zitierung *f.*
almanac Almanach *m.*
alpha character Alpha-Zeichen *n.*
alpha date Datum *n.* in Buchstaben
alpha format Zeichenformat *n.*
alpha shift Buchstabenumschalttaste *f.*
alphabet Alphabet *n.*
alphabet extender Alphabeterweiterung *f.*
alphabet key Buchstabentaste *f.*
alphabet name Alphabetname *m.*
alphabet of symbols Symbolalphabet *n.*
alphabetic alphabetisch *adj.*
alphabetic character Buchstabe *m.*, alphabetisches Zeichen *n.*
alphabetic character set alphabetischer Zeichensatz *m.*
alphabetic code alphabetischer Code *m.*
alphabetic coding alphabetische Codierung *f.*
alphabetic collating Alphabetmischeinrichtung *f.*
alphabetic date Datum *n.* in Buchstaben

alphabetic equivalent alphabetische Ergänzung *f.*
alphabetic field Alphabetfeld *n.*
alphabetic field limit Alphabetfeldbegrenzung *f.*
alphabetic keyboard alphanumerische Tastatur *f.*
alphabetic notation alphabetische Notation *f.*
alphabetic order alphabetische Reihenfolge *f.*, alphabetische Ordnung *f.*
alphabetic receive Alphabetempfang *m.*
alphabetic sequence alphabetische Reihenfolge *f.*
alphabetic shift Alphaumschaltung *f.*
alphabetic sorting Alphabetsortierung *f.*
alphabetic storage Alphabetspeichereinrichtung *f.*
alphabetical alphabetisch *adj.*
alphabetical arrangement alphabetische Ordnung *f.*
alphabetical bibliography alphabetische Bibliographie *f.*
alphabetical catalog alphabetischer Katalog *m.*
alphabetical-classed catalog Gruppenschlagwortkatalog *m.*
alphabetical code alphabetischer Code *m.*
alphabetical coding alphabetische Codierung *f.*
alphabetical division alphabetische Einteilung *f.*
alphabetical extension alphabetische Unterteilung *f.*
alphabetical index alphabetisches Register *n.*

alphabetical index of places alphabetisches Ortsregister *n.*
alphabetical list of subject headings alphabetisches Schlagwortverzeichnis *n.*
alphabetical notation alphabetische Notation *f.*
alphabetical register alphabetisches Register *n.*
alphabetical subject catalog alphabetischer Sachkatalog *m.*
alphabetical subject collocation alphabetische Sachordnung *f.*
alphabetical subject index alphabetisches Schlagwortverzeichnis *n.*
alphabetical thesaurus alphabetischer Thesaurus *m.*
alphabetico-classed catalog alphabetischer Gruppenschlagwortkatalog *m.*
alphabetico-classed heading alphabetisch geordneter Klassentitel *m.*
alphabetico-classed index alphabetisch geordnetes Register *n.*
alphabetico-directed catalog alphabetischer Schlagwortkatalog *m.*
alphabetics Alphabetik *f.*
alphabetization Alphabetisierung *f.*, alphabetische Ordnung *f.*
alphabetize/to alphabetisieren *vrb.*, alphabetisch ordnen *vrb.*
alphameric alphanumerisch *adj.*
alphameric block checking Zeichenzulässigkeitsprüfung *f.*
alphanumeric alphanumerisch *adj.*

alphanumeric area alphanumerischer Tastenbereich *m.*
alphanumeric character alphanumerisches Zeichen *n.*
alphanumeric code alphanumerischer Code *m.*
alphanumeric control alphanumerische Steuerung *f.*
alphanumeric data alphanumerische Daten *pl.*
alphanumeric edited character alphanumerisches Druckaufbereitungszeichen *n.*
alphanumeric keyboard alphanumerische Tastatur *f.*
alphanumeric notation alphanumerische Notation *f.*
alphanumeric replacement alphanumerischer Ersatzwert *m.*
alphanumerical number alphanumerische Nummer *f.*
alter operation Eingabeoperation *f.*
alteration Änderung *f.*
alteration switch Umschalter *m.*
altering technische Änderung *f.*
alternate coding key Codetaste *f.*
alternate collating sequence wechselnde Sortierfolge *f.*
alternate file Ersatzdatei *f.*
alternate function Alternativfunktion *f.*
alternate function key Taste *f.* mit wechselnder Funktion
alternate index Alternativindex *m.*
alternate key Alternativschlüssel *m.*
alternating field Wechselfeld *n.*

alternating header wechselnde Kopfzeile *f.*
alternative channel Ersatzkanal *m.*
alternative location alternative Klassifikation *f.*
alternative relation Alternativrelation *f.*
alternative school library Ausweichschulbibliothek *f.*
alternative title Untertitel *m.*, Alternativsachtitel *m.*
alternative version verschiedene Lesarten *pl.*, Textvariante *f.*
alternatives Alternativen *pl.*
aluminium industry library Bibliothek *f.* der Aluminiumindustrie
alumni association Ehemaligenverband *m.*
alumni publication Veröffentlichung *f.* der Ehemaligen
amalgamate Symbol *n.* mit Sinnvariationen
amateur recording Amateuraufnahme *f.*
ambiguity Mehrdeutigkeit *f.*
ambiguous reference mehrdeutige Bezugnahme *f.*
amend/to berichtigen *vrb.*, verbessern *vrb.*
amendment Novellierung *f.*, Berichtigung *f.*, Verbesserung *f.*
amendment file Änderungsdatei *f.*
amendment record Änderungsdatensatz *m.*
American studies Amerikanistik *f.*
Americanistics Amerikanistik *f.*

amount Betrag *m.*
amount shift Anzahl *f.* der verschobenen Stellen
amplified class erweiterte Klasse *f.*
anagram Anagramm *n.*
analet zusammengesetzte Notation *f.*
analog analog *adj.*
analog computer Analogcomputer *m.*
analysis Analyse *f.*
analysis method Auswertungsmethode *f.*
analysis of covariance Covarianzanalyse *f.*
analysis of the grammatical form grammatikalische Analyse *f.*
analysis of variance Varianzanalyse *f.*
analyst Analytiker *m.*
analytical bibliography analytische Bibliographie *f.*
analytical catalog Aufsatzkatalog *m.*
analytical classification analytische Klassifikation *f.*
analytical description analytische Aufnahme *f.*
analytical entry Stücktitelaufnahme *f.*
analytical index analytisches Register *n.*
analytical relation analytische Beziehung *f.*
analytical statistics analytische Statistik *f.*
analytical subdivision besondere Anhängezahlen *pl.*
analytical subject entry analytische Titelaufnahme *f.*

analytical survey Übersichtsbericht *m.*, Literaturbericht *m.*
analytico-synthetical classification analytisch-synthetische Klassifikation *f.*
anaphoric expression anaphorischer Ausdruck *m.*
ancillary subject Hilfsgröße *f.*
AND UND
AND connector UND-Verbindungsoperator *m.*
AND element UND-Glied *n.*
AND operation UND-Verknüpfung *f.*, Konjunktion *f.*
AND relationship UND-Beziehung *f.*
AND rule UND-Regel *f.*
AND symbol UND-Symbol *n.*
Anglistics Anglistik *f.*
Anglo-American Cataloging Rules anglo-amerikanische Katalogisierungsregeln *pl.*
animal husbandry school library Viehzuchtschulbibliothek *f.*
animation Animation *f.*
annals Annalen *pl.*, Jahrbücher *pl.*
annex Anhang *m.*, Anbau *m.*
anniversary issue Jubiläumsausgabe *f.*
annotate/to kommentieren *vrb.*, anmerken *vrb.*
annotated bibliography kommentierte Bibliographie *f.*
annotated catalog kommentierter Katalog *m.*
annotated edition kommentierte Ausgabe *f.*
annotation Anmerkung *f.*, Kommentierung *f.*, Anmerkung *f.*

annotation routine Beschriftungsroutine *f.*
annotator Kommentator *m.*
announcement Veröffentlichung *f.*, Bekanntmachung *f.*
announcement bulletin Neuerscheinungsliste *f.*
annual Jahrbuch *n.*
annual changeover Jahresabschluß *m.*
annual conference Jahreskonferenz *f.*
annual congress Jahreskongreß *m.*
annual index Jahresverzeichnis *n.*
annual meeting Jahresversammlung *f.*
annual publication Jahrbuch *n.*, jährliche Veröffentlichung *f.*
annual report Jahresbericht *n.*
annual review Jahresrückblick *m.*
annual subscription Jahresabonnement *n.*
annual survey Jahreserhebung *f.*
anomalous state of knowledge ungewöhnlicher Wissensstand *m.*
anonymous anonym *adj.*, ohne Namen *pl.*
anonymous author ungenannter Verfasser *m.*
anonymous entry anonymer Eintrag *m.*
answer book Lösungsbuch *n.*
answer-passage retrieval Abschnittsretrieval *n.*
answer processing Antwortkontrolle *f.*
answer sheet Auswertungsformular *n.*
answer signal Beginnzeichen *n.*
answering machine Anrufbeantworter *m.*
antedate/to vordatieren *vrb.*, vorausdatieren *vrb.*
anterior subdivision vorgesetzte Unterteilung *f.*
anteriorizing symbol Vorsetzzeichen *n.*
anthology Anthologie *f.*
anticipatory post-coordination vorwegnehmende Postkoordination *f.*
antiquarian bookshop Antiquariat *n.*
antiquarian catalog Antiquariatskatalog *m.*
antiquated rückständig *adj.*
antonym Antonym *n.*, Gegensatz *m.*
antonymic relation Gegensatzbeziehung *f.*
aperture Öffnung *f.*
aperture card Filmlochkarte *f.*
aperture punched card Filmlochkarte *f.*
apostrophe editing apostrophgesteuerte Druckaufbereitung *f.*
apparent storage virtueller Speicher *m.*
appeal Revision *f.*
appears shortly erscheint demnächst
appearance Erscheinungsbild *f.*
append/to ketten *vrb.*
appendage Anhang *m.*
appendix Anhang *m.*, Appendix *m.*, Nachtrag *m.*
applicability Anwendungsmöglichkeit *f.*, Übertragbarkeit *f.*

applicant Bewerber *m.*
application Anwendung *f.*, Antrag *m.*, Verwendung *f.*
application area Anwendungsgebiet *n.*
application blank Bewerbungsformular *n.*
application buffer Anwendungspuffer *m.*
application card Aufnahmeformular *n.*
application combination Verbindung *f.* von Anwendungen
application control area Anwendungssteuerungsbereich *m.*
application control block Anwendungssteuerblock *m.*
application control code Anwendungssteuerungscode *m.*
application control structure Anwendungssteuerungsstruktur *f.*
application customizer Steuerprogramm *n.*
application data area Anwendungsdatenbereich *m.*
application data structure Anwendungsdatenstruktur *f.*
application database Anwendungsdatenbank *f.*
application description manual Anwendungsbeschreibung *f.*
application design Anwendungsentwurf *m.*
application development Anwendungsentwicklung *f.*
application entity Anwendungsinstanz *f.*
application file Benutzerkartei *f.*
application form Bewerbungsformular *n.*
application function routine Anwendungsfunktionsroutine *f.*
application group name Anwendungsgruppenname *m.*
application information service Anwendungsprogramminformationsdienst *m.*
application instructions Ausführungsbestimmungen *pl.*
application manual Anwendungsbeschreibung *f.*
application password Anwendungskennwort *n.*
application process Anwendungsprozeß *m.*
application program Anwendungsprogramm *n.*
application program identification Anwendungsprogrammidentifikation *f.*
application programmer Anwendungsprogrammierer *m.*
application questionnaire Bewerbungsfragebogen *m.*
application specialist Anwendungsspezialist *m.*
application structure Anwendungsstruktur *f.*
application system Anwendungssystem *n.*
applications program library Anwendungsprogrammbibliothek *f.*
applied angewandt *adj.*
appointment Termin *m.*
apportion/to zuteilen *vrb.*, aufteilen *vrb.*
apportionment Zuteilung *f.*, Umlage *f.*, Aufteilung *f.*
apportionment of notation

Symbolverteilung *f.*
appose/to aufdrucken *vrb.*
appraisal Bewertung *f.*, Begutachtung *f.*
appreciate/to anerkennen *vrb.*
apprentice Auszubildender *m.*
apprenticeship Ausbildungsjahre *pl.*, Ausbildungszeit *f.*
approach Methode *f.*, Verfahren *n.*, Lösungsvorschlag *m.*, Ansatz *m.*
approach term Suchwort *n.*
appropriate technology geeignete Technologie *f.*
appropriation Zweckbestimmung *f.*
approval Genehmigung *f.*, Bestätigung *f.*
approval copy Ansichtsexemplar *n.*
approval order Ansichtsbestellung *f.*
approve/to anerkennen *vrb.*
approximation Näherung *f.*
approximation method Annäherungsverfahren *n.*
appurtenance Zugehörigkeit *f.*
appurtenance relation Zugehörigkeitsbeziehung *f.*
appurtenance term Zugehörigkeitsbegriff *m.*
aptitude test Eignungstest *m.*
aquaria library Aquariumsbibliothek *f.*
arabesque Arabeske *f.*
arbitrary access wahlfreier Zugriff *m.*, Direktzugriff *m.*
arbitrary sign natürliches Zeichen *n.*
archaic term veralteter Begriff *m.*
archeology Archäologie *f.*

architectural history Baugeschichte *f.*, Architekturgeschichte *f.*
architecture Architektur *f.*, Bauwesen *n.*
archival archivarisch *adj.*, urkundlich *adj.*
archival documents Archivalien *pl.*, Archivgut *n.*
archival film Archivfilm *m.*
archival science Archivkunde *f.*
archival source Archivquelle *f.*
archival storage Ablage *f.* im Archiv
archivalia Archivalien *pl.*, Archivgut *n.*
archive Archiv *n.*, Dokumentensammlung *f.*, Urkundensammlung *f.*
archive/to archivieren *vrb.*
archive collection Archivbestand *m* .
archive material Archivmaterial *n.*, Archivgut *n.*
archive officer Archivbeamter *m.*
archive procedure Archivierungsprozedur *f.*
archive science Archivwissenschaft *f.*
archive type Archivierungsart *f.*
archives Archiv *n.*, Archivgut *n.*
archives administration Archivverwaltung *f.*
archivist Archivar *m.*
archivistics Archivwesen *n.*
area Bereich *m.*, Suchgebiet *n.*, Fläche *f.*, Zone *f.*
area address Bereichsadresse *f.*
area bibliographer Länderreferent *m.*
area boundary Bereichsgrenze *f.*

area concept Bereichskonzept *n.*

area definition Bereichsdefinition *f.*

area identification Bereichsbezeichnung *f.*

area material Regionalia *pl.*

area name Bereichsname *m.*

area of notation Bereich *m.* einer Notation

area of search Suchbereich *m.*

area planning Raumplanung *f.*

area protection feature Speicherbereichsschutz *m.*

area search Grobrecherche *f.*

area variable Bereichsvariable *f.*

argument Inhaltsangabe *f.*, Problemstellung *f.*, Argument *n.*, Parameter *m.*

argument association Parameterzuordnung *f.*

arithmetic expression arithmetischer Ausdruck *m.*

arithmetic instruction arithmetischer Befehl *m.*

arithmetic mean arithmetisches Mittel *n.*

arithmetic operand arithmetischer Operand *m.*

arithmetic operation arithmetische Operation *f.*

arithmetic operator arithmetischer Operator *m.*

arithmetic register Rechenregister *n.*

arithmetic relation arithmetische Relation *f.*

arithmetic subroutine arithmetisches Unterprogramm *n.*

arithmetic unit Rechenwerk *n.*

arithmetical rechnerisch *adj.*

arithmetical instruction arithmetischer Befehl *m.*

armarian Klosterbibliothekar *m.*

armed forces library Militärbibliothek *f.*, Bibliothek *f.* der Streitkräfte

armorial Wappenbuch *n.*

army library Bibliothek *f.* des Heeres

Arnesen classification Arnesen-Klassifikation *f.*

arrange/to ordnen *vrb.*

arrange/to a text einen Text anpassen *vrb.*, bearbeiten *vrb.*, umarbeiten *vrb.*

arrangement Anordnung *f.*, Klassierung *f.*, Ablage *f.*

arrangement by size Aufstellung *f.* nach dem Format

arrangement of a library Aufstellordnung *f.* einer Bibliothek

arrangement of subjects Sachgebietsordnung *f.*

arrangement of the bookracks Regalaufstellung *f.*

arrangement of the bookshelves Regalbrettanordnung *f.*

array Bereich *m.*, Feld *n.*, Matrix *f.*, klassifikatorische Reihe *f.*

array declaration Bereichsvereinbarung *f.*

array file Feldgruppendatei *f.*

array index Feldgruppenindex *m.*

array index error Feldgruppenindexfehler *m.*

array processor Vektorrechner *m.*

array variable Anordnungsvariable *f.*

arrearages Rückstände *pl.*

arrears letter Mahnung *f.*
arrears letter fee Mahngebühr
f.
art Kunst *f.*
art bibliography Kunstbibliographie *f.*
art collection Kunstsammlung *f.*
art library Kunstbibliothek *f.*
art original Original *n.* eines
Kunstwerkes
art print Kunstdruck *m.*
art school library Kunsthochschulbibliothek *f.*
art search Recherche *f.* zum
Stand der Technik
article Artikel *m.*, Aufsatz *m.*
artifact Artefakt *n.*
**artificial characteristics of divi-
sion** künstliche Einteilungsmerkmale *pl.*
artificial classification künstliche Klassifikation *f.*
artificial intelligence künstliche
Intelligenz *f.*
artificial language Kunstsprache *f.*
artificial line künstliche Leitung
f.
artificial word Kunstwort *n.*
as a loan leihweise *adj.*
ask/to for a book ein Buch bestellen *vrb.*
aspect beschreibender Ausdruck
m.
aspect-based method aspektgestütztes Verfahren *n.*
aspect card Sichtlochkarte *f.*
aspect card system Sichtlochkartensystem *n.*
aspect classification Aspektklassifikation *f.*
assemblage Kopplung *f.*

assemble/to assemblieren *vrb.*,
umwandeln *vrb.*, zusammentragen *vrb.*
assembler Assembler *m.*
assembly Versammlung *f.*,
Montage *f.*, Baugruppe *f.*
assembly language Assembliersprache *f.*
assembly line Fließband *n.*
assembly program Assembler
m.
assembly time Umwandlungszeit *f.*
assess/to abschätzen *vrb.*, veranschlagen *vrb.*
assign/to zuweisen *vrb.*, anweisen *vrb.*, zuordnen *vrb.*
assigned angewiesen *adj.*, bestimmt *adj.*
assignment Zuweisung *f.*, Anweisung *f.*, Anordnung *f.*
assignment name Zuordnungsname *m.*
assignment status Zuordnungsstatus *m.*
assignment symbol Zuordnungszeichen *n.*
assistant documentalist Dokumentationsassistent *m.*
assistant editor Herausgeberassistent *m.*
assistant librarian Bibliotheksassistent *m.*
assistantship Assistenz *f.*
associate librarian stellvertretender Bibliotheksdirektor *m.*
associated data set zugeordnete Datei *f.*
associated file verbundene Datei *f.*
associated libraries Verbundbibliotheken *pl.*

association Vereinigung *f.*, Assoziation *f.*, Zuordnung *f.*, Verband *m.*

association of documents Verwandtschaft *f.* von Dokumenten

association of terms Verwandtschaft *f.* von Benennungen

association trials Verwandtschaftshinweis *m.*

associative indexing assoziative Indexierung *f.*

associative memory Assoziativspeicher *m.*

associative processor Assoziativprozessor *m.*

associative relation Assoziationsrelation *f.*

associative storage Assoziativspeicher *m.*

assumption Annahme *f.*, Übernahme *f.*

assurance Zusicherung *f.*, Garantie *f.*

asterisk Sternchen *n.*

asterisk/to mit Sternchen versehen *vrb.*

asterisk address Sternadresse *f.*

astronautics Astronautik *f.*

astronomy Astronomie *f.*

astrophysics Astrophysik *f.*

asymmetric asymmetrisch *adj.*

asynchronous asynchron *adj.*

asynchronous balanced mode Mischbetrieb *m.*

asynchronous transmission asynchrone Übertragung *f.*

asyndetic index Register *n.* ohne Verweise

at a reduced price zu ermäßigtem Preis

at end condition bei Endebedin-gung

at end phrase bei Endeangabe

at intervals absatzweise *adv.*

at object time zur Zeit der Programmausführung

atlas Atlas *m.*, Kartenwerk *n.*

atlas size Atlasformat *n.*, Planoformat *n.*

attach/to anschließen *vrb.*

attached processing unit Anschlußprozessor *m.*

attached processor Anschlußprozessor *m.*

attachment Anschluß *m.*, Zusatzgerät *n.*

attachment accessory Anschlußelement *n.*

attachment approval Anschlußgenehmigung *f.*

attachment charge Anschlußgebühr *f.*

attachment identification Anschlußkennung *f.*

attachment independence Anschlußunabhängigkeit *f.*

attachment point Anschaltpunkt *m.*

attend/to überwachen *vrb.*, beaufsichtigen *vrb.*, betreuen *vrb.*

attendance Besuch *m.*, Dienst *m.*, Anwesenheit *f.*

attendance card Stempelkarte *f.*

attendance recorder Stempeluhr *f.*

attendance register Anwesenheitsliste *f.*

attendance time Anwesenheitszeit *f.*

attendant Bibliotheksgehilfe *m.*

attended unter Aufsicht

attended operation Bedienerbe-

trieb *m.*
attended time Betriebszeit *f.*
attention Abruf *m.*, Achtung *f.*,
Unterbrechung *f.*
attention exit Abrufausgang *m.*
attention identifier Hinweiszeichen *n.*
attention interruption Abrufunterbrechung *f.*
attention key Unterbrechungstaste *f.*, Abruftaste *f.*
attention note Hinweis *m.*
attention routine Anforderungsbehandlung *f.*
attitude Einstellung *f.*
attitude change Einstellungsänderung *f.*
attribute Attribut *n.*, Kennzeichen *n.*, Merkmal *n.*
attribute character Attributzeichen *n.*
attribute value Attributwert *m.*
attributed author mutmaßlicher
Verfasser *m.*
attributive relation attributive
Beziehung *f.*
auction Versteigerung *f.*, Auktion *f.*
auction/to versteigern *vrb.*
auction catalog Auktionskatalog *m.*
auction house Auktionshaus *n.*
auctioneer Auktionator *m.*, Versteigerer *m.*
audibility Hörbarkeit *f.*, Verständlichkeit *f.*
audio archive Tonträgerarchiv
n.
audio-cartridge Tonbandkassette *f.*
audio cassette Tonkassette *f.*
audio disc Schallplatte *f.*

audio library Schallarchiv *n.*
audio player Plattenspieler *m.*
audio recorder Tonbandgerät *n.*
audio recording Tonaufzeichnung *f.*
audio response unit Sprachausgabeeinheit *f.*
audio tape Tonband *n.*
audio-visual aids audiovisuelle
Hilfsmittel *pl*
audio-visual center audiovisuelles Zentrum *n.*
audio-visual document audiovisuelles Dokument *n.*
audio-visual material audiovisuelles Material *n.*
audio-visual media audiovisuelle Medien *pl.*
audio-visual presentation Ton-
Bild-Schau *f.*
auditing Rechnungsprüfung *f.*
auditor Rechnungsprüfer *m.*
**augmented alphabetical subject
index** erweitertes alphabetisches Sachregister *n.*
augmented edition erweiterte
Ausgabe *f.*
augmented KWIC index erweiterter KWIC-Index *m.*
augmented KWOC index erweiterter KWOC-Index *m.*
augmented transition network
erweitertes Übergangsnetzwerk *n.*
AUSMARC australisches
MARC *n.*
authentic authentisch *adj.*, echt
adj., verbürgt *adj.*
authentication Echtheitsbescheinigung *f.*
author Autor *m.*, Schriftsteller
m., Verfasser *m.*

author abstract Autorenreferat
n.
author authority file Autorennormdatei *f.*, Verfasserna-
mennormdatei *f.*
author bibliography Biobibliographie *f.*, Personalbibliographie *f.*
author card Verfasserkarte *f.*
author catalog Autorenkatalog
m., Verfasserkatalog *m.*, alphabetischer Katalog *m.*
author entry Verfassereintrag
m.
author fullness vollständiger
Verfassername *m.*
author heading Verfassereintrag *m.*
author index Autorenregister
n., Verfasserverzeichnis *n.*
author list Verfassernamenver-
zeichnis *n.*
author mark Verfassersignatur
f.
author notation Verfassersignatur *f.*
author number Verfassersignatur *f.*
author of the preface Verfasser
m. des Vorworts
author statement Verfasserangabe *f.*
author-title added entry Ver-
fasser- und Sachnebeneintrag
m.
author-title catalog Verfasser-
und Sachkatalog *m.*
author-title index Verfasser-
und Sachregister *n.*
authority Behörde *f.*, Berechtigung *f.*
authority code Benutzercode

m., Berechtigungscode *m.*
authority file Normdatei *f.*, Zugriffsberechtigungsdatei *f.*
authority level Benutzerrecht *n.*
authority list kontrollierte
Schlagwortliste *f.*
authorization Autorisierung *f.*,
Zugriffsberechtigung *f.*
authorization checking Autorisierungsprüfung *f.*
authorize/to berechtigen *vrb.*
authorized edition autorisierte
Ausgabe *f.*
authorized file zugriffsberechtigte Datei *f.*
authorized installer Hersteller
m.
authorized library autorisierte
Bibliothek *f.*
authorized program autorisiertes Programm *n.*
authorized receiver Empfangsbevollmächtigter *m.*
authorized rights of use autorisierte Benutzerrechte *pl.*
authorized user autorisierter
Benutzer *m.*
authorized version autorisierte
Version *f.*
authorship Autorenschaft *f.*
author's abstract Autorenreferat *n.*
author's copy Handexemplar
n., Autorenexemplar *n.*, Belegexemplar *n.*
author's correction Autorenkorrektur *f.*
author's right Urheberrecht *n.*
author's summary Zusammenfassung *f.* des Verfasser
auto abstract automatisch erstelltes Referat *n.*

auto abstracting automatische Referaterstellung *f.*
auto answering automatische Anrufbeantwortung *f.*
auto centred automatisch zentriert *adj.*
auto encoding automatische Indexierung *f.* nach Stichworthäufigkeit
auto extracting automatische Referaterstellung *f.*
auto index automatisch erstelltes Register *n.*
auto indexing automatische Indexierung *f.*
auto link automatisches Verbinden *n.*
autobiographer Autobiograph *m.*, Selbstbiograph *m.*
autobiographic autobiographisch *adj.*
autobiography Autobiographie *f.*, Selbstbiographie *f.*
autoduplication automatisches Duplizieren *n.*
autograph Originalhandschrift *f.*, Urschrift *f.*, Autograph *n.*, Autogramm *n.*, Unterschrift *f.*
autograph/to signieren *vrb.*, unterschreiben *vrb.*
autograph document signed eigenhändig geschriebenes, signiertes Dokument
autographed by the author mit eigenhändiger Unterschrift des Verfassers
autographed copy signiertes Exemplar *n.*
autography Autographie *f.*, Handschrift *f.*
automate/to automatisieren *vrb.*

automated circulation system automatisches Ausleihverbuchungssystem *n.*
automated data medium maschinenlesbarer Datenträger *m.*
automated data processing automatische Datenverarbeitung *f.*
automated encyclopaedia elektronische Enzyklopädie *f.*
automated language processing maschinelle Sprachverarbeitung *f.*
automated microfiche terminal automatisiertes Microfichegerät *n.*
automated operator automatisiertes Bedienerprogramm *n.*
automatic maschinell *adj.*, automatisch *adj.*
automatic abstracting maschinelle Referateerstellung *f.*, automatische Referaterstellung *f.*
automatic backup automatische Sicherung *f.*
automatic book delivery automatische Buchauslieferung *f.*
automatic carriage automatischer Vorschub *m.*
automatic cataloging maschinelle Katalogerstellung *f.*, maschinelle Katalogisierung *f.*
automatic classification automatische Klassifikation *f.*
automatic command automatischer Befehl *m.*
automatic control selbsttätige Regelung *f.*
automatic controller Regelgerät *n.*

automatic correction automatische Korrektur *f.*
automatic data editing automatische Datenbearbeitung *f.*
automatic data input automatische Dateneingabe *f.*
automatic data processing maschinelle Datenverarbeitung *f.*, automatische Datenverarbeitung *f.*
automatic dictionary elektronisches Wörterbuch *n.*
automatic dissemination automatische Verteilung *f.*
automatic duplication automatisches Duplizieren *n.*
automatic field automatisches Feld *n.*
automatic formatting automatische Formatierung *f.*
automatic indexing maschinelle Registererstellung *f.*, automatische Indexierung *f.*
automatic indexing technique maschinelles Indexierungsverfahren *n.*
automatic key generation automatische Schlüsselerzeugung *f.*
automatic order generation automatisches Bestellwesen *n.*
automatic process automatischer Ablauf *m.*
automatic programming automatische Programmierung *f.*
automatic query adjustment automatische Rechercheoptimierung *f.*
automatic recall automatischer Rückruf *m.*
automatic restart automatischer Wiederanlauf *m.*

automatic revision automatischer Prüfgang *m.*
automatic routing automatische Laufwerksteuerung *f.*
automatic scan automatisches Suchen *n.*
automatic searching maschinelle Recherche *f.*
automatic sentence extraction automatische Satzextraktion *f.*
automatic skipping automatisches Springen *n.*
automatic storage automatischer Speicher *m.*
automatic subject indexing automatische Sacherschließung *f.*
automatic term control automatische Begriffskontrolle *f.*
automatic text analysis automatische Textanalyse *f.*
automatic text processing automatische Textverarbeitung *f.*
automatic thesaurus construction automatische Thesauruserstellung *f.*
automatic translation automatische Übersetzung *f.*
automatic variant generation automatische Erzeugung *f.* von Varianten
automatic voice recognition automatische Spracherkennung *f.*
automatic word link automatische Wortwiederholung *f.*
automation Automation *f.*, Automatisierung *f.*
automation of library Bibliotheksautomatisierung *f.*

auxiliary zusätzlich *adj.*
auxiliary conjunction Hilfskonjunktion *f.*
auxiliary descriptor Hilfsdeskriptor *m.*
auxiliary facilities Hilfseinrichtungen *pl.*
auxiliary number Anhängezahl *f.*, Hilfszahl *f.*
auxiliary processor Hilfsprozessor *m.*
auxiliary schedule Hilfsschema *n.*, Hilfstafel *f.*
auxiliary stack Ausweichmagazin *n.*
auxiliary storage Hintergrundspeicher *m.*
auxiliary store Hilfsspeicher *m.*

auxiliary syndesis Hilfsverweise *pl.*
auxiliary table Hilfstafel *f.*
AV materials audio-visuelle Materialien *pl.*
availability Verfügbarkeit *f.*
availability table Verfügbarkeitstabelle *f.*
available lieferbar *adj.*, verfügbar *adj.*
available time Benutzerzeit *f.*
available unit queue Warteschlange *f.* verfügbarer Einheiten
average Durchschnitt *m.*
average access time durchschnittliche Zugriffszeit *f.*

B

b-tree B-Baum *m.*
back Buchrücken *m.*
back/to a book den Buchrücken abpressen *vrb.*
back board Rückendeckel *m.*
back cover Rückendeckel *m.*
back-end processor Back-End-Prozessor *m.*
back file bereits erschienene Ausgaben
back issue bereits erschienene Ausgaben
back label Rückenschild *n.*
back liner Buchrückenpresse *f.*

back lining Hinterklebepapier *n.*
back lining paper Hinterklebepapier *n.*
back margin Bundsteg *m.*, innerer Papierrand *m.*
back mark Flattermarke *f.*
back numbers bereits erschienene Ausgaben
back of a book Buchrücken *m.*
back of the page Rückseite *f.*
back out/to rückbuchen *vrb.*, zurücksetzen *vrb.*
back reference Rückverweisung *f.*

back rounding Buchrückenrunden *n.*
back tab key Tabulatorrücktaste *f.*
back title Rückentitel *m.*
backbone Buchrücken *m.*
background Hintergrund *m.*
background job Hintergrundjob *m.*
background material Hintergrundmaterial *n.*, Quellenangabe *f.*
background processing Hintergrundverarbeitung *f.*
background program Hintergrundprogramm *n.*
background reader Hintergrundleser *m.*
background reflexion Reflexionsvermögen *n.* des Papiers
backing hammer Buchbindehammer *m.*
backing storage Hintergrundspeicher *m.*
backing up Widerdruck *m.*, Sicherung *f.*
backlog Rückstand *m.*
backorder code Rückstandsschlüssel *m.*
backslide Gleitblock *m.*, Zettelstütze *f.*
backspace/to rücksetzen *vrb.*
backspace character Rücksetzzeichen *n.*
backspace code Rücksetzcode *m.*
backspace key Rücksetztaste *f.*
backtracking method automatische Rückverfolgung *f.*
backup Datensicherung *f.*
backup/to sichern *vrb.*
backup computer Ersatzrechner *m.*
backup copy Sicherungskopie *f.*
backup file Sicherungsdatei *f.*
backup frequency Sicherungshäufigkeit *f.*
backup library Sicherungsbibliothek *f.*
backup operating procedure Ausweichbetriebsprozedur *f.*
backup procedure Datensicherungsprozedur *f.*
backup processing Datensicherungsverfahren *n.*
backup system Sicherungssystem *n.*
backup volume Sicherungsdatenträger *m.*
backward rückwärts *adj.*
backward channel Hilfskanal *m.*
backward processing Rückwärtsverarbeitung *f.*
backward reference Rückbezugsname *m.*, Rückhinweis *m.*
backward supervision Rückwärtssteuerung *f.*
bad break Hurenkind *n.*
bad copy schlechtes Manuskript *n.*
bad letter beschädigter Buchstabe *m.*
bad spot Bandfehlstelle *f.*
badge Abzeichen *n.*, Ausweiskarte *f.*, Ausweis *m.*
badge column Ausweisspalte *f.*
badge number Ausweisnummer *f.*
badge reader Ausweisleser *m.*
badge security Ausweisschutz *m.*
badly trimmed verschnitten *adj.*
bag binding Beutelbuch *n.*

balance of goods and services Leistungsbilanz *f.*
balanced tree B-Baum *m.*
band chart Banddiagramm *n.*
bank Speicherbereich *m.*
bank library Bankbibliothek *f.*
banking system Bankwesen *n.*
banner Banner *n.*, Schlagzeile *f.*
bar chart Balkendiagramm *n.*
bar code Strichcode *m.*
bar code lable Strichcodeetikett *n.*
bar code reader Strichcodeleser *m.*
bar code scanner Strichcodeleser *m.*
bar coding Strichcodierung *f.*
barefoot librarian Barfußbibliothekar *m.*
barrier Schranke *f.*
barring Sperre *f.*
barring feature Sperreinrichtung *f.*
barring reliability Sperrsicherheit *f.*
barring table Sperrtabelle *f.*
Barrow method Barrow-Verfahren *n.*
base Basis *f.*, Grundzahl *f.*
base address Basisadresse *f.*, Bezugsadresse *f.*
base identifier Basisbezeichner *m.*
base line Grundlinie *f.*, Schriftlinie *f.*
base notation Radixschreibweise *f.*
base number Basiszahl *f.*
base of notation Notationsbasis *f.*
base of symbolism Symbolenalphabet *n.*

base register Basisregister *n.*
based on bezogen auf *adj.*, zeigerbezogen *adj.*
based storage zeigerbezogener Speicher *m.*
based variable zeigerbezogene Variable *f.*
basic grundlegend *adj.*
basic access method Basiszugriffsmethode *f.*
basic agreement Rahmenabkommen *n.*
basic catalog Grundkatalog *m.*, Hauptkatalog *m.*
basic charge Grundgebühr *f.*
basic class Grundklasse *f.*
basic coding Basiscodierung *f.*
basic competency elementare Fähigkeit *f.*, grundsätzliche Zuständigkeit *f.*
basic concept Grundbegriff *m.*
basic configuration Regelausstattung *f.*
basic console Systemkonsole *f.*
basic contract Rahmenvertrag *m.*
basic data exchange Basisdatenaustausch *m.*
basic edit Standardaufbereitung *f.*
basic entry Basiseintrag *m.*
basic entry card Stammkarte *f.*
basic field Datenfeld *n.*
basic field description Datenfeldbeschreibung *f.*
basic focus Hauptfacettenunterteilung *f.*
basic function Grundfunktion *f.*, Standardfunktion *f.*
basic index Basisregister *n.*
basic information unit Nachrichtenelement *n.*

basic instruction set Standardbefehlsvorrat *m.*
basic operation Basisoperation
f.
basic price Grundpreis *m.*
basic programming support
Programmiergrundunterstützung *f.*
basic requirement Grundbedarf
m.
basic right Grundrecht *n.*
basic square Grundschreibfeld
n.
basic storage Basisspeicher *m.*
basic system Basissystem *n.*
basic training Grundausbildung
f.
basis Grundlage *f.*
basis for discussion Diskussionsgrundlage *f.*
basis of division Untergliederungsgesichtspunkt *m.*
basis of subdivision Unterteilungsgesichtspunkt *m.*
bastard title Schmutztitel *m.,*
Vortitel *m.*
batch Gruppe *f.,* Schub *m.,*
Stapel *m.*
batch accumulator Zwischensummenzähler *m.*
batch communication Stapelübertragung *f.*
batch data exchange Stapeldatenaustausch *m.*
batch data transfer Stapeldatenübertragung *f.*
batch environment Stapelumgebung *f.*
batch file Stapelverarbeitungsdatei *f.*
batch function Stapelfunktion *f.*
batch initiation Stapelinitiie-

rung *f.*
batch input Stapelbetriebseingabe *f.*
batch interface file Schnittstellendatei *f.* für Stapelverarbeitung
batch job Stapeljob *m.*
batch message Stapelnachricht
f.
batch mode Stapelbetrieb *m.*
batch mode data processing
Stapelverarbeitung *f.*
batch number Stapelnummer *f.*
batch numbering Stapelnumerierung *f.*
batch print function Stapeldruckfunktion *f.*
batch processing Stapelverarbeitung *f.*
batch processing program Stapelverarbeitungsprogramm *n.*
batch program Stapelverarbeitungsprogramm *n.*
batch retrieval Satzzugriff *m.*
batch system Stapelverarbeitungssystem *n.*
batch test Stichprobenprüfung
f.
batch transmission Stapelübertragung *f.*
batching Stapelverarbeitung *f.*
batten card Sichtlochkarte *f.*
baud Baud *n.*
bay Abteilung *f.,* Nische *f.,* Zwischenraum *m.*
beam Lesestrahl *m.*
begin Beginn *m.,* Start *m.*
begin/to beginnen *vrb.,* starten
vrb.
begin bracket Startklammer *f.*
begin column Anfangsspalte *f.*
begin field code Feldanfangs-

code *m*.
begin statement Beginnanweisung *f*.
beginning Entstehung *f*., Anfang *m*.
beginning file label Dateianfangskennsatz *m*.
beginning number Anfangsnummer *f*.
beginning of tape marker Bandanfangsmarke *f*.
behavior Verhalten *n*.
bell-shaped curve Glockenkurve *f*.
belles lettres Belletristik *f*.
bench press Spindelpresse *f*.
benchmark Fixpunkt *m*.
benchmark run Vergleichslauf *m*.
benchmark test Vergleichstest *m*.
benefit Nutzen *m*.
benefit-cost analysis Nutzen-Kosten-Analyse *f*.
bequest Hinterlassenschaft *f*., Vermächtnis *n*., Nachlaß *m*.
bequest inventory Nachlaßverzeichnis *n*.
Berne convention Berner Urheberrechtsabkommen *n*.
Berne copyright union Berner Urheberrechtsvereinigung *f*.
bespeak/to a book ein Buch reservieren *vrb*.
bestseller Bestseller *m*.
biannual Halbjahresschrift *f*.
bias Ausrichtung *f*., systematischer Fehler *m*.
bias address Distanzadresse *f*.
bias relation Richtungsbeziehung *f*.
bias test Distanzprüfung *f*.

biblioclasm Büchervernichtung *f*.
biblioclast Büchervernichter *m*.
bibliognost Buchkundiger *m*.
bibliogony Herstellung *f*. von Büchern
bibliographer Bibliograph *m*., Buchwissenschaftler *m*.
bibliographic bibliographisch *adj*.
bibliographic checking Bibliographieren *n*., Vorakzession *f*.
bibliographic citation bibliographische Angaben *pl*.
bibliographic control bibliographische Kontrolle *f*.
bibliographic coupling bibliographische Kopplung *f*.
bibliographic database Literaturdatenbank *f*., bibliographische Datenbank *f*.
bibliographic description bibliographische Beschreibung *f*.
bibliographic documentation Literaturdokumentation *f*.
bibliographic element bibliographisches Element *n*.
bibliographic entry bibliographischer Eintrag *m*.
bibliographic indexing Literaturerschließung *f*.
bibliographic information system Literaturinformationssystem *n*.
bibliographic instruction bibliographische Anleitung *f*.
bibliographic note bibliographische Annotation *f*.
bibliographic record Titelaufnahme *f*.
bibliographic reference bibliographischer Nachweis *m*.,

Literaturnachweis *m.*
bibliographic retrieval bibliographisches Retrieval *n.*
bibliographic service Literaturdienst *m.*, bibliographischer Dienst *m.*
bibliographic unit bibliographische Einheit *f.*
bibliographic verification bibliographische Ermittlung *f.*, Bibliographieren *n.*
bibliographical cataloging bibliographisch getreue Titelaufnahme *f.*
bibliographical center bibliographisches Zentrum *n.*
bibliographical classification Bibliotheksklassifikation *f.*
bibliographical description bibliographische Beschreibung *f.*
bibliographical ghost vermutete Ausgabe *f.*
bibliographical guide bibliographischer Führer *f.*
bibliographical index bibliographisches Verzeichnis *n.*
bibliographical information bibliographische Auskunft *f.*
bibliographical inquiry bibliographische Abfrage *f.*, bibliographische Suchanfrage *f.*, bibliographische Suche *f.*
bibliographical monograph Fachbibliographie *f.*, Spezialbibliographie *f.*
bibliographical resource bibliographische Quelle *f.*
bibliographical strip Inhaltsfahne *f.*
bibliographical unit bibliographische Einheit *f.*
bibliography Quellenverzeichnis *n.*, Bibliographie *f.*, Buchkunde *f.*
bibliography of bibliographies Bibliographie *f.* der Bibliographien
biblioklept Bücherdieb *m.*
bibliology Theorie *f.* der Bibliographie
bibliomania Bibliomanie *f.*
bibliomaniac Bibliomane *m.*, Büchernarr *m.*
bibliometric distribution bibliometrische Verteilung *f.*
bibliometrics Bibliometrie *f.*
bibliopegist Buchbinder *m.*
bibliopegy Buchbindekunst *f.*
bibliophile Bücherfreund *m.*, Bibliophile *m.*
bibliotherapy Bibliotherapie *f.*
bibliothics Handschriftenanalyse *f.*
bid Angebot *n.*
bid/to bieten *vrb.*
bid documents Ausschreibungsunterlagen *pl.*
bid retry Aufrufwiederholung *f.*
bidirectional print Vor- und Rückwärtsdrucken *n.*
bidirectional transfer Zweirichtungsübertragung *f.*
biennial Zweijahresschrift *f.*
biennial budget Zweijahreshaushalt *m.*
bifurcate classification dichotomische Klassifikation *f.*
bilaminated zweischichtig *adj.*
bilingual zweisprachig *adj.*
bilingual dictionary zweisprachiges Wörterbuch *n.*
bill Rechnung *f.*
bill/to eine Rechnung ausstellen *vrb.*

billable time Benutzungszeit *f.*
billboard Anschlagtafel *f.*
billet Billett *n.*
billet-doux Liebesbrief *m.*
billing Rechnungslegung *f.*
billing data Rechnungsdatum *n.*
billing file Rechnungsdatei *f.*
bimonthly zweimonatlich *adj.*,
Zweimonatsschrift *f.*
binary binär *adj.*, dual *adj.*
binary character Binärzeichen
n.
binary code Binärcode *m.*
binary-coded decimal code binärcodierte Dezimalzifferndarstellung *f.*
binary-coded notation binärcodierte Darstellung *f.*
binary control Binärsteuerung
f.
binary counter Binärzähler *m.*
binary digit Binärziffer *f.*, Bit *n.*
binary display Binäranzeige *f.*
binary element Binärelement *n.*,
Binärzeichen *n.*
binary element string Binärelementenkette *f.*
binary indexing Binärindexierung *f.*
binary input unit Binäreingabeeinheit *f.*
binary instruction Binärinstruktion *f.*
binary item Binärfeld *n.*
binary notation Binärschreibweise *f.*, Binärsystem *n.*
binary number Binärzahl *f.*,
Dualzahl *f.*
binary numeral Binärzahl *f.*
binary operation Binäroperation *f.*
binary operator Binäroperator

m.
binary output unit Binärausgabeeinheit *f.*
binary overflow binärer Überlauf *m.*
binary point Binärkomma *n.*
binary recording mode Binärschreibweise *f.*
binary scale Binärsystem *n.*
binary search Binärsuche *f.*
binary signal Binärsignal *n.*
binary system Binärsystem *n.*
binary term weighting binäre
Deskriptorgewichtung *f.*
binary time interval binäres
Zeitintervall *n.*
binary zero Binärnull *f.*
bind/to einbinden *vrb.*, einspeichern *vrb.*, verknüpfen *vrb.*,
zuordnen *vrb.*, anbinden *vrb.*
bind/to in boards kartonieren
vrb.
bind/to in paper covers broschieren *vrb.*
bind/to with cord verschnüren
vrb.
binder Buchbinder *m.*, Mappe *f.*
binder's block Prägestempel *m.*
binder's cloth Buchbinderleinwand *f.*
binder's coin Prägestempel *m.*
binder's die Prägestempel *m.*
binder's glue Buchbinderleim
m.
binder's knife Buchbindermesser *n.*
binder's leaves Vorsatzblätter
pl.
binder's stamp Prägestempel
m.
binder's title Buchbindertitel
m., Titelaufdruck *m.* bei Ein-

bänden
bindery Buchbinderei *f.*
binding Binden *n.*, Buchbinden *n.*, Einband *m.*
binding art Buchbindekunst *f.*
binding book Buchbinderjournal *n.*
binding case Einbanddecke *f.*
binding cord Buchbinderschnur *f.*
binding department Hausbinderei *f.*
binding design Einbandgestaltung *f.*
binding edge Einheftkante *f.*
binding in paper covers Broschur *f.*
binding machine Buchbindereimaschine *f.*
binding pattern Einbandmuster *n.*
binding press Buchbinderpresse *f.*
binding record Buchbinderjournal *n.*
binding register Buchbinderjournal *n.*
binding sample Einbandmuster *n.*
binding saw Fuchsschwanz *m.*
binding sheet Anweisung *f.* für den Buchbinder
binding slip Anweisung *f.* für den Buchbinder
binding specimen Einbandmuster *n.*
binding thread Heftfaden *m.*
binding title Einbandtitel *m.*
binding wire Heftdraht *m.*
binding with a folding flap Klappenband *m.*
binding with yapp edges Beu-

telbuch *n.*
binding workman Buchbindergeselle *m.*
binomial distribution Binomialverteilung *f.*
bio-bibliographical catalog biobibliographischer Katalog *m.*
bio-bibliography Biobibliographie *f.*, Personalbibliographie *f.*
biochemistry Biochemie *f.*
biographee Biographierte *m.*
biographer Biograph *m.*
biographic biographisch *adj.*
biographic lexicon biographisches Lexikon *n.*
biographical biographisch *adj.*
biographical data biographische Daten *pl.*
biographical sketch Lebensabriß *m.*
biography Biographie *f.*
biography file biographisches Archiv *n.*
biology Biologie *f.*
biomedicine Biomedizin *f.*
biophysics Biophysik *f.*
biotechnology Biotechnik *f.*
bipartite graph zweiteiliger Graph *m.*
bit Binärziffer *f.*, Bit *n.*
bit assignment Bitzuordnung *f.*
bit capacity Übertragungsgeschwindigkeit *f.*
bit combination Bitkombination *f.*
bit density Bitdichte *f.*
bit manipulation Bitverarbeitung *f.*
bit position Bitstelle *f.*, Bitposition *f.*
bit rate Übertragungsge-

schwindigkeit *f.*
bit stream Bitstrom *m.*
bit string searching
Bitfolgensuche *f.*
biweekly Zweiwochenschrift *f.*
black box Black Box *f.*
black face Fettschrift *f.*
black ink Druckerschwärze *f.*
blackboard Wandtafel *f.*
blacklisted user ausgeschlossener Benutzer *m.*
blackout Gesamtausfall *m.*
blank Leerzeichen *n.*, Leerstelle *f.*, Leerseite *f.*
blank address Leeradresse *f.*
blank after Löschen *n.* nach Ausgabe
blank after print Löschen *n.* nach dem Drucken
blank card Leerkarte *f.*
blank character Leerzeichen *n.*
blank column Leerspalte *f.*
blank cover titelloser Umschlag *m.*
blank dummy Blindband *m.*
blank form Vordruck *m.*
blank leaf Leerblatt *n.*
blank line Leerzeile *f.*
blank out/to löschen *vrb.*
blank page Leerseite *f.*
blank paper Blankopapier *n.*
blank sheets unbedruckte Bogen *pl.*
blank space Leerzeichen *n.*, Leerstelle *f.*
blank transfer Leerübertragung *f.*
blank truncation Leerstellenabschneidung *f.*
blank volume Zwischenraum *m.*
blanked order Dauerauftrag *m.*
blanked reference Sammelver-

weis *m.*
blanking interval Austastlücke *f.*
blind blocking Blindpressung *f.*
blind crossreference Fehlverweisung *f.*
blind out/to ausblenden *vrb.*
blink/to blinken *vrb.*
blink field Blinkfeld *n.*
blip Bildmarke *f.*
blob Schreibmarke *f.*
block Block *m.*, Satz *m.*, Klischee *n.*
block/to blocken *vrb.*
block address Blockadresse *f.*
block book Inkunabel *f.*, Holztafeldruck *m.*
block by block blockweise *adj.*
block character Blockzeichen *n.*
block check Blockprüfung *f.*
block check character Blockprüfzeichen *n.*
block count Blockanzahl *f.*
block diagram Blockdiagramm *n.*
block format Satzaufbau *m.*
block indexing Blockindexierung *f.*
block length Blocklänge *f.*
block letters Blockschrift *f.*
block multiplexing Blockmultiplexverarbeitung *f.*
block name Speicherbereichsname *m.*
block of print Druckblock *m.*
block processor Blockprozessor *m.*
block search Satzsuchlauf *m.*
block securing Blocksicherungsverfahren *n.*
block size Blockgröße *f.*
block time out Blockzeitbegren-

zung *f.*
block transfer Blockübertragung *f.*
blocked data geblockte Daten *pl.*
blocked record geblockter Satz *m.*
blocking Blockung *f.*, Verdichtung *f.*
blocking factor Blockungsfaktor *m.*
blocking of data Datenblockung *f.*
blocking signal Sperrsignal *n.*
blow-up Vergrößerung *f.*
blue print Blaupause *f.*
blurb Waschzettel *m.*, Buchwerbung *f.*
board Platine *f.*, Steckkarte *f.*, Karton *m.*, Entscheidungsorgan *n.*
boards Deckel *pl.*
body Hauptteil *m.*
body line Grundlinie *f.*, Textzeile *f.*
body of book Buchinhalt *m.*, Buchtext *m.*
body of the entry Buchdruckspezifikation *f.*
body-punched aspect card Sichtlochkarte *f.*
body-punched card Lochkarte *f.*
body-punched feature card Sichtlochkarte *f.*
bold fett *adj.*
bold face halbfett *adj.*
bold type fette Schrift *f.*
book Buch *n.*
book/to verbuchen *vrb.*
book acquisition Literaturbeschaffung *f.*
book archive Bucharchiv *n.*

book art Buchkunst *f.*
book auction Buchauktion *f.*
book automobile Bücherbus *m.*, Autobücherei *f.*
book backing paper Hinterklebepapier *n.*
book boat Bücherboot *n.*, schwimmende Bibliothek *f.*
book brace Bücherstütze *f.*
book budget Erwerbungsetat *m.*
book buying Buchkauf *m.*
book car Bücherbus *m.*, Autobücherei *f.*
book card Buchkarte *f.*
book carrier Buchförderanlage *f.*
book case Futteral *n.*, Schuber *m.*, Schutzhülle *f.*
book catalog Bandkatalog *m.*
book chest Bücherkiste *f.*
book choice Bücherauswahl *f.*
book classification Bibliotheksklassifikation *f.*
book club Buchklub *m.*
book collecting policy Erwerbungspolitik *f.*
book collection Buchbestand *m.*
book collector Büchersammler *m.*
book coupon Büchergutschein *m.*
book craft Buchgewerbe *n.*
book cutting machine Buchschneidemaschine *f.*
book demand Literaturanforderung *f.*
book design Buchgestaltung *f.*
book display Buchauslage *f.*
book elevator Bücheraufzug *m.*
book end Bücherstütze *f.*
book exchange Buchmesse *f.*
book exhibition Buchausstellung *f.*

book exposition Bücherausstellung f.
book face Buchschrift f.
book fair Buchmesse f.
book form index Register n. in Buchform
book format Buchformat n.
book funds Erwerbungsetat m.
book gilding Buchvergoldung f.
book guard Buchsicherung f.
book hand Buchschrift f.
book history Buchgeschichte f.
book hoist Bücheraufzug m.
book illustration Buchillustration f.
book illustrator Buchillustrator m.
book in sheets Buch n. in Rohbogen
book indexing Buchindexierung f.
book issue system Buchausgabesystem n.
book jacket Lesehülle f., Schutzumschlag m., Schutzdecke f.
book jobber Buchgroßhändler m.
book jobbing Buchgroßhandel m.
book lift Bücheraufzug m.
book maintenance Buchpflege f.
book manufacture Buchherstellung f.
book-mark Lesezeichen n.
book-marker Lesezeichen n.
book market Büchermarkt m.
book mobile library Bücherbus m., Autobücherei f.
book museum Büchermuseum n.
book number Buchzeichen n., Signatur f.

book on loan entliehenes Buch n.
book order suggestion Anschaffungsvorschlag m.
book piracy Raubdruck m.
book pocket Buchtasche f.
book processing Geschäftsgang m.
book production Buchproduktion f.
book promotion Buchwerbung f.
book publicity Buchwerbung f.
book publishing Verlagswesen n.
book-read belesen adj.
book requests Buchwünsche pl.
book rest Lesepult n.
book restoration Buchrestaurierung f.
book review Buchbesprechung f., Rezension f., Buchkritik f.
book reviewing Buchbesprechungswesen n.
book selection Literaturauswahl f.
book shelving Buchaufstellung f.
book size Buchgröße f.
book slide Bücherbrett n. mit Schiebeeinrichtung
book slip Buchkarte f.
book stand Aufstellplatz m.
book stock Buchbestand m.
book supply Literaturangebot n., Literaturversorgung f.
book support Bücherstütze f.
book tag Buchrückenschild n.
book tally Büchergutschein m.
book token Büchergutschein m.
book trade Buchhandel m.
book trade bibliography Buch-

handelsbibliographie *f.*
book trade fair Buchmesse *f.*
book trade journal Buchhändlerzeitschrift *f.*
book trolly Bücherwagen *m.*
book wagon Bücherbus *m.*, Autobücherei *f.*
book wholesaler Buchgroßhändler *m.*
book worm Bücherwurm *m.*
bookbinder Buchbinder *m.*
bookcase Bücherschrank *m.*
bookform catalog Bandkatalog *m.*
booklet Büchlein *n.*
booklist Bücherliste *f.*
bookmobile Bücherbus *m.*, Autobücherei *f.*
bookplate Exlibris *n.*
bookrack Büchergestell *n.*
books-by-mail service Buchversand *m.*
books from abroad ausländische Bücher *pl.*
books in print Verzeichnis *n.* lieferbarer Bücher
books preserving library Archivbibliothek *f.*
bookseller Buchhändler *m.*
bookselling Bücherverkauf *m.*
bookshelf Bücherbrett *n.*
bookshop Buchhandlung *f.*
bookstack Büchergestell *n.*
bookstacks Büchermagazin *n.*
bookstall Bücherstand *m.*
bookstore Buchhandlung *f.*
Boolean Boolesch *adj.*
Boolean algebra Boolesche Algebra *f.*
Boolean character Boolesches Zeichen *n.*
Boolean complementation

Boolesche Komplementierung *f.*
Boolean data item Boolesches Datenfeld *n.*
Boolean expression Boolescher Ausdruck *m.*
Boolean factor Boolescher Faktor *m.*
Boolean function Boolesche Funktion *f.*
Boolean logic Boolesche Logik *f.*
Boolean operation Boolesche Operation *f.*
Boolean operator Boolescher Operator *m.*
Boolean retrieval Boolesches Retrieval *n.*
boot/to laden *vrb.*, starten *vrb.*
bootstrap Urlader *m.*
border Einfassung *f.*, Umrahmung *f.*
border-punched card Randlochkarte *f.*
borrow/to entleihen *vrb.*
borrow/to a book ein Buch entleihen *vrb.*
borrowed entliehen *adj.*
borrowed concept entlehnter Begriff *m.*
borrower Entleiher *m.*
borrower's card Leihschein *m.*
borrower's file Benutzerkartei *f.*
borrower's identification card Leihkarte *f.*
borrower's index Benutzerkartei *f.*
borrower's register Benutzerkartei *f.*
borrower's ticket Leihschein *m.*
borrowing data Entleihdaten *pl.*

borrowing data recording Entleihverbuchung *f.*
borrowing information Entleihinformation *f.*
borrowing period Leihfrist *f.*
botanical garden library Bibliothek *f.* eines botanischen Gartens
both way wechselseitig *adj.*
both-way communication beidseitige Datenübermittlung *f.*
both-way operation Duplexbetrieb *m.*
bottleneck Engpaß *m.*
bottom Boden *m.,* Unterteil *n.*
bottom line Fußzeile *f.*
bottom margin unterer Seitenrand *m.*
bottom margin text Fußzeilentext *m.*
bottom note Fußnote *f.*
bottom of the page Fußsteg *m.*
bottom row untere Zeile *f.*
bottom-up search Bottom-up-Suche *f.*
bought-in cataloging Fremdkatalogisierung *f.*
bound gebunden *adj.,* Grenze *f.*
bound book gebundenes Buch *n.*
bound form Affix *n.*
bound in boards kartoniert *adj.*
bound in paper covers broschiert *adj.*
bound in vellum Pergamenteinband *m.*
bound term unselbständiges Schlagwort *n.*
bound volume gebundenes Buch *n.,* gebundener Band *m.*
boundary Grenze *f.*
boundary alignment Begrenzungszuordnung *f.*

boundary function Grenzfunktion *f.*
boundary node Begrenzungsknoten *m.*
bounded variable begrenzte Variable *f.*
bow bracket geschwungene Klammer *f.*
bowdlerize/to bereinigen *vrb.*
bowdlerized edition bereinigte Ausgabe *f.*
box Schreibfeld *n.,* Behälter *m.*
boxhead umrandete Überschrift *f.*
boxheading umrandete Überschrift *f.*
brace geschwungene Klammer *f.*
bracket Klammer *f.*
bracket/to einklammern *vrb.*
Bradford´s law of scatter Bradfords Gesetz *n.* der Streuung
braille Blindenschrift *f.*
braille library Blindenbücherei *f.*
branch Verzweigung *f.,* Zweigstelle *f.*
branch/to verzweigen *vrb.*
branch address Verzweigungsadresse *f.*
branch instruction Verzweigungsbefehl *m.*
branch library Filialbibliothek *f.,* Bibliothekszweigstelle *f.,* Zweigbibliothek *f.*
branch line Abzweigleitung *f.*
branch of study Fachrichtung *f.*
branch point Verzweigungspunkt *m.*
branch supervisor Leiter *m.* der Filialbibliothek

branching Verzweigung *f.*
branching operation Verzweigungsoperation *f.*
break Verbindungsabbruch *m.*, Absatz *m.*
break/to unterbrechen *vrb.*, abschalten *vrb.*
break character Trennzeichen *n.*, Unterstreichungszeichen *n.*
break off Abbruch *m.*
break off/to abbrechen *vrb.*
break point bedingter Programmstopp *m.*, Schnittpunkt *m.*
break scan code Unterbrechungscode *m.*
break time Unterbrechungszeit *f.*
breakdown Gliederung *f.*, Ausfall *m.*
breaking period Abschaltzeit *f.*
brevity of notation Notationskürzel *n.*
brief cataloging Kurztitelkatalogisierung *f.*
Brillouin distribution Brillouin'sche Verteilung *f.*
British Council library Bibliothek *f.* des British Council
broad classification Grobklassifikation *f.*
broadband communication Breitbandkommunikation *f.*
broadcast corporation archive Rundfunkarchiv *n.*
broadcast videotex Videotext *m.* einer Sendeanstalt
broadcasting Rundfunk *m.*
broadcasting corporation Rundfunkanstalt *f.*
broadcasting library Rundfunkbibliothek *f.*

broader term Oberbegriff *m.*
broadsheet Einblattdruck *m.*, Plakatdruck *m.*
broadside Einblattdruck *m.*, Plakatdruck *m.*
brochure Broschüre *f.*
Browne system Browne'sches System *n.*
browsability freie Suchmöglichkeit *f.*
browse/to durchsuchen *vrb.*, blättern *vrb.*, suchen *vrb.*
browsing Suchen *n.*, Suchlauf *m.*
browsing collection Nahbereichsbestand *m.*
Brussels system universelle Dezimalklassifikation *f.*
bubble memory Magnetblasenspeicher *m.*
budget Haushalt *m.*, Etat *m.*
budget account Haushaltstitel *m.*
budget problem Finanzierungsproblem *n.*
budget regulations Haushaltsordnung *f.*
budgetary control Haushaltsüberwachung *f.*
budgeting Haushaltsführung *f.*
buffer Puffer *m.*, Zwischenspeicher *m.*
buffer/to zwischenspeichern *vrb.*
buffer address Pufferadresse *f.*
buffer allocation Pufferzuordnung *f.*
buffer chaining Pufferkettung *f.*
buffer data Pufferdaten *pl.*
buffer deallocation Pufferfreigabe *f.*
buffer expansion Puffererwei-

terung *f.*
buffer limit Pufferbegrenzung *f.*
buffer list Pufferliste *f.*
buffer loop Pufferschleife *f.*
buffer main storage Pufferhauptspeicher *m.*
buffer order Pufferbefehl *m.*
buffer overrun Pufferüberlauf
m.
buffer pointer Pufferzeiger *m.*
buffer pool Puffervorrat *m.*
buffer program Pufferprogramm *n.*
buffer segment Puffersegment
n.
buffer shift Pufferverlagerung
f.
buffer size Puffergröße *f.*
buffer storage Pufferspeicher
m., Zwischenspeicher *m.*
buffer store Pufferspeicher *m.*
buffer unit Puffereinheit *f.*
build/to aufbauen *vrb.*
built-in procedures eingebaute
Prozeduren *pl.*
bulk Menge *f.*
bulk eraser Löschmagnet *m.*
bulk loader Ladeprogramm *n.*
bulk print Drucken *n.* großer
Mengen
bulk storage Massenspeicher
m.
bulletin Bulletin *n.*
bulletin board Anschlagbrett *n.*
bulletin of new books Neuerscheinungsliste *f.*
bump storage nichtadressierba-

rer Hilfsspeicher *m.*
bureau Amt *n.*
burst/to reißen *vrb.,* trennen
vrb.
burst mode Stoßbetrieb *m.*
burst transmission gebündelte
Übertragung *f.*
burster Trenneinrichtung *f.*
bus Bus *m.,* Übertragungsweg
m.
bus-out check Gültigkeitsfehler
m.
business administration Betriebswirtschaft *f.*
business archives Firmenarchiv
n.
business database Wirtschaftsdatenbank *f.*
business information Firmeninformation *f.*
business law Wirtschaftsrecht
n.
business year Geschäftsjahr *n.*
busy belegt *adj.*
busy signal Besetztzeichen *n.*
buzz Störung *f.*
by-name gleichnamig *adj.*
by-name entry Eintrag *f.* unter
dem Vornamen
by paragraphs absatzweise
adv.
by steps absatzweise *adv.*
bypass/to übergehen *vrb.*
bypass field geschütztes Feld *n.*
byte Byte *n.*
byte boundary Bytegrenze *f.*
byte index Byteindex *m.*

C

cabinet size Querformat *n.*
cable Kabel *n.*
cable television Kabelfernsehen
n.
cable transmission Kabelübertragung *f.*
calculation Berechnung *f.*
calculation basis Kalkulationsbasis *f.*
calculation program Tabellenkalkulationsprogramm *n.*
calculator Rechenmaschine *f.*,
Rechner *m.*
calendar Kalender *m.*, chronologisch geordnete Dokument-
liste *f.*
calendar/to verzeichnen *vrb.*
call card Bestellschein *m.*, Bestellvordruck *m.*
call for tender Ausschreibung *f.*
call mark Standortnummer *f.*
call number Standortnummer
f., Signatur *f.*
call number formulation Signaturbildung *f.*
call slip Bestellschein *m.*, Bestellzettel *m.*
call slip for a loan Leihschein *m.*
called line identification Anschlußkennung *f.*
called station gerufene Station *f.*
calligraph Kalligraph *m.*
calligrapher Kalligraph *m.*
calligraphic kalligraphisch *adj.*

calligraphic types Schönschrift *f.*
calligraphist Kalligraph *m.*
calligraphy Kalligraphie *f.*
calling card Besucherkarte *f.*,
Visitenkarte *f.*
calling up Abruf *m.*
campaign Aktion *f.*
cancel/to streichen *vrb.*, ausstreichen *vrb.*, durchstreichen
vrb., annullieren *vrb.*, abbestellen *vrb.*
cancel/to a loan die Ausleihe
zurückbuchen *vrb.*, die Buchung löschen *vrb.*, die Buchung austragen *vrb.*
cancel/to a subscription ein
Abonnement abbestellen *vrb.*
cancel character Löschzeichen
n., Ungültigkeitszeichen *n.*
candidate descriptor Deskriptorkandidat *m.*
canonical kanonisch *adj.*
canonical class kanonische Unterklasse *f.* einer Hauptklasse
canonical order formale Ordnung *f.*
canonical sequence kanonische
Reihenfolge *f.*
canton library Kantonalbibliothek *f.*
capability Leistungsvermögen
n.
capacity of a notation Kapazität *f.* einer Notation

capital Großbuchstabe *m.*, Versal *m.*
capital letter Großbuchstabe *m.*, Versal *m.*
capitalism Kapitalismus *m.*
capitalization Großschreibung *f.*
capitalize/to großschreiben *vrb.*
caption Bildunterschrift *f.*, Tabellenüberschrift *f.*, Untertitel *m.*
caption title Kapitelüberschrift *f.*
card Karteikarte *f.*
card cabinet Karteikartenkasten *m.*
card catalog Zettelkatalog *m.*, Karteikatalog *m.*, Kartei *f.*
card charging Zusammenstellung *f.* von Buch- und Leserkarte
card charging system Buchkartensystem *n.*
card deck Kartenstapel *m.*
card division Karteikartenabteilung *f.*
card drawer Karteikartenschubfach *n.*
card face Karteikartenvorderseite *f.*
card feed Karteikartenzuführung *f.*
card file Kartei *f.*
card holder Benutzer *m.*
card index Kartei *f.*, Zettelkatalog *m.*, Register *n.* auf Karteikarten
card manuscript Zettelmanuskript *n.*
card service Karteikartenabteilung *f.*
card slip Bestellschein *m.*

card tray Katalogkasten *m.*
card union catalog Zentralkatalog *m.* auf Karten
cardboard Kartonpapier *n.*
cardex Zeitschriftenkontrollsystem *n.*
care of books Pflege *f.* der Bücher
career Werdegang *m.*
Carnegie library Carnegiebibliothek *f.*
Carolingian monastic library karolingische Klosterbibliothek *f.*
carrel Arbeitsnische *f.*
carriage return character Wagenrücklaufzeichen *n.*
Cartesian product kartesisches Produkt *n.*
cartobibliography Kartenbibliographie *f.*
cartographer Kartograph *m.*, Landkartenzeichner *m.*, Kartenzeichner *m.*
cartographic material kartographisches Material *n.*, Landkarten *pl.*, Bilder *pl.*, Luftbilder *pl.*, Atlanten *pl.*
cartography Kartographie *f.*, Landkartenkunde *f.*
cartology Kartenkunde *f.*
cartoon Zeichentrickfilm *m.*
cartridge Kartusche *f.*, Patrone *f.*
cartulary Urkundenbuch *n.*, Urkundenregister *n.*
case Behälter *m.*, Kasten *m.*
case binding englische Broschur *f.*
case grammar Kasusgrammatik *f.*
case studies Fallstudien *pl.*

casebook Fallsammlung *f.*
cased englische Broschur *f.*
cash discount Skonto *n.*
casing englische Broschur *f.*
cassation Ungültigkeitserklärung *f.*
cassette Kassette *f.*
catalog Katalog *m.*, Bibliothekskatalog *m.*
catalog/to katalogisieren *vrb.*
catalog card Katalogkarte *f.*
catalog card copy Laufzettel *m.*
catalog card mailing service Katalogkartenversand *m.*
catalog card service Katalogkartendienst *m.*
catalog code Katalogisierungsregel *f.*
catalog construction Katalogerstellung *f.*
catalog data Katalogdaten *pl.*
catalog database Katalogdatenbank *f.*
catalog department Katalogabteilung *f.*
catalog drawer Katalogschublade *f.*
catalog editing Katalogrevision *f.*
catalog entry Katalogeintrag *m.*, Titelaufnahme *f.*
catalog in book-form Bandkatalog *m.*, Katalog *m.* in Buchform
catalog maintenance Katalogpflege *f.*
catalog of books in print Verzeichnis *n.* lieferbarer Bücher
catalog of periodicals Zeitschriftenkatalog *m.*
catalog of persons and places Namenskatalog *m.*

catalog of serial works Zeitschriftenkatalog *m.*
catalog revision Katalogrevision *f.*
catalog tray Karteikartenschubfach *n.*
catalog use Katalogbenutzung *f.*
catalog user Katalogbenutzer *m.*
catalog with pasted-in slips Katalog *m.* mit aufgeklebten Titelstreifen
cataloged procedure katalogisiertes Verfahren *n.*
cataloger Katalogsachbearbeiter *m.*, Katalogbearbeiter *m.*
cataloger´s slip Laufzettel *m.*
cataloging Katalogisierung *f.*, Katalogwesen *n.*, Katalogisieren *n.*
cataloging agency Katalogisierungsstelle *f.*
cataloging code Katalogisierungsregeln *pl.*
cataloging database Katalogisierungsdatenbank *f.*
cataloging department Katalogisierungsabteilung *f.*
cataloging in publication Vorauskatalogisierung *f.*
cataloging in source Vorauskatalogisierung *f.*
cataloging problems Katalogprobleme *pl.*
cataloging room Katalogisierungsraum *m.*
cataloging rules Regeln *pl.* zur Katalogisierung
cataloging system Katalogisierungssystem *n.*
cataloging technique Katalogi-

sierungstechnik *f.*
catch letter Leitbuchstabe *m.*
catchword Stichwort *n.*
catchword catalog Stichwortkatalog *m.*
catchword entry Stichworteintrag *m.*
catchword index Stichwortregister *n.*
catchword indexing Stichwortindexierung *f.*
catchword title Stichworttitel
m., Kurztitel *m.*
categorial relation kategoriale
Beziehung *f.*
categorial table Hilfstafel *f.*
categorization Kategorisierung
f.
category Kategorie *f.*, Begriffsklasse *f.*
catering school library Gastronomieschulbibliothek *f.*
cathedral library Kirchenbibliothek *f.*
cathode-ray tube Kathodenstrahlröhre *f.*, Bildschirm *m.*
causation Kausalbeziehung *f.*
CD-ROM drive CD-ROM-
Laufwerk *n.*
ceased publications eingestellte
Reihe *f.*, unvollständige Reihe
f.
censor Schrifttumsprüfer *m.*,
Zensor *m.*
censor/to zensieren *vrb.*
censorship Zensur *f.*
census statistische Erhebung *f.*,
Zensus *m.*
center Zentrum *n.*
center margin Bundsteg *m.*
center notes Anmerkungen *f.*
zwischen Textspalten

central archive Zentralarchiv *n.*
central catalog Zentralkatalog
m., Hauptkatalog *m.*, Gesamtkatalog *m.*
central collection Kernbestand
m.
central lending library zentrale
Leihbücherei *f.*
central library Zentralbücherei
f., Zentralbibliothek *f.*
central memory Zentralspeicher
m.
central office Zentralstelle *f.*
central processing unit Zentraleinheit *f.*
central processor Zentraleinheit
f.
central shelflist zentrale Standortliste *f.*
central special library zentrale
Fachbibliothek *f.*
centralization Zentralisierung *f.*
centralized cataloging Zentralkatalogisierung *f.*
centralized depository zentralisierte Aufbewahrung *f.*
centralized interloan zentralisierter Leihverkehr *m.*
**centralized on-line circulation
control** zentrale Online-Ausleihkontrolle *f.*
centralized system zentralisiertes System *n.*
centred heading zentriertes
Hauptschlagwort *n.*
certificate Urkunde *f.*, Zeugnis
n., Bescheinigung *f.*, Gutachten *n.*, Zertifikat *n.*, Beglaubigung *f.*
certification of librarian Diplom *n.* eines Bibliothekars
chain Kette *f.*, Begriffsleiter *f.*

chain classification Kettenklassifikation *f.*

chain indexing Kettenindexierung *f.*

chain procedure Methode *f.* der Kettenindexierung

chaining Adressverkettung *f.*

chaining of records Datensatzverkettung *f.*

chaining search Suche *f.* mit Folgeadressen

chairman Obmann *m.*, Diskussionsleiter *m.*

chamber of commerce Handelskammer *f.*

chamber of commerce library Handelskammerbibliothek *f.*

chancellor Rektor *m.*

change Änderung *f.*

change/to class mark umsignieren *vrb.*

change-over Übergang *m.*

changeable änderbar *adj.*

changed title abgeänderter Titel *m.*

channel Kanal *m.*, Übertragungskanal *m.*

channel study Untersuchung *f.* von Kanälen zur Informationsübertragung

chapeau allgemeiner Titel *m.*

Chapin Charts Chapin-Diagramm *n.*

chapter Kapitel *n.*

chapter heading Kapitelüberschrift *f.*

character Zeichen *n.*, Schriftzeichen *n.*

character area Zeichenfeld *n.*

character boundary Zeichenbegrenzung *f.*

character check Zeichenkon-

trolle *f.*

character coding Zeichencodierung *f.*

character comparison Zeichenabgleich *m.*

character density Zeichendichte *f.*

character distance Zeichenabstand *m.*

character encoder Klarschriftcodierer *m.*

character generator Zeichengenerator *m.*

character height Zeichenhöhe *f.*

character position Zeichenstelle *f.*

character reader Zeichenleser *m.*, Klarschriftleser *m.*

character recognition Zeichenerkennung *f.*

character register Zeichenregister *n.*

character sensing field Lesefeld *n.*

character sensing strip Lesestreifen *m.*

character set Zeichenvorrat *m.*, Zeichensatz *m.*

character spacing Zeichenmittenabstand *m.*

character string Zeichenkette *f.*

character subset Teilmenge *f.* eines Zeichenvorrats

character validity check Zeichengültigkeitskontrolle *f.*

character width Zeichenbreite *f.*

characteristic charakteristische Eigenschaft *f.*, Charakteristikum *n.*, Merkmal *n.*; Kennziffer *f.*

characteristic dimension Merkmalsdimension *f.*

characteristic of division Untergliederungsgesichtspunkt *m.*
characteristic of origin Herkunftsmerkmal *n.*
characteristic of purpose Anwendungsmerkmal *n.*
characteristic value Kennwert *m.*
charge Ausleihverbuchung *f.*, Eintragung *f.* einer Entleihung
charge/to a book eine Buchausleihe verbuchen *vrb.*
charge card Leihschein *m.*
charge/to out ausleihen *vrb.*
charge slip Leihschein *m.*
charging Ausleihverbuchung *f.*
charging card Leihschein *m.*
charging desk Bücherausgabetheke *f.*
charging file Ausleihkartei *f.*
charging slip Buchkarte *f.*
charging system Ausleihverbuchungssystem *n.*
chart Graphik *f.*, Karte *f.*, Diagramm *f.*
charta Urkunde *f.*
charter Gründungsurkunde *f.*
chartered librarian diplomierter Bibliothekar *m.*
chartulary Urkundenbuch *n.*, Urkundenregister *n.*
check Kontrolle *f.*, Prüfung *f.*, Scheck *m.*, Revision *f.*
check/to abhaken *vrb*, abstreichen *vrb.*, prüfen *vrb.*
check character Prüfzeichen *n.*
check digit Prüfziffer *f.*
check list Kontrolliste *f.*
check out/to austesten *vrb.*
check out routine Ausscheidungsverfahren *n.*
checking Bestandsprüfung *f.*

checking card Nachweiskarte *f.*
checking counter Kontrolltisch *m.*
checkpoint Kontrollpunkt *m.*
chemical cipher ziffermäßige Notation *f.* für chemische Verbindungen
chemical formula chemische Formel *f.*
chemical industry Chemiewirtschaft *f.*
chemical information Chemieinformation *f.*
chemistry Chemie *f.*
chi-square test Chiquadrattest *m.*
chief cataloger Leiter *m.* der Katalogabteilung
chief editor Hauptschriftleiter *m.*, Chefredakteur *m.*
chief librarian Bibliotheksdirektor *m.*, Bibliotheksleiter *m.*
chief source of information Hauptinformationsquelle *f.*
children's and juvenile librarianship Kinder- und Jugendbibliothekswesen *n.*
children's book Kinderbuch *n.*, Jugendbuch *n.*
children's cultural center Kinderkulturzentrum *n.*
children's department Kinderabteilung *f.*, Jugendabteilung *f.*
children's library Kinderbücherei *f.*, Jugendbücherei *f.*, Kinderbibliothek *f.*
children's library work Kinderbibliotheksarbeit *f.*
children's literature Kinderlektüre *f.*, Kinderliteratur *f.*
children's theater Kindertheater *n.*

Chinese style Broschur *f.* mit
Umschlagdeckel
chip Chip *m.*
chirography Handschrift *f.*
chiropractic school library Chiropraktikerschulbibliothek *f.*
choice of library Bibliothekswahl *f.*
choice of terms Begriffswahl *f.*
chorus score Partitur *f.*
chronicle Chronik *f.*
chronicler Chronist *m.*
chronological descriptor chronologischer Deskriptor *m.*
chronological division chronologische Unterteilung *f.*
chronological filing system
chronologische Ordnung *f.*
von Dokumenten
chronological order chronologische Ordnung *f.*
chronological subdivision chronologische Unterteilung *f.*
chronology Chronologie *f.*
church archive Kirchenarchiv *n.*
church library Kirchenbibliothek
f., Dombibliothek *f.*
cinefilm Film *m.*
circuit noise Leitungsgeräusch *n.*
circular Rundschreiben *n.*, Zirkular *n.*
circular routing unkontrollierte
Ausleihe *f.*
circulate/to ausleihen *vrb.*
circulating book Leihbuch *n.*
circulating library Leihbibliothek *f.*
circulation Ausleihe *f.*, Auflage
f.
circulation/acquisitions ratio
Erwerb-Ausleih-Quote *f.*
circulation card Leihschein *m.*

circulation control Auflagenkontrolle *f.*, Ausleihkontrolle
f., Entleihkontrolle *f.*
circulation data Leihdaten *pl.*
circulation department Leihstelle *f.*
circulation desk Bücherausgabetheke *f.*
circulation file Ausleihkartei *f.*
circulation record Ausleihkartei
f., Ausleihregister *n.*, Rundlaufplan *m.*
circulation restriction Ausleihbeschränkung *f.*
circulation rules Ausleihbestimmungen *pl.*
circulation statistics Ausleihstatistik *f.*
circulation system Entleihsystem *n.*
circulation transaction Ausleihvorgang *m.*
circulation work Ausleihbetrieb
m., Ausleihe *f.*
circumstances Sachverhalt *m.*
circus library Zirkusbibliothek *f.*
citation Zitat *n.*, Literaturangabe *f.*
citation analysis Zitatanalyse *f.*
citation frequency Zitierhäufigkeit *f.*
citation index Zitierregister *m.*,
Zitierindex *m.*
citation indexing Zitierindexierung *n.*
citation network Zitiernetzwerk
n.
citation order of facets Facettenfolge *f.*
citation pattern Zitiermuster *n.*
citation search Zitatensuche *f.*
cite/to zitieren *vrb.*

city library Großstadtbibliothek
f., Stadtbibliothek *f.*
civil code Zivilgesetzbuch *n.*
claim Mahnung *f.*, Anspruch *m.*
claim/to anfordern *vrb.*, anmahnen *vrb.*
claims adjustment Schadenregulierung *f.*
class Klasse *f.*, Fach *n.*, Gruppe
f., Sachgebiet *n.*
class/to klassieren *vrb.*
class book Schulbuch *n.*
class catalog systematischer
Katalog *m.*
class description Klassenbezeichnung *f.*
class heading Gruppenschlagwort *n.*
class letter alphabetisches No-
tationszeichen *n.*
class mark Klassennummer *f.*,
Signatur *f.*
class-mate Klassenmitglied *n.*
class media center Klassenmediothek *f.*
class-membership relation
Klasse-Objektbeziehung *f.*
class name Klassenbezeichnung
f.
class number Klassennummer
f., Signatur *f.*
class relation Beziehung *f.* zwischen Klassen
class term Klassenbezeichnung
f.
classed catalog systematischer
Katalog *m.*
classic klassisch *adj.*, ausgezeichnet *adj.*, erstklassig *adj.*
classical author Klassiker *m.*
classical edition klassische Ausgabe *f.*, Standardausgabe *f.*

classical studies Altertumswissenschaft *f.*
classifiable klassifizierbar *adj.*
classification Klassifikation *f.*,
Typisierung *f.*, Klassifizierung
f., Einstufung *f.*
classification by dichotomy dichotomische Klassifikation *f.*
classification by size Aufstellung *f.* nach dem Format
classification code Klassifikationsregel *f.*
classification method Klassifikationsverfahren *n.*
classification number Klassifikationsnummer *f.*, Signatur *f.*
classification of documents Dokumentenklassifizierung *f.*
classification problem Klassifikationsproblem *n.*
classification research Klassifikationsforschung *f.*
classification schedule Klassifikationsschema *n.*, Klassifikationstafel *f.*
classification scheme Klassifikationsschema *n.*
classification system Klassifikationssystem *n.*
classification table Klassifikationsschema *n.*, Klassifikationstafel *f.*
classification theory Klassifikationstheorie *f.*
classificationist Entwickler *m.*
einer Klassifikation
classificatory structure klassifikatorische Struktur *f.*
classified arrangement systematische Aufstellung *f.*
classified catalog systematischer Katalog *m.*

classified document Verschlußsache f.
classified file systematisches
Archiv n.
classified filing system systematische Anordnung f. von
Dokumenten
classified index systematisches
Register n.
classified list of concepts systematische Begriffsliste f.
classified order systematische
Ordnung f.
classified sequence systematische Reihenfolge f.
classified subject catalog systematischer Sachkatalog m.
classifier Klassifikator m.
classify/to klassifizieren vrb.,
als geheim kennzeichnen vrb.
classifying Klassifizieren n.,
Eingruppierung f.
classing Klassieren n.
classroom Unterrichtsraum m.
classroom library Klassenzimmerbibliothek f.
clause Klausel f.
clear/to löschen vrb.
clear area nicht beschriftete
Oberfläche f.
clear band nicht beschriftete
Oberfläche f.
clearance Zugangserlaubnis f.,
Zugangsberechtigung f.
clearing house Clearinghaus n.
clerical assistant Bürokraft f.
clerical operations Büroarbeiten pl.
clerical staff Büropersonal n.
cliche Klischee n.
client Benutzer m., Leser m.,
Kunde m.

clientele Benutzer pl., Leser pl.
climatization Klimatisierung f.
clinical medical librarianship
klinisch-medizinisches Bibliothekswesen f.
clinical treatment report Krankenblatt n.
clip Büroklammer f.
clipping Zeitungsausschnitt m.
clipping archive Ausschnittarchiv n., Presseausschnittarchiv
n.
clipping bureau Zeitungsausschnittbüro n.
clipping file Zeitungsausschnittsammlung f.
clipping service Zeitungsausschnittdienst m.
cloakroom Garderobe f.
clock Taktgeber m.
close/to schließen vrb.
close classification Feinklassifikation f.
close/to down abschließen vrb.
close statement Dateiabschlußanweisung f.
closed geschlossen adj.
closed-access collection magazinierter Bestand m.
closed-access library Magazinbibliothek f.
closed-access material Magazingut n.
closed array geschlossene Reihe
f.
closed counter lending Schalterausleihe f.
closed entry abgeschlossene
Aufnahme f.
closed loan counter Schalter m.
closed loop geschlossene
Schleife f.

closed shelves Magazin *n.*
closed stack Magazin *n.*
closed subroutine geschlossenes Unterprogramm *n.*
closed system geschlossenes System *n.*
cloth bound Leineneinband *m.*
club Verein *m.*
club library Vereinsbibliothek *f.*
clump Gruppe *f.*
cluster Cluster *n.*
cluster analysis Clusteranalyse *f.*
cluster sample Klumpenstichprobe *f.*
cluster search Clustersuche *f.*
clustering Clusterbildung *f.*, Gruppenbildung *f.*, Klassenbildung *f.*
co-author Koautor *m.*, Mitverfasser *m.*
co-authorship Mehrfachautorenschaft *f.*
co-editor Mitherausgeber *m.*
co-extensive term Bezeichnung *f.* mit gleichem Begriffsinhalt
co-publishing Gemeinschaftsveröffentlichung *f.*
coacervate ungeordnete Dokumentsammlung *f.*
cocitation Kozitation *f.*
code Code *m.*, Schlüssel *m.*, Regelwerk *n.*
code/to codieren *vrb.*, verschlüsseln *vrb.*
code comparison Stichwortvergleich *m.*
code converter Codeumsetzer *m.*
code element Codeelement *n.*
code position Lochstelle *f.*
code representation Codeelement *n.*
code set Menge *f.* der Codeele-

mente, Zeichenvorrat *m.*
code translator Decodierer *m.*
code value Codeelement *n.*
codebook Codebuch *n.*
coded abstract codiertes Referat *n.*
coded bibliographical reference codierte bibliographische Daten *pl.*
coded character set Codetabelle *f.*, codierter Zeichenvorrat *m.*
codex Kodex *m.*
coding Kodierung *f.*, Codierung *f.*
coding scheme Codierschlüssel *m.*
coffee house library Kaffeehausbibliothek *f.*
cognitive kognitiv *adj.*
cognitive processes kognitive Prozesse *pl.*
cognitive science Kognitionswissenschaft *f.*
cognitive structures kognitive Strukturen *pl.*
coil binding Spiralbindung *f.*
coin-operated equipment Gerät *n.* mit Münzautomat
coincidence Übereinstimmung *f.*
coincidence hole card Sichtlochkarte *f.*
collaborator Mitarbeiter *m.*
collate/to durchblättern *vrb.*, mischen *vrb.*, abgleichen *vrb.*, zuordnen *vrb.*
collating machine Zusammentragmaschine *f.*
collating marks Flattermarken *pl.*, hintere Anlegemarke *f.*
collating sequence Sortierfolge *f.*
collating table Zusammentragetisch *m.*

collation Textvergleich *m.*
collator Kartenmischer *m.*
collectanea ausgewählte Werke
pl.
collected edition Sammelausgabe *f.*
collected works gesammelte
Werke *pl.*
collecting policy Erwerbungspolitik *f.*
collection Sammlung *f.*, Bestand *m.*, Dokumentsammlung *f.*
collection analysis Bestandsanalyse *f.*
collection catalog Bestandskatalog *m.*
collection completeness Bestandsvollständigkeit *f.*
collection coverage Bestandsabdeckung *f.*
collection currency Bestandsaktualität *f.*
collection development Bestandsentwicklung *f.*, Bestandsaufbau *m.*
collection emphasis Sammelschwerpunkt *m.*, Bestandsschwerpunkt
collection evaluation Bestandsbewertung *f.*
collection growth Bestandswachstum *n.*
collection guide Bestandsverzeichnis *f.*
collection improvement Bestandsergänzung *f.*
collection item Sammelobjekt *n.*
collection items Sammelgut *n.*
collection main field Sammelschwerpunkt *m.*
collection maintenance Bestandspflege *f.*
collection management Bestandsverwaltung *f.*
collection number Bestandsnummer *f.*
collection of poems Gedichtsammlung *f.*
collection overlap Bestandsüberschneidung *f.*
collection profile Bestandsprofil *n.*
collection science Bestandswissenschaft *f.*
collection size Bestandsgröße *f.*, Bestandsumfang *m.*
collection type Bestandstyp *m.*
collection utilization Bestandsnutzung *f.*
collective biography Sammelbiographie *f.*
collective cataloging Sammelkatalogisierung *f.*
collective entry Sammeleintrag *m.*
collective term Sammelbezeichnung *f.*
collective title Sammeltitel *m.*
collective work Sammelwerk *n.*
collector Sammler *m.*
collector's edition Liebhaberausgabe *f.*
college Hochschule *f.*
college archive Hochschularchiv *n.*
college bookshop Hochschulbuchhandlung *f.*
college library Hochschulbibliothek *f.*
college of physical education Sporthochschule *f.*
college publication Hochschulschrift *f.*

collocation Zusammenstellung
f.
colloquial language Umgangssprache *f.*
colloquium Kolloquium *n.*
colon Doppelpunkt *m.*
colon classification Facettenklassifikation *f.*
colophon Kolophon *m.*, Schlußtitel *m.*
color coding Stichwörter *pl.* mit
Farbzeichen
color film Farbfilm *m.*
color microfiche Farbmikrofiche *m.*
color microfilm Farbmikrofilm
m.
color monitor Farbbildschirm
m.
color photocopy Farbkopie *f.*
color printing Farbdruck *m.*
colored pencil Buntstift *m.*
column Spalte *f.*, Kolumne *f.*
column arrangement Spaltenanordnung *f.*
column chart Säulendiagramm
n.
column width Spaltenbreite *f.*
combination Kombination *f.*
combination card Verbundkarte
f.
combination coding kombi-
nierte Randlochung *f.*
combination of morphemes
Wortverbindung *f.*
combination order of facets Facettenformel *f.*
combined file kombinierte Datei
f.
combined number zusammen-
gesetzte Zahl *f.*
comic strips Bildergeschichten

pl.
comma Komma *n.*
command Kommando *n.*,
Befehl *m.*
command-driven befehlsge-
steuert *adj.*
command language Befehls-
sprache *f.*, Abfragesprache *f.*
command mode Kommando-
modus *m.*
commemorative sermon Ge-
denkrede *f.*
commemorative volume Festschrift *f.*, Gedenkschrift *f.*
comment Stellungnahme *f.*,
Bemerkung *f.*
commentary Erläuterung *f.*,
Kommentar *m.*
commerce Handel *m.*
commerce library wirtschaftswissenschaftliche Bibliothek *f.*
commercial kommerziell *adj.*,
gewerblich *adj.*
commercial archive Wirt-
schaftsarchiv *n.*
commercial books Handelsbücher *pl.*
commercial documentation
Wirtschaftsdokumentation *f.*
commercial information Wirtschaftsinformation *f.*
commercial library Handelsbibliothek *f.*, kaufmännische
Bibliothek *f.*, gebührenpflichtige Leihbücherei *f.*
commercial publisher kommerzieller Verlag *m.*
commission Kommission *f.*,
Provision *f.*
committee Komitee *n.*
common auxiliaries allgemeine
Anhängezahlen *pl.*

common command language
allgemeine Abfragesprache *f.*
common facet allgemeine Facette *f.*
common language Umgangssprache *f.*
common machine language einheitliche Maschinensprache *f.*
common subdivisions allgemeine Anhängezahlen *pl.*
common technical language
Fachsprache *f.*
common title Gesamttitel *m.*
communal library Gemeindebücherei *f.*
communication Kommunikation *f.*
communication analysis Kommunikationsanalyse *f.*
communication center Kommunikationszentrum *n.*
communication channel Übertragungskanal *m.*
communication control character Übertragungssteuerzeichen *n.*
communication cost Übertragungskosten *pl.*
communication culture Kommunikationskultur *f.*
communication engineering
Nachrichtentechnik *f.*
communication format Austauschformat *n.*
communication medium Kommunikationsmittel *n.*
communication networks
Kommunikationsnetzwerke *pl.*
communication patterns Kommunikationsmuster *pl.*
communication policy Kommunikationspolitik *f.*

communication process Kommunikationsprozeß *m.*
communication research Kommunikationsforschung *f.*
communication satellite Nachrichtensatellit *m.*
communication science Kommunikationswissenschaft *f.*
communication system Kommunikationssystem *n.*
communication technique
Kommunikationstechnik *f.*
communication technology
Kommunikationstechnik *f.*
communication theory Kommunikationstheorie *f.*
communicative grammar kommunikative Grammatik *f.*
communicative value Kommunikationswert *m.*
communicator Kommunikator *m.*
community Gemeinde *f.*
community college library Gemeindehochschulbibliothek *f.*
community hospital library
Gemeindekrankenhausbibliothek *f.*
community information Bürgerinformation *f.*
community information service
Bürgerinformationsdienst *m.*
community librarianship Gemeindebibliothekswesen *n.*
community library Gemeindebibliothek *f.*
compact shelving Kompaktregalanlage *f.*
compact storage Kompaktregal *n.*, Rotationsregal *n.*
company Unternehmen *n.*, Firma *f.*

company archiv Betriebsarchiv
n.
company directory Firmenadreßbuch *n.*
company library Firmenbibliothek *f.*
company publication Firmenschrift *f.*
comparability Vergleichbarkeit
f.
comparative vergleichend *adj.*
comparative librarianship vergleichende Bibliothekswissenschaft *f.*
comparative relation Vergleichsbeziehung *f.*
comparator Vergleichseinrichtung *f.*
compare/to vergleichen *vrb.*
comparison Gegenüberstellung
f., Vergleich *m.*
compatibility Verträglichkeit *f.*,
Kompatibilität *f.*
compatibility problem Kompatibilitätsproblem *n.*
compendium Abriß *m.*, Grundriß *m.*, Kompendium *n.*, Kurzfassung *f.*
compensation Vergütung *f.*
competition Wettbewerb *m.*,
Konkurrenz *f.*
compilation Sammlung *f.*, Zusammenstellung *f.*
compile/to zusammenstellen
vrb., übersetzen *vrb.*, kompi-
lieren *vrb.*, umwandeln *vrb.*
compiler Compiler *m.*, Übersetzer *m.*
compiling program Compilerprogramm *n.*
complementary education Zusatzausbildung *f.*

complementary studies Zusatzstudium *n.*
complete abgeschlossen *adj.*
complete bibliography vollständige Bibliographie *f.*
complete chain vollständige
Kette *f.*
complete edition Gesamtausgabe *f.*, vollständige Ausgabe
f.
complete series vollständige
Reihe *f.*
complete work Gesamtwerk *n.*
complete works gesammelte
Werke *pl.*
completed abgeschlossen *adj.*
completed series abgeschlossene Reihe *f.*
completeness Vollständigkeit *f.*
completion Fertigstellung *f.*
complex-structured thesaurus
komplex strukturierter Thesaurus *m.*
complex system komplexes System *n.*
complex term Mehrwortbegriff
m.
complexity Komplexität *f.*
complimentary copy Freiexemplar *n.*
compo Schriftsetzer *m.*
component Bestandteil *m.*,
Komponente *f.*
component of a term Bestandteil *m.* einer Bezeichnung
compose/to setzen *vrb.*
composing machine Setzmaschine *f.*
composite book Sammelwerk *n.*
composite classification synthetische Klassifikation *f.*
composite heading zusammen-

gesetztes Schlagwort *n.*
composite subject synthetisches Objekt *n.*
composite volume Sammelband *m.*
composite work Sammelwerk *n.*
composition Satz *m.*
composition computer Satzrechner *m.*
compositor Setzer *m.*
compound Kompositum *n.*
compound catchwords zusammengesetzte Stichworte *pl.*
compound heading zusammengesetztes Schlagwort *n.*
compound name Doppelname *m.*
compound number zusammengesetzte Zahl *f.*
compound subject heading zusammengesetztes Schlagwort *n.*
compound subject name zusammengesetztes Schlagwort *n.*
compound term Mehrwortbegriff *m.*
compound word Kompositum *n.*
comprehensive bibliography vollständige Bibliographie *f.*
comprehensive relation Umfassungsrelation *f.*
comprehensive school Gesamtschule *f.*
comprehensive school library Gesamtschulbibliothek *f.*
comprehensive term Gesamtbegriff *m.*
comprehensiveness Reichhaltigkeit *f.*
compression Verdichtung *f.*,

Kompression *f.*
compulsory deposit Pflichtablieferung *f.*
computation Berechnung *f.*
computational linguistics Computerlinguistik *f.*
computer Computer *m.*
computer-aided rechnerunterstützt *adj.*, computergestützt *adj.*, computerunterstützt *adj.*
computer-aided composition Computersatz *m.*
computer-aided indexing computergestützte Indexierung *f.*
computer-aided instruction computerunterstützter Unterricht *m.*
computer-aided learning computerunterstütztes Lernen *n.*
computer-aided translation computergestützte Übersetzung *f.*
computer-aided union cataloging computergestützte Verbundkatalogisierung *f.*
computer architecture Rechnerarchitektur *f.*
computer-based circulation system computergestütztes Ausleihsystem *n.*
computer-based information elektronisch gespeicherte Information *f.*
computer center Computerzentrum *n.*
computer criminality Computerkriminalität *f.*
computer graphics grafische Datenverarbeitung *f.*, Computergraphik *f.*
computer instruction Maschinenbefehl *m.*

computer language Computersprache *f.*

computer literacy Computerkenntnisse *pl.*

computer network Rechnernetz *n.*, Rechnerverbundnetzwerk *n.*, Computerverbund *m.*, Computernetzwerk *n.*

computer network system Rechnerverbundsystem *n.*

computer-oriented language maschinenorientierte Programmiersprache *f.*

computer printout Computerausdruck *m.*

computer program Computerprogramm *n.*

computer programming Programmierung *f.*

computer science Informatik *f.*

computer scientist Informatiker *m.*

computer services Computerdienste *pl.*

computer technology Computertechnik *f.*, Computertechnologie *f.*

computer vision computergestützte Bildverarbeitung *f.*

computer word Maschinenwort *n.*

computerized monitoring automatische Überwachung *f.*

computerized ordering automatisches Bestellwesen *n.*

computerized thesaurus elektronischer Thesaurus *m.*

computerized translation maschinelle Übersetzung *f.*

computerized typesetting Computersatz *m.*

computerized updating auto-

matische Aktualisierung *f.*

concealed classification verborgene Klassifikation *f.*

concentration Konzentration *f.*

concentration ratio Konzentrationsquote *f.*

concentrator Konzentrator *m.*

concept Begriff *m.*

concept analysis Begriffsanalyse *f.*

concept array Begriffsreihe *f.*

concept chain Begriffsleiter *f.*

concept-coordinate index gleichordnendes Register *n.*

concept coordination Begriffskoordination *f.*, Gleichordnung *f.* von Begriffen

concept definition Begriffsdefinition *f.*

concept indexing begriffsorientierte Indexierung *f.*

concept organization Begriffseinteilung *f.*

concept relation Begriffsrelation *f.*

conception Vorstellung *f.*, Auffassung *f.*

conceptual analysis Begriffsanalyse *f.*

conceptual method begriffliches Verfahren *n.*

conceptual representation begriffliche Darstellung *f.*

concertina fold Harmonikafalz *m.*, Leporellofalz *m.*, Zickzackfalz *m.*

concise dictionary Handwörterbuch *n.*

conclusion Schlußfolgerung *f.*, Zusammenfassung *f.*

concomitant begleitend *adj.*, zusammengehend *adj.*

concord Vereinbarung f., Abkommen n.
concordance Konkordanz f.
concrete concept konkreter Begriff m.
condensation Verdichtung f.
condensed book Buch n. in Kurzfassung
condensed edition Kurzausgabe f.
condition Erhaltungszustand m.
conditional branch bedingte Verzweigung f.
conditional instruction bedingter Befehl m.
conditional jump bedingte Verzweigung f.
conference Konferenz f., Tagung f.
conference paper Konferenzbeitrag m., Vortrag m., Tagungsbeitrag m.
conference proceedings Tagungsbericht m.
confession magazine Konfessionsmagazin n.
confidential documents vertrauliche Dokumente pl.
confidential file vertrauliche Dokumente pl.
configuration Konfiguration f.
conflation Verschmelzung f.
conformation Formgebung f., Gestaltung f.
congress Kongreß m., Tagung f.
congress report Kongreßausschußbericht m.
congressional committee report Kongreßausschußbericht n.
conjunction Konjunktion f.
conjunctive konjunktiv adj.

conjunctive search Recherche f. mit Booleschen Operatoren
connect time Anschaltzeit f., Verbindungszeit f.
connecting symbol Verbindungszeichen n.
connection Zusammenhang m.
connective catalog Katalog m. mit durch Verweise verbundenen Schlagwörtern, syndetischer Katalog m.
connective index Register n. mit durch Verweise verbundenen Schlagwörtern, syndetisches Register n.
connector Konnektor m.
connotation Nebenbedeutung f., Begriffsinhalt m.
connotative meaning konnotative Bedeutung f.
consensus übereinstimmende Meinung f.
conservatory Musikhochschule f.
conservatory library Musikhochschulbibliothek f.
consideration Berücksichtigung f.
consignment Ansichtssendung f.
consistency Konsistenz f.
consistency of indexing Indexierungskonsistenz f.
consistorial archive Konsistorialarchiv n.
console Bedienerplatz m.
consolidated index kumuliertes Register n.
consolidated information zusammengefaßte Information f.
constituent Bestandteil m., Zubehör n.
constituent term Bestandteil m.

einer Bezeichnung
constitution Verfassung *f.*
constitutional law Verfassungsrecht *n.*
constitutional state Rechtsstaat
m.
constraint Einschränkung *f.*,
Begrenzung *f.*
construction Erstellung *f.*
consultant Gutachter *m.*, Berater *m.*
consumer Verbraucher *m.*, Nutzer *m.*
consumer education Nutzerschulung *f.*
contact copy Kontaktkopie *f.*
contact librarian Verbindungsbibliothekar *m.*
contemporary history Zeitgeschichte *f.*
content Inhalt *m.*
content-addressable memory
Assoziativspeicher *m.*
content analysis Inhaltsanalyse
f.
content title inhaltsbeschreibender Titel *m.*
contents Inhalt *m.*, Inhaltsverzeichnis *n.*
contents card Übersichtszettel
m.
contents list Inhaltsverzeichnis
n.
contents list bulletin laufende
Zeitschrifteninhaltsübersicht *f.*
contents note Inhaltsangabe *f.*
contents page Seite *f.* des Inhaltsverzeichnises
contents sheet Seite *f.* des Inhaltsverzeichnises
context Kontext *m.*
context operator Kontextope-

rator *m.*
context-free grammer kontextfreie Grammatik *f.*
context-free term kontextfreier
Begriff *m.*
contextual definition Anwendungsdefinition *f.*, Gebrauchsdefinition *f.*
contingency Zufall *m.*, Zufälligkeit *f.*
contingency table Kontingenztabelle *f.*
contingent zufällig *adj.*
continuation Weiterführung *f.*,
Fortsetzung *f.*
continuation card Fortsetzungskarte *f.*
continuation list Fortsetzungsliste *f.*
continuation order fortlaufende
Bestellung *f.*
continuation record Fortsetzungskartei *f.*, Verzeichnis *n.*
der Fortsetzungswerke
continuation register Verzeichnis *n.* der Fortsetzungswerke
continuation volume Fortsetzungsband *m.*
continuations Folgen *pl.*, Reihenwerke *pl.*
continuations check-list Verzeichnis *n.* der Reihenwerke
continuing education Weiterbildung *f.*
continuous kontinuierlich *adj.*
continuous form Endlosformular *n.*
continuous pagination durchlaufende Numerierung *f.*
continuous text Fließtext *m.*
contract Vertrag *m.*
contribution Beitrag *m.*, Zu-

schuß *m.*
contribution to a discussion
Diskussionsbeitrag *m.*
contributor Mitarbeiter *m.*
control Steuerung *f.*
control character Steuerzeichen
n.
control code Prüfcode *m.*
control function Kontrollfunktion *f.*
control group Kontrollgruppe *f.*
control number Prüfziffer *f.*
control operation Kontrollfunktion *f.*
control panel Konsole *f.*,
Schalttafel *f.*
control register Steuerbefehlsregister *n.*
control sequence Befehlsfolge
f., Programmablauf *m.*
control symbol Steuerzeichen *n.*
control system Steuersystem *n.*
control transfer instruction
Sprungbefehl *m.*
control unit Steuereinheit *f.*
controlled circulation kontrollierte Ausleihe *f.*
controlled circulation journal
Zeitschrift *f.* mit kontrollierter
Auflage
controlled index Register *n.* mit
kontrolliertem Vokabular
controlled index term kontrolliertes Schlagwort *n.*
controlled indexing Indexierung *f.* mit kontrolliertem Vokabular
controlled term list kontrollierte Schlagwortliste *f.*
controlled vocabulary kontrolliertes Vokabular *n.*
controlling body Führungs-

gremium *n.*
controversial kontrovers *adj.*
controversial material umstrittenes Material *n.*
convention Konvention *f.*
conventional konventionell *adj.*
conventional cataloging konventionelle Katalogisierung *f.*
conventional meaning konventionalisierte Bedeutung *f.*
conventional sign konventionalisiertes Zeichen *n.*
conventional title Sammeltitel
m.
conventional titles heading
Schlagwort *n.* für Sammeltitel
convergence Annäherungstendenz *f.*
convergency theory Konvergenztheorie *f.*
conversation Gespräch *n.*
conversational flow Gesprächsfluß *m.*
conversational language Dialogsprache *f.*
conversion Konvertierung *f.*
conversion of information Datenkonvertierung *f.*, Datenumsetzung *f.*
conversion program Konvertierungsprogramm *n.*
convert/to konvertieren *vrb.*
converter Konverter *m.*, Umsetzer *m.*
conveyer Fließband *n.*
conveyer belt Förderband *n.*
cooccurrance paralleles Vorkommen *n.*
cookery book Kochbuch *n.*
cooperation Zusammenarbeit
f., Kooperation *f.*
cooperation agreement Koope-

rationsvereinbarung *f.*
cooperative genossenschaftlich *adj.*
cooperative acquisition gemeinsame Erwerbung *f.*
cooperative association Genossenschaft *f.*
cooperative cataloging gemeinsame Katalogisierung *f.*, Katalogisierungsverbund *m.*
cooperative cataloging system Katalogisierungsverbundsystem *n.*
cooperative movement library Genossenschaftsbibliothek *f.*
coordinate classes gleichgeordnete Klassen *pl.*
coordinate index gleichordnendes Register *n.*
coordinate indexing gleichordnende Indexierung *f.*
coordinate relation Gleichordnungsbeziehung *f.*
coordinates Koordinaten *pl.*
coordination Gleichordnung *f.*, Koordinierung *f.*
copier Kopiergerät *n.*
copy Abschrift *f.*, Abzug *m.*, Exemplar *n.*, Kopie *f.*, Druckvorlage *f.*, Manuskript *n.*
copy/to abbilden *vrb.*, ablichten *vrb.*, abzeichnen *vrb.*, abschreiben *vrb.*, kopieren *vrb.*
copy card Kopierkarte *f.*
copy cataloging Fremddatenübernahme *f.*, Fremdkatalogisierung *f.*
copy deadline Redaktionsschluß *m.*
copy letter Exemplarsignatur *f.*
copy machine Kopiergerät *n.*
copy reader Korrektor *m.*

copy service Kopierdienst *m.*
copy slip Laufzettel *m.*
copying technology Kopiertechnik *f.*
copyist Kopist *m.*
copyright Urheberrecht *n.*
copyright date Datum *n.* des Urheberrechts
copyright duration Schutzfrist *f.*
copyright library Pflichtexemplarbibliothek *f.*
copyright of a title Titelschutz *m.*
core book Basiswerk *n.*
core collection Kernbestand *m.*
core document Kerndokument *n.*
core library Kernbibliothek *f.*
core memory Hauptspeicher *m.*
core publication Kernveröffentlichung *f.*
corporate author Mitautor *m.*, Koautor *m.*
corporate body Körperschaft *f.*
corporate entry Körperschaftseintrag *m.*
corporate heading Körperschaftseintrag *m.*
corporate periodical Firmenzeitschrift *f.*
corpus Textsammlung *f.*, Korpus *m.*
correct fehlerfrei *adj.*
correct/to berichtigen *vrb.*, verbessern *vrb.*
correct/to proofs Korrektur lesen *vrb.*
correct spelling Rechtschreibung *f.*
correctional institution library Bibliothek *f.* einer Besserungs-

anstalt

corrector Korrektor *m.*
correlation Korrelation *f.*
correlation coefficient Korrelationskoeffizient *m.*
correlation table Korrelationstabelle *f.*
correlative korrelativ *adj.*
correlative index korrelatives Register *n.*
correlative indexing korrelative Indexierung *f.*
correspondence Briefwechsel *m.*
correspondence course Fernstudium *n.*
correspondence lesson Lehrbrief *m.*
correspondent Zeitungskorrespondent *m.*
corrigenda Druckfehlerberichtigung *f.*
cosine Kosinus *m.*
cost Kosten *pl.*
cost-benefit analysis Kosten-Nutzen-Analyse *f.*
cost covering Kostendeckung *f.*
cost-effectiveness analysis Kosten-Leistungsanalyse *f.*
cost evaluation Kostenbewertung *f.*
cost sensitivity Kostensensitivität *f.*
cost sensitivity analysis Kostensensitivitätsanalyse *f.*
Council of Ministers Ministerrat *m.*
country authority file Ländernormdatei *f.*
country circulation auswärtiger Leihverkehr *m.*
country lending auswärtiger Leihverkehr *m.*
country of publication Erscheinungsland *n.*
country planning Landesplanung *f.*
county Landkreis *m.*
county archive Bezirksarchiv *n.*, Kreisarchiv *n.*
county board Kreistag *m.*
county court Kreisgericht *n.*
county hospital Kreiskrankenhaus *n.*
county law library Bezirksrechtsbibliothek *f.*
county library Bezirksbibliothek *f.*, Kreisbibliothek *f.*
county supplement library Kreisergänzungsbücherei *f.*
coupon Gutschein *m.*
course Lehrgang *m.*, Kurs *m.*
court library Hofbibliothek *f.*, Gerichtsbibliothek *f.*, Hofbibliothek *f.*
cover Bucheinband *m.*, Abdeckung *f.*, Umschlag *m.*
cover/to abdecken *vrb.*
cover picture Umschlagbild *n.*
cover title Umschlagtitel *m.*
coverage Berichterstattung *f.*, inhaltliche Abdeckung *f.*, Dokumentationsbereich *m.*, Abdeckung *f.*
coverage of demand Bedarfsdeckung *f.*
coverage ratio Abdeckungsquote *f.*
crash Absturz *m.*
crash recovery Wiederanlauf *m.*
creator Schöpfer *m.*
credit Gutschrift *f.*
credit system Kreditwesen *n.*
criminal law Strafrecht *n.*

criminalistics Kriminalistik *f.*
criterion Kriterium *n.*
critic Kritiker *m.*, Rezensent *m.*
critical bibliography kritische
Bibliographie *f.*
critical indexing kritische Indexierung *f.*
critical reading kritisches Lesen
n.
critical review Rezension *f.*, Besprechung *f.*
criticism Kritik *f.*, Rezension *f.*
cross catalog Kreuzkatalog *m.*
cross classification Mehrfacheinordnung *f.* einer Klasse
cross compiler Cross-Compiler
m.
cross-file searching datenbankübergreifende Recherche *f.*
cross head Zwischenüberschrift
f.
cross out/to ausstreichen *vrb.*,
annullieren *vrb.*, durchstreichen *vrb.*
cross reference Verweis *m.*
cross word Kreuzworträtsel *n.*
CRT terminal Bildschirm *m.*
crumpled zerknüllt *adj.*, zerknittert *adj.*
cryptography Kryptographie *f.*
cubicle Arbeitsnische *f.*
cue word Stichwort *n.*
cultural agreement Kulturabkommen *n.*
cultural assets Kulturgut *n.*
cultural center Kulturzentrum
n.
cultural pattern Kulturform *f.*
cultural policy Kulturpolitik *f.*
cultural work Kulturarbeit *f.*
cumulate/to kumulieren *vrb.*
cumulation Kumulation *f.*

cumulative kumulierend *adj.*
cumulative bibliography kumulative Bibliographie *f.*
cumulative book index kumuliertes Bücherverzeichnis *n.*
cumulative book list kumuliertes Bücherverzeichnis *n.*
cumulative catalog kumulierter
Katalog *m.*, Gesamtkatalog
m.
cumulative index kumuliertes
Register *n.*
cumulative volume bandweise
Kumulierung *f.*
currency Währung *f.*
current awareness bulletin
Schnellinformationsdienst *m.*
current awareness service
Schnelldienst *m.*, Schnellinformationsdienst *m.*
current bibliography laufende
Bibliographie *f.*
current contents bulletin laufende Zeitschriftinhaltsüber-
sicht *f.*
current contents service Zeitschrifteninhaltsdienst *m.*
current national bibliography
laufende Nationalbibliographie *f.*
current number laufende Nummer *f.*
current publication survey
Überwachung *f.* der laufenden
Veröffentlichungen
curriculum Lehrplan *m.*, Studienplan *m.*
cursor Cursor *m.*, Schreibmarke *f.*
curves Klammern *pl.*
customer Kunde *m.*
customer number Nutzerken-

nung *f*.
cut in note Anmerkung *f*.
cutter classification Cutter-
  Klassifikation *f*., Expansivklassifikation *f*.
cutter number Cutter-Notation
  f.

cutter table Cutter-Tafel *f*.
cutting Zeitungsausschnitt *m*.
cybernetics Kybernetik *f*.
cycle time Zykluszeit *f*.
cyclic index permutiertes Register *n*.
cyclopaedia Enzyklopädie *f*.

D

daily täglich *adj*.
daily entering-up tägliche Eintragung *f*.
daily newspaper Tageszeitung
  f.
daily paper Tageszeitung *f*.
daisywheel printer Typenraddrucker *m*.
damaged letter beschädigter
  Buchstabe *m*.
damp Feuchtigkeit *f*.
damp-spotted wasserfleckig
  adj.
damp stains Wasserflecken *pl*.
dash Gedankenstrich *m*.
data Daten *pl*.
data acquisition Datenerfassung *f*.
data analysis Datenanalyse *f*.
data bank Datenbank *f*.
data bus Datenbus *m*.
data capture Datenerfassung *f*.
data capture terminal Datenerfassungsgerät *n*.
data carrier Datenträger *m*.

data cell Datenzelle *f*.
data center Datenzentrum *n*.
data code Datencode *m*.
data collection Datenerfassung
  f.
data collection system Datensammelsystem *n*.
data communication Datenkommunikation *f*., Datenaustausch *m*., Datenübertragung
  f.
data compilation Datenzusammenstellung *f*.
data compression Datenverdichtung *f*.
data conversion Datenkonversion *f*., Datenumsetzung *f*.
data converter Datenumsetzer
  m.
data cut-off Datenausschluß *m*.
data definition language Datendefinitionssprache *f*.
data description language Datenbeschreibungssprache *f*.
data dictionary Datenbeschrei-

bungskatalog *m.*, Datenverzeichnis *n.*, Feldnamenerklärung *f.*
data display Datenanzeige *f.*
data documentation Datendokumentation *f.*
data editing Datenaufbereitung
f.
data element Datenelement *n.*
data encryption Datenverschlüsselung *f.*
data entry Dateneingabe *f.*,
Dateneintrag *m.*, Daten-
erfassung *f.*
data entry of documents Dokumenterfassung *f.*
data evaluation Datenbewertung *f.*
data field Datenfeld *n.*
data file Datenbestand *m.*
data files Datendateien *pl.*
data flow Datenfluß *m.*
data flowchart Datenflußplan
m.
data flowdiagram Datenflußplan *m.*
data format Datenformat *n.*
data gathering Datenerfassung
f.
data hierarchy Datenhierarchie
f.
data independence Datenunabhängigkeit *f.*
data input Dateneingabe *f.*
data input sheet Datenerfassungsblatt *n.*
data inquiry Datenabfrage *f.*
data integrity Datensicherheit
f., Datenintegrität *f.*
data link escape character Da-
tenübertragungsumschalt-
zeichen *n.*

data management system Datenverwaltungssystem *n.*
data manipulation language
Datenmanipulationssprache *f.*
data medium Datenträger *m.*
data models Datenmodelle *pl.*
data multiplexer Datenmultiplexer *m.*
data network Datennetz *n.*
data object Datenobjekt *n.*
data organization Datenorganisation *f.*
data output Datenausgabe *f.*
data overrun Datenverlust *m.*
data ownership Dateneigentumsrechte *pl.*
data preparation Datenvorbereitung *f.*
data processing Datenverarbeitung *f.*
data processing center Rechenzentrum *n.*
data processing equipment
Datenverarbeitungsanlage *f.*
data processing machine Datenverarbeitungsanlage *f.*
data processing network Datenverarbeitungsnetz *n.*
data processing system Datenverarbeitungssystem *n.*
data processor Prozessor *m.*
data protection Datenschutz *m.*
data quality Datenqualität *f.*
data queue Datenwarteschlange *f.*
data record Datensatz *m.*
data reduction Datenverdichtung *f.*
data representation Datenrepräsentation *f.*
data retrieval Datenretrieval *n.*
data security Datensicherheit *f.*

data set geordnete Datenmenge *f.*, Datei *f.*

data set identifier Dateikennzeichen *n.*

data signaling rate Übertragungsgeschwindigkeit *f.*

data sink Datensenke *f.*

data source Datenquelle *f.*

data standard Datennorm *f.*

data station Datenstation *f.*

data storage Datenspeicher *m.*

data storage and retrieval system Datenspeicher- und Retrievalsystem *n.*

data storage unit Datenspeichereinheit *f.*

data stream Datenstrom *m.*

data structure Datenstruktur *f.*

data table Datentabelle *f.*

data terminal Datenstation *f.*, Datenendeinrichtung *f.*

data track Datenspur *f.*

data traffic Datenverkehr *m.*

data transfer Datenübertragung *f.*

data transfer rate Datenübertragungsrate *f.*

data transformation Datenumsetzung *f.*

data transmission Datenübertragung *f.*

data transmission block Datenübertragungsblock *m.*

data unit Dateneinheit *f.*

database Datenbank *f.*, Datenbasis *f.*

database access Datenbankzugriff *m.*

database computer Datenbankmaschine *f.*

database description Datenbankbeschreibung *f.*

database design Datenbankaufbau *m.*, Datenbankentwurf *m.*

database directory Datenbankverzeichnis *n.*

database inquiry Datenbankrecherche *f.*

database integrity Datenbankintegrität *f.*

database language Datenbanksprache *f.*

database machine Datenbankmaschine *f.*

database management system Datenbankmanagementsystem *n.*

database model Datenbankmodell *n.*

database network Datenbanknetzwerk *n.*

database producer Datenbankproduzent *m.*

database recovery Datenbankwiederherstellung *f.*

database selection Datenbankauswahl *f.*

database system Datenbanksystem *n.*

database vendor Datenbankanbieter *m.*

date due Ablauftermin *m.*, Rückgabetermin *m.*

date field Datumsfeld *n.*

date file Fristkartei *f.*

date guide Leitkarte *f.* in der Fristkartei

date key Terminierungsschlüssel *m.*

date label Fristzettel *m.*, Friststreifen *m.*

date of borrowing Ausleihdatum *n.*

date of entry Eingangsdatum *n.*
date of issue Ausgabedatum *n.*, Entleihdatum *n.*
date of printing Druckjahr *n.*
date of publication Veröffentlichungsdatum *n.*
date of receipt Eingangsdatum *n.*
date of return Rückgabedatum *n.*
date record Fristkartei *f.*
date schedule Terminplan *m.*
date slip Fristzettel *m.*, Friststreifen *m.*
date stamp Datumsstempel *m.*
dating Datierung *f.*
day book Tagebuch *n.*
deacquisition Aussonderung *f.*
dead key Tottaste *f.*
dead letter unzustellbarer Brief *m.*, toter Buchstabe *m.*
deadline Abgabefrist *f.*, Termin *m.*, Frist *f.*
deadlock Stillstand *m.* im Funktionsablauf
dealer Buchhändler *m.*
debit Soll *n.*
debug/to austesten *vrb.*, Fehler beseitigen *vrb.*
debugging Fehlerbeseitigung *f.*, Programmkorrektur *f.*
debugging run Testlauf *m.*
decay/to zerfallen *vrb.*
decentralization Dezentralisierung *f.*
decimal classification Dezimalklassifikation *f.*
decimal digit Dezimalziffer *f.*
decimal division Dezimalunterteilung *f.*
decimal fraction notation Dezimalbruchnotation *f.*

decimal notation Dezimalnotation *f.*
decimal number Dezimalzahl *f.*
decimal numeral dezimales Numeral *n.*
decimal numeration dezimale Numerierung *f.*
decimal point Dezimalpunkt *m.*, Dezimalkomma *n.*
decision Entscheidung *f.*, Beschluß *m.*
decision analysis Entscheidungsanalyse *f.*
decision making Entscheidungsprozeß *m.*
decision support Entscheidungshilfe *f.*
decision support system entscheidungsunterstützendes System *n.*
decision table Entscheidungstabelle *f.*
decision trees Entscheidungsbäume *pl.*
deck Büchergeschoß *n.*, Stapel *m.*, Magazinebene *f.*
deckle edge Büttenrand *m.*
declaration Vereinbarung *f.*, Erklärung *f.*
declassify/to freigeben *vrb.*
declination Deklination *f.*
decode/to entschlüsseln *vrb.*
decoder Decoder *m.*, Entschlüßler *m.*
decoding Entschlüsselung *f.*, Decodierung *f.*
decreasing concreteness abnehmende Konkretheit *f.*
decreasing extension abnehmender Umfang *m.*
decree Verordnung *f.*, Erlaß *m.*
dedicated line Standleitung *f.*

dedication Widmung *f*.
dedication copy Widmungsexemplar *n*.
deduction Deduktion *f*.
deductive text analysis deduktive Textanalyse *f*.
deduping Dublettenbereinigung
f.
deed Akte *f*.
deep indexing tiefes Indexieren
n., ausführliches Indexieren *n*.
deep structure Tiefenstruktur *f*.
default format Standardformat
n.
defaulter säumiger Bibliotheksbenutzer *m*.
defective defekt *adj*., unvollständig *adj*.
defective copy defektes Exemplar *n*., unvollständiges Exemplar *n*.
defendant Verteidiger *m*.
definition Abgrenzung *f*., Definition *f*., Begriffsbestimmung
f.
definition by context Anwendungsdefinition *f*., Gebrauchsdefinition *f*.
definition by extension Umfangsdefinition *f*.
**definition by genus and diffe-
rence** Inhaltsdefinition *f*.
definition by genus and species
Inhaltsdefinition *f*.
definition by intension Inhaltsdefinition *f*.
definitive edition endgültige
Ausgabe *f*.
definitive relation Definitionsbeziehung *f*.
definor Begriffseinschränkung
f.

del Löschzeichen *n*.
delay line storage Laufzeitspeicher *m*.
delayed search technique Methode *f*. der verzögerten Suche
delete/to streichen *vrb*., löschen
vrb.
delete character Löschzeichen
n.
delete key Löschtaste *f*.
deletion character Löschzeichen
n.
deletion mark Tilgungszeichen
n.
deletion record Ersatzregister
n.
delimitation Abgrenzung *f*.
delimiter Trennzeichen *n*.
delimiter character Begrenzungszeichen *n*.
delimiter key Kennzeichentaste
f.
deliver/to abgeben *vrb*., ausliefern *vrb*.
delivery Zustellung *f*., Übergabe
f., Abgabe *f*., Lieferung *f*., Sendung *f*., Versand *m*.
delivery contract Liefervertrag
m.
delivery date Lieferdatum *n*.
delivery desk Bücherausgabetheke *f*.
delivery fee Zustellgebühr *f*.
delivery obligation Ablieferungspflicht *f*.
delivery of documents Dokumentauslieferung *f*.
delivery room Ausleihe *f*., Leihstelle *f*., Bücherausgabestelle *f*.
delivery service Zustelldienst *m*.
demand-distributed collection
nach Bedarf *m*. verteilter Be-

stand
demand for employees Arbeitskräftebedarf *m.*
demand study Bedarfsuntersuchung *f.*
demography Demographie f.
demonstration Vorführung *f.*
denominational public library konfessionelle öffentliche Bücherei *f.*
denotation Begriffsumfang *m.*
denotative meaning denotative Bedeutung *f.*
density Dichte *f.*, Schreibdichte *f.*
density of use ranking Benutzungshäufigkeitsrangliste *f.*
dental library zahnmedizinische Bibliothek *f.*
department Fachbereich *m.*, Abteilung *f.*
department library Fachbereichsbibliothek *f.*, Institutsbibliothek *f.*
department of printed books Druckschriftenabteilung *f.*
departmental section Fachreferat *n.*
dependency grammar Dependenzgrammatik *f.*
dependent auxiliary unselbständige Ergänzungszahl *f.*
dependent facet abhängige Facette *f.*
deposit Kaution *f.*, Dauerleihgabe *f.*
deposit/to hinterlegen *vrb.*
deposit collection Depotsammlung *f.*
deposit copy Freiexemplar *n.*, Pflichtexemplar *n.*
deposit library Depotbibliothek *f.*
deposit loan Dauerleihgabe *f.*
deposit slip Einzahlungsbeleg *m.*
deposit station Nebenstelle *f.* einer Bücherei, Stützpunktbücherei *f.*
depository library Archivbibliothek *f.*, Pflichtexemplarbibliothek *f.*, Depotbibliothek *f.*
deprecated term nichtzugelassene Bezeichnung *f.*
depth interview Tiefeninterview *n.*
depth of analysis Analysetiefe *f.*
depth of indexing Indexierungstiefe *f.*, Indexierungsgenauigkeit *f.*
deputy librarian stellvertretender Bibliothekar *m.*
derivative Ableitung *f.*
derived cataloging Fremdkatalogisierung *f.*
derived word abgeleitetes Wort *n.*
descending figure tiefstehende Ziffer *f.*
description Beschreibung *f.*, Katalogaufnahme *f.*, Titelaufnahme *f.*
description of invention Erfindungsbeschreibung *f.*
descriptive abstract deskriptives Referat *n.*
descriptive bibliography deskriptive Bibliographie *f.*
descriptive catalog Formalkatalog *m.*
descriptive cataloging Formalkatalogisierung *f.*, alphabetische Katalogisierung *f.*
descriptive cataloging rules

Titelaufnahmeregeln *pl.*, Regeln *pl.* für die formale Erfassung, Regeln *pl.* zur alphabetischen Katalogisierung
descriptive entry Titelaufnahme *f.*
descriptive statistics beschreibende Statistik *f.*
descriptor Schlagwort *n.*, Deskriptor *m.*
descriptor association list Deskriptorenassoziationsliste *f.*
descriptor authority file Schlagwortnormdatei *f.*
descriptor authority list Standardschlagwortliste *f.*
descriptor language Deskriptorensprache *f.*
descriptor network Deskriptorennetzwerk *n.*
descriptor term Deskriptor *m.*
desiderata Desiderate *pl.*
desiderata book Desiderienbuch *n.*
desiderata list Desiderienliste *f.*
design Entwurf *m.*
designation Bezeichnung *f.*
designation of function Funktionsbezeichnung *f.*
desk Schreibtisch *m.*
desktop computer Arbeitsplatzrechner *m.*
desktop publishing Desktop Publishing *n.*
destructive read löschendes Lesen *n.*
detailed design detaillierter Entwurf *m.*
determinant Determinante *f.*
deterministic deterministisch *adj.*
detour Umweg *m.*

development Entwicklung *f.*
development department Entwicklungsabteilung *f.*
development program Entwicklungsplan *m.*
development system Entwicklungssystem *n.*
device control character Gerätesteuerzeichen *n.*
Dewey decimal classification Dewey-Dezimalklassifikation *f.*
diacritical marks diakritische Zeichen *pl.*
diacritical points diakritische Zeichen *pl.*
diagnostic program Diagnoseprogramm *n.*
diagonal slash Schrägstrich *m.*
diagram Diagramm *n.*, Schaubild *n.*
dial access telefonischer Zugang *m.*
dial-up/to wählen *vrb.*
dial-up line Wählleitung *f.*
dialect Dialekt *m.*, Idiom *n.*
dialog Dialog *m.*
dialog language Dialogsprache *f.*
dialog mode Dialogmodus *m.*
dialog system Dialogsystem *n.*
diary Tagebuch *n.*
diazo microform Diazomikrofiche *m.*
dichotomize/to binär klassifizieren *vrb.*
dichotomized classification Binärklassifikation *f.*
dichotomous division dichotomische Einteilung *f.*
dichotomy Dichotomie *f.*
dictionary Wörterbuch *n.*

dictionary catalog Kreuzkatalog *m*.
dictionary database Wörterbuchdatenbank *f*.
dictionary index Wörterbuchverzeichnis *n*.
dictionary of descriptors Thesaurus *m*.
dictionary of foreign terms Fremdwörterbuch *n*.
dictionary word lexikographisches Wort *n*.
didactics Didaktik *f*.
Diethelm classification Diethelm-Klassifikation *f*.
difference Untergliederungsgesichtspunkt *m*., Unterteilungsgesichtspunkt *m*., Unterschied *m*.
differential analyzer Analogrechner *m*.
differential facet Unterscheidungsfacette *f*.
differentiation logische Unterteilung *f*.
diffuse gestreut *adj*., verstreut *adj*.
diffuse/to diffundieren *vrb*., zerstreuen *vrb*.
diffusion of innovation Verbreitung *f*. einer Innovation
diffusion transfer process Diffusionsverfahren *n*.
digest Auswahl *f*., Abriß *m*., Überblick *m*.
digit Ziffer *f*.
digit character Ziffernzeichen *n*.
digit error Zeichenfehler *m*.
digit key Zifferntaste *f*.
digit number Zahl *f*.
digit place Zifffernstelle *f*.
digital digital *adj*.

digital computer Digitalrechner *m*.
digital data Digitaldaten *pl*.
digital data processing system digitales Datenverarbeitungssystem *n*.
digital data transmission digitale Datenübermittlung *f*.
digital differential analyser Digital-Differentialanalysator *m*.
digital network digitales Netzwerk *n*.
digital notation Ziffernnotation *f*.
digital optical disk optische Speicherplatte *f*.
digital output control Digitalausgabesteuerung *f*.
digital recording digitale Aufnahme *f*.
digital representation digitale Darstellung *f*.
digital search tree digitaler Suchbaum *m*.
digital signal digitales Signal *n*.
digitize/to digitalisieren *vrb*.
dimension Dimension *f*.
dimensional relation Dimensionsrelation *f*.
dimensionality Dimensionalität *f*.
diocesan archive Diözesanarchiv *n*.
diocesan library Diözesanbibliothek *f*.
diorama Diorama *n*.
diploma Diplom *n*.
diploma examination Diplomexamen *n*., Diplomprüfung *f*.
diplomatics Urkundenlehre *f*.
diptych Diptychon *n*.

direct access Direktzugriff *m.*
direct access storage Direktzugriffsspeicher *m.*
direct address direkte Adresse *f.*, direkte Adressierung *f.*
direct application Direktbestellung *f.*
direct code Direktschlüssel *m.*
direct communication direkte Kommunikation *f.*
direct cost Einzelkosten *pl.*
direct cost analysis Einzelkostenanalyse *f.*
direct documentation direkte Dokumentation *f.*
direct file direkte Datei *f.*, gestreute Datei *f.*
direct file organization direkte Dateiorganisation *f.*, gestreute Dateiorganisation *f.*
direct input Direkteingabe *f.*
direct lending Direktausleihe *f.*
direct positive Direktpositiv *n.*
direct recording Direktaufnahme *f.*
direction for use Gebrauchsanweisung *f.*
director of library Bibliotheksdirektor *m.*
directory Verzeichnis *n.*, Adreßbuch *n.*
directory entry Verzeichniseintrag *m.*
directory file Verzeichnisdatei *f.*
dirty data fehlerhafte Daten *pl.*
disambiguation Disambiguierung *f.*, Vereindeutigung *f.*
disassemble/to abbauen *vrb.*
discard/to ausrangieren *vrb.*, ausscheiden *vrb.*
discards Ausschuß *m.*, Makulatur *f.*

discharge Entladung *f.*
discharge/to books die Ausleihe zurückbuchen *vrb.*, die Buchung löschen *vrb.*, die Buchung austragen *vrb.*
discharging desk Bücherausgabetheke *f.*
discipline Disziplin *f.*
discography Schallplattenverzeichnis *n.*
disconnect/to abschalten *vrb.*
disconnection Verbindungsabbruch *m.*
discontinuance Abbruch *m.*
discontinue/to a subscription ein Abonnement abbestellen *vrb.*
discontinue notice Kündigung *f.* eines Abonnements
discount Abzug *m.*, Rabatt *m.*
discrete diskret *adj.*
discrete data digitale Daten *pl.*
discrete representation diskrete Darstellung *f.*
discrete signal digitales Signal *n.*
discrete universe selbständiges Universum *n.*
discriminant Diskriminante *f.*
discriminant analysis Diskriminanzanalyse *f.*
discriminant function Diskriminanzfunktion *f.*
discrimination value Diskriminanzwert *m.*
discussible diskutabel *adj.*
discussion Diskussion *f.*
discussion participant Diskussionsteilnehmer *m.*
disjunction Disjunktion *f.*, ODER-Verknüpfung *f.*
disk Platte *f.*, Magnetplatte *f.*

disk address Plattenadresse f.
disk allocation Magnetplattenzuordnung f.
disk cartridge Plattenkasette f.
disk checking Plattenprüfung f.
disk controller Plattensteuereinheit f.
disk drive Plattenlaufwerk n.
disk error Plattenfehler m.
disk file Plattendatei f., Plattenspeicher m.
disk file name Plattendateiname m.
disk pack Plattenstapel m.
disk storage Plattenspeicher m.
diskette Diskette f.
diskette drawer Diskettenschublade f.
diskette drive Diskettenlaufwerk n.
diskette envelope Diskettenschutzhülle f.
diskette input device Diskettenleser m.
diskette interchangeability Diskettenaustauschbarkeit f.
diskette patch Diskettenänderungsprogramm n.
dislocation Versetzung f.
dismantle/to abbauen vrb.
dispatch/to abfertigen vrb.
displacement Umwandlung f.,
Verschiebung f.
display Anzeige f., Datensichtgerät n., Bildschirmeinheit f.
display/to anzeigen vrb.
display device Sichtgerät n.,
Anzeigegerät n.
display field Anzeigefeld n.
display format Bildschirmformat n.
display screen Bildschirm m.,

Datensichtgerät n.
display stand Aufstellplatz m.
display technique Ausgabetechnik f.
display unit Ausgabegerät n.
display work Akzidenzdruck m.
disposal Ausscheiden n.
dispose/to ausscheiden vrb.,
ausrangieren vrb.
dissemination of information
Verteilung f. von Informationen
dissemination of knowledge
Wissensvermittlung f.
dissemination service Verteildienst m.
dissertation Dissertation f.,
Doktorarbeit f.
dissipation Verzettelung f.
distance education Fernstudium n.
distinct klar adj.
distributed data processing verteilte Datenverarbeitung f.
distributed database verteilte
Datenbank f.
distributed system verteiltes
System n.
distribution Verteilung f., Zusendung f.
distribution curve Verteilungskurve f.
district Stadtbezirk m., Landkreis m.
district authority Kreisverwaltung f.
district library Bezirksbücherei
f., Bezirksbibliothek f., Stadtbezirksbibliothek f.
divide/to a word ein Wort trennen vrb.
divided catalog Einzelkatalog m.

division Sektion *f.*
division by date chronologische
Einteilung *f.*
division head Abteilungsleiter
m.
divisional librarian Abteilungsleiter *m.*
divisional library Abteilungsbibliothek *f.*
doctoral dissertation Dissertation *f.*, Doktorarbeit *f.*
document Urkunde *f.*, Dokument *n.*, Schriftstück *n.*
document/to dokumentieren
vrb.
document analysis Dokumentanalyse *f.*
document center Dokumentationsstelle *f.*
document classification Dokumentklassierung *f.*
document cluster Dokumentcluster *n.*
document collection Doku-
mentbestand *m.*, Urkundenbestand *m.*
document copying Kopierverfahren *n.*
document cover Aktendeckel *m.*
document date Dokumentda-
tum *n.*
document delivery Dokumentlieferung *f.*
document description Dokumentbeschreibung *f.*
document directory Dokumentenverzeichnis *n.*
document distribution Dokumentverteilung *f.*
document entry Dokumenteintrag *m.*
document error Dokumentfeh-

ler *m.*
document examination Dokumentprüfung *f.*
document exchange Doku-
mentaustausch *m.*
document filing Dokumentablage *f.*
document flow Dokumentfluß
m.
document frequency Doku-
menthäufigkeit *f.*
document handling system Dokumentenverarbeitungssystem
n.
document identification Dokumentnachweise *m.*
document index Dokumentenverzeichnis *n.*
document modification Dokumentmodifizierung *f.*
document name Dokument-
name *m.*
document number Dokument-
nummer *f.*, Exemplarnummer
f.
document originator Doku-
menturheber *m.*
document output Dokument-
ausgabe *f.*
document owner Dokument-
besitzer *m.*
document processing Doku-
mentverarbeitung *f.*
document profile Dokumentprofil *n.*
document ranking Dokumentrangreihung *f.*
document restauration Urkundenrestaurierung *f.*
document retrieval Dokumentretrieval *n.*
document space Dokumenten-

raum *m.*
document storage Dokumentenspeicher *m.*
document storage file Dokumentspeicherdatei *f.*
document supply Literaturversorgung *f.*
document type Dokumentart *f.*
documentalist Dokumentar *m.*
documentalists conference Dokumentartag *m.*
documentary dokumentarisch *adj.*
documentary classification dokumentarische Klassifikation *f.*
documentary film Dokumentarfilm *m.*
documentary language Dokumentationssprache *f.*
documentary photograph Dokumentaraufnahme *f.*
documentary play Dokumentarstück *n.*
documentary unit dokumentarische Bezugseinheit *f.*, Dokumentationseinheit *f.*
documentation Dokumentationswesen *n.*, Dokumentation *f.*
documentation center Dokumentationszentrum *n.*, Dokumentationsstelle *f.*
documentation department Dokumentationseinrichtung *f.*
documentation file Dokumentationsdatei *f.*
documentation language Dokumentationssprache *f.*
documentation methodology Dokumentationsmethodik *f.*
documentation of institutions

Institutionendokumentation *f.*
documentation relevancy Dokumentationswürdigkeit *f.*
documentation system Dokumentationssystem *n.*
documentation technique Dokumentationsverfahren *n.*
documents Schriftgut *n.*
docuterm Deskriptor *m.* mit Rollenindikator
dodger Handzettel *m.*
dog´s ear Eselsohr *n.*
domestic trade Binnenhandel *m.*
donation Geschenk *n.*, Schenkung *f.*
donation book Spendenverzeichnis *n.*
donor Schenker *m.*, Stifter *m.*
door label Türschild *n.*
dossier Akte *f.*
dotted line punktierte Linie *f.*
double entry Doppeleintrag *m.*
double-faced shelf freistehendes Bücherregal *n.*
double-layered zweischichtig *adj.*
double register doppeltes Merkband *n.*
double-row coding mehrreihige Kerblochmarkierung *f.*
double-tracked zweigleisig *adj.*
doubtful authorship zweifelhafte Autorenschaft *f.*
doubtful ownership zweifelhaftes Eigentum *n.*
downgrade/to teilweise freigeben *vrb.*
downloading Downloading *n.*, Herunterladen *n.*
downstroke Abstrich *m.*
draft Entwurf *m.*, Skizze *f.*, Konzept *n.*

draft/to entwerfen *vrb.*
drama and music school library Theater- und Musikschulbibliothek *f.*
draw/to zeichnen *vrb.*
drawing Zeichnung *f.*
Driver-Mock model Driver-Mock-Modell *n.*
drop-down title Kapitelüberschrift *f.*
drop-in Störsignal *n.*
drop-out Signalausfall *m.*
dropping fraction Auswurfsmenge *f.*
drum Trommelspeicher *m.*
dual card Verbundkarte *f.*
dual use duale Nutzung *f.*
due Abgabe *f.*
due back fällig *adj.*
due date Fälligkeitsdatum *n.*
due for return fällig *adj.*
dumb terminal dummes Terminal *n.*
dummy Vertreter *m.*, Hilfsgröße *f.*
dummy data set Pseudodatei *f.*
dummy field Blindfeld *n.*
dummy variable Hilfsvariable *f.*
dummy volume Musterband *m.*, Probeband *m.*
dump Speicherauszug *m.*
dump file Speicherauszugsdatei *f.*
duplex method Duplexmethode *f.*
duplicate Doppel *n.*, Dublette *f.*, Zweitexemplar *n.*
duplicate/to reproduzieren *vrb.*, duplizieren *vrb.*
duplicate checking Dublettenkontrolle *f.*
duplicate entry Doppeleintrag *m.*
duplicate list Dublettenliste *f.*
duplicate record Dublette *f.*
duplicate title Doppeltitel *m.*
duplicating machine Vervielfältigungsgerät *n.*
duplication Vervielfältigung *f.*
duplication of coverage Verdopplung *f.* der inhaltlichen Abdeckung
duplicity Duplizität *f.*
duty Abgabe *f.*
duty-free abgabenfrei *adj.*
dye-line copy Lichtpause *f.*, Diazokopie *f.*
dynamic allocation dynamische Zuordnung *f.*
dynamic document space dynamischer Dokumentraum *m.*
dynamic storage dynamischer Speicher *m.*
dynamic subroutine dynamisches Unterprogramm *n.*
dynamic system dynamisches System *n.*
dynamics Dynamik *f.*

E

e-measure E-Maß *n.*
early history Frühgeschichte *f.*
early imprints Frühdrucke *pl.*,
Inkunabeln *pl.*
easy book Bilderbuch *n.*
easy-to-use benutzerfreundlich
adj.
ecclesiastical library Kirchenbibliothek *f.*
economic analysis Wirtschaftlichkeitsanalyse *f.*
economic efficiency Wirtschaftlichkeit *f.*
economic factor Wirtschaftsfaktor *m.*
economics Wirtschaftswissenschaften *pl.*, Volkswirtschaftlehre *f.*
economics library wirtschaftswissenschaftliche Bibliothek *f.*
economics of information Informationsökonomie *f.*
economy Wirtschaft *f.*
economy measure Sparmaßnahme *f.*
edge decoration Schnittverzierung *f.*
edge detection Randerkennung *f.*
edge gilding Randvergoldung *f.*
edge-notched card Randlochkarte *f.*
edge-punched card Randlochkarte *f.*
edit/to zur Veröffentlichung fer-

tigmachen *vrb.*, zum Drucken
aufbereiten *vrb.*, redigieren
vrb., edieren *vrb.*, herausgeben
vrb.
edited herausgegeben *adj.*
editing Druckaufbereitung *f.*
editio princeps Erstausgabe *f.*,
Originalausgabe *f.*
edition Ausgabe *f.*, Auflage *f.*
edition size Auflagenhöhe *f.*
editor Herausgeber *m.*,
Schriftleiter *m.*, Lektor *m.*
editorial Leitartikel *m.*
editorial board Herausgebergremium *n.*
editorial processing redaktionelle Bearbeitung *f.*
educated gebildet *adj.*
education Bildung *f.*, Ausbildung *f.*
education center Bildungszentrum *f.*
education grant Ausbildungsbeihilfe *f.*
education system Bildungswesen *n.*
educational broadcasting Bildungsfernsehen *n.*
educational film Lehrfilm *m.*
educational institution Bildungsstätte *f.*
educational institution library
Bibliothek *f.* einer Bildungseinrichtung

educational material Lehrmaterial *n.*
educational media Lehrmittel *pl.*
educational policy Bildungspolitik *f.*
educational radio Schulfunk *m.*
educational research Bildungsforschung *f.*
educational television Bildungsfernsehen *n.*
educational theory Bildungstheorie *f.*
educational trip Studienreise *f.*
edulcorate/to reinigen *vrb.*
effect relation Wirkungsbeziehung *f.*
effectiveness Leistung *f.*, Leistungsfähigkeit *f.*
effectiveness indicator Leistungsindikator *m.*
effectivity Effektivität *f.*
efficiency Wirkungsgrad *m.*, Effizienz *f.*
efficiency control Effizienzkontrolle *f.*
eject/to auswerfen *vrb.*
elaboration Ausarbeitung *f.*
elective core course Wahlpflichtfach *n.*
electrical engineering Elektrotechnik *f.*
electronic bulletin board elektronisches "Schwarzes Brett" *n.*
electronic data processing elektronische Datenverarbeitung *f.*
electronic document delivery elektronischer Dokumentversand *m.*
electronic document storage

elektronische Dokumentspeicherung *f.*
electronic mail elektronische Post *f.*
electronic publishing elektronisches Publizieren *n.*
electronic reading machine elektronisches Lesegerät *n.*
electronic spreadsheet elektronisches Arbeitsblatt *n.*
electronics Elektronik *f.*
element Element *n.*
elementary school Grundschule *f.*
elementary school library Grundschulbibliothek *f.*
elementary term Bedeutungselement *n.*
elimination factor Eliminierungsfaktor *m.*
elliptical elliptisch *adj.*
elliptical title elliptischer Titel *m.*
elucidated erklärt *adj.*
emblem book Emblembuch *n.*
emigration Übersiedlung *f.*
emitter Sender *m.*
emmorphosis Unsicherheitsreduktion *f.*
emperor´s library kaiserliche Bibliothek *f.*
empirical empirisch *adj.*
empirical study empirische Untersuchung *f.*
employee Arbeitnehmer *m.*
employer Arbeitgeber *m.*
employment Beschäftigung *f.*, Arbeit *f.*, Arbeitsstelle *f.*
employment contract Arbeitsvertrag *m.*
empty symbol Leersymbol *n.*
emulate/to emulieren *vrb.*

emulation Emulation *f.*
emulator Emulator *m.*
enciphered data verschlüsselte Daten *pl.*
enclosure Anlage *f.*, Beilage *f.*
encode/to codieren *vrb.*
encoded abstract codiertes Referat *n.*
encoded question verschlüsselte Suchanfrage *f.*
encoder Codeumsetzer *m.*
encoding Codierung *f.*, Verschlüsselung *f.*
encryption Verschlüsselung *f.*
encyclopaedia Enzyklopädie *f.*
end in itself Selbstzweck *m.*
end marker Endemarke *f.*
end of file Dateiende *n.*
end of file label Dateiendekennsatz *m.*
end of tape marker Bandendemarke *f.*
end of transmission character Übertragungsendezeichen *n.*
end sheet Schmutzblatt *n.*
end user Benutzer *m.*
end user searching Endbenutzerrecherche *f.*
ending Flexionsendung *f.*
ending dictionary Endungswörterbuch *n.*
endowed library Stiftungsbibliothek *f.*
energy Energie *f.*
energy facet Energiefacette *f.*
engineering college Ingenieurhochschule *f.*
engineering college library Ingenieurhochschulbibliothek *f.*
engineering library ingenieurwissenschaftliche Bibliothek *f.*

engineering science Ingenieurwissenschaft *f.*
engineering standards committee Fachnormenausschuß *m.*
engineers education Ingenieurausbildung *f.*
engraved title page Kupfertitel *m.*
engraver Graveur *m.*
enlarged edition erweiterte Ausgabe *f.*
enlargement Vergrößerung *f.*
enquiry Suchanfrage *f.*, Abfrage *f.*
enquiry character Abfragezeichen *n.*
enriched alphabetical subject index erweitertes alphabetisches Sachregister *m.*
enrollment Eintragung *f.*, Anmeldung *f.*
ensemble Ganze *n.*
enter/to eingeben *vrb.*
enter/to into the index indexieren *vrb.*
enter/to under the subject verschlagworten *vrb.*
entering Eintragung *f.*
enterprise Unternehmen *n.*, Großbetrieb *m.*
entitled betitelt *adj.*
entity Entität *f.*
entropy Entropie *f.*
entry Eintrag *m.*, Aufnahme *f.*
entry description Buchungstext *m.*
entry for a single item of a series Stücktitel *m.*
entry sequence Zugangsfolge *f.*
entry word Schlagwort *n.*, Registereintrag *m.*

enumerate/to übersichtlich aufstellen *vrb.*

enumerative bibliography aufzählende Bibliographie *f.*

enumerative classification aufzählende Klassifikation *f.*

enumerative notation aufzählende Notation *f.*

environment Umgebung *f.*, Umfeld *n.*

environmental information system Umweltinformationssystem *n.*

environmental planning Umweltplanung *f.*

environmental pollution Umweltverschmutzung *f.*

environmental protection Umweltschutz *m.*

environmental research Umweltforschung *f.*

ephemera Ephemera *pl.*, kurzlebige Zeitschrift *f.*, Eintagsmaterialien *pl.*

epigraph Motto *n.*, Sinnspruch *m.*, Epigraph *n.*

episcopal library bischöfliche Bibliothek *f.*

epistemology Erkenntnistheorie *f.*

epitome Zusammenfassung *f.*

epitomize/to zusammenfassen *vrb.*

eponym Eponym *m.*, Namensgeber *m.*

equal mark Gleichheitszeichen *n.*

equal sign Gleichheitszeichen *n.*

equalization Entzerrung *f.*

equation evaluation Gleichungsberechnung *f.*

equipment Maschine *f.*, Gerät *n.*, Ausstattung *f.*

equivalence Äquivalenz *f.*

equivalence association Zuordnung *f.* durch Äquivalenz

equivalence category Äquivalenzkategorie *f.*

equivalence operation Äquivalenzoperation *f.*

equivalence relation Äquivalenzrelation *f.*

equivalent characteristics gleichwertige Merkmale *pl.*

equivalent term Äquivalenzbezeichnung *f.*

equivocality Eindeutigkeit *f.*

equivocation gleichlautender Informationsgehalt *m.*

era Zeitalter *n.*

erasable storage löschbarer Speicher *m.*

erase head Löschkopf *m.*

erase/to ausblenden *vrb.*, löschen *vrb.*

eraser Löscheinrichtung *f.*

erotic publication Erotikum *n.*

errata Druckfehlerberichtigungen *pl.*

error Fehler *m.*

error bucket Fehlersammelbereich *m.*

error-checking code Fehlerprüfcode *m.*

error control Fehlerüberwachung *f.*

error correction Fehlerkorrektur *f.*

error debugging Fehlersuche *f.*

error-detecting code Fehlererkennungscode *m.*

error flag Fehlerkennzeichen *n.*

error lock Fehlerverriegelung *f.*
error rate Fehlerhäufigkeit *f.*
error recovery Fehlerkorrektur *f.*
escape character Codeumschaltung *n.*
escape sequence ESC-Folge *f.*
esotericism Esoterik *f.*
essay Aufsatz *m.*, Essay *m.*, Abhandlung *f.*
essential character of division wesentliches Unterteilungsmerkmal *n.*
establish/to erstellen *vrb.*
estimate Schätzung *f.*, Voranschlag *m.*, Gutachten *n.*
estimate/to abschätzen *vrb.*
ethnology Völkerkunde *f.*
etymological dictionary etymologisches Wörterbuch *n.*
evaluate/to bewerten *vrb.*
evaluation Bewertung *f.*, Begutachtung *f.*
evaluation factor Bewertungsfaktor *m.*
evaluation measure Bewertungskennziffer *f.*
evaluation of information Wertbestimmung *f.* einer Information
evaluation study Bewertungsuntersuchung *f.*
Evangelical Lutheran Church library Bibliothek *f.* der Evangelisch-Lutherischen Kirche
even gerade *adj.*
evening newspaper Abendzeitung *f.*
evening school Volkshochschule *f.*
event Veranstaltung *f.*, Fall *m.*,

Ereignis *n.*
every day language Umgangssprache *f.*
evolutionary order Ordnung *f.* vom Einfachen zum Komplexen
exact classification Feinklassifikation *f.*
examination Abgangsprüfung *f.*
examination copy Probeexemplar *n.*
examination method Untersuchungsmethode *f.*
examination report Untersuchungsbericht *m.*
exams regulations Prüfungsordnung *f.*
exception Ausnahmebedingung *f.*
exception log Vorgangsdatei *f.*
excerpt Exzerpt *m.*
excerpt/to exzerpieren *vrb.*
exchange Austausch *m.*, Vermittlung *f.*, Tausch *m.*, Schriftentausch *m.*
exchange arrangement Tauschvereinbarung *f.*
exchange center Tauschstelle *f.*
exchange department Tauschstelle *f.*
exchange format Austauschformat *n.*
exchange list Tauschliste *f.*
exchange magnetic tape Austauschmagnetband *n.*
exchange of experience Erfahrungsaustausch *m.*
exchange service Vermittlungsdienst *m.*
exclusive reference exklusive Referenz *f.*

exclusiveness Exklusivität *f*.
executable ausführbar *adj*.
execute/to aktivieren *vrb*.,
ausführen *vrb*.
execution processor Ausführungsprozessor *m*.
execution time Ausführungszeit *f*.
executive Führungskraft *f*.
executive board Vorstand *m*.
executive program Supervisor
m.
executor message Meldung *f*.
des Steuerprogramms
exemption from charges Gebührenfreiheit *f*.
exemption from fees Gebührenfreiheit *f*.
exhausted edition vergriffene
Ausgabe *f*.
exhaustive division Tiefenunterteilung *f*.
exhaustive indexing Tiefenindexierung *f*.
exhaustivity Indexierungstiefe
f.
exhaustivity of indexing Indexierungstiefe *f*.
exhibition Ausstellung *f*.
exhibition catalog Ausstellungskatalog *m*.
exhibition collection Ausstellungssammlung *f*.
exit Ausgang *m*.
expandability Ausweitungsfähigkeit *f*.
expander Erweiterung *f*.
expansion Anwachsen *n*. des
Bestandes
expansive classification Expansivklassifikation *f*.
experience Erfahrung *f*.

experience of application Anwendungserfahrung *f*.
experiment Experiment *n*.
**experimental retrieval collec-
tion** experimenteller Retrievalbestand *m*.
experimental school Laborschule *f*.
experimental study Experimentaluntersuchung *f*.
expert Gutachter *m*.
expert commission Fachkommmission *f*.
expert file Expertendatei *f*.
expert opinion Gutachten *n*.
expert system Expertensystem
n.
expiration date Verfallsdatum
n., Ablauffrist *f*.
expire/to ablaufen *vrb*.
explained erklärt *adj*., erläutert *adj*.
explanatory dictionary Definitionswörterbuch *n*., Glossar
n.
explanatory guide card Kommentarkarte *f*.
explanatory note Kommentierung *f*.
explanatory reference Verweis
m. mit Erklärung
explicandum undefinierter Begriff *m*.
explicatum exakte Begriffsbestimmung *f*., exakte Definition *f*.
explicite explizit *adj*.
export Export *m*.
exportability Exportfähigkeit *f*.
express information service
Schnellinformationsdienst *m*.
expression Ausdruck *m*.

expressive notation semantische Notation *f.*, strukturierte Notation
expunge/to löschen *vrb.*
expurgate/to bereinigen *vrb.*
expurgated edition bereinigte Ausgabe *f.*
extend/to a loan die Leihfrist verlängern *vrb.*, eine Ausleihe erneuern *vrb.*
extended Boolean strategy erweiterte Boolesche Suchstrategie *f.*
extension Begriffsumfang *m.*, Nebenanschluß *m.*, Anbau *m.*
extension by composition Begriffsbestand *m.*
extension by resemblance Begriffsumfang *m.*
extension card Fortsetzungskarte *f.*
extension library service Erwachsenenbildung *f.* durch Veranstaltungen in der Bibliothek

extensional definition Umfangsdefinition *f.*
external data set externe Datei *f.*
external file externe Datei *f.*
external reader auswärtiger Bibliotheksbenutzer *m.*
external storage Hilfsspeicher *m.*
extra Handeinband *m.*
extra copy Mehrstück *n.*, Wiederholungsstück *n.*
extra partition data set sequentielle Datei *f.*
extract/to exzerpieren *vrb.*, herausnehmen *vrb.*, isolieren *vrb.*
extracted article Sonderdruck *m.*
extraction of terms Stichwortbildung *f.*
extracts ausgewählte Werke *pl.*
extrinsic characteristics Beziehungsmerkmale *pl.*

F

fable Fabel *f.*
face Buchstabenbild *n.*
face-to-face communication direkte Kommunikation *f.*
faced rule fette Linie *f.*
facet Facette *f.*

facet analysis Facettenanalyse *f.*
facet formula Facettenformel *f.*
facet indicator Facettenindikator *m.*

facet order Facettenfolge *f.*, Facettenordnung *f.*
faceted classification Facettenklassifikation *f.*
facilities Betriebsmittel *pl.*
facility Fertigkeit *f.*
facsimile Faksimile *n.*
facsimile catalog Faksimilekatalog *m.*
facsimile edition Faksimileausgabe *f.*
facsimile transmission Übermittlung *f.* per Fax
facsimile transmitter Telekopierer *m.*
fact Sachverhalt *m.*, Tatsache *f.*
fact retrieval Faktenretrieval *n.*
factor analysis Faktorenanalyse *f.*
factoring Zerlegung *f.*, Faktorisierung *f.*
factory Industriebetrieb *m.*
facts Fakten *pl.*
factual database Faktendatenbank *f.*
faculty library Institutsbibliothek *f.*, Fakultätsbibliothek *f.*
faculty paper Fachbereichsschrift *f.*, Fakultätsschrift *f.*
failure Ausfall *m.*, fehlerhafte Funktion *f.*
failure rate Ausfallquote *f.*
fair Messe *f.*
fair copy Reinschrift *f.*
fake Fälschung *f.*
faked nachgedruckt *adj.*
fall meeting Herbstsitzung *f.*
fallout ratio Abfallquote *m.*
false combination falsche Kombination *f.*
false data falsche Daten *pl.*
false drop Fehlselektion *f.*

false retrieval fehlerhafter Informationsnachweis *m.*
false sorts falsche Kombination *f.*
familiarizing Einarbeitung *f.*
family library Familienbibliothek *f.*
family name Familienname *m.*
family record book Familienbuch *n.*
farming Landwirtschaft *f.*
Farradane´s relational indexing system relationales Indexierungssystem *n.* nach Farradane
fascism Faschismus *m.*
fascist Faschist *m.*
fast memory Schnellspeicher *m.*
fastener Halter *m.*, Verschluß *m.*
fat-face type fetter Buchstabe *m.*
fault Fehler *f.*
fault time Ausfallzeit *f.*
faulty fehlerhaft *adj.*
faulty margin fehlerhafter Rand *m.*
feasibility analysis Machbarkeitsanalyse *f.*
feasibility study Machbarkeitsstudie *f.*
feature Merkmal *n.*, Einrichtung *f.*
feature card system Sichtlochkartensystem *n.*
feature heading Begriffsbezeichnung *f.*
federal administration Bundesverwaltung *f.*
federal archive Bundesarchiv *n.*
federal government Bundesregierung *f.*

federal library Bundesbibliothek
f.
federal ministry Bundesministerium *n.*
**federal program on informa-
tion and documentation** IuD
Programm *n.*
federation Verband *m.*, Vereinigung *f.*, Assoziation *f.*
fee Gebühr *f.*
fee schedule Gebührenordnung
f.
feed Transport *m.*, Zuführung
f., Vorschub *m.*
feed/to anlegen *vrb.*
feed holes Transportlöcher *pl.*
feedback Rückkopplung *f.*
feedback control rückgekoppelte Steuerung *f.*
feeder Zuführeinrichtung *f.*
fellowship Forschungsstipendium *n.*
fence Scheinglied *n.*
fenced notation aufzählende
Notation *f.*
festival Festival *n.*
festschrift Festschrift *f.*
fetch Abruf *m.*
fetch/to lesen *vrb.*
fetch protection Lesesperre *f.*
fetch routine Zugriffsroutine *f.*
fiber optic transmission Lichtleiterübertragung *f.*
fiche Mikrofiche *m.*
fiction Dichtung *f.*, Prosaliteratur *f.*, Romanliteratur *f.*, Belletristik *f.*
field Feld *n.*
field addressing Feldadressierung *f.*
field code Feldschlüssel *m.*
field content Feldinhalt *m.*

field definition Feldbestimmung
f.
field definition character Feldanfangszeichen *n.*
field definition specification
Felddefinitionsanweisung *f.*
field dependence Feldabhängigkeit *f.*
field display Feldanzeige *f.*
field independence Feldunabhängigkeit *f.*
field indicator Feldbezugszahl *f.*
field label Dateikennsatz *m.*
field length Feldlänge *f.*
field mark Feldmarke *f.*
field number Feldnummer *f.*
field of applications Einsatzgebiet *n.*
field of knowledge Fachgebiet
n., Wissensgebiet *n.*
field of work Tätigkeitsbereich
m.
field separator Feldtrennzeichen *n.*
field size Feldlänge *f.*
field tag Feldmarke *f.*
field trip Studienfahrt *f.*, Ausflug *m.*
field validation Feldprüfung *f.*
field work Feldarbeit *f.*
figure Abbildung *f.*, Ziffer *f.*
file Datei *f.*, Akte *f.*
file/to abheften *vrb.*, einfügen
vrb., einlegen *vrb.*, einordnen
vrb., einreihen *vrb.*
file access Dateizugriff *m.*
file architecture Dateiorganisation *f.*
file attribute Dateiattribut *n.*
file cabinet Aktenschrank *m.*
file card Karteikarte *f.*
file change Dateiänderung *f.*

file connection Dateiverbindung *f.*
file constant Dateikonstante *f.*
file conversion Dateiumsetzung *f.*
file creation Dateierstellung *f.*
file description Dateibeschreibung *f.*
file descriptor document Dateibeschreibungsdokument *n.*
file dust Aktenstaub *m.*
file expiration date Dateiverfallsdatum *n.*
file expression Dateiausdruck *m.*
file handling Dateihandhabung *f.*
file header label Dateianfangskennsatz *m.*
file identifier Dateikennung *f.*
file label Dateikennsatz *m.*
file layout Dateianordnung *f.*
file maintenance Dateipflege *f.*
file management Dateiverwaltung *f.*
file mark Dateikennzeichen *n.*
file number Aktenzeichen *n.*
file organization Dateiorganisation *f.*
file packing Belegungsdichte *f.*
file processing Dateiverarbeitung *f.*
file protection Dateischutz *m.*
file reorganization Dateireorganisation *f.*
file scan Datensuchen *n.*
file separator Dateitrennzeichen *n.*
file set Dateimenge *f.*
file setup Dateiaufbau *m.*
file size Dateigröße *f.*
file structure Dateistruktur *f.*

file updating Dateipflege *f.*
files Akten *pl.*
filing Anordnung *f.*, Ablage *f.*
filing cabinet Aktenschrank *m.*
filing case Karteikasten *m.*
filing character Ordnungszeichen *n.*
filing code Ablageregeln *pl.*
filing criterion Ordnungskriterium *n.*
filing department Registratur *f.*
filing holes Abheftlöcher *pl.*
filing medium Ordnungsgesichtspunkt *m.*
filing method Ablageverfahren *n.*
filing of cards Karteikarteneinordnung *f.*
filing of cards by subject schlagwortorientierte Karteikarteneinordnung *f.*
filing order Reihenfolge *f.*
filing plan Aktenplan *m.*
filing qualifier Ordnungshilfe *f.*
filing room Aktenarchiv *n.*
filing rules Ordnungsregeln *pl.*
filing section Ordnungsgruppe *f.*
filing sequence Ordnungsfolge *f.*
filing shelf Aktenständer *m.*
filing slip Karteikarte *f.*
filing system Ablagesystem *n.*
filing unit Ordnungseinheit *f.*
filing word Schlagwort *n.*, Registereintrag *m.*
fill character Füllzeichen *n.*
filler Füllzeichen *n.*
film Verfilmung *f.*, Film *m.*
film/to verfilmen *vrb.*
film archive Filmarchiv *n.*
film library Filmothek *f.*

film rights Verfilmungsrechte *pl.*

film sort aperture card Mikrofilmlochkarte *f.*

film strip Filmstreifen *m.*

final authoritative edition Ausgabe *f.* letzter Hand

final character Schlußzeichen *n.*

final control element Stellglied *n.*

final destination Zielort *m.*

final examination Abschlußprüfung *f.*

final form Endfassung *f.*

final form document Originaldokument *n.*

final inspection Endprüfung *f.*

final letter Endbuchstabe *m.*, Schlußbuchstabe *m.*

final proof letzter Revisionsabzug *m.*

final proposition Schlußsatz *m.*

final report Schlußbericht *m.*

final revise letzter Revisionsabzug *m.*

final route Kennzahlweg *m.*

final title strip Nachspann *m.*

final total Endsumme *f.*

finance Finanzen *pl.*, Finanzwesen *n.*

financial analysis Finanzanalyse *f.*

financial budget kurzfristiger Finanzplan *m.*

financial needs Geldbedarf *m.*

financial press Wirtschaftspresse *f.*

financial year Geschäftsjahr *n.*

find/to finden *vrb.*

finding list Suchliste *f.*, Findbuch *n.*

findings Untersuchungsergeb-

nis *n.*

fine Mahngebühr *f.*

finger alphabet Taubstummenalphabet *n.*

finished abgeschlossen *adj.*

finishing tool Prägestempel *m.*

finite state automaton endlicher Automat *m.*

fire prevention Brandschutz *m.*

fire prevention technology Brandschutztechnik *f.*

firm Unternehmen *n.*

firm library Firmenbibliothek *f.*

firm order Festbestellung *f.*

first copy Erstexemplar *n.*

first correction Erstkorrektur *f.*

first edition Erstdruck *m.*, Erstausgabe *f.*

first indention erste Einrückung *f.*

first normal form erste Normalform *f.*

first word entry Eintrag *m.* unter dem ersten Titelwort

fiscal law Steuerrecht *n.*

fiscal law documentation Steuerrechtsdokumentation *f.*

fiscal year Finanzjahr *n.*

Fisher's discriminant function Diskriminanzfunktion *f.* nach Fisher

fixed cost fixe Kosten *pl.*

fixed cycle operation fester Arbeitszyklus *m.*

fixed field festes Feld *n.*

fixed field coding Festfeldcodierung *f.*

fixed-format data Daten *pl.* mit festem Format

fixed head schneller Zugriff *m.*

fixed-length record Satz *m.* fester Länge

fixed location ortsfeste Aufstellung *f.*

fixed numbering Feststellennummerierung *f.*

fixed point arithmetic Festkommaarithmetik *f.*

fixed point representation Festkommadarstellung *f.*

fixed shelves nichtverstellbare Regalbretter *pl.*

fixed storage Festspeicher *m.*

fixing Fixierung *f.*

flag Kennzeichen *n.*, Markierung *f.*, Anzeige *f.*, Kartenreiter *m.*, Klappe *f.*

flat-bed equipment Flachbettgerät *n.*

flat-bed printing Flachdruck *m.*

flap blurb Klappentext *m.*

flat impression Abzug *m.* ohne Zurichtung

flat proof Probeabzug *m.*

flat pull Abzug *m.* ohne Zurichtung

flat stiching Blockheftung *f.*

flat visible index Flachkartei *f.*, Sichtkartei *f.*

flexibility Erweiterungsfähigkeit *f.*, Flexibilität *f.*

flexibility of a chain Erweiterungsfähigkeit *f.* einer Kette

flexible disk Diskette *f.*

flexible fastening flexible Heftung *f.*

flexible notation flexible Notation *f.*

flexible sewing flexible Heftung *f.*

flexional symbols Flexionssymbole *pl.*

flier Flugblatt *n.*

floating-point arithmetic Gleit-kommaarithmetik *f.*

floating-point base Gleitkommabasis *f.*

floating-point comparison Gleitkommavergleich *m.*

floating-point computation Gleitkommarechnung *f.*

floating-point constant Gleitkommakonstante *f.*

floating-point number Gleitkommazahl *f.*

floating-point operand Gleitkommaoperand *m.*

floating-point representation Gleitkommadarstellung *f.*

floating-point routine Gleitkommaprogramm *n.*

floating-point subroutine Gleitkommaunterprogramm *n.*

floating register Gleitkommaregister *n.*

floating replacement gleitende Ersetzung *f.*

floating speed Stellgeschwindigkeit *f.*

floating storage address gleitende Hauptspeicheradressierung *f.*

floppy disk Diskette *f.*

flow camera Durchlaufkamera *f.*

flow chart Flußdiagramm *n.*

flow chart symbol Flußdiagrammsymbol *n.*

flow diagram Flußdiagramm *n.*

flow direction Flußrichtung *f.*

flow line Flußlinie *f.*

flow of information Informationsfluß *m.*

flow proposal Arbeitsvorschlag *m.*

flush left Flattersatz *m.* links

ausgeschlossen
flush paragraph Flattersatz *m*.
flush right Flattersatz *m*. rechts
ausgeschlossen
fly back time Rücklaufzeit *f*.
fly-leaf Vorsatzblatt *n*., fliegendes Blatt *n*.
fly title Vortitel *m*., Schmutztitel *m*.
focus Fokus *m*.
foil Folie *f*.
fold Falz *m*.
fold/to falten *vrb*.
folded leaflet Faltblatt *n*., Faltprospekt *m*.
folded table Falttabelle *f*.
folder Faltbroschur *f*., Faltprospekt *m*., Aktenumschlag *m*., Mappe *f*.
folding Zeichenumsetzung *f*., Faltung *f*., Falzung *f*.
foliate/to Seiten numerieren *vrb*.
foliation Blattnumerierung *f*., Blattzahl *f*.
folio Seitenzahl *f*., Bogenformat *n*., Foliant *m*.
follow/to copy nach Manuskript setzen *vrb*.
follow-up notice wiederholte Mahnung *f*., zweite Mahnung *f*.
font Schriftsatz *m*., Schriftart *f*.
font change character Schriftartänderungszeichen *n*.
font size Schrifthöhe *f*.
foot Fußsteg *m*.
foot line Fußzeile *f*.
foot margin unterer Seitenrand *m*.
foot note Fußnote *f*.
foot of the page Fußsteg *m*.

for reference only nur zur Benutzung *f*. in der Bibliothek
for review zur Ansicht *f*.
foreign books ausländische Bücher *pl*.
foreign information service Auslandsinformationsdienst *m*.
foreign language Fremdsprache *f*.
foreign language education Fremsprachenausbildung *f*.
foreign language publisher´s library Bibliothek *f*. fremdsprachlicher Verlage
foreign language teaching Fremdsprachenunterricht *m*.
foreign materials ausländische Materialien *pl*.
forel Buchhülle *f*.
forename entry Eintrag *m*. unter dem Vornamen
foreseeable abschätzbar *adj*.
forest Forst *m*.
forestry Forstwesen *n*., Forstwirtschaft *f*.
foreword Vorwort *n*., Geleitwort *n*.
forgery Fälschung *f*.
form Formular *n*., Formblatt *n*.
form entry Formaleintrag *m*.
form feed Formularvorschub *m*.
form of catalog Katalogform *f*.
form set Belegsatz *m*.
form skip Formularvorschub *m*.
form subdivision formale Unterteilung *f*.
form title Vordruckbenennung *f*.
formal parameter Formalparameter *m*.

formal relation formale Beziehung f.

format Format n.

format change Formatwechsel m.

format compiler Formatumwandler m.

format control Formatkontrolle f., Formatsteuerung f.

format database Formatdatenbank f.

format description Formatbeschreibung f.

format effector Formatsteuerzeichen n.

format entry Eingabeformat n.

format entry name Eingabeformatname m.

format entry unit Eingabeformateinheit f.

format error Formatfehler m.

format feature Formatspeicherung f.

format file Formatdatei f.

format identification field Formatidentifikationsfeld n.

format identifier Formatkennzeichen n.

format instruction Formatinstruktion f.

format item Formatangabe f.

format language Formatiersprache f.

format line Formatzeile f.

format record Steuerinformation f.

format secondary Formatsekundärausdruck m.

format selection Formatauswahl f.

format selector Formatwähler m.

format set Formatgruppe f.

format specification Formatangabe f.

format string Formatzeichenfolge f.

formatted data transfer formatierter Datentransfer m.

formatted diskette formatierte Diskette f.

formatted display formatierte Anzeige f.

formatted record formatgebundener Datensatz m.

formatter Formatierungsprogramm n.

formatting Textgliederung f., Formatgestaltung f., Formatierung f.

forms entry Formulareingabe f.

forms guide Formularführung f.

formula Formel f.

formula counter Formelzähler m.

fortnightly periodical vierzehntägige Zeitschrift f.

forward vorwärts adv.

forward direction Vorwärtsrichtung f.

forward recovery time Durchlaßverzögerungszeit f.

forward space/to vorsetzen vrb.

forward supervising Vorwärtssteuerung f.

forwarding system Nachsendesystem n.

foundation Stiftung f., Grundlage f.

fraction Bruch m.

fraction format Dezimalstellenformat n.

fractional exponent gebrochener Exponent *m*.
fractional scanning schrittweise
Abtastung *f*.
fragment Fragment *n*.
fragmentation Zerstückelung *f*.
fragmenting Kennwortanalyse
f.
frame Rahmen *m*.
frame index Rahmenindex *m*.
frame number Rahmennummer
f.
frame record Rahmensatz *m*.
fraudulent access betrügerischer Zugang *m*.
free frei *adj*.
free/to freigeben *vrb*.
free acquisition kostenfreie Erwerbung *f*.
free copy Freiexemplar *n*.
free element freies Element *n*.
free endpaper Endblatt *n*.
free format freies Format *n*.
free format data formatfreie
Daten *pl*.
free indexing freie Indexierung
f.
free library gebührenfreie Bibliothek *f*.
free materials kostenlose Materialien *pl*.
free of charge kostenlos *adj*.,
unentgeltlich *adj*., gebührenfrei *adj*.
free running Durchlaufbetrieb *m*.
free text Freitext *m*.
free text search Freitextrecherche *f*., Freitextsuche *f*.
freedom of access to information Informationsfreiheit *f*.
freedom of information Informationsfreiheit *f*.

freedom of science Wissenschaftsfreiheit *f*.
freedom to read Lesefreiheit *f*.
freelance editing freiberufliche
redaktionelle Arbeit *f*.
freelance indexing freiberufliches Indexieren *n*.
freelancer freier Mitarbeiter *m*.
frequency Häufigkeit *f*., Frequenz *f*.
frequency analysis Häufigkeitsuntersuchung *f*.
frequency dictionary Häufigkeitswörterbuch *n*.
frequency distribution Häufigkeitsverteilung *f*.
frequency of publication Erscheinungsweise *f*., Periodizität *f*.
friends of the library Freunde
pl. der Bibliothek
front-end processor Vorrechner
m.
frontispiece Titelbild *n*.
fugitive facts file Kurzzeitdokumentation *f*.
fugitive material Kurzzeitinformationen *pl*.
full cap Großbuchstabe *m*.
full cataloging bibliographisch
getreue Aufnahme *f*.
full description Haupteintrag
m.
full-face rule fette Linie *f*.
full-face type fetter Buchstabe
m.
full page plate ganzseitige Tafel *f*.
full point Punkt *m*.
full score Partitur *f*.
full size Planoformat *n*.
full stop Punkt *m*.

full text Volltext *m*.
full text database Volltextdatenbank *f*.
full text processing Volltextverarbeitung *f*.
full text retrieval Volltextretrieval *n*.
full text searching Volltextrecherche *f*., Volltextsuche *f*.
full text storage Volltextspeicherung *f*.
full time employment Vollzeitarbeit *f*.
full title Haupttitel *m*.
fully qualified name vollgekennzeichneter Name *m*.
function Funktion *f*.
function chart Funktionsübersicht *f*.
function code Funktionscode *m*.
function definition Funktionsdefinition *f*.
function designator Funktionsbezeichner *m*.
function file Funktionsdatei *f*.
function key Funktionstaste *f*.
function of the library Bibliotheksaufgaben *pl*.
function reference Funktionsaufruf *m*.
function request Funktionsan-

forderung *f*.
functional building Zweckbau *m*.
functional character Funktionszeichen *n*.
functional characteristic Funktionsbeschreibung *f*.
functional dependency funktionale Abhängigkeit *f*.
functional guidance funktionelle Berichtswege *f*.
functional unit Funktionseinheit *f*.
fund Budget *n*.
fund/to finanzieren *vrb*.
fundamental category Fundamentalkategorie *f*.
funding Finanzierung *f*.
funds Haushaltsmittel *pl*.
funds transfer Mitteltransfer *m*.
furnishment Möblierung *f*.
further copy Mehrstück *n*., Wiederholungsstück *n*.
fuse Sicherung *f*.
future Zukunft *f*.
futurology Zukunftsforschung *f*., Futurologie *f*.
fuzzy set unscharfe Menge *f*.
fuzzy set theory Theorie *f*. der unscharfen Menge

G

galley proof Korrekturabzug
m.
galley slave Schriftsetzer m.
gaol library Gefängnisbibliothek f.
gap Zwischenraum m., Lücke f.
gap character Füllzeichen n.
gap scatter Spaltlagen-
streuung f.
gardening school Gärtner-
schule f.
gateway Übergang m., Ein-
gang m.
gateway facility Gatewayeinrichtung f.
gather/to zusammentragen
vrb.
gathered write sammelndes
Schreiben n.
gathering Bogen m., Bogensatz m., Lage f.
gathering machine Zusammentragmaschine f.
gazette Amtsblatt n., Staatsanzeiger m.
gazetter Ortslexikon n., Ortsregister n.
general bibliography allgemeine Bibliographie f.
general bookstore Sortimentsbuchhandlung f.
general catalog Hauptkatalog
m.
general chart Übersichtsblatt

n.
general classification allgemeine Klassifikation f.
general classification scheme
Universalklassifikations-
schema n.
general cross reference allgemeiner Verweis m.
general education Allgemeinbildung f.
general heading allgemeines
Schlagwort n.
general index Gesamtregister
n.
general information manual
Handbuch n. für allgemeine
Informationen
general information reference
generischer Verweis m.
general library Universalbibliothek f.
general meeting Mitgliederversammlung f.
general plenary meeting Mitgliedervollversammlung f.
general-purpose computer
Universalrechner m.
general-purpose program Universalprogramm n.
general reference allgemeiner
Verweis m.
general register allgemeines
Register n.
general relation allgemeine

Beziehung *f.*
general semantics allgemeine Semantik *f.*
general storage Hauptspeicher *m.*
general system theory allgemeine Systemtheorie *f.*
general term gemeinsprachliche Bezeichnung *f.*
general usage allgemeine Verwendung *f.*
general user Normalbenutzer *m.*
generalization Verallgemeinerung *f.*
generalized sequential access method allgemeine sequentielle Zugriffsmethode *f.*
generate/to generieren *vrb.*
generated address errechnete Adresse *f.*
generating function erzeugende Funktion *f.*
generation Generierung *f.*, Generation *f.*
generation data group Gruppe *f.* von Dateigenerationen
generation data set Dateigeneration *f.*, Dateigenerierung *f.*
generation language Generierungssprache *f.*
generation number Erstellungsnummer *f.*, Dateikennungszahl *f.*
generation phase Umwandlungsphase *f.*
generative grammar generative Grammatik *f.*
generator Generator *m.*
generic generisch *adj.*
generic assignment capability

Selbstzuordnungseigenschaft *f.*
generic chain generische Kette *f.*
generic characteristic generisches Merkmal *n.*
generic coding generische Codierung *f.*
generic concept Allgemeinbegriff *m.*
generic entry allgemeiner Eintrag *m.*
generic heading generisches Schlagwort *n.*
generic name Gattungsname *m.*
generic posting generische Aufnahme *f.*
generic relation Abstraktionsrelation *f.*, generische Relation *f.*, Oberbegriffs-/ Unterbegriffsbeziehung *f.*
generic structure generische Struktur *f.*
generic term allgemeine Bezeichnung *f.*, Gattungsname *m.*, Oberbegriff *m.*, Hauptbegriff *m.*, Gesamtbegriff *m.*
genus Genus *m.*, Geschlecht *n.*, Oberbegriff *m.*
genus-species relation Abstraktionsrelation *f.*, generische Relation *f.*, Oberbegriffs-/ Unterbegriffsbeziehung *f.*
genus-species system Oberbegriffs-/ Unterbegriffssystem *n.*
geochemistry Geochemie *f.*
geographer Geograph *m.*
geographic geographisch *adj.*
geographic arrangement geographische Ordnung *f.*

geographic filing method geographische Ordnung *f*.
geographical catalog geographischer Katalog *m*.
geographical division geographische Einteilung *f*.
geographical group geographische Gruppe *f*.
geographical order geographische Ordnung *f*.
geographical subdivisions geographische Unterteilungen *pl*.
geographical survey map Generalstabskarte *f*.
geography Geographie *f*.
geological geologisch *adj*.
geologist Geologe *m*.
geology Geologie *f*.
geometry Geometrie *f*.
geophysics Geophysik *f*.
Germanic languages and literature study Germanistik *f*.
get/to field Feld lesen *vrb*.
get file Holdatei *f*.
get-up Ausstattung *f*.
ghost edition vermutete Ausgabe *f*.
gift Schenkung *f*., Geschenk *n*.
gift and exchange department Geschenk- und Tauschstelle *f*.
gift edition Geschenkausgabe *f*.
gilt edge Goldschnitt *m*.
given name entry Eintrag *m*. unter dem Vornamen
global global *adj*.
global checking Globalprüfung *f*.
global processor globaler Hauptprozessor *m*.
global storage globaler

Speicher *m*.
global title globaler Name *m*.
globe Globus *m*.
gloss Glosse *f*.
glossary Glossar *n*., Wörterverzeichnis *n*.
glossy paper Hochglanzpapier *n*.
GO TO statment Sprungbefehl *m*.
goal Ziel *n*.
Goffman´s epidemic theory Goffmans epidemische Theorie *f*.
Goffman´s indirect retrieval method indirekte Retrievalmethode *f*. nach Goffman
going down of subscriptions Abonnementsrückgang *m*.
goods Ware *f*.
gothic gothische Schrift *f*.
government archive Regierungsarchiv *n*.
government department library Regierungsstellenbibliothek *f*.
government library Staatsbibliothek *f*.
government publications amtliche Druckschriften *pl*., amtliche Veröffentlichungen *pl*.
governmental staatlich *adj*.
governmental agency Regierungsstelle *f*.
gradation by speciality Anordnung *f*. mit zunehmender Klassenspezialisierung
grade Papierbeschaffenheit *f*., Grad *m*., Prüfungsergebnis *n*.
grade down absteigende Sortierung *f*.
grade up aufsteigende Sortie-

rung *f.*

gradual stufenweise *adj.*

graduate Absolvent *m.*, Akademiker *m.*

graduate from/to absolvieren *vrb.*

graduate library school Bibliotheksschule *f.* für Graduierte

graduated graduiert *adj.*

graduated librarian Diplombibliothekar *m.*

grammage Grammgewicht *n.*

grammar Grammatik *f.*

grammar rules grammatikalische Regeln *pl.*

grammars Grammatikmodelle *pl.*

grammatical analysis grammatikalische Analyse *f.*

grammatical formalism grammatikalischer Formalismus *m.*

grammatical models grammatische Modelle *pl.*

grammmar school library Gymnasialbibliothek *f.*

gramophone record Schallplatte *f.*

gramophone records library Schallplattenarchiv *n.*, Phonothek *f.*

grant Zuschuß *m.*

graph graphische Darstellung *f.*, Graph *m.*, Schaubild *n.*

graph structure Struktur *f.* eines Graphen

graph theory Graphentheorie *f.*

grapheme Graphem *n.*

graphic graphisch *adj.*

graphic art collection Graphothek *f.*

graphic character Schriftzeichen *n.*

graphic check Zeichenprüfung *f.*

graphic data graphische Daten *pl.*

graphic device Bildschirmeinheit *f.*

graphic display Graphikbildschirm *n.*

graphic display program Programm mit graphischer Anzeige *n.*

graphic information graphische Information *f.*

graphic input graphische Eingabe *f.*

graphic record graphischer Datensatz *m.*

graphic representation graphische Darstellung *f.*

graphic representation of a classification graphische Darstellung *f.* einer Klassifikation

graphical methods Methoden *pl.* der graphischen Darstellung

graphical symbol graphisches Zeichen *n.*, Bildzeichen *n.*

graphics access method graphische Zugriffsmethode *f.*

graphics device graphisches Gerät *n.*

graphics display graphische Darstellung *f.*

graphics monitor graphischer Bildschirm *m.*

graphics output graphische Ausgabe *f.*

graphics printer Graphikdrucker *m.*

graphics terminal Graphik-

schirm *m.*
grey literature graue Literatur
f.
grid Raster *n.*, Gitternetz *n.*
grid density Rasterfeinheit *f.*
grid point Rasterpunkt *m.*
grid position Rasterpunkt *m.*
grid square Planquadrat *n.*
groove Falz *m.*, Nut *f.*, Rinne *f.*
group Gruppe *f.*, Eingruppierung *f.*
group addressing Gruppenadressierung *f.*
group communication Gruppenkommunikation *f.*
group data set Gruppendatei *f.*
group indication Gruppenkennzeichnung *f.*, Gruppenanzeige *f.*
group interview Gruppendiskussion *f.*
group item Datengruppe *f.*
group mark Gruppenmarke *f.*
group name Gruppenname *m.*
group notation Gruppennotation *f.*
group number Gruppennummer *f.*
group processing Gruppenverarbeitung *f.*
group record Gruppensteuersatz *m.*
group relation Gruppenbeziehung *f.*
group separator Gruppentrennzeichen *n.*
group term Bezeichnung *f.* einer Begriffsgruppe
grouping Gruppierung *f.*
growing demand steigende
Nachfrage *f.*
growth Wachstum *n.*

growth limitation Wachstumsbegrenzung *f.*
growth of knowledge Wissenszuwachs *m.*
growth of periodicals Zeitschriftenzuwachs *m.*
growth of stock Bestandsvermehrung *f.*, Bestandszuwachs
m.
growth pattern Wachstumsmuster *n.*
growth rate Zuwachsrate *f.*
guarantee Bürgschaft *f.*, Sicherheit *f.*
guarantee/to sicherstellen *vrb.*
guarantor Bürge *m.*
guard Ansetzfalz *m.*
guard-book catalog Bandkatalog *m.*, Katalog *m.* in Registerform
guard digit Schutzziffer *f.*
guard sheet kleines Deckblatt
n.
guard signal Ausblendsignal *n.*
guarding Fälzeln *n.*
guidance Anweisung *f.*
guidance character Führungszeichen *n.*
guidance indicator Führungsanzeige *f.*
guide Führung *f.*, Anleitung *f.*,
Leitfaden *m.*
guide/to führen *vrb.*
guide book Führer *m.*, Reiseführer *m.*
guide card Leitkarte *f.*
guide edge Bezugskante *f.*,
Führungsrand *m.*
guide hole Führungsloch *n.*, Fixierungsloch *n.*
guide slip Laufzettel *m.*
guide to operation Bediener-

handbuch *n.*
guide to the literature Literaturführer *m.*
guideline Richtlinie *f.*
guideline assistance Orientierungshilfe *f.*

guiding word Leitwort *n.*
guillotine Papierschneidemaschine *f.*
gymnasium library Gymnasialbibliothek *f.*, Sportbibliothek *f.*

H

habilitation Habilitation *f.*
half-adder Halbaddierer *m.*
half-adjust/to aufrunden *vrb.*
half-backspace lever Halbschritthebel *m.*
half binding Halbband *m.*
half-byte Halbbyte *n.*
half channel Halbkanal *m.*
half controllable connection halbgesteuerte Schaltung *f.*
half correction Aufrundung *f.*
half cycle Halbschritt *m.*
half duplex halbduplex *adj.*
half-duplex channel Halbduplexkanal *m.*
half-duplex communication line Halbduplexleitung *f.*
half-duplex facilities Halbduplexübertragungsweg *m.*
half-duplex operation Halbduplexbetrieb *m.*
half-duplex transmission Wechselbetrieb *m.*
half-fat halbfett *adj.*
half-frame Halbbildschaltung *f.*

half index down Tiefstellen *n.*
half index up Hochstellen *n.*
half-line spacing Halbzeilenschaltung *f.*
half-monthly halbmonatlich *adj.*
half-path Halbpfad *m.*
half space Halbschritt *m.*
half-space key Halbschritttaste *f.*
half-speed capability halbe Geschwindigkeit *f.*
half-subtractor Halbsubtrahierer *m.*
half title Schmutztitel *m.*, Vortitel *m.*
half tone Grauwert *m.*, Halbton *m.*
half-volume Halbband *m.*
half-yearly halbjährlich *adj.*
halfword Halbwort *n.*
halfword constant Halbwortkonstante *f.*
halfword operand Halbwortoperand *m.*
halfword parameter Halb-

wortparameter *m.*
halt Halt *m.*, Stopp *m.*
halt code Haltcode *m.*
halt identifier Haltkennzeichnung *f.*
halt indicator Haltanzeiger *m.*
halt instruction Haltinstruktion *f.*
halt procedure Stoppver-
zeichnis *n.*
halted unterbrochen *adj.*
halted function unterbrochene
Funktion *f.*
hammer Hammer *m.*
hand Hand *f.*, Handschrift *f.*
hand alphabet Taubstummenalphabet *n.*
hand atlas Taschenatlas *m.*
hand calculator Taschenrechner *m.*
hand-feed Handzuführung *f.*
hand-list Büchernachweisliste
f.
hand-made paper Büttenpa-
pier *n.*
hand-operated punched card
Handlochkarte *f.*
hand over/to aushändigen *vrb.*
hand-press Handpresse *f.*
hand print Schreibschrift *f.*
hand set handgesetzt *adj.*,
Handsatz *m.*
hand sorting Handauswahl *f.*
hand tooling Handprägung *f.*
handbill Rechnung *f.*
handbook Handbuch *n.*
handing back a book Buchrückgabe *f.*
handing in a book Buchrückgabe *f.*
handle/to bearbeiten *vrb.*,
handhaben *vrb.*

handler Programm *n.*
handling Behandlung *f.*, Bearbeitung *f.*, Abwicklung *f.*
handling charge Bearbeitungsgebühr *f.*
handling time Abwicklungszeit
f., Materialtransportzeit *f.*
handprinting Blockschrift *f.*
hands-on training Praktikum *n.*
handset Handapparat *m.*
handshaking Quittungsbetrieb
m.
handwriting Handschrift *f.*,
Schrift *f.*, handgeschrieben
adj.
hang-up Aufhängen *n.*
hanging attribute hängendes
Attribut *n.*
hanging figure tiefstehende
Ziffer *f.*
hanging indention Einzug *m.*
hard copy Ausdruck *m.*, Papierkopie *f.*
hard copy document schriftliches Dokument *n.*
hard copy log Systemdatei *f.*
hard copy printer Drucker *m.*
hard disk Magnetplatte *f.*,
Festplatte *f.*
hard machine check harter
Maschinenfehler *m.*
hard stop harter Stopp *m.*
hard wait state permanenter
Wartestatus *m.*
hard-sectored hartsektoriert
adj.
hardware Hardware *f.*, Geräteausstattung *f.*
hardware assignment Gerätezuweisung *f.*
hardware assistance Maschinenunterstützung *f.*

hardware buffer Hardware-puffer *m.*, Festspeicher *m.*
hardware check Hardwarefehler *m.*
hardware instruction retry Hardwareinstruktionswiederholung *f.*
hardware malfunction Maschinenfehler *m.*
hardware representation maschinengebundene Darstellung *f.*
hardware switch Maschinenschalter *m.*
hardwired controller festverdrahtete Steuerung *f.*
harmonized standards harmonisierte Normen *pl.*
has been adapted from bearbeitet nach *adj.*
hash coding Hashcodierung *f.*
hash function Hashfunktion *f.*
hash table Hashtabelle *f.*
hash total Kontrollsumme *f.*
hash total field Kontrollsummenfeld *n.*
hatch Schalter *m.*
hatch/to schraffieren *vrb.*
hatch system Schalterausleihe *f.*
haul Transportweg *m.*
head Kopf *m.*, Magnetkopf *m.*, Untertitel *m.*, Überschrift *f.*
head carriage assembly Kopfträgereinheit *f.*
head exchange Zentralvermittlung *f.*
head gap Kopfabstand *m.*
head librarian Bibliotheksdirektor *m.*
head load/to Magnetkopf laden *vrb.*

head load solenoid Kopflademagnet *m.*
head loading zone Kopfladebereich *m.*
head margin Kopfsteg *m.*
head of catalog division Leiter *m.* der Katalogabteilung
head of department Abteilungsleiter *m.*
head of the page Kopf *m.* einer Buchseite
head office Hauptbüro *n.*, Leitstelle *f.*, Zentralstelle *f.*
head positioning system Kopfpositionierungssystem *n.*
head selection time Kopfauswahlzeit *f.*
head stack Mehrspurkopf *m.*
headband Kapitalband *n.*
headcap Häubchen *n.*
headed buffer Vorsatzpuffer *m.*
header Kennsatz *m.*, Vorsatz *m.*
header card Leitkarte *f.*, Hauptkarte *f.*
header entry Vorsatz *m.*
header form Kopfformular *n.*
header information Vorsatzinformation *f.*
header label Anfangskennsatz *m.*
header length Leitsatzlänge *f.*
header line Kopfzeile *f.*
header margin text Kopfzeilentext *m.*
header portion Vorsatz *m.*
header program Kopfprogramm *n.*
header record Bandkennsatz *m.*, Vorlaufkarte *f.*
header segment Vorsatzseg-

ment *n.*

header specification Vorlaufbestimmung *f.*

header statement Kopfanweisung *f.*

header table Kopftabelle *f.*

heading Überschrift *f.*, Schlagwort *n.*, Registereintrag *m.*,
Haupteintrag *m.*

heading message Leitnachricht
f.

headline Schlagzeile *f.*, Banner
n., Titelzeile *f.*

headquarter Hauptverwaltung
f., Zentrale *f.*, Generaldirektion *f.*

health certificate ärztliches
Attest *n.*

health insurance identity card
Krankenversicherungskarte *f.*

heat output Wärmeabgabe *f.*

heat sink Kühlprofil *n.*

heavy print Fettdruck *m.*

helical schraubenförmig *adj.*

help Hilfe *f.*, Bedienerhilfe *f.*

help area Hilfebereich *m.*

help area definition Definition
f. des Hilfebereiches

help definition specification
Hilfebereichsbestimmung *f.*

help display Bedienerhilfsanzeige *f.*

help format Hilfeformat *n.*

help menu Bedienerhilfemenu
n.

help subcommand Hilfsunterbefehl *m.*

help text Hilfetext *m.*

helpful sequence aufklärende
Reihenfolge *f.*

heuristic heuristisch *adj.*

heuristic approach heuristische

Näherung *f.*

heuristic dispatching heuristische Auswahl *f.*

heuristic method heuristische
Methode *f.*

heuristics Heuristik *f.*

hexadecimal hexadezimal *adj.*

hexadecimal notation hexadezimale Notation *f.*

**hexadecimal numbering sys-
tem** Hexadezimalsystem *n.*

hexadecimal representation
hexadezimale Darstellung *f.*

hidden bibliography versteckte
Bibliographie *f.*

hidden line verborgene Linie *f.*

hidden variable verborgene
Variable *f.*

hierarchic hierarchisch *adj.*

hierarchic file hierarchische
Datei *f.*

hierarchic network hierachisches Netz *n.*

hierarchical classification hierarchische Klassifikation *f.*

hierarchical clustering hierarchisches Klassieren *n.*

hierarchical database model
hierarchisches Datenbankmodell *n.*

**hierarchical direct access me-
thod** hierarchisch direkte Zugriffsmethode *f.*

**hierarchical-indexed sequen-
tial access method** hierarchisch indexsequentielle Zugriffsmethode *f.*

hierarchical linkage hierarchische Verbindung *f.*

hierarchical notation hierarchische Notation *f.*

hierarchical path hierarchi-

scher Pfad *m.*
hierarchical queue hierarchische Reihe *f.*
hierarchical reference hierarchischer Verweis *m.*
hierarchical relation hierarchische Beziehung *f.*
**hierarchical sequential access
method** hierarchisches Zugriffsverfahren *n.*
hierarchical structure hierarchische Struktur *f.*
hierarchical tree hierarchischer
Baum *m.*
hierarchy Hierarchie *f.*
hierarchy storage Hierarchiespeicher *m.*
high-glazed paper Hochglanzpapier *n.*
high-intensity display Intensivanzeige *f.*
high level Großsignal *n.*
high-level language höhere
Programmiersprache *f.*
high light erhöhte Helligkeit *f.*
high-order position höchste
Stelle *f.*
high-order zeros führende
Nullen *pl.*
high-priority record queue
Warteschlange *f.* für Programme mit hoher Priorität
high resolution hohe Auflösung
f.
high school Oberschule *f.*,
Gymnasium *n.*
high school library Gymnasialbibliothek *f.*
**high-speed accumulating
counter** Hochgeschwindigkeitsaddierzähler *m.*
high-speed buffer Hochge-

schwindigkeitspufferspeicher
m.
high-speed channel Hochleistungskanal *m.*
high-speed data transfer
Hochgeschwindigkeitsüber-
tragung *f.*
high-speed printer Schnelldrucker *m.*
high-speed skip schneller
Sprung *m.*
high-speed stop Sofortstopp *m.*
high-speed storage Speicher
m. mit schnellem Zugriff
high-speed store Schnellspeicher *m.*
high-usage route Querweg *m.*
Higher Administrative Court
Oberverwaltungsgericht *n.*
higher education Hochschulausbildung *f.*
higher education librarianship
Hochschulbibliothekswesen *n.*
higher education system Hochschulwesen *n.*
highlight wichtiges Ereignis *n.*,
Hauptmerkmal *n.*
highlight/to hervorheben *vrb.*
highway Vielfachleitung *f.*,
Zeitmultiplexleitung *f.*
hiking guide Wanderbuch *n.*
hinge Scharnier *n.*, Falz *m.*
hint Hinweis *m.*, Lernhilfe *f.*
histogram Histogramm *n.*
historical bibliography Buchgeschichte *f.*
historical cartography Geschichtskartographie *f.*
historical data Vergangenheitsdaten *pl.*
historical order historische
Reihenfolge *f.*

historical research Geschichtsforschung *f.*
historical subdivisions zeitliche
Unterteilungen *pl.*
historical value Anschaffungswert *m.*
historiography Historiographie *f.*, Geschichtsschreibung
f.
history Geschichte *f.*, Aufzeichnung *f.*, Protokoll *n.*, Geschichtswissenschaft *f.*
history book Geschichtsbuch *n.*
history card Leitkarte *f.*
history data set Dokumentardatei *f.*
history file Ablage *f.*, Statistikdatei *f.*, Protokolldatei *f.*
history of art Kunstgeschichte
f.
history of literature Literaturgeschichte *f.*
history overflow file Protokollüberlaufdatei *f.*
hit Treffer *m.*
hit on the fly printer Drucker
m. mit fliegendem Abdruck
hit rate Trefferquote *f.*
hit ratio Trefferquote *f.*
hitchless stoßfrei *adj.*
hitherto unpublished ungedruckt *adj.*, unveröffentlicht
adj.
hold/to anhalten *vrb.*, belegt
halten *vrb.*
hold area Zwischenspeicher
m., Suchergebnisbereich *m.*
hold buffer Haltespeicher *m.*
hold-file Wiedervorlage *f.*
hold function Festhaltefunktion *f.*
hold-off interval Freihaltezeit

f.
hold page queue Warteschlange *f.* reservierter Seiten
hold print Druckerhalt *m.*
hold status Haltestatus *m.*
hold time Haltezeit *f.*
holding Bestand *m.*
holding analysis Bestandsanalyse *f.*
holding file Verarbeitungsdatei
f.
holding list Bestandsliste *f.*
hole Loch *n.*
hollow hohl *adj.*
hollow-back binding Einband
m. mit hohlem Rücken
hologram Hologramm *n.*
holographic memory holographischer Speicher *m.*
holography Holographie *f.*
home Ausgangsstellung *f.*,
Grundstellung *f.*
home address Spuradresse *f.*
home binding Hausbinderei *f.*
home computer Heimcomputer
m.
home-data channel Lokaldatenkanal *m.*
home lending Ausleihe *f.*
home-loop operation Lokalverarbeitung *f.*
home market Binnenmarkt *m.*
home mode Lokalmodus *m.*
home position Grundstellung *f.*
home reading department
Leihstelle *f.*
home record Haussatz *m.*
home register Lokaldatenregister *n.*
home row Grundstellung *f.*
home trade Binnenhandel *m.*
homing in Grundstellung brin-

gen
homogeneity Homogenität *f.*
homogeneous homogen *adj.*
homograph Homograph *n.*
homologous homolog *adj.*
homonym Homonym *n.*
homonymous homonym *adj.*
homonymy Homonymie *f.*
homophonous homophon *adj.*
homostasis stabiler Zustand *m.*
homothetic figures ähnliche
Muster *pl.*
homotopic homotop *adj.*
homotopic abstract begleitendes Selbstreferat *n.*
hook-on brackets Schaltsteg *m.*
hook-up/to anschliessen *vrb.*
hook-up machine Ergänzungsmaschine *f.*
hopper Kartenmagazin *n.*
hopper control Magazinsteuerung *f.*
hopper input station Stapelzuführstation *f.*
horizontal control Horizontalsteuerung *f.*
horizontal deflection Horizontalablenkung *f.*
horizontal drive horizontale
Steuerung *f.*
horizontal fine adjustment horizontale Feineinstellung *f.*
horizontal keyboard horizontale Tastatur *f.*
horizontal pointer horizontaler Adreßzeiger *m.*
horizontal return horizontaler
Rücklauf *m.*
horizontal skip Zeilensprung
m.
horizontal spacing Zeichendichte *f.*

horizontal tabulating Horizontaltabulierung *f.*
horizontal tabulation Horizontaltabulator *m.*
horizontal transport Horizontalvorlauf *m.*
horologe Zeitmessgerät *n.*
horology Zeitmessung *f.*
horsing Korrekturlesen *n.* ohne
Vorleser
hose Schlauch *m.*
hospital Krankenhaus *n.*
hospital information system
Krankenhausinformations-
system *n.*
hospital library Krankenhausbibliothek *f.*, Krankenhausbücherei *f.*
hospitality Erweiterungsfähigkeit *f.*, Flexibilität *f.*
hospitality of notation Erweiterungsfähigkeit *f.* der Notation
host Hostcomputer *m.*, Hauptrechner *m.*, Leitrechner *m.*,
Host *m.*, Datenbankbetreiber
m.
host access method zentrale
Zugriffsmethode *f.*
host computer Hostcomputer
m., Hauptrechner *m.*, Leitrechner *m.*, gastgebender
Rechner *m.*, Wirtsrechner *m.*,
Datenbankrechner *m.*
host conversational zentraler
Datenverkehr *m.*
host language Wirtssprache *f.*
host master key Hauptschlüssel *m.*
host node zentraler Knoten *m.*
host processor Hauptrechner
m., Leitrechner *m.*, Zentral-

rechner *m.*, gastgebender Rechner *m.*, Wirtsrechner *m.*

host subarea Hauptrechnerunterbereich *m.*

host system zentrales System *n.*, Hostsystem *n.*, Rechnersystem *n.*

host transaction manager Hosttransaktionsverwalter *m.*

hot unter Spannung stehend *adj.*

hot job Eiljob *m.*

hot junction spannungsführende Verbindung *f.*

hot start Schnellstart *m.*

hot type Bleisatz *m.*, Heißsatz *m.*

hot writer Schnelldrucker *m.*

hot zone Ausschließzone *f.*

hourly charge Stundensatz *m.*

hourly rate Stundensatz *m.*

hours of opening Öffnungszeiten *pl.*

house corrections Erstkorrektur *f.*

household Privathaushalt *m.*

housing shroud Kartensockel *m.*

hub Buchse *f.*

human information processing menschliche Informationsverarbeitung *f.*

human-oriented language menschlich orientierte Sprache *f.*

humanities Geisteswissenschaften *pl.*

humidity Feuchtigkeit *f.*, Luftfeuchtigkeit *f.*

hybrid hybrid *adj.*

hybrid computer Hybridrechner *m.*

hybrid input matching point Hybrideingabegruppe *f.*

hybrid input terminal Hybrideingabeanschlußblock *m.*

hydroelectricity Hydroelektrik *f.*

hyperbola Hyperbel *f.*

hyperbolic hyperbolisch *adj.*

hypertext Hypertext *m.*

hyphen Bindestrich *m.*, Trennungszeichen *n.*

hyphenate/to ein Wort trennen *vrb.*

hyphenated catchwords zusammengesetzte Stichworte *pl.*

hyphenation Silbentrennung *f.*

hyphenless justification ungetrennter Blocksatz *m.*

hypotaxis Hypotaxe *f.*, Unterordnung *f.*

hypotenuse Hypotenuse *f.*

hypothesis Hypothese *f.*

I

iconic document Bilddokument *n.*

iconographic archive Bildarchiv *n.*

iconography Ikonographie *f.*, Bildbeschreibung *f.*

idea Konzeption *f.*

ideal capacity Betriebsoptimum *n.*, Kapazitätsoptimum *n.*

identical copy Duplikat *n.*

identical equation identische Gleichung *f.*

identification Identifikation *f.*, Identifizierung *f.*

identification burst Schriftkennung *f.*

identification card Benutzerkarte *f.*

identification card holder Benutzer *m.*

identification character Identifikationszeichen *n.*

identification field Kennzeichnungsfeld *n.*

identification guide Bestimmungsbuch *n.*

identification number Kennnummer *f.*, Identifizierungsnummer *f.*

identification of cause Kennzeichnung *f.* der Ursache

identification qualifier Kennzeichnungsmerkmal *n.*

identification storage Kennungsspeicher *m.*

identification verification Identifikationsprüfung *f.*

identifier Name *m.*, Bezeichnung *f.*, Kennungsgeber *m.*, freies Schlagwort *n.*

identifier field Kennzeichenfeld *n.*

identifier list Namensliste *f.*, Liste *f.* freier Schlagwörter

identifier tag Code *m.*

identify/to erkennen *vrb.*, identifizieren *vrb.*

identifying code Identifikationscode *f.*

identifying label Kennsatz *m.*

identity Identität *f.*

identity element Einzelelement *n.*

identity gate Identitätsglied *n.*, Identitätsbedingung *f.*

ideogram Ideogramm *n.*, Begriffszeichen *n*

ideographic heading ideographisches Schlagwort *n.*, künstliches Schlagwort *n.*

ideography Ideographie *f.*, Schrift *f.* mit Begriffszeichen

idiom Idiom *n.*

idle/to leerlaufen *vrb*

idle capacity ungenutzte Kapazität *f.*

idle character Leerzeichen *n.*

idle condition Freizustand *m.*
idle current Blindstrom *m.*
idle frame leerer Rahmen *m.*
idle insertion Leerzeicheneinfügung *f.*
idle interval stromlose Zeit *f.*
idle plant expenses Stillstandskosten *pl.*
idle state Leerlaufstatus *m.*
idle time Leerlaufzeit *f.*
IF-AND-ONLY-IF element
Äquivalenzbedingung *f.*
IF-AND-ONLY-IF operation
Äquivalenzoperation *f.*
IF-clause WENN-Bedingung *f.*
IF-statement WENN-Anwei-
sung *f.*
IF-THEN element Folgebedingung *f.*
IF-THEN gate Folgeschaltung
f.
ignore/to übergehen *vrb.*, auslassen *vrb.*
ignore character Annullierungszeichen *n.*, Ungültigkeitszeichen *n.*
ignore option Übergehangabe
f.
illative folgernd *adj.*, schlies-
send *adj.*
illuminate/to beleuchten *vrb.*,
illuminieren *vrb.*, ausmalen
vrb.
illuminated manuscript ausgemalte Handschrift *f.*, handkolorierte Handschrift *f.*, illuminierte Handschrift *f.*
illumination Beleuchtung *f.*,
Ausmalung *f.* einer Handschrift
illustrate/to illustrieren *vrb.*
illustrated illustriert *adj.*

illustrated dictionary Bildwörterbuch *n.*, illustriertes Wörterbuch *n.*
illustrated edition illustrierte
Ausgabe *f.*
illustration Abbildung *f.*, Illustration *f.*
illustrative illustrativ *adj.*
illustrator Illustrator *m.*
image Bild *n.*, Abbildung *f.*,
Darstellungsformat *n.*, Wiedergabe *f.*
image area Bildfeld *n.*, Bildbereich *m.*
image communication Bild-
kommunikation *f.*
image content Bildinhalt *m.*
image copy utility Kopierprogramm *n.*
image database Bilddatenbank
f.
image defect Abbildungsfehler
m.
image dissection Bildzerlegung
f.
image dissector Bildzerleger
m.
image mode Bildmodus *m.*
image processing Bildverarbeitung *f.*
image scale Abbildungsmaßstab *m.*
image statement Formatvereinbarung *f.*
image storage Bildspeicher *m.*
image theory Abbildtheorie *f.*
image transmission Bildübertragung *f.*
imaginary imaginär *adj.*
imaginary number Imaginärzahl *f.*
imaginary part Imaginärteil *m.*

immediate access unmittelbarer Zugriff *m*.

immediate addressing unmittelbare Adressierung *f*.

immediate cancel sofortiger Abbruch *m*.

immediate checkpoint sofortige Prüfpunktschreibung *f*.

immediate configuration restart unverzögerter Konfigurationswiederanlauf *m*.

immediate data Direktdaten *pl*.

immediate database Datenbank *f*. für Dialogverarbeitung

immediate instruction Direktbefehl *m*.

immediate logical unit sofort ausführbare logische Einheit *f*.

immediate operand Direktoperand *m*.

immediate operation Direktoperation *f*.

immediate skip Sofortvorschub *m*.

immediate state unmittelbarer Status *m*.

immediate subordinate unmittelbar untergeordnet *adj*.

immediate-to-storage format Direktspeicherformat *n*.

impact Anschlag *m*., Auswirkung *f*.

impact measurement Wirkungsmessung *f*.

impact printer mechanischer Drucker *m*.

impact resistance Schlagzähigkeit *f*.

imperative sentence unbeding-

ter Programmsatz *m*.

imperative statement unbedingte Anweisung *f*.

imperfect copy defektes Exemplar *n*.

imperfection Fehlordnung *f*., Störstelle *f*.

imperial court library kaiserliche Hofbibliothek *f*.

implement/to einführen *vrb*., implementieren *vrb*., durchführen *vrb*., ausführen *vrb*.

implementation Implementierung *f*., Einführung *f*., Durchführung *f*., Ausführung *f*.

implementation stage Implementierungsphase *f*.

implementor Hersteller *m*.

implication Implikation *f*.

implicit implizit *adj*.

implicit address implizite Adresse *f*.

implicit close impliziter Dateiabschluß *m*.

implicit declaration implizite Vereinbarung *f*.

implicit differentiation implizite Differentiation *f*.

implicit function implizite Funktion *f*.

implicit location unspezifische Lokalisation *f*.

implicit opening implizite Eröffnung *f*.

implied implizit *adj*.

implied address implizite Adresse *f*.

implied association implizite Typzuordnung *f*.

implied attribute implizites Attribut *n*.

implied length implizite Länge *f*.

import/to einführen *vrb.*, zurückladen *vrb.*
import bookshop Importbuchhandlung *f.*
import tax Einfuhrsteuer *f.*
importance Tragweite *f.*
importance measure Bedeu-
tungsmaß *n.*
impose/to ausschießen *vrb.*
imposing scheme Ausschießschema *n.*
imposition Ausschießen *n.*
impress Stempel *m.*
impression Anschlag *m.*, unveränderter Nachdruck *m.*,
Auflage *m.*
impression indicator Auf-
schlagsstärkeregler *m.*
imprint Druck *m.*, Aufdruck *m.*,
Druckvermerk *m.*, Erscheinungsvermerk *m.*, Impressum
n., Abdruck *m.*
imprint position Beschriftungsstelle *f.*
imprinter Eindruckvorrichtung
f.
improper feeding Störung *f.* in
der Zuführung
improved edition verbesserte
Auflage *f.*, verbesserte Ausgabe *f.*
improved response time verbesserte Antwortzeit *f.*
improved revision Textkorrektur *f.*
improvement Verbesserung *f.*
improvement proposal Verbesserungsvorschlag *m.*
impulse Impuls *m.*
impulse/to auslösen *vrb.*, erregen *vrb.*
in boards kartoniert *adj.*

in book form in Buchform
in cipher chiffriert *adj.*
in classified order systematisch
geordnet *adj.*
in code chiffriert *adj.*
in curves in runden Klammern
in-depth indexing Tiefenindexierung *f.*
in-house betriebsintern *adj.*,
innerbetrieblich *adj.*
in-house information innerbetriebliche Information *f.*
in-house journal hausinterne
Zeitschrift *f.*
in-house material hausinternes
Material *n.*
in-house network innerbe-
triebliches Computernetz *n.*
in-house system hausinternes
System *n.*, innerbetriebliches
System *n.*
in-line processing gleichzeitige
Verarbeitung *f.*
in one column einspaltig *adj.*
in parenthesis in runden Klammern
in parts heftweise *adj.*, in Lie-
ferungen
in-plant printer Hausdruckerei
f.
in pointed brackets in spitzen
Klammern
in press in Druck
in print lieferbar *adj.*
in process in Bearbeitung
in round brackets in runden
Klammern
in sheets ungebunden *adj.*
in-source cataloging Vorauskatalogisierung *f.*
in-source indexing Vorausindexierung *f.*, Eigeninde-

xierung *f.*
in square brackets in eckigen
Klammern
in stock auf Lager, vorrätig
adj.
in-storage list im Hauptspeicher gehaltene Liste *f.*
in-stream procedure In-Stream-Prozedur *f.*
in strict alphabetical order in
streng alphabetischer Reihenfolge
in subject order systematisch
geordnet
in type abgesetzt *adj.*
in use in Benutzung, benutzt
adj.
inactive inaktiv *adj.*
inactive frame inaktiver Rahmen *m.*
inactive line inaktive Leitung *f.*
inactive station inaktive Datenstation *f.*
inaugural dissertation Habilitationsschrift *f.*
inboard file Innerborddatei *f.*
inbound data Eingabedaten *pl.*
inbound request processing
Verarbeitung *f.* von ankommenden Anforderungen
incident record Ereignisprüfpunktsatz *m.*
incident report technischer Arbeitsbericht *m.*
incidental characteristic unwesentliche Eigenschaft *f.*
incidental charges Nebenkosten *pl.*
incidental time sonstige Zeit *f.*
incircle Innenkreis *m.*
include/to einschließen *vrb.*,
enthalten *vrb.*

include line Einfügungszeile *f.*
include mode Einfügemodus *m.*
include statement Einfügungsanweisung *f.*
inclusion Implikation *f.*, Einschluß *m.*
inclusive notation Bereichsangabe *f.*
inclusive relation Einschlußbeziehung *f.*
income Einnahme *f.*, Umsatz
m., Einkommen *n.*
incoming eingehend *adj.*, ankommend *adj.*
incoming group Eingangsgruppe *f.*
incoming line ankommende
Leitung *f.*
incompatible unverträglich
adj.
incomplete unvollständig *adj.*,
defekt *adj.*
incomplete mapping unvollständige Kartographie *f.*
inconsistency Unstimmigkeit *f.*
inconsistent nicht übereinstimmend *adj.*
**incorporation of entries in a
catalog** Einordnung *f.* der Titelaufnahme
incorrect length falsche Länge
f., falsche Satzlänge *f.*, Längenfehler *m.*
incorrect spelling Falschschreibung *f.*
increase Erhöhung *f.*, Zunahme *f.*
increase in efficiency Leistungssteigerung *f.*
increase of charges Gebührenerhöhung *f.*
increase of stock Bestandszu-

wachs *m.*
increasing concreteness zunehmende konkrete Beschaffenheit *f.*
increasing function steigende Funktion *f.*
increment Zuwachs *m.*, Inkrement *n.*, Wertzuwachs *m.*, Schritt *m.*, Belegvorschub *m.*
increment document Dokumentvorschub *m.*
increment size Inkrementgröße *f.*
incremental backup Zuwachssicherung *f.*
incremental computer Inkrementalrechner *m.*
incremental coordinates Kettenmaß *n.*
incremental dimension Kettenmaß *n.*
incremental representation inkrementale Darstellung *f.*
incrementing Belegvorschub *m.*, Vorschub *m.*
incunabula cataloging Inkunabelkatalogisierung *f.*
incunabula collection Inkunabelsammlung *f.*
incunabulum Inkunabel *f.*, Wiegendruck *m.*
indefinite unbestimmt *adj.*
indemnity Schadenersatzleistung *f.*, Entschädigung *f.*, Abfindung *f.*
indent/to einrücken *vrb.*, einziehen *vrb.*
indentation Einrückung *f.*, Einzug *m.*
indentation convention Einrückungsregel *f.*
indentation guideline Einrüc-

kungsrichtlinie *f.*
indented eingerückt *adj.*, eingezogen *adj.*
indention Einrückung *f.*, Einzug *m.*
independence Datenunabhängigkeit *f.*
independent access method unabhängige Zugriffsmethode *f.*
independent auxiliary selbständige Anhängezahl *f.*
independent data communication unabhängige Datenübermittlung *f.*
independent research library unabhängige Forschungsbibliothek *f.*
independent school library unabhängige Schulbibliothek *f.*
independent utility program unabhängiges Dienstprogramm *n.*
indeterminate unbestimmter Ausdruck *m.*
index Register *n.*, Index *m.*
index /to indexieren *vrb.*, ein Register anlegen *vrb.*, verzeichnen *vrb.*
index access hole Indexloch *n.*
index analyser Indexanalysator *m.*
index built Indexerstellung *f.*
index card Karteikarte *f.*
index component Indexkomponente *f.*
index control entry Indexeintragung *f.*
index data item Indexfeld *n.*
index database Indexdatenbank *f.*
index detection Indexerkennung *f.*

index development indicator
Anzeige *f.* der Indexentwicklung

index end position letzte Indexstelle *f.*

index entry Indexeintrag *m.*,
Registereintrag *m.*

index field Indexfeld *n.*

index file Indexdatei *f.*, Registerdatei *f.*

index in book-form Register *n.*
in Buchform

index key Indexschlüssel *m.*

index level Indexstufe *f.*, Indexkomponente *f.*

index link entry Indexverbindungseintrag *m.*

index list Indexliste *f.*

index map Übersichtskarte *f.*

index mark Indexmarke *f.*

index marker Indexpunkt *m.*

index name Indexname *m.*

index of films Filmverzeichnis
n.

index of periodicals Zeitschriftenregister *n.*

index of persons Personenregister *n.*

index of places Ortsregister *n.*

index point Indexpunkt *m.*

index record Indexsatz *m.*

index replication Indexwiederholung *f.*

index return unveränderliche
Zeilenschaltung *f.*

index selection Adresse *f.*

index sequential access indexsequentieller Zugriff *m.*

index sequential organization
indexsequentielle Dateiorganisation *f.*

index set Indexgruppe *f.*

index term Registereintrag *m.*,
Indexeintrag *m.*

index vocabulary Inde-
xierungssprache *f.*, Dokumentationssprache *f.*

index volume Registerband *m.*

index word Indexwort *n.*

indexed indexiert *adj.*

indexed access method Indexzugriffsverfahren *n.*

indexed file indexsequentielle
Datei *f.*

indexed instruction Instruktion
f. mit Indexadresse

indexed organization indexierte Dateiorganisation *f.*

indexed search Indexsuchverfahren *n.*

indexed sequential data set indexsequentielle Datei *f.*

indexed sequential file indexsequentielle Datei *f.*

indexed sequential storage
Speicher *m.* mit indexsequentiellem Zugriff

indexer Indexierer *m.*

indexing Registererstellung *f.*,
Inhaltserschließung *f.*, Erschließung *f.*, Bestandserschließung *f.*, Indexierung *f.*

indexing consistency Indexierungskonsistenz *f.*

indexing criteria Indexierungskriterien *pl.*

indexing density Indexierungsbreite *f.*

indexing department Indexierungsabteilung *f.*

indexing exhaustivity Indexierungstiefe *f.*

indexing feature Indexregister
n.

indexing language Indexierungssprache *f.*, Dokumentationssprache *f.*
indexing process Erschlies-
sungsprozeß *m.*
indexing rules Erschließungsregeln *pl.*
indexing sequence Reihenfolge
f. der Indexeinträge
indexing service Indexierungsdienst *m.*
indexing specificity Indexierungsspezifizität *f.*
indexing standard Indexierungsnorm *f.*
indexing system Indexierungssystem *n.*
indexing technique Indexierungsverfahren *n.*
indexing term Indexterm *m.*,
Indexeintrag *m.*
indicate/to anzeigen *vrb.*, hinweisen *vrb.*
indication Kennzeichen *n.*,
Meldung *f.*
indicative abstract Kurzreferat
n., indikatives Referat *n.*
indicative entry indikative Beschreibung *f.*
**indicative-informative ab-
stract** indikativ-informatives
Referat *n.*
indicator Indikator *m.*, Anzeige
f., Bezugszahl *f.*
indirect indirekt *adj.*
indirect access indirekter Zugriff *m.*
indirect communication indirekte Kommunikation *f.*
indirect data address list indirekte Datenadressliste *f.*
indirect documentation indi-

rekte Dokumentation *f.*
indirect entry invertierter Eintrag *m.*
indirect instruction indirekter
Befehl *m.*
indirect material Hilfsmaterial
n.
indirect operation indirekte
Operation *f.*
indirect study indirekte Benutzeruntersuchung *f.*
indirectly accessible storage
Speicher *m.* mit indirektem
Zugriff
individual author Einzelautor
m.
individual bibliography Personalbibliographie *f.*
individual concept Individualbegriff *m.*
individual control Einzelsteuerung *f.*
individual library Privatbibliothek *f.*
induction Induktion *f.*
industrial data processing industrielle Datenverarbeitung
f.
industrial library Industriebibliothek *f.*, Firmenbibliothek *f.*
industrial medicine Arbeitsmedizin *f.*
industrial plant Industriebetrieb *m.*
industrialized countries Industrieländer *pl.*
industry Industrie *f.*
industry code Branchenschlüssel *m.*
ineffective wirkungslos *adj.*,
erfolglos *adj.*, unwirksam
adj., unwirtschaftlich *adj.*

inefficiency Unwirksamkeit *f.*, Unwirtschaftlichkeit *f.*
inequality Ungleichung *f.*
inferior character tiefstehende Ziffer *f.*
inferior figure tiefstehende Ziffer *f.*
inferior letter tiefstehender Buchstabe *m.*
infima species kleinste Untergruppe *f.*, kleinste Unterteilung *f.*
infinite set unendliche Menge *f.*
infix Infix *n.*
influence quality Einflußgröße *f.*, Störgröße *f.*
influence relation Einflußbeziehung *f.*
informatics Informatik *f.*
information Information *f.*, Informationen *pl.*
information analysis Informationsanalyse *f.*
information analysis center Informationsanalysezentrum *n.*
information analyst Informationsanalytiker *m.*
information and documentation Informations- und Dokumentationswesen *n.*
information and documentation service Informations- und Dokumentationsdienst *m.*
information area Informationsfeld *n.*
information banks Informationsbanken *pl.*
information barrier Informationsschranke *f.*
information broker Informa-

tionsbroker *m.*
information brokerage Informationsvermittlung *f.*
information capacity Informationskapazität *f.*
information card Leitkarte *f.*, Titelübersicht *f.*
information carrier Informationsträger *m.*
information center IuD-Stelle *f.*, Beratungsstelle *f.*, Informationszentrum *n.*, Informationsstelle *f.*
information channel Informationskanal *m.*, Datenkanal *m.*
information collecting Informationsbeschaffung *f.*
information communicating system Informationsaustauschsystem *n.*
information consultation Informationsberatung *f.*
information content Informationsgehalt *m.*
information counseling Informationsberatung *f.*
information demand Informationsbedarf *m.*
information density Informationsdichte *f.*
information department Informationsabteilung *f.*
information desk Informationsschalter *m.*, Auskunft *f.*
information dispensing Informationsausgabe *f.*
information dissemination Informationsverbreitung *f.*
information economy Informationsökonomie *f.*
information elements Informationselemente *pl.*

information enquiry Informationssuche *f.*

information entropy Informationsentropie *f.*

information ethics Informationsethik *f.*

information evaluation Informationsbewertung *f.*

information exchange Informationsaustausch *m.*

information explosion Informationsflut *f.*, Informationsexplosion *f.*

information feedback system Informationsrückkopplungssystem *n.*

information field Datenfeld *n.*

information flow Informationsfluß *m.*

information flow analysis Informationsflußanalyse *f.*

information format Informationsformat *n.*

information frame Informationsrahmen *m.*

information function Informationsfunktion *f.*

information gain Informationsgewinn *m.*

information gathering Informationsbeschaffung *f.*, Informationssammlung *f.*

information gathering patterns Informationsbeschaffungsmuster *n.*

information handling Informationsbearbeitung *f.*

information industry Informationsindustrie *f.*

information interest Informationsinteresse *n.*

information language Dokumentationssprache *f.*

information law Informationsrecht *n.*

information linguistics Informationslinguistik *f.*

information loss Informationsverlust *m.*

information management Informationsmanagement *n.*

information market Informationsmarkt *m.*

information marketing Informationsmarketing *n.*

information medium Informationsträger *m.*, Informationsmedium *n.*

information message Übertragungszeichenfolge *f.*, Benutzernachricht *f.*

information needs Informationsbedürfnisse *pl.*

information network Informationsverbund *m.*, Informationsnetz *n.*

information officer Informationsbeauftragte *m.*

information overload Informationsüberlastung *f.*

information paper Nachrichtenblatt *n.*

information planning Informationsplanung *f.*

information policy Informationspolitik *f.*

information presentation Informationspräsentation *f.*

information problem Informationsproblem *n.*

information process Informationsprozeß *m.*

information processing Informationsverarbeitung *f.*, Datenverarbeitung *f.*, Nachrichtenverarbeitung *f.*

information producer Informationsproduzent *m.*

information product Informationsprodukt *n.*

information professional Informationsfachmann *m.*

information psychology Informationspsychologie *f.*

information request Suchanfrage *f.*

information requirements Informationsanforderungen *pl.*

information resource management Informationsmanagement *n.*

information retrieval Information Retrieval *n.*, Informationswiedergewinnung *f.*

information retrieval by subject sachorientiertes Information Retrieval *n.*

information retrieval language Informationsrecherchesprache *f.*, Information Retrievalsprache *f.*

information retrieval machine Datenbankcomputer *m.*

information retrieval system Information Retrievalsystem *n.*, Informationswiedergewinnungssystem *n.*, Informationsrecherchesystem *n.*

information science Informationswissenschaft *f.*

information scientist Informationswissenschaftler *m.*

information seeking behavior Informationssuchverhalten *n.*

information selection system Information Retrievalsystem *n.*

information separator Trennzeichen *n.*

information service Auskunftsdienst *m.*, Informationsdienst *m.*

information society Informationsgesellschaft *f.*

information source Informationsquelle *f.*, Nachrichtenquelle *f.*, Fundstelle *f.*

information specialist Informationsfachkraft *f.*, Informationsspezialist *m.*, Fachdokumentar *m.*

information storage and retrieval Informationsspeicherung *f.* und -wiedergewinnung *f.*

information store Informationsspeicher *m.*

information supply Informationsangebot *n.*, Informationsversorgung *f.*

information system Informationssystem *n.*

information technology Informationstechnik *f.*

information theory Informationstheorie *f.*

information track Informationsspur *f.*

information trade Informationshandel *m.*

information transfer Informationstransfer *m.*

information transmission system Informationsübertragungssystem *n.*

information type Informationstyp *m.*

information unit Informationseinheit *f.*

information use Informationsgebrauch *m*.
information utilization Informationsnutzung *f*.
information utility Informationswert *m*.
information work Informationstätigkeit *f*.
informative abstract informatives Referat *n*., ausführliches
Referat *n*.
informatory informativ *adj*.
informetrics Informetrie *f*.
infrastructure Infrastruktur *f*.
infringement of copyright Urheberrechtsverletzung *f*.
inherited error mitgeschleppter Fehler *m*.
inhibit input Sperreingang *m*.
initial Anfangsbuchstabe *m*.,
Initiale *f*.
initial call Anfangsaufruf *m*.
initial display Startmenü *n*.
initial inventory Anfangsbestand *m*.
initial letter Anfangsbuchstabe
m., Initiale *f*.
initial line Startzeile *f*.
initial mode Einleitungsmodus
m.
initial parameter Anfangsparameter *m*.
initial point Dateianfangspunkt *m*.
initial procedure Anfangsprozedur *f*.
initial selection einleitende
Adreßselektion *f*.
initial setup Einschalten *n*.
initial test routine Anfangstestroutine *f*.
initialization Initialisierung *f*.

initialization procedure Initialisierungsablauf *m*.
initialization step Initialisierungsschritt *m*.
initialize/to initialisieren *vrb*.,
vorbereiten *vrb*., einleiten
vrb.
initialize statement Initialisierungsanweisung *f*.
initializer Initialisierungsprogramm *n*.
initially created erstmalig erstellt
initials Anfangsbestand *m*.
initiate/to aufrufen *vrb*.
initiation Initialisierung *f*.
initiator Initiator *m*.
initiator procedure Initiatorprozedur *f*.
ink Druckfarbe *f*., Schreibtinte
f.
ink jet printer Tintenstrahldrucker *m*.
ink ribbon Farbband *n*.
inlet Eingang *m*.
inner city library Innenstadtbibliothek *f*.
inner endpaper Vorsatzblatt *n*.,
Endblatt *n*.
inner form innere Form *f*.
inner margin Bundsteg *m*., innerer Papierrand *m*.
innovation Innovation *f*.
innovation counseling Innovationsberatung *f*.
inoperable time nicht nutzbare
Zeit *f*.
inoperative funktionsunfähig
adj.
input Eingabe *f*.
input/to eingeben *vrb*.
input allowed freie Eingabe *f*.

input and error listing Eingabe- und Fehlerprotokoll *n*.
input buffer Eingabepuffer *m*.
input capacity Eingabekapazität *f*.
input card Eingabekarte *f*.
input channel Eingangskanal *m*.
input command Eingabebefehl *m*.
input configuration Eingangskonfiguration *f*.
input control unit Eingabesteuereinheit *f*.
input data Eingabedaten *pl*.
input data set Eingabedatei *f*.
input data translation Umsetzung *f*. der Eingabedaten
input device Erfassungsgerät *n*., Eingabegerät *n*.
input error checking Prüfung *f*. auf Eingabefehler
input field Eingabefeld *n*.
input file Eingabedatei *f*.
input job queue Eingabewarteschlange *f*.
input label Eingabekennsatz *m*.
input language Eingabesprache *f*.
input medium Eingabemedium *n*.
input operation Eingabeoperation *f*.
input/ output Ein-/ Ausgabe *f*.
input/ output channel Ein-/ Ausgabekanal *m*.
input/ output device Ein-/ Ausgabeeinheit *f*.
input/ output file Ein-/ Ausgabedatei *f*.
input/ output model Ein-/ Ausgabemodell *n*.

input/ output process Ein-/ Ausgabeprozeß *m*., radiale Übertragung *f*.
input/ output processor Ein-/ Ausgabeprozessor *m*.
input/ output register Ein-/ Ausgaberegister *n*.
input/ output statement Ein-/ Ausgabeanweisung *f*.
input/ output unit Ein-/ Ausgabeeinheit *f*.
input process Eingabe *f*.
input program Eingabeprogramm *n*.
input prompting character Eingabeabfragezeichen *n*.
input queue Eingabewarteschlange *f*.
input rate Eingabegeschwindigkeit *f*.
input routine Eingabeprogramm *n*.
input sequence number Eingabefolgenummer *f*.
input specification Eingabespezifikation *f*.
input state Eingabemodus *m*.
input storage Eingabespeicher *m*.
input time interval Eingabezeit *f*.
input transfer rate Eingaberate *f*.
input unit Eingabeeinheit *f*.
inquiry Erhebung *f*., Suche *f*., Abfrage *f*., Suchanfrage *f*., Anfrage *f*.
inquiry command Abfragebefehl *m*., Abfrageanweisung *f*.
inquiry file Abfragedatei *f*.
inquiry operation Abfrageauswahl *f*.

inquiry processing Abfragebearbeitung f.
inquiry request Abfrageanforderung f.
inquiry specifier Abfrageparameter m.
inquiry unit Abfrageeinheit f.
inscribe/to beschriften vrb.
inscribed copy signiertes
Exemplar n.
inscription Inschrift f.
insert Einsatz m., Einfügung
f.., Beilage f.
insert/to einfügen vrb., einstecken vrb., einwerfen vrb.,
einschieben vrb.
insert/to after einfügen vrb.
nach
insert/to an extra entry einen
neuen Eintrag einfügen vrb.
insert character Einfügezeichen n.
insert mode Einfügemodus m.
inserted card Einschaltkarte f.
inserted leaf Einschaltblatt n.
inserting Einfügen n.
insertion Einfügung f., Einschiebung f.
insertion character Einfügezeichen n.
insertion in a text Texteinfügung f.
insertion of a new heading
Einfügung f. eines neuen
Schlagwortes
insertion sequence Einschiebungsfolge f.
inset Beilage f.
inset map Nebenkarte f.
inset plates Abbildungen pl.
außerhalb eines Textes
insetting Einschalten n.

inside cover Deckelinnenseite
f.
inside title Innentitel m.
inspection Untersuchung f.
inspection characteristic Prüfmerkmal n.
inspection copy Ansichts-
exemplar n.
inspection instruction Prüfanweisung f.
install/to installieren vrb.
installation Aufstellung f.,
Montage f., Installation f.
installation standard Installationsvorgabe f.
installed user program installiertes Benutzerprogramm n.
institute Institut n.
institute and society library
Instituts- und Gesellschafts-
bibliothek f.
institute library Institutsbibliothek f.
institution Institution f., Anstalt f.
institutional library Anstaltsbibliothek f.
instruction Unterricht m.,
Ausbildung f., Befehl m., Instruktion f., Anweisung f.
instruction address register
Befehlsfolgeregister n., Instruktionsadreßregister n.
instruction booklet Bedienungsanleitung f.
instruction code Befehlscode
m.
instruction counter Befehlszähler m., Instruktionszähler
m.
instruction cycle Instruktionsphase f.

instruction decoder Befehlsdecodierer *m.*
instruction execution Befehlsausführungsphase *f.*
instruction fetch Befehlsabruf
m.
instruction for use Gebrauchsanweisung *f.*
instruction format Befehlsstruktur *f.*
instruction list Befehlsliste *f.*
instruction manual Bedienungshandbuch *n.*
instruction modifier Ergänzung *f.*
instruction processing unit Befehlsverarbeitungseinheit *f.*
instruction processor unit Befehlsprozessor *m.*
instruction register Befehlsregister *n.*
instruction repertoire Befehlsvorrat *m.*
instruction set Befehlsvorrat
m.
instruction sheet Merkblatt *n.*
instruction statement Befehlsanweisung *f.*, Befehlseinzelschritt *m.*
instruction word Befehlswort
n.
instructional material Lehrmaterial *n.*, Unterrichtsmaterial
n.
instructional method Lehrmethode *f.*
instructor Ausbilder *m.*, Lehrer
m.
instrument Gerät *n.*, Instrument *n.*
instrumental relation instrumentelle Beziehung *f.*

insurance Versicherung *f.*
insurance business Versicherungswesen *n.*
insurance contract Versicherungsvertrag *m.*
insurance policy Versicherungspolice *f.*
intake Neuerwerbung *f.*
integer Ganzzahl *f.*, ganzzahlig *adj.*
integer attribute ganzzahliges
Attribut *n.*
integer constant ganzzahlige
Konstante *f.*
integer editing Ganzzahlaufbereitung *f.*
integer number Ganzzahl *f.*
integer part ganzzahliger Teil
m.
integer solution ganzzahlige
Lösung *f.*
integral Integral *n.*
integral action controller Integralregler *m.*
integral part ganzzahliger Teil
m.
integral value Integralwert *m.*
integrated angegliedert *adj.*,
eingebaut *adj.*
integrated circuit integrierter
Schaltkreis *m.*
**integrated communications
adapter** Direktanschluß *m.*
für Datenfernverarbeitung
integrated control unit integrierte Steuereinheit *f.*
integrated data processing integrierte Datenverarbeitung
f.
integrated dictionary system
integriertes Wörterbuchsystem *n.*

integrated direct access storage integrierter Direktzugriffsspeicher *m.*

integrated directory sytem integriertes Verzeichnissystem *n.*

integrated file adapter Direktanschluß *m.*

integrated keyboard integrierte Tastatur *f.*

integrated word processing integrierte Textverarbeitung *f.*

integrating network integrierendes Netzwerk *n.*

integration Integration *f.*

integration by parts partielle Integration *f.*

integration model Integrationsmodell *n.*

integration policy Integrationspolitik *f.*

integration process Integrationsprozeß *m.*

integrative level Komplexitätsniveau *n.*

integrity Integrität *f.*, Sicherheit *f.*, Datenintegrität *f.*

integrity of data Datenvollständigkeit *f.*

intellectual freedom geistige Freiheit *f.*

intellectual level geistiges Niveau *n.*

intellectual property geistiges Eigentum *n.*

intelligence Intelligenz *f.*

intelligence report Geheimdienstbericht *m.*

intensified display Intensivanzeige *f.*

intension Begriffsinhalt *m.*

intensional definition Inhaltsdefinition *f.*

intensity Helligkeit *f.*

intensity level Helligkeitsstufe *f.*

intent of a document Ziel *n.* eines Dokuments, Zweck *m.* eines Dokuments

inter-block time cut Zwischenblockzeitbegrenzung *f.*

inter-library comparison Bibliotheksvergleich *m.*

inter-library lending auswärtiger Leihverkehr *m.*, Fernleihe *f.*, aktiver Leihverkehr *m.*

inter-library loan Fernleihbestellung *f.*, auswärtiger Leihverkehr *m.*, Fernleihe *f.*

inter-operation time Übergangszeit *f.*

inter-operator connection unmittelbarer Sprechweg *m.*

interaction Wechselwirkung *f.*, Interaktion *f.*

interaction time Interaktionszeit *f.*

interactive dialoggestützt *adj.*, interaktiv *adj.*, im Dialogbetrieb

interactive data entry Dialogerfassung *f.*

interactive data processing Dialogdatenverarbeitung *f.*

interactive debug interaktiver Testmonitor *m.*

interactive facility Dialogfähigkeit *f.*

interactive format interaktiver Aufbau *m.*

interactive front end Dialogdatenerfassung *f.*

interactive inquiry Dialogrecherche *f.*

interactive mode Dialogbetrieb *m.*

interactive operation Interaktion *f.*, Wechselwirkung *f.*

interactive processing Dialogverarbeitung *f.*

interactive retrieval interaktives Retrieval *n.*, Informationssuche *f.* im Dialog

interactive searching interaktive Suche *f.*

intercalate/to einfügen *vrb.*, einschieben *vrb.*

intercalation Einfügen *n.* eines neuen Schlagwortes

interchange Wechsel *m.*

interchange format Austauschformat *n.*

interchange point Übergabestelle *f.*

interchange record separator Satzbegrenzung *f.*

interchangeability Austauschbarkeit *f.*

interchangeable accessory austauschbares Zubehör *n.*

interconnect/to verknoten *vrb.*

interconnecting cable Verbindungskabel *f.*

interdisciplinary fachübergreifend *adj.*

interdisciplinary information center interdisziplinäres Informationszentrum *n.*

interdisciplinary subject interdisziplinäres Thema *n.*

interdisciplinary subjects interdisziplinäre Sachgebiete *pl.*

interest profile Interessenprofil *n.*, Interessenliste *f.*

interests record Interessenliste

f.

interface Schnittstelle *f.*, Anschlußstelle *f.*

interface/to anschließen *vrb.*, verbinden *vrb.*

interface adaptor Schnittstellenanpassung *f.*

interface control word Schnittstellensteuerwort *n.*

interface information Schnittstelleninformation *f.*

interference Störung *f.*, Überlagerung *f.*

interference time Verlustzeit *f.*

interfering signals Störspannung *f.*

interfile/to einordnen *vrb.*

interim archive Zwischenarchiv *n.*

interim report vorläufiger Bericht *m.*, Zwischenbericht *m.*

interim results Zwischenbilanz *f.*

interindexer consistency Interindexiererkonsistenz *f.*

interior design Raumgestaltung *f.*

interlanguage facility Sprachverbindung *f.*

interleaf Durchschuß *m.*, Zwischenblatt *n.*

interleave/to überlappen *vrb.*, verzahnen *vrb.*, einschießen *vrb.*

interleaves eingeschossene Bogen *pl.*

interlinear zwischen den Zeilen

interlinear spacing Zeilenabstand *m.*

interlock Verschluß *m.*, Verriegelung *f.*

intermediar Informationsver-

mittler *m.*
intermediate/to vermitteln
vrb.
intermediate copy Zwischenkopie *f.*
intermediate data Zwischenergebnis *n.*
intermediate file Zwischendatei *f.*
intermediate grade Mittelstufe *f.*
intermediate information Zwischeninformation *f.*
intermediate master Zwischenoriginal *n.*
intermediate storage Zwischenspeicher *m.*
intermediate text Zwischentext *m.*
intermeshing Vermaschung *f.*
internal intern *adj.*
internal connection Innenverbindung *f.*
internal file Interndatei *f.*
internal reader interner Leser *m.*
internal revenue office Finanzamt *m.*
internal stock circulation Ausleihe *f.* des internen Bestandes
internal storage interner Speicher *m.*, Zentralspeicher *m.*
international bibliography internationale Bibliographie *f.*
international catalog card internationale Katalogkarte *f.*
international exchange of publications internationaler Schriftenaustausch *m.*
international law internationales Recht *n.*
international standard inter-

nationale Norm *f.*
international standard book number internationale Standardbuchnummer *f.*
international standard serial number internationale Standardseriennummer *f.*
interpolate/to interpolieren *vrb.*, durchblättern *vrb.*, abgleichen *vrb.*, zuordnen *vrb.*
interpolation Interpolation *f.*
interpolation in array Interpolation *f.* einer Reihe
interpolator Kartenmischer *m.*
interpret/to interpretieren *vrb.*
interpreter Interpreter *m.*
interpreter function Interpreterfunktion *f.*
interpreting Interpretation *f.*
interpretive code Interpretercode *m.*
interpretive program Interpreterprogramm *n.*
interprocessor communication Rechnerkommunikation *f.*
interrecord gap Satzlücke *f.*, Satzzwischenraum *m.*
interrecord separator Satztrennzeichen *n.*
interrelation Wechselbeziehung *f.*
interrogate/to rückfragen *vrb.*
interrogation Rückfrage *f.*, Aufforderung *f.*
interrogation mark Fragezeichen *n.*
interrupt Unterbrechung *f.*
interrupt/to unterbrechen *vrb.*
interrupt controller Unterbrechungssteuerung *f.*
interrupt mode Unterbrechungsmodus *m.*

interrupt priority Unterbrechungspriorität *f.*

interrupt request Unterbrechungsanforderung *f.*

interrupt service routine Unterbrechungssteuerprogramm *n.*

interrupt signal Unterbrechungssignal *n.*

interruptable instruction unterbrechbare Instruktion *f.*

interrupting time Abschaltzeit *f.*

interruption Unterbrechung *f.*

interruption action Unterbrechungsaktion *f.*

interruption code Unterbrechungscode *m.*

interruption condition Unterbrechungsbedingung *f.*

interruption network Unterbrechungsnetzwerk *n.*

interruption pending anstehende Unterbrechung *f.*

interruption priority level Vorrangsunterbrechungsebene *f.*

interruption supervision Unterbrechungsüberwachung *f.*

intersection Schnittpunkt *m.*

intersection data Schnittdaten *pl.*, Intersektionsdaten *pl.*

interurban circulation auswärtiger Leihverkehr *m.*

interurban lending auswärtiger Leihverkehr *m.*

interval control program Zeitintervallkontrollprogramm *n.*

interval password Intervallkennwort *n.*

interval timer Zeitgeber *m.*, Intervallzeitgeber *m.*

interval timer interrupt Intervallzeitgeberunterbrechung *f.*

intervention Eingriff *m.*

intervention required Eingriff *m.* erforderlich

interview Interview *n.*

intracompany innerbetrieblich *adj.*

intrafacet connector Intrafacettenkonnektor *m.*

intrafacet relations Intrafacettenrelationen *pl.*

intrafield check feldinterne Prüfung *f.*

intrapartition Intrapartition *f.*

intrapartition data set interne Datei *f.*

intrapartition destination Übergangsspeicher *m.*

intrarecord sequence field Datensatzsortierfeld *n.*

intrasystem systemintern *adj.*

intrinsic characteristic Eigenmerkmal *n.*, inhärentes Merkmal *n.*

intrinsic conduction Eigenleitung *f.*

intrinsic error Grundfehler *m.*

intrinsic relation intrinsische Relation *f.*, Beziehung *f.* des Enthaltenseins

introduction Einleitung *f.*, Einführung *f.*

introductory course Einführungskurs *m.*

invalid ungültig *adj.*

invalid access action ungültiger Zugriff *m.*

invalid address ungültige Adresse *f.*

invalid choice ungültige Auswahl *f.*

invalid combination of charac-

ter ungültige Zeichenkombination *f.*
invalid entry ungültige Eingabe *f.*
invalid error status ungültiger Fehlerstatus *m.*
invalid field ungültiges Feld *n.*
invalid key ungültige Taste *f.*
invalid name ungültiger Name *m.*
invalid operation fehlerhafte Operation *f.*, ungültige Operation *f.*
invalid program diskette ungültige Programmdiskette *f.*
invalid reception ungültiger Empfang *m.*
invention Erfindung *f.*
inventory Bestandsverzeichnis *n.*, Inventar *n.*
inventory database Bestandsdatenbank *f.*
inventory file Bestandsdatei *f.*
inverse umgekehrt *adj.*, reziprok *adj.*, invers *adj.*
inverse document frequency inverse Dokumenthäufigkeit *f.*
inversion Inversion *f.*, Richtungswechsel *m.*
inversion of heading Umkehrung *f.* der natürlichen Wortfolge
inversion of titles Titelinversion *f.*
invert/to umkehren *vrb.*, invertieren *vrb.*
inverted commas Anführungszeichen *pl.*, Hochkommata *pl.*
inverted compound term invertierter Mehrwortbegriff *m.*
inverted coordinate indexing

invertiertes gleichordnendes Indexieren *n.*
inverted entry invertierter Eintrag *m.*
inverted file invertierte Datei *f.*, invertierte Liste *f.*
inverted heading invertiertes Schlagwort *n.*
inverted number invertierte Zahl *f.*
inverted title Titelinversion *f.*
investigation Ermittlung *f.*
invisible college informelle Gruppe von Wissenschaftlern
invitation Aufruf *m.*
invitation delay Aufrufsverzögerung *f.*
invitation list Aufrufsliste *f.*
invite/to aufrufen *vrb.*
invocation Aufruf *m.*
invoice Rechnung *f.*
invoice/to in Rechnung stellen *vrb.*
invoke/to aufrufen *vrb.*
irrecoverable error nichtbehebbarer Fehler *m.*
irreducibility Unreduzierbarkeit *f.*
irreducible unreduzierbar *adj.*
irregular unregelmäßig *adj.*, irregulär *adj.*
irrelevance Irrelevanz *f.*
isolate Isolat *n.*, Grundbestandteil *m.*, Bedeutungselement *n.*, Einzelklasse *f.*, Singularklasse *f.*
isolate/to entkoppeln *vrb.*, abgrenzen *vrb.*,
isolated location geschützter Speicherplatz *m*
issue Auflagenhöhe *f.*, Ausgabe *f.*

issue/to ausleihen *vrb.*
issue desk Bücherausgabetheke *f.*
issue guide Leitkarte *f.*
issue slip Leihschein *m.*
issue statistic Ausleihstatistik *f.*
issue tray Leihkasten *m.*
issued ausgeliehen *adj.*, verliehen *adj.*
issuing department Leihstelle *f.*
issuing system Ausleihsystem *n.*
italic kursiv *adj.*, Kursivschrift *f.*, Schrägschrift *f.*
italics Kursivschrift *f.*, Schrägschrift *f.*
item Datenfeld *n.*, Feld *n.*, Element *n.*, Artikel *m.*, Betrachtungseinheit *f.*, Posten *m.*, Einheit *f.*, Eintrag *m.*, Objekt *n.*, Dateneinheit *f.*, Informationseinheit *f.*

item entry Dokumenteintrag *m.*, Deskriptoreintrag *m.*
item identification Bestandsnachweis *m.*
item master file Artikelstammdatei *f.*
item match list Auslieferungsliste *f.*
item of information Informationseinheit *f.*
itemize/to spezifizieren *vrb.*
items on loan entliehene Objekte *pl.*
iterate/to wiederholen *vrb.*, iterieren *vrb.*
iteration index Iterationsindex *m.*
iterative partitioning iterative Partitionierung *f.*
iterative search iterative Suche *f.*

J

Jaccard coefficient Jaccard-Koeffizient *m.*
jack Stecker *m.*, Buchse *f.*
jack panel Steckkarte *f.*
jacket Umschlag *m.*, Mikrofilmtasche *f.*
jacket blurb Klappentext *m.*
jackplug Telefonstecker *m.*
jail library Gefängnisbibliothek *f.*

jam Kartenstau *m.*, Papierstau *m.*
jamming Papierstau *m.*
Japanese vellum Japanpapier *m.*
Jesuit archive Archiv *n.* der Jesuiten
Jesuit college library Bibliothek *f.* eines Jesuitenkollegs
jet printer Tintenstrahldrucker

m.
job Auftrag *m.*, Job *m.*, Beschäftigung *f.*
job accounting Auftragsabrechnung *f.*, Jobabrechnung *f.*
job batch Jobstapel *m.*
job begin Auftragsbeginn *m.*
job control document Auftragsbegleitdokument *n.*
job control information Auftragssteuerungsinformation *f.*
job control language Kommandosprache *f.*, Jobkontrollsprache *f.*
job control record Jobkontrollsatz *m.*
job control statement Jobkontrollanweisung *f.*
job controlling Auftragssteuerung *f.*
job cycle Jobzyklus *m.*
job definition Jobdefinition *f.*
job description Auftragsanweisung *f.*, Stellenbeschreibung *f.*, Berufsbild *n.*
job end Auftragsende *n.*
job file Jobdatei *f.*
job flow Jobfluß *m.*
job identification Auftragskennzeichen *n.*, Jobidentifikation *f.*
job indicator Jobbezugszahl *f.*
job initiation Jobeinleitung *f.*
job input device Jobeingabegerät *n.*
job interrupt Jobunterbrechung *f.*
job library Jobbibliothek *f.*
job logging Auftragsprotokoll *n.*
job management Aufgabenver-

waltung *f.*
job market Arbeitsmarkt *m.*
job name Jobname *m.*
job-oriented terminal aufgabenspezifische Datenstation *f.*
job output device Jobausgabegerät *n.*
job printing Akzidenzdruck *m.*
job processing Jobverarbeitung *f.*
job profil Jobprofil *n.*
job queue entry Jobwarteschlangeneintrag *m.*
job satisfaction Arbeitszufriedenheit *f.*
job scheduler Auftragsverwaltungsprogramm *n.*
job select switch Jobauswahlschalter *m.*
job sequence Auftragsabfolge *f.*
job step Auftragsstufe *f.*
job stream Auftragsabfolge *f.*
job subject Auftragsleistung *f.*
job termination Jobbeendigung *f.*
jobber Buchhändler *m.*
jobbing house Akzidenzdruckerei *f.*
jobbing work Akzidenzdruck *m.*
joggle/to anschlagen *vrb.*
join/to verbinden *vrb.*
join operation kartesische Verknüpfungsoperation *f.*
joint Falz *m.*, Verbindung *f.*
joint author Koautor *m.*, Mitverfasser *m.*
joint catalog Zentralkatalog *m.*
joint editor Mitherausgeber *m.*
journal Journal *n.*, Tageszeitung *f.*, Tagebuch *n.*, Zeitschrift *f.*
journal acquisition Zeitschrif-

tenerwerbung *f*.
journal article Zeitungsartikel
m.
journal article title Zeitungsartikeltitel *m*.
journal citation Zitierrate *f*.
von Zeitschriften
journal influence Einfluß *m*.
von Zeitschriften
journal of transactions Transaktionsprotokoll *n*.
journal subscription Zeitschriftenbestellung *f*.
journalese Zeitungsstil *m*.
journalism Journalismus *m*.,
Pressewesen *n*., Publizistik *f*.
journalist Journalist *m*.
journalize/to in ein Tagebuch
eintragen *vrb*.
joystick Steuerknüppel *m*.
judgement Beurteilung *f*., Urteil *n*.
jump Sprung *m*.
jump instruction Sprungbefehl
m.
jumper Brücke *f*.
jumps partition key Sprungtaste *f*.
junction Anschluß *m*., Verbin-

dung *f*., Übergang *m*.
junctor Koppler *m*.
junior college library Bibliothek
f. eines Junior-College
junior high school Realschule *f*.
junior library Kinderbücherei
f., Kinderbibliothek *f*.
junk Ausschuß *m*.
jurisprudence Rechtswissenschaft *f*.
just issued soeben erschienen
adj.
just published soeben erschienen *adj*.
justice Justiz *f*.
justification Justierung *f*., Ausrichtung *f*.
justified right-hand margin
rechtsbündig ausgerichtet *adj*.
justify/to ausrichten *vrb*., ausschließen *vrb*.
juvenile book Jugendbuch *n*.
juvenile book department Jugendbuchabteilung *f*.
juvenile book week Jugendbuchwoche *f*.
juvenile literature Jugendliteratur *f*.

K

keep/to aufbewahren *vrb*., bewahren *vrb*.
keep up-to-date/to fortschrei-

ben *vrb*., auf den neuesten
Stand bringen *vrb*., auf dem
neuesten Stand halten *vrb*.

kern Überhang *m.*
kerned letter überhängender
Buchstabe *m.*
key Schlüssel *m.*, Taste *f.*, Identifikator *m.*
key area Schlüsselfeld *n.*
key-button Tastenknopf *m.*
key contact time Tastenwirkdauer *f.*
key control Tastensteuerung *f.*
key-controlled tastengesteuert
adj.
key-controlled protection
schlüsselgesteuerter Speicherschutz *m.*
key description Tastenbeschreibung *f.*
key entry area Eintastbereich
m.
key field Schlüsselfeld *n.*
key figure Schlüsselzahl *f.*
key form Hauptformular *n.*
key heading Überschrift *f.* für
Schlüsselfeld
key identification Schlüsselkennzeichnung *f.*
key in/to eingeben *vrb.*
key in data set Satzschlüssel *m.*
key indexed access method
Schlüsselindexzugriffsmethode *f.*
key length Schlüssellänge *f.*
key limit Schlüsselgrenze *f.*
key location Schlüssellage *f.*
key log Schlüsselschalter *m.*,
Betriebsschloß *n.*
key of reference Bezugsschlüssel *m.*
key operating Tastenbetätigung *f.*
key operating time Tastenbetätigungsdauer *f.*

key-pointer Schlüsselhinweisfeld *n.*
key publication Schlüsselwerk
f.
key punch Locher *m.*
key range Schlüsselbereich *m.*
key row Tastenreihe *f.*
key sequence Schlüsselfolge *f.*
key-sequenced data set Datei *f.*
in Schlüsselfolge
key-sequenced file Datei *f.* in
Schlüsselfolge
key station Erfassungsstelle *f.*
key stroke Tastenanschlag *m.*
key symbol Tastensymbol *n.*
key title Schlüsseltitel *m.*
key to sectional map Übersichtskarte *f.*
key to the signs used Legende
f., Zeichenerklärung *f.*
key-to-type system Taste-
Druck-System *n.*
key touch Tastenanschlag *m.*
key verification Schlüsselüberprüfung *f.*
keyboard Tastatur *f.*
keyboard arrangement Zeichenanordnung *f.* der Tastatur, Tastenanordnung *f.*
keyboard attachment Direktanschluß *m.* der Tastatur
keyboard change Tastaturwechsel *m.*
keyboard-controlled tastaturgesteuert *adj.*, tastengesteuert *adj.*
keyboard correction Fehlerkorrektur *f.* über Tastatur
keyboard difference Tastaturunterschied *m.*
keyboard file Tastaturdatei *f.*
keyboard graphic druckbares

Zeichen *n.*

keyboard inquiry Tastaturabfrage *f.*

keyboard lock-up Tastaturblockierung *f.*

keyboard modul Tastatur *f.*

keyboard printer Terminaldrucker *m.*

keyboard programming manuelle Programmierung *f.*

keyboard punch Locher *m.*

keyboard request Abruftaste *f.*

keyboard scanning Tastenauswahl *f.*

keyboard stroke Tastenanschlag *m.*

keyboard substitution Tastaturänderung *f.*

keyboardless printer Schreibwerk *n.* ohne Tastatur

keyed direct access Direktzugriff *m.* mit Schlüssel

keyed sequential access sequentieller Zugriff *m.* in Schlüsselfolge

keying Eintasten *n.*

keying mistake Tippfehler *m.*

keypad Tastatur *f.*

keypad area Tastaturbereich *m.*

keypunch Locher *m.*

keysort Schlüsselsortierung *f.*

keytop Tastenknopf *m.*

keyword Schlüsselwort *n.*, Stichwort *n.*, Kennwort *n.*

keyword-and-context index KWAC-Index *m.*

keyword catalog Stichwortkatalog *m.*

keyword-in-context index KWIC-Index *m.*

keyword-in-title indexing

KWIT-Indexierung *f.*

keyword indexing Stichwortindexierung *f.*

keyword list Stichwortliste *f.*

keyword operand Schlüsselwortoperand *m.*

keyword-out-of-context index KWOC-Index *m.*

keyword-out-of-context indexing KWOC-Indexierung *f.*

keyword parameter Schlüsselwortparameter *m.*

kill/to abbrechen *vrb.*

kilobaud Kilobaud *n.*

kilobyte Kilobyte *n.*

kind Art *f.*

kind of letter Schriftart *f.*

kind of type Schriftart *f.*

kinds of catalogs Katalogarten *pl.*

kinds of libraries Bibliothekstypen *pl.*

kinetic relation kinetische Beziehung *f.*

King's library Bibliothek *f.* des Königs

kit Nachrüstsatz *m.*, Satz *m.*

knowledge Gelernte *n.*, Wissen *n.*

knowledge acquisition Wissenserwerb *m.*

knowledge base Wissensbasis *f.*

knowledge-based system wissensbasiertes System *n.*

knowledge database Wissensbank *f.*

knowledge engineering Wissensingenieurwesen *n.*

knowledge field Wissensgebiet *n.*

knowledge in a specialized field Fachwissen *n.*

knowledge presentation Wissensdarstellung *f.*
knowledge representation Wissensrepräsentation *f.*

knowledge transfer Wissenstransfer *m.*
known problems database Datenbank *m.* bekannter Fehler

L

label Marke *f.*, Kennsatz *m.*, Merkmal *n.*, Hinweisschild *n.*, Papierschildchen *n.*, Anweisungsname *m.*, Kennzeichnung *f.*, Bezeichnung *f.*, Aufkleber *m.*, Etikett *n.*, Marke *f.*
label/to kennzeichnen *vrb.*, bezeichnen *vrb.*
label area Kennsatzbereich *m.*
label constant Markenkonstante *f.*
label group Kennsatzgruppe *f.*
label handling routine Kennsatzroutine *f.*
label holder Etikettenhalter *m.*, Schilderhalter *m.*
label identifier Kennsatzkennzeichen *n.*
label information Kennsatzinformation *f.*
label information area Kennsatzinformationsbereich *m.*
label name Kennsatzname *m.*
label number Kennsatznummer *f.*
label printer Etikettendrucker *m.*
label processing Kennsatzver-

arbeitung *f.*
label processor error message Label-Prozessorfehlernachricht *f.*
label processor input data set Label-Prozessoreinheit *f.*
label processor output Label-Prozessorausgabe *f.*
label record Kennsatz *m.*
label sector Kennsatzsektor *m.*
label set Kennsatzfamilie *f.*, Kennsatzgruppe *f.*
label storage area Kennsatzspeicherbereich *m.*
label track Kennsatzspur *f.*
label variable Markenvariable *f.*
labelled tag beschrifteter Anhänger *m.*
labelling Kennzeichnung *f.*, Etikettieren *n.*
labor certificate Arbeitserlaubnis *f.*
labor law Arbeitsrecht *n.*
labor market Arbeitsmarkt *m.*
labor union Gewerkschaft *f.*
labor union archive Gewerkschaftsarchiv *n.*

labor union library Gewerkschaftsbibliothek *f.*
lack Mangel *m.*
lacuna Lücke *f.*, Zwischenraum *m.*
lag Verzögerung *f.*, Abstand *m.*, Lücke *f.*
land register Grundbuch *n.*
language Sprache *f.*
language and literature library sprach- und literaturwissenschaftliche Bibliothek *f.*
language atlas Sprachatlas *m.*
language barrier Sprachbarriere *f.*
language comprehension Sprachverdichtung *f.*
language course Sprachkurs *m.*
language data processing Sprachdatenverarbeitung *f.*
language development Sprachentwicklung *f.*
language generation Sprachgenerierung *f.*
language laboratory Sprachlabor *n.*
language pattern Sprachmuster *n.*
language processing Sprachverarbeitung *f.*
language processor Sprachprozessor *m.*, Übersetzer *m.*
language school Sprachschule *f.*
language school library Sprachschulbibliothek *f.*
language statement Sprachanweisung *f.*
language subdivision sprachliche Unterteilung *f.*
language tape Sprachkassette *f.*
language test Sprachprüfung *f.*
language theory Sprachtheorie *f.*
language translation Übersetzung *f.*
language translator Übersetzer *m.*
language understanding system sprachverstehendes System *n.*
lap-size computer tragbarer Computer *m.*
large-capacity storage Großhauptspeicher *m.*
large edition Massenauflage *f.*
large face grobe Schrift *f.*, grober Schnitt *m.*
large folio Großfolio *n.*
large format Großformat *n.*
large library Großbibliothek *f.*
large print Großdruck *m.*
large-sized großformatig *adj.*
large system Großsystem *n.*
laser Laser *m.*
laser disk Laserplatte *f.*
laser enclosure geschlossener Laser *m.*
laser memory Laserspeicher *m.*
laser printer Laserdrucker *m.*
laser scanner Laserskanner *m.*
laser vision Laserbild *n.*
last access date letztes Zugriffsdatum *n.*
last copy Archivexemplar *n.*
last issue letzte Ausgabe *f.*
last-record indicator Anzeiger *m.* des letzten Satzes
last-record pointer Hinweisadresse *f.* zum letzten Satz
last years Lebensabend *m.*
latch elektronischer Schalter

m.

latch/to abschalten *vrb.*, sperren *vrb.*

latch-down key einrastbare Taste *f*.

late charges Mahngebühren *pl.*

late exception recognition späte Ausnahmeerkennung *f*.

latency Wartezeit *f*.

latency time Zugriffswartezeit *f*.

latest end date spätester Endtermin *m*.

latest estimate neueste Vorausschätzung *f*.

latest finish date spätester Fertigstellungstermin *m*.

latest start date spätester Starttermin *m*.

lattice Netzwerk *n*.

lattice structure Gitterstruktur *f*.

launching cost Anlaufkosten *pl.*

law Recht *n.*, Gesetz *n*.

law gazette Gesetzblatt *n*.

law library juristische Bibliothek *f*.

law of contract Vertragsrecht *n*.

law of nature Naturgesetz *n*.

law school library Bibliothek *f*. der juristischen Fakultät

layer Schicht *f.*, Belag *m*.

layout Gestaltung *f*. von Veröffentlichungen, Layout *n.*, Entwurf *m*.

layout character Formatsteuerzeichen *n*.

layout editor Layoutredakteur *m*.

layout format Formataufbau *m.*, Formatentwurf *m*.

layout instruction Layoutanweisung *f*.

layout procedure Anordnungsprozedur *f*.

lead Netzkabel *n*.

lead/to anführen *vrb.*, leiten *vrb*.

lead time Durchlaufzeit *f*.

lead typesetting Bleisatz *m*.

leaded durchschossen *adj*.

leaded matter gesperrter Satz *m*.

leader Vorspannstreifen *m.*, Startband *n*.

leader record Vorsatz *m*.

leader strip Startband *n*.

leader writer Leitartikelschreiber *m*.

leaders punktierte Linie *f*.

leading Durchschuß *m.*, Blindmaterial *n*.

leading dial Durchschußwähler *m*.

leading edge Führungskante *f*.

leading end Bandanfang *m*.

leading graphics führende Zeichen *pl.*, voreingestellte Zeichen *pl.*

leading sign Führungszeichen *n.*, Vorzeichen *n*.

leading string character Wortanfangszeichen *n*.

leads Durchschüsse *pl.*

leaf Blatt *n*.

leaf number Blattzahl *f*.

leaflet Faltblatt *n.*, Flugblatt *n*.

learned gelehrt *adj*.

learned library Studienbibliothek *f.*, Forschungsbibliothek *f*.

learned publication wissenschaftliche Veröffentlichung *f*.

learner Auszubildender *m.*
learning Gelehrsamkeit *f.*, Wissen *n.*
learning environment Lernumgebung *f.*
least effort geringster Widerstand *m.*
least significant bit niederwertigstes Bit *n.*
least term kleinstes Glied *n.*
leather binding Ledereinband *m.*
lectorate Lektorat *n.*, Dozentur *f.*
lecture Vortrag *m.*, Lehrveranstaltung *f.*, Vorlesung *f.*, Kolleg *n.*
lectureship Dozentur *f.*, Lektorat *n.*
ledger Hauptbuch *n.*, Register *n.*
ledger card Karteikarte *f.*
ledger catalog Katalog *m.* in Registerform, Bandkatalog *m.*
left adjusted linksbündig *adj.*
left column number linke Stelle *f.*
left-hand margin Anfangsanschlag *m.*
left-hand zero führende Null *f.*
left justification Linksausrichtung *f.*
left justified linksbündig *adj.*
left margin Anfangsrand *m.*, linker Schreibrand *m.*
left margin control linke Randsteuerung *f.*
left oblique Schrägstrich *m.*
left parenthesis Klammer *f.* auf, öffnende Klammer *f.*
left part linke Seite *f.*
legal gesetzlich *adj.*, gültig *adj.*
legal authority Justizbehörde *f.*
legal data processing juristi-

sche Datenverarbeitung *f.*
legal database Rechtsdatenbank *f.*
legal deposit Pflichtablieferung *f.*
legal deposit library Pflichtexemplarbibliothek *f.*
legal deposit material Pflichtablieferungsmaterial *n.*
legal deposit regulations Pflichtablieferungsbestimmungen *pl.*
legal document Akte *f.*
legal documentation Rechtsdokumentation *f.*
legal file Gesetzessammlung *f.*
legal memorandum rechtskräftiges Dokument *n.*
legal problems Rechtsfragen *pl.*
legal research Rechtsinformationssuche *f.*
legal service library Rechtsberatungsbibliothek *f.*
legend Bildunterschrift *m.*, Erklärung *f.*, Legende *f.*
legibility Lesbarkeit *f.*
legible lesbar *adj.*
legislator Gesetzgeber *m.*
legislature library Legislativbibliothek *f.*
lemma Lemma *n.*, Kurztitel *m.*
lemmatization Lemmatisierung *f.*
lend/to ausleihen *vrb.*
lender Ausleiher *m.*
lending Leihverkehr *m.*
lending area Leihverkehrsregion *f.*
lending collection Ausleihbestand *m.*
lending data Leihdaten *pl.*
lending department Buchaus-

gabe *f.*, Leihstelle *f.*
lending desk Ausleihtheke *f.*
lending form Leihschein *m.*
lending library Leihbibliothek *f.*
lending record Leihvermerk *m.*
lending rules Leihverkehrsordnung *f.*
lending service Verleihdienst *m.*
lending stock Ausleihbestand *m.*
lending survey Ausleihschätzung *f.*
lending system Ausleihverfahren *n.*
length Länge *f.*
length code Längenschlüssel *m.*
length field Längenfeld *n.*
length modifier Längenschlüssel *m.*
length of form Formatbreite *f.*
length record Satzlänge *f.*
length specification Längenangabe *f.*
lengthwise Hochformat *n.*,
längsgerichtet *adj.*
lens Leuchtknopf *m.*, Linse *f.*
lent ausgeliehen *part.*, verliehen *part.*
less than sign Kleiner-als-Zeichen *n.*
less-structured data system
schwach strukturiertes Datensystem *n.*
lessen/to verringern *vrb.*
lessons Unterricht *m.*
let in/to einschleusen *vrb.*
let out/to ausschleusen *vrb.*
letter Schriftzeichen *n.*, Buchstabe *m.*, Brief *m.*
letter-by-letter buchstabenweise *adj.*
letter-by-letter arrangement
buchstabenweise Sortierung

f.
letter folder Ablagemappe *f.*
letter key Buchstabentaste *f.*
letter key row Buchstabentastenreihe *f.*
letter-quality print Schönschriftdruck *m.*
letter shift Buchstabenumschaltung *f.*
letter spacing Sperrdruck *m.*
letter string Buchstabenfolge *f.*
letter tray Ablagekorb *m.*
letter type Buchstabentyp *m.*
letterhead Briefkopf *m.*
lettering Titeldrucken *n.*, Beschriftung *f.*
letterpress composition Bleisatz *m.*
letterpress printer Buchdrucker
m.
letterpress printing Buchdruck
m., Hochdruck *m.*
level Stufe *f.*, Ordnung *f.*,
Ebene *f.*, Niveau *n.*
level control Einrücksteuerung
f.
level field Kontrollfeld *n.*
level identifier Stufenkennung
f.
level indicator Stufenbezeichnung *f.*
level number Ebenennummer *f.*
level of efficiency Leistungsgrad *m.*
level of integration Integrationsgrad *m.*
level of knowledge Wissensniveau *n.*
level of organization Organisationsniveau *n.*
level regulator Niveauregler
m.

level structure Ebenenaufbau *m.*

level switching Ebenenumschaltung *f.*

levels of measurement Meßniveau *n.*

lever Hebel *m.*

lexeme Lexem *n.*

lexical lexikalisch *adj.*

lexical analysis lexikalische Analyse *f.*

lexical content lexikalischer Inhalt *m.*

lexical distortion lexikalische Verzerrung *f.*

lexical meaning lexikalische Bedeutung *f.*

lexical process lexikalischer Prozeß *m.*

lexicographer Lexikograph *m.*

lexicography Lexikographie *f.*

lexicology Lexikologie *f.*

lexicon Lexikon *n.*

lexigraphy Wortschrift *f.*

liable verantwortlich *adj.*

liaison work Verbindungsarbeit *f.*

librarian Bibliothekar *m.*

librarian association Bibliothekarsverband *m.*

librarian´s day Tag *m.* des Bibliothekars

librarianship Bibliothekswesen *n.*

library Bücherei *f.*, Bibliothek *f.*, Programmbibliothek *f.*

library act Bibliotheksgesetz *n.*

library administration Büchereiverwaltung *f.*, Bibliotheksverwaltung *f.*

library adviser Fachstellenbibliothekar *f.*

library association Bibliotheksverband *m.*

library automation Bibliotheksautomatisierung *f.*

library board Bibliotheksausschuß *m.*

library budget Bibliotheksetat *m.*

library building Bibliotheksbau *m.*, Bibliotheksgebäude *n.*

library card Lesekarte *f.*, Benutzerausweis *m.*

library chaining Verketten *n.* von Bibliotheken

library charge Bibliotheksgebühr *f.*

library classification bibliothekarische Klassifikation *f.*, Bibliotheksklassifikation *f.*

library clerk Bibliotheksangestellter *m.*

library collection Bibliotheksbestand *f.*

library commission Bibliothekskommission *f.*

library committee Bibliotheksausschuß *m.*

library computer center Bibliotheksrechenzentrum *n.*

library conference Bibliothekskonferenz *f.*

library congress Bibliothekskongreß *m.*

library consultant Bibliotheksberater *m.*

library council Bibliotheksrat *m.*

library counseling center Fachstelle *f.*

library directory Bibliotheksverzeichnis *n.*

library economy Bibliotheks-

wirtschaft *f.*
library education Bibliotheksausbildung *f.*
library equipment Bibliotheksausstattung *f.*, Bibliothekseinrichtung *f.*
library evaluation Bibliotheksbewertung *f.*
library fee Bibliotheksgebühr *f.*
library for the blind Blindenbibliothek *f.*
library function Bibliotheksfunktion *f.*
library history Bibliotheksgeschichte *f.*
library information Bibliotheksinformation *f.*
library information system
Bibliotheksinformationssystem *n.*
library institute Bibliotheksinstitut *n.*
library legislation Bibliotheksrecht *n.*
library maintenance Bibliothekswartung *f.*
library management Bibliotheksverwaltung *n.*
library manager Bibliotheksmanager *m.*
library material Bibliotheksmaterial *n.*
library name Bibliotheksname
m.
library network Bibliotheksnetz *n.*, Bibliotheksverbund
m., Bibliotheksnetzwerk *n.*
library of congress Kongreßbibliothek *f.*
library of programs Programmbibliothek *f.*
library option Bibliotheksop-

tion *f.*
library organization Bibliotheksorganisation *f.*
library orientation Bibliothekseinführung *f.*
library periodical bibliothekarische Fachzeitschrift *f.*
library personnel Bibliothekspersonal *n.*
library planning Bibliotheksplanung *f.*
library policy Bibliothekspolitik
f.
library publicity Bibliothekswerbung *f.*
library regulation Bibliotheksordnung *f.*
library research Bibliotheksforschung *f.*
library rules Bibliotheksordnung *f.*
library school Bibliotheksschule
f.
library science Bibliothekswissenschaft *f.*
library service Bibliotheksdienst *m.*
**library service for the old peo-
ple** Altenbücherdienst *m.*
library skill bibliothekarische
Fachkenntnis *f.*
library staff Bibliotheksmitarbeiter *pl.*
library standard Bibliotheksnorm *f.*, Bibliotheksstandard
m.
library statistics Bibliotheksstatistik *f.*
library stock Bibliotheksbestand *m.*
library subroutine Bibliotheksprogramm *n.*

library supply agency bibliothekarische Einkaufszentrale *f.*

library supply center Einkaufszentrale *f.*

library survey Bibliotheksumfrage *f.*

library system Bibliothekssystem *n.*

library technician Bibliothekstechniker *m.*

library technology Bibliothekstechnik *f.*

library tour Bibliotheksführung *f.*

library track Hinweisspur *f.*

library trustees Bibliotheksverwaltungsrat *m.*

library use Bibliotheksbenutzung *f.*

library user Büchereibenutzer *m.*, Bibliotheksbenutzer *m.*

library week Woche *f.* der Bibliothek

library work Bibliotheksarbeit *f.*

license Approbation *f.*, Lizenz *f.*, Lizenzgebühr *f.*

license/to lizenzieren *vrb.*

license agreement Nutzungsvertrag *m.*, Lizenzabkommen *m.*

license program Lizenzprogramm *n.*

licensed lizenziert *adj.*

licensee Lizenznehmer *m.*

licenser Lizenzgeber *m.*

licensing Lizenzerteilung *f.*

life-span Lebensdauer *f.*

lift/to heben *vrb.*

lift key Hebeplattenkontrolle *f.*

lift-off correction Korrektur *f.*

durch Abheben

lift-off tape Korrekturband *n.*

ligature Doppelbuchstabe *m.*

light fiction Trivialliteratur *f.*

light output Lichtemission *f.*

light pen Lichtstift *m.*

light pen attachment Lichtstiftanschluß *m.*

light pen attention Lichtstiftabruf *m.*

light pen detection Lichtstifterkennung *f.*

light pen hit Lichtstifterkennung *f.*

light pen input Lichtstifteingang *m.*

light pen mode Lichtstiftmodus *m.*

light pen strike Lichtstifterkennung *f.*

light pen switching Lichtstiftschalter *m.*

light pen tracking Lichtstiftverfolgung *f.*

light sensing device Photozelle *f.*

light-sensitive lichtempfindlich *adj.*

light-wave cable Glasfaserkabel *n.*

lighted beleuchtet *adj.*

lighted message Leuchtanzeige *f.*

lightface Dünndruck *m.*

lighting Beleuchtung *f.*

lighting of the library Bibliotheksbeleuchtung *f.*

like gleich *adj.*

like attribute Gleichheitsattribut *n.*

limit Grenzwert *m.*

limit/to begrenzen *vrb.*

limit priority Grenzvorrang
m., Schwellpriorität *f.*
limit value Grenzwert *m.*
limitation Einschränkung *f.,*
Beschränkung *f.*
limitation of growth Wachstumsbegrenzung *f.*
limited begrenzt *adj.*
limited cataloging Kurztitelaufnahme *f.*
limited edition begrenzte Auflage *f.*
limited entry row begrenzte
Zeilen *pl.*
limited interchangeability begrenzte Austauschbarkeit *f.*
limiter Begrenzer *m.*
limiting deviations Grenzabweichungen *pl.*
limiting facility Begrenzungseinrichtung *f.*
limiting level Aussteuerungsgrenze *f.*
limiting value Grenzwert *m.*
line Leitung *f.,* Zeile *f.,* Linie *f.*
line/to linieren *vrb.*
line adapter Leitungsanschluß
m.
line addressing Zeilenadressierung *f.*
line base adapter Leitungsanschluß *m.*
line beginning Zeilenanfang *m.*
line-by-line zeilenweise *adj.*
line cancel character Zeilenlöschzeichen *n.*
line charge Leitungsgebühr *f.*
line check Leitungsprüfung *m.*
line circuit Übertragung *f.*
line communication network
Liniennetz *n.*
line continuation Zeilenfortset-

zung *f.*
line control Leitungssteuerung
f., Übertragungssteuerung *f.*
line control character Leitungssteuerzeichen *n.*
line control discipline Leitungsprozedur *f.*
line control signal Leitungssteuerzeichen *n.*
line control specification
Druckzeilenbestimmung *f.*
line current Netzstrom *m.*
line data area Leitungsdatenbereich *m.*
line data channel Ferndatenkanal *m.*
line end signal Zeilenendsignal
n.
line entry Leitungseingang *m.*
line error Leitungsfehler *m.*
line expand Zeilenerweiterung
f., Zeilenverlängerung *f.*
line feed Zeilenschaltung *f.,*
Zeilenvorschub *m.*
line feed character Zeilenvorschubzeichen *n.*
line finder mark Zeilenmarkierung *f.*
line format Zeilenformat *n.*
line format change Zeilenformatwechsel *m.*
line generator Vektorgenerator *m.*
line group data set Leitungsgruppendatei *f.*
line height Zeilenhöhe *f.*
line identification Kennzeichnung *f.* der Anschlußleitungen
line key Linientaste *f.*
line length Zeilenlänge *f.*
line limit Zeilenlänge *f.*
line loop operation Fernverar-

beitung *f*.
line loss Leitungsdämpfung *f*.
line mark Zeilenkennzeichnung
f.
line motion control system
Streckensteuerung *f*.
line number Zeilennummer *f*.,
Leitungsnummer *f*.
line occupancy Leitungsbelegung *f*.
line of access Vorschublinie *f*.
line of communication Kommunikationskanal *m*.
line off/to Leitung abhängen
vrb.
line pitch Zeilenabstand *m*.
line position indicator Zeilenanzeiger *m*.
line posting Zeileneinstellung *f*.
line printer Zeilendrucker *m*.
line printer attachment Anschluß *m*. für Zeilendrucker
line rag Einschubrahmen *m*.
line return Zeilenwiederholung
f.
line ruler Liniereinrichtung *f*.
line scanner Zeilenabtaster *m*.
line separation vertikaler
Druckzonenabstand *m*.
line separator Zeilentrennsymbol *n*.
line sequence Signalfolge *f*.
line set Leitungsanschluß *m*.
line skip Zeilensprung *m*.
line skipping Zeilenvorschub *m*.
line space Zeilenabstand *m*.
line space key Zeilenschalttaste
f.
line space lever Zeilenabstandhebel *m*.
line space preset key Zeilenabstandsvoreinsteller *m*.

line space selector Zeilenabstandeinsteller *m*.
line space set key Zeilenabstandeinsteller *m*.
line spacer Zeilenschalter *m*.
line spacing Zeilentransport
m., Zeilenschaltung *f*., Zeilenabstand *m*.
line speed Übertragungsgeschwindigkeit *f*.
line speed options Übertra-
gungsgeschwindigkeitswahl
f.
line splitter Kanalaufteiler *m*.
line start Zeilenanfang *m*.
line statistic Leitungsstatistik *f*.
line supervision Leitungsüberwachung *f*.
line switch Hauptschalter *m*.
line switching Leitungsvermittlung *f*.
line termination Leitungsabbruch *m*.
line time out Leitungszeitsperre *f*.
line trace Leitungsprotokoll *n*.
line traffic Leitungsverkehr *m*.
line transfer Leitungsumschaltung *f*.
line transfer switch manueller
Leitungsumschalter *m*.
line transmission error Übertragungsfehler *m*.
line transport Zeilenschritt *m*.
line type Leitungsart *f*.
line unit Leitungseinheit *f*.
line-up Leitungseinschaltung *f*.
line voltage Netzspannung *f*.
line weight Schriftstärke *f*.
linear linear *adj*.
linear classification Linearklassifikation *f*.

linear file lineare Datei *f*.
linear list lineare Liste *f*.
linear model lineares Modell *n*.
linear notation lineare Notation *f*.
linear optimization lineare Optimierung *f*.
linear programming lineare Programmierung *f*.
linear scan lineare Abtastung *f*.
linearity Linearität *f*.
linearity error Linearitätsfehler *m*.
linearize/to linearisieren *vrb*.
lined gedeckt *adj*.
linguistic linguistisch *adj*.
linguistic ambiguity linguistische Mehrdeutigkeit *f*.
linguistic analysis linguistische Analyse *f*.
linguistic data processing linguistische Datenverarbeitung *f*.
linguistic method linguistisches Verfahren *n*.
linguistic processor linguistischer Prozessor *m*.
linguistic thesaurus linguistischer Thesaurus *m*.
linguistics Linguistik *f*., Sprachwissenschaft *f*.
link Verbindungselement *n*., Beziehung *f*.
link address Verkettungsadresse *f*.
link circuit Verbindungsleitung *f*.
link connection Verbindung *f*.
link edit/to verbinden *vrb*.
link editor Bindeprogramm *n*.
link field Kettfeld *n*.
link header Verbindungsvor-

satz *m*.
link in the chain Glied *n*. der Kette
link indicator Verbindungsindikator *m*.
link protocol Übermittlungsvorschrift *f*., Verbindungsprotokoll *n*.
link station Verbindungsstation *f*.
link test Verbindungstest *m*.
link to program Programmverbindung *f*.
linkage Verbindung *f*., Verkettung *f*.
linkage convention Richtlinien *pl*. der Programmverbindung
linkage symbol Programmverbindungssymbol *n*.
linked subroutine verbundenes Unterprogramm *n*.
linker Binder *m*.
linking Kopplung *f*.
linking sequence Folge *f*. von Bindebefehlen
list Liste *f*.
list/to auflisten *vrb*.
list-directed listengesteuert *adj*.
list-directed input/output listengesteuerte Ein-/Ausgabe *f*.
list-directed transmission listengesteuerte Übertragung *f*.
list field Druckfeld *n*.
list file Listdatei *f*.
list identifier Listenkennung *f*.
list item Listenelement *n*.
list name Listenname *m*.
list of abbreviations Abkürzungsverzeichnis *n*., Liste *f*. der Abkürzungen

list of contents Inhaltsangabe *f.*
list of illustrations Verzeichnis
n. der Abbildungen
list of recommended books
Buchempfehlungsliste *f.*
list of terms Begriffsliste *n.*
list off Sammelgang *m.*
list processing Listenverarbeitung *f.*
list selection Listenauswahl *f.*
listen-in extension Mithörstelle *f.*
listen-in set Mithörapparat *m.*
listing Liste *f.*, Bericht *m.*
listing control instruction Listensteuerbefehl *m.*
literacy literarische Bildung *f.*
literal wörtlich *adj.*, Literal *n.*
literal constant Literalkonstante *f.*
literal pool Literalbereich *m.*
literal translation wortgetreue
Übersetzung *f.*
literalism Buchstabenglaube
m., wirklichkeitstreue Wiedergabe *f.*
literality wörtliche Bedeutung
f.
literalize/to wörtlich wiedergeben *vrb.*
literally wörtlich *adv.*, Wort
für Wort
literary literarisch *adj.*
literary activity literarische
Tätigkeit *f.*
literary criticism Literaturkritik
f.
literary language literarische
Sprache *f.*
literary periodical literarische
Zeitschrift *f.*
literary review literarische

Renzension *f.*
literary studies Literaturwissenschaft *f.*
literate literarisch *adj.*, literarisch Gebildeter *m.*
literature Schrifttum *n.*,
Literatur *f.*
literature analyst Literaturauswerter *m.*
literature and language library
literatur- und sprachwissenschaftliche Bibliothek *f.*
literature documentation Literaturdokumentation *f.*
literature growth Literaturzuwachs *m.*
literature guide Literaturführer *m.*
literature review Literaturbesprechung *f.*
literature search Literatursuche *f.*, Literaturrecherche *f.*
lithography Lithographie *f.*
little magazine Illustrierte *f.*
live test Test *m.* unter Einsatzbedingungen
live wire Leitung *f.* unter
Spannung
load Belastung *f.*, Belegung *f.*,
Einspannen *n.*
load/to laden *vrb.*, erstellen
vrb., belegen *vrb.*
load format Ladeformat *n.*
load indicator Ladeanzeiger *m.*
load member Ladeeintragung
f.
load mode Laden *n.*
load module Lademodul *n.*
load module library Ladebibliothek *f.*
load point Ladepunkt *m.*, Ladeadresse *f.*

load procedure Ladeverfahren
n.
loader Ladeprogramm *n.*
loading Laden *n.*
loading capacity Belastbarkeit
f.
loading factor Lastfaktor *m.*
loan Ausleihe *f.*, Leihgabe *f.*
loan/to ausleihen *vrb.*
loan collection Ausleihbestand
m., Leihbestand *m.*
loan data Leihdaten *pl.*
loan department Leihstelle *f.*
loan desk Bücherausgabetheke
f.
loan fee Leihgebühr *f.*
loan library Ausleihbibliothek *f.*
loan library rules Leihordnung
f.
loan period Leihfrist *f.*
loan record Ausleihkartei *f.*
loan register Ausleihregister *n.*
loan service Verleih *m.*
loan statistic Leihstatistik *f.*
loan system Ausleihverfahren
n.
loanable items entleihbare
Objekte *pl.*
loans work Ausleihbetrieb *m.*
local lokal *adj.*
local address lokale Adresse *f.*
local area network lokales
Netzwerk *n.*
local authority Kommunalbehörde *f.*
local bibliography Ortsbibliographie *f.*
local catalog Lokalbestandskatalog *m.*
local circulation Ortsleihe *f.*
local clustering lokales Clustern *n.*

local command lokaler Befehl
m.
local data Lokaldaten *pl.*
local destination lokaler Bestimmungsort *m.*
local device lokale Einheit *f.*
local key lokaler Schlüssel *m.*
local lending Ortsleihe *f.*
local link Endfeld *n.*
local list geographische Unterteilung *f.*
local loans Ortsleihe *f.*
local output lokale Ausgabe *f.*
local processor lokaler Hauptprozessor *m.*
local storage lokaler Speicher
m.
local subdivision geographische Unterteilung *f.*
local system lokales System *n.*
local title lokaler Name *m.*
localization Eingrenzung *f.*
localize/to eingrenzen *vrb.*
locate/to lokalisieren *vrb.*
location Speicherzelle *f.*,
Standort *m.*
location chart Belegungsplan
m.
location code Standortcode *m.*
location counter Adreßzähler
m.
location data Standortdaten
pl.
location identification Standortkennung *f.*
location index Standortregister *n.*, Fundortregister *n.*
location mark Standortnummer *f.*
location name Subsystemname
m.
location number Ortsschlüssel

m.
location of a book Standort *m*.
eines Buches
locator Zeiger *m*., Fundstellenangabe *f*.
locator qualification Zeigerkennzeichnung *f*.
locator variable Zeigervariable
f.
lock Datensperre *f*., Verriegelung *f*.
lock/to sperren *vrb*., verriegeln
vrb.
lock bar knob Verriegelungsknopf *m*.
lock key Sperrtaste *f*.
lock manager Sperrverwaltung *f*.
lock mode Sperrmodus *m*.,
Verriegelungsmodus *m*.
lock out/to abwerfen *vrb*.
lock phrase Sperrangabe *f*.
locked function verdeckte
Funktion *f*.
locked name gesperrter Name
m.
locked record gesperrter Satz
m.
locker Schließfach *n*.
locking Verriegelung *f*.
locking mechanism Verriegelungsmechanismus *m*.
locking rod Schließstange *f*.
lodging house Wohnheim *n*.
log Logbuch *n*., Protokoll *n*.
log/to protokollieren *vrb*., aufzeichnen *vrb*.
log data set Protokolldatei *f*.
log file Protokolldatei *f*.
log in/to sich anmelden *vrb*.
log message Logbuchaufzeichnung *f*.

log off/to abmelden *vrb*.
log on/to anmelden *vrb*.
log out/to sich abmelden *vrb*.
log utility Protokollausführung
f.
logarithm Logarithmus *m*.
logbook Schiffstagebuch *n*.
logger Protokolliereinrichtung
f.
logging Aufzeichnen *n*., Protokollieren *n*.
logging device Protokolliverein-
heit *f*.
logging file Protokolldatei *f*.
logging of faults Fehlerprotokollierung *f*.
logic Logik *f*.
logic analyser Logikanalysator
m.
logic control Verknüpfungssteuerung *f*.
logic diagram Logikdiagramm
n.
logic element logisches Element *n*., logisches Symbol *n*.
logic function Schaltfunktion *f*.
logic symbol Schaltsymbol *n*.
logical logisch *adj*., Boolesch
adj.
logical add Disjunktion *f*.
logical address logische
Adresse *f*.
logical analysis logische Einteilung *f*.
logical beginning logischer Dateianfang *m*.
logical comparision Identitätsvergleich *m*.
logical configuration logische
Konfiguration *f*.
logical connective logische
Verknüpfung *f*.

logical database logische Datenbank *f.*
logical data structures logische Datenstrukturen *pl.*
logical design logischer Entwurf *m.*
logical difference logische Differenz *f.*
logical disjunct Boolesche Disjunktion *f.*
logical error logischer Fehler *m.*
logical expression Boolescher Ausdruck *m.*
logical factor Boolescher Faktor *m.*
logical file organization logische Dateiorganisation *f.*
logical flowchart logisches Flußdiagramm *n.*
logical indicator logischer Anzeiger *m.*
logical instruction logischer Befehl *m.*, logische Instruktion *f.*
logical line logische Zeile *f.*
logical link logische Verbindung *f.*
logical loop logische Schleife *f.*
logical operand Boolescher Operand *m.*
logical operation logische Operation *f.*, logische Verknüpfung *f.*
logical operator logischer Operator *m.*, Boolescher Operator *m.*
logical order logische Reihenfolge *f.*
logical product logisches Produkt *n.*, Konjunktion *f.*
logical record logischer Satz

m.
logical relation logische Relation *f.*
logical relationship logische Verknüpfung *f.*
logical sequence logische Ordnung *f.*
logical storage logischer Speicher *m.*
logical sum logische Summe *f.*, Disjunktion *f.*
logical unit logische Einheit *f.*
logical value boolescher Wert *m.*
logical variable logische Variable *f.*
long-term planning langfristige Planung *f.*
long-term subscription Langzeitabonnement *m.*
look ahead Vorgriff *m.*
look-ahead field Vorgriffsfeld *n.*
look-ahead record Vorgriffssatz *m.*
loop Schleife *f.*, Programmschleife *f.*
loop control Schleifensteuerung *f.*
loop cycle Schleifendurchlauf *m.*
loop network Ringnetz *n.*
loop signalling Schleifenkennzeichen *n.*
loop system Ringsystem *n.*
loop test Testschleife *f.*
looping Schleifenbildung *f.*
loose-leaf binding Loseblattbindung *f.*
loose-leaf book Loseblattsammlung *f.*
loose-leaf format Loseblatt-

form *f.*
loss Dämpfung *f.,* Verlust *m.*
loss parameter Verlustrate *f.*
lost vergessen *adj.,* verloren
adj.
lost significance Genauigkeitsverlust *m.*
lost time Verlustzeit *f.*
Lotka´s law Lotkas Gesetz *n.*
loudspeaker Lautsprecher *m.*
lower bound untere Grenze *f.*

lower case Kleinschreibung *f.*
lower case character Kleinbuchstabe *m.*
lower grades Unterstufe *f.*
lowering Tiefstellung *f.*
lumbecking Klebebindung *f.*
Lutheran Church Library Bibliothek *f.* der Lutherischen
Kirche
luxury binding Luxuseinband
m.

M

machine abstract maschinelles
Referat *n.*
machine abstracting maschinelles Referieren *n.*
machine address absolute
Adresse *f.*
machine-aided intelligence
künstliche Intelligenz *f.*
machine code Maschinencode
f.
machine dictionary Computerwörterbuch *n.*
machine error Machinenfehler
m.
machine failure Machinenaus-
fall *m.*
machine indexing maschinelle
Indexierung *f.*
machine instruction Maschinenbefehl *m.*
machine instruction code Ma-

schinenbefehlscode *m.*
machine language Maschinensprache *f.*
machine learning Maschinenlernen *n.*
machine literature searching
maschinelle Literaturrecherche *f.*
machine malfunction Maschinenstörung *f.*
machine-oriented language
maschinenorientierte Pro-
grammiersprache *f.*
machine program Maschinenprogramm *n.,* Steuerpro-
gramm *n.*
machine readability Maschinenlesbarkeit *f.*
machine-readable maschinenlesbar *adj.*
machine-readable catalog ma-

schinenlesbarer Katalog *m*.
machine-readable code maschinenlesbarer Code *m*.
machine-readable data file maschinenlesbare Datei *f*.
machine-readable dictionary maschinenlesbares Wörterbuch *n*.
machine-readable information maschinenlesbare Information *f*.
machine retrieval system maschinelles Retrievalsystem *n*.
machine serial number Maschinennummer *f*.
machine sorting maschinelle Sortierung *f*.
machine speed Maschinengeschwindigkeit *f*.
machine standard Maschinenstandard *m*.
machine status Maschinenstatus *m*.
machine time Maschinenzeit *f*.
machine translation maschinelle Übersetzung *f*.
machine word Maschinenwort *n*.
macro Makro *n*.
macro analysis Makroanalyse *f*.
macro call Makroaufruf *m*.
macro definition Makrodefinition *f*.
macro expansion Makroauflösung *f*.
macro generation Makrogenerierung *f*.
macro generator Makrogenerator *m*.
macro instruction Makrobefehl *m*.

macro library Makrobibliothek *f*.
macro preprocessing Makrovorverarbeitung *f*.
macro processor Makroumwandler *m*.
macrodocuments Makrodokumente *pl*.
macrothesaurus Makrothesaurus *m*., Dachthesaurus *m*.
magazine Zeitschrift *f*.
magazine box Zeitschriftenschachtel *f*.
magazine case Zeitschriftenfach *n*.
magazine room Zeitschriftenlesesaal *m*.
magnetic magnetisch *adj*.
magnetic bubble memory magnetischer Blasenspeicher *m*.
magnetic card Magnetkarte *f*.
magnetic card storage Magnetkartenspeicher *m*.
magnetic card unit Magnetkarteneinheit *f*.
magnetic character reader Magnetschriftenleser *m*.
magnetic core Magnetspeicher *m*.
magnetic disk Magnetplatte *f*.
magnetic disk storage Magnetplattenspeicher *m*.
magnetic drum Magnettrommel *f*.
magnetic drum storage Magnettrommelspeicher *m*.
magnetic encode station magnetische Codiereinrichtung *f*.
magnetic film Magnetfilm *m*.
magnetic film storage Magnetfilmspeicher *m*.
magnetic head Magnetkopf *m*.

magnetic ink Magnettinte *f.*
magnetic ink character recognition magnetische Zeichenerkennung *f.*
magnetic recording magnetische Aufzeichnung *f.*
magnetic storage magnetischer Speicher *m.*
magnetic strip Magnetstreifen *m.*
magnetic strip card reader Magnetkartenleser *m.*
magnetic strip reader Magnetstreifenleser *m.*
magnetic strip recording Magnetstreifenaufzeichnung *f.*
magnetic strip storage Magnetstreifenspeicher *m.*
magnetic surface Speicherfläche *f.*
magnetic tape Magnetband *n.*
magnetic tape cassette Magnetbandkassette *f.*
magnetic tape file Banddatei *f.*
magnetic tape information service Magnetbandinformationsdienst *m.*
magnetic tape leader Streifenvorspann *m.*
magnetic tape reader Magnetbandlesegerät *n.*
magnetic tape sound record Tonaufnahme *f.* auf Magnetband
magnetic tape storage Magnetbandspeicher *m.*
magnetic tape unit Magnetbandeinheit *f.*
magnetic tape writer Magnetbandschreibkopf *m.*
magnetic thin film magnetische Dünnschicht *f.*

magnetic thin film storage magnetischer Dünnschichtspeicher *m.*
magnetic track Magnetspur *f.*
magnetic verification station magnetische Prüfeinheit *f.*
magnetic wand reader Lesestift *m.* für Magnetetiketten
magnetic wire Magnetdraht *m.*
magnify/to vergrößern *vrb.*
mail Post *f.*, Postsendung *f.*
mail-coach Postkutsche *f.*
mail order Postversand *m.*
mail order firm Versandhaus *n.*
mail questionnaire schriftliche Befragung *f.*
mail service Versand *m.*
mail train Postzug *m.*
mailbag Postbeutel *m.*
mailbox Briefkasten *m.*
mailcard Posthandwagen *m.*
mailer Adressiermaschine *f.*, Frankiermaschine *f.*
mailgram Telebrief *m.*
mailing costs Portokosten *pl.*
mailing list Versandliste *f.*
mailing tube Versandrolle *f.*
mailman Postbote *m.*, Briefträger *m.*
main author Hauptverfasser *m.*
main card Hauptkarte *f.*
main catalog Hauptkatalog *m.*, Gesamtkatalog *m.*
main class Hauptklasse *f.*
main control unit Hauptsteuereinheit *f.*
main data area Hauptdatenbereich *m.*
main device scheduler Hauptsteuereinheit *f.*

main entry Haupteintrag *m.*
main entry card Hauptein-
tragskarte *f.*
main field Schwerpunkt *m.*
main file Hauptdatei *f.*
main heading Hauptschlag-
wort *n.*
main library Hauptbibliothek
f., Zentralbibliothek *f.*
main line Hauptanschluß *m.*
main memory Hauptspeicher
m.
main problem Kernproblem *n.*
main processor Hauptprozessor *m.*
main program Hauptpro-
gramm *n.*
main purpose Schwerpunkt-
thema *n.*
main schedule Haupttafel *f.*,
Hauptschema *n.*
main shelf list Zentralkatalog
m.
main station Hauptstelle *f.*
main storage Hauptspeicher
m.
main storage controller
Hauptspeichersteuereinheit *f.*
main storage database Hauptspeicherdatenbank *f.*
main storage dump Haupt-
speicherauszug *m.*
main storage processor
Hauptspeicherprozessor *m.*
main storage region Hauptspeicherbereich *m.*
main storage size Hauptspeichergröße *f.*
main storage unit Hauptspeichereinheit *f.*
main title Haupttitel *m.*
main title page Haupttitelblatt

n.
mainframe Großrechner *m.*
mainline program Hauptprogramm *n.*
mains Stromnetz *n.*
mains supply Netzstromversorgung *f.*
mains voltage Netzspannung
f.
maintain/to warten *vrb.*, pflegen *vrb.*
maintainability Wartbarkeit *f.*
maintenance Wartung *f.*, Instandhaltung *f.*
maintenance charges War-
tungskosten *pl.*
maintenance service War-
tungsdienst *m.*
maintenance time Wartungszeit *f.*
major hauptsächlich *adj.*, vorrangig *adj.*
major application area Hauptanwendungsgebiet *n.*
major control field Hauptkontrollfeld *n.*
major cycle Hauptzyklus *m.*,
Hauptschleife *f.*
major field Hauptfeld *n.*
major field of study Hauptfach
n.
major loop Hauptschleife *f.*
major node Hauptknoten *m.*
major structure Hauptstruktur
f.
major study Fachstudium *n.*
major time slice Hauptzeitscheibe *f.*
majority Mehrheit *f.*
make ready time Vorberei-
tungszeit *f.*
making an inventory Inventa-

risierung *f.*, Bestandsaufnahme *f.*
malfunction fehlerhafte Funktion *f.*
malfunction indicator Störungsanzeiger *m.*
malfunction time Störungsdauer *f.*
man-hour Arbeitsstunde *f.*
man-machine communication
Mensch-Maschine-Kommu-
nikation *f.*
man-machine dialog Mensch-
Maschine-Dialog *m.*
man-machine interface
Mensch-Maschine-Schnitt-
stelle *f.*
management Unternehmensführung *f.*, Management *n.*
**management information sy-
stem** Managementinforma-
tionssystem *n.*
management school library
betriebswirtschaftliche Hochschulbibliothek *f.*
management service Verwaltungsfunktion *f.*
manager Manager *m.*
mandatory obligatorisch *adj.*,
zwingend *adj.*
mandatory date Festtermin *m.*
**Mandelbrot-Zipf-Bradford
distribution** Verteilung *f.* nach
Mandelbrot, Zipf und Bradford
manipulation Manipulation *f.*
manpower Arbeitskräfte *pl.*,
Manpower *f.*
manpower budget Personalbudget *n.*
manpower management Personalverwaltung *f.*

manpower scheduling Personalplanung *m.*
manual Leitfaden *m.*, Benutzungsanweisung *f.*, Handbuch *n.*, manuell *adj.*
manual alphabet Taubstummenalphabet *n.*
manual catalog konventioneller Katalog *m.*
manual cataloging konventionelle Katalogisierung *f.*
manual control Handsteuerung *f.*
manual data input manuelle
Dateneingabe *f.*
manual entry manuelle Eingabe *f.*
manual function manuelle
Funktion *f.*
manual indexing manuelle Indexierung *f.*
manual input manuelle Eingabe *f.*
manual keyboard entry Eingabe *f.* über die Tastatur
manual programming manuelle Programmierung *f.*
manual scan manuelles Suchen
n.
manual searching konventionelle Suche *f.*
manual selection Handauswahl *f.*, manuelle Selektion *f.*
manual system manuelles System *n.*
manufacturing Herstellung *f.*,
Produktion *f.*
**manufacturing data genera-
tion** Generierung *f.* der Produktionsdaten
manufacturing time Produktionszeit *f.*

manuscript Handschrift *f.*, Manuskript *n.*
manuscript card handschriftlicher Zettel *m.*
manuscript catalog Handschriftenkatalog *m.*
manuscript cataloging Handschriftenkatalogisierung *f.*
manuscript collection Handschriftenbestand *m.*, Handschriftensammlung *f.*
manuscript department Handschriftenabteilung *f.*
manuscript preservation Handschriftenkonservierung *f.*
manuscripts archive Literaturarchiv *n.*
map Abbild *n.*, Bildschirmformat *n.*, Karte *f.*
map/to abbilden *vrb.*, adressieren *vrb.*
map collection Kartensammlung *f.*
map department Kartenabteilung *f.*
map file Kartenarchiv *n.*
map library Kartothek *f.*
map reading Kartenlesen *n.*
map reading instrument Kartenleser *m.*
map stand Kartenständer *m.*
map stock Kartenbestand *m.*
mapping Kartenaufnahme *f.*, Abbildung *f.*, Muster *n.*
margin Rand *m.*, Kantenabstand *m.*
margin adjust zone Randausgleichszone *f.*
margin alignment Randausgleich *m.*
margin control Randsteuerung *f.*
margin indicator Randanzeiger *m.*
margin line number Zeilennumerierung *f.*
margin position Randeinstellung *f.*
margin release/to Rand lösen *vrb.*
margin release key Randlöser *m.*
margin reset key Randsetzer *m.*
margin set/to Rand einstellen *vrb.*
margin set left Randeinsteller *m.* links
margin stop Randbegrenzer *m.*
margin stop indicator Randzeiger *m.*
marginal figure Zeilenzähler *m.*
marginal note Randnote *f.*, Randbemerkung *f.*
mark Kennzeichen *n.*, Markierung *f.*
mark/to anmerken *vrb.*, markieren *vrb.*
mark area Markierungsbereich *m.*
mark off/to abzeichnen *vrb.*
mark reader Belegleser *m.*
mark recognition Markierungserkennung *f.*
mark scanning optischer Markierungsleser *m.*
marked sheet Markierungsbeleg *m.*
marker Markierer *m.*, Trennzeichen *n.*
market analysis Marktanalyse *f.*

market information Marktinformation f.
market opportunities Marktchancen pl.
market report Marktbericht m.
market research Marktforschung f.
market review Marktübersicht f.
market situation Marktsituation f.
marketing Vertrieb m., Absatz m., Marketing n.
marketing manager Vertriebsleiter m.
marketing policy Vertriebspolitik f.
marking Abzeichen n., Markierung f., Standortbezeichnung f.
marshalling sequence Sortierfolge f.
mask Maske f., Schablone f., Abdeckung f.
mask/to maskieren vrb.
mask statement Maskenanweisung f.
mass communication Massenkommunikation f.
mass data Massendaten pl.
mass media Massenmedien pl.
mass production Massenproduktion f.
mass sequential insertion Massenzugang m.
mass storage Massenspeicher m.
mass storage control Massenspeichersteuerung f.
mass storage facility Massenspeichereinheit f.
mass storage file Massenspeicherdatei f.

mass storage system Massenspeichersystem n.
mass storage volume Massenspeicherdatenträger m.
master Vorlage f.
master bookbinder Buchbindemeister m.
master card Leitkarte f., Stammkarte f.
master catalog Hauptkatalog m., Zentralkatalog m.
master console Hauptkonsole f., Systemkonsole f.
master controller Führungsregler m.
master data Stammdaten pl.
master data sheet Leitblatt n.
master display station Leitbildschirm m.
master document Schlüsseldokument n., Ursprungsbeleg m.
master file Stammdatei f.
master file inquiry Abfrage f. der Stammdatei
master file key name Hauptdateischlüsselname m.
master format Standardformat n.
master index Hauptindex m.
master key Hauptschlüssel m.
master password Hauptkennwort n.
master program Hauptprogramm n.
master record Hauptsatz m., Stammsatz m.
master station Hauptstation f.
master tape Mutterband n.
master track Hauptspeicherindex m.
masthead Zeitschriftenkopf m., Titelleiste f.

match Übereinstimmung *f.*,
Gleichheit *f.*
match/to vergleichen *vrb.*, abgleichen *vrb.*
match code Vergleichsschlüssel
m.
match field Vergleichsfeld *n.*
match level Vergleichsebene *f.*
matched übereinstimmend *adj.*
matching Vergleich *m.*
matching record indicator Vergleichsanzeiger *m.*
matching records übereinstimmende Sätze *pl.*
material Werkstoff *m.*, materiell *adj.*, Material *n.*
material budget Sachmittel *pl.*,
Materialbudget *n.*
material code Materialschlüssel *m.*
material control Materialkontrolle *f.*
material cost Materialkosten
pl.
material costing Materialkostenermittlung *f.*
material data Werkstoffdaten
pl.
material database Werkstoffdatenbank *f.*
material due date Materialstichtag *m.*
material need Materialbedarf
m.
material on order bestelltes
Material *n.*
material record Materialsatz
m.
material requirement Materialbedarf *m.*
material research Werkstofforschung *f.*

material status Materialstatus
m.
mathematical method mathematisches Verfahren *n.*
mathematical model mathematisches Modell *n.*
mathematical order formale
Ordnung *f.*
mathematics Mathematik *f.*
matrix Matrix *f.*
matrix keyboard Maskentastatur *f.*
matrix memory Matrixspeicher *m.*
matrix name Matrixname *m.*
matrix notation Matrizenschreibweise *f.*
matrix printer Matrixdrucker
m.
matrix row Matrizenzeile *f.*
matrix storage Matrixspeicher
m.
matter Gegenstand *m.*, Stoff
m., Materie *f.*
maximal maximal *adj.*
maximal word size maximale
Wortlänge *f.*
maximize/to maximieren *vrb.*
maximum Maximum *n.*
maximum capacity Höchstkapazität *f.*
maximum float value maximale Pufferzeit *f.*
maximum idle time maximale
Leerzeit *f.*
maximum length maximale
Länge *f.*
maximum performance
Höchstleistung *f.*
maximum print line maximale
Druckzeile *f.*
maximum value Maximalwert

m.

mean durchschnittlich *adj.*, Mittelwert *m.*

mean deviation mittlerer Fehler *m.*

mean frequency mittlere Häufigkeit *f.*

mean time between failures mittlerer Ausfallabstand *m.*

mean value Mittelwert *m.*

meaning Bedeutung *f.*, semantischer Gehalt *m.*

measure Maß *n.*, Maßnahme *f.*

measure/to messen *vrb.*

measure of information Informationsmaß *n.*, Informationsgehalt *m.*

measurement Messung *f.*

measuring instrument Meßgerät *n.*

mechanical charging mechanisches Buchungsverfahren *n.*

mechanical dictionary Computerwörterbuch *n.*

mechanical documentation maschinelle Dokumentation *f.*

mechanical engineering Maschinenbau *m.*

mechanical keyboard mechanische Tastatur *f.*

mechanical linkage mechanische Verbindung *f.*

mechanical selection automatische Selektion *f.*

mechanical translation maschinelle Übersetzung *f.*

mechanism Mechanismus *m.*

mechanized classification maschinelle Klassifizierung *f.*

mechanized documentation maschinelle Dokumentation *f.*

mechanized index maschinelles

Register *n.*

media center Medienzentrum *n.*, Mediothek *f.*

media resource center Mediothek *f.*

median Median *m.*

medical library medizinische Bibliothek *f.*

medical school library medizinische Hochschulbibliothek *f.*

medicine Medizin *f.*

medium Medium *n.*, durchschnittlich *adj.*

medium resolution mittlere Auflösung *f.*

medium-sized library Bibliothek *f.* mittlerer Größe

medium system System *n.* mittlerer Größe

meeting Tagung *f.*

meeting place Tagungsort *m.*

meeting point Treffpunkt *m.*

megabyte Megabyte *n.*

megacycle Megahertz *n.*

member Mitglied *n.*, Element *n.*

member state Mitgliedsland *n.*

membership Mitgliedschaft *f.*

memorandum Notiz *f.*, Verzeichnis *n.*, Memorandum *n.*, Denkschrift *f.*

memorial Denkmal *f.*

memorial library Gedenkbibliothek *f.*

memorial place Gedenkstätte *f.*

memorial volume Festschrift *f.*, Gedenkschrift *f.*

memory Speicher *m.*, Hauptspeicher *m.*

memory address register Speicheradreßregister *n.*

memory cell Speicherelement *n.*

memory device Speicher *m.*, Speichereinheit *f.*

memory display Speicheranzeige *f.*

memory dump Speicherauszug *m.*

memory element Speicherelement *n.*

memory expansion Hauptspeichererweiterung *f.*

memory function Speicherfunktion *f.*

memory management Speicherverwaltung *f.*

memory map Speicherabzug *m.*

memory modification Speicheränderung *f.*

memory parity check Speicherparitätsprüfung *f.*

memory parity error Speicherparitätsfehler *m.*

memory pointer Basisregister *n.*

memory protect Speicherschutz *m.*

memory read command Hauptspeicherlesebefehl *m.*

memory read cycle Speicherlesezyklus *m.*

memory size Speichergröße *f.*

memory typewriter Speicherschreibmaschine *f.*

memory write command Hauptspeicherschreibbefehl *m.*

menu Menü *n.*

menu-driven menügesteuert *adj.*

menu selection Menüauswahl *f.*

merge/to mischen *vrb.*, abgleichen *vrb.*

merge pass Mischlauf *m.*

merger Zusammenschluß *m.*

mesh Eingriff *m.*

message Nachricht *f.*, Meldung *f.*

message buffering facility gepufferte Nachrichtenverwaltung *f.*

message channel Nachrichtenkanal *m.*

message character Nachrichtenzeichen *n.*

message control program Nachrichtensteuerprogramm *n.*

message control statement Nachrichtensteueranweisung *f.*

message count Nachrichtenzähler *m.*

message data set Nachrichtendatei *f.*

message delete option Nachrichtenlöschoption *f.*

message display unit Nachrichtenanzeigeeinheit *f.*

message editing Nachrichtenaufbereitung *f.*

message error record Nachrichtenfehlersatz *m.*

message field Nachrichtenfeld *n.*

message file Nachrichtendatei *f.*

message format Nachrichtenformat *n.*

message header Nachrichtenkopf *m.*

message identification code

Nachrichtenkennzeichnungsnummer *f.*
message identifier Nachrichtenkennzeichnung *f.*
message indicator Nachrichtenanzeiger *m.*
message input descriptor
Nachrichteneingabedeskriptor *m.*
message length Nachrichtenlänge *f.*
message mode Nachrichtenmodus *m.*
message output descriptor
Nachrichtenausgabedeskriptor *m.*
message priority Nachrichtenpriorität *f.*
message processing Nachrichtenverarbeitung *f.*
message queue Nachrichtenwarteschlange *f.*
message routing Nachrichtenvermittlung *f.*
message scheduling Nachrichtensteuerung *f.*
message set Nachrichtengruppe *f.*
message sink Nachrichtensenke *f.*
message source Nachrichtenquelle *f.*
message structure Nachrichtenstruktur *f.*
message switching Nachrichtenverteilung *f.*
message system Nachrichtensystem *n.*
message text Nachrichtentext
m.
message unit Nachrichteneinheit *f.*

message waiting time Nachrichtenwartezeit *f.*
metagraphy Transliteration *f.*,
Umschrift *f.*
metalanguage Metasprache *f.*
metallurgy Metallurgie *f.*,
Hüttenwesen *n.*
metaphrase wortgetreue
Übersetzung *f.*
meteorology Meteorologie *f.*
meter Zähler *m.*
meter time Benutzungszeit *f.*
method Methode *f.*
method of marking Aufzeichnungsverfahren *n.*
methodical systematisch *adj.*
methodics Methodik *f.*
Methodist Church Library Bibliothek *f.* der Methodistischen Kirche
metropolitan Umland *n.*
metropolitan library Kreisbibliothek *f.*
micro computer Mikrocomputer *m.*
micro-image Mikrobild *n.*
microcard Mikrokarte *f.*
microcard reader Mikrokartenleser *m.*
microcode Mikroprogramm *n.*
microcomputer Mikrocomputer *m.*
microcontroller Mikroprozessorsteuerung *f.*
microcopy Mikrokopie *f.*
microdocuments Mikrodokumente *pl.*
microelectronics Mikroelektronik *f.*
microfiche Mikroplanfilm *m.*,
Mikrofiche *m.*
microfiche edition Ausgabe *f.*

auf Mikrofiche
microfiche reader Mikrofichelesegerät *n.*
microfiche technology Mikroplanfilmtechnik *f.*
microfilm Mikrofilm *m.*
microfilm collection Mikrofilmsammlung *f.*
microfilm equipment Mikrofilmgerät *n.*
microfilm reader Mikrofilmleser *m.*
microfilm record-office Mikrofilmarchiv *n.*
microfilm strip Mikrofilmstreifen *m.*
microfilm technology Mikrofilmtechnik *f.*
microfilming Mikroverfilmung
f.
microform Mikrobildspeicher
m., Mikroform *f.*
micrography Mikrographie *f.*
micromodule Mikromodul *n.*
microphone Mikrophon *n.*
microprocessor Mikroprozessor *m.*
microprogram Mikroprogramm *n.*
microprogram execution Mikroprogrammablauf *m.*
microprogram memory Mikroprogrammspeicher *m.*
microprogrammability Mikroprogrammierbarkeit *f.*
microprogrammable computer
mikroprogrammierbarer
Rechner *m.*
microprogramming Mikroprogrammierung *f.*
micropublication Mikrofilmpublikation *f.*

microsecond Mikrosekunde *f.*
microsyncronization Mikrosynchronbetrieb *m.*
microthesaurus Mikrothesaurus *m.*, Hilfsthesaurus *m.*
middle Mitte *f.*, Einlage *f.*
middle-grade staff gehobener
Dienst *m.*
middle letter row Buchstabentastenreihe *f.*
middle school library Bibliothek *f.* einer Realschule
middle-sized mittelgroß *adj.*
migrating Übergang *m.*
migration Systemumstellung *f.*
migration path Übergangspfad
m.
military academy library Bibliothek *f.* einer Militärakademie
**military administration of
justice** Militärjustiz *f.*
military affairs Militärwesen
n.
military archive Kriegsarchiv
n.
military files Militärakten *pl.*
military record-office Militärarchiv *n.*
millisecond Millisekunde *f.*
miner's institute library
Knappschaftsbibliothek *f.*
mineralogist Mineraloge *m.*
mineralogy Mineralogie *f.*
miniature Miniatur *f.*
miniaturization Miniaturisierung *f.*
minicomputer mittlere Datentechnik *f.*, Minicomputer *m.*
minidisk Miniplatte *f.*
minifloppy disk Minidiskette *f.*
minimal cataloging Kurztitel-

aufnahme *f.*, verkürzte Katalogisierung *f.*
minimum Minimum *n.*
minimum access programming Bestzeitprogrammierung *f.*
minimum delay coding Bestzeitcodierung *f.*, Bestzeitprogrammierung *f.*
minimum run time Mindestbearbeitungszeit *f.*
mining academy Bergakademie *f.*
mining and steel university Montanuniversität *f.*
mining industry Bergbau *m.*
mining school library Bergbauhochschulbibliothek *f.*
Minister of Culture Kultusminister *m.*
Ministry of Culture Kultusministerium *n.*
ministry Ministerium *n.*
minor Unterbegriff *m.*, Untergruppe *f.*
minor control Untergruppenkontrolle *f.*
minor control change Untergruppentrennung *f.*
minor control field Untergruppenkontrollfeld *n.*
minor cycle Nebenzyklus *m.*, Nebenschleife *f.*
minor field Unterfeld *n.*
minor loop Nebenschleife *f.*
minor node Nebenknoten *m.*
minor structure Unterstruktur *f.*
minor time slice Nebenzeitscheibe *f.*
minus minus *prep.*
minus sign Minuszeichen *n.*
minute Minute *f.*

minute/to protokollieren *vrb.*
minute classification detaillierte Klassifikation *f.*
minutely genau *adj.*
minuteness Genauigkeit *f.*
minutes Protokoll *n.*, Minuten *pl.*
minutes total Gesamtzeit *f.*
misalignment Ausrichtungsfehler *m.*, Falschausrichtung *f.*
misapplication falsche Anwendung *f.*, Mißbrauch *m.*
miscalculate/to falsch berechnen *vrb.*
miscalculation Rechenfehler *m.*
miscellaneous verschiedenes *adj.*
miscellaneous data recorder gemischte Datenaufzeichnung *f.*
miscellaneous time sonstige Zeit *f.*
misclassification Falschklassifikation *f.*
misdate/to falsch datieren *vrb.*
misdirect/to falsch adressieren *vrb.*
misentry Falscheingabe *f.*
misfeed Transportfehler *m.*, Zuführungsfehler *m.*
mishandle/to falsch handhaben *vrb.*
misinform/to falsch informieren *vrb.*
misinformation Fehlinformation *f.*
misinterpret/to falsch auswerten *vrb.*
misinterpretation Falschauswertung *f.*
mismanagement Mißmanage-

ment *n.*
mismatch Nichtübereinstimmung *f.*, Abweichung *f.*
misplace/to verstellen *vrb.*
misprint Druckfehler *m.*
miss/to verfehlen *vrb.*, verpassen *vrb.*
miss ratio Fehlquote *f.*
misses Auslassungen *pl.*
misshelving falsche Regalordnung *f.*
missing abgängig *adj.*, fehlend *adj.*
missing issue fehlende Ausgabe *f.*
missing number fehlende Nummer *f.*
missing page interrupt Fehlseitenunterbrechung *f.*
mission Mission *f.*, Aufgabe *f.*
mission-oriented thesaurus aufgabenbezogener Thesaurus *m.*, Fachthesaurus *m.*
missionary school library Missionsschulbibliothek *f.*
missionary society archive Missionsarchiv *n.*
misspelling Tippfehler *m.*, Schreibfehler *m.*
mistake Fehler *m.*, Irrtum *m.*
miswrite/to falsch schreiben *vrb.*
mix/to mischen *vrb.*
mixed alphabetical catalog Kreuzkatalog *m.*
mixed data set gemischte Dateien *pl.*
mixed entry row gemischte Eingabezeile *f.*
mixed environment gemischte Systemauslegung *f.*
mixed function gemischte

Funktion *f.*
mixed notation gemischte Notation *f.*, Mischnotation *f.*
mnemonic notation mnemotechnische Notation *f.*
mnemonic symbol mnemotechnisches Zeichen *n.*
mobile library Autobücherei *f.*, Bibliothek *f.* auf Rädern, Fahrbibliothek *f.*
mobility Beweglichkeit *f.*, Tragbarkeit *f.*
mock title Schmutztitel *m.*, Vortitel *m.*
modal command modaler Befehl *m.*
modal length häufigste Länge *f.*
mode Betriebsart *f.*, Modus *m.*
mode field Betriebsartenfeld *n.*
mode indicator Betriebszustandsanzeige *f.*
mode level field Betriebsartenfeld *n.*
mode of operation Betriebsart *f.*, Betriebsweise *f.*
mode of recording Aufzeichnungsverfahren *n.*
mode of transmission Übertragungsart *f.*
mode register Betriebsartenregister *n.*
mode selector Betriebsartenwähler *m.*
model Modell *n.*
model application Modellanwendung *f.*
model library Modellbibliothek *f.*
model library competition Modellbibliothekswettbewerb *m.*
model profile Modellprofil *n.*

model select Modellauswahl *f.*
model statement Modellanweisung *f.*
modem Modem *n.*
modifiable änderbar *adj.*
modifiable keyboard erweiterbare Tastatur *f.*
modification Umwandlung *f.*, Änderung *f.*
modification fee Änderungsgebühr *f.*
modified data geänderte Daten *pl.*
modified data indicator Veränderungsanzeiger *m.*
modifier Modifikator *m.*
modifier register Indexregister *n.*
modify/to anpassen *vrb.*, modifizieren *vrb.*, ändern *vrb.*
modular check Modularprüfung *f.*
modularity Modularität *f.*
modulation Modulation *f.*
modulation index Modulationsindex *m.*
modulator Modulator *m.*
module Modul *n.*
molecular biology Molekularbiologie *f.*
molecular data Molekulardaten *pl.*
moment Augenblick *m.*, Zeitpunkt *m.*
momentary key Einzeltaste *f.*
monadic einstellig *adj.*
monadic operation monadische Operation *f.*
monastery library Klosterbibliothek *f.*, Konventsbibliothek *f.*
monastic library Klosterbiblio-

thek *f.*
monitor Monitor *m.*, Bildschirm *m.*
monitor/to überwachen *vrb.*
monitor mode Monitormodus *m.*
monitor program Überwachungsprogramm *n.*
monitor type Bildschirmart *f.*
monitoring Überwachung *f.*, Mithören *n.*
monitoring feature Überwachungseinrichtung *f.*
monitoring procedure Überwachungsprozedur *f.*
monodimensional classification eindimensionale Klassifikation *f.*
monograph Monographie *f.*
monographic issue Monographie *f.*
monographic series Schriftenreihe *f.*
monographs in series Schriftenreihe *f.*
monohierarchical classification monohierarchische Klassifikation *f.*
monolingual einsprachig *adj.*
monosemantic monosem *adj.*, eindeutig *adj.*
monovalent term eindeutige Benennung *f.*
month Monat *m.*
monthly monatlich *adj.*
monthly periodical monatliche Zeitschrift *f.*
monthly publication monatliche Veröffentlichung *f.*
morale index Meinungsindex *m.*
Mormon Church library Bi-

bliothek *f.* der Mormonenkirche
morning paper Morgenzeitung
f.
morpheme Morphem *n.*, Wortelement *n.*
morpheme-word Stammwort
n.
morphological analysis morphologische Analyse *f.*
morphological components
morphhologische Bestandteile *pl.*
morphological process morphologisches Verfahren *n.*
morphology Morphologie *f.*
morphosyntactic analysis morphosyntaktische Analyse *f.*
mosaic printer Mosaikdrucker
m.
mosque library Moscheebibliothek *f.*
motion-picture Film *m.*
motion-picture database Filmdatenbank *m.*
motion-picture studies Filmwissenschaft *f.*
motion-picture title Filmtitel
m.
mount/to montieren *vrb.*, befestigen *vrb.*
mountable einbaubar *adj.*
mouse Maus *f.*
movable location bewegliche
Aufstellung *f.*
move/to übertragen *vrb.*, verschieben *vrb.*
move/to column Spalte versetzen *vrb.*
move mode Übertragungsmodus *m.*
move/to text Text versetzen *vrb.*

moveable picture book Klappbilderbuch *n.*, Leporello *n.*
movie Spielfilm *m.*
moving head disk Wechselplatte *f.*
muliple volume set mehrbändiges Werk *n.*
multi-access Mehrfachzugriff
m.
multi-address computer Mehradreßrechner *m.*
multi-address instruction
Mehradreßbefehl *m.*
multi-address service Rundschreiben *n.*
multi-aspect classification polydimensionale Klassifikation
f.
multi-aspect indexing koordinierte Indexierung *f.*
multi-column file mehrspaltige
Datei *f.*
multi-media center Multimediazentrum *n.*
multi-media material Multimediamaterial *n.*
multi-operation Multioperation *f.*
multi-station system Mehrplatzsystem *n.*
multi-tag Mehrfachkennzeichnung *f.*
multi-tagged mehrfach gekennzeichnet *adj.*
multi-track tape Mehrspurband *n.*
multi-unit file Datei *f.* auf
mehreren Einheiten
multi-user computer Mehrbenutzerrechner *m.*
multicharacter input Mehrzeicheneingabe *f.*

multicollinearity Multikollinearität *f.*
multicomputer system Mehrrechnersystem *n.*
multidimensional mehrdimensional *adj.*
multidimensional classification mehrdimensionale Klassifikation *f.*
multidimensional mapping mehrdimensionale Kartographie *f.*
multidimensional scaling mehrdimensionale Skalierung *f.*
multifacetted classification Facettenklassifikation *f.*
multifile processing Mehrdateienverarbeitung *f.*
multifile volume Mehrdateienträger *m.*, Mehrdateienband *n.*
multifunction key Mehrfunktionstaste *f.*
multifunction unit Mehrfachfunktionseinheit *f.*
multilevel mehrstufig *adj.*, indirekt *adj.*
multilevel address indirekte Adresse *f.*
multilevel indexing multihierarchische Indexierung *f.*
multilevel interrupt mehrstufige Programmunterbrechung *f.*
multiline display mehrzeilige Anzeige *f.*
multiline field Mehrzeilenfeld *n.*
multiline function mehrzeilige Funktion *f.*
multiline print Mehrzeilen-

druck *m.*
multilingual multilingual *adj.*
multilingual dictionary mehrsprachiges Wörterbuch *n.*
multilingual package Fremdsprachenausgleicher *m.*
multilingual-printed catalog mehrsprachig gedruckter Katalog *m.*
multilingual subject indexing mehrsprachige Verschlagwortung *f.*
multilingual thesaurus mehrsprachiger Thesaurus *m.*
multilingual translation aid mehrsprachige Übersetzungshilfe *f.*
multinational character set multinationaler Zeichensatz *m.*
multipart form Durchschreibeformular *n.*
multiphase program Mehrphasenprogramm *n.*
multiple mehrfach *adj.*
multiple access Mehrfachzugriff *m.*
multiple access system Mehrfachzugriffsystem *n.*
multiple address instruction Multiadreßbefehl *m.*
multiple address message Rundschreiben *n.*
multiple authorship Mehrfachautorenschaft *f.*
multiple choice Mehrfachauswahl *f.*
multiple column control Mehrspaltensucher *m.*
multiple computer system Mehrrechnersystem *n.*
multiple connection Vielfach-

schaltung *f.*
multiple copy Duplikat *n.*
multiple database search
Mehrdatenbanksuche *f.*
multiple display Mehrfachanzeige *f.*
multiple entry Mehrfacheintrag *m.*
multiple index file mehrfachindexierte Datei *f.*
multiple index support mehrfache Zugriffswege *pl.*
multiple library support Unterstützung *f.* mehrerer Bibliotheken
multiple programming Mehrprogrammbetrieb *m.*
multiple register to storage
Vielfachregister *n.* zum Speichern
multiple regression multiple
Regression *f.*
multiple terminal access Mehrfachterminalzugriff *m.*
multiple usage Mehrfachbenutzung *f.*
multiplex/to multiplexen *vrb.*
multiplex channel Multiplexkanal *m.*
multiplex mode Multiplexmodus *m.*
multiplexer Multiplexer *m.*
multiplicand Multiplikand *m.*
multiplication Multiplikation *f.*
multiplication factor Vervielfachungsfaktor *m.*
multiplicity Vielfachheit *f.*
multiplier Multiplikator *m.*
multiply/to multiplizieren *vrb.*
multipoint connection Mehrpunktverbindung *f.*
multiport register Register *n.*

mit Mehrfachzugriff
multiprocessing Simultanverarbeitung *f.*
multiprocessing system Simultanverarbeitungssystem *n.*,
Mehrprozessorensystem *n.*
multiprogramming Mehrprogrammbetrieb *m.*
multiprogramming system
Mehrprogrammsystem *n.*
multiscan Multiscan *n.*
multistructured mehrfach
strukturiert *adj.*
multistructured file mehrfachstrukturierte Datei *f.*
multisystem Mehrrechnersystem *n.*
multisystem network Mehrrechnersystemnetzwerk *n.*
multitask operation Multitaskoperation *f.*
multitasking Multitasking *n.*
**multivariate analysis of va-
riance** multivariate Varianzanalyse *f.*
multivolume data set Mehrdatenträgerdatei *f.*
multivolume file Mehrdatenträgerdatei *f.*
multivolume publication mehrbändige Veröffentlichung *f.*
multivolume work mehrbändiges Werk *n.*
municipal archive Gemeindearchiv *n.*, Kommunalarchiv *n.*
municipal bibliography Stadtbibliographie *f.*
municipal library Stadtbücherei *f.*, Stadtbibliothek *f.*, Gemeindebücherei *f.*
museum Museum *n.*
museum documentation Mu-

seumsdokumentation *f.*
museum library Museumsbibliothek *f.*
music and drama school library Musik- und Theaterhochschulbibliothek *f.*
music archive Musikarchiv *n.*
music cataloging Musikkatalogisierung *f.*
music department Musikabteilung *f.*
music documentation center Musikdokumentationszentrum *n.*
music format musikalische Ausgabeform *m.*
music information center Mu-

sikinformationszentrum *n.*
music librarian musikwissenschaftlicher Bibliothekar *m.*
music librarian education Musikbibliothekarsausbildung *f.*
music library Musikbibliothek *f.*, Musikbücherei *f.*
music magazine Musikzeitschrift *f.*
music paper Notenpapier *n.*
music school Musikschule *f.*
music video Musikvideo *n.*
musical notation musikalische Notation *f.*
musicology Musikwissenschaft *f.*

N

name Name *m.*, symbolische Adresse *f.*
name/to benennen *vrb.*
name authority file verbindliche Namensliste *f.*, Namennormdatei *f.*
name catalog Verfasserkatalog *m.*, Nominalkatalog *m.*
name entry Verfassereintrag *m.*
name field Namensfeld *n.*
name index Namensregister *n.*
name pallet Namensstempel *m.*
name reference Namensver-

weisung *f.*
named benannt *adj.*
named common block benannter gemeinsamer Speicherbereich *m.*
named constant benannte Konstante *f.*
named file benannte Datei *f.*
named system benanntes System *n.*
naming convention Benennungsregel *f.*, Namenskonvention *f.*
nanosecond Nanosekunde *f.*
narrative description erklä-

rende Beschreibung *f.*
narrow catchword Unterbegriff *m.*
narrower term Unterbegriff *m.*
national archive Staatsarchiv *n.*
national bibliography Nationalbibliographie *f.*
national biography Nationalbiographie *f.*
national certification system nationales Kennzeichnungssystem *n.*
national exchange nationaler Austausch *m.*
national information system nationales Informationssystem *n.*
national library Nationalbibliothek *f.*
national literature Nationalliteratur *f.*
national museum Nationalmuseum *n.*
national product Sozialprodukt *n.*
national standard nationale Norm *f.*
native einheimisch *adj.*
native character set maschineneigener Zeichenvorrat *m.*
native language Muttersprache *f.*
natural natürlich *adj.*
natural binary code reiner Binärcode *m.*
natural characteristic of division natürliches Merkmal *n.*
natural classification natürliche Klassifikation *f.*
natural language natürliche Sprache *f.*

natural language access natürlichsprachiger Zugriff *m.*
natural language processing natürlichsprachige Verarbeitung *f.*
natural language queries natürlichsprachige Suchanfragen *pl.*
natural language search natürlichsprachige Suche *f.*
natural number natürliche Zahl *f.*
natural science library naturwissenschaftliche Bibliothek *f.*
natural sign natürliches Zeichen *n.*
natural unit natürliche Einheit *f.*
natural word order natürliche Wortfolge *f.*
nature conservation Naturschutz *m.*
nature protection Naturschutz *m.*
nautical chart Seekarte *f.*
nautical school library Seefahrtsschulbibliothek *f.*
NCR paper Durchschreibepapier *n.*
near-synonym Quasisynonym *n.*
near-synonymity Quasisynonymie *f.*
near-synonymous quasisynonym *adj.*
neatline Kartenfeldbegrenzung *f.*
need Bedarf *m.*
needle Nadel *f.*, Sortiernadel *f.*
needle-operated punch card Nadellochkarte *f.*
negate/to negieren *vrb.*

negated verneint *adj.*
negation Negation *f.*, Verneinung *f.*
negative Negativ *n.*, negativ *adj.*
negative acknowledge character negatives Empfangsanzeigezeichen *n.*
negative entry Eingabe *f.* negativer Zahlen
negative feedback negative Rückkopplung *f.*
negative number negative Zahl *f.*
negative relation Ausschlußrelation *f.*, Ausschlußbeziehung *f.*
negative response negative Antwort *f.*
negotiation Verhandlung *f.*
nest/to verschachteln *vrb.*
nested geschachtelt *adj.*
nested command procedure geschachtelte Befehlsprozedur *f.*
nested procedure geschachtelte Prozedur *f.*
nested structure geschachtelte Struktur *f.*
nesting Verschachtelung *f.*
nesting store Kellerspeicher *m.*, Stapelspeicher *m.*
net Netz *n.*, netto *adj.*
net published price Nettoladenpreis *f.*
network Netz *n.*, Netzwerk *n.*
network address Netzwerkadresse *f.*, Anschlußnummer *f.*
network analog Netzmodell *n.*
network analyser Netzwerkanalysator *m.*
network analysis Netzplantechnik *f.*
network architecture Netzarchitektur *f.*
network calculator Netzwerkanalysator *m.*
network configuration Netzwerkkonfiguration *f.*
network control Netzwerksteuerung *f.*
network control mode Netzwerksteuermodus *m.*
network control program Netzwerksteuerprogramm *n.*
network coordinator Netzwerkkoordinator *m.*
network database model Netzwerkdatenbankmodell *n.*
network-dependent netzabhängig *adj.*
network description Netzwerkbeschreibung *f.*
network design Netzwerkentwurf *m.*
network document distribution Netzwerkdokumentverteilung *f.*
network file Netzplandatei *f.*
network-independent netzunabhängig *adj.*
network job processing Netzwerkjobverarbeitung *f.*
network level Netzebene *f.*
network management Netzwerkmanagement *n.*
network name Netzwerkname *m.*
network number Netznummer *f.*
network operation support program Netzbedienungsprogramm *n.*
network-oriented netzorien-

tiert *adj.*
network plan Netzplan *m.*
network preparation Netzplanerstellung *f.*
network priority Netzpriorität
f.
network protocol Netzwerkprotokoll *n.*
network resource Netzwerkelement *n.*
network resource dictionary
Netzwerkressourcenver-
zeichnis *n.*
network services Netzwerkverwaltung *f.*
network size Netzplangröße *f.*
network solicitor Netzwerkaufrufprogramm *n.*
network structure Netzstruktur *f.*
network technique Netzplantechnik *f.*
network topology Netzwerktopologie *f.*, Netzwerkarchitektur *f.*
network transformation rules
Netzwerktransformationsregeln *pl.*
network unit Netzwerkeinheit
f.
networked vernetzt *adj.*
networking Vernetzung *f.*,
Netzwerkbetrieb *m.*
neutral neutral *adj.*
never-ending program haupt-
speicherresidentens Pro-
gramm *n.*
new neu *adj.*
new book display Neuerwerbungsauslage *f.*
new books Neuerscheinungen
pl.

new building Neubau *m.*
new edition Neuausgabe *f.*
new establishment Neugründung *f.*
new line Zeilenvorschub *m.*
new line character Zeilenvorschubzeichen *n.*
new line key Zeilenvorschubtaste *f.*
new paragraph neuer Absatz
m.
new publications Neuerscheinungen *pl.*
new regulation Neuregelung *f.*
new series neue Reihe *f.*
new string neue Zeichenfolge *f.*
new titles Neuerscheinungen
pl.
news Nachrichten *pl.*
news bulletin Informationsbrief *m.*
news magazine Nachrichtenmagazin *n.*
news release Presseinformation *f.*
news service Nachrichtendienst *m.*
news stand Zeitungskiosk *m.*
newsletter Informationsbrief
m., Rundbrief *m.*
newspaper Zeitung *f.*, Tageszeitung *f.*
newspaper article Zeitungsartikel *m.*
newspaper collection Zeitungsbestand *m.*, Zeitungssammlung *f.*
newspaper cutting Zeitungsausschnitt *m.*
newspaper database Pressedatenbank *f.*
newspaper documentation

Zeitungsdokumentation *f.*
newspaper holder Zeitungshalter *m.*
newspaper indexing Zeitungserschließung *f.*
newspaper kiosk Zeitungskiosk
m.
newspaper publishers' library
Zeitungsverlagsbibliothek *f.*
newspaper room Zeitungsleseraum *m.*
newspaper stand Zeitungsregal *n.*
newspaper stick Zeitungshalter
m.
newsprint Zeitungspapier *n.*
next executable sentence nächster auszuführender Satz *m.*
next executable statement
nächste auszuführende An-
weisung *f.*
next record nächster Datensatz *m.*
next-record field Folgesatzsuchfeld *n.*
next-sentence phrase Folgesatzangabe *f.*
nickname Beiname *m.*
night service Nachtschaltung *f.*
nil Null *f.*
nil return Fehlanzeige *f.*
niladic nullstellig *adj.*
no assignment keine Arbeit *f.*
no date ohne Jahresangabe *f.*
no growth policy Nullwachstumspolitik *f.*
no match keine Übereinstimmung *f.*
no operation kein Betrieb *m.*
no place ohne Ortsangabe *f.*
no response keine Antwort *f.*
no sharing keine gemeinsame

Benutzung *f.*
no station address Sperradresse *f.*
node Netzknoten *m.*, Knoten
m.
node error program Knotenfehlerprogramm *n.*
node initialization block Knoteninitialisierungsblock *m.*
node name Knotenname *m.*
node operator Knotenbediener
m.
node splitting Knotenteilung *f.*
node-to-node routing function
Knoten-zu-Knoten Leitfunktion *f.*
node type Knotentyp *m.*
noise Ballast *m.*, Rauschen *n.*,
Störsignal *n.*
noise factor Rauschfaktor *m.*,
Ballastfaktor *m.*
noise figure Rauschkennziffer
f.
noise immunity Störfestigkeit
f.
noise ratio Ballastquote *f.*
noise signal Rauschsignal *n.*
noisefree störungsfrei *adj.*
noiseless störungsfrei *adj.*
nomenclature Nomenklatur *f.*,
Namensverzeichnis *n.*, Benennungssystem *n.*
nominal nominell *adj.*
nomogram Nomogramm *n.*
non-addressable storage nichtadressierbarer Speicher *m.*
non-ask type Ausgabe ohne
Anfrage
non-authorized translation
nichtautorisierte Übersetzung
f.
non-book material Nicht-

Buch-Material *n.*
non-book trade publications graue Literatur *f.*
non-chargeable gebührenfrei *adj.*
non-computational nicht berechenbar *adj.*
non-connected storage nichtzusammenhängender Speicher *m.*
non-controllable nichtbeeinflußbar *adj.*
non-conventional material nichtkonventionelles Material *n.*
non-descriptor Nicht-Deskriptor *m.*
non-destructive read nichtlöschendes Lesen *n.*
non-detailed list Summenliste *f.*
non-dialled connection Sofortverbindung *f.*
non-display nichtanzeigbar *adj.*, Anzeigeunterdrückung *f.*
non-equivalence Antivalenz *f.*, Ungleichwertigkeit *f.*
non-erasable nichtlöschbar *adj.*
non-erasable storage Festspeicher *m.*
non-escaping key Tottaste *f.*
non-essential nichtessentiell *adj.*
non-executable nichtausführbar *adj.*
non-executable statement nichtausführbare Anweisung *f.*
non-hierarchical relation nichthierarchische Beziehung *f.*

non-home record Überlaufsatz *m.*
non-interchangeable accessory nichtaustauschbares Zubehör *n.*
non-lending collection Präsenzbestand *m.*
non-linear nichtlinear *adj.*
non-local global *adj.*
non-locking Entriegelung *f.*
non-magnetic nichtmagnetisch *adj.*
non-negative integer nichtnegative Zahl *f.*
non-numeric nichtnumerisch *adj.*
non-numeric data processing nichtnumerische Datenverarbeitung *f.*
non-numerical character nichtnumerisches Zeichen *n.*
non-pageable nichtauslagerbar *adj.*
non-parametric statistics nichtparametrische Statistik *f.*
non-print nichtdruckbar *adj.*, Drucksperrimpuls *m.*
non-print key Nichtdrucktaste *f.*
non-programmable nichtprogrammierbar *adj.*
non-prompting mode Nichtabfragemodus *m.*
non-qualified book unqualifiziertes Buch *n.*
non-readable nichtlesbar *adj.*
non-recoverable unbehebbar *adj.*
non-recovery unbehebbarer Fehler *m.*
non-relevant nichtrelevant

adj.
non-resident nichtresident *adj.*
non-resident reader auswärtiger Bibliotheksbenutzer *m.*
non-scannable nichtlesbar *adj.*
non-sequenced information nichtfolgegebundene Information *f.*
non-sharable nicht gemeinsam benutzbar
non-shared channel nicht gemeinsam benutzter Kanal *m.*
non-shared system ungeteiltes System *n.*
non-significant nichtsignifikant *adj.*
non-standard nichtstandardisiert *adj.*
non-standard job Nichtstandardjob *m.*
non-standard label Nichtstandardkennsatz *m.*
non-stop durchgehend *adj.*
non-swappable storage nichtauslagerbarer Speicherbereich *m.*
non-systematic unsystematisch *adj.*
non-temporary data set nichttemporäre Datei *f.*
non-valid ungültig *adj.*
non-varying fest *adj.*, konstant *adj.*
non-verify ohne Prüfung
nonfiction Sachbuch *n.*
nonprofit nichtkommerziell *adj.*, Gemeinnützigkeit *f.*
nonprofit organization library Bibliothek *f.* einer gemeinnützigen Einrichtung
NOR WEDER-NOCH-Bedingung *f.*

normal normal *adj.*, typisch *adj.*
normal condition normale Bedingung *f.*
normal distribution Normalverteilung *f.*
normal execution sequence normale Ausführungsreihenfolge *f.*
normal file objektbezogene Datei *f.*
normal flow Normaldatenfluß *m.*
normal form Normalform *f.*
normal operation Normalbetrieb *m.*
normal priority normale Priorität *f.*
normal sequence normale Fortsetzung *f.*
normal text Klarschrift *f.*
normalization Normalisierung *f.*
normalize/to normalisieren *vrb.*
normalized normalisiert *adj.*
normalized evaluation measure normalisierte Bewertungskennziffer *f.*
normalized form normalisierte Form *f.*
normalized precision normalisierte Präzision *f.*
normalized recall normalisierter Recall *m.*
NOT NICHT-Bedingung *f.*
NOT-AND element NICHT-UND-Glied *n.*
NOT condition NICHT-Bedingung *f.*
NOT operation NICHT-Operation *f.*

not for sale nicht zu verkaufen
not of immediate interest inaktuell *adj.*
not out noch nicht erschienen
not topical inaktuell *adj.*
not yet published noch nicht erschienen
notation Notation *f.*, Bezeichnungsweise *f.*
notational base Notationsbasis *f.*
notational system Notationssystem *n.*
notch Kerbe *f.*
notched card Kerblochkarte *f.*
notching pliers Kerbzange *f.*
note Note *f.*, Anmerkung *f.*, Notiz *f.*
note/to aufzeichnen *vrb.*
notebook Notizbuch *n.*
notes Banknoten *pl.*
notice Notiz *f.*, Anzeige *f.*, Kündigung *f.*, Mitteilung *f.*,Nachricht *f.*, Bekanntmachung *f.*, Anschlag *m.*, Ankündigung *f.*
notice/to bemerken *vrb.*, beachten *vrb.*
notice board Anschlagbrett *n.*, Schwarzes Brett *n.*
notice period Kündigungsfrist *f.*
notification Benachrichtigung *f.*, Verständigung *f.*
notify/to benachrichtigen *vrb.*
notion Begriff *m.*, Vorstellung *f.*
notional overlap begriffliche Überschneidung *f.*
nought Null *f.*, Nichts *n.*
nought state Nullzustand *m.*
noun Substantiv *n.*

noun phrase Nominalphrase *f.*
novel Roman *m.*
novelette Novelle *f.*
novelty ratio Neuheitsquote *f.*
novelty search Neuheitsrecherche *f.*
nuclear energy technology Kernenergietechnik *f.*
nuclear research Nuklearforschung *f.*
nuclear technology Kerntechnik *f.*, Atomtechnik *f.*
null Null *f.*
null character Nullzeichen *n.*
null character string Leerzeichenkette *f.*
null entry Nulleintrag *m.*
null line Leerzeile *f.*
null output message Leerausgabenachricht *f.*
null response Leerantwort *f.*
null statement Leeranweisung *f.*
null string Leerzeichenkette *f.*
null token Nullzeichen *n.*
number Nummer *f.*, Zahl *f.*
number/to numerieren *vrb.*, zählen *vrb.*
number format Zahlenformat *n.*
number of digits Ziffernanzahl *f.*
number of volumes Bandzahl *f.*
number position Ziffernstelle *f.*
number representation Zahlendarstellung *f.*
number sign Nummernzeichen *n.*
number/to the pages paginieren *vrb.*, Seiten numerieren *vrb.*
numbered numeriert *adj.*

numbered copy numeriertes
Exemplar *n.*
numbered data set numerierte
Datei *f.*
numbered leaves numerierte
Blätter *pl.*
numbering Numerierung *f.*
numbering machine Numerator *m.*
numbering of blank lines Leerzeilennumerierung *f.*
numbering of sections Bogenzählung *f.*
numbering system Zahlensystem *n.*
numbering technique Nummerungstechnik *f.*
numeral Numeral *n.*
numeral position numerische
Position *f.*
numeral row Zifferntastenreihe *f.*
numeration Zahlendarstellung
f.
numeric numerisch *adj.*
numeric area numerischer Bereich *m.*
numeric character numerisches
Zeichen *n.*
numeric character data numerische Zeichendaten *pl.*
numeric character set numerischer Zeichensatz *m.*
numeric code numerischer
Code *m.*
numeric constant numerische
Konstante *f.*
numeric data numerische Daten *pl.*

numeric data code numerischer
Datencode *m.*
numeric database numerische
Datenbank *f.*
numeric field numerisches Datenfeld *n.*
numeric input field numerisches Eingabefeld *n.*
numeric key Zifferntaste *f.*
numeric keyboard numerische
Tastatur *f.*
numeric literal numerisches Literal *n.*
numeric mode numerischer
Modus *m.*
numeric notation numerische
Notation *f.*, Ziffernnotation *f.*
numeric operator numerischer
Operator *m.*
numeric ranging numerische
Bandbreite *f.*
numeric representation numerische Darstellung *f.*
numeric shift numerische Umschaltung *f.*
numeric word numerisches
Wort *n.*
numerical numerisch *adj.*
numerical capacity Zahlenbereich *m.*
numerical control numerische
Steuerung *f.*
numerical data numerische
Daten *pl.*
nursing school library Krankenpflegeschulbibliothek *f.*
nutrition science Ernährungswissenschaft *f.*

O

obituary Nachruf *m.*, Todesanzeige *f.*
object Maschinenprogramm *n.*, Objekt *n.*, Abbildungsgegenstand *m.*
object code Objektcode *m.*
object language Objektsprache *f.*, Zielsprache *f.*
object library Objektbibliothek *f.*
object library directory Objektbibliotheksverzeichnis *n.*
object module Objektmodul *n.*
object name Objektname *m.*
object program Objektprogramm *n.*, Maschinenprogramm *n.*
object time Programmlaufzeit *f.*
objective Zielsetzung *f.*, Lernziel *n.*
objective function Zielfunktion *f.*
objectives Zielvorgaben *pl.*
obligatory copy Pflichtexemplar *n.*
oblique schräg *adj.*, Schrägstrich *m.*
oblique/to schrägstellen *vrb.*
oblique stroke Schrägstrich *m.*
obliterate/to löschen *vrb.*
obliteration Löschung *f.*
oblong format Querformat *n.*, Breitformat *n.*

obscure term mehrdeutiger Begriff *m.*
observation Beobachtung *f.*
observed value Beobachtungswert *m.*
obsolescence technische Veralterung *f.*, Obsoleszenz *f.*, Veralten *n.*
obsolete material veraltetes Material *n.*
obsolete term veralteter Begriff *m.*
obtain/to document Dokument abrufen *vrb.*
occasional user Gelegenheitsnutzer *m.*
occupation Tätigkeit *f.*, Beruf *m.*, Beschäftigung *f.*
occupational classification Berufsgliederung *f.*
occupational school library Berufsschulbibliothek *f.*
occurrence Auftreten *n.*
oceanographic biology Meeresbiologie *f.*
oceanographic research Meeresforschung *f.*
oceanography Ozeanographie *f.*
octal oktal *adj.*
octal digit Oktalziffer *f.*
octal notation Oktalnotation *f.*
octal number Oktalzahl *f.*
octavo Oktav *n.*

odd ungerade *adj.*, einzeln *adj.*
odd copy Einzelexemplar *n.*
odd-even check Paritätsprüfung *f.*
odd-numbered page rechte Seite *f.*, ungerade Seitenzahl *f.*
odd numbers ungerade Zahlen *pl.*
odd page rechte Seite *f.*, ungerade Seitenzahl *f.*
odd parity ungerade Parität *f.*
odd part Einzelband *m.*
odd volume Einzelband *m.*
off-state Sperrzustand *m.*
OFF status ausgeschaltet *adj.*
off time Fehlzeit *f.*
offer Angebot *n.*
offer/to aufschalten *vrb.*, anbieten *vrb.*
office Amt *n.*, Dienststelle *f.*, Büro *n.*
office automation Büroautomation *f.*
office automation system Bürosystem *n.*
office communication Bürokommunikation *f.*
office communication system Bürokommunikationssystem *n.*
office computer Bürocomputer *m.*
office hours Dienstzeit *f.*, Dienststunden *pl.*, Öffnungszeit *f.*
office organization Büroorganisation *f.*
office-oriented büroorientiert *adj.*
office technology Bürotechnik *f.*
official bulletin Amtsblatt *n.*
official catalog Dienstkatalog

m.
official document amtliches Schriftstück *n.*
official journal Amtsblatt *n.*
official publication amtliche Druckschrift *f.*
official title Amtsbezeichnung *f.*
offline offline *adj.*, systemunabhängig *adj.*
offline data entry systemunabhängige Erfassung *f.*
offline field total systemunabhängige Feldsumme *f.*
offline mode Offlinemodus *m.*
offline operation Offlinebetrieb *m.*
offline output systemunabhängige Ausgabe *f.*
offline processing Offlineverarbeitung *f.*
offline search Offline-Suche *f.*
offline storage Offlinespeicher *m.*
offline test Offlinetest *m.*
offprint Sonderdruck *m.*
offset Offsetdruck *m.*
old books antiquarische Bücher *pl.*
old stock alter Bestand *m.*
omission marks Auslassungspunkte *pl.*
omit/to auslassen *vrb.*
omit line Ausschlußzeile *f.*
omitted fehlend *adj.*
omnibus review Sammelreferat *n.*
omnibus volume Sammelband *m.*
on a word basis wortweise *adj.*
on approbation zur Ansicht *f.*
on approval zur Ansicht *f.*

on-demand-publishing Veröffentlichung *f.* auf Anfrage
on expiration nach Ablauf *m.*
on loan leihweise *adj.*, ausgeliehen *adj.*, verliehen *adj.*
on-order file Bestelldatei *f.*
on-order list Bestelliste *f.*
ON status eingeschaltet *adj.*
on the record aktenkundig *adj.*
one-level address direkte Adresse *f.*
one-level description einstufige Titelaufnahme *f.*
one-to-one relationship Eins-zu-Eins Beziehung *f.*
one-track specialist Fachidiot *m.*
ongoing costs laufende Kosten *pl.*
online online *adj.*, systemabhängig *adj.*
online access Onlinezugriff *m.*
online application Onlineanwendung *f.*
online bibliography Onlinebibliographie *f.*
online catalog Onlinekatalog *m.*
online cataloging Onlinekatalogisierung *f.*
online computer system Onlinecomputersystem *n.*
online connection Onlineanschluß *m.*
online data entry Onlineerfassung *f.*, systemabhängige Erfassung *f.*
online data processing Onlinedatenverarbeitung *f.*
online document ordering Onlineliteraturbestellung *f.*
online field total systemabhängige Feldsumme *f.*
online information retrieval Onlineretrieval *n.*
online information service Onlineinformationsdienst *m.*
online inquiry system Onlineabfragesystem *n.*
online operation Onlinebetrieb *m.*
online ordering Onlinebestellung *f.*
online problem solving Onlineproblemlösung *f.*
online processing Onlineverarbeitung *f.*
online public access catalog Onlinebenutzerkatalog *m.*
online query system Onlineabfragesystem *n.*
online retrieval Onlineretrieval *n.*
online search services Onlinerecherchedienst *m.*
online searching Onlinesuche *f.*
online storage Onlinespeicher *m.*
online system Onlinesystem *n.*
online test Onlinetest *m.*
online test system Onlinetestsystem *n.*
online union catalog Onlinegesamtkatalog *m.*
online user group Onlinebenutzergruppe *f.*
online vendor Datenbankanbieter *m.*
only edition einzige Ausgabe *f.*
opaque copy Aufsichtskopie *f.*
OPEN statement Dateieröffnungsanweisung *f.*
open/to öffnen *vrb.*
open access freier Zugang *m.*

open-access area Freihandbereich *m.*

open-access library Freihandbibliothek *f.*

open counter Ausleihtheke *f.*

open data file geöffnete Datei *f.*

open-end question offene Frage *f.*

open-ended mit Erweiterungsmöglichkeit *f.*

open entry Aufnahme *f.* mit Fortsetzungskarte *f.*

open loop offene Schleife *f.*

open stack Freihandmagazin *n.*, Freihandaufstellung *f.*

open-stack borrowing Freihandausleihe *f.*

open-stack classification Freihandsystematik *f.*

open-stack collection Freihandbestand *m.*

open subroutine offenes Unterprogramm *n.*

open system offenes System *n.*

open systems interconnection Kommunikation *f.* offener Systeme

opening hours Öffnungszeiten *pl.*

operable time Nutzzeit *f.*

operand Operand *m.*

operand field Operandfeld *n.*

operate/to arbeiten *vrb.*, betreiben *vrb.*

operating characteristic Arbeitsweise *f.*, technische Angabe *f.*

operating cost Betriebskosten *pl.*

operating error Bedienungsfehler *m.*

operating instruction Bedienungsanweisung *f.*

operating language Betriebssprache *f.*

operating mode Arbeitsweise *f.*, Betriebsart *f.*

operating procedure Bedienungsablauf *m.*

operating space Darstellungsfläche *f.*

operating speed Ablaufgeschwindigkeit *f.*

operating state Betriebsstatus *m.*

operating system Betriebssystem *n.*

operating time Betriebszeit *f.*

operation Operation *f.*, Arbeitsgang *m.*, Vorgang *m.*

operation analysis Arbeitsstudie *f.*

operation checkout Funktionsprüfung *f.*

operation code Systemcode *m.*

operation control Systemsteuerung *f.*

operation control language Systemsteuersprache *f.*

operation duration Arbeitsgangdauer *f.*

operation exception Systemausnahmebedingung *f.*

operation field Operationsfeld *n.*

operation flowchart Arbeitsflußdiagramm *n.*

operation group Funktionsgruppe *f.*

operation priority Arbeitsgangpriorität *f.*

operation register Operationsregister *n.*

operation status Operationsstatus *m.*
operation time Betriebszeit *f.*, Bearbeitungszeit *f.*
operational funktionsfähig *adj.*
operational design operationaler Entwurf *m.*
operational guidance Bedienerführung *f.*
operational reliability Betriebszuverlässigkeit *f.*
operationals Betriebskosten *pl.*
operations analysis Unternehmensforschung *f.*
operations guide Bedienungsanleitung *f.*
operations research Unternehmensforschung *f.*
operations scheduling Arbeitsvorbereitung *f.*
operations unit Rechenwerk *n.*
operator Operator *m.*, Bediener *m.*
operator command Bedienerbefehl *m.*
operator console unit Abfrageplatz *m.*
operator control command Bedienersteuerbefehl *m.*
operator control function Bedienersteuerfunktion *f.*
operator control panel Bedienerkonsole *f.*
operator desk Vermittlungsplatz *m.*, Abfrageplatz *m.*
operator guidance Bedienerführung *f.*
operator input field Bedienereingabefeld *n.*
operator intervention Bedienereingriff *m.*
operator keyboard console

Operatoreingabetastatur *f.*
operator-oriented system bedienerorientiertes System *n.*
operator response field Bedienerantwortfeld *n.*
operator´s access code Bedienerzugriffscode *m.*
operator security Bedienerabsicherung *f.*
opinion Meinung *f.*
opposite page gegenüberliegende Seite *f.*
optical character reader optischer Belegleser *m.*, Klarschriftleser *m.*
optical character recognition optische Zeichenerkennung *f.*
optical coincidence optische Übereinstimmung *f.*
optical disk Bildplatte *f.*
optical encoder optischer Codeumsetzer *m.*
optical fiber Glasfaserkabel *n.*
optical fiber transmission Glasfaserübertragung *f.*
optical font optisch lesbare Schrift *f.*
optical industry optische Industrie *f.*
optical mark reader optischer Markierungsleser *m.*
optical page reader optischer Seitenleser *m.*
optical reader optischer Belegleser *m.*
optical scanner optischer Belegleser *m.*
optical storage optischer Speicher *m.*
optical videodisk Bildplatte *f.*
optics Optik *f.*
optimal performance optimale

Leistung *f.*
optimal size optimale Größe *f.*
optimizer Optimierer *m.*
optimum inventory Optimalbestand *m.*
option Zusatz *m.*, Ergänzungsangabe *f.*, Auswahl *f.*
option code Auswahlcode *m.*
option field Optionsfeld *n.*, Zusatzfeld *n.*
option instruction Erweiterungsanweisung *f.*
option list Eingabeliste *f.*
option number Auswahlnummer *f.*
option table Optionstabelle *f.*
optional wahlweise *adj.*
optional file Wahldatei *f.*
optional pause instruction bedingter Stoppbefehl *m.*
optional stop bedingter Halt
m.
optional stop instruction bedingter Stoppbefehl *m.*
optional word Wahlwort *n.*
options Auswahlmöglichkeiten
pl.
OR ODER
OR connector ODER-Verbindungsoperator *m.*
OR element ODER-Glied *n.*
OR gate ODER-Schaltung *f.*
OR operation ODER-Verknüpfung *f.*, Disjunktion *f.*
OR relationship ODER-Beziehung *f.*
OR rule ODER-Regel *f.*
order Ordnung *f.*, Auftrag *m.*,
Befehl *m.*, Reihenfolge *f.*, Bestellung *f.*
order/to ordnen *vrb.*, einreihen
vrb., bestellen *vrb.*

order book Bestellbuch *n.*
order/to by merging einordnen
vrb. durch Mischen
order card Bestellkarte *f.*
order catalog Bestellkatalog
m.
order cataloging Bestellkatalogisierung *f.*
order code Anweisungscode *m.*
order department Erwerbungsabteilung *f.*
order entry Auftragseingang
m.
order file Auftragsbestand *m.*
order form Bestellvordruck *m.*,
Bestellformular *n.*
order inquiry Auftragsabfrage
f.
order number Auftragsnummer *f.*
order of operation Reihenfolge
f. der Operationen
order point Bestellpunkt *m.*
order priority Auftragspriorität *f.*
order procedures Bestellvorgang *m.*
order processing Auftragsabwicklung *f.*
order record Auftragssteuersatz *m.*, Bestellnachweis *m.*
order request Bestellwunsch *m.*
order sequence Anweisungsfolge *f.*
order set Satzgruppe *f.*
ordering time Bestellzeit *f.*
orders-outstanding file Bestelldatei *f.*
ordinal data Ordinaldaten *pl.*
ordinal notation lineare Notation *f.*
ordinal scale Ordinalskala *f.*

ordinary symbol allgemeines Symbol *n.*
ordinary version gewöhnliche Lesart *f.*
organic structure organische Struktur *f.*
organization Organisation *f.*
organization table Organigramm *n.*
organizational chart Organigramm *n.*
organize/to organisieren *vrb.*
organized geordnet *adj.*
organized database geordnete Datenbank *f.*
organizer Organisator *m.*
orient/to ausrichten *vrb.*, orientieren *vrb.*
orientation Ausrichtung *f.*
oriented ausgerichtet *adj.*
origin Nullpunkt *m.*, Ursprung *m.*
origin address field Absenderadressenfeld *n.*
origin element field Absenderelementfeld *n.*
origin system Eingabesystem *n.*
original original *adj.*, Original *n.*, Vorlage *f.*
original cataloging Erstkatalogisierung *f.*
original costs Ursprungskosten *pl.*
original document Urbeleg *m.*, Originaldokument *n.*
original edition Originalausgabe *f.*, Erstausgabe *f.*
original position Ausgangsstellung *f.*
original sources Originalquellen *pl.*
original statement Originalan-

weisung *f.*
original text Urtext *m.*
original title originalsprachlicher Titel *m.*
original version Originalfassung *f.*
originality Originalität *f.*, Echtheit *f.*
originate/to verursachen *vrb.*
origination Erfindung *f.*
origination address field logische Herkunftsadresse *f.*
originative erfinderisch *adj.*
originator Urheber *m.*, Erfinder *m.*, Absender *m.*
orthographic orthographisch *adj.*
orthography Rechtschreibung *f.*
other title information Sachtitelzusatz *m.*
out verliehen *adj.*, ausgeliehen *adj.*
out of date veraltet *adj.*, rückständig *adj.*
out of line nicht ausgerichtet *adj.*
out of order außer Betrieb *m.*, gestörte Reihenfolge *f.*
out of print vergriffen *adj.*
out of print edition vergriffene Ausgabe *f.*
out of stock nicht vorrätig *adj.*, nicht auf Lager *adj.*
out of work außer Betrieb *m.*, arbeitslos *adj.*
out plant system außerbetriebliches System *n.*
outage Ausfall *m.*
outbound code Ausgabecode *m.*
outer form äußere Form *f.*
outline Gliederung *f.*, Abriß *m.*

outline formatting Abschnittskennzeichnung *f.*
outlook Zukunftsperspektive *f.*
output Ausgabe *f.*, Ausgang *m.*
output/to ausgeben *vrb.*
output area Ausgabebereich *m.*
output block Ausgabebereich
m.
output buffer Ausgabepuffer
m.
output capacity Ausgabekapazität *f.*
output channel Ausgangskanal
m.
output class Ausgabeklasse *f.*
output configuration Ausgangskonfiguration *f.*
output control character Ausgabekontrollzeichen *n.*
output data Ausgabedaten *pl.*
output device Ausgabegerät *n.*
output display Ausgabeanzeige
f.
output element Ausgabeglied
n.
output file Ausgabedatei *f.*
output format Ausgabeformat
n.
**output-format specification
sheet** Ausgabeformatspezifizierungsblatt *n.*
output formatting Ausgabeformatierung *f.*
output indicator Ausgabeanzeiger *m.*
output interface Ausgabe-
schnittstelle *f.*
output label Ausgabekennsatz
m.
output language Ausgabesprache *f.*
output line Ausgabezeile *f.*

output listing Ausgabeliste *f.*
output mode Ausgabemodus
m.
output operation Ausgabeoperation *f.*
output process Ausgabeprozeß
m.
output program Ausgabeprogramm *n.*
output queue Ausgabewarteschlange *f.*
output rate Ausgabegeschwindigkeit *f.*
output record Ausgabesatz *m.*
output request Ausgabeanforderung *f.*
output routine Ausgabeprogramm *n.*
output section Ausgabebereich
m.
output sequence number Ausgabefolgenummer *f.*
output signal Ausgabesignal *n.*
output specification Ausgabebestimmung *f.*
output state Ausgabestatus *m.*
output storage Ausgabespeicher *m.*
output time interval Ausgabezeit *f.*
output transfer rate Ausgaberate *f.*
output unit Ausgabeeinheit *f.*
output work queue Ausgabewarteschlange *f.*
outset Anfang *m.*
outside source auswärtige
Quelle *f.*
outside user auswärtiger Benutzer *m.*
overall costs Gesamtkosten *pl.*
overdue fee Säumnisgebühr *f.*

overdue fine Mahngebühr *f*.
overdue material überfälliges Material *n*.
overdue notice Mahnung *f*.
overflow Überlauf *m*.
overflow condition Überlaufbedingung *f*.
overflow field Überlauffeld *n*.
overflow indicator Überlaufanzeige *f*.
overflow line Überlaufzeile *f*.
overflow page Überlaufseite *f*.
overflow record Überlaufsatz *m*.
overflow track Überlaufspur *f*.
overhead Aufwand *m*., Gemeinkosten *pl*.
overhead projector Overheadprojektor *m*., Tageslichtprojektor *m*.
overlap überlappung *f*., Überschneidung *f*.
overlap/to überlappen *vrb*.,

überschneiden *vrb*.
overlap measure Überschneidungskennziffer *f*.
overlay Überlagerung *f*.
overlay name Vordruckmaskenname *m*.
overlay program Überlagerungsprogramm *n*.
overload Bereichsüberschreitung *f*.
overload capacity Überlastfaktor *m*.
overloading Überlastung *f*.
overprinting Mehrfachdruck *m*.
override/to überschreiten *vrb*.
overrun Überlauf *m*.
overrun time Überlaufzeit *f*.
oversized book Buch *n*. im Überformat
overwrite/to überschreiben *vrb*.

P

pace/to dosieren *vrb*.
pacing Schrittsteuerung *f*., Dosierung *f*.
pack Stapel *m*.
pack/to packen *vrb*.
pack feed/to einlegen *vrb*.
pack feed slot Stapelzuführung *f*.
pack of cards Kartenstapel *m*.

package Programmpaket *n*.
packed gepackt *adj*.
packed card Sammelkarte *f*.
packed data field gepacktes Datenfeld *n*.
packed field gepacktes Feld *n*.
packed format gepacktes Format *n*.
packed keys gepackte Schlüssel

pl.
packed mode gepackte Form *f.*
packed print zone gepackter Druckbereich *m.*
packed transmission gepackte Übertragung *f.*
packet Paket *n.*, Datenpaket *n.*
packet-mode operation Paketübermittlung *f.*
packet-switched network Paketvermittlungsnetz *n.*
packet switching Paketvermittlung *f.*
packing Konfektionierung *f.*
packing density Zeichendichte *f.*
packing factor Verdichtungsfaktor *m.*
packing slip Lieferschein *m.*
packing technology Verpackungstechnik *f.*
pad Block *m.*, Puffer *m.*
pad/to auffüllen *vrb.*
pad character Auffüllzeichen *n.*
padded binding gefütterter Einband *m.*
padding Auffüllen *n.*
padding byte Füllbyte *n.*
paedagogy Erziehungswissenschaft *f.*
page Seite *f.*
page/to seitenweise überlagern *vrb.*, blättern *vrb.*
page-access exception Seitenzugriffsfehler *m.*
page address Seitenadresse *f.*
page-at-a-time printer Seitendrucker *m.*
page back/to zurückblättern *vrb.*
page body Seitenrumpf *m.*
page buffer Seitenspeicher *m.*

page buffer storage Seitenspeicher *m.*
page capacity count Seitenkapazitätszähler *m.*
page catalog Bandkatalog *m.*
page control Seitensteuerung *m.*
page control block Seitensteuerblock *m.*
page counter Seitenzähler *m.*
page data Seitendaten *pl.*
page data set Seitendatei *f.*
page depth Seitenlänge *f.*
page description Seitenbeschreibung *f.*
page display Seitenanzeige *f.*
page down/to vorwärtsblättern *vrb.*
page end indicator Seitenendanzeige *f.*
page fault Fehlseitenbedingung *f.*
page fault interrupt Fehlseitenunterbrechung *f.*
page fix entry Seitenfixierungseintrag *m.*
page fixing Seitenfixierung *f.*
page footing Fußzeile *f.*
page format Seitenformat *n.*
page format change Seitenformatwechsel *m.*
page frame Seitenrahmen *m.*
page frame table Seitenrahmentabelle *f.*
page heading Seitenkopf *m.*, Kopfzeile *f.*, Seitenüberschrift *f.*
page image Seitenbild *n.*
page in/to seitenweise einlagern *vrb.*
page-in operation Seiteneinlagerung *f.*

page index Seitenindex *m*.
page key Seitenstopptaste *f*.
page layout Seitengestaltung
f., Textanordnung *f*.
page length control feature
Formularlängensteuerung *f*.
page limit Seitenbegrenzung *f*.
page locking Seitenfixierung *f*.
page make-up Umbruch *m*.
page migration Seitenmigration *f*.
page mode seitenweise Übertragung *f*.
page number Seitenzahl *f*.,
Seitennummer *f*.
page number increment Seitennumerierschritt *m*.
page numbering Seitennumerierung *f*.
page option Seitenvorschubangabe *f*.
page out/to auslagern *vrb*.
page-out operation Seitenauslagerung *f*.
page overflow Seitenüberlauf
m.
page pool Seitenspeicher *m*.,
Seitenvorrat *m*.
page printer Seitendrucker *m*.
page proof Umbruchkorrektur
f.
page read mode seitenweises
Lesen *n*.
page reclamation Seitenreaktivierung *f*., Seitenrückforderung *f*.
page reference Seitenverweis
m.
page replacement Seitenersetzung *f*.
page slot Seitenfach *n*.
page-size option Seitenlän-

genangabe *f*.
page state Seitenstatus *m*.
page stealing Seitenentzug *m*.
page storage Seitenspeicher *m*.
page supervisor Seitensupervisor *m*.
page table Seitentabelle *f*.
page through/to durchblättern
vrb.
page transfer Seitenübetragung *f*.
page-transition exception Seitenübertragungsfehler *m*.
page turning Seitenwechsel *m*.
page up/to zurückblättern *vrb*.
page wait Seitenwartestatus
m.
page write mode seitenweises
Schreiben *n*.
pageable auslagerbar *adj*.
paginate/to paginieren *vrb*.
paginate document Seitenumbruchdokument *n*.
paginating machine Paginiermaschine *f*.
pagination Paginierung *f*.,
Seitennumerierung *f*.
paging Paginierung *f*., Seitennumerierung *f*., Personensuchen *n*.
paging area memory Seitenspeicher *m*.
paging data set Seitendatei *f*.
paging demand Seitenanforderung *f*.
paging device Seitenspeichergerät *n*.
paging operation Seitenwechseloperation *f*.
paging status Seitenwechselstatus *m*.
paging supervisor Seitensu-

pervisor *m.*
pair Paar *n.*
pair generation Paarbildung *f.*
pair production Paarbildung *f.*
paired parentheses paarweises Klammern *n.*
paired segment gepaartes Segment *n.*
palette Palette *f.*
pamphlet Broschüre *f.*, Flugschrift *f.*
pamphlet box Broschürenbehälter *m.*
pamphlet volume Sammelband *m.*
Pan Soviet State Library Allunionsbibliothek *f.*
panel Panel *n.*, Schalttafel *f.*, Format *n.*, Maske *f.*
panel data set Maskendatei *f.*
panel description Formatbeschreibung *f.*
panel discussion Podiumsdiskussion *f.*
panel formatting Formatgestaltung *f.*
panel management Formatmanagement *n.*
panel member Diskussionsteilnehmer *m.*
paper Papier *n.*, Abhandlung *f.*
paper bail Papierhalter *m.*
paper carrier Papierführung *f.*
paper cassette Blattmagazin *n.*
paper clip Büroklammer *f.*
paper cutter Papierschneider *m.*
paper direction Papierrichtung *f.*
paper dispenser Blattspender *m.*
paper drawer Papierfach *n.*

paper feed Papiertransport *m.*, Papierzuführung *f.*
paper form Blattformular *n.*
paper goods Papierwaren *pl.*
paper guide Formularführung *f.*
paper holder Papierhalter *m.*
paper insert Papiereinlage *f.*
paper jam Papierstau *m.*
paper length Papierlänge *f.*
paper line Papierbahn *f.*
paper path Papierpfad *m.*
paper permanence Papierhaltbarkeit *f.*
paper restauration Papierrestaurierung *f.*
paper separator Papiertrenner *m.*
paper sheet support Papierstütze *f.*
paper shredder Reißwolf *m.*
paper side guides Papierstapelbegrenzer *m.*
paper size Formulargröße *f.*
paper skip Papiervorschub *m.*
paper stand Papierablage *f.*
paper supply Papierzuführung *f.*
paper support Papierauflage *f.*
paper tape Lochstreifen *m.*
paper throw Papiervorschub *m.*
paper tray Papierbehälter *m.*
paperback Broschur *f.*, Paperback *n.*
paperless papierlos *adj.*
paperless information system papierloses Informationssystem *n.*
paperwork Schreibarbeiten *pl.*
paperwork management Schriftgutverwaltung *f.*

papyrus Papyrus *m.*
papyrus collection Papyrussammlung *f.*
paradigm Paradigma *n.*
paradigmatic relation paradigmatische Beziehung *f.*
paragraph Paragraph *m.*, Absatz *m.*
paragraph control Absatzsteuerung *f.*
paragraph header Absatzüberschrift *f.*
paragraph indention Absatzeinrückung *f.*
paragraph key Absatztaste *f.*
paragraph mark Absatzzeichen
n.
paragraph name Paragraphenname *m.*
parallel parallel *adj.*, simultan
adj.
parallel/to parallel betreiben
vrb.
parallel access Parallelzugriff
m.
parallel adder paralleles Addierwerk *n.*
parallel addition parallele Addition *f.*
parallel balance Quersummenkontrolle *f.*
parallel by bit bitparallel *adj.*
parallel by character zeichenparallel *adj.*
parallel connection Parallelschaltung *f.*
parallel counter Synchronzähler *m.*
parallel data parallele Datenübertragung *f.*
parallel data adapter Mehrkanalanschluß *m.*

parallel data extension Mehrkanalerweiterung *f.*
parallel data timeout Mehrkanalzeitsperre *f.*
parallel input Paralleleingabe
f.
parallel interface parallele
Schnittstelle *f.*
parallel link Parallelverbindung *f.*
parallel mode Parallelbetrieb
m.
parallel numbering system Parallelnummernsystem *n.*
parallel operation Parallelbetrieb *m.*
parallel processing Parallelverarbeitung *f.*
parallel processors Vektorrechner *m.*
parallel register Parallelregister *n.*
parallel section paralleler Unterbereich *m.*
parallel-serial parallel-seriell
adj.
parallel storage Parallelspeicher *m.*
parallel title Parallelsachtitel
m.
parallel transfer signal Parallelübertragungssignal *n.*
parallel transmission Parallelübertragung *f.*
parameter Parameter *m.*
parameter card Parameterkarte *f.*
parameter delimiter Parameterbegrenzer *m.*
parameter descriptor Parameterbeschreiber *m.*
parameter estimation Parame-

terschätzung *f.*
parameter list Parameterliste
f.
parameter passing Parameterübergabe *f.*
parameterize/to parametrisieren *vrb.*
parametric instruction parametrisierter Befehl *m.*
parametric procedure parametrisierte Prozedur *f.*
parametric program parametrisiertes Programm *n.*
parametric statistics parametrische Statistik *f.*
paraphrase Paraphrase *f.,*
Umschreibung *f.*
parataxis Beiordnung *f.,* Nebenordnung *f.*
parchment Pergament *n.*
parent body übergeordnete
Körperschaft *f.*
parent-child relation Eltern-
Kind-Relation *f.*
parent class übergeordnete
Klasse *f.*
parent disk Originalplatte *f.*
parent institution Trägerinstitution *f.*
parenthesis runde Klammer *f.*
parenthesize/to in Klammer
setzen *vrb.*
parenthesized expression in
Klammern gesetzter Ausdruck
m.
parish bulletin Gemeindeblatt
n.
parish church library Pfarrkirchenbibliothek *f.*
parish library Pfarrbücherei *f.*
parish register Gemeinderegister *n.*

parity Parität *f.*
parity bit Paritätsbit *n.,* Prüfbit
n.
parity check Paritätsprüfung *f.*
parity error Paritätsfehler *m.*
parliament Parlament *n.*
parliament archive Parlamentsarchiv *n.*
parliamentary parlamentarisch *adj.*
parliamentary library Parlamentsbibliothek *f.*
parliamentary paper Parlamentsschrift *f.*
parse/to grammatikalisch analysieren *vrb.*
parser Syntaxanalysator
parsing Syntaxanalyse *f.*
part Teil *n.*
part number Teilenummer *f.*
part of a volume Teilband *m.*
part of number Ziffernteil *n.*
part term Teilbegriff *m.*
part-time employment Teilzeitarbeit *f.*
part-whole relation Teil-Ganze-Relation *f.*
part work Fortsetzungswerk *n.*
partial teilweise *adj.*
partial answer processing Teilantwortkontrolle *f.*
partial carry Teilübertragung
f.
partial channel Teilkanal *m.*
partial clustering partielle
Klassenbildung *f.*
partial correlation partielle
Korrelation *f.*
**partial database reorganiza-
tion** partielle Datenbankreorganisation *f.*
partial dependency partielle

Abhängigkeit *f.*
partial failure Teilausfall *m.*
partial key Teilschlüssel *m.*
partial match partielle Übereinstimmung *f.*
partial operating time Teilbetriebszeit *f.*
partial page Teilseite *f.*
partial system simulator Teilsystemsimulator *m.*
partial title Sekundärtitel *m.*
partially qualified name teilweise spezifizierter Name *m.*
participant Teilnehmer *m.*, Gesprächspartner *m.*
participant observation teilnehmende Beobachtung *f.*
participate/to teilnehmen *vrb.*, mitwirken *vrb.*
participation Partizipation *f.*, Beteiligung *f.*, Teilnahme *f.*, Mitwirkung *f.*
particle of relation Beziehungsverbindung *f.*
particularity Besonderheit *f.*
partition Partition *f.*, Unterteilung *f.*
partition allocation Partitionszuordnung *f.*
partition distribution Partitionsaufteilung *f.*
partition priority Partitionspriorität *f.*
partitioned data set untergliederte Datei *f.*
partitioned file untergliederte Datei *f.*
partitioned index untergliederter Index *m.*
partitioned key untergliederter Schlüssel *m.*
partitive relation Teil-Ganze-

Relation *f.*, partitive Relation *f.*
partitive term partitive Benennung *f.*
party Partei *f.*
party archive Parteiarchiv *n.*
party convention Parteitag *m.*
pass Arbeitsgang *m.*, Durchlauf *m.*
pass/to absolvieren *vrb.*, ablaufen *vrb.*, durchlaufen *vrb.*
pass-band Durchlaßbereich *m.*
pass for press druckfertig *adj.*
passage retrieval Abschnittsretrieval *n.*
passed data set weitergereichte Datei *f.*
passive fault passiver Fehler *m.*
password Kennwort *n.*, Paßwort *n.*
password protection Kennwortdateischutz *m.*
password security Kennwortkontrolle *f.*
past Vergangenheit *f.*
past due überfällig *adj.*
paste/to kleben *vrb.*
patch Korrektur *f.*
patch/to korrigieren *vrb.*, einfügen *vrb.*
patch area Korrekturbereich *m.*
patch panel Schalttafel *m.*
patent Patent *n.*
patent abstracts Patentabstract *n.*
patent application Patentanmeldung *f.*
patent attorney Patentanwalt *m.*
patent bulletin Patentblatt *n.*

patent claim Patentanspruch *m*.

patent classification Patentklassifikation *f*.

patent database Patentdatenbank *f*.

patent depository Patentschriftenauslegestelle *f*.

patent document Patentdokument *n*.

patent documentation Patentdokumentation *f*.

patent information Patentinformation *f*.

patent information center Patentinformationszentrum *n*.

patent information service Patentinformationsdienst *m*.

patent information system Patentinformationssystem *n*.

patent law Patentrecht *f*.

patent library Patentbibliothek *f*., Patentbücherei *f*.

patent literature Patentliteratur *f*.

patent office Patentamt *n*.

patent records Patentakten *pl*.

patent rights Schutzrecht *n*.

patent search Patentrecherche *f*.

patent specification Patentschrift *f*.

path Pfad *m*., Zugriffspfad *m*., Zweig *m*.

path analysis Pfadanalyse *f*.

path control Pfadsteuerung *m*.

path control network Pfadsteuerungsnetzwerk *n*.

path entry Pfadeintragung *f*.

path finding Wegsuche *f*.

path information unit Pfadinformationseinheit *f*.

path major node Pfadhauptknoten *m*.

path of integration Integrationspfad *m*.

path switch Programmablaufschalter *m*.

path table Pfadtabelle *f*.

patient library Patientenbibliothek *f*.

patron Benutzer *m*.

patron registration Benutzeranmeldung *f*.

patron registration card Benutzerkarte *f*.

patron registration file Benutzerdatei *f*.

pattern Muster *n*., Schema *n*.

pattern detection Mustererkennung *f*.

pattern generator Zeichengenerator *m*.

pattern recognition Mustererkennung *f*.

PAUSE statement HALT-Befehl *m*.

pause Pause *f*., Halt *m*.

pause instruction Haltbefehl *m*.

payment by installments Ratenzahlung *f*.

peak capacity Höchstleistungsgrenze *f*.

peak load Spitzenbelastung *f*.

peak point Scheitelpunkt *m*.

peculiarity Besonderheit *f*.

pedagogics Pädagogik *f*.

peek/to nachsehen *vrb*.

peek-a-boo Sichtprüfung *f*., Blickkontrolle *f*.

peek-a-boo card Sichtlochkarte *f*.

peep-hole card Sichtlochkarte

f.

peer review Expertenbegutachtung *f.*
pen Feder *f.*
pen name Pseudonym *n.*
pen recording instrument Tintenschreiber *m.*
pencil Bleistift *m.*
percent key Prozenttaste *f.*
percentage distribution method Methode *f.* der prozentualen Verteilung
perfect abgeschlossen *adj.*
perfect binding Klebebindung *f.*
perforated perforiert *adj.*, gelocht *adj.*
perforated tape Lochstreifen *m.*
perforation Perforation *f.*
perforator Perforiermaschine *f.*, Locher *m.*
perform/to durchführen *vrb.*, ausführen *vrb.*
PERFORM statement DURCHLAUF-Befehl *m.*
performance Leistung *f.*, Leistungsniveau *n.*
performance efficiency Leistungsgrad *m.*
performance evaluation Leistungsbewertung *f.*
performance factors Leistungsfaktoren *pl.*
performance function Zielfunktion *f.*
performance level Leistungsstufe *f.*
performance measurement Leistungsmessung *f.*
performance objective Leistungsziel *n.*
performance rate Leistungsgrad *m.*
performance specification Leistungsangabe *f.*
performance standard Leistungsstandard *m.*, Qualitätsnorm *f.*
perimeter shelves Wandregal *n.*
period Periode *f.*, Zeitraum *m.*
period definition Periodendefinition *f.*
period division Zeitunterteilung *f.*
period subdivision Zeitschlüssel *m.*
periodic function periodische Funktion *f.*
periodic reporting periodische Auswertung *f.*
periodical Zeitschrift *f.*, Periodikum *n.*
periodical accession record Zeitschriftenzugangsnachweis *m.*
periodical article Zeitschriftenaufsatz *m.*
periodical bibliography periodische Bibliographie *f.*, Zeitsschriftenbibliographie *f.*
periodical cataloging Zeitschriftenkatalogisierung *f.*
periodical circulation Zeitschriftenzirkulation *f.*
periodical database Zeitschriftendatenbank *f.*
periodical display shelves Zeitschriftenregal *n.*
periodical fund Zeitschriftenetat *m.*, Zeitschriftenerwerbungsetat *m.*
periodical holding list Zeitschriftenliste *f.*
periodical holding system Zeit-

schriftenverwaltungsystem *n*.
periodical holdings Zeitschriftenbestand *m*.
periodical index Zeitschrifteninhaltsbibliographie *f*.
periodical publication periodische Veröffentlichung *f*.
periodical publisher Zeitschriftenverleger *m*.
periodical rack Zeitschriftenregal *n*.
periodical receipt record Zeitschriftenzugangsnachweis *m*.
periodical room Zeitschriftenlesesaal *m*.
periodicals checklist Zeitschriftenverzeichnis *n*.
periodicals collection Zeitschriftenbestand *m*.
periodicals department Zeitschriftenabteilung *f*.
periodicals directory Zeitschriftenverzeichnis *n*.
periodicals indexing Zeitschriftenauswertung *f*.
periodicity Periodizität *f*.
peripheral control unit Ein-
/Ausgabesteuereinheit *f*.
peripheral equipment Peripherieausstattung *f*.
peripheral node peripherer
Knoten *m*.
peripheral storage peripherer
Speicher *m*.
peripheral transfer periphere
Übertragung *f*.
peripheral unit periphere Einheit *f*.
peripherals Peripheriegeräte
pl.
permanence Haltbarkeit *f*.
permanent entry permanente

Eintragung *f*.
permanent file permanente
Datei *f*.
permanent loan Dauerleihe *f*.
permanent post feste Stelle *f*.,
Planstelle *f*.
permanent record film Archivfilm *m*.
permanent segment permanentes Segment *n*.
permanent storage Festspeicher *m*.
permitted term zugelassene
Benennung *f*.
permutation Permutation *f*.
permutation index permutiertes Register *n*.
permutation technique Permutationsverfahren *n*.
permute/to permutieren *vrb*.
permuted index permutiertes
Register *n*.
permuted title index permutiertes Titelregister *m*.
perpetual inventory file laufende Bestandskartei *f*.
personal persönlich *adj*.
personal computer Arbeitsplatzrechner *m*., Tischcomputer *m*.
personal data personenbezogene Daten *pl*.
personal file Personalakte *f*.
personal heading Personenschlagwort *n*.
personal identifier Personalkennzeichen *n*.
personnel Personal *n*., Mitarbeiter *pl*.
personnel administration Personalverwaltung *f*.
personnel costs Personalkosten

pl.
personnel file Personalkartei *f.*
personnel information system Personalinformationssystem *n.*
personnel policy Personalpolitik *f.*
pertinency Pertinenz *f.*, Relevanz *f.*
pertinency factor Relevanzfaktor *m.*
pertinency ratio Relevanzmaß *n.*
petrochemical library petrochemische Bibliothek *f.*
petrochemistry Petrochemie *f.*
pharmaceutical pharmazeutisch *adj.*
pharmacology Pharmakologie *f.*
pharmacy Pharmazie *f.*
phase Phase *f.*
phase modulation Phasenmodulation *f.*
phase name Phasenname *m.*
phase relation Phasenbeziehung *f.*
phasing Phasenlage *f.*
philanthropic library philanthropische Bibliothek *f.*
philology Philologie *f.*, Sprachwissenschaft *f.*
philosophy Philosophie *f.*
phone number Rufnummer *f.*
phone survey Telefonbefragung *f.*
phoneme Phonem *n.*
phonetic phonetisch *adj.*
phonetic alphabet Lautschrift *f.*
phonetic components phonetische Bestandteile *pl.*
phonetic conversion phoneti-

sche Umsetzung *f.*
phonetic encoding phonetische Verschlüsselung *f.*
phonetic key phonetischer Schlüssel *m.*
phonetic writing Lautschrift *f.*
phonetics Phonetik *f.*
phonogram Tonaufzeichnung *f.*
phonorecord Schallaufnahme *f.*
photo Foto *n.*
photo archive Bildarchiv *n.*
photo document sensor Fotozelle *f.*
photocomposition Lichtsatz *m.*
photocopy Photokopie *f.*, Fotokopie *f.*
photocopying machine Fotokopiergerät *n.*
photocopying service Fotokopierdienst *m.*
photocopying system Fotokopiersystem *n.*
photoelectric reader fotoelektrischer Leser *m.*
photoelectric scanning fotoelektrisches Skannen *n.*
photograph Fotographie *f.*
photographic archives Fotoarchiv *n.*
photographic department Fotostelle *f.*
photographic library Fotoarchiv *n.*
photolithography Fotolithographie *f.*
photomask Fotomaske *f.*
photomechanical fotomechanisch *adj.*
photomontage Fotomontage *f.*
photosensing mark optisch les-

bare Markierung *f.*
photosensitive lichtempfindlich
adj.
photosetting Lichtsatz *m.*, Fotosatz *m.*
photosetting equipment Fotosatzanlage *f.*
phototype output Lichtsatzausgabe *f.*
phototype technology Lichtsatztechnik *f.*
phototype unit Lichtsatzanlage
f.
phrase Wortgruppe *f.*, Satzteil
m.
phrase book Sprachführer *m.*
phrase structure grammar
Phrasenstrukturgrammatik *f.*
phraseologie Ausdrucksweise
f.
physical access control Zugangskontrolle *f.*
physical access level physische
Zugriffsebene *f.*
physical address physische
Adresse *f.*
physical block physischer Block
m.
physical connection physische
Verbindung *f.*
physical control unit physische
Steuereinheit *f.*
physical data structure physische Datenstruktur *f.*
physical database physische
Datenbank *f.*
physical database record physischer Datenbanksatz *m.*
physical description technische
Beschreibung *f.*
physical dimension Abmessung
f.

physical file physische Datei *f.*
physical life Nutzungsdauer *f.*,
technische Nutzungsdauer *f.*
physical line Leitung *f.*
physical link physische Verbindung *f.*
physical make-up physische
Ausstattung *f.*
physical model physisches Modell *n.*
physical organization physikalische Organisation *f.*
physical page physische Seite *f.*
physical paging physischer Seitenwechsel *m.*
physical pointer physikalischer
Zeiger *m.*
physical quantity physikalische
Größe *f.*
physical record physischer Satz
m.
physical segment physisches
Segment *n.*
physical structure physischer
Aufbau *m.*
physical terminal physische
Datenstation *f.*
physical transmission physikalische Übertragung *f.*
physical unit physische Einheit
f.
physics Physik *f.*
pick/to anregen *vrb.*, heraussuchen *vrb.*
pick time Ansprechzeit *f.*
pick up/to lesen *vrb.*
picker failure Zugriffsfehler *m.*
pictogram Piktogramm *n.*
pictography Bilderschrift *f.*
pictorial database Bilddatenbank *f.*
pictorial query language

Bildabfragesprache *f.*
picture Abbildung *f.*, Bild *n.*,
Maske *f.*
picture agency Bildagentur *f.*
picture archive Bildarchiv *n.*
picture archiving Bildarchivierung *f.*
picture book Bilderbuch *n.*
picture character Maskenzeichen *n.*
picture check Maskenprüfung *f.*
picture collection Bildbestand
m., Bildsammlung *f.*
picture element Bildelement *n.*
picture index Bildindex *m.*
picture library Bildarchiv *n.*
picture specification Maskenspezifikation *f.*
picture string Maskenzeichenfolge *f.*
pictured maskiert *adj.*
pie chart Kreisdiagramm *n.*
piece good Schnitteil *n.*
pigeonhole Ablagefach *n.*
pile of documents Aktenstoß *m.*
pilot application Pilotanwendung *f.*
pilot card Steuerkarte *f.*
pilot issue Nullnummer *f.*
pilot line Fertigungslinie *f.*
pilot project Pilotprojekt *n.*,
Modellversuch *m.*
pilot run Testlauf *m.*
pilot selector Leitselektor *m.*
pilot study Vorstudie *f.*, Pilotstudie *f.*
pin Kontaktstift *m.*
pin-compatible steckerkompatibel *adj.*
pin name Anschlußbezeichnung
f.
pinboard Stecktafel *f.*

pinpoint/to hinweisen *vrb.*
pipeline processor Vektorrechner *m.*
pipelining Befehlsverknüpfung
f.
pitch Abstand *m.*, Schreibdichte
f., Teilung *f.*
pitch escapement Schrittschaltung *f.*
pitch group Teilungsgruppe *f.*
pixel Bildpunkt *m.*
place Ort *m.*
place holder Platzhalter *m.*
place holder record Platzhaltersatz *m.*
place index Ortsregister *n.*
place name Ortsbezeichnung *f.*
place of publication Erscheinungsort *m.*, Verlagsort *m.*
place value Stellenwert *m.*
plaintext Klartext *m.*
plan Plan *m.*
plane Ebene *f.*, eben *adj.*
plane coordinates ebene Koordinaten *pl.*
planetarium Planetarium *n.*
planishing plate Auflageplatte
f.
planning Planung *f.*
planning cost accounting Plan-
kostenrechnung *f.*
planning exposure Planungsunsicherheit *f.*
planning guide Planungshandbuch *n.*
planning system Planungssystem *n.*
planning worksheet Planungsblatt *n.*
plant Betrieb *m.*, Werk *n.*, Fabrik *f.*
plastic sheet Plastikfolie *f.*

plate 190

plate Photoplatte *f.*, Druckstock *m.*, Klischee *n.*
plausibility Plausibilität *f.*
plausibility check Plausibilitätsprüfung *f.*
play back Wiedergabe *f.*
play review Theaterkritik *f.*
playbill Programmheft *n.*
playbill collection Theaterzettelsammlung *f.*
plenary meeting Vollversammlung *f.*
plenary session Plenarsitzung *f.*
plot Diagramm *n.*
plot/to zeichnen *vrb.*
plotter Zeichengerät *n.*
plotting size Zeichenfläche *f.*
plural Plural *m.*, mehrfach *adj.*
plus plus *prep.*
plus sign Pluszeichen *n.*
pneumology Pneumologie *f.*
pocket Ablagefach *n.*
pocket book Taschenbuch *n.*
pocket calculator Taschenrechner *m.*
pocket dictionary Taschenwörterbuch *n.*
podium Podium *n.*
poem Gedicht *n.*
poetic form Gedichtform *f.*
poetry Lyrik *f.*
point Punkt *m.*
point/to zeigen *vrb.*
point of contact Berührungspunkt *m.*
point of interruption Unterbrechungspunkt *m.*
point of intersection Schnittpunkt *m.*
point out/to hinweisen *vrb.*
point setting Kommaeinstellung *f.*
point shifting Kommaverschiebung *f.*
point size Schriftgröße *f.*
pointer Hinweisadresse *f.*, Zeiger *m.*
pointer qualification Zeigerkennzeichnung *f.*
pointer structure Zeigerstruktur *f.*
pointer variable Zeigervariable *f.*
poisson distribution Poissonverteilung *f.*
poke/to speichern *vrb.*
polar exploration Polarforschung *f.*
policy Politik *f.*
political science Politologie *f.*
politics Politik *f.*
poll/to aufrufen *vrb.*, abrufen *vrb.*
polling Sendeaufruf *m.*
polling character Sendeaufrufzeichen *n.*
polling delay Abrufverzögerung *f.*
polling interval Sendeaufrufintervall *n.*
polling mode Abrufbetrieb *m.*
polling pass Abrufdurchlauf *m.*
polling signal Datenabrufsignal *n.*
polling technique Datenabrufverfahren *n.*
polyglot mehrsprachig *adj.*
poly-hierarchical classification polyhierarchische Klassifikation *f.*
poly-hierarchy Polyhierarchie *f.*
polynomial Polynom *n.*, poly-

nomial *adj.*
polysemy Polysemie *f.*, Mehrdeutigkeit *f.*
polysyllabic mehrsilbig *adj.*
polytechnic library Bibliothek *f.*
einer technischen Hochschule
polytechnical polytechnisch
adj.
polyvalence Mehrwertigkeit *f.*
polyvalent mehrwertig *adj.*
pool Pool *m.*
pool of volumes Datenträgergruppe *f.*
pooled konzentriert *adj.*, zusammengefaßt *adj.*
pooled library zusammengefaßte Bibliothek *f.*
pooling Zusammenschluß *m.*
pop music Popmusik *f.*
popular library Volksbücherei
f.
popularized populärwissenschaftlich *adj.*
population Bestand *m.*,
Grundgesamtheit *f.*
pornographic stock pornographischer Bestand *m.*
port Anschluß *m.*, Port *m.*
portability Portabilität *f.*,
Tragbarkeit *f.*
portable portabel *adj.*, tragbarer Computer *m.*
portable computer tragbarer
Computer *m.*
portable file übertragbare
Datei *f.*
portable reader tragbares Lesegerät *n.*
portfolio Mappe *f.*
portrait Porträt *n.*
position Stelle *f.*, Position *f.*,
Stellung *f.*

position/to positionieren *vrb.*
position encoder Stellungsgeber *m.*
position indicator Positionsanzeiger *m.*
position pointer Positionszei-
ger *m.*
positional representation Stellenschreibweise *f.*
positioning time Positionierungszeit *f.*
positive positive *adj.*
positive feedback positive
Rückkopplung *f.*
positive response positive Antwort *f.*
possibility Möglichkeit *f.*
possible purchase file Vormerkdatei *f.*
post/to eintragen *vrb.*
post box Postfach *n.*
post card Postkarte *f.*
post clerk Postbeamter *m.*
post collection Briefkastenleerung *f.*
post-editing Nachbereitung *f.*
post master Postamtsleiter *m.*
post money order Postanweisung *f.*
post number Folgenummer *f.*
post office Postamt *n.*
postage Postgebühr *f.*
postage charge Postgebühr *f.*
postcoordinate indexing postkoordinierte Indexierung *f.*
postcoordination Postkoordination *f.*
postdate/to nachdatieren *vrb.*
postdated nachdatiert *adj.*
postedit/to nachredigieren
vrb., druckfertig machen *vrb.*
postediting Nachredaktion *f.*

poster Plakat *n*.
poster collection Plakatsammlung *f*.
postfix Suffix *n*.
postgraduate course Fortbildungsveranstaltung *f*.
postgraduate education Fortbildung *f*.
posthumous edition posthume Ausgabe *f*.
posting Buchung *f*., Aufnahme *f*.
posting card Buchungskarte *f*.
posting date Buchungsdatum *n*.
posting key Buchungsschlüssel *m*.
postmark Poststempel *m*.
postnormalization Nachnormalisierung *f*.
postprocessing Nachbearbeitung *f*.
potential potentiell *adj*., möglich *adj*., Potential *n*.
power Strom *m*., Netzteil *n*., Arbeitsleistung *f*.
power consumption Stromverbrauch *m*.
power failure Stromausfall *m*.
power outage Netzausfall *m*.
power source Stromquelle *f*.
power supply Stromversorgung *f*.
power window automatisches Fenster *n*.
practical training Praktikum *n*.
practice Praxis *f*., Erfahrung *f*.
practice/to üben *vrb*.
practicability Durchführbarkeit *f*.
practice-intensive übungsintensiv *adj*.

practice-related praxisbezogen *adj*.
practitioner Praktiker *m*.
pragmatical value Erfahrungswert *m*.
pragmatics Pragmatik *f*.
pre-edit/to vorredigieren *vrb*.
pre-editing Vorredaktion *f*.
preapply/to vorbeugen *vrb*.
precataloging Vorauskatalogisierung *f*.
precedence Vorrang *m*.
preceding record vorausgehender Datensatz *m*.
precharge/to vorladen *vrb*.
precision Präzision *f*.
precision ratio Präzionsmaß *n*.
preconditioning time Anpassungszeit *f*.
preconfigure/to vorkonfigurieren *vrb*.
preconfigured system definition vorkonfigurierte Systemdefinition *f*.
precoordinate indexing präkoordinierte Indexierung *f*.
precoordination Präkoordination *f*.
predefined phrase vordefinierter Ausdruck *m*.
predefined process vordefinierter Vorgang *m*.
predetermined vorkalkuliert *adj*.
predicate calculus Prädikatenlogik *f*.
prediction Voraussage *f*., Prognose *f*.
preempt/to verhindern *vrb*.
preexecution time Ladezeit *f*.
preface Geleitwort *n*., Vorwort *n*.

preferential relation Präferenzrelation *f.*
preferred term Vorzugsbenennung *f.*
prefix Präfix *n.*, Vorsilbe *f.*
preformat/to vorformatieren *vrb.*
pregenerate/to vorgenerieren *vrb.*
preliminaries Präliminarien *pl.*
preliminary vorläufig *adj.*, Einleitung *f.*
preliminary announcement Voranzeige *f.*
preliminary cataloging vorläufiges Katalogisieren *n.*
preliminary draft Vorentwurf *m.*
preliminary edition vorläufige Ausgabe *f.*
preliminary notice Voranzeige *f.*
preliminary program vorläufiges Programm *n.*
preliminary report Vorbericht *m.*
prelims Präliminarien *pl.*
premature unfertig *adj.*, vorzeitig *adj.*
preparation Vorbereitung *f.*, Vorbearbeitung *f.*
preparation time Vorbereitungszeit *f.*
prepare/to initialisieren *vrb.*
prepayment Vorauszahlung *f.*
preposition Präposition *f.*
prepotent vorherrschend *adj.*
preprint Vorabdruck *m.*
preprocessing Vorverarbeitung *f.*
prepublication Vorveröffentlichung *f.*

prepublication cataloging Vorabkatalogisierung *f.*
prepublication order Vorbestellung *f.*
prerequisite Voraussetzung *f.*
preschool Vorschule *f.*
preselector Vorwähler *m.*
present worth Zeitwert *m.*
presentation Darstellung *f.*, Präsentation *f.*
presequenced vorsortiert *adj.*
preservation Konservierung *f.*
preserved context index system PRECIS
preset voreingestellt *adj.*
preset key Voreinsteller *m.*
presetting Einstellen *n.*
presidential library Präsidentenbibliothek *f.*
press Pressewesen *n.*, Presse *f.*
press/to drucken *vrb.*, betätigen *vrb.*, drücken *vrb.*
press agency Nachrichtenagentur *f.*
press archive Pressearchiv *n.*
press archivist Pressearchivar *m.*
press clipping Zeitungsausschnitt *m.*
press conference Pressekonferenz *f.*
press copy Rezensionsexemplar *n.*
press cutting Zeitungsausschnitt *m.*
press library Pressebibliothek *f.*
press proof Schlußkorrektur *f.*
press release Presseinformation *f.*
press stand Zeitungsstand *m.*
pressure Druck *m.*
prestore/to vorspeichern *vrb.*

presumptive instruction unmodifizierter Befehl *m*.
pretest Voruntersuchung *f*., Übungsprüfung *f*.
prevent/to verhindern *vrb*.
preview Vorschau *f*.
previous vorherig *adj*.
price Preis *m*.
price increase Preissteigerung *f*.
price index Preisindex *m*.
price policy Preispolitik *f*.
primary primär *adj*., Erstkarte *f*.
primary access Primärzugriff *m*.
primary application program Primäranwendungsprogramm *n*.
primary bibliography Primärbibliographie *f*.
primary card Erstkarte *f*.
primary distribution direkte Verteilung *f*.
primary document Primärdokument *n*.
primary entry point Primäreingangsstelle *f*.
primary extent Primärbereich *m*.
primary file Erstkartendatei *f*.
primary index Primärindex *m*.
primary information source Primärinformationsquelle *f*.
primary input Primäreingabe *f*.
primary key Primärschlüssel *m*.
primary keyword primäres Schlagwort *n*.
primary literature Primärliteratur *f*.
primary material Primärmaterial *n*.

primary meaning Hauptbedeutung *f*.
primary processing unit Primärzentraleinheit *f*.
primary publication Primärveröffentlichung *f*.
primary request Primäranforderung *f*.
primary school Grundschule *f*.
primary school library Grundschulbibliothek *f*., Grundschulbücherei *f*.
primary sources Primärquellen *pl*.
primary station Primärstation *f*.
primary storage Primärspeicher *m*.
primary supervisor Primärsupervisor *m*.
primary system control facility primäre Systemsteuerungseinrichtung *f*.
primary track Primärspur *f*.
primary volume Primärdatenträger *m*.
prime area Hauptbereich *m*.
prime data area Hauptdatenbereich *m*.
prime index Primärindex *m*.
prime key Primärschlüssel *m*.
prime record key primärer Datensatzschlüssel *m*.
primitive expression einfacher Ausdruck *m*.
primitive function Elementarfunktion *f*.
principal author Hauptverfasser *m*.
principal register Standardregister *m*.
principle Gesetz *n*.

principle of order Ordnungsprinzip *n*.
print Abdruck *m*., Kopie *f*.,
Ausdruck *m*.
print/to abdrucken *vrb*., drucken *vrb*.
print buffer Druckpuffer *m*.
print chain Druckkette *f*.
print control character Drucksteuerzeichen *n*.
print data set Druckdatensatz
m.
print error Druckfehler *m*.
print file Druckdatei *f*.
print format Druckformat *n*.
print formatter Druckformatierer *m*.
print house Druckerei *f*.
print job Druckjob *m*.
print key Drucktaste *f*.
print line Druckzeile *f*.
print mode Druckmodus *m*.
print out Ausdruck *m*.
print output Druckausgabe *f*.
print queue Druckerwarteschlange *f*.
print space Satzspiegel *m*.
print span Druckbreite *f*.
print speed Druckgeschwindigkeit *f*.
print storage Druckspeicher *m*.
print unit Druckeinheit *f*.
print wheel Typenrad *n*.
printable abdruckbar *adj*.,
druckfähig *adj*.
printable item druckfähiges
Datenfeld *n*.
printed gedruckt *adj*.
printed catalog gedruckter Katalog *m*.
printed form Vordruck *m*.
printed matter Drucksache *f*.

printed music Musikalien *pl*.
printed music collection Musikalienbestand *m*.
printer Drucker *m*.
printer graphics druckbare Zeichen *pl*.
printer overflow Seitenüberlauf *m*.
printer overrun Drucküberlauf
m.
printing Abdruck *m*., Drucken
n.
printing area Druckzone *f*.
printing block Druckstock *m*.,
Klischee *n*.
printing cycle Druckzyklus *m*.
printing industry Druckindustrie *f*.
printing machine Druckmaschine *f*.
printing method Druckverfahren *n*.
printing office Druckerei *f*.
printing on demand Druck *m*.
nach Bedarf
printing rate Druckgeschwindigkeit *f*.
printing technology Drucktechnik *f*.
printing width Zeilenbreite *f*.
printout Ausdruck *m*.
priority Priorität *f*.
priority assignment Priorit ä-
tenzuordnung *f*.
priority change Priorit ätsände-
rung *f*.
priority control Vorrangssteuerung *f*.
priority indicator Priorit ätsan-
zeige *f*.
priority of access Zugriffspriorität *f*.

priority processing Vorrangsverarbeitung *f.*
priority queue Prioritätswarteschlange *f.*
priority table Prioritätstabelle *f.*
prison library Gefängnisbibliothek *f.*
privacy Vertraulichkeit *f.*, Privatsphäre *f.*
privacy protection Daten-
schutz *m.*
private privat *adj.*
private archive Privatarchiv *n.*
private circulation nicht im
Buchhandel
private collection Privatsammlung *f.*
private library Privatbibliothek
f.
private sector Privatwirtschaft
f.
private storage privater Speicher *m.*
private volume privater Datenträger *m.*
privileged command bevor-
rechtigter Befehl *m.*
privileged instruction bevorrechtigter Befehl *m.*
probabilistic indexing probabilistische Indexierung *f.*
probabilistic retrieval probabilistisches Retrieval *n.*
probability Wahrscheinlichkeit
f.
probability calculus Wahrscheinlichkeitsrechnung *f.*
probability curve Wahrscheinlichkeitskurve *f.*
probability of failure Ausfallwahrscheinlichkeit *f.*
probability of relevance Rele-

vanzwahrscheinlichkeit *f.*
probable author mutmaßlicher
Verfasser *m.*
probable deviation wahr-
scheinlicher Fehler *m.*
problem Problem *n.*
problem data Problemdaten *pl.*
problem description Problembeschreibung *f.*
problem determination Problembestimmung *f.*
problem logging Problemaufzeichnung *f.*
problem-oriented language
problemorientierte Programmiersprache *f.*
problem recovery Problembehebung *f.*
problem reporting Störungsbericht *m.*
problem sequence number Problemfolgenummer *f.*
problem solution Problemlösung *f.*
problem state Problemstatus
m.
problem tracking Problemverfolgung *f.*
procedural definition Ablaufdefinition *f.*
procedural language verfahrensorientierte Programmiersprache *f.*
procedural statement Befehl
m., Instruktion *f.*
procedure Verfahren *n.*, Ablauf
m., Prozedur *f.*
procedure area Prozedurenbereich *m.*
procedure command Prozedurbefehl *m.*
procedure control expresssions

Prozedursteuerbedingungen *pl.*
procedure heading Prozedurkopf *m.*
procedure identifier Prozedurname *m.*
procedure level Prozedurebene *f.*
procedure library Prozedurbibliothek *f.*
procedure manual Dienstanweisung *f.*
procedure member Prozedureintragung *f.*
procedure name Prozedurname *m.*
procedure-oriented language verfahrensorientierte Programmiersprache *f.*
procedure processor Prozedurprozessor *m.*
procedure reference Prozeduraufruf *m.*
procedure start Prozeduraufruf *m.*
procedure statement Prozeduranweisung *f.*
procedure step Prozedurschritt *m.*
procedure subprogram Prozedurunterprogramm *n.*
procedures Arbeitsvorgänge *pl.*
proceed/to fortsetzen *vrb.*
proceeding Vorgehen *n.*
proceedings Tagungsliteratur *f.*, Kongreßbericht *m.*, Tagungsbericht *m.*
process Prozeß *m.*, Vorgang *m.*
process/to abarbeiten *vrb.*, abfertigen *vrb.*, bearbeiten *vrb.*, verarbeiten *vrb.*
process chart Flußdiagramm *n.*
process control Prozeßsteue-

rung *f.*
process data Prozeßdaten *pl.*
process engineering Verfahrenstechnik *f.*
process entry Prozeßeintrag *m.*
process identification Prozeßidentifikation *f.*
process interrupt Programmunterbrechung *f.*
process model Prozeßmodell *n.*
process of documentation Dokumentationsprozeß *m.*
process queue Verarbeitungswarteschlange *f.*
process simulation Prozeßsimulation *f.*
process slip Bearbeitungszettel *m.*, Laufzettel *m.*
process stamp Kontrollstempel *m.*
process variable Prozeßvariable *f.*
processibility Verarbeitbarkeit *f.*
processing Aufbereitung *f.*, Entwicklung *f.*, Verarbeitung *f.*
processing cost Verarbeitungskosten *pl.*
processing department technische Abteilung *f.*
processing depth Verarbeitungstiefe *f.*
processing fee Bearbeitungsgebühr *f.*
processing information Verarbeitungshinweis *m.*
processing level Verarbeitungsstufe *f.*
processing limit Verarbeitungslimit *n.*
processing option Verarbei-

tungsoption *f.*
processing overlap Verarbeitungsüberlappung *f.*
processing parameter Verarbeitungsparameter *m.*
processing program Programm *n.* in Verarbeitung
processing request Verarbeitungsanforderung *f.*
processing service Verarbeitungsservice *m.*
processing system Verarbeitungssystem *n.*
processing time Verarbeitungszeit *f.*
processing unit Zentraleinheit *f.*
processor Prozessor *m.*
processor address space Prozessoradreßbereich *m.*
processor check Rechnerprüfung *f.*
processor controller Prozessorsteuereinheit *f.*
processor identification Rechneridentifikation *f.*
processor main storage Prozessorhauptspeicher *m.*
processor module Prozessormodul *n.*
processor profile Prozessorprofil *n.*
processor storage Hauptspeicher *m.*
processor storage allocation Hauptspeicherzuordnung *f.*
processor storage utilization Hauptspeicherbenutzung *f.*
processor unit Prozessoreinheit *f.*
procurement Beschaffung *f.*
procurement policy Beschaf-

fungspolitik *f.*
produce/to abbilden *vrb.*, produzieren *vrb.*
producer Produzent *m.*
product Ware *f.*, Produkt *n.*
product description Warenbeschreibung *f.*, Produktbeschreibung *f.*
product directory Bezugsquellennachweis *m.*
product information Produktinformation *f.*
product requirements specification Pflichtenheft *n.*
production Fertigung *f.*, Produktion *f.*
production capacity Produktionskapazität *f.*
production cost Herstellungskosten *pl.*, Produktionskosten *pl.*
production data Betriebsdaten *pl.*
production rules Produktionsregeln *pl.*
production time Produktionszeit *f.*
productive relation Herstellungsbeziehung *f.*
productivity Produktivität *f.*
profession Beruf *m.*
professional fachlich *adj.*
professional association Berufsverband *m.*
professional association publication Berufsverbandspublikation *f.*
professional book Fachbuch *n.*
professional education Fachausbildung *f.*
professional ethics Berufsethos *n.*

professional experience Berufserfahrung *f.*
professional information center Berufsinformationszentrum *n.*
professional meeting Fachtagung *f.*
professional prospect Berufsaussicht *f.*
professional school Fachschule *f.*
professional school certificate Fachschulabschluß *m.*
professional school examination Fachschulprüfung *f.*
professional school librarianship Fachschulbibliothekswesen *n.*
professional school library Fachschulbibliothek *f.*
professional skill test Facharbeiterprüfung *f.*
professional training center Berufsbildungszentrum *n.*
professionalism Professionalisierung *f.*
professor Hochschullehrer *m.*
professorship Lehrstuhl *m.*
profile Profil *n.*
profit Gewinn *m.*
profit maximization Gewinnmaximierung *f.*
program Arbeitsprogramm *n.*, Programm *n.*
program/to programmieren *vrb.*
program access code Programmzugriffscode *m.*
program access facility Programmschnittstelle *f.*
program access key Zugriffsschlüssel *m.*

program architecture Programmstruktur *f.*
program attention key Programmabruftaste *f.*
program check Programmprüfung *f.*
program code Programmcode *m.*
program coding Programmierung *f.*
program control Programmsteuerung *f.*
program control data Programmsteuerungsdaten *pl.*
program control program Programmverwaltung *f.*
program control table Transaktionstabelle *f.*
program-controlled interruption programmgesteuerte Unterbrechung *f.*
program counter Befehlszähler *m.*
program cycle Programmzyklus *m.*
program data set Programmdatei *f.*
program date Programmdatum *n.*
program debugging Programmfehlersuche *f.*
program definition Programmbeschreibung *f.*
program-dependent function programmabhängige Funktion *f.*
program description Programmbeschreibung *f.*
program design Programmentwurf *m.*
program development process Programmentwicklungspro-

zeß *m.*

program development system
Programmentwicklungssystem *n.*

program diskette Programmdiskette *f.*

program documentation Programmdokumentation *f.*

program execution Programmausführung *f.*

program exit Programmausgang *m.*

program fetch Programmabruf *m.*

program field Programmfeld *n.*

program file Programmdatei *f.*

program file name Programmdateiname *m.*

program flow Programmablauf *m.*

program function key Programmfunktionstaste *f.*

program function keyboard programmierbare Funktionstastatur *f.*

program generation Programmgenerierung *f.*

program generation language Programmgenerierungssprache *f.*

program generator Programmgenerator *m.*

program identification Programmkennzeichnung *f.*

program identification number Programmkennzeichnungsnummer *f.*

program-independent function programmunabhängige Funktion *f.*

program indicator Programm-

anzeiger *m.*

program information code Programminformationscode *m.*

program interface Programmschnittstelle *f.*

program interruption Programmunterbrechung *f.*

program item Programmelement *n.*

program language Programmiersprache *f.*

program level Programmebene *f.*

program library Programmbibliothek *f.*

program load Programmladen *n.*

program loader Programmlader *m.*

program loop Programmschleife *f.*

program maintenance Programmwartung *f.*, Programmpflege *f.*

program management Programmverwaltung *f.*

program mask Programmaske *f.*

program memory Programmspeicher *m.*

program mode Programmodus *m.*

program number Programmnummer *f.*

program-oriented routines programmorientierte Routinen *pl.*

program pack Programmplatte *f.*

program part Programmteil *n.*

program patch Programmän-

derung *f.*
program phase Programmphase *f.*
program production time Programmlaufzeit *f.*
program request Programmaufruf *m.*
program reset Programmgrundstellung *f.*
program residence time Programmverweilzeit *f.*
program restart Programmwiederanlauf *m.*
program run Programmablauf *m.*
program section Programmabschnitt *m.*
program segment Programmsegment *n.*
program selection Programmauswahl *f.*
program shift Programmwechsel *m.*
program source Quellprogramm *n.*
program specification Programmspezifikation *f.*
program start key Programmstarttaste *f.*
program step Programmschritt *m.*
program storage Programmspeicher *m.*
program support Programmunterstützung *f.*
program test time Programmtestzeit *f.*
program text Programmtext *m.*
program time out Programmzeitsperre *f.*
program unit Programmein-

heit *f.*
programmable programmierbar *adj.*
programmable read-only memory programmierbarer Festspeicher *m.*
programmable terminal programmierbares Terminal *n.*
programmed check programmierte Prüfung *f.*
programmed instruction programmierter Unterricht *m.*
programmed stop programmierter Halt *m.*
programmer Programmierer *m.*
programmer's guide Programmieranleitung *f.*
programmer's manual Programmierhandbuch *n.*
programming Programmierung *f.*
programming aid Programmierhilfe *f.*
programming effort Programmieraufwand *m.*
programming error Programmierfehler *m.*
programming flowchart Programmablaufplan *m.*
programming language Programmiersprache *f.*
programming note Programmierhinweis *m.*
programming support Programmierunterstützung *f.*
programming system Programmiersystem *n.*
progress Weiterentwicklung *f.*, Fortschritt *m.*
progress field Fortschrittsfeld *n.*

progress report Tätigkeitsbericht *m.*, Fortschrittsbericht *m.*

progressing fortschreitend *adj.*

progressive zukunftsorientiert *adj.*, fortschreitend *adj.*, zunehmend *adj.*

project Vorhaben *n.*, Projektierung *f.*, Projekt *n.*

project control network Projektüberwachungsplan *m.*

project database Projektdatenbank *f.*

project documentation Projektdokumentation *f.*, Forschungsdokumentation *f.*

project library Projektbibliothek *f.*

project manager Projektmanager *m.*

project number Projektnummer *f.*

project planning Projektplanung *f.*

project report Projektbericht *m.*

project target date Projektendtermin *m.*

projecting Projektieren *n.*

projector Projektor *m.*

promotion Förderung *f.*

prompt Systemnachricht *f.*, Eingabeaufforderung *f.*

prompt line Bedienerführungszeile *f.*

prompting Bedienerführung *f.*

prompting message Eilnachricht *f.*

proof Nachweis *m.*, Probeabzug *m.*

proof copy Entwurf *m.*

proof feature Schreibsicherung *f.*

proof mark Korrekturzeichen *n.*

proof print Andruck *m.*

proof pulling Korrekturabzug *m.*

proof reader Korrektur *f.*

proof reading Korrekturlesen *n.*

proof sheet Korrekturanweisung *f.*

propagate/to propagieren *vrb.*

propagated error mitlaufender Fehler *m.*

propagation delay Laufzeitverzögerung *f.*

propagation time Laufzeit *f.*

proper name Eigenname *m.*

property Eigenschaft *f.*

proportional step Proportionalschritt *m.*

propose/to anregen *vrb.*

prosecution Verfolgung *f.*, Durchführung *f.*

prospective bibliography prospektive Bibliographie *f.*

protect password security Kennwortsicherheit *f.*

protected access geschützter Zugriff *m.*

protected copy geschützte Kopie *f.*

protected data field geschütztes Datenfeld *n.*

protected file geschützte Datei *f.*

protected location geschützter Speicherplatz *m.*

protected queue area geschützter Warteschlangenbereich *m.*

protected storage geschützter Speicher *m.*

protection Schutz *m*.
protection action Schutzmaßnahme *f*.
protection of data Datenschutz
m.
protection of data privacy Datenschutz *m*.
protective disk Schutzplatte *f*.
protocol Protokoll *n*.
prototype Prototyp *m*.
provide/to liefern *vrb*., bereitstellen *vrb*.
provincial library Provinzbibliothek *f*.
provision Bereitstellung *f*.
provisional edition vorläufige
Ausgabe *f*.
pseudoclassification Pseudoklassifikation *f*.
pseudodata entry Pseudodateneintrag *m*.
pseudoinstruction Pseudobe-
fehl *m*.
pseudonym Pseudonym *n*.
pseudorecord Pseudosatz *m*.,
Scheinsatz *m*.
psychiatry Psychiatrie *f*.
psychogram Psychogramm *n*.
psychologist Psychologe *m*.
psychology Psychologie *f*.
psychotherapy Psychotherapie
f.
public allgemein *adj*.
public access allgemeine Zugriffsberechtigung *f*.
public access catalog Publikumskatalog *m*.
public administration öffentliche Verwaltung *f*.
public author Urheber *m*., Herausgeber *m*.
public catalog Benutzerkatalog

m.
public document amtliche Veröffentlichung *f*.
public health Gesundheitswesen *n*.
public information office Pressestelle *f*.
public law Staatsrecht *n*., öffentliches Recht *n*.
public librarianship öffentliches Bibliothekswesen *n*.
public library öffentliche Bibliothek *f*., Volksbibliothek *f*.,
Bürgerbücherei *f*.
public network öffentliches
Netz *n*.
public record office Archiv *n*.
public relations Öffentlichkeitsarbeit *f*.
public research library öffentliche wissenschaftliche Bibliothek *f*.
public services öffentlicher
Dienst *m*.
public switched network öffentliches Wählnetz *n*.
public utilities öffentliche
Dienstleistungen *pl*.
public volume freier Datenträger *m*.
publication Veröffentlichung *f*.
publication date Erscheinungsdatum *n*., Veröffentlichungsdatum *n*.
publication exchange Schriftenaustausch *m*.
publication language Veröffentlichungssprache *f*.
publication price Ladenpreis *m*.
publication type Publikationsform *f*.
publicity Werbung *f*.

publicity edition Werbeausgabe
f.
publish/to herausgeben *vrb.*,
verlegen *vrb.*, publizieren *vrb.*
published documents veröffentlichte Dokumente *pl.*
publisher Verleger *m.*
publisher's editor Verlagslektor *m.*
publishing Verlagswesen *n.*,
Drucksache *f.*
publishing bookshop Verlagsbuchhandlung *f.*
publishing contract Verlagsvertrag *m.*
publishing house Verlag *m.*,
Verlagshaus *n.*
pull Probeabzug *m.*
pull/to ziehen *vrb.*
pull out/to herausziehen *vrb.*
pull through/to durchziehen
vrb.
pulp Papierstoff *m.*
pulp/to einstampfen *vrb.*
pulse Impuls *m.*
punch Locher *m.*
punch/to lochen *vrb.*
punch card Lochkarte *f.*
punched gelocht *adj.*
punched card Lochkarte *f.*

punched tape Lochstreifen *m.*
punctuation Zeichensetzung *f.*
punctuation mark Satzzeichen
n.
purchase Kauf *m.*
purchase/to kaufen *vrb.*
purchase suggestion Anschaffungsvorschlag *m.*, Bestellwunsch *m.*
purchasing key Erwerbungsschlüssel *m.*
pure rein *adj.*
pure notation reine Notation *f.*
purge/to löschen *vrb.*
pursue/to verfolgen *vrb.*
purview Zuständigkeitsbereich
m.
push Druck *m.*, Schub *m.*
push/to drücken *vrb.*
push button Drucktaste *f.*
push-in/to einstecken *vrb.*
pushdown stack Kellerspeicher
m.
pushpin Reißzwecke *f.*
put/to ausgeben *vrb.*, setzen
vrb., stellen *vrb.*
put/to in custody sicherstellen
vrb.
putting into service Inbetriebnahme *f.*

Q

qualification Qualifikation *f.*, Kennzeichnung *f.*, Bedingung *f.*
qualificatory qualifizierend *adj.*
qualified qualifiziert *adj.*
qualified book qualifiziertes Buch *n.*
qualified compound key qualifizierter Verbundschlüssel *m.*
qualified data name gekennzeichneter Datenname *m.*
qualified heading gekennzeichnetes Schlagwort *n.*
qualified librarian ausgebildeter Bibliothekar *m.*
qualified name qualifizierter Name *m.*, gekennzeichneter Name *m.*
qualifier Spezifikator *m.*, Qualifikator *m.*
qualify/to qualifizieren *vrb.*, ausbilden *vrb.*, sich eignen *vrb.*
qualifying connective Kennzeichnerbindewort *n.*
qualifying element qualifizierender Zusatz *m.*
qualitative qualitativ *adj.*
quality Qualität *f.*
quality assurance Qualitätssicherung *f.*
quality capability Qualitätsfähigkeit *f.*

quality characteristic Qualitätsmerkmal *n.*
quality control Qualitätskontrolle *f.*
quality standard Qualitätsstandard *m.*
quality test Qualitätsprüfung *f.*
quantification Quantifizierung *f.*
quantify/to quantifizieren *vrb.*
quantitative quantitativ *adj.*
quantitative data quantitative Daten *pl.*
quantity Quantität *f.*, Menge *f.*, Größe *f.*
quantity discount Mengenrabatt *m.*
quantity key Mengenschlüssel *m.*
quantity on hand Lagerbestand *m.*
quantity on order Bestellbestand *m.*
quantity ordered bestellte Menge *f.*, Auftragsmenge *f.*
quantity standard Mengenvorgabe *f.*
quantity variance Mengenabweichung *f.*
quantize/to quantifizieren *vrb.*
quarterly Vierteljahreschrift *f.*
quarto Quartband *m.*, Quartformat *n.*
quasi-synonym Quasisynonym

n.

quasi-synonymy Quasisynonymie *f.*

query Anfrage *f.*, Frage *f.*, Abfrage *f.*, Suchanfrage *f.*

query/to fragen *vrb.*, abfragen *vrb.*

query analysis Suchanfragenanalyse *f.*

query-by-example Abfrage *f.* mittels Beispiel

query classification Suchanfragenklassifizierung *f.*

query-dependent abfrageabhängig *adj.*

query document similarity Suchanfragen-Dokument-Ähnlichkeit *f.*

query expansion Suchanfragenerweiterung *f.*

query expression Abfragebefehl *m.*

query formulation Suchanfragenbildung *f.*

query language Abfragesprache *f.*

query modification Suchanfragenmodifizierung *f.*

query optimization Suchanfragenoptimierung *f.*

query reformulation Suchanfragenreformulierung *f.*

query representation Suchanfragenrepräsentation *f.*

query specification Suchanfragenspezifikation *f.*

query splitting Suchanfragenteilung *f.*

query station Abfragestation *f.*

query term Suchbegriff *m.*

query term weights Suchbegriffsgewichtung *f.*

query vector Suchanfragenvektor *m.*

question Frage *f.*, Problem *n.*

question/to fragen *vrb.*

question-answering retrieval system Frage-Antwort-Retrievalsystem *n.*

question-answering system Frage-Antwort-System *n.*

question file Fragedatei *f.*

question group Lernelement *n.*

question mark Fragezeichen *n.*

questioning Befragung *f.*

questionnaire Fragebogen *m.*

questionnaire design Fragebogenentwurf *m.*

questionnaire survey schriftliche Befragung *f.*

queue Warteschlange *f.*

queue/to einreihen *vrb.*, Warteschlange bilden *vrb.*

queue control block Warteschlangensteuerblock *m.*

queue element Warteschlangenelement *n.*

queue name Warteschlangenname *m.*

queue space Pufferbereich *m.*

queue time Wartezeit *f.*

queued in Warteschlange eingereiht *adj.*

queued access method erweiterte Zugriffstechnik *f.*

queuing Warteschlangenbildung *f.*

queuing theory Warteschlangentheorie *f.*

quick access Schnellzugriff *m.*

quick-access storage Schnellspeicher *m.*

quick closedown Schnellabschluß *m.*

quick reference book Nachschlagewerk *n*.
quick reference chart Nachschlagetafel *f*.
quiesce/to stillegen *vrb*.
quiesce state interner Wartestatus *m*.
quiet ruhig *adj*., geräuscharm

adj.
quota sample Quotenstich-
probe *f*.
quotation Zitat *n*.
quotation mark Anführungszeichen *n*.
quote/to zitieren *vrb*.
quotient Quotient *m*.

R

rack Fach *n*., Gestell *n*.
rack adapter Einschub *m*.
rack enclosure Gehäuse *n*.
radial transfer Radialübertragung *f*.
radical change Umwälzung *f*.
radical sign Wurzelzeichen *n*.
radio Rundfunk *m*.
radio license fee Rundfunkgebühren *pl*.
radio station Funkhaus *n*.
radix Wurzel *f*.
ragged-right setting Flattersatz *m*.
railway library Eisenbahnbibliothek *f*.
raise/to auslösen *vrb*.
raising hochstellen *vrb*.
random access wahlfreier Zugriff *m*.
random access memory Di-
rektzugriffsspeicher *m*.
random access storage Direktzugriffsspeicher *m*.

random addressing wahlfreie
Adressierung *f*.
random by key wahlweise *adj*.
nach Schlüssel
random disturbance Rauschstörung *f*.
random error Zufallsfehler *m*.
random failure Zufallsauswahl
f.
random file wahlfreier Dateizugriff *m*.
random number Zufallszahl *f*.
random processing wahlfreie
Verarbeitung *f*.
random sample Zufallsstichprobe *f*.
random seek wahlfreier Zugriff *m*.
random sequence Zufallsfolge
f.
randomization Randomisie-
rung *f*.
randomizing Randomisieren *n*.
range Tragweite *f*., Bereich *m*.,

Regalreihe *f.*
range/to klassifizieren *vrb.*,
ordnen *vrb.*
range aisle Regalgang *m.*
range check Bereichsprüfung *f.*
range of applications Einsatzmöglichkeit *f.*
range of error Fehlerbereich
m.
range of unbalanced error asymetrischer Fehlerbereich *m.*
rank Rang *m.*
rank/to hierarchisch anordnen
vrb.
rank order Rangordnung *f.*
ranking in eine Rangordnung *f.*
bringen
rapid memory Schnellzugriffsspeicher *m.*
rapid reading Schnellesen *n.*
rapid response time hohe Antwortgeschwindigkeit *f.*
rare literature schwer zugängliche Literatur *f.*
raster Raster *n.*
raster display Rasterbildschirm
m.
raster pattern storage Zeichenspeicher *m.*
raster scan Zeilenabtastung *f.*
raster unit Rastereinheit *f.*
rate Rate *f.*
rate/to bewerten *vrb.*
rating Bewertung *f.*
rating committee Gutachterausschuß *m.*
ratio Kennzahl *f.*, Verhältnis *n.*
ratio scale Rationalskala *f.*
rational number rationale Zahl
f.
rationalization Rationalisierung *f.*

raw data Rohdaten *pl.*
raw material Rohstoff *m.*,
Rohmaterial *n.*
raw speed Grundgeschwindigkeit *f.*
reaction Reaktion *f.*
reaction time Reaktionszeit *f.*
read/to lesen *vrb.*
read access time Lesezugriffszeit *f.*
read backward/to rückwärtslesen *vrb.*
read buffer Eingabepuffer *m.*
read check Leseprüfung *f.*
read command Lesebefehl *m.*
read cycle Lesezyklus *m.*
read cycle time Lesezykluszeit
f.
read data stream Lesedatenfolge *f.*
read emitter Leseimpulsgeber
m.
read head Lesekopf *m.*
read hopper Kartenmagazin *n.*
read interrupt Empfangsunterbrechung *f.*
read mode Lesemodus *m.*
read off/to ablesen *vrb.*
read-only disk schreibgeschützte Platte *f.*
read-only flag Schreibsperrenanzeige *f.*
read-only instruction Festspeicherbefehl *m.*
read-only memory Festspeicher *m.*
read-only storage Festspeicher
m.
read out Sichtanzeige *f.*, Auslesen *n.*
read out/to auslesen *vrb.*
read out control Auslesesteue-

rung *f.*
read password Lesepaßwort *n.*
read request Leseanforderung
f.
READ statement LESE-Anweisung *f.*
read window Lesefenster *m.*
read/write head Lese-
/Schreibkopf *m.*
read/write memory Lese-
/Schreibspeicher *m.*
read/write speed Lese-
/Schreibgeschwindigkeit *f.*
readability Ablesbarkeit *f.*, Lesbarkeit *f.*
readable ablesbar *adj.*, lesbar
adj.
reader Leser *m.*, Lektor *m.*
reader adapter Lesersteuerung
f.
reader admission Benutzerzulassung *f.*
reader advisory Leserberatung
f.
reader instruction Benutzerschulung *f.*
reader-printer Rückvergrößerungsgerät *n.*
reader procedure Leseprozedur *f.*
reader queue Lesewarteschlange *f.*
reader registration Benutzeranmeldung *f.*
reader task Leseroutine *f.*
reader's proof Hauskorrektur
f.
reader's request Benutzerwunsch *m.*
reader's slip Bestellschein *m.*
readership Leserschaft *f.*, Leser
pl.

readership survey Leserumfrage *f.*
readers' advisory work Leserberatung *f.*
readers' assistance Leserberatung *f.*
readers' guide Lesehinweise
pl.
reading Lesung *f.*, Lesen *n.*
reading assignment Leseanweisung *f.*
reading behavior Leseverhalten *n.*
reading clientele Leserschaft *f.*,
Benutzerschaft *f.*
reading club Leseclub *m.*
reading custom Lesegewohnheit *f.*
reading desk Lesepult *n.*
reading frequency Lesehäufigkeit *f.*
reading program Leseerziehung *f.*
reading promotion Leseförderung *f.*
reading room Lesehalle *f.*, Bücherhalle *f.*,Lesesaal *m.*
reading room collection Lesesaalbestand *m.*
reading society Lesegesellschaft *f.*
reading survey Leserumfrage
f.
readjustment Umstellung *f.*
ready betriebsbereit *adj.*
ready for data Übertragungsbereitschaft *f.*
ready for press druckfertig *adj.*
ready for receiving Empfangsbereitschaft *f.*
ready for sending Sendebereitschaft *f.*

ready indicator Bereitschaftsanzeige *f.*
ready reference collection
Handbibliothek *f.*
ready reference holdings Auskunftsbestand *m.*
ready state Laufbereitschaft *f.*
ready to read lesebereit *adj.*
ready to receive Empfangsbereitschaft *f.*
real real *adj.*
real address reale Adresse *f.*
real memory Realspeicher *m.*
real number reale Zahl *f.*
real partition reale Partition *f.*
real storage realer Speicher *m.*
real storage address reale
Speicheradresse *f.*
real time Echtzeit *f.*
real time computer system
Echtzeitcomputersystem *n.*
real time input Echtzeiteingabe
f.
real time operation Echtzeitbetrieb *m.*
real time output Echtzeitausgabe *f.*
real time processing Echtzeitverarbeitung *f.*
realization Verwirklichung *f.*,
Realisierung *f.*
realize/to realisieren *vrb.*
realized profit realisierter Gewinn *m.*
rear Rückseite *f.*
rear document insertion manuelle Einzelblattzuführung *f.*
rear panel Rückansicht *f.*
rearrange/to umordnen *vrb.*
reasonableness check Plausibilitätsprüfung *f.*
reassemble/to reorganisieren

vrb.
reassembling Reorganisation *f.*
reassign/to neu zuordnen *vrb.*
reattachment Wiederanschluß
m.
rebuilding Wiederaufbau *m.*
recabling Neuverkabelung *f.*
recalibrate/to nachjustieren
vrb.
recalibrate command Nullstellungsbefehl *m.*
recall Abruf *m.*, Recall *m.*,
Rückruf *m.*
recall/to abrufen *vrb.*, zurückrufen *vrb.*, zurückfordern *vrb.*
recall factor Trefferquote *f.*
recall measure Recallmaß *n.*
recall ratio Trefferquote *f.*
recalling Zurückholen *n.*
recap/to zusammenfassen *vrb.*
recase/to neubinden *vrb.*
recataloging Rekatalogisierung *f.*, Neukatalogisierung *f.*
receipt Empfang *m.*, Quittung
f.
receipt confirmation Empfangsbestätigung *f.*
receivable fällig *adj.*, zulässig
adj.
receive/to empfangen *vrb.*
receive buffer Empfangspuffer
m.
receive count Empfangszähler
m.
receive diskette Empfangsdiskette *f.*
receive interrupt Empfangsunterbrechung *f.*
receive mode Empfangsmodus
m.
receive timer Empfangsüberwachung *f.*

received data Empfangsdaten
pl.
received data present Empfangsdatenkennzeichnung *f.*
receiver Empfänger *n.*
receiving Empfang *m.*
receiving field Empfangsfeld *n.*
receiving terminal Empfangsstation *f.*
reception Empfang *m.*
recess Unterbrechung *f.*
recessed eingelassen *adj.*
recipient Empfänger *m.*
recipient number Empfängernummer *f.*
reciprocal reziprok *adj.*
reclaim/to zurücknehmen *vrb.*
reclamation Rückforderung *f.*
reclassification Neuklassifizierung *f.*
recode/to umschlüsseln *vrb.*
recognition Anerkennung *f.*,
Erkennung *f.*
recognition control block Erkennungssteuerblock *m.*
recognition table Zeichenerkennungstabelle *f.*
recognition table error Zeichenerkennungstabellenfehler
m.
recognize/to anerkennen *vrb.*
recommendation Empfehlung
f.
recomposition Neusatz *m.*
reconciliation Abstimmung *f.*
recondition/to überholen *vrb.*
reconditioning Generalüberholung *f.*
reconfiguration Umgestaltung
f.
reconstruction Neuaufbau *m.*
record Datensatz *m.*, Aufzeich-

nung *f.*, Titelaufnahme *f.*,
Satz *m.*
record/to erfassen *vrb.*, aufzeichnen *vrb.*, registrieren
vrb.
record address Satzadresse *f.*
record address file Satzadreßdatei *f.*
record area Datensatzbereich
m.
record block Satzblock *m.*
record boundary Satzgrenze *f.*
record chain Satzkette *f.*
record checking Satzprüfung *f.*
record code specification Satzartbestimmung *f.*
record count Satzanzahl *f.*
record counter Satzzähler *m.*
record definition field Satzbeschreibungsfeld *n.*
record delete function Satzannullierungsfunktion *f.*
record density Aufzeichnungsdichte *f.*
record description Datensatzbeschreibung *f.*
record format Satzformat *n.*
record format descriptor Satzformatbeschreiber *m.*
record gap Satzzwischenraum
m.
record identification field
Satzkennzeichnungsfeld *n.*
record insert Satzeinfügung *f.*
record key Satzschlüssel *m.*
record label Satzkennung *f.*
record layout Satzaufbau *m.*
record length Satzlänge *f.*
record library Phonothek *f.*
record mark Satzmarke *f.*
record mode Satzmodus *m.*
record name Satzname *m.*

record number Satznummer *f.*,
Zeilennummer *f.*
record office Verwaltungsarchiv *n.*, Aktenarchiv *n.*,Archiv
n.
record-oriented file satzorientierte Datei *f.*
record overflow Satzüberlauf
m.
record position Satzposition *f.*
record program Satzprogramm *n.*
record replacement Satzersetzung *f.*
record segment Satzsegment
n.
record selection Datensatzauswahl *f.*
record separator Satztrennzeichen *n.*
record sequence number Satzfolgenummer *f.*
record set Satzgruppe *f.*
record sheet Erfassungsblatt *n.*
record specifier Satzparameter
m.
record transmission satzweise
Übertragung *f.*
record type Satzart *f.*
record variable Satzvariable *f.*
recorded aufgezeichnet *adj.*
recorded information aufgezeichnete Information *f.*
recorded time Erfassungszeitraum *m.*
recorder Aufnahmegerät *n.*
recording Aufzeichnen *n.*
recording area Aufzeichnungsfeld *n.*
recording density Aufzeichnungsdichte *f.*
recording device Aufzeich-

nungseinrichtung *f.*
recording head Schreibkopf *m.*
recording instrument Registriergerät *n.*
recording line Schreibzeile *f.*
recording medium Tonträger
m., Datenträger *m.*
recording mode Schreibverfahren *n.*
recording technique Aufnahmetechnik *f.*
records management Schriftgutverwaltung *f.*
recount/to nachzählen *vrb.*
recover/to wiederanlaufen
vrb., wiederherstellen *vrb.*
recoverable behebbar *adj.*, rekonstruierbar *adj.*
recoverable catalog wiederherstellbarer Katalog *m.*
recoverable error wiederherstellbarer Fehler *m.*
recoverable transaction wiederherstellbare Transaktion *f.*
recovery Wiederherstellung *f.*,
Fehlerbehebung *f.*
recovery area Sicherungsbereich *m.*
recovery management Fehlerbeseitigung *f.*
recovery procedure Wiederherstellungsverfahren *n.*
recovery time Erholzeit *f.*
recreate/to wiederherstellen
vrb.
recreation Wiederherstellung *f.*
recreational reading Lesen *n.*
zur Entspannung
recruitment Personalbeschaffung *f.*
recur/to sich wiederholen *vrb.*
recursion Rekursion *f.*

recursive rekursiv *adj.*
recursive function rekursive
Funktion *f.*
recursive procedure rekursive
Prozedur *f.*
recursive routine rekursives
Unterprogramm *n.*
recycle/to regenerieren *vrb.*
redaction Ausgabe *f.*, Redaktion *f.*
redefine/to neudefinieren *vrb.*
redefined field neudefiniertes
Feld *n.*
redesign Neuentwurf *m.*
reduce/to reduzieren *vrb.*, verkleinern *vrb.*
reduced loan period verkürzte
Leihfrist *f.*
reducible reduzierbar *adj.*, zurückführbar *adj.*
reduction Verkleinerung *f.*,
Kürzung *f.*
reduction factor Verkleinerungsfaktor *m.*
reduction of charges Gebührenermäßigung *f.*
reduction ratio Verkleinerungsfaktor *m.*
redundancy Redundanz *f.*
redundancy check Redundanzprüfung *f.*
redundant redundant *adj.*
reel Band *n.*, Rolle *f.*, Spule *f.*
reel capacity Bandkapazität *f.*
reenlarge/to rückvergrößern
vrb.
reenlargement Rückvergrößerung *f.*
reenter/to rückverzweigen
vrb.
reenterable wiederverwendbar, simultan benutzbar *adj.*

reenterable program simultan
benutzbares Programm *n.*
reentrant program simultan
benutzbares Programm *n.*
reentry point Rücksprungstelle
f.
refer/to verweisen *vrb.*
refer option Bezugsangabe *f.*
referee Gutachter *m.*
reference Bezugnahme *f.*, Verweis *m.*
reference address Bezugsadresse *f.*
reference block Hauptsatz *m.*,
Nachschlagewerk *n.*, Präsenzexemplar *n.*
reference card Verweiskarte *f.*
reference character Verweiszeichen *n.*, Kennzeichen *n.*
reference code Referenzcode
m.
reference collection Auskunftsapparat *m.*, Präsenzbibliothek
f.
reference data Hinweise *pl.*
reference database Referenzdatenbank *f.*, Hinweisdatenbank *f.*
reference database system Referenzsystem *n.*
reference department Informationszentrum *n.*
reference desk Auskunftsbereich *m.*, Auskunft *f.*
reference field Bezugsfeld *n.*
reference librarian Auskunftsbibliothekar *m.*
reference library Präsenzbibliothek *f.*
reference manual Handbuch *n.*
reference mark Anmerkungszeichen *n.*

reference number Aktenzeichen
n.
reference retrieval Dokumentnachweisretrieval *n.*
reference retrieval system Dokumentnachweissystem *n.*
reference service Auskunftsdienst *m.*
reference work Nachschlagewerk *n.*
references Quellenverzeichnis
n.
referral Nachweis *m.*
referral center Informationsvermittlungsstelle *f.*
referral service Nachweisdienst *m.*
refine/to verfeinern *vrb.*
refinement Verfeinerung *f.*
refit/to überholen *vrb.*
reflect/to widerspiegeln *vrb.*
reflection Reflexion *f.*
reflex copy Reflexkopie *f.*
reformat/to neuformatieren
vrb.
reformation Neugestaltung *f.*
refresh/to auffrischen *vrb.*
refresh memory Wiederholspeicher *m.*
refreshable wiederherstellbar
adj.
refund Kostenerstattung *f.*,
Rückgabe *f.*, Rückerstattung *f.*
refuse/to ablehnen *vrb.*
regenerate/to regenerieren
vrb.
region Region *f.*
regional lokal *adj.*, regional
adj.
regional and city library Re-
gional- und Stadtbücherei *f.*
regional archive Regionalar-

chiv *n.*
regional bibliography Regionalbibliographie *f.*
regional catalog Regionalkatalog *m.*
regional depository regionale
Aufbewahrung *f.*
regional edition Regionalausgabe *f.*
regional geography Landeskunde *f.*
regional library Bereichsbibliothek *f.*, Regionalbibliothek *f.*
regional media center regionales Medienzentrum *n.*
regional union catalog regionaler Zentralkatalog *m.*
register Register *n.*, Verzeichnis *n.*
register/to erfassen *vrb.*, eintragen *vrb.*, registrieren *vrb.*
registered eingetragen *adj.*
registered borrower eingetragener Benutzer *m.*
registered design Gebrauchsmuster *n.*
registered trade-mark eingetragenes Warenzeichen *n.*
registration Erfassung *f.*, Registrierung *f.*, Anmeldung *f.*
registration fee Einschreibgebühr *f.*
registration file Benutzerdatei
f.
regression Regression *f.*
regression analysis Regressionsanalyse *f.*
regression coefficient Regressionskoeffizient *m.*
regressive rückläufig *adj.*
regular regelmäßig *adj.*, vorschriftsmäßig *adj.*

regulation Vorschrift *f.*
reimpression Nachdruck *m.*
reinforced verstärkt *adj.*
reject/to ablehnen *vrb.*, zurückweisen *vrb.*
rejection Zurückweisung *f.*
related term verwandter Begriff *m.*
relation Beziehung *f.*, Relation *f.*, Vergleich *m.*
relation character Beziehungszeichen *n.*
relation indicator Beziehungsindikator *m.*
relational algebra Relationenalgebra *f.*
relational analysis Beziehungsanalyse *f.*
relational data model relationales Datenmodell *n.*
relational database relationale Datenbank *f.*
relational database system relationales Datenbanksystem *n.*
relational indexing Beziehungsindexierung *f.*
relational operator Vergleichsoperator *m.*
relationship Verknüpfung *f.*, Beziehung *f.*
relationship data Verknüpfungsdaten *pl.*
relative address relative Adresse *f.*
relative addressing relative Adressierung *f.*
relative error relativer Fehler *m.*
relative file relative Datei *f.*
relative frequency relative Häufigkeit *f.*

relative key relativer Schlüssel *m.*
relative record relativer Datensatz *m.*
relator Relator *m.*
release Freigabe *f.*, Freigabeversion *f.*
release/to freigeben *vrb.*
release bar Auslösetaste *f.*
relegate/to aussondern *vrb.*
relegation Aussonderung *f.*
relevance Relevanz *f.*
relevance assessment Relevanzbewertung *f.*
relevance factor Relevanzfaktor *m.*
relevance feedback Relevanzrückmeldung *f.*, Relevanzfeedback *n.*
relevance ranking Relevanzrangliste *f.*
relevance ratio Relevanzquote *f.*
relevance weight Relevanzgewicht *n.*
relevant relevant *adj.*
relevant in documentation dokumentationswürdig *adj.*
reliability Verläßlichkeit *f.*, Zuverlässigkeit *f.*
reliability data Zuverlässigkeitsangabe *f.*
reliable zuverlässig *adj.*
relief printing Buchdruck *m.*
religious body archive Archiv *n.* einer Glaubensgemeinschaft
religious body library Bibliothek *f.* einer Glaubensgemeinschaft
reload/to laden *vrb.*
reloadable wiederladbar *adj.*

reloadable control storage ladbarer Kontrollspeicher *m.*
relocatability Verschiebbarkeit *f.*
relocatable verschiebbar *adj.*
relocatable address verschiebbare Adresse *f.*
relocatable format verschiebbares Format *n.*
relocate/to verschieben *vrb.*
relocation Verschiebung *f.*, Umstellung *f.*
relocation dictionary Verschiebungsverzeichnis *n.*
remainder Rest *m.*
remainder/to verramschen *vrb.*, billig abgeben *vrb.*
remainders Restauflage *f.*
remaining restlich *adj.*
remake Neuauflage *f.*
remark Bemerkung *f.*
reminder Gedächtnisstütze *f.*, Mahnung *f.*
remittance Überweisung *f.*
remodeling Umbau *m.*
remote fern *adj.*, entfernt *adj.*
remote access Datenfernzugriff *m.*, Fernzugriff *m.*
remote administration Fernverwaltung *f.*
remote batch processing Stapelfernverarbeitung *f.*
remote communications unit Übertragungseinheit *f.*
remote computing Fernverarbeitung *f.*
remote control Fernsteuerung *f.*
remote-controlled ferngesteuert *adj.*
remote copier Fernkopierer *m.*
remote data transmission Da-

tenfernübertragung *f.*
remote diagnosis Ferndiagnose *f.*
remote display Fernanzeige *f.*
remote identification Fernkennung *f.*
remote indication Fernanzeige *f.*
remote installation Außenstelle *f.*
remote location Außenstelle *f.*
remote maintenance Fernwartung *f.*
remote processing Datenfernverarbeitung *f.*
remote station entfernt stehende Datenstation *f.*
remote supervision Fernüberwachung *f.*
remote terminal entfernt stehende Datenstation *f.*
remote transaction Ferntransaktion *f.*
remote workstation entfernt stehende Datenstation *f.*
removable disk Wechselplatte *f.*
removal Austausch *m.*, Umzug *m.*
removal slip Ersatzzettel *m.*
remove/to austauschen *vrb.*, entfernen *vrb.*
rename/to umbenennen *vrb.*, neubenennen *vrb.*
renewal Erneuerung *f.*, Verlängerung *f.*
rental collection gewerbliche Leihbibliothek *f.*
rental library kommerzielle Leihbücherei *f.*, gewerbliche Leihbibliothek *f.*
renumber/to neunumerieren

vrb.

reopened search neu gestartete Suche *f.*

reorder/to umordnen *vrb.*, nachbestellen *vrb.*

reorganization Neuorganisation *f.*

reorganize/to reorganisieren *vrb.*

repair/to reparieren *vrb.*

repair service Kundendienst *m.*

repeat/to wiederholen *vrb.*

repeat function Dauerfunktion *f.*

repeat key Dauertaste *f.*

repeat option Wiederholangabe *f.*

repeater Entzerrer *m.*, Verstärker *m.*

repetition Wiederholung *f.*

repetitive addressing Wiederholungsadressierung *f.*

repetitive printing Folgekartenbeschriftung *f.*

repetitive specification Wiederholungsspezifikation *f.*

replace/to ersetzen *vrb.*, verändern *vrb.*, austauschen *vrb.*

replaceable austauschbar *adj.*

replacement Austausch *m.*, Ersetzung *f.*

replacement character Ersetzungszeichen *n.*

replacement copy Ersatzexemplar *n.*

replenish/to auffüllen *vrb.*

replicate/to wiederholen *vrb.*

replication Wiederholung *f.*

replicator Wiederholangabe *f.*

reply/to antworten *vrb.*

report Report *m.*, Liste *f.*, Bericht *m.*, Auswertung *f.*, Stu-

die *f.*

report file Listendatei *f.*

report format Listenformat *n.*

report line Berichtszeile *f.*, Listenzeile *f.*

report on experiences Erfahrungsbericht *m.*

report preparation Berichterstellung *f.*

report program generator Listprogrammgenerator *f.*

reporting module Listmodul *n.*

reposition indicator Positionsanzeiger *m.*

reposition/to neupositionieren *vrb.*

repositioning Umpositionierung *f.*

repository library Speicherbibliothek *f.*, Außenmagazin *n.*

represent/to darstellen *vrb.*

representation Abbild *n.*, Abbildung *f.*, Darstellung *f.*

representative Beauftragter *m.*, Vertreter *m.*

repressible condition unterdrückbare Bedingung *f.*

reprint Nachdruck *m.*, Neudruck *m.*

reprocessing Wiederaufbereitung *f.*

reproduce/to abdrucken *vrb.*, kopieren *vrb.*, vervielfältigen *vrb.*

reproduction Abbild *n.*, Abbildung *f.*, Wiedergabe *f.*, Reproduktion *f.*

reprogrammable neuprogrammierbar *adj.*

reprogrammable controller neuprogrammierbare Steuerung *f.*

reprogramming Neuprogrammierung *f.*
reprography Reprographie *f.*
republication Wiederveröffentlichung *f.*
request Anfrage *f.*
request/to anfragen *vrb.*, anfordern *vrb.*, erfordern *vrb.*
request for repeat Wiederholungsaufforderung *f.*
request key Anforderungstaste
f.
required program erforderliches Programm *n.*
required reading Pflichtliteratur *f.*
requirement Anforderung *f.*
Erfordernis *n.*, Bedingung *f.*
requisition Anforderung *f.*
rereading Lesewiederholung *f.*
rerouting Weiterschaltung *f.*
rerun Wiederholungslauf *m.*
rerun time Wiederholungszeit
f.
reschedule/to verschieben *vrb.*
research and development
Forschung *f.* und Entwicklung
f.
research center Forschungszentrum *n.*
research commission Forschungsbeirat *m.*
research department Forschungsabteilung *f.*
research institute Forschungsinstitut *n.*
research library wissenschaftliche Bibliothek *f.*, Forschungsbibliothek *f.*
research paper Forschungsbericht *m.*
research problem Forschungs-

aufgabe *f.*
research project Forschungsprojekt *n.*
research report Forschungsbericht *m.*
research result Forschungsergebnis *m.*
research work Forschungsarbeit *f.*
researcher Forscher *m.*
reserve/to reservieren *vrb.*
reserve capacity Reservekapazität *f.*
reserved identifier reservierter
Name *m.*
reserved word reserviertes
Wort *n.*
reset/to rücksetzen *vrb.*, löschen *vrb.*
reset instruction Löschbefehl
m.
reset key Rücksetztaste *f.*
reset time Nachstellzeit *f.*
resetting Neusatz *m.*
reshape/to regenerieren *vrb.*
reshelve/to zurückstellen *vrb.*
residence time Verweilzeit *f.*,
Verweildauer *f.*
resident speicherresident *adj.*
resident file speicherresidente
Datei *f.*
resident program speicherresidentes Programm *n.*
residential area Wohngebiet *n.*
residual restlich *adj.*
resolution Beschluß *m.*, Auflösung *f.*
resolution time Auflösungszeit
f.
resolver Koordinatenwandler
m.
resource Betriebsmittel *n.*,

Hilfsmittel *n.*
resource center Medienzentrum *n.*
resource sharing gemeinsame Nutzung *f.* der Betriebsmittel
resources documentation Quellendokumentation *f.*
respond/to beantworten *vrb.*
responded output bestätigte Ausgabe *f.*
response Rückmeldung *f.*, Antwort *f.*
response message antwortabhängige Nachricht *f.*
response mode Antwortmodus *m.*
response time Antwortzeit *f.*
response unit Antworteinheit *f.*
responsibility Zuständigkeit *f.*, Verantwortung *f.*
restart/to wiederanlaufen *vrb.*
restart condition Wiederanlaufbedingung *f.*
restart data set Wiederanlaufdatei *f.*
restart instruction Wiederanlaufbefehl *m.*
restart procedure Wiederanlaufverfahren *n.*
restorable change rückführbare Änderung *f.*
restoration Restaurierung *f.*
restoration studio Restaurierungswerkstatt *f.*
restore/to restaurieren *vrb.*, umspeichern *vrb.*
restorer Restaurator *m.*
restricted access beschränkter Zugang *m.*
restriction of growth Wachstumsbeschränkung *f.*
restructure Neukonstruktion *f.*

result Ergebnis *n.*, Resultat *n.*
resume/to wiederaufnehmen *vrb.*
retail bookseller Buchhändler *m.*
retail price Ladenpreis *m.*
retailer Händler *m.*
retention period Aufbewahrungsfrist *f.*
retraining Umschulung *f.*
retrieval Retrieval *n.*, Wiederauffinden *n.*
retrieval effectiveness Retrievaleffektivität *f.*
retrieval efficiency Retrievaleffizienz *f.*
retrieval evaluation Retrievalbewertung *f.*
retrieval language Recherchesprache *f.*, Retrievalsprache *f.*, Abfragesprache *f.*
retrieval process Retrievalprozeß *m.*
retrieval ratio Nachweisquote *f.*
retrieval run Suchlauf *m.*
retrieval strategy Retrievalstrategie *f.*
retrieval system Retrievalsystem *n.*
retrieval techniques Retrievalverfahren *pl.*
retrieve/to wiedergewinnen *vrb.*, heraussuchen *vrb.*
retro active notation rückläufige Notation *f.*
retrospective Retrospektive *f.*
retrospective bibliography Sammelbibliographie *f.*
retrospective conversion Umstellung *f.* des Altbestandes
retrospective search retro-

spektive Suche *f.*, retrospektive Recherche *f.*
retry Wiederholung *f.*
return Rückführung *f.*
return/to zurückkehren *vrb.*, zurückspringen *vrb.*
return address Rücksprungadresse *f.*
return code Rückmeldecode *m.*
return key Rücklauftaste *f.*
return register Rücksprungregister *n.*
returned value Rückgabewert *m.*
returns Remittenden *pl.*
retype/to neuschreiben *vrb.*
reunification Wiedervereinigung *f.*
reusable mehrfach benutzbar *adj.*
reusable file mehrfach benutzbare Datei *f.*
reusable routine mehrfach benutzbares Programm *n.*
revaluation Neubewertung *f.*
revalue/to neu adressieren *vrb.*
reverification Prüfwiederholung *f.*, Neuprüfung *f.*
reversal Umschlag *m.*
reversal function Umkehrfunktion *f.*
reverse rückwärts *adj.*, entgegengesetzt *adj.*
reverse extract Rückübertragung *f.*
reverse printer bidirektionaler Drucker *m.*
reversible umkehrbar *adj.*
review Revision *f.* , Buchbesprechung *f.*, Rezension *f.*
review/to nachprüfen *vrb.*, re-

zensieren *vrb.*
review article Buchbesprechung *f.*
review copy Rezensionsexemplar *n.*
review periodical Rezensionszeitschrift *f.*
reviewer Rezensent *m.*
revise/to überarbeiten *vrb.*
revised edition überarbeitete Auflage *f.*
revised form Neufassung *f.*
reviser Korrektor *m.*
revision Korrektur *f.*
revoke/to aufheben *vrb.*, widerrufen *vrb.*
revolution archive Revolutionsarchiv *n.*
rewind/to rückspulen *vrb.*
rewind control Rückspulsteuerung *f.*
rewind key Rückspultaste *f.*
rewind time Rückspulzeit *f.*
rewinding Rückspulen *n.*
ribbon Farbband *n.*
right rechts *adj.*, richtig *adj.*
right margin set key rechter Randsteller *m.*
right of publication Verlagsrecht *n.*
right of reproduction Abdruckrecht *n.*
right truncation Rechtsmaskierung *f.*, Rechtstrunkierung *f.*
rise time Anlaufzeit *f.*
road map Straßenkarte *f.*
role indicator Rollenindikator *m.*
roll/to rollen *vrb.*
roll down Bild *n.* abwärts
roll in/to einspeichern *vrb.*
roll key Bildtaste *f.*

roll microfilm Rollfilm *m*.
roll paper Rollenpapier *n*.
roll up Bild *n*. aufwärts
roller Laufrolle *f*.
rolling Bilddurchlauf *m*.
Roman Catholic Church Library Bibliothek *f*. der römisch-katholischen Kirche
roman numeral römische Ziffern *pl*.
Romance languages and literatures Romanistik *f*.
room Raum *m*.
root Wurzel *f*., Wortstamm *m*.
root dictionary Wortstammwörterbuch *n*.
root-word Stammwort *n*.
roster Dienstplan *m*.
rotate/to rotieren *vrb*.
rotated entry rotierter Eintrag *m*.
rotated index Rotationsregister *n*., rotiertes Register *n*.
rotation Umdrehung *f*.
round/to runden *vrb*.
rounding Rundung *f*.
rounding error Rundungsfehler *m*.
route Leitweg *m*.
router Nachrichtenführer *m*.
routine Programm *n*.

routing Weiterleitung *f*.
routing of periodicals Zeitschriftenumlauf *m*.
routings Umläufe *pl*., Arbeitsfolge *f*.
row Zeile *f*.
row format Zeilenformat *n*.
royal library königliche Bibliothek *f*.
royalty Honorar *n*., Lizenzgebühr *f*.
rubber Gummi *m*.
rubber tape Isolierband *n*.
rule Regel *f*.
ruled liniert *adj*.
ruler Lineal *n*.
run Lauf *m*., Programmausführung *f*.
run duration Laufzeit *f*.
run length Lauflänge *f*.
run out/to auslaufen *vrb*., ablaufen *vrb*.
run through Durchlauf *m*.
run time Bearbeitungszeit *f*., Laufzeit *f*.
running number laufende Nummer *f*.
running title Kolumnentitel *m*.
rural library Dorfbibliothek *f*.
rush-order Eilauftrag *m*.

S

safe geschützt *adj.*, sicher *adj.*, Tresor *m.*
safeguard Sicherung *f.*
safety Sicherheit *f.*
safety film Sicherheitsfilm *m.*
sailors´ library Seemannsbibliothek *f.*
sale Absatz *m.*, Verkauf *m.*
sales catalog Verkaufskatalog *m.*
sales manager Verkaufsleiter *m.*
sales order Verkaufsauftrag *m.*
sales tax Umsatzsteuer *f.*
sales terms Verkaufsbedingungen *pl.*
same area gemeinsamer Bereich *m.*
sample Stichprobe *f.*
sample bias systematischer Stichprobenfehler *m.*
sample consignment Ansichtssendung *f.*
sample file Musterdatei *f.*
sample issue Probeheft *n.*, Probeausgabe *f.*
sample size Stichprobengröße *f.*
sample survey Stichprobenerhebung *f.*
sampler Abtaster *m.*
sampling Stichprobenbildung *f.*
sampling error Stichprobenfehler *m.*

sampling method Stichprobenverfahren *n.*
satchel Buchtasche *f.*
satellite Satellit *m.*
satellite computer Satellitenrechner *m.*
satellite processor Satellitenrechner *m.*
satellite station Außenstelle *f.*
satellite television Satellitenfernsehen *n.*
satellite transmission Satellitenübertragung *f.*
save/to sichern *vrb.*, speichern *vrb.*
save area Schutzbereich *m.*, Sicherungsbereich *m.*
save indicator Sicherungsanzeige *f.*
saving Einsparung *f.*
scale Skala *f.*, Skalierung *f.*, Maßstab *m.*
scale/to messen *vrb.*
scale down/to maßstabsgerecht verkleinern *vrb.*
scale of charges Gebührenordnung *f.*
scale unit Maßeinheit *f.*
scale up/to maßstabsgerecht vergrößern *vrb.*
scaling Skalieren *n.*, Normierung *f.*
scan/to abtasten *vrb.*, rastern *vrb.*, suchen *vrb.*

scan/to abtasten *vrb.*, rastern *vrb.*, suchen *vrb.*
scannable area Lesebereich *m.*
scanner Skanner *m.*, Lesegerät *n.*
scanning Zeichenabtastung *f.*
scanning field Abtastbereich *m.*
scanning speed Abtastgeschwindigkeit *f.*
scanning technique Abtasttechnik *f.*
scatter/to streuen *vrb.*
scatter diagram Streuungsbild *f.*
scattered read gestreutes Lesen *n.*
scattering Streuung *f.*
schedule Plan *m.*, Tabelle *f.*, Übersicht *f.*, Zeitplan *m.*
schedule/to planen *vrb.*, bereitstellen *vrb.*
scheduled planmäßig *adj.*
scheduled date Plantermin *m.*, geplanter Termin *m.*
scheduled maintenance geplante Wartung *f.*
scheduler Steuerprogramm *n.*
scheduling Zeitplanung *f.*, Disposition *f.*
scheme Schema *n.*, Datenbankschema *n.*
scholar Gelehrter *m.*
scholarly gelehrt *adj.*
scholarly library wissenschaftliche Spezialbibliothek *f.*
scholarly publication wissenschaftliche Veröffentlichung *f.*
scholarship Stipendium *n.*
school Schule *f.*, Schulhaus *n.*
school book Schulbuch *n.*
school certificate Abgangszeugnis *n.*
school leaver Abgänger *m.*
school librarian Schulbibliothekar *m.*
school librarianship Schulbibliothekswesen *n.*
school library Schulbibliothek *f.*, Schulbücherei *f.*
school media center Schulmediothek *f.*
school of commerce Handelshochschule *f.*
science Wissenschaft *f.*, Naturwissenschaft *f.*
science fiction utopischer Roman *m.*, Zukunftsroman *m.*
science librarian wissenschaftlicher Bibliothekar *m.*
science of fine arts Kunstwissenschaft *f.*
science of law Rechtswissenschaft *f.*
science of literature Literaturwissenschaft *f.*
scientific and technical information Fachinformation *f.*
scientific and technical information center Fachinformationszentrum *n.*
scientific and technical information policy Fachinformationspolitik *f.*
scientific and technical information program Fachinformationsprogramm *n.*
scientific and technical information system Fachinformationssystem *n.*
scientific communication wissenschaftliche Kommunikation *f.*
scientific council Wissenschaftsrat *m.*

scientific information wissenschaftliche Information *f.*
scientific meeting Fachkonferenz *f.*
scientific systematization wissenschaftliche Systematisierung *f.*
scientist Wissenschaftler *m.*
scientometrics Scientometrie *f.*
scope Bereich *m.*, Gültigkeitsbereich *m.*
scope note Erläuterung *f.*
score Punktzahl *f.*, Testergebnis *n.*
score/to bewerten *vrb.*
scoring sheet Auswertungsformular *n.*
scramble/to verschlüsseln *vrb.*
scratch area Arbeitsbereich *m.*
scratchpad Notizblock *m.*
screen Bildschirm *m.*, Anzeige *f.*
screen-based bildschirmorientiert *adj.*
screen cursor Positionsanzeige *f.*
screen design Bildschirmentwurf *m.*
screen diagonal Bildschirmdiagonale *f.*
screen dot Rasterpunkt *m.*
screen field Bildschirmfeld *n.*
screen handling Bildschirmhandhabung *f.*
screen image Bildschirmformat *n.*
screen layout Bildschirmaufteilung *f.*
screen pattern Bildschirmraster *n.*
screen record Bildschirmsatz *m.*

screen resolution Bildschirmauflösung *f.*
screen window Bildschirmfenster *n.*
screening Rastern *n.*, Sieben *n.*
screw Schraube *f.*
script Manuskript *n.*
scroll/to verschieben *vrb.*, blättern *vrb.*
scroll backward/to rückwärtsschieben *vrb.*
scroll forward/to vorwärtsschieben *vrb.*
scrollable rollfähig *adj.*, blätterfähig *adj.*
search Suche *f.*, Recherche *f.*, Suchanfrage *f.*
search/to suchen *vrb.*, recherchieren *vrb.*
search aid Suchhilfe *f.*
search argument Suchargument *n.*
search control word Suchsteuerwort *n.*
search criteria Suchkriterien *pl.*
search cycle Suchschleife *f.*
search field Suchfeld *n.*
search instrument Recherchemittel *n.*
search key Suchbegriff *m.*
search logic Suchlogik *f.*
search mode Suchmodus *m.*
search order Suchreihenfolge *f.*, Suchauftrag *m.*
search procedure Suchverfahren *n.*
search process Suchvorgang *m.*
search profile Suchprofil *n.*
search query Suchfrage *f.*
search report Suchbericht *m.*

search request Suchanfrage *f.*
search request form Suchanfragenformular *n.*
search result Rechercheergebnis *n.*
search strategy Suchstrategie *f.*, Recherchestrategie *f.*
search term Suchbegriff *m.*
search time Suchzeit *f.*
search tree Suchbaum *m.*
search word Suchwort *n.*
searcher Rechercheur *m.*, Searcher *m.*
seat Sitzplatz *m.*
secondary sekundär *adj.*
secondary author Mitverfasser *m.*
secondary bibliography Sekundärbibliographie *f.*
secondary data Sekundärdaten *pl.*
secondary document Sekundärdokument *n.*
secondary entry Nebeneintrag *m.*
secondary failure Folgeausfall *m.*
secondary index Sekundärindex *m.*
secondary input Sekundäreingabe *f.*
secondary keyword Sekundärschlüsselwort *n.*
secondary literature Sekundärliteratur *f.*
secondary processing sequence Sekundärverarbeitungsfolge *f.*
secondary program Sekundärprogramm *n.*
secondary publication Sekundärpublikation *f.*, Sekundär-

veröffentlichung *f.*
secondary storage Sekundärspeicher *m.*
secondary title Untertitel *m.*
secondary use Sekundärnutzung *f.*
secrecy Geheimhaltung *f.*
secret document Geheimdokument *n.*
section Abschnitt *m.*, Paragraph *m.*, Kapitel *n.*, Sektion *f.*
section control Abschnittsteuerung *f.*
section header Kapitelüberschrift *f.*
sector Sektor *m.*, Plattensektor *m.*
sector address Sektoradresse *f.*
sector identifier Sektorkennung *f.*
sectoral information center Bereichsinformationszentrum *n.*
secure sicher *adj.*, geschützt *adj.*
secured file geschützte Datei *f.*
security Sicherheit *f.*, Datensicherheit *f.*
security check Sicherheitsprüfung *f.*
security code Sicherheitscode *m.*
security feature Kennwortschutz *m.*
security file Sicherheitsdatei *f.*
see also reference siehe-auch-Verweisung *m.*
see page siehe Seite
see reference siehe-Verweisung *m.*
seek/to suchen *vrb.*, positionieren *vrb.*
seek address Suchadresse *f.*

seek command Suchbefehl *m*.
seek error Positionierungsfehler *m*.
seek time Suchzeit *f.*, Positionierzeit *f*.
segment Segment *n.*, Abschnitt *m*.
segmentation Untergliederung *f.*, Segmentierung *f*.
segmented segmentiert *adj*.
seize/to belegen *vrb*.
select/to auswählen *vrb*.
select group Auswahlgruppe *f*.
selectable function Auswahlfunktion *f*.
selected bibliography Auswahlbibliographie *f*.
selecting Auswählen *n*.
selection Selektion *f.*, Auswahl *f*.
selection catalog Auswahlkatalog *m*.
selection check Auswahlprüfung *f*.
selection field Auswahlfeld *n*.
selection of documents Dokumentauswahl *f*.
selection policy Bestandspolitik *f*.
selection step Auswahlschritt *m*.
selection time Auswahlzeit *f*.
selective selektiv *adj*.
selective bibliography Auswahlbibliographie *f*.
selective cataloging Auswahlkatalogisierung *f*.
selective dissemination of information Standardprofildienst *m.*, Profildienst *m*.
selective dump selektiver Speicherauszug *m*.

selective list Auswahlverzeichnis *n*.
selector Wähler *m*.
selector pen Auswahlstift *m*.
self-censorship Selbstzensur *f*.
self-check Funktionstest *m*.
self-checking selbstprüfend *adj*.
self-citation Eigenzitat *n*.
self-defining data selbstdefinierende Daten *pl*.
self-help Selbsthilfe *f*.
self-loading selbstladend *adj*.
self-renewal automatische Verlängerung *f*.
self-resetting selbstzurücksetzend *adj*.
self-service Selbstbedienung *f*.
sell/to verkaufen *vrb*.
selling price Verkaufspreis *m*.
semantic analysis semantische Analyse *f*.
semantic change Bedeutungswandel *m*.
semantic factoring semantische Begriffszerlegung *f*.
semantic information content semantischer Informationsgehalt *m*.
semantic model semantisches Modell *n*.
semantic network semantisches Netz *n*.
semantic relation semantische Beziehung *f*.
semantics Semantik *f*.
semester Semester *n*.
semiannual halbjährlich *adj.*, Halbjahresschrift *f*.
semiautomatic halbautomatisch *adj*.
semiconductor Halbleiter *m*.

semimonthly halbmonatlich *adj.*, Halbmonatsschrift *f.*
seminar report Seminarbericht *m.*
seminary library Seminarbibliothek *f.*
semiotics Semiotik *f.*
senate library Senatsbibliothek *f.*
send/to versenden *vrb.*
send request Sendeanforderung *f.*
sending Senden *n.*
sense Prüfung *f.*
sense condition Prüfbedingung *f.*
sense/to fühlen *vrb.*, abtasten *vrb.*, prüfen *vrb.*
sense data Prüfdaten *pl.*
sensitive sichtbar *adj.*, empfindlich *adj.*
sensitivity Empfindlichkeit *f.*, Sensitivität *f.*
sensor Meßfühler *m.*, Sensor *m.*
sensor-based computer Prozeßrechner *m.*
sentence Satz *m.*, Programmsatz *m.*
sentence analysis Satzanalyse *f.*
sentence key Satzstopptaste *f.*
sentence structure Satzstruktur *f.*
separable programming separierbare Programmierung *f.*
separate clause Trennsymbol *n.*
separating character Trennzeichen *n.*
separation Trennung *f.*
separator Trennzeichen *n.*, Separator *m.*, Begrenzer *m.*
separator line Trennlinie *f.*
sequence Reihenfolge *f.*, Sortierfolge *f.*
sequence checking Folgekontrolle *f.*, Folgeprüfung *f.*
sequence number Folgenummer *f.*, Satznummer *f.*
sequence processor Ablaufschaltwerk *n.*
sequence set Folgegruppe *f.*, Folgestufe *f.*
sequenced information folgegebundene Information *f.*
sequential sequentiell *adj.*
sequential access sequentieller Zugriff *m.*
sequential access storage Speicher *m.* mit sequentiellem Zugriff
sequential addressing sequentielle Adressierung *f.*
sequential control Ablaufsteuerung *f.*
sequential file sequentielle Datei *f.*
sequential processing sequentielle Verarbeitung *f.*
sequential search sequentielle Suche *f.*
serial seriell *adj.*, fortlaufend *adj.*, Sammelwerk *n.*
serial access serieller Zugriff *m.*
serial access memory Speicher *m.* mit seriellem Zugriff
serial catalog Zeitschriftenkatalog *m.*
serial cataloging Zeitschriftenkatalogisierung *f.*
serial holdings Zeitschriftenbestand *m.*

serial input serielle Eingabe *f.*
serial interface serielle Schnittstelle *f.*
serial number Seriennummer *f.*
serial printer serieller Drucker *m.*
serial search serielles Suchen *n.*
serial transfer serielle Übertragung *f.*
serialization Serialisierung *f.*, Durchnumerierung *f.*
serialize/to serialisieren *vrb.*
serials department Zeitschriftenstelle *f.*
series Serie *f.*, Reihe *f.*, Folge *f.*, Schriftenreihe *f.*
series of lectures Vortragsreihe *f.*
series publication Serie *f.*
series title Serientitel *m.*
serve/to betreuen *vrb.*
service Dienstleistung *f.*, Wartung *f.*, Dienst *m.*
service industries Dienstleistungsgewerbe *n.*
service life Nutzungsdauer *f.*
service order Dienstleistungsauftrag *m.*
service point Servicestelle *f.*
service program Dienstprogramm *n.*
service routine Dienstprogramm *n.*
services enterprise Dienstleistungsbetrieb *m.*
session Sitzung *f.*, Arbeitsabschnitt *m.*
set Menge *f.*, Set *m.*, Satz *m.*
set/to setzen *vrb.*, einstellen *vrb.*
set identifier Satzkennzeichnung *f.*
set off abgesetzt *adj.*
set theory Mengenlehre *f.*
set up/to absetzen *vrb.*, aufbauen *vrb.*, installieren *vrb.*
set-up time Anlaufzeit *f.*
setting Einstellung *f.*, Einstellen *n.*
setting accuracy Einstellgenauigkeit *f.*
sexuality Sexualität *f.*
shape/to formen *vrb.*
share/to gemeinsam benutzen *vrb.*
shared gemeinsam benutzt *adj.*
shared cataloging gemeinsame Katalogisierung *f.*
shared data gemeinsam benutzte Daten *pl.*
shared file gemeinsam benutzte Datei *f.*
shared line Gemeinschaftsanschluß *m.*
sheet Blatt *n.*, Bahn *f.*
sheet feeder Einzelblattzuführung *f.*
shelf Regal *n.*
shelf arrangement Regalanordnung *f.*, Regalaufstellung *f.*
shelf catalog Standortkatalog *m.*
shelf list Standortkatalog *m.*
shelf mark Signatur *f.*, Standortnummer *f.*
shelf number Signatur *f.*, Standortnummer *f.*
shell Schale *f.*
shell document konstantes Textdokument *n.*
shelve/to ins Regal stellen *vrb.*
shield Abschirmung *f.*

shield/to abschirmen *vrb.*
shift Umschaltung *f.*, Versetzen *n.*, Schieben *n.*
shift/to umschalten *vrb.*
shift interlock Umschaltfeststeller *m.*
shift key Umschalttaste *f.*
shift lock Feststeller *m.*
shift motion Umschalthöhe *f.*
shift unlock/to Umschaltung lösen *vrb.*
shifting Verschiebung *f.*
ship/to versenden *vrb.*
ship library Schiffsbibliothek *f.*
short-entry cataloging Kurztitelaufnahme *f.*
short film Kurzfilm *m.*
short loan collection Kurzleihbestand *m.*
short period loan Kurzleihe *f.*
short report Kurzbericht *m.*
short story Kurzgeschichte *f.*
short survey Abriß *m.*
short-title catalog Kurztitelkatalog *m.*
shortcut Abkürzung *f.*
shorten/to abkürzen *vrb.*
shortened abgekürzt *adj.*
shorthand Kurzschrift *f.*
show/to anzeigen *vrb.*
show-case Vitrine *f.*
show/to graph Diagramm anzeigen *vrb.*
shut off/to abschalten *vrb.*
shutdown Stillegung *f.*
side Rand *m.*, Seite *f.*
sight check Sichtprüfung *f.*
sign Zeichen *n.*
sign/to unterzeichnen *vrb.*
sign off/to beenden *vrb.*, abmelden *vrb.*
sign-off command Abmeldebe-

fehl *m.*
sign on/to anmelden *vrb.*
sign-on menu Startmenü *n.*
sign-on procedure Eröffnungsprozedur *f.*
signal Signal *n.*
signal buzzer Summer *m.*
signal sequence Signalfolge *f.*
signal shaping Signalumsetzer *m.*
signal tone Signalfrequenz *f.*
signal transformation Signalumsetzer *m.*
signalling Signalisierung *f.*
signalling exchange Zeichenaustausch *m.*
signalling system Zeichenaustauschsystem *n.*
signature Unterschrift *f.*, Signatur *f.*
signature/to unterschreiben *vrb.*
signed mit Vorzeichen *n.*
significance Bedeutung *f.*, Signifikanz *f.*, Stellenwert *m.*
significance test Signifikanztest *m.*
significant signifikant *adj.*
signify/to bezeichnen *vrb.*
similarity measure Ähnlichkeitsmaß *n.*
similarity relation Ähnlichkeitsbeziehung *f.*
simple einfach *adj.*
simple term einfacher Begriff *m.*
simplex mode Simplexbetrieb *m.*
simplicity Einfachheit *f.*
simplified cataloging vereinfachte Titelaufnahme *f.*
simplify/to vereinfachen *vrb.*

simulate/to simulieren *vrb.*
simulated künstlich *adj.*, simuliert *adj.*
simulated load function simulierte Ladefunktion *f.*
simulation Simulation *f.*
simulator Simulator *m.*
simultaneity Gleichzeitigkeit *f.*
simultaneous simultan *adj.*, gleichzeitig *adj.*
simultaneous access Parallelzugriff *m.*
simultaneous computer Parallelrechner *m.*
simultaneous mode Simultanbetrieb *m.*
simultaneous operation Simultanbetrieb *m.*
single column einspaltig *adj.*
single device Einzelgerät *n.*
single document Einzelbeleg *m.*
single error Einzelfehler *m.*
single key stroke Einzelanschlag *m.*
single-level einstufig *adj.*
single-level file einstufige Datei *f.*
single-line einzeilig *adj.*
single precision einfache Genauigkeit *f.*
single-sided einseitig *adj.*
single-space einzeilig *adj.*
single-stage einstufig *adj.*
single station Einzelstation *f.*
single terminal Einzelstation *f.*
situation Situation *f.*
size Größe *f.*, Umfang *m.*, Format *n.*
sketch Abriß *m.*
sketch/to abzeichnen *vrb.*
skill Fertigkeit *f.*, Fähigkeit *f.*, Kenntnis *f.*, Qualifikation *f.*

skilled gelernt *adj.*
skip Übergehen *n.*, Sprung *m.*, Vorschub *m.*
skip/to springen *vrb.*
skip field Sprungfeld *n.*
skip instruction Sprungbefehl *m.*
skip key Sprungtaste *f.*, Tabulatortaste *f.*
slanted mark schräge Markierung *f.*
slash Schrägstrich *m.*
slave mode Empfangsmodus *m.*
slave station Nebenstation *f.*
Slavic languages and literature Slawistik *f.*
slide Diapositiv *n.*
small and medium-sized enterprises Klein- und Mittelbetriebe *pl.*
small library Kleinbibliothek *f.*
small town library Kleinstadtbibliothek *f.*
social legislation Sozialrecht *n.*
social pedagogy Sozialpädagogik *f.*
social psychology Sozialpsychologie *f.*
social science Sozialwissenschaft *f.*
social sciences Gesellschaftswissenschaften *pl.*
social security Sozialversicherung *f.*
social security legislation Sozialversicherungsrecht *n.*
social work Sozialarbeit *f.*
socialism Sozialismus *m.*
society Verband *m.*, Gesellschaft *f.*
society and club library Gesell-

schafts- und Vereinsbibliothek
f.
sociological gesellschaftswissenschaftlich *adj.*, soziologisch *adj.*
sociology Soziologie *f.*
soft copy Bildschirmausgabe *f.*
software Programm *n.*, Software *f.*
software documentation Softwaredokumentation *f.*
software engineering Softwareentwicklung *f.*
software package Softwarepaket *n.*, Programmpaket *n.*
solicit/to abrufen *vrb.*, anfordern *vrb.*
solicit operation Abrufoperation *f.*
solid-state research Festkörperforschung *f.*
sort/to sortieren *vrb.*
sort field Sortierfeld *n.*
sort file Sortierdatei *f.*
sort order Sortierfolge *f.*
sort program Sortierprogramm *n.*
sort run Sortierlauf *m.*
sorted sortiert *adj.*
sorter Sortierer *m.*, Sortierprogramm *n.*
sorting Sortierung *f.*
sorting program Sortierprogramm *n.*
sound archive Schallarchiv *n.*
sound library for the blind Blindenhörbücherei *f.*
sound record Tonaufnahme *f.*
sound recording Schallaufzeichnung *f.*
source Herkunft *f.*, Quelle *f.*,
Ursprung *m.*

source book Quellenwerk *n.*
source data Ursprungsdaten
pl.
source database Faktendatenbank *f.*
source descriptor Quellendeskriptor *m.*
source document Originaldokument *n.*, Quellendokument *n.*
source documentation Faktendokumentation *f.*
source key Quellenschlüssel *m.*
source language Quellsprache
f., Ausgangssprache *f.*
source language file Quellprogrammdatei *f.*
source material Quellenmaterial *n.*
source program Quellprogramm *n.*
source thesaurus Quellenthesaurus *m.*
space Leerzeichen *n.*, Zwischenraum *m.*
space allocation Leerbereichszuordnung *f.*
space bar Leertaste *f.*
space character Leerzeichen *n.*
space check Leerspaltenprüfung *f.*
space key Leertaste *f.*
space line Leerzeile *f.*
space research Weltraumforschung *f.*, Raumforschung *f.*
space utilization Raumnutzung
f.
spaced gesperrt *adj.*
spaced out gesperrt gedruckt
adj.
spacing chart Entwurfsblatt *n.*
spare extra *adj.*, frei *adj.*
spare capacity freie *adj.* Kapa-

zität

spare part Ersatzteil *n.*
spare time Freizeit *f.*
speaker Diskussionsredner *m.*
special archive Facharchiv *n.*
special bibliography Fachbibliographie *f.*
special catalog Fachkatalog *m.*
special character Sonderzeichen *n.*
special classification Spezialklassifikation *f.*
special classification scheme Spezialklassifikationsmodell *n.*
special collection Sondersammlung *f.*, Spezialbestand *m.*, Spezialsammlung *f.*
special department Sonderabteilung *f.*
special dictionary Fachwörterbuch *n.*
special education Spezialbildung *f.*
special feature Zusatzeinrichtung *f.*
special heading Zusatzüberschrift *f.*
special issue Sonderheft *n.*, Sondernummer *f.*
special library Spezialbibliothek *f.*, Fachbibliothek *f.*, wissenschaftliche Spezialbibliothek *f.*
special library network Fachbibliotheksnetz *n.*
special publishing house Fachverlag *m.*
special register Sonderregister *n.*
special school Sonderschule *f.*
special subject collection Son-

dersammelgebiet *n.*
special subject collection library Sondersammelgebietsbibliothek *f.*
special subject literature Sondersammelgebietsliteratur *f.*
special symbol key Sonderzeichentaste *f.*
special training Spezialausbildung *f.*
speciality Spezialgebiet *n.*
specialized classification Fachklassifikation *f.*
specialized union catalog Fachzentralkatalog *f.*
species Unterbegriff *m.*
specific spezifisch *adj.*
specific heading spezifisches Schlagwort *n.*
specific text component Textbaustein *m.*
specification Spezifikation *f.*, Spezifizierung *f.*
specification sheet Beschreibungsblatt *n.*
specification test Abnahmeprüfung *f.*
specificator Spezifikator *m.*
specificity Genauigkeit *f.*
specifier Spezifikationszeichen *n.*
specify/to beschreiben *vrb.*, spezifizieren *vrb.*
specimen Probedruck *m.*
specimen copy Belegexemplar *n.*
specimen copy deposit Belegexemplarabgabe *f.*
speech Sprechweise *f.*, Rede *f.*
speech analysis Sprachanalyse *f.*
speech pattern recognition

Spracherkennung *f.*
speed change control Geschwindigkeitsumschalter *m.*
speed reading Schnellesen *n.*
spell/to buchstabieren *vrb.*
spell aid Rechtschreibhilfe *f.*
spell verify Rechtschreibprüfung *f.*
spelling Schreibweise *f.*
spelling check Korrekturhilfe *f.*
spill/to überlaufen *vrb.*
spill file Überlaufdatei *f.*
spill volume Reservedatenträger *m.*
spine labelling Buchrückenbeschriftung *f.*
splice/to verbinden *vrb.*, kleben *vrb.*
split/to aufspalten *vrb.*, splitten *vrb.*
split screen geteilter Bildschirm *m.*
splitting Spaltung *f.*, Teilung *f.*
spoken book Literaturkassette *f.*
spool Spulbetrieb *m.*, Bandspule *f.*
spooling Spulbetrieb *m.*, Zwischenspeicherung *f.*
sport Sport *m.*
sport report Sportbericht *m.*
sports library Sportbibliothek *f.*
spread Ausbreitung *f.*
spread/to ausbreiten *vrb.*
spreadsheet Arbeitsblatt *n.*
spring meeting Frühjahrstreffen *n.*
square Quadrat *n.*, Rechteck *n.*, quadratisch *adj.*
square bracket eckige Klammer *f.*
square root Quadratwurzel *f.*

stability Stabilität *f.*
stabilization Stabilisierung *f.*
stabilizing Stabilisieren *n.*
stable stabil *adj.*
stack Stapel *m.*
stack/to puffern *vrb.*, stapeln *vrb.*
stack accessories Regalzubehör *n.*
stack collection Magazinbestand *m.*
stack feeder Stapelzuführung *f.*
stack job processing sequentielle Verarbeitung *f.*
stacker Ablagefach *n.*
stacking Magazinierung *f.*
stacks Magazin *n.*
staff Personal *n.*
staff development Personalentwicklung *f.*
staff exchange Personalaustausch *m.*
staff library Personalbibliothek *f.*
staff requirement Personalbedarf *m.*
staff-user interaction Personal-Nutzer-Interaktion *f.*
staff-user ratio Personal-Nutzer-Quote *f.*
staffing level Besetzungsniveau *n.*
stage Phase *f.*, Stufe *f.*
stage/to speichern *vrb.*, zwischenspeichern *vrb.*
stage device Zwischenspeichereinheit *f.*
staging Abstufen *n.*
staging error Zwischenspeicherfehler *m.*
staging library Zwischen-

speicherbibliothek *f.*
stand-alone selbständig *adj.*
stand-alone computing system selbständiger Rechner *m.*
stand-alone device Einzelstation *f.*
stand-alone program selbständiges Programm *n.*
stand-alone text editing selbständige Textbearbeitung *f.*
stand-alone utility selbständiges Hilfsprogramm *n.*
stand-by Bereitschaft *f.*, Reserve *f.*, einsatzbereit *adj.*
stand-by computer Reserverechner *m.*
stand-by equipment Reserveausrüstung *f.*
stand-by system Bereitschaftssystem *n.*
stand-by time Wartezeit *f.*
standard Standard *m.*, Norm *f.*
standard book numbering Standardbuchnummernkennzeichnung *f.*
standard capacity Normalkapazität *f.*
standard classification Einheitsklassifikation *f.*
standard contract Mustervertrag *m.*
standard data format Standarddatenformat *n.*
standard file Standarddatei *f.*
standard input record Standardeingabesatz *m.*
standard paragraph Textbaustein *m.*
standard profile Standardprofil *n.*
standard serial numbering Standardseriennummern-

kennzeichnung *f.*
standard size Normalformat *n.*
standard software Standardsoftware *f.*
standard specification Normblatt *n.*
standard time Vorgabezeit *f.*
standard value Richtwert *m.*
standardization Normung *f.*, Vereinheitlichung *f.*, Standardisierung *f.*
standardization committee Normenausschuß *m.*
standing order Abonnement *n.*
start Beginn *m.*, Start *m.*, Anfang *m.*
start/to beginnen *vrb.*, starten *vrb.*
start character Startzeichen *n.*
start key Starttaste *f.*
start-up procedure Inbetriebnahme *f.*
start-up time Anlaufzeit *f.*
starting character Startzeichen *n.*
starting point Ansatzpunkt *m.*
state Zustand *m.*, Bundesland *n.*
state/to melden *vrb.*, festlegen *vrb.*
state administration Landesverwaltung *f.*
state archive Staatsarchiv *n.*, Landesarchiv *n.*
state authority Landesbehörde *f.*
state government Landesregierung *f.*
state government publication Landesveröffentlichung *f.*
state history Landesgeschichte *f.*

state indicator Statusanzeige f.
state information system Landesinformationssystem n.
state library Staatsbibliothek f., Landesbibliothek f.
state museum Landesmuseum n.
state of development Entwicklungsstand m.
state of the art analysis Istanalyse f.
state of the art report Bericht m. zum Stand der Technik, Literaturüberblick m.
state parliament Landesparlament n.
state parliament library Landtagsbibliothek f.
statement Anweisung f., Bericht m., Bestimmung f.
statement identifier Anweisungsbezeichnung f.
static statisch adj.
static buffer allocation statische Pufferzuordnung f.
static charge statische Aufladung f.
static dump statischer Speicherauszug m.
static file statische Datei f.
static input statische Eingabe f.
static memory statischer Speicher m.
static relocation statische Verschiebung f.
static storage statischer Speicher m.
statics Statik f.
station Anlage f., Datenstation f.
station/to aufstellen vrb., unterbringen vrb.

stationary stationär adj.
stationery Bürobedarf m., Schreib- und Papierwaren pl.
statistical analysis statistische Analyse f.
statistical bibliography statistische Bibliographie f.
statistical data statistische Daten pl.
statistical sampling statistische Stichprobenziehung f.
statistical survey statistische Untersuchung f.
statistical technique statistisches Verfahren n.
statistics Statistik f.
status Status m., Zustand m.
status indication Statusanzeige f.
status indicator Statusanzeiger m.
status information Statusinformation f.
status modification Statusveränderung f.
status report Zwischenbericht m.
statute Satzung f., Statut n.
statute book Gesetzbuch n.
statutory copy Pflichtexemplar n.
stem Stamm m., Wortstamm m.
stem dictionary Stammwörterbuch n.
stencil Vervielfältigungsmatrize f.
stencil base paper Matrizenfolie f.
stencil printing Durchdruck m.
step Schritt m., Ablaufschritt m.

step-by-step schrittweise *adj.*
step-by-step operation Einzelschrittbetrieb *m.*
step counter Schrittzähler *m.*
step-over Zeilensprung *m.*
still picture Festbild *n.*
stock control Bestandskontrolle *f.*
stock of books Bücherbestand *m.*
stock revision Bestandsrevision *f.*
stocktaking Inventur *f.*
stop Stopp *m.*, Stoppcode *m.*
stop condition Haltbedingung *f.*
stop control Stopptaste *f.*
stop element Stoppsignal *n.*
stop instruction Stoppbefehl *m.*
stop key Stopptaste *f.*
stop sequence Stopproutine *f.*
stop status Stoppstatus *m.*
storage Speicher *m.*, Speicherung *f.*, Lagerung *f.*
storage allocation Speicherzuweisung *f.*
storage area Speicherbereich *m.*
storage block Speicherblock *m.*
storage capacity Speicherkapazität *f.*
storage control unit Speichersteuereinheit *f.*
storage cushion Reservespeicher *m.*
storage cycle time Speicherzykluszeit *f.*
storage data register Speicherdatenregister *n.*
storage density Speicherdichte *f.*
storage device Speicher *m.*

storage dump Speicherauszug *m.*
storage expansion Speichererweiterung *f.*
storage extension Speichererweiterung *f.*
storage file Speicherdatei *f.*
storage location Speicherstelle *f.*, Speicheradresse *f.*
storage management Speicherverwaltung *f.*
storage medium Speichermedium *n.*
storage organization Speicherorganisation *f.*
storage problem Speicherproblematik *f.*
storage select key Speicherwahltaste *f.*
storage size Speichergröße *f.*
storage stack Speicherstapel *m.*
storage time Speicherzeit *f.*
storage unit Speichereinheit *f.*
store/to speichern *vrb.*
stored gespeichert *adj.*
stored program gespeichertes Programm *n.*
story Geschichte *f.*
storybook Geschichtenbuch *n.*
storyteller Geschichtenerzähler *m.*
strategy Strategie *f.*
stream Datenstrom *m.*
stream file Datenstromdatei *f.*
string Kette *f.*, Reihe *f.*, Folge *f.*
string data Zeichenfolge *f.*
string search Zeichenkettensuche *f.*
strip Streifen *m.*
stroke Schrägstrich *m.*
structural abstract Strukturre-

ferat *n.*
structural change Strukturwandel *m.*
structural components strukturelle Bauteile *pl.*
structural formula Strukturformel *f.*
structural principle Strukturprinzip *n.*
structure Struktur *f.*
structure chart Struktogramm
n.
structure member Strukturglied *n.*
structure variable Strukturvariable *f.*
structured data strukturierte
Daten *pl.*
structured notation strukturierte Notation *f.*
structured programming
strukturierte Programmie-
rung *f.*
structuring Gliederung *f.*,
Strukturierung *f.*
student Student *m.*, Absolvent
m.
students´ library Schülerbücherei *f.*, Studentenbücherei *f.*
studies Studium *n.*
studies of dramaturgy Theaterwissenschaft *f.*
study Studie *f.*
study/to studieren *vrb.*
study group Arbeitsgemeinschaft *f.*
study room Arbeitsraum *m.*
study time Studienzeit *f.*
sub-section Untersektion *f.*
suballocate/to abteilen *vrb.*
subarea Teilbereich *m.*
subclass Unterklasse *f.*

subcommand Unterbefehl *m.*
subfield Unterfeld *n.*, Teilfeld
n.
subgroup Untergruppe *f.*
subheading Unterschlagwort
n., Nebeneintrag *m.*
subhost Verbundrechner *m.*,
Nebenrechner *m.*
subject Subjekt *n.*, Betreff *m.*,
Fachgebiet *n.*, Thema *n.*,
Lehrgebiet *n.*, Gesprächsthema *n.*, Abbildungsgegenstand
m.
subject analysis inhaltliche Erschließung *f.*, Inhaltserschließung *f.*
subject area Sachbereich *m.*,
Sachgebiet *n.*
subject authority file verbindliche Schlagwortliste *f.*
subject bibliography Fachbibliographie *f.*
subject catalog Schlagwortkatalog *m.*, Sachkatalog *m.*
subject cataloging Sachkatalogisierung *f.*
subject classification Sachklassifikation *f.*, Sachgruppeneinteilung *f.*
subject classification scheme
Fachordnung *f.*
subject coverage Fachgebietsabdeckung *f.*
subject cross reference Sachverweisung *f.*
subject dictionary Fachwörterbuch *n.*
subject entry Schlagworteintrag *m.*
subject field Sachgebiet *n.*
subject heading Schlagwort *n.*
subject heading list kontrollier-

te Schlagwortliste *f.*
subject index Schlagwortregister *n.*, Sachregister *n.*, Schlagwortverzeichnis *n.*
subject indexing Sacherschließung *f.*, Schlagwortindexierung *f.*
subject indexing method Sacherschließungsmethode *f.*
subject indexing model Sacherschließungsmodell *n.*
subject indexing system Sacherschließungssystem *n.*
subject inquiry Sachsuche *f.*
subject name Fachgebietsbezeichnung *f.*
subject order Sachgebietsordnung *f.*
subject-oriented fachgebietsorientiert *adj.*
subject-oriented thesaurus Fachthesaurus *m.*, Spezialthesaurus *m.*
subject reference Schlagwortverweisung *f.*
subject search Sachrecherche *f.*
subject section Fachgruppe *f.*
subject specialist Fachreferent *m.*
subject to charges gebührenpflichtig *adj.*
subject word Schlagwort *n.*
subordinate untergeordnet *adj.*
subordinate concept Unterbegriff *m.*
subordinate field untergeordnetes Feld *n.*
subprocedure Unterprozedur *f.*
subprogram Unterprogramm *n.*
subroutine Unterprogramm *n.*
subroutine procedure Unter-

programmprozedur *f.*
subscribe/to abonnieren *vrb.*, subskribieren *vrb.*
subscriber Teilnehmer *m.*, Abonnent *m.*
subscript Index *m.*
subscripted subskribiert *adj.*
subscripted data indizierte Daten *pl.*
subscripting Subskribierung *f.*
subscription Subskription *f.*, Abonnement *n.*
subscription length Abonnementdauer *f.*
subscription library Leihbibliothek *f.*
subscription rate Abonnementpreis *m.*
subscription renewal Abonnementerneuerung *f.*
subsequence field Ergänzungsfeld *n.*
subsidiary untergeordnet *adj.*, stellvertretend *adj.*
subsidiary edition Nebenausgabe *f.*
subsidize/to subventionieren *vrb.*
substitute/to ersetzen *vrb.*, austauschen *vrb.*
substitution Veränderung *f.*, Substitution *f.*
substitution character Ersatzzeichen *n.*
substring Unterkette *f.*, Zeichenteilfolge *f.*
subsystem Subsystem *n.*, Teilsystem *n.*
subtitle Untertitel *m.*
subtract/to subtrahieren *vrb.*
successor Nachfolger *m.*
successor function Nachfolge-

funktion *f.*
successor title Folgetitel *m.*
suffix Suffix *n.*
suggestion Vorschlag *m.*
suitable passend *adj.*
sum/to addieren *vrb.*
sum up/to zusammenfassen
vrb.
summarize/to zusammenfassen *vrb.*
summary Zusammenfassung *f.,*
Überblick *m.,* Resumee *n.,*
Abriß *m.*
summer Summierer *m.*
supervisor Supervisor *m.,* Vorgesetzter *m.*
supervisory program Kontrollprogramm *n.*
supervisory routine Kontrollprogramm *n.*
supplier Lieferant *m.,* Anbieter
m.
suppliers´ plant Lieferungswerk *n.*
supplies Zubehör *n.*
supply Versorgung *f.,* Bereitstellung *f.*
support Unterstützung *f.*
support/to unterstützen *vrb.*
support program Unterstützungsprogramm *n.*
surface Oberfläche *f.*
surrounding area Randfeld *n.*
survey Umfrage *f.,* Befragung
f., Erhebung *f.,* Datenerhebung *f.*
survival function Bestandsfunktion *f.*
suspend/to suspendieren *vrb.,*
unterbrechen *vrb.*
suspend time Suspendierungszeit *f.*

swap/to austauschen *vrb.,*
überlagern *vrb.*
swap data set Tauschdatei *f.*
swap in/to einlagern *vrb.*
swap out/to auslagern *vrb.*
swapping area Auslagerungsbereich *m.*
switch Schalter *m.*
switch/to umschalten *vrb.,*
vermitteln *vrb.*
switch code Umschaltcode *m.*
switch off/to abschalten *vrb.,*
ausschalten *vrb.*
switch on/to anschalten *vrb.*
syllabic notation Silbennotation *f.*
syllable Silbe *f.*
syllable hyphen Silbentrennzeichen *n.*
symbol Symbol *n.*
symbol dictionary Symbolverzeichnis *n.*
symbol key Symboltaste *f.*
symbolic address symbolische
Adresse *f.*
symbolic coding symbolische
Codierung *f.*
symbolic file symbolische Datei
f.
symbolic instruction symbolischer Befehl *m.*
symbolic language symbolische
Programmiersprache *f.*
symbolic program symbolisches Programm *n.*
symmetric symmetrisch *adj.*
symposium Symposium *n.*
syndetic syndetisch *adj.*
synergistic zusammenwirkend
adj.
synonym Synonym *n.*
synopsis Autorenreferat *n.*

syntactic analysis syntaktische
Analyse *f.*
syntactic indexing syntaktische
Indexierung *f.*
syntactic network syntaktisches Netz *n.*
syntactics Syntaktik *f.*
syntax Syntax *f.*
syntax error Syntaxfehler *m.*
synthesis Synthese *f.*
synthetic classification synthetische Klassifikation *f.*
synthetic relations synthetische
Relationen *pl.*
system System *n.*
system access panel Systemzugriffskonsole *f.*
system administration Systemverwaltung *f.*
system analysis Systemanalyse
f.
system application Systemanwendung *f.*
system backup Systemsicherung *f.*
system call Systemaufruf *m.*
system command Systembefehl
m.
system control program Systemsteuerprogramm *n.*
system data analyser Systemdatenanalysator *m.*
system data set Systemdatei *f.*
system definition Systemdefinition *f.*
system description Systembeschreibung *f.*
system design Systemplanung
f., Systementwurf *m.*, Systemgestaltung *f.*
system documentation Systemdokumentation *f.*

system effectiveness Systemeffektivität *f.*
system effort Systemaufwand
m.
system environment Systemumgebung *f.*
system error Systemfehler *m.*
system evaluation Systembewertung *f.*
system failure Systemausfall
m.
system flowchart Systemablaufplan *m.*
system function Systemfunktion *f.*
system generation Systemgenerierung *f.*
system identification Systemidentifikation *f.*
system initialization Systeminitialisierung *f.*
system input unit Systemeingabeeinheit *f.*
system introduction Systemeinführung *f.*
system library Systembibliothek *f.*
system lock Systemsperre *f.*
system log Systemprotokoll *n.*
system output unit Systemausgabeeinheit *f.*
system performance data Systemleistungsdaten *pl.*
system production time Systemzeit *f.*
system programming error Systemprogrammierfehler *m.*
system relevance Systemrelevanz *f.*
system reset Systemgrundstellung *f.*
system restart Systemwieder-

anlauf *m.*
system security Systemsicherheit *f.*
system simulator Systemsimulator *m.*
system support program Systemsteuerprogramm *n.*
system test time Systemtestzeit
f.
system testing Systemtest *m.*
system unit Zentraleinheit *f.*
system-user interface System-
Nutzer-Schnittstelle *f.*
system utility program Systemdienstprogramm *n.*
system variable Systemvariable *f.*
system verification Programmsystemprüfung *f.*
systematic arrangement syste-

matische Ordnung *f.*
systematic bibliography systematische Bibliographie *f.*
systematic catalog systematischer Katalog *m.*
systematic failure systematischer Ausfall *m.*
systematic thesaurus systematischer Thesaurus *m.*
systematics Systematik *f.*
systems analysis Systemanalyse *f.*
systems design Systementwurf
m.
systems engineer Systemberater *m.*
systems interconnection Systemverbund *m.*
systems management Systemsteuerung *f.*

T

t-test t-Test *m.*
tab Tabulator *m.*
tab key Tabulatortaste *f.*
table Tisch *m.*, Tabelle *f.*
table delimiter Tabellenbegrenzer *m.*
table entry Tabelleneintrag *m.*
table function Tabellenfunktion
f.
table item Tabelleneintrag *m.*
table modification Tabellenänderung *f.*

table of addresses Adreßtabelle
f.
table of contents Inhaltsverzeichnis *n.*
table search Tabellensuche *f.*
tabular query language tabellarische Abfragesprache *f.*
tabulate/to tabellieren *vrb.*
tabulate key Tabuliertaste *f.*
tag Kennzeichen *n.*, Etikett *n.*
tail margin Fußsteg *m.*
takeover policy Übernahme-

politik *f*.
talent Fertigkeit *f*.
talking book Buchkassette *f*.
tally Zähler *m*.
tally/to auszählen *vrb*.
tape Magnetband *n*., Band *n*.
tape cassette Bandkassette *f*.
tape control Bandsteuereinheit
f.
tape deck Bandlaufwerk *n*.
tape density Banddichte *f*.
tape drive Bandlaufwerk *n*.
tape end retainer Bandendebe-
festiger *m*.
tape error Bandfehler *m*.
tape file Banddatei *f*.
tape library Bandarchiv *n*.
tape mark Bandmarke *f*.
tape reader Bandleser *m*.
tape recording Bandaufnahme *f*.
tape reel Bandrolle *f*.
tape service Magnetbanddienst *m*.
tape speed Bandgeschwindigkeit *f*.
tape start Bandanlauf *m*.
tape storage Bandspeicher *m*.
tape track Bandspur *f*.
tape unit Bandeinheit *f*.
target Einsatzziel *n*., Ziel *n*.
target descriptor Zieldeskriptor *m*.
target language Zielsprache *f*.,
Objektsprache *f*.
target program Zielprogramm *n*.
target reference Zielbezugnahme *f*.
target table Eingabetabelle *f*.
task Aufgabe *f*., Auftrag *m*.
task command Aufgabenbefehl
m.
task control Auftragssteuerung

f.
task force Arbeitsgruppe *f*.,
Projektgruppe *f*.
task sharing Funktionsteilung
f.
tax Steuer *f*.
taxonomy Taxonomie *f*.
teacher Lehrkraft *f*.
teacher college library Bibliothek *f*. einer Pädagogischen
Hochschule
teacher-librarian Lehrbibliothekar *m*.
teacher training Lehrerbildung
f.
teaching Unterricht *m*.
teaching aid Lehrmittel *pl*.
teaching by mail Fernunterricht *m*.
teaching method Unterrichtsmethode *f*.
team of specialists Fachgruppe
f.
teamwork Gemeinschaftsarbeit *f*., Gruppenarbeit *f*.
technical fachlich *adj*.
technical bibliography Fachbibliographie *f*.
technical book Fachbuch *n*.
technical communication Fachkommunikation *f*.
technical consultant technischer Berater *m*.
technical dictionary Fachwörterbuch *n*.
technical discussion Fachgespräch *n*.
technical journal Fachblatt *n*.,
Fachzeitschrift *f*.
technical language Fachsprache *f*.
technical lecture Fachreferat *n*.

technical library Fachbibliothek
f.
technical literature Fachliteratur *f.*
technical question Fachfrage *f.*
technical reference manual
technisches Handbuch *n.*
technical report Fachbericht
m., Forschungsbericht *m.*
technical services technische
Abteilung *f.*
technical specification technische Spezifikation *f.*
technical support technische
Unterstützung *f.*
technical term Fachausdruck
m., Fachwort *n.*, Fachbegriff
m.
technical text Fachtext *m.*
technical translator Fachübersetzer *m.*
technician Techniker *m.*
technochemistry Chemotechnik *f.*
technology Technik *f.*, Technologie *f.*
technology assessment Technologiefolgenabschätzung *f.*
technology limitations technologische Grenzen *pl.*
technology policy Technologiepolitik *f.*
technology transfer Technologietransfer *m.*
tele-education Fernstudium *n.*
telecode Fernschreibschlüssel
m.
telecommunication Telekommunikation *f.*
telecommunication equipment
Fernmeldeanlage *f.*
telecommunication line Über-

tragungsleitung *f.*
telecommunication network
Telekommunikationsnetz-
werk *n.*
telecommunication system Telekommunikationssystem *n.*
telecommunications Fernmeldewesen *n.*
teleconference Telekonferenz *f.*
teleconnection Verbindungsaufbau *m.*
telecontrol Fernsteuerung *f.*
telecopier Telekopierer *m.*
telecopy Telekopie *f.*
telediagnosis Ferndiagnose *f.*
telefacsimile transmission Telefax-Übermittlung *f.*
telefax Telekopie *f.*
telefax service Telefaxdienst
m.
telefax technique Telekopierverfahren *n.*
teleordering Fernbestellung *f.*
telephone Telephon *n.*
telephone directory Fernsprechverzeichnis *n.*, Telefonbuch *n.*
telephone line Fernsprechleitung *f.*
telephone number Telephon-
nummer *f.*
telephone service Fernsprechdienst *m.*
telephone set Telephonapparat
m.
telephone subscriber Fernsprechteilnehmer *m.*
teleprint Fernschreiben *n.*
teleprinter Fernschreiber *m.*
teleprocessing Datenfernverarbeitung *f.*
telescript/to fernschreiben *vrb.*

teletex Teletext *m.*
teletex service Teletextdienst *m.*
teletext Videotext *m.*
teletype/to fernschreiben *vrb.*
teletypewriter Fernschreiber *m.*
television Fernsehen *n.*
television journalist Fernsehjournalist *m.*
television production Fernsehproduktion *f.*
telework Telearbeit *f.*
telex Telex *n.*
telex service Telexdienst *m.*
telex system Fernschreibsystem *n.*
temperature Temperatur *f.*
temperature-sensitive temperaturempfindlich *adj.*
template Schablone *f.*
temporary temporär *adj.*, vorläufig *adj.*
temporary cataloging provisorische Katalogisierung *f.*
temporary contract befristeter Vertrag *m.*
temporary disk temporäre Platte *f.*
temporary file temporäre Datei *f.*
temporary library Temporärbibliothek *f.*
temporary personnel Aushilfspersonal *n.*
temporary stop vorübergehende Unterbrechung *f.*
temporary storage Zwischenspeicher *m.*
temporary store Puffer *m.*
tendency Tendenz *f.*
tender Angebot *n.*

tentative provisorisch *adj.*
term Bezeichnung *f.*, Benennung *f.*, Begriff *m.*
term adjacency Begriffsverkettung *f.*
term association Begriffsassoziation *f.*
term classification Begriffsklassifikation *f.*
term conflation Begriffsverschmelzung *f.*
term discrimination value Begriffsdiskriminanzwert *m.*
term entry Registereintrag *m.*
term extraction Begriffsextraktion *f.*
term formation Benennungsbildung *f.*
term frequency Begriffshäufigkeit *f.*
term independency Begriffsunabhängigkeit *f.*
term list Benennungsliste *f.*, Vokabularliste *f.*
term location Begriffsposition *f.*
term of delivery Lieferfrist *f.*
term phrase Mehrwortbegriff *m.*
term relevance factor Begriffsrelevanzfaktor *m.*
term similarity Begriffsähnlichkeit *f.*
term specificity Begriffsspezifität *f.*
term weighting Begriffsgewichtung *f.*
terminal Terminal *n.*, Datenstation *f.*
terminal cost Grenzkosten *pl.*
terminal error Abbruchfehler *m.*

terminal installation Datenstation *f.*
terminal interface Geräteschnittstelle *f.*
terminal list table Datenstationstabelle *f.*
terminal mode Datenstationsmodus *m.*
terminal node Netzknoten *m.*
terminate/to beenden *vrb.*
terminating point Endstelle *f.*
termination Beendigung *f.*
terminological control terminologische Kontrolle *f.*
terminologist Terminologe *m.*
terminology Fachsprache *f.*, Terminologie *f.*
terminology database Terminologiedatenbank *f.*
terminology research Terminologieforschung *f.*, Fachsprachenforschung *f.*
terminology work Terminologiearbeit *f.*
terms of delivery Lieferbedingungen *pl.*
terms of payment Zahlungsbedingungen *pl.*
terrestrial terrestrisch *adj.*
territorial authority Gebietskörperschaft *f.*
tertiary database tertiäre Datenbank *f.*
test Erprobungsphase *f.*
test/to prüfen *vrb.*, testen *vrb.*
test bench Prüfstand *m.*
test button Testlauftaste *f.*
test character Prüfkennzeichen *n.*
test chart Testvorlage *f.*
test command Testbefehl *m.*
test instruction Prüfanweisung

f.
test method Prüfverfahren *n.*
test mode Testbetrieb *m.*
test program Prüfprogramm *n.*
test request key Testabfragetaste *f.*
test result Untersuchungsergebnis *n.*
test run Testlauf *m.*
test specification Prüfspezifikation *f.*
testing Prüfen *n.*
testing character Prüfzeichen *n.*
text Text *m.*
text access Textzugriff *m.*
text analysis Textanalyse *f.*
text compression Textverdichtung *f.*
text database Textdatenbank *f.*
text editing Textbearbeitung *f.*
text field Satzspiegel *m.*
text file Textdatei *f.*
text formatting Textformatierung *f.*
text module Textbaustein *m.*
text processing Textverarbeitung *f.*
text processing program Textverarbeitsprogramm *n.*
text retrieval system Textretrievalsystem *n.*
text searching Textsuche *f.*
text storage Textspeicherung *f.*
textbook Schulbuch *n.*, Lehrbuch *n.*
textbook collection Schulbuchsammlung *f.*
textbook supply Lehrbuchversorgung *f.*
textual database Textdatenbank *f.*

theater Theater *n.*
theater archive Theaterarchiv *n.*
theater museum Theatermuseum *n.*
thematic index Sachregister *n.*
thematical thesaurus Querschnittsthesaurus *m.*
theological school library Bibliothek *f.* einer theologischen Fakultät
theology Theologie *f.*
theory Theorie *f.*
thermographic printer thermographischer Drucker *m.*
thermography Thermographie *f.*
thesaurus Thesaurus *m.*, Wortschatz *m.*
thesaurus class Thesaurusklasse *f.*
thesaurus construction Thesauruskonstruktion *f.*, Thesauruserstellung *f.*
thesaurus content Thesaurusinhalt *m.*
thesaurus evaluation Thesaurusbewertung *f.*
thesaurus format Thesaurusformat *n.*
thesaurus index Thesaurusregister *n.*
thesaurus-like thesaurusartig *adj.*
thesaurus research Thesaurusforschung *f.*
thesaurus structure Thesaurusstruktur *f.*
thesaurus updating Thesauruspflege *f.*
thesis akademische Arbeit *f.*, Diplomarbeit *f.*

thickness copy Musterband *m.*
thin-film memory Dünnschichtspeicher *m.*
threshold Schwelle *f.*
through switching Durchschalten *n.*
throughput Durchsatz *m.*
throughput time Durchlaufzeit *f.*
thumb index Griffregister *n.*
tick off/to abhaken *vrb.*
tie line Mietleitung *f.*, Querverbindung *f.*
tilde Tilde *f.*
time Zeit *f.*, Dauer *f.*
time/to zeitlich bestimmen *vrb.*
time analysis Zeitanalyse *f.*
time dependency Zeitabhängigkeit *f.*
time-dependent zeitabhängig *adj.*
time division Zeitmultiplexverfahren *n.*
time-independent zeitunabhängig *adj.*
time interval Zeitintervall *n.*
time-lag Zeitverzögerung *f.*
time of day Uhrzeit *f.*, Tageszeit *f.*
time off Fehlzeit *f.*
time-out Zeitlimitüberschreitung *f.*
time program control Zeitplanregelung *f.*
time-scheduling Terminplanung *f.*
time sharing Zeitscheibenverarbeitung *f.*
time slicing Zeitscheibenverfahren *n.*
time study Zeitstudie *f.*
time value Zeitfaktor *m.*

timer Zeitgeber *m.*
timesharing service Dialogteilnehmerdienst *m.*
timetable Dienstplan *m.*, Fahrplan *m.*
timing Zeitberechnung *f.*, Abstimmung *f.*
title Sachtitel *m.*, Titel *m.*,
Name *m.*
title and author catalog Titel-
Autor-Katalog *m.*
title area Titelfeld *n.*
title card Titelvorlage *f.*
title catalog Titelkatalog *m.*,
Sachtitelkatalog *m.*
title change Titeländerung *f.*
title construction Ansetzung *f.*
eines Titels
title edition Titelausgabe *f.*
title entry Titeleintrag *m.*
title frame Titelbild *n.*
title generation Ansetzung *f.*
eines Titels
title-leaf Titelblatt *n.*
title page Titelseite *f.*
title proper Hauptsachtitel *m.*
title space Titelfeld *n.*
title strip Titelsichtleiste *f.*
token Zeichen *n.*, Zeichenfolge
f.
token fee Schutzgebühr *f.*
token passing Token-Passing-
Verfahren *n.*
tolerance Toleranz *f.*
tolerated term zugelassene Benennung *f.*
toll Fernsprechgebühr *f.*
toll network Fernsprechnetz *n.*
toner Toner *m.*
tools Hilfsmittel *pl.*, Werkzeuge *pl.*
top Anfang *m.*, Oberteil *n.*,

Oberseite *f.*, Kopf *m.*
top margin oberer Rand *m.*,
Kopfsteg *m.*
top row obere Zeile *f.*
top side obere Seite *f.*
topic Gesprächsthema *n.*, Thematik *f.*
topical bibliography Sachbibliographie *f.*
topical heading Schlagwort *n.*
topical subdivision Unterschlagwort *n.*
topographical index Ortsregister *n.*
total Endsumme *f.*
total line Summenzeile *f.*
total memory Gesamtspeicher
m.
total processing time Gesamtbearbeitungszeit *f.*
total response time Gesamtantwortzeit *f.*
total running time Gesamtlaufzeit *f.*
total survey Vollerhebung *f.*
touch key Sensortaste *f.*
touch screen Sensorbildschirm
m.
touch-screen terminal berührungssensitiver Bildschirm *m.*
tourism Tourismus *m.*
town archive Stadtarchiv *n.*
town library Stadtbibliothek *f.*
toxicological information center Giftinformationszentrum
n.
toxicological substances Giftstoffe *pl.*
toxicology Toxikologie *f.*
trace Ablaufverfolgung *f.*
trace/to verfolgen *vrb.*
tracing Nebeneintragsvermerk

m.
track Spur *f.*
track identifier Spurkennzeichnung *f.*
tracking Informationsverfolgung *f.*
trade Handel *m.*
trade directory Firmenadreßbuch *n.*, Firmenverzeichnis *n.*
trade journal Handelsblatt *n.*
trade literature gewerbliche
Literatur *f.*, Handelsliteratur
f.
trade report Handelsbericht *m.*
trade union library Gewerkschaftsbibliothek *f.*
trademark Warenzeichen *n.*
trademark law Warenzeichenrecht *n.*
trademark name Markenname
m.
trademark rights Schutzrecht
n.
tradition Tradition *f.*, Überlieferung *f.*
traffic Straßenverkehr *m.*
traffic capacity Verkehrsleistung *f.*
traffic museum Verkehrsmuseum *n.*
traffic system Verkehrswesen
n.
trailer Nachsatz *m.*
train library Zugbibliothek *f.*
trained gelernt *adj.*
trainee Lehrling *m.*
trainer Ausbilder *m.*
training Ausbildung *f.*
training center Ausbildungsstätte *f.*
training course Ausbildungskurs *m.*

training method Ausbildungsmethode *f.*
training schedule Ausbildungsplan *m.*
transaction Bewegung *f.*,
Transaktion *f.*, Vorgang *m.*
transaction data Bewegungsdaten *pl.*, Vorgangsdaten *pl.*
transaction date Bewegungsdatum *n.*
transaction documentation
Vorgangsdokumentation *f.*
transaction error Übertragungsfehler *m.*, Transaktionsfehler *m.*
transaction identification
Transaktionsidentifikation *f.*
transaction management
Transaktionsmanagement *n.*
transaction record Bewegungssatz *m.*
transborder data flow grenzüberschreitender Datenfluß
m.
transcribe/to umschreiben *vrb.*,
transkribieren *vrb.*
transcription Abschrift *f.*,
Transkription *f.*, Übertragung
f., Umschrift *f.*
transfer/to übertragen *vrb.*
transfer check Übertragungskontrolle *f.*
transfer key Übertragungstaste *f.*
transfer list Transferliste *f.*
transfer rate übertragungsrate
f.
transfer signal übertragunsgsignal *n.*
transfer time übertragungszeit
f.
transferability Übertragbarkeit

f.

transferred meaning übertragene Bedeutung *f.*

transferred term übertragene Bezeichnung *f.*

transform/to umsetzen *vrb.*, umwandeln *vrb.*

transformation Umsetzung *f.*, Umwandlung *f.*

transformational generative grammar generative Transformationsgrammatik f.

transformational grammar Transformationsgrammatik *f.*

transformer Umformer *m.*, Transformator *m.*

transient area Übertragungsbereich *m.*

transient data Übertragungsdaten *pl.*

transient number Übertragungsnummer *m.*

transistor Transistor *m.*

transit Übergang *m.*

transition Überleitung *f.*

transition time Übergangszeit *f.*

transitional regulations Übergangsregelung *f.*

translate/to übersetzen *vrb.*

translating program Übersetzungsprogramm *n.*

translation Übersetzung *f.*

translation science Übersetzungswissenschaft *f.*

translation service Übersetzungsdienst *m.*

translator Übersetzer *m.*

transliterate/to transkribieren *vrb.*, umschreiben *vrb.*

transliteration Transliteration *f.*

transmission Übermittlung *f.*, Übertragung *f.*

transmission control Übertragungssteuerung *f.*

transmission error Übertragungsfehler *m.*

transmission line Übertragungsleitung *f.*

transmission priority Übertragungspriorität *f.*

transmission rate Übertragungsrate *f.*

transmission sequence Übertragungsfolge *f.*

transmission speed Übertragungsgeschwindigkeit *f.*

transmit/to senden *vrb.*, übertragen *vrb.*

transmittal record Übertragungssatz *m.*

transmitted data übertragene Daten *pl.*

transmitter Sender *m.*

transparent transparent *adj.*, codeunabhängig *adj.*

transport Transport *m.*

transport time Transportzeit *f.*

transportation Verkehrswesen *n.*

transportation system Transportwesen *n.*

transportation technology Verkehrstechnik *f.*

trap Auffangvorrichtung *f.*

trap/to auffangen *vrb.*

travelling library Reisebibliothek *f.*

travelog Reisebericht *m.*

treatise Abhandlung *f.*

treatment Behandlung *f.*

tree Baum *m.*

tree structure Baumstruktur *f.*

trend Entwicklungstendenz *f.*,
Tendenz *f.*, Trend *m.*
trial-and-error method Versuch-Irrtum-Verfahren *n.*
trial run Probelauf *m.*
trial subscription Probeabonnement *n.*
tribal information center Stammesinformationszentrum *n.*
trigger Trigger *m.*, Auslöseimpuls *m.*
trigger program Triggerprogramm *n.*
trim/to beschneiden *vrb.*
troubleshoot/to Fehler suchen
vrb.
troubleshooting Fehlersuche *f.*
true echt *adj.*, wahr *adj.*, zutreffend *adj.*
truncate/to abschneiden *vrb.*,
maskieren *vrb.*
truncated maskiert *adj.*
truncated search key maskierter Suchbegriff *m.*
truncation Abschneiden *n.*, Runden *n.*, Weglassen *n.*, Maskierung *f.*
truncation error Rundungsfehler *m.*
truth Wahrheit *f.*
truth table Wahrheitstabelle *f.*
truth value Wahrheitswert *m.*
tuning Optimierung *f.*, Abstimmung *f.*
tuning control Abstimmung *f.*
turn/to drehen *vrb.*
turn off/to abschalten *vrb.*
turn on/to anschalten *vrb.*
turnaround Richtungsänderung *f.*, Umschaltung *f.*
turnaround time Verweilzeit *f.*,
Durchlaufzeit *f.*

turnkey schlüsselfertig *adj.*
turnkey system schlüsselfertiges System *n.*
turnover Umschlag *m.*, Umsatz *m.*
tutorial Lernmaterial *n.*,
Übung *f.*
two-columned zweispaltig *adj.*
type Typ *m.*, Datentyp *m.*
type/to maschineschreiben
vrb., tippen *vrb.*
type charge Druckkosten *pl.*
type-in time Eingabezeit *f.*
type key Schreibtaste *f.*
type-out time Ausdruckzeit *f.*
type size Schriftgrad *m.*
type style Schriftart *f.*
type wheel Typenrad *n.*
type wheel printer Typenraddrucker *m.*
typescript maschinengeschriebene Veröffentlichung *f.*, Typoskript *n.*
typeset/to setzen *vrb.*
typesetter Schriftsetzer *m.*,
Setzer *n.*
typesetting Satz *m.*, Satzherstellung *f.*
typesetting computer Satzrechner *m.*
typesetting machine Setzmaschine *f.*
type-setting technique Setzverfahren *n.*
typewidth Schriftbreite *f.*
typewriter Schreibmaschine *f.*
typing error Tippfehler *m.*
typing speed Schreibgeschwindigkeit *f.*
typist Schreibkraft *f.*
typographer Typograph *m.*
typographer design Satzbild *n.*

typography Druckbild *n.*, Typographie *f.*

typology Typologie *f.*

U

ultimate class kleinste Unterteilung *f.*
ultimate constituent Wortelement *n.*
ultrasound Ultraschall *m.*
umbrella network Sternnetz *n.*
unabridged ungekürzt *adj.*, unverkürzt *adj.*
unaligned unausgerichtet *adj.*
unattended ohne Aufsicht *f.*
unattended mode bedienerloser Modus *m.*
unattended operation automatisches Einschalten *n.*
unattended printing bedienerloses Drucken *n.*
unattended receive bedienerloser Empfang *m.*
unattended time Ruhezeit *f.*
unattended transmit bedienungsloses Senden *n.*
unauthorized edition nichtautorisierte Ausgabe *f.*
unauthorized file gesperrte Datei *f.*
unavailability Totzeit *f.*
unavailable nicht verfügbar *adj.*
unavailable time Ausfallzeit *f.*
unbalanced unsymmetrisch *adj.*
unblanked sichtbar *adj.*

unblocked ungeblockt *adj.*
unblocked record ungeblockter Satz *m.*
unbound ungebunden *adj.*
unbuffered ungepuffert *adj.*
uncatalog/to entkatalogisieren *vrb.*
uncertain unbestimmt *adj.*
unchangeable nicht auswechselbar *adj.*, unveränderlich *adj.*
unchecked unkontrolliert *adj.*
unclassified ungeordnet *adj.*
uncoded uncodiert *adj.*
uncommitted nicht festgeschrieben *adj.*
unconditional unbedingt *adj.*, bedingungslos *adj.*
unconditional jump unbedingter Sprungbefehl *m.*
unconditional statement unbedingte Anweisung *f.*
unconditional table bedingungslose Tabelle *f.*
unconnected nicht angeschlossen *adj.*
unconnected terminal nicht angeschlossene Datenstation *f.*
uncontrollable unkontrollierbar *adj.*

uncontrolled ungesteuert *adj.*, unkontrolliert *adj.*

uncontrolled vocabulary nichtstandardisiertes Vokabular *n.*

undated undatiert *adj.*

undefined undefiniert *adj.*, unbestimmt *adj.*

undefined record undefinierter Satz *m.*

undefined symbol undefiniertes Symbol *adj.*

underdeveloped rückständig *adj.*

underflow Unterlauf *m.*

undergraduate collection Lehrbuchsammlung *f.*

undergraduate library Lehrbuchsammlung *f.*

undergraduate text Lehrbuch *n.*

underline/to unterstreichen *vrb.*, betonen *vrb.*

underscore/to unterstreichen *vrb.*

underscore character Unterstreichungszeichen *n.*

undetermined coefficient unbestimmter Koeffizient *m.*

unemployment Arbeitslosigkeit *f.*

unequal ungleich *adj.*

unequal margin fehlerhafter Rand *m.*

unformatted character string formatfreie Zeichenfolge *f.*

unformatted data transfer formatfreier Datentransfer *m.*

unformatted display unformatierte Anzeige *f.*

unformatted mode formatfreier Modus *m.*

unformatted record format-

freier Datensatz *m.*

unformatted write statement formatfreie Schreibanweisung *f.*

unicum Unikat *n.*

unidimensional eindimensional *adj.*

unidimensional classification eindimensionale Klassifikation *f.*

unification Vereinheitlichung *f.*

uniform einheitlich *adj.*

uniform filing system einheitliches Ablagesystem *n.*

uniform numbering einheitliche Numerierung *f.*

uniform title Einheitssachtitel *m.*

uninterruptable unterbrechungsfrei *adj.*

union Verband *m.*, Verbund *m.*

union catalog Gesamtkatalog *m.*, Zentralkatalog *m.*, Verbundkatalog *m.*

union catalog of periodicals Zeitschriftenzentralkatalog *m.*

union cataloging Verbundkatalogisierung *f.*

union list Gesamtverzeichnis *n.*

union list of periodicals Gesamtzeitschriftenverzeichnis *n.*

union list of serials Gesamtzeitschriftenverzeichnis *n.*

uniprocessor Einzelrechner *m.*

unique eindeutig *adj.*, einzigartig *adj.*

unique call number Individualsignatur *f.*

unique copy einziges Exemplar

n., Unikat *n.*
unique file Einzeldatei *f.*
unique identification number Satznummer *f.*
uniquely defined eindeutig definiert *adj.*
unit Einheit *f.*, Gerät *n.*, Endgerät *n.*
unit card Stammkarte *f.*, Einheitskarte *f.*
unit check Einheitenprüfung *f.*
unit control word Einheitenschlüssel *m.*
unit cost Stückkosten *pl.*
unit number Einheitennummer *f.*
unit of data transfer Datenübertragungseinheit *f.*
unit of time Zeiteinheit *f.*
unit process Elementarprozeß *m.*
unit selection Einheitenauswahl *f.*
unit separator Gruppentrennzeichen *n.*
unit sets Schnelltrennsatz *m.*
uniterm Uniterm *m.*
uniterm indexing Unitermindexierung *f.*
uniterm system Unitermsystem *n.*
units of memory Speichereinheiten *pl.*
units position Ziffernstelle *f.*
universal access allgemeiner Zugriff *m.*
universal bibliography Universalbibliographie *f.*
universal character set universeller Zeichensatz *m.*
universal classification Universalklassifikation *f.*
universal decimal classification Universaldezimalklassifikation *f.*
universal element Universaleingang *m.*
universal instruction set universeller Befehlssatz *m.*
universal library Universalbibliothek *f.*
universal match character Maskierungszeichen *n.*
university Hochschule *f.*, Universität *f.*
university archive Hochschularchiv *n.*
university bibliography Hochschulbibliographie *f.*
university directory Hochschulverzeichnis *n.*
university education Hochschulausbildung *f.*
university institute Hochschulinstitut *n.*
university library Universitätsbibliothek *f.*, Hochschulbibliothek *f.*
university press Universitätsverlag *m.*
university publication Hochschulschrift *f.*
university student Hochschulstudent *m.*
unjustified setting Flattersatz *m.*
unknown quantity unbekannte Größe *f.*
unknown term unbekannte Bezeichnung *f.*
unlabelled nicht markiert *adj.*
unlabelled file Datei *f.* ohne Kennsätze
unlatch/to entriegeln *vrb.*
unlatched unverriegelt *adj.*

unlimited unbegrenzt *adj.*
unload/to ausladen *vrb.*
unloading Entladen *n.*
unlock/to entsperren *vrb.*, lösen *vrb.*
unmatched nicht übereinstimmend *adj.*
unnamed control section unbenannte Steuersektion *f.*
unnormalized nicht normalisiert *adj.*
unnumbered unnumeriert *adj.*
unpack/to entpacken *vrb.*
unpaged unpaginiert *adj.*
unprinted leaf Leerblatt *n.*
unpublished unveröffentlicht *adj.*
unqualified unqualifiziert *adj.*
unqualified call nichtqualifizierter Aufruf *m.*
unreadable unlesbar *adj.*
unrecognizable unauffindbar *adj.*, nicht erkennbar *adj.*
unrecoverable error nicht behebbarer Fehler *m.*
unrecoverable transaction nicht wiederherstellbare Transaktion *f.*
unreturned book nicht zurückgegebenes Buch *n.*
unscannable unlesbar *adj.*
unsigned ohne Vorzeichen *n.*
unsigned number vorzeichenlose Zahl *f.*
unsolicited unaufgefordert *adj.*
unsolicited message unerwartete Nachricht *f.*
unsorted unsortiert *adj.*
unsought heading unerwartetes Stichwort *n.*
unspanned record nichtsegmentierter Satz *m.*

unstable labil *adj.*
unsubscripted reference nicht indizierte Bezugnahme *f.*
unsupported document nicht unterstütztes Dokument *n.*
untagged nicht gekennzeichnet *adj.*
untitled unbetitelt *adj.*, ohne Titel *m.*, titellos *adj.*
untrimmed copy unbeschnittenes Exemplar *n.*
untrimmed size Rohformat *n.*
unused page freie Seite *f.*, Leerseite *f.*
unused setup freier Aufbau *m.*
unverified unbestätigt *adj.*
unwanted signal Störsignal *n.*
unweighted unbewertet *adj.*
unwind/to abwickeln *vrb.*
up-arrow aufwärtsgerichteter Pfeil *m.*
up-to-date auf dem neuesten Stand, aktuell *adj.*
update/to fortschreiben *vrb.*, aktualisieren *vrb.*
update command statement Fortschreibungsanweisung *f.*
update intent geplante Aktualisierung *f.*
update mark Aktualisierungskennzeichen *n.*
update operator Aktualisierungsoperator *m.*
update password Aktualisierungskennwort *n.*
update run Aktualisierungslauf *m.*
update statement Aktualisierungsanweisung *f.*
update transaction Aktualisierungstransaktion *f.*
updated edition aktualisierte

Ausgabe *f.*
updating Aktualisierung *f.*,
Fortschreibung *f.*
updating run Aktualisierungslauf *m.*
upgrade/to ausbauen *vrb.*, erweitern *vrb.*, befördern *vrb.*
upgrade set Aktualisierungsdaten *pl.*
upline subsystem Sekundärsystem *n.*
upper obere *adj.*
upper bound obere Grenze *f.*
upper case character Großbuchstabe *m.*
upper class Oberschicht *f.*
upper fold oberer Falz *m.*
upper letter Großbuchstabe *m.*
upper limiting value oberer
Grenzwert *m.*
upper shift key Umschalttaste
f.
upper side Oberseite *f.*
upright format Hochformat *n.*
uptime Betriebszeit *f.*
urban history Stadtgeschichte
f.
urban library Stadtbücherei *f.*,
Stadtbibliothek *f.*
usability Verwendbarkeit *f.*
usable nutzbar *adj.*
usable area Nutzfläche *f.*
usable line lenght nutzbare Zeilenlänge *f.*
usage Auslastung *f.*, Verwendung *f.*
usage analysis Benutzungsanalyse *f.*
usage code Verwendungscode
m.
usage condition Benutzungsbedingung *f.*

usage contract Benutzungsverhältnis *n.*
usage frequency Benutzungsfrequenz *f.*
USE BENUTZE-Verweis *m.*
use Benutzung *f.*, Anwendung
f.
use analysis Benutzungsanalyse *f.*
use study Benutzungsstudie *f.*
USED FOR BENUTZT-FÜR-
Verweis *m.*
used equipment gebrauchte
Maschine *f.*
usefulness Brauchbarkeit *f.*
user Benutzer *m.*, Endbenutzer
m., Anwender *m.*
user access mode Benutzerzugriffsmodus *m.*
user analysis Benutzerforschung *f.*
user association Nutzergemeinschaft *f.*
user attribute data set Benutzermerkmaldatei *f.*
user authorization Benutzerberichtigung *f.*
user behavior Benutzerverhalten *n.*
user benefit Benutzernutzen *m.*
user catalog Benutzerkatalog
m.
user class of service Benutzerklasse *f.*
user control Benutzerkontrolle
f.
user cost Benutzerkosten *pl.*
user data Benutzerdaten *pl.*
user data file Benutzerdatendatei *f.*
user data set Benutzerdatendatei *f.*

user-defined benutzerdefiniert *adj.*

user-defined keyboard programmierbare Tastatur *f.*

user demand Benutzerbedarf *m.*

user-driven benutzergesteuert *adj.*

user education Benutzerschulung *f.*

user effort Benutzeraufwand *m.*

user fees Benutzungsgebühren *pl.*

user field Benutzerfeld *n.*

user friendliness Benutzerfreundlichkeit *f.*

user friendly benutzerfreundlich *adj.*

user group Nutzergruppe *f.*

user guide Benutzerhandbuch *n.*

user habits Benutzergewohnheiten *pl.*

user help desk Benutzerhilfe *f.*

user identification Benutzeridentifizierung *f.*

user identity Benutzerkennung *f.*

user information need Benutzerinformationsbedürfnis *n.*

user inquiry Endnutzerrecherche *f.*

user interest Benutzerinteresse *n.*

user interface Benutzeroberfläche *f.*

user label Benutzerkennsatz *m.*

user library Benutzerbibliothek *f.*

user library directory Benutzerbibliotheksverzeichnis *n.*

user load Benutzeranzahl *f.*

user manual Benutzerhandbuch *n.*

user menu Benutzermenu *n.*

user message table Benutzernachrichtentabelle *f.*

user name Benutzername *m.*

user-named vom Benutzer benannt

user needs Benutzerbedürfnisse *pl.*

user-oriented benutzerorientiert *adj.*

user participation Benutzerbeteiligung *f.*

user profile Benutzerprofil *n.*

user program Anwendungsprogramm *n.*

user relevance response Benutzerrelevanzangabe *f.*

user report Anwenderbericht *m.*

user security verification Benutzerautorisierungskontrolle *f.*

user statistics Benutzerstatistik *f.*

user study Benutzerstudie *f.*

user survey Benutzerumfrage *f.*

user-system interaction Benutzer-System-Interaktion *f.*

user terminal Benutzerterminal *n.*

user training Benutzerausbildung *f.*

user types Benutzertypen *pl.*

users Benutzergruppe *f.*, Benutzerkreis *m.*

usual gebräulich *adj.*, üblich *adj.*

utility Hilfsprogramm *n.*,

Dienstprogramm *n*.
utility function Hilfsprogrammfunktion *f*.
utility measure Nutzenkennziffer *f*.
utility program Dienstpro-

gramm *n*.
utility routine Dienstprogramm *n*.
utilization Verwendung *f*.,
Nutzung *f*.

V

vacancy Leerstelle *f*., Lücke *f*.
vacant unbesetzt *adj*.
vacate/to leeren *vrb*.
vacuous leer *adj*.
vacuousness Leere *f*.
vacuum Vakuum *n*.
vademecum Vademecum *n*.
valence Wertigkeit *f*.
valid gültig *adj*., zulässig *adj*.
validate/to bewerten *vrb*.,
prüfen *vrb*.
validate file Kontrollsatzdatei
f.
validation Gültigkeitsprüfung
f.
validity Gültigkeit *f*.
validity bit Gültigkeitsbit *n*.
validity check Gültigkeitsprüfung *f*.
validity error Gültigkeitsfehler
m.
validity search Gültigkeitsrecherche *f*.
value Wert *m*.
value added Zusatznutzen *m*.
value assignment Wertzuwei-

sung *f*.
value attribute Wertattribut *n*.
value of information Informationswert *m*.
value separator Werttrennsymbol *n*.
valuer Gutachter *m*.
vanish/to verschwinden *vrb*.
variable Variable *f*., variabel
adj.
variable adjustment Verändern
n. einer Größe
variable block format variables
Blockformat *n*.
variable cost variable Kosten
pl.
variable data variable Daten
pl.
variable field variables Feld *n*.
variable format variables Format *n*.
variable identifier variabler
Name *m*.
variable input area variabler
Eingabebereich *m*.
variable length variable Länge

f.
variable length record Satz *m.*
variabler Länge
variable record format variables Satzformat *n.*
variable record length variable Satzlänge *f.*
variable symbol variables Zeichen *n.*
variable text variabler Text *m.*
variable word length variable Wortlänge *f.*
variance Varianz *f.*
variance analysis Varianzanalyse *f.*
variant abweichend *adj.*
variant edition abweichende Ausgabe *f.*
variant reading Lesart *f.*
variant spelling Schreibart *f.*
variant title Nebentitel *m.*
variate Zufallsvariable *f.*
variation Variation *f.*
variation from standard Abweichung *f.* vom Standard
variety Vielfalt *f.*
vary/to variieren *vrb.*
vary off/to abhängen von *vrb.*
vary on/to anhängen *vrb.*, aktivieren *vrb.*
vary sensing variierbare Leseempfindlichkeit *f.*
varying veränderbar *adj.*, variierbar *adj.*
vector Vektor *m.*
vector analysis Vektoranalysis *f.*
vector constant Vektorkonstante *f.*
vector generator Vektorgenerator *m.*
vector graphics Vektorgraphik

f.
vector processor Vektorrechner *m.*
vector similarity vektorielle Ähnlichkeit *f.*
vectored zeigergesteuert *adj.*
vectorial vektoriell *adj.*
vellum Transparentpapier *n.*, Pergament *n.*
velocity Geschwindigkeit *f.*
vendor Lieferant *m.*
venn diagram Venn-Diagramm *n.*
ventilation Lüftung *f.*
verb Verb *n.*
verbal verbal *adj.*
verbal indexing Schlagwortindexierung *f.*
verbatim wörtlich *adj.*
verification Prüfung *f.*
verification code Prüfcode *m.*
verification message Prüfnachricht *f.*
verification routine Prüfroutine *f.*
verified geprüft *adj.*
verified database geprüfte Datenbank *f.*
verifier Prüfgerät *n.*
verify/to prüfen *vrb.*, kontrollieren *vrb.*, verifizieren *vrb.*
verify mode Prüfmodus *m.*
verify operation Prüfoperation *f.*
verifying program Prüfprogramm *n.*
version Version *f.*, Ausgabe *f.*
verso Rückseite *f.*
vertical alignment vertikale Ausrichtung *f.*
vertical control Vertikalsteuerung *f.*

vertical feed vertikale Zuführung f.
vertical file Hängekartei f.
vertical format control vertikale Formatsteuerung f.
vertical keyboard vertikale Tastatur f.
vertical pointer vertikaler Adreßzeiger m.
vertical redundancy check vertikale Redundanzprüfung f.
vertical spacing Zeilenvorschub m.
vertical tab table Vertikaltabulatorentabelle f.
vertical tabulating vertikal Tabulieren n.
vertical tabulation Vertikaltabulator m.
vertical tabulation character vertikales Tabulierzeichen n.
vertical tabulator key Vertikaltabuliertaste f.
veterinary medicine Tiermedizin f.
vice chancellor Prorektor m.
video archiv Bildarchiv n.
video camera Videokamera f.
video cassette Videokassette f.
video catalog Videokatalog m.
video clip Videoclip m.
video communication Videokommunikation f.
video conference Videokonferenz f.
video display Bildausgabe f., Bildschirm m.
video display unit Bildschirm m.
video generator Bildgenerator m.
video recorder Videorecorder

m.
video recording Bildaufzeichnung f.
video scanner Bildleser m.
video screen Bildschirm m.
video tape Videoband n.
video technology Videotechnik f.
video telephone Bildtelephon n.
video terminal Bildschirm m.
video work-station Bildschirmarbeitsplatz m.
videocast Videotext m.
videodisk Bildplatte f.
videotext Videotext m.
videotext page Videotextseite f.
view Sicht f.
view/to betrachten vrb., einsehen vrb.
view source Quellenanzeige f.
view storage Bildspeicher m.
viewdata Bildschirmtext m.
viewer Zuschauer m.
viewpoint Standpunkt m.
vignette Vignette f.
vinculum Strich m.
virgin fabrikneu adj.
virgin medium nichtinitialisierter Datenträger m.
virgule Komma n.
virtual virtuell adj.
virtual address virtuelle Adresse f.
virtual address area virtueller Adreßraum m.
virtual addressing virtuelle Adressierung f.
virtual computer virtueller Rechner m.
virtual device virtuelle Einheit

f.
virtual disk virtuelle Platte f.
virtual drive virtuelles Laufwerk n.
virtual instruction virtuelle Instruktion f.
virtual line virtuelle Leitung f.
virtual logical unit virtuelle logische Einheit f.
virtual machine virtueller Rechner m.
virtual memory virtueller Speicher m.
virtual mode virtueller Modus m.
virtual operating system virtuelles Betriebssystem n.
virtual partition virtuelle Partition f.
virtual storage virtueller Speicher m.
virtual storage access method virtuelles Speicherzugriffsverfahren n.
virtual storage size virtuelle Speichergröße f.
virtual timer virtueller Zeitgeber m.
virtual transfer address virtuelle Übertragungsadresse f.
virtual unit virtuelle Einheit f.
virtual unit address virtuelle Einheitenadresse f.
virtual volume virtueller Datenträger m.
virtual wait time virtuelle Wartezeit f.
visible sichtbar adj.
visible file Sichtkartei f.
visible indicator Schauzeichen n.
visual sichtbar adj.

visual control Sichtkontrolle f.
visual display Sichtanzeige f.
visual display device Sichtgerät n.
visual input control visuelle Eingabekontrolle f.
visual scanner optisches Lesegerät n.
visual test Sichtprüfung f.
vocabulary Vokabular n., Wörterverzeichnis n., Wortgut n.
vocabulary control terminologische Kontrolle f.
vocabulary matching terminologischer Abgleich m.
vocational fachlich adj.
vocational college Fachhochschule f.
vocational college act Fachhochschulgesetz n.
vocational college education Fachhochschulausbildung f.
vocational college library Fachhochschulbibliothek f.
vocational school Berufsschule f.
vocational school library Berufsschulbibliothek f.
voice Stimme f.
voice analysis Stimmanalyse f.
voice entry Spracheingabe f.
voice output Sprachausgabe f.
voice processing Sprachverarbeitung f., Verarbeitung f. gesprochener Sprache
voice recognition Spracherkennung f.
voice recognition unit Spracherkennungsgerät n.
voice recording set Sprachaufzeichnungsgerät n.
voice synthesizer Sprachgene-

rator *m.*
void leer *adj.*, Zeichenfehlstelle
f.
void key Stornotaste *f.*
volatile flüchtig *adj.*
volatile information veränderliche Information *f.*
volatile memory flüchtiger
Speicher *m.*
voltage Spannung *f.*
volume Band *m.*, Datenträger
m.
volume clean-up Datenträgerlöschen *n.*

volume entry Datenträgereintrag *m.*
volume label Bandanfangskennsatz *m.*
volume number Bandnummer
f.
volume security Datenträgerschutz *m.*
volume table of contents Datenträgerinhaltsverzeichnis *n.*
voucher Beleg *m.*, Buchungsunterlage *f.*, Gutschein *m.*
voucher date Belegdatum *n.*
voucher record Belegsatz *m.*

W

wage adjustment Lohnausgleich *m.*
wait/to warten *vrb.*
wait call Warteaufruf *m.*
wait condition Wartebedingung *f.*
wait control Wartesteuerung *f.*
wait indicator Warteanzeiger
m.
wait list Warteschlange *f.*
wait loop Warteschleife *f.*
wait state Wartestatus *m.*
wait time Wartezeit *f.*
waiting line Warteschlange *f.*
waiting list Vormerkliste *f.*
waiting state Wartestatus *m.*
waiting time Wartezeit *f.*
wall catalog Wandkatalog *m.*

wand Lesestift *m.*
want file Wunschliste *f.*
want list Wunschliste *f.*
warm restart Warmstart *m.*
warm start Warmstart *m.*
warming-up time Anwärmzeit
f.
warn/to alarmieren *vrb.*
warning indicator Warnanzeige *f.*
warning mark Warnstreifen *m.*
warning message Warnmeldung *f.*
warpage Verwerfung *f.*
warranty Garantie *f.*
waste instruction Leeroperation *f.*
waste paper Altpapier *n.*

waste sheet Fehldruck *m*.
water mark Wasserzeichen *n*.
water-resistant wasserfest *adj*.
watt Watt *n*.
wattage Stromverbrauch *m*., Leistung *f*.
wave guide Lichtwellenleiter *m*.
way Art *f*.
weak interrupt schwache Unterbrechung *f*.
weak sight Sehschwäche *f*.
wear Abnutzung *f*., Verschleiß *m*.
wearout failure Verschleiß *m*., Ausfall *m*.
web Papierrolle *f*., Endlospapier *n*.
weed/to aussortieren *vrb*.
weeding Bestandsrevision *f*.
week Woche *f*.
weekly wöchentlich *adj*.
weekly paper Wochenschrift *f*.
weight Stellenwert *m*., Gewicht *n*.
weighted average gewichteter Durchschnitt *m*.
weighted data gewichtete Daten *pl*.
weighted indexing gewichtete Indexierung *f*.
weighted retrieval gewichtetes Retrieval *n*.
weighting Gewichtung *f*.
weighting factor Gewichtungsfaktor *m*.
weighting function Gewichtungsfunktion *f*.
wheel Rad *n*., Scheibe *f*.
wheel printer Typenraddrucker *m*.
WHEN option WENN-Bedin-

gung *f*.
WHILE option SOLANGE-Bedingung *f*.
whole edition Gesamtauflage *f*.
whole-part relation Bestandsrelation *f*., Teil-Ganze-Relation *f*.
wholesale Großhandel *m*.
wholesale bookseller Kommissionsbuchhändler *m*.
wide area network überregionales Netz *n*.
wide band Breitband *n*.
width Breite *f*., Dicke *f*.
wild branch fehlerhafte Verweisung *f*.
wind up/to aufwickeln *vrb*.
window Fenster *n*., Ausschnitt *n*
window form Fortsetzungsformular *n*.
window size Fenstergröße *f*.
wire Draht *m*.
wire communication drahtgebundene Kommunikation *f*.
wire printer Matrixdrucker *m*.
wire size Drahtquerschnitt *m*.
wire stitching Drahtheftung *f*.
wired verdrahtet *adj*.
wireless drahtlos *adj*.
wireless telephone station drahtloses Telephon *n*.
wireless transmission drahtlose Übertragung *f*.
wiring Verdrahtung *f*., Schaltung *f*.
wiring diagram Schaltbild *n*.
withdraw/to zurücknehmen *vrb*., entnehmen *vrb*.
withdrawal Entnahme *f*., Rückzug *m*.
withdrawals register Abgangsbuch *n*.

without charge gebührenfrei *adj*.
without competition konkurrenzlos *adj*.
without date ohne Jahresangabe *f*.
without indention ohne Einrückung *f*.
without pagination nicht numeriert *adj*.
women's profession Frauenberuf *m*.
word Wort *n*.
word buffer Wortpuffer *m*.
word by word wörtlich *adj*., wortweise *adj*.
word combination Wortkombination *f*., Wortverbindung *f*.
word constant Wortkonstante *f*.
word element Wortelement *n*.
word family Wortfamilie *f*.
word frequency Worthäufigkeit *f*.
word frequency analysis Worthäufigkeitsanalyse *f*.
word group Wortgruppe *f*.
word index Wortregister *n*.
word length Wortlänge *f*.
word mark Wortmarke *f*.
word order Wortfolge *f*.
word processing Textverarbeitung *f*.
word processing equipment Textverarbeitungssystem *n*.
word processor Textverarbeitungssystem *n*., Schreibautomat *m*.
word separator Wortbegrenzer *m*.
word separator character Wortbegrenzungszeichen *n*.

word size Wortlänge *f*.
word spacing Wortzwischenraum *m*.
word time Wortzeit *f*.
word underline Wortunterstreichung *f*.
word underscore Wortunterstreichung *f*.
work Arbeit *f*.
work/to arbeiten *vrb*.
work area Arbeitsbereich *m*., Rechenfeld *n*.
work creation program Arbeitsbeschaffungsprogramm *n*.
work day Arbeitstag *m*.
work disk Arbeitsplatte *f*.
work file Arbeitsdatei *f*.
work report Tätigkeitsbericht *m*., Arbeitsbericht *m*.
work station Arbeitsplatzrechner *m*., Datenstation *f*.
work station buffer Datenstationspuffer *m*.
work station controller Datenstationssteuerung *f*.
work tape Arbeitsband *n*.
work track Arbeitsspur *f*.
work unit Arbeitseinheit *f*.
workers' librarianship Arbeiterbibliothekswesen *n*.
workers' library Arbeiterbibliothek *f*.
workers' movement Arbeiterbewegung *f*.
working area Arbeitsbereich *m*.
working class Arbeiterklasse *f*.
working conditions Arbeitsbedingungen *pl*.
working environment Arbeitsumgebung *f*.
working group Arbeitsgemein-

schaft *f.*, Arbeitskreis *m.*
working hours Arbeitszeit *f.*
working instructions Arbeitsanweisung *f.*
working process Arbeitsprozeß
m.
working register Arbeitsregister *n.*
working set Arbeitsbereich *m.*,
Arbeitsteil *m.*
working storage Arbeitsspeicher *m.*
working technique Arbeitstechnik *f.*
workload Arbeitsbelastung *f.*
workplace Arbeitsplatz *m.*
works Werke *pl.*
works in progress Reihe *f.*,
Fortsetzungswerk *n.*
worksheet Arbeitsblatt *n.*
workshop Seminar *n.*, Werk-
statt *f.*
workshop report Werkstattbericht *m.*
workspace Arbeitsbereich *m.*
workspace identification Arbeitsbereichsidentifikation *f.*
world bibliography Universalbibliographie *f.*, Weltbibliographie *f.*
worn abgenutzt *adj.*, zerlesen
adj.
wrap/to springen *vrb.*
wrap around/to umbrechen
vrb.
wrap around file Umlaufdatei
f.
wrap connection Steckkontakt
m.
wrap test Schleifenprüfung *f.*
write/to schreiben *vrb.*, beschreiben *vrb.*

write access time Schreibzugriffszeit *f.*
write command Schreibbefehl
m.
write control character
Schreibbefehlsteuerzeichen *n.*
write cycle Schreibzyklus *m.*
write data stream Schreibdatenfolge *f.*
write enable ring Schreibring *m*
write error Schreibfehler *m.*
write head Schreibkopf *m.*
write in/to einlesen *vrb.*
write-link Schreibverbindung
f.
write lockout Schreibsperre *f.*
write mode Schreibmodus *m.*
write off/to ausrangieren *vrb.*
write operation Schreiboperation *f.*
write protect error Schreibschutzfehler *m.*
write protect field Schreibschutzfeld *n.*
write protection Schreibschutz
m.
write-read cycle time Schreib-
/Lesezeit *f.*
writeable beschreibbar *adj.*
writer Schriftsteller *m.*
writing field Schreibfeld *n.*
writing line Schreiblinie *f.*
written form Schriftbild *n.*
written line Schriftzeile *f.*
written music Musikhandschriften *pl.*
wrong falsch *adj.*
wrong diskette falsche Diskette *f.*
wrong length record falsche
Satzlänge *f.*
wrong-reading seitenverkehrt

X

x-axis x-Achse *f.*
x-coordinate Abszissenwert *m.*
x-skip x-Sprung *m.*
x-y-plotter x-y-Schreiber *m.*

xerographic printer xerographischer Drucker *m.*
xerography Xerographie *f.*

Y

y-axis y-Achse *f.*, Ordinate *f.*
y-coordinate Ordinatenwert *m.*
yard Yard *n.*
year Jahr *n.*, Jahrgang *m.*
year-to-date Stichtag *m.*, ausgelaufen *adj.*
year under review Berichtsjahr *n.*
yearbook Jahrbuch *n.*
yearly jährlich *adj.*
yellow/to vergilben *vrb.*

yellow journal Boulevardzeitschrift *f.*
yellow pages gelbe Seiten *pl.*
yellow press Boulevardpresse *f.*
yellowed vergilbt *adj.*
yield Ausbeute *f.*, Erfolgsrate *f.*
young people´s edition Jugendausgabe *f.*
youth library Kinderbücherei *f.*, Jugendbücherei *f.*, Jugendbibliothek *f.*

Z

zero Null *f.*, Nullpunkt *m.*
zero-access storage Schnellspeicher *m.*
zero address Nulladresse *f.*
zero address instruction adressenloser Befehl *m.*
zero adjust Nulleichung *f.*
zero adjuster Nullpunkteinsteller *m.*
zero argument Nullargument
n.
zero check Nullkontrolle *f.*
zero compression Nullauslassung *f.*
zero control Nullkontrolle *f.*
zero correction Nullpunktkorrektur *f.*
zero displacement Nullpunktverschiebung *f.*
zero division Nulldivision *f.*
zero elimination Nullelimination *f.*
zero error Nullpunktabweichung *f.*
zero fill Nulleinsteuerung *f.*
zero float Nullspanne *f.*
zero growth Nullwachstum *n.*
zero growth policy Nullwachstumspolitik *f.*

zero indicator Nullanzeiger *m.*
zero insert Nulleinsteuerung *f.*
zero insertion Nulleinsteuerung *f.*
zero level Nullebene *f.*
zero node Nullknoten *m.*
zero offset Nullpunktverschiebung *f.*
zero out/to auf Null setzen
vrb.
zero point Nullpunkt *m.*
zero position Nullstellung *f.*
zero shift Nullpunktverschiebung *f.*
zero suppression Nullunterdrückung *f.*
zero test Nullprüfung *f.*
zerodivide Nulldivision *f.*
zerodivide condition Nulldivisionsbedingung *f.*
zerofill/to mit Nullen füllen
vrb.
zeroize/to mit Nullen füllen
vrb.
zip code Postleitzahl *f.*
Zipf´s law Zipfsches Gesetz *n.*
zone Zone *f.*
zoo library Zoobibliothek *f.*

Deutsch/ Englisch

A

abarbeiten *vrb.* process/to
abbauen *vrb.* disassemble/to,
dismantle/to
abbestellen *vrb.* cancel/to
Abbild *n.* representation, reproduction, map
abbilden *vrb.* produce/to,
copy/to, map/to
Abbildtheorie *f.* image theory
Abbildung *f.* representation,
reproduction, figure, illustration, image, mapping, picture
Abbildungen *pl.* außerhalb eines Textes inset plates
Abbildungsfehler *m.* image
defect
Abbildungsgegenstand *m.*
subject, object
Abbildungsmaßstab *m.* image
scale
abbrechen *vrb.* break off/to,
abort/to, kill/to
Abbruch *m.* discontinuance,
break off
Abbruchfehler *m.* terminal
error
Abbruchscode *m.* abnormal
end code
abdecken *vrb.* cover/to
Abdeckung *f.* cover, coverage,
mask
Abdeckungsquote *f.* coverage
ratio
Abdruck *m.* print, printing, im-

print
abdruckbar *adj.* printable
abdrucken *vrb.* reproduce/to,
print/to
Abdruckrecht *n.* right of reproduction
Abendzeitung *f.* evening
newspaper
Abfallquote *m.* fallout ratio
abfertigen *vrb.* process/to,
dispatch/to
Abfindung *f.* indemnity
Abfrage *f.* enquiry, inquiry,
query
Abfrage *f.* der Stammdatei
master file inquiry
Abfrage *f.* mittels Beispiel
query-by-example
abfrageabhängig *adj.* query-
dependent
Abfrageanforderung *f.* inquiry
request
Abfrageanweisung *f.* inquiry
command
Abfrageauswahl *f.* inquiry
operation
Abfragebearbeitung *f.* inquiry
processing
Abfragebefehl *m.* inquiry
command, query expression
Abfragedatei *f.* inquiry file
Abfrageeinheit *f.* inquiry unit
abfragen *vrb.* query/to
Abfrageparameter *m.* inquiry

specifier
Abfrageplatz *m.* operator console unit, operator desk
Abfragesprache *f.* command language, query language, retrieval language
Abfragestation *f.* query station
Abfragezeichen *n.* enquiry character
Abgabe *f.* delivery, due, duty
Abgabefrist *f.* deadline
abgabenfrei *adj.* duty-free
Abgänger *m.* school leaver
abgängig *adj.* missing
Abgangsbuch *n.* withdrawals register
Abgangsprüfung *f.* examination
Abgangszeugnis *n.* school certificate
abgeänderter Titel *m.* changed title
abgeben *vrb.* deliver/to
abgekürzt *adj.* shortened, abbreviated
abgeleitetes Wort *n.* derived word
abgenutzt *adj.* worn
abgeschlossen *adj.* perfect, finished, complete, completed
abgeschlossene Aufnahme *f.* closed entry
abgeschlossene Reihe *f.* completed series
abgesetzt *adj.* set off, in type
abgleichen *vrb.* collate/to, interpolate/to, match/to, merge/to
abgrenzen *vrb.* isolate/to
Abgrenzung *f.* definition, delimitation
abhaken *vrb.* check/to, tick

off/to
Abhandlung *f.* treatise, paper, essay
abhängen von *vrb.* vary off/to
abhängige Facette *f.* dependent facet
abheften *vrb.* file/to
Abheftlöcher *pl.* filing holes
Abkommen *n.* agreement, concord
abkürzen *vrb.* shorten/to, abridge/to, abbreviate/to
Abkürzung *f.* shortcut, abbreviation, abridgment
Abkürzungsverzeichnis *n.* list of abbreviations
Ablage *f.* arrangement, filing, history file
Ablage *f.* **im Archiv** archival storage
Ablagefach *n.* pigeonhole, pocket, stacker
Ablagekorb *m.* letter tray
Ablagemappe *f.* letter folder
Ablageregeln *pl.* filing code
Ablagesystem *n.* filing system
Ablageverfahren *n.* filing method
Ablauf *m.* procedure
Ablaufdefinition *f.* procedural definition
ablaufen *vrb.* run out/to, expire/to, pass/to
Ablauffrist *f.* expiration date
Ablaufgeschwindigkeit *f.* operating speed
Ablaufschaltwerk *n.* sequence processor
Ablaufschritt *m.* step
Ablaufsteuerung *f.* sequential control
Ablauftermin *m.* date due

Ablaufverfolgung f. trace
ablehnen vrb. refuse/to, reject/to
Ableitung f. derivative
ablesbar adj. readable
Ablesbarkeit f. readability
ablesen vrb. read off/to
ablichten vrb. copy/to
Ablieferungspflicht f. delivery obligation
Abmeldebefehl m. sign-off command
abmelden vrb. log off/to, sign off/to
Abmessung f. physical dimension
Abnahmeprüfung f. specification test
abnehmende Konkretheit f. decreasing concreteness
abnehmender Umfang m. decreasing extension
abnormale Bedingung f. abnormal condition
abnormales Ende n. abnormal end, abnormal ending
Abnutzung f. wear
Abonnement n. standing order, subscription
Abonnement abbestellen vrb. cancel/to a subscription, discontinue/to a subscription
Abonnementdauer f. subscription length
Abonnementerneuerung f. subscription renewal
Abonnementpreis m. subscription rate
Abonnementsrückgang m. going down of subscriptions
Abonnent m. subscriber
abonnieren vrb. subscribe/to
Abriß m. short survey, sketch, summary, compendium, digest, outline
Abruf m. recall, calling up, attention, fetch
Abrufausgang m. attention exit
Abrufbetrieb m. polling mode
Abrufdurchlauf m. polling pass
abrufen vrb. recall/to, poll/to, solicit/to
Abrufoperation f. solicit operation
Abruftaste f. attention key, keyboard request
Abrufunterbrechung f. attention interruption
Abrufverzögerung f. polling delay
Absatz m. break, marketing, paragraph, sale
Absatzeinrückung f. paragraph indention
Absatzsteuerung f. paragraph control
Absatztaste f. paragraph key
Absatzüberschrift f. paragraph header
absatzweise adv. by paragraphs, by steps, at intervals
Absatzzeichen n. paragraph mark
abschalten vrb. disconnect/to, break/to, latch/to, shut off/to, switch off/to, turn off/to
Abschaltzeit f. interrupting time, breaking period
abschätzbar adj. foreseeable, assessable
abschätzen vrb. estimate/to, assess/to
abschirmen vrb. shield/to
Abschirmung f. shield
abschließen vrb. close/to down

Abschlußprüfung *f.* final examination
Abschneiden *n.* truncation
abschneiden *vrb.* truncate/to
Abschnitt *m.* section, segment
Abschnittskennzeichnung *f.* outline formatting
Abschnittsretrieval *n.* answer-passage retrieval, passage retrieval
Abschnittsteuerung *f.* section control
abschreiben *vrb.* copy/to
Abschrift *f.* transcription, copy
Absender *m.* originator
Absenderadressenfeld *n.* origin address field
Absenderelementfeld *n.* origin element field
absetzen *vrb.* set up/to
absolute Adresse *f.* absolute address, machine address
absolute Adressierung *f.* absolute addressing
absolute Koordinate *f.* absolute coordinate
absolute Verzögerung *f.* absolute delay
absoluter Ausdruck *m.* absolute expression, absolute term
absoluter Fehler *m.* absolute error
absoluter Punkt *m.* absolute point
absolutes Symbol *n.* absolute symbol
Absolvent *m.* student, graduate
absolvieren *vrb.* pass/to, graduate from/to
Abstand *m.* lag, pitch
Abstandsoperator *m.* adja-cency operator
absteigende Sortierung *f.* grade down
Abstimmung *f.* reconciliation, timing, tuning, tuning control
Abstimmungsprogramm *n.* adjustment program
Abstract *n.* abstract
abstraktes Symbol *n.* abstract symbol
Abstraktion *f.* abstraction
Abstraktionsrelation *f.* abstraction relation, generic relation, genus-species relation
abstreichen *vrb.* check/to
Abstrich *m.* downstroke
Abstufen *n.* staging
Absturz *m.* crash
Abszissenwert *m.* x-coordinate
Abtastbereich *m.* scanning field
abtasten *vrb.* scan/to, sense/to
Abtaster *m.* sampler
Abtastgeschwindigkeit *f.* scanning speed
Abtasttechnik *f.* scanning technique
abteilen *vrb.* suballocate/to
Abteilung *f.* bay, department
Abteilungsbibliothek *f.* divisional library
Abteilungsleiter *m.* head of department, division head, divisional librarian
abweichend *adj.* variant
abweichende Ausgabe *f.* variant edition
Abweichung *f.* mismatch
Abweichung *f.* **vom Standard** variation from standard
abwerfen *vrb.* lock out/to

abwickeln *vrb.* unwind/to
Abwicklung *f.* handling
Abwicklungszeit *f.* handling
time
Abzeichen *n.* marking, badge
abzeichnen *vrb.* sketch/to,
mark off/to, copy/to
Abzug *m.* copy, discount
Abzug *m.* **ohne Zurichtung** flat
impression, flat pull
Abzweigleitung *f.* branch line
Achtung *f.* attention
Adapter *m.* adapter
adaptives Speicherelement *n.*
adaptive device
adaptives System *n.* adaptive
control system
addieren *vrb.* add/to, sum/to
Addierwerk *n.* adder
Addition *f.* addition
Additionstaste *f.* add key
Additionsübertrag *m.* add
carry
Additionszeit *f.* add time
additives Attribut *n.* additive
attribute
Adreßanhängung *f.* address
enable
Adressat *m.* addressee
Adreßaufkleber *m.* address
label
Adreßausgabe *f.* address out
Adreßbereich *m.* address
range, address space
Adreßblock *m.* addressing
module
Adreßbuch *n.* directory
Adreßdatei *f.* address file
Adreßdrucker *m.* address
printer
Adresse *f.* address, index
selection

Adressenbildung *f.* address
generation
Adressenliste *f.* address list
adressenlose Instruktion *f.* addressless instruction
adressenloser Befehl *m.* zero
address instruction
Adressenschreibung *f.* address
printing
Adressenteil *m.* address part
Adreßfeld *n.* address field
Adreßformat *n.* addressing
format
Adreßgenerierung *f.* address
generation
adressierbarer Speicher *m.*
addressable storage
Adressierbarkeit *f.* addressability
adressieren *vrb.* map/to
Adressiermaschine *f.* mailer
Adressiersystem *n.* addressing
system
Adressierung *f.* addressing
Adressierungsart *f.* addressing
mode
Adressierungsfehler *m.* ad-
dressing exception
Adressierungssignal *n.* ad-
dressing signal
Adressierungstechnik *f.* ad-
dress management, addressing technique
Adreßindex *m.* address index
Adreßkonstante *f.* address
constant
Adreßleitung *f.* address line
Adreßmarke *f.* address marker
Adreßmodifikation *f.* address
modification
Adreßposition *f.* address posi-
tion

Adreßraum *m.* address space
Adreßrechnung *f.* address adjustment, address computation
Adreßregister *m.* address register
Adreßsatz *m.* address record
Adreßschalter *m.* address switch
Adreßschlüssel *m.* address reference number
Adreßschlüsselregister *n.* address key register
Adreßspeicher *m.* address storage
Adreßspur *f.* address track
Adreßstecker *m.* address plug
Adreßstopp *m.* address stop
Adreßtabelle *f.* address table, table of addresses
Adreßumsetzung *f.* address translation
Adreßumwandlung *f.* address conversion
Adreßvergleich *m.* address comparison
Adreßverkettung *f.* chaining
Adreßwert *m.* address value
Adreßzähler *m.* location counter
Adreßzeichen *n.* address character
Adreßzeile *f.* address line
Affix *n.* affix, bound form
Agrarwissenschaft *f.* agricultural science, agronomy
ähnliche Figuren *pl.* homothetic figures
Ähnlichkeitsbeziehung *f.* similarity relation
Ähnlichkeitsmaß *n.* similarity measure

Akademie *f.* academy
Akademiker *m.* graduate
akademisch *adj.* academic
akademische Arbeit *f.* thesis
Akkommodationswahrscheinlichkeit *f.* accommodation factor
akkreditiert *adj.* accredited
Akkumulator *m.* accumulator
akkumulieren *vrb.* accumulate /to
akkumulierter Fehler *m.* accumulated error
Akronym *n.* acronym
Akte *f.* deed, dossier, file, legal document
Aktenarchiv *n.* record office, filing room
Aktendeckel *m.* document cover
aktenkundig *adj.* on the record
Aktenplan *m.* filing plan
Aktenschrank *m.* file cabinet, filing cabinet
Aktenständer *m.* filing shelf
Aktenstaub *m.* file dust
Aktenstoß *m.* pile of documents
Aktenumschlag *m.* folder
Aktenzeichen *n.* file number, reference number
Aktion *f.* campaign, action
Aktionsanzeige *f.* action indicator
Aktionsnachricht *f.* action message
aktiv *adj.* active
aktive Benutzerbibliothek *f.* active user library
aktive Datei *f.* active data set, active file
aktive Datenstation *f.* active

station
aktive Folgenummer *f.* active
sequence number
aktive Leitung *f.* active line
aktive Nachrichtendatei *f.* active message members
aktive Seite *f.* active page
aktive Verbindungsstrecke *f.*
active link
aktiver Bereich *m.* active partition
aktiver Fehler *m.* active fault
aktiver Leihverkehr *m.* interlibrary lending
aktiver Seitenrahmen *m.* active page frame
aktiver Status *m.* active state
aktives Format *n.* active format
aktivieren *vrb.* activate/to, execute/to, vary on/to
aktiviert *adj.* active
aktivierte Datei *f.* activated file
Aktivierung *f.* activation
Aktivität *f.* activity
Aktivitätsstufe *f.* activity level
Aktivitätsverhältnis *n.* activity ratio
aktualisieren *vrb.* update/to
aktualisierte Ausgabe *f.* updated edition
Aktualisierung *f.* updating
Aktualisierungsanweisung *f.*
update statement
Aktualisierungsdaten *pl.* upgrade set
Aktualisierungskennwort *n.*
update password
Aktualisierungskennzeichen *n.*
update mark
Aktualisierungslauf *m.* update

run
Aktualisierungstransaktion *f.*
update transaction
Aktualität *f.* actuality
aktuell *adj.* up-to-date
Akustikkoppler *m.* acoustic coupler
akustischer Speicher *m.*
acoustic storage
Akzeptanz *f.* acceptance
akzeptieren *vrb.* accept/to
Akzession *f.* acquisition unit
Akzessionierung *f.* accessioning
Akzessionsjournal *n.* accession book, accession register
Akzessionsnummer *f.* accession number
Akzessionsordnung *f.* accession order
Akzidenzdruck *m.* display work, job printing, jobbing work
Akzidenzdruckerei *f.* jobbing house
alarmieren *vrb.* warn/to
Album *n.* album
Algebra *f.* algebra
algebraische Linguistik *f.* algebraic linguistics
algorithmische Sprache *f.* algorithmic language
Algorithmus *m.* algorithm
alle Rechte vorbehalten all rights reserved
allgemein *adj.* public
Allgemeinbegriff *m* . generic concept
Allgemeinbildung *f.* general education
allgemeine Abfragesprache *f.*
common command language

allgemeine Anhängezahlen *pl.*
common subdivisions, common auxiliaries
allgemeine Bezeichnung *f.* generic term
allgemeine Beziehung *f.* general relation
allgemeine Bibliographie *f.* general bibliography
allgemeine Facette *f.* common facet
allgemeine Klassifikation *f.* general classification
allgemeine Semantik *f.* general semantics
allgemeine sequentielle Zugriffsmethode *f.* generalized sequential access method
allgemeine Systemtheorie *f.* general system theory
allgemeine Verwendung *f.* general usage
allgemeine Zugriffsberechtigung *f.* public access
allgemeiner Eintrag *m.* generic entry
allgemeiner Titel *m.* chapeau
allgemeiner Verweis *m.* general cross reference, general reference
allgemeiner Zugriff *m.* universal access
allgemeines Register *n.* general register
allgemeines Schlagwort *n.* general heading
allgemeines Symbol *n.* ordinary symbol
Allunionsbibliothek *f.* Pan Soviet State Library
Almanach *m.* almanac
Alpha-Zeichen *n.* alpha-character

acter
Alphabet *n.* alphabet
Alphabetempfang *m.* alphabetic receive
Alphabeterweiterung *f.* alphabet extender
Alphabetfeld *n.* alphabetic field
Alphabetfeldbegrenzung *f.* alphabetic field limit
Alphabetik *f.* alphabetics
alphabetisch *adj.* alphabetic, alphabetical
alphabetisch geordneter Klassentitel *m.* alphabetico-classed heading
alphabetisch geordnetes Register *n.* alphabetico-classed index
alphabetisch ordnen *vrb.* alphabetize/to
alphabetische Bibliographie *f.* alphabetical bibliography
alphabetische Codierung *f.* alphabetic coding, alphabetical coding
alphabetische Einteilung *f.* alphabetical division
alphabetische Ergänzung *f.* alphabetic equivalent
alphabetische Katalogisierung *f.* descriptive cataloging
alphabetische Notation *f.* alphabetic notation, alphabetical notation
alphabetische Ordnung *f.* alphabetical arrangement, alphabetic order, alphabetizatic
alphabetische Reihenfolge *f.* alphabetic order, alphabetic sequence
alphabetische Sachordnung *f.*

alphabetical subject collocation
alphabetische Unterteilung *f.*
alphabetical extension
alphabetischer Code *m.* alphabetic code, alphabetical code
**alphabetischer Gruppen-
schlagwortkatalog** *m.* alphabetico-classed catalog
alphabetischer Katalog *m.* alphabetical catalog, author
catalog
alphabetischer Sachkatalog *m.*
alphabetical subject catalog
**alphabetischer Schlagwortka-
talog** *m.* alphabetico-directed
catalog
alphabetischer Thesaurus *m.*
alphabetical thesaurus
alphabetischer Zeichensatz *m.*
alphabetic character set
**alphabetisches Notationszei-
chen** *n.* class letter
alphabetisches Ortsregister *n.*
alphabetical index of places
alphabetisches Register *n.* alphabetical index, alphabetical
register
**alphabetisches Schlagwort-
verzeichnis** *n.* alphabetical
list of subject headings, alphabetical subject index
alphabetisches Zeichen *n.* alphabetic character
alphabetisieren *vrb.* alpha-
betize / to
Alphabetisierung *f.* alphabetization
Alphabetmischeinrichtung *f.*
alphabetic collating
Alphabetname *m.* alphabetname

Alphabetsortierung *f.* alphabetic sorting
Alphabetspeichereinrichtung *f.*
alphabetic storage
alphanumerisch *adj.* alphameric, alphanumeric
alphanumerische Daten *pl.* alphanumeric data
alphanumerische Notation *f.*
alphanumeric notation
alphanumerische Nummer *f.*
alphanumerical number
alphanumerische Steuerung *f.*
alphanumeric control
alphanumerische Tastatur *f.*
alphabetic keyboard, alphanumeric keyboard
alphanumerischer Code *m.* alphanumeric code
alphanumerischer Ersatzwert
m. alphanumeric replacement
**alphanumerischer Tastenbe-
reich** *m.* alphanumeric area
**alphanumerisches Druckaufbe-
reitungszeichen** *n.* alphanumeric edited character
alphanumerisches Zeichen *n.*
alphanumeric character
Alphaumschaltung *f.* alphabetic shift
als geheim kennzeichnen *vrb.*
classify / to
Altenbücherdienst *m.* library
service for the old people
alter Bestand *m.* old stock
alternative Klassifikation *f.*
alternative location
Alternativen *pl.* alternatives
Alternativfunktion *f.* alternate
function
Alternativindex *m.* alternate

index
Alternativrelation *f.* alternative relation
Alternativsachtitel *m.* alternative title
Alternativschlüssel *m.* alternate key
Altertumswissenschaft *f.* classical studies
Alterung *f.* aging
Altpapier *n.* waste paper
Amateuraufnahme *f.* amateur recording
Amerikanistik *f.* American studies, Americanistics
Amt *n.* office, bureau
amtliche Druckschriften *pl.* government publications, official publications
amtliche Veröffentlichung *f.* public document
amtliche Veröffentlichungen *pl.* government publications
amtliches Schriftstück *n.* official document
Amtsbezeichnung *f.* official title
Amtsblatt *n.* official bulletin, gazette, official journal
Anagramm *n.* anagram
analog *adj.* analog
Analogcomputer *m.* analog computer
Analogrechner *m.* differential analyzer
Analyse *f.* analysis
Analysetiefe *f.* depth of analysis
Analytiker *m.* analyst
analytisch-synthetische Klassifikation *f.* analytico-synthetical classification

analytische Aufnahme *f.* analytical description
analytische Beziehung *f.* analytical relation
analytische Bibliographie *f.* analytical bibliography
analytische Klassifikation *f.* analytical classification
analytische Statistik *f.* analytical statistics
analytische Titelaufnahme *f.* analytical subject entry
analytisches Register *n.* analytical index
anaphorischer Ausdruck *m.* anaphoric expression
Anbau *m.* extension, addition, annex
anbieten *vrb.* offer/to
Anbieter *m.* supplier
anbinden *vrb.* bind/to
Anbindung *f.* acquiring
änderbar *adj.* modifiable, changeable
ändern *vrb.* modify/to
Änderung *f.* modification, change, alteration
Änderungsdatei *f.* amendment file
Änderungsdatensatz *m.* amendment record
Änderungsgebühr *f.* modification fee
Änderungslauf *m.* updating run
Andruck *m.* proof print
Aneinanderreihung *f.* von Symbolen juxtaposition of symbols
anerkennen *vrb.* recognize/to, accept/to, appreciate/to, approve/to
Anerkennung *f.* recognition,

admission
Anfang *m.* start, outset, beginning, top
Anfangsanschlag *m.* left-hand margin
Anfangsaufruf *m.* initial call
Anfangsbestand *m.* initial inventory, initials
Anfangsbuchstabe *m.* initial, initial letter
Anfangskennsatz *m.* header label
Anfangsnummer *f.* beginning number
Anfangsparameter *m.* initial parameter
Anfangsprozedur *f.* initial procedure
Anfangsrand *m.* left margin
Anfangsspalte *f.* begin column
Anfangstestroutine *f.* initial test routine
anfordern *vrb.* claim/to, request /to, solicit/to
Anforderung *f.* requirement, requisition
Anforderungsbehandlung *f.* attention routine
Anforderungstaste *f.* request key
Anfrage *f.* query, inquiry, request
anfragen *vrb.* request/to
anführen *vrb.* lead/to
Anführung *f.* allusion
Anführungszeichen *n.* quotation mark, inverted commas
Angebot *n.* bid, offer, tender
angegliedert *adj.* integrated
angewandt *adj.* applied
angewiesen *adj.* assigned
Anglistik *f.* Anglistics

anglo-amerikanische Katalogisierungsregeln *pl.* Anglo-American Cataloging Rules
anhalten *vrb.* hold/to
Anhang *m.* annex, appendage, appendix
anhängen *vrb.* vary on/to
Anhängezahl *f.* auxiliary number
Animation *f.* animation
ankommend *adj.* incoming
ankommende Leitung *f.* incoming line
Ankündigung *f.* notice
Anlage *f.* enclosure, station
Anlaufkosten *pl.* launching cost
Anlaufzeit *f.* rise time, set-up time, start-up time
anlegen *vrb.* feed/to
Anleitung *f.* guide
anmahnen *vrb.* claim/to
anmelden *vrb.* log on/to, sign on/to
Anmeldung *f.* enrollment, registration
anmerken *vrb.* mark/to, annotate/to
Anmerkung *f.* cut in note, annotation, annotation, note
Anmerkungen *pl.* **zwischen Textspalten** center notes
Anmerkungszeichen *n.* reference mark
Annäherungstendenz *f.* convergence
Annäherungsverfahren *n.* approximation method
Annahme *f.* acceptance, assumption
Annalen *pl.* annals
annehmen *vrb.* accept/to
annehmende Datenstation *f.*

accepting station
annullieren *vrb.* cancel/to,
cross out/to
Annullierungszeichen *n.* ignore character
anonym *adj.* anonymous
anonymer Eintrag *m.* anonymous entry
Anordnung *f.* arrangement, assignment, filing
Anordnung *f.* **mit zunehmender Klassenspezialisierung** gradation by speciality
Anordnungsprozedur *f.* layout procedure
Anordnungsvariable *f.* array variable
anpassen *vrb.* modify/to
Anpassungsfähigkeit *f.* adaptability, *f.* adaptiveness
Anpassungszeit *f.* preconditioning time
anpaßbar *adj.* adaptable
Anpaßbarkeit *f.* adaptability
anregen *vrb.* propose/to, pick/to
Anrufbeantworter *m.* answering machine
Ansatz *m.* approach
Ansatzpunkt *m.* starting point
anschaffen *vrb.* acquire/to
Anschaffung *f.* acquisition
Anschaffungsetat *m.* acquisition budget
Anschaffungsvorschlag *m.* book order suggestion, purchase suggestion
Anschaffungswert *m.* historical value
anschalten *vrb.* switch on/to, turn on/to
Anschaltnetz *n.* access net-

work
Anschaltpunkt *m.* attachment point
Anschaltzeit *f.* connect time
Anschlag *m.* impact, impression, notice
Anschlagbrett *n.* bulletin board, notice board
anschlagen *vrb.* joggle/to
Anschlagtafel *f.* billboard
anschließen *vrb.* hook-up/to, attach/to, interface/to
Anschluß *m.* adapter, attachment, junction, port
Anschluß *m.* **für Zeilendrucker** line printer attachment
Anschlußbezeichnung *f.* pin name
Anschlußelement *n.* attachment accessory
Anschlußgebühr *f.* attachment charge
Anschlußgenehmigung *f.* attachment approval
Anschlußkennung *f.* attachment identification, called line identification
Anschlußnummer *f.* network address
Anschlußprozessor *m.* attached processing unit, attached processor
Anschlußstelle *f.* interface
Anschlußunabhängigkeit *f.* attachment independence
Anschriftenverzeichnis *n.* address directory
Anschriftfeld *n.* address field
Ansetzfalz *m.* guard
Ansetzung *f.* **eines Titels** title construction, title generation
Ansichtsbestellung *f.* approval

order
Ansichtsexemplar *n.* approval
copy, inspection copy
Ansichtssendung *f.* sample
consignment, consignment
Ansprechzeit *f.* pick time
Anspruch *m.* claim
Anstalt *f.* institution
Anstaltsbibliothek *f.* institu-
tional library
anstehende Unterbrechung *f.*
interruption pending
Anthologie *f.* anthology
Antiquariat *n.* antiquarian
bookshop
Antiquariatskatalog *m.* anti-
quarian catalog
antiquarische Bücher *pl.* old
books
Antivalenz *f.* non-equivalence
Antonym *n.* antonym
Antrag *m.* application
Antwort *f.* response
antwortabhängige Nachricht *f.*
response message
Antworteinheit *f.* response
unit
antworten *vrb.* reply/to
Antwortkontrolle *f.* answer
processing
Antwortmodus *m.* response
mode
Antwortzeit *f.* response time
Anwachsen *n.* **des Bestandes**
expansion
Anwärmzeit *f.* warming-up
time
anweisen *vrb.* assign/to
Anweisung *f.* assignment,
guidance, instruction, statement
Anweisung *f.* **für den Buchbin-**

der binding sheet, binding slip
Anweisungsbezeichnung *f.*
statement identifier
Anweisungscode *m.* order
code
Anweisungsfolge *f.* order se-
quence
Anweisungsname *m.* label
Anwender *m.* user
Anwenderbericht *m.* user
report
Anwendung *f.* use, application
Anwendungsbeschreibung *f.*
application description
manual, application manual
Anwendungsdatenbank *f.* ap-
plication database
Anwendungsdatenbereich *m.*
application data area
Anwendungsdatenstruktur *f.*
application data structure
Anwendungsdefinition *f.* con-
textual definition, definition
by context
Anwendungsdienst *m.* application service
Anwendungsentwicklung *f.*
application development
Anwendungsentwurf *m.* application design
Anwendungserfahrung *f.* experience of application
Anwendungsfragebogen *m.*
application questionnaire
Anwendungsfunktionsroutine
f. application function
routine
Anwendungsgebiet *n.* application area
Anwendungsgruppenname *m.*
application group name
Anwendungsinstanz *f.* appli-

cation entity

Anwendungskennwort *n.* application password

Anwendungsmerkmal *n.* characteristic of purpose

Anwendungsmöglichkeit *f.* applicability

Anwendungsprogramm *n.* application program, user program

Anwendungsprogrammbibliothek *f.* applications program library

Anwendungsprogrammidentifikation *f.* application program identification

Anwendungsprogrammierer *m.* application programmer

Anwendungsprogramminformationsdienst *m.* application information service

Anwendungsprozeß *m.* application process

Anwendungspuffer *m.* application buffer

Anwendungsspezialist *m.* application specialist

Anwendungssteuerblock *m.* application control block

Anwendungssteuerungsbereich *m.* application control area

Anwendungssteuerungscode *m.* application control code

Anwendungssteuerungsstruktur *f.* application control structure

Anwendungsstruktur *f.* application structure

Anwendungssystem *n.* application system

Anwesenheit *f.* attendance

Anwesenheitsliste *f.* attend-

ance register

Anwesenheitszeit *f.* attendance time

Anzahl *f.* **der verschobenen Stellen** amount shift

Anzeige *f.* display, flag, indicator, notice, screen

Anzeige *f.* **der Indexentwicklung** index development indicator

Anzeigefeld *n.* display field

Anzeigegerät *n.* display device

anzeigen *vrb.* display/to, indicate/to, show/to

Anzeigenblatt *n.* advertising journal

Anzeiger *m.* **des letzten Satzes** last-record indicator

Anzeigeunterdrückung *f.* nondisplay

apostrophgesteuerte Druckaufbereitung *f.* apostrophe editing

Appendix *m.* appendix

Approbation *f.* licence

Aquariumsbibliothek *f.* aquaria library

Äquivalenz *f.* equivalence

Äquivalenzbedingung *f.* IF-AND-ONLY-IF element

Äquivalenzbezeichnung *f.* equivalent term

Äquivalenzkategorie *f.* equivalence category

Äquivalenzoperation *f.* equivalence operation, IF-AND-ONLY-IF operation

Äquivalenzrelation *f.* equivalence relation

Arabeske *f.* arabesque

Arbeit *f.* work, employment

arbeiten *vrb.* operate/to,

work/to
arbeitende Rechenanlage *f.* active computer
Arbeiterbewegung *f.* workers' movement
Arbeiterbibliothek *f.* workers' library
Arbeiterbibliothekswesen *n.* workers' librarianship
Arbeiterklasse *f.* working class
Arbeitgeber *m.* employer
Arbeitnehmer *m.* employee
Arbeitsabschnitt *m.* session
Arbeitsanweisung *f.* working instructions
Arbeitsband *n.* work tape
Arbeitsbedingungen *pl.* working conditions
Arbeitsbelastung *f.* workload
Arbeitsbereich *m.* scratch area, work area, working area, working set, workspace
Arbeitsbereichsidentifikation *f.* workspace identification
Arbeitsbericht *m.* work report
Arbeitsbeschaffungsprogramm *n.* work creation program
Arbeitsblatt *n.* worksheet, spreadsheet
Arbeitsdatei *f.* work file
Arbeitseinheit *f.* work unit
Arbeitserlaubnis *f.* labor certificate
Arbeitsflußdiagramm *n.* operation flowchart
Arbeitsfolge *f.* routings
Arbeitsgang *m.* operation, pass
Arbeitsgangdauer *f.* operation duration
Arbeitsgangpriorität *f.* operation priority

Arbeitsgemeinschaft *f.* working group, study group
Arbeitsgruppe *f.* task force
Arbeitskräfte *pl.* manpower
Arbeitskräftebedarf *m.* demand for employees
Arbeitskreis *m.* working group
Arbeitsleistung *f.* power
arbeitslos *adj.* out of work
Arbeitslosigkeit *f.* unemployment
Arbeitsmarkt *m.* labor market, job market
Arbeitsmedizin *f.* industrial medicine
Arbeitsnische *f.* carrel, cubicle
Arbeitsplatte *f.* work disk
Arbeitsplatz *m.* workplace
Arbeitsplatzrechner *m.* desktop computer, personal computer, work station
Arbeitsprogramm *n.* program, agenda
Arbeitsprozeß *m.* working process
Arbeitsraum *m.* study room
Arbeitsrecht *n.* labor law
Arbeitsregister *n.* working register
Arbeitsspeicher *m.* working storage
Arbeitsspur *f.* work track
Arbeitsstelle *f.* employment
Arbeitsstudie *f.* operation analysis
Arbeitsstunde *f.* man-hour
Arbeitstag *m.* work day
Arbeitstechnik *f.* working technique
Arbeitsteil *m.* working set
Arbeitsumgebung *f.* working environment

Arbeitsvertrag *m.* employment contract
Arbeitsvorbereitung *f.* operations scheduling
Arbeitsvorgänge *pl.* procedures
Arbeitsvorschlag *m.* flow proposal
Arbeitsweise *f.* operating characteristic, operating mode
Arbeitszeit *f.* working hours
Arbeitszufriedenheit *f.* job satisfaction
Archäologie *f.* archeology
Architektur *f.* architecture
Architekturgeschichte *f.* architecural history
Archiv *n.* archive, archives, public record office, record office
Archiv *n.* **der Jesuiten** Jesuit archive
Archiv *n.* **einer Glaubensgemeinschaft** religious body archive
Archivalien *pl.* archival documents, archivalia
Archivar *m.* archivist
archivarisch *adj.* archival
Archivbeamter *m.* archive officer
Archivbestand *m* archive collection
Archivbibliothek *f.* books preserving library, depository library
Archivexemplar *n.* last copy
Archivfilm *m.* archival film, permanent record film
Archivgut *n.* archival function, archivalia, archive material, archives
archivieren *vrb.* archive/to

Archivierungsart *f.* archive type
Archivierungsprozedur *f.* archive procedure
Archivkunde *f.* archival science
Archivmaterial *n.* archive material
Archivquelle *f.* archival source
Archivverwaltung *f.* archives administration
Archivwesen *n.* archivistics
Archivwissenschaft *f.* archive science
Argument *n.* argument
Argumentenverzeichnis *n.* argument list
arithmetische Operation *f.* arithmetic operation
arithmetische Relation *f.* arithmetic relation
arithmetischer Ausdruck *m.* arithmetic expression
arithmetischer Befehl *m.* arithmetic instruction, arithmetical instruction
arithmetischer Operand *m.* arithmetic operand, arithmetic operator
arithmetisches Mittel *n.* arithmetic mean
arithmetisches Unterprogramm *n.* arithmetic subroutine
Arnesen-Klassifikation *f.* Arnesen classification
Art *f.* kind, way
Artefakt *n.* artifact
Artikel *m.* article, determiner, item
Artikelstammdatei *f.* item master file
ärztliches Attest *n.* health certificate

aspektgestütztes Verfahren n.
aspect-based method
Aspektklassifikation f. aspect
classification
Assembler m. assembler, assembly program
assemblieren vrb. assemble/to
Assembliersprache f. assembly
language
Assistenz f. assistantship
Assoziation f. association, federation
Assoziationsrelation f. associative relation
assoziative Indexierung f. associative indexing
Assoziativprozessor m. associative processor
Assoziativspeicher m. associative memory, associative
storage, content-addressable
memory
Astronautik f. astronautics
Astronomie f. astronomy
Astrophysik f. astrophysics
asymetrischer Fehlerbereich m.
range of unbalanced error
asymmetrisch adj. asymmetric
asynchron adj. asynchronous
asynchrone Übertragung f. a-
synchronous transmission
Atlanten pl. cartographic
material
Atlas m. atlas
Atlasformat n. atlas size
Atomtechnik f. nuclear technology
Attribut n. attribute
attributive Beziehung f. attributive relation
Attributwert m. attribute
value

Attributzeichen n. attribute
character
audiovisuelle Hilfsmittel pl.
audio-visual aids
audiovisuelle Materialien pl.
AV materials
audiovisuelle Medien pl.
audio-visual media
audiovisuelles Dokument n.
audio-visual document
audiovisuelles Material n.
audio-visual material
audiovisuelles Zentrum n.
audio-visual center
auf dem neuesten Stand up-
to-date
auf dem neuesten Stand halten
vrb. keep up-to-date/to
auf den neuesten Stand bringen vrb. keep up-to-date/to
auf Lager in stock
auf Null setzen vrb. zero
out/to
aufbauen vrb. build/to, set up
/to
Aufbereitung f. processing
aufbewahren vrb. keep/to
Aufbewahrungsfrist f. retention period
Aufdruck m. imprint
aufdrucken vrb. appose/to
auffangen vrb. trap/to
Auffangvorrichtung f. trap
Auffassung f. conception
Aufforderung f. interrogation
auffrischen vrb. refresh/to
Auffüllen n. padding
auffüllen vrb. pad/to,
replenish /to
Auffüllzeichen n. pad
character
Aufgabe f. mission, task

Aufgabenbefehl *m.* task command

aufgabenbezogener Thesaurus *m.* mission-oriented thesaurus

aufgabenspezifische Datenstation *f.* job-oriented terminal

Aufgabenverwaltung *f.* job management

aufgegangen in absorbed by

aufgezeichnet *adj.* recorded

aufgezeichnete Information *f.* recorded information

Aufhängen *n.* hang-up

aufheben *vrb.* revoke/to

aufklärende Reihenfolge *f.* helpful sequence

Aufkleber *m.* adhesive label, label

Auflage *f.* circulation, edition, impression

Auflagenhöhe *f.* edition size, issue

Auflagenkontrolle *f.* circulation control

Auflageplatte *f.* planishing plate

auflisten *vrb.* list/to

Auflösung *f.* resolution

Auflösungszeit *f.* resolution time

Aufnahme *f.* entry, posting, affiliation

Aufnahme *f.* **mit Fortsetzungskarte** open entry

Aufnahmeformular *n.* application card

Aufnahmegerät *n.* recorder

Aufnahmetechnik *f.* recording technique

Aufnahmevermerk *m.* admission record

Aufruf *m.* invitation, invocation

aufrufen *vrb.* initiate/to, invite /to, invoke/to, poll/to

Aufrufsliste *f.* invitation list

Aufrufsverzögerung *f.* invitation delay

Aufrufwiederholung *f.* bid retry

aufrunden *vrb.* half-adjust/to

Aufrundung *f.* half correction

Aufsatz *m.* article, essay

Aufsatzkatalog *m.* analytical catalog

aufschalten *vrb.* offer/to

aufschieben *vrb.* adjourn/to

Aufschlagsstärkeregler *m.* impression indicator

Aufsichtskopie *f.* opaque copy

aufspalten *vrb.* split/to

aufsteigende Sortierung *f.* grade up

aufstellen *vrb.* station/to

Aufstellordnung *f.* **einer Bibliothek** arrangement of a library

Aufstellplatz *m.* book stand, display stand

Aufstellung *f.* installation

Aufstellung *f.* **nach dem Format** arrangement by size, classification by size

aufteilen *vrb.* apportion/to

Aufteilung *f.* apportionment

Auftrag *m.* job, order, task

Auftragsabfolge *f.* job sequence, job stream

Auftragsabfrage *f.* order inquiry

Auftragsabrechnung *f.* job accounting

Auftragsabwicklung *f.* order processing

Auftragsanweisung *f.* job description

Auftragsbeginn *m.* job begin
Auftragsbegleitdokument *n.*
job control document
Auftragsbestand *m.* order file
Auftragseingang *m.* order
entry
Auftragsende *n.* job end
Auftragskennzeichen *n.* job
identification
Auftragsleistung *f.* job subject
Auftragsmenge *f.* quantity ordered
Auftragsnummer *f.* order
number
Auftragspriorität *f.* order priority
Auftragsprotokoll *n.* job
logging
Auftragssteuersatz *m.* order
record
Auftragssteuerung *f.* job controlling, task control
Auftragssteuerungsinformation *f.* job control information
Auftragsstufe *f.* job step
Auftragsverwaltungsprogramm *n.* job scheduler
Auftreten *n.* occurrence
Aufwand *m.* overhead
aufwärtsgerichteter Pfeil *m.*
up-arrow
aufwickeln *vrb.* wind up/to
aufzählende Bibliographie *f.*
enumerative bibliography
aufzählende Klassifikation *f.*
enumerative classification
aufzählende Notation *f.* enumerative notation, fenced
notation
Aufzeichnen *n.* logging, recording
aufzeichnen *vrb.* log/to, note

/to, record/to
Aufzeichnung *f.* history, record
Aufzeichnungsdichte *f.* record
density, recording density
Aufzeichnungseinrichtung *f.*
recording device
Aufzeichnungsfeld *n.* recording area
Aufzeichnungsverfahren *n.*
method of marking, mode of
recording
Augenblick *m.* moment
Auktion *f.* auction
Auktionator *m.* auctioneer
Auktionskatalog *m.* auction
catalog
Ausarbeitung *f.* elaboration
ausbauen *vrb.* upgrade/to
Ausbeute *f.* yield
ausbilden *vrb.* qualify/to
Ausbilder *m.* trainer, instructor
Ausbildung *f.* training,
instruction, education
Ausbildungsbeihilfe *f.* education grant
Ausbildungsjahre *pl.* apprenticeship
Ausbildungskurs *m.* training
course
Ausbildungsmethode *f.*
training method
Ausbildungsplan *m.* training
schedule
Ausbildungsstätte *f.* training
center
Ausbildungszeit *f.* apprenticeship
ausblenden *vrb.* blind out/to,
erase/to
Ausblendsignal *n.* guard signal
ausbreiten *vrb.* spread/to

Ausbreitung *f.* spread
Ausdruck *m.* expression, hard copy, print, printout
Ausdrucksweise *f.* phraseologie
Ausdruckzeit *f.* type-out time
Ausfall *m.* breakdown, failure, outage, wearout failure
Ausfallquote *f.* failure rate
Ausfallwahrscheinlichkeit *f.* probability of failure
Ausfallzeit *f.* fault time, unavailable time
Ausflug *m.* field trip
ausführbar *adj.* executable
ausführen *vrb.* execute/to, implement/to, perform/to
ausführliches Indexieren *n.* deep indexing
ausführliches Referat *n.* informative abstract
Ausführung *f.* implementation
Ausführungsbestimmungen *pl.* application instructions
Ausführungsprozessor *m.* execution processor
Ausführungsroutine *f.* action module
Ausführungszeit *f.* execution time
Ausgabe *f.* edition, issue, output, redaction, version
Ausgabe *f.* **auf Mikrofiche** microfiche edition
Ausgabe *f.* **letzter Hand** final authoritative edition
Ausgabe *f.* **ohne Anfrage** non-ask type
Ausgabeanforderung *f.* output request
Ausgabeanzeige *f.* output display

Ausgabeanzeiger *m.* output indicator
Ausgabebereich *m.* output area, output block, output section
Ausgabebestimmung *f.* output specification
Ausgabecode *m.* outbound code
Ausgabedatei *f.* output file
Ausgabedaten *pl.* output data
Ausgabedatum *n.* date of issue
Ausgabeeinheit *f.* output unit
Ausgabefolgenummer *f.* output sequence number
Ausgabeformat *n.* output format
Ausgabeformatierung *f.* output formatting
Ausgabeformatspezifizierungsblatt *n.* output-format specification sheet
Ausgabegerät *n.* output device, display unit
Ausgabegeschwindigkeit *f.* output rate
Ausgabeglied *n.* output element
Ausgabekapazität *f.* output capacity
Ausgabekennsatz *m.* output label
Ausgabeklasse *f.* output class
Ausgabekontrollzeichen *n.* output control character
Ausgabeliste *f.* output listing
Ausgabemodus *m.* output mode
Ausgabeoperation *f.* output operation
Ausgabeprogramm *n.* output program, output routine

Ausgabeprozeß *m.* output process
Ausgabepuffer *m.* output buffer
Ausgaberate *f.* output transfer rate
Ausgabesatz *m.* output record
Ausgabesignal *n.* output signal
Ausgabespeicher *m.* output storage
Ausgabesprache *f.* output language
Ausgabestatus *m.* output state
Ausgabetechnik *f.* display technique
Ausgabewarteschlange *f.* output queue, output work queue
Ausgabezeile *f.* output line
Ausgabezeit *f.* output time interval
Ausgang *m.* exit, output
Ausgang *m.* **bei Programmabbruch** abnormal termination exit
Ausgangskanal *m.* output channel
Ausgangskonfiguration *f.* output configuration
Ausgangsschnittstelle *f.* output interface
Ausgangssprache *f.* source language
Ausgangsstellung *f.* home, original position
ausgeben *vrb.* output/to, put/to
ausgebildeter Bibliothekar *m.* qualified librarian
ausgelaufen *adj.* year-to-date
ausgeliehen *adj.* issued, lent, on loan, out
ausgemalte Handschrift *f.* illu-

minated manuscript
ausgerichtet *adj.* oriented
ausgeschaltet *adj.* OFF status
ausgeschlossener Benutzer *m.* blacklisted user
ausgewählte Werke *pl.* collectanea, extracts
ausgezeichnet *adj.* classic
aushändigen *vrb.* hand over/to
Aushilfspersonal *n.* temporary personnel
Auskunft *f.* information desk, reference desk
Auskunftsapparat *m.* reference collection
Auskunftsbereich *m.* reference desk
Auskunftsbestand *m.* ready reference holdings
Auskunftsbibliothekar *m.* reference librarian
Auskunftsdienst *m.* reference service, information service
ausladen *vrb.* unload/to
auslagerbar *adj.* pageable
auslagern *vrb.* page out/to, swap out/to
Auslagerungsbereich *m.* swapping area
ausländische Bücher *pl.* books from abroad, foreign books
ausländische Materialien *pl.* foreign materials
Auslandsinformationsdienst *m.* foreign information service
auslassen *vrb.* ignore/to, omit/to
Auslassungen *pl.* misses
Auslassungspunkte *pl.* omission marks
Auslastung *f.* usage

Auslastungsgrad *m.* activity level

auslaufen *vrb.* run out/to

Ausleihbeschränkung *f.* circulation restriction

Ausleihbestand *m.* lending collection, lending stock, loan collection

Ausleihbestimmungen *pl.* circulation rules

Ausleihbetrieb *m.* circulation work, loans work

Ausleihbibliothek *f.* circulating library, loan library

Ausleihdatum *n.* date of borrowing

Ausleihe *f.* circulation, circulation work, delivery room, home lending, loan

Ausleihe *f.* **des internen Bestandes** internal stock circulation

Ausleihe erneuern *vrb.* extend/to a loan

Ausleihe zurückbuchen *vrb.* cancel/to a loan, discharge/to books

ausleihen *vrb.* charge/to out, circulate/to, issue/to, lend/to, loan/to

Ausleiher *m.* lender

Ausleihkartei *f.* charging file, circulation file, circulation record, loan record

Ausleihkontrolle *f.* circulation control

Ausleihregister *n.* circulation record, loan register

Ausleihschätzung *f.* lending survey

Ausleihstatistik *f.* circulation statistics, issue statistic

Ausleihsystem *n.* issuing system

Ausleihtheke *f.* lending desk, open counter

Ausleihverbuchung *f.* charge, charging

Ausleihverbuchungssystem *n.* charging system

Ausleihverfahren *n.* loan system, lending system

Ausleihvorgang *m.* circulation transaction

Auslesen *n.* read out

auslesen *vrb.* read out/to

Auslesesteuerung *f.* read out control

ausliefern *vrb.* deliver/to

Auslieferungsliste *f.* item match list

Auslöseimpuls *m.* trigger

auslösen *vrb.* impulse/to, raise/

Auslösetaste *f.* release bar

ausmalen *vrb.* illuminate/to

Ausmalung *f.* **einer Handschrift** illumination

Ausnahmebedingung *f.* exception

ausrangieren *vrb.* discard/to, dispose/to, write off/to

Ausrichtbereich *n.* alignment area

ausrichten *vrb.* adjust/to, justify/to, orient /to

Ausrichtung *f.* alignment, bias, justification, orientation

Ausrichtungsfehler *m.* misalignment

ausschalten *vrb.* switch off/to

Ausscheiden *n.* disposal

ausscheiden *vrb.* discard/to, dispose/to

Ausscheidungsverfahren *n.* check out routine

Ausschießen *n.* imposition
ausschießen *vrb.* impose/to
Ausschießschema *n.* imposing
scheme
ausschleusen *vrb.* let out/to
ausschließen *vrb.* justify/to
Ausschließzone *f.* hot zone
Ausschlußbeziehung *f.* negative relation
Ausschlußrelation *f.* negative
relation
Ausschlußzeile *f.* omit line
Ausschnitt *m.* window
Ausschnittarchiv *n.* clipping
archive
Ausschreibung *f.* call for tender
Ausschreibungsunterlagen *pl.*
bid documents
Ausschuß *m.* discards, junk
aussondern *vrb.* relegate/to
Aussonderung *f.* deacquisition,
relegation
aussortieren *vrb.* weed/to
Ausstattung *f.* get-up, equipment
Ausstellung *f.* exhibition
Ausstellungskatalog *m.* exhibition catalog
Ausstellungssammlung *f.* exhibition collection
Aussteuerungsgrenze *f.* limiting level
ausstreichen *vrb.* cancel/to,
cross out/to
Austastlücke *f.* blanking interval
Austausch *m.* exchange, removal, replacement
austauschbar *adj.* replaceable
austauschbares Zubehör *n.* interchangeable accessory
Austauschbarkeit *f.* interchangeability

austauschen *vrb.* remove/to,
replace/to, substitute/to,
swap/to
Austauschformat *n.* communication format, interchange
format, exchange format
Austauschmagnetband *n.*
exchange magnetic tape
austesten *vrb.* check out/to,
debug/to
australisches MARC *n.* AUSMARC
Auswahl *f.* digest, option,
selection
Auswahlbibliographie *f.* selected bibliography, selective
bibliography
Auswahlcode *m.* option code
Auswählen *n.* selecting
auswählen *vrb.* select/to
Auswahlfeld *n.* selection field
Auswahlfunktion *f.* selectable
function
Auswahlgruppe *f.* select group
Auswahlkatalog *m.* selection
catalog
Auswahlkatalogisierung *f.* selective cataloging
Auswahlmöglichkeiten *pl.* options
Auswahlnummer *f.* option
number
Auswahlprüfung *f.* selection
check
Auswahlschritt *m.* selection step
Auswahlstift *m.* selector pen
Auswahlverzeichnis *n.* selective list
Auswahlzeit *f.* selection time
auswärtige Quelle *f.* outside
source
auswärtiger Benutzer *m.* out-

side user
auswärtiger Bibliotheksbenutzer *m.* external reader, nonresident reader
auswärtiger Leihverkehr *m.* country circulation, country lending, interlibrary lending, interlibrary loan, interurban circulation, interurban lending
Ausweichbetriebsprozedur *f.* backup operating procedure
Ausweichmagazin *n.* auxiliary stack
Ausweichschulbibliothek *f.* alternative school library
Ausweis *m.* badge
Ausweiskarte *f.* badge
Ausweisleser *m.* badge reader
Ausweisnummer *f.* badge number
Ausweisschutz *m.* badge security
Ausweisspalte *f.* badge column
Ausweitungsfähigkeit *f.* expandability
auswerfen *vrb.* eject/to
Auswertung *f.* report
Auswertungsformular *n.* answer sheet, scoring sheet
Auswertungsmethode *f.* analysis method
Auswirkung *f.* impact
Auswurfsmenge *f.* dropping fraction
auszählen *vrb.* tally/to
Auszubildender *m.* apprentice, learner
Außenmagazin *n.* repository library
Außenstelle *f.* remote installation, remote location, satellite station
außer Betrieb *m.* out of order, out of work
außerbetriebliches System *n.* out plant system
äußere Form *f.* outer form
authentisch *adj.* authentic
Autobiograph *m.* autobiographer
Autobiographie *f.* autobiography
autobiographisch *adj.* autobiographic
Autobücherei *f.* book automobile, book car, book library, book mobile library, book wagon, bookmobile, mobile library
Autogramm *n.* autograph
Autograph *n.* autograph
Autographie *f.* autography
Automation *f.* automation
automatisch *adj.* automatic
automatisch erstelltes Referat *n.* auto abstract
automatisch erstelltes Register *n.* auto index
automatisch zentriert *adj.* auto centred
automatische Aktualisierung *f.* computerized updating
automatische Begriffskontrolle *f.* automatic term control
automatische Buchauslieferung *f.* automatic book delivery
automatische Datenbearbeitung *f.* automatic data editing
automatische Dateneingabe *f.* automatic data input
automatische Datenverarbei-

tung *f.* automated data processing, automatic data processing

automatische Erzeugung *f.* **von Varianten** automatic variant generation

automatische Formatierung *f.* automatic formatting

automatische Indexierung *f.* auto indexing, automatic indexing

automatische Klassifikation *f.* automatic classification

automatische Korrektur *f.* automatic correction

automatische Laufwerksteuerung *f.* automatic routing

automatische Programmierung *f.* automatic programming

automatische Rechercheoptimierung *f.* automatic query adjustment

automatische Referaterstellung *f.* automatic abstracting, auto extracting

automatische Rückverfolgung *f.* backtracking method

automatische Rufbeantwortung *f.* auto answering

automatische Sacherschließung *f.* automatic subject indexing

automatische Satzextraktion *f.* automatic sentence extraction

automatische Schlüsselerzeugung *f.* automatic key generation

automatische Selektion *f.* mechanical selection

automatische Sicherung *f.* automatic backup

automatische Spracherkennung *f.* automatic voice recognition

automatische Textanalyse *f.* automatic text analysis

automatische Textverarbeitung *f.* automatic text processing

automatische Thesauruserstellung *f.* automatic thesaurus construction

automatische Übersetzung *f.* automatic translation

automatische Überwachung *f.* computerized monitoring

automatische Verlängerung *f.* self-renewal

automatische Verteilung *f.* automatic dissemination

automatische Wortwiederholung *f.* automatic word link

automatischer Ablauf *m.* automatic process

automatischer Befehl *m.* automatic command

automatischer Prüfgang *m.* automatic revision

automatischer Rückruf *m.* automatic recall

automatischer Speicher *m.* automatic storage

automatischer Vorschub *m.* automatic carriage

automatischer Wiederanlauf *m.* automatic restart

automatisches Ausleihverbuchungssystem *n.* automated circulation system

automatisches Bestellwesen *n.* automatic order generation, computerized ordering

automatisches Duplizieren *n.*
autoduplication, automatic
duplication

automatisches Einschalten *n.*
unattended operation

automatisches Feld *n.* automatic field

automatisches Fenster *n.*
power window

automatisches Springen *n.*
automatic skipping

automatisches Suchen *n.* automatic scan

automatisches Verbinden *n.*
auto link

automatisieren *vrb.* automate
/to

automatisiertes Bedienerprogramm *n.* automated operator

automatisiertes Microfichegerät *n.* automated microfiche
terminal

Automatisierung *f.* automation

Autor *m.* author

Autorenexemplar *n.* author's
copy

Autorenkatalog *m.* author catalog

Autorenkorrektur *f.* author's
correction

Autorennormdatei *f.* author
authority file

Autorenreferat *n.* author abstract, author's abstract, synopsis

Autorenregister *n.* author
index

Autorenschaft *f.* authorship

autorisierte Ausgabe *f.* authorized edition

autorisierte Benutzerrechte *pl.*
authorized rights of use

autorisierte Bibliothek *f.* authorized library

autorisierte Version *f.* authorized version

autorisierter Benutzer *m.* authorized user

autorisiertes Programm *n.* authorized program

Autorisierung *f.* authorization

Autorisierungsprüfung *f.* authorization checking

B

B-Baum *m.* balanced tree, b-tree
Back-End-Prozessor *m.* back-end processor
Bahn *f.* sheet
Balkendiagramm *n.* bar chart
Ballast *m.* noise
Ballastfaktor *m.* noise factor
Ballastquote *f.* noise ratio
Band *m.* volume, reel, tape
Bandanfang *m.* leading end
Bandanfangskennsatz *m.* volume label
Bandanfangsmarke *f.* beginning of tape marker
Bandanlauf *m.* tape start
Bandarchiv *n.* tape library
Bandaufnahme *f.* tape recording
Banddatei *f.* magnetic tape file, tape file
Banddiagramm *n.* band chart
Banddichte *f.* tape density
Bandeinheit *f.* tape unit
Bandendemarke *f.* end of tape marker
Bandendenbefestiger *m.* tape end retainer
Bandfehler *m.* tape error
Bandfehlstelle *f.* bad spot
Bandgeschwindigkeit *f.* tape speed
Bandkapazität *f.* reel capacity
Bandkassette *f.* tape cassette

Bandkatalog *m.* book catalog, bookform catalog, catalog in book-form, guard-book catalog, ledger catalog
Bandkennsatz *m.* header record
Bandlaufwerk *n.* tape deck, tape drive
Bandleser *m.* tape reader
Bandmarke *f.* tape mark
Bandnummer *f.* volume number
Bandrolle *f.* tape reel
Bandspeicher *m.* tape storage
Bandspule *f.* spool
Bandspur *f.* tape track
Bandsteuereinheit *f.* tape control
bandweise Kumulierung *f.* cumulative volume
Bandzahl *f.* number of volumes
Bankbibliothek *f.* bank library
Banknoten *pl.* notes
Bankwesen *n.* banking system
Banner *n.* banner, headline
Barfußbibliothekar *m.* barefoot librarian
Barrow-Verfahren *n.* Barrow method
Basis *f.* base
Basisadresse *f.* base address
Basisbezeichner *m.* base identifier

Basiscodierung *f.* basic coding
Basisdatenaustausch *m.* basic data exchange
Basiseintrag *m.* basic entry
Basisoperation *f.* basic operation
Basisregister *n.* base register, basic index, memory pointer
Basisspeicher *m.* basic storage
Basissystem *n.* basic system
Basiswerk *n.* core book
Basiszahl *f.* base number
Basiszugriffsmethode *f.* basic access method
Baud *n.* baud
Baugeschichte *f.* architectural history
Baugruppe *f.* assembly
Baum *m.* tree
Baumstruktur *f.* tree structure
Bauwesen *n.* architecture
beachten *vrb.* notice/to
beantworten *vrb.* respond/to
bearbeiten *vrb.* arrange/to, handle/to
Bearbeiter *m.* adapter, adaptor
bearbeitet nach *adj.* has been adapted from
Bearbeitung *f.* adaptation, handling
Bearbeitungsgebühr *f.* handling charge, processing fee
Bearbeitungszeit *f.* operation time, run time
Bearbeitungszettel *m.* process slip
beaufsichtigen *vrb.* attend/to
Beauftragter *m.* representative
Bedarf *m.* need
Bedarfsdeckung *f.* coverage of demand
Bedarfsuntersuchung *f.* demand study
Bedeutung *f.* meaning, significance
Bedeutungselement *n.* elementary term, isolate
Bedeutungsmaß *n.* importance measure
Bedeutungswandel *m.* semantic change
Bediener *m.* operator
Bedienerabsicherung *f.* operator security
Bedienerantwortfeld *n.* operator response field
Bedienerbefehl *m.* operator command
Bedienerbetrieb *m.* attended operation
Bedienereingabefeld *n.* operator input field
Bedienereingriff *m.* operator intervention
Bedienerführung *f.* operational guidance, operator guidance, prompting
Bedienerführungszeile *f.* prompt line
Bedienerhandbuch *n.* guide to operation
Bedienerhilfe *f.* help
Bedienerhilfemenu *n.* help menu
Bedienerhilfsanzeige *f.* help display
Bedienerkonsole *f.* operator control panel
bedienerloser Empfang *m.* unattended receive
bedienerloser Modus *m.* unattended mode

bedienerloses Drucken *n.* unattended printing
bedienerorientiertes System *n.* operator-oriented system
Bedienerplatz *m.* console
Bedienersteuerbefehl *m.* operator control command
Bedienersteuerfunktion *f.* operator control function
Bedienerzugriffscode *m.* operator´s access code
Bedienungsablauf *m.* operating procedure
Bedienungsanleitung *f.* instruction booklet, operations guide
Bedienungsanweisung *f.* operating instruction
Bedienungsfehler *m.* operating error
Bedienungshandbuch *n.* instruction manual
bedienungsloses Senden *n.* unattended transmit
bedingte Verzweigung *f.* conditional branch, conditional jump
bedingter Befehl *m.* conditional instruction
bedingter Halt *m.* optional stop
bedingter Programmstopp *m.* break point
bedingter Stoppbefehl *m.* optional pause instruction, optional stop instruction
Bedingung *f.* qualification, requirement
bedingungslos *adj.* unconditional
bedingungslose Tabelle *f.* unconditional table

Beeinflussungsbeziehung *f.* affective relation
beenden *vrb.* sign off/to, terminate/to
Beendigung *f.* termination
Befehl *m.* command, instruction, order, procedural statement
Befehlsabruf *m.* instruction fetch
Befehlsadresse *f.* address instruction
Befehlsanweisung *f.* instruction statement
Befehlsausführungsphase *f.* instruction execution
Befehlscode *m.* instruction code
Befehlsdecodierer *m.* instruction decoder
Befehlseinzelschritt *m.* instruction statement
Befehlsfolge *f.* control sequence
Befehlsfolgeregister *n.* instruction address register
befehlsgesteuert *adj.* command-driven
Befehlsliste *f.* instruction list
Befehlsprozessor *m.* instruction processor unit
Befehlsregister *n.* instruction register
Befehlssprache *f.* command language
Befehlsstruktur *f.* instruction format
Befehlsverarbeitungseinheit *f.* instruction processing unit
Befehlsverknüpfung *f.* pipelining
Befehlsvorrat *m.* instruction

repertoire, instruction set
Befehlswort *n.* instruction word
Befehlszähler *m.* instruction counter, program counter
befestigen *vrb.* mount/to
befördern *vrb.* upgrade/to
Befragung *f.* questioning, survey
befristeter Vertrag *m.* temporary contract
Beginn *m.* begin, start
Beginnanweisung *f.* begin statement
beginnen *vrb.* begin/to, start/to
Beginnzeichen *n.* answer signal
Beglaubigung *f.* certificate
begleitend *adj.* concomitant
begleitendes Selbstreferat *n.* homotopic abstract
Begleitmaterial *n.* accompanying material
begrenzen *vrb.* limit/to
Begrenzer *m.* limiter, separator
begrenzt *adj.* limited
begrenzte Auflage *f.* limited edition
begrenzte Austauschbarkeit *f.* limited interchangeability
begrenzte Zeilen *pl.* limited entry row
Begrenzung *f.* constraint
Begrenzungsadresse *f.* address limit
Begrenzungseinrichtung *f.* limiting facility
Begrenzungsknoten *m.* boundary node
Begrenzungszeichen *n.* delim-

iter character
Begrenzungszuordnung *f.* boundary alignment
Begriff *m.* concept, notion, term
begriffliche Darstellung *f.* conceptual representation
begriffliche Überschneidung *f.* notional overlap
begriffliches Verfahren *n.* conceptual method
Begriffsähnlichkeit *f.* term similarity
Begriffsanalyse *f.* concept analysis, conceptual analysis
Begriffsassoziation *f.* term association
Begriffsbestand *m.* extension by composition
Begriffsbestimmung *f.* definition
Begriffsbezeichnung *f.* feature heading
Begriffsdefinition *f.* concept definition
Begriffsdiskriminanzwert *m.* term discrimination value
Begriffseinschränkung *f.* definor
Begriffseinteilung *f.* concept organization
Begriffsextraktion *f.* term extraction
Begriffsgewichtung *f.* term weighting
Begriffshäufigkeit *f.* term frequency
Begriffsinhalt *m.* connotation, intension
Begriffsklasse *f.* category
Begriffsklassifikation *f.* term classification

Begriffskoordination *f.* concept co-ordination
Begriffsleiter *f.* chain, concept chain
Begriffsliste *n.* list of terms
begriffsorientierte Indexierung *f.* concept indexing
Begriffsposition *f.* term location
Begriffsreihe *f.* concept array
Begriffsrelation *f.* concept relation
Begriffsrelevanzfaktor *m.* term relevance factor
Begriffsspezifität *f.* term specificity
Begriffsumfang *m.* denotation, extension by resemblance, extension
Begriffsunabhängigkeit *f.* term independency
Begriffsverkettung *f.* term adjacency
Begriffsverschmelzung *f.* term conflation
Begriffswahl *f.* choice of terms
Begriffszeichen *n.* ideogram
Begutachtung *f.* appraisal, evaluation
Behälter *m.* box, case
Behandlung *f.* handling, treatment
behebbar *adj.* recoverable
Behörde *f.* authority
Behördenbibliothek *f.* administrative library
behördliche Datenverarbeitung *f.* administrative data processing
bei Endeangabe at end phrase
bei Endebedingung at end condition

beidseitige Datenübermittlung *f.* both-way communication
Beilage *f.* enclosure, insert, inset
Beiname *m.* nickname
Beiordnung *f.* addition, parataxis
Beirat *m.* advisory council
Beitrag *m.* contribution
Bekanntmachung *f.* announcement, notice
Belag *m.* layer
Belastbarkeit *f.* loading capacity
Belastung *f.* load
Beleg *m.* voucher
Belegdatum *n.* voucher date
belegen *vrb.* load/to, seize/to
Belegexemplar *n.* advertising copy, author´s copy, specimen copy
Belegexemplarabgabe *f.* specimen copy deposit
Belegleser *m.* mark reader
Belegnummer *f.* advertising copy
Belegsatz *m.* form set, voucher record
belegt *adj.* busy
belegt halten *vrb.* hold/to
Belegung *f.* load
Belegungsdichte *f.* file packing
Belegungsplan *m.* location chart
Belegvorschub *m.* incrementing, increment
belesen *adj.* book-read
beleuchten *vrb.* illuminate/to
beleuchtet *adj.* lighted
Beleuchtung *f.* illumination, lighting
Belletristik *f.* fiction, belles lettres

bemerken

bemerken *vrb.* notice/to
Bemerkung *f.* remark, comment
benachbarte Verbindungsstation *f.* adjacent link station
benachbarter Begriff *m.* adjacent term
benachbarter Kanal *m.* adjacent channel
benachrichtigen *vrb.* notify/to
Benachrichtigung *f.* notification
benannt *adj.* named
benannte Datei *f.* named file
benannte Konstante *f.* named constant
benannter gemeinsamer Speicherbereich *m.* named common block
benanntes System *n.* named system
benennen *vrb.* name/to
Benennung *f.* term
Benennungsbildung *f.* term formation
Benennungsliste *f.* term list
Benennungsregel *f.* naming convention
Benennungssystem *n.* nomenclature
BENUTZE-Verweis *m.* USE
Benutzer *m.* card holder, client, end user, identification card holder, patron, user, clientele
Benutzer-System-Interaktion *f.* user-system interaction
Benutzeranmeldung *f.* patron registration, reader registration
Benutzeranzahl *f.* user load
Benutzeraufwand *m.* user effort
Benutzerausbildung *f.* user training
Benutzerausweis *m.* library card
Benutzerautorisationskontrolle *f.* user security verification
Benutzerbedarf *m.* user demand
Benutzerbedürfnisse *pl.* user needs
Benutzerberatung *f.* advice to users
Benutzerberichtigung *f.* user authorization
Benutzerbeteiligung *f.* user participation
Benutzerbibliothek *f.* user library
Benutzerbibliotheksverzeichnis *n.* user library directory
Benutzercode *m.* authority code
Benutzerdatei *f.* patron registration file, registration file
Benutzerdaten *pl.* user data
Benutzerdatendatei *f.* user data file, user data set
benutzerdefiniert *adj.* user-defined
Benutzerfeld *n.* user field
Benutzerforschung *f.* user analysis
benutzerfreundlich. *adj.* easy-to-use, user friendly
Benutzerfreundlichkeit *f.* user friendliness
benutzergesteuert *adj.* user-driven
Benutzergewohnheiten *pl.* user habits

Benutzergruppe *f.* users
Benutzerhandbuch *n.* user guide, user manual
Benutzerhilfe *f.* user help desk
Benutzeridentifizierung *f.* user identification
Benutzerinformationsbedürfnis *n.* user information need
Benutzerinteresse *n.* user interest
Benutzerkarte *f.* admission card, identification card, patron registration card
Benutzerkartei *f.* application file, borrower's file, borrower's index, borrower's register
Benutzerkatalog *m.* public catalog, user catalog
Benutzerkennsatz *m.* user label
Benutzerkennung *f.* user identity
Benutzerklasse *f.* user class of service
Benutzerkontrolle *f.* user control
Benutzerkosten *pl.* user costs
Benutzerkreis *m.* users
Benutzermenu *n.* user menu
Benutzermerkmaldatei *f.* user attribute data set
Benutzernachricht *f.* information message
Benutzernachrichtentabelle *f.* user message table
Benutzername *m.* user name
Benutzernutzen *m.* user benefit
Benutzeroberfläche *f.* user interface
benutzerorientiert *adj.* user-

oriented
Benutzerprofil *n.* user profile
Benutzerrecht *n.* authority level
Benutzerrelevanzangabe *f.* user relevance response
Benutzerrelevanzquote *f.* acceptance rate
Benutzerschaft *f.* reading clientele
Benutzerschulung *f.* reader instruction, user education
Benutzerstatistik *f.* user statistics
Benutzerstudie *f.* user study
Benutzerterminal *n.* user terminal
Benutzertypen *pl.* user types
Benutzerumfrage *f.* user survey
Benutzerverhalten *n.* user behavior
Benutzerwunsch *m.* reader's request
Benutzerzeit *f.* available time
Benutzerzugriffsmodus *m.* user access mode
Benutzerzulassung *f.* reader admission
BENUTZT-FÜR-Verweis *m.* USED FOR
Benutzung *f.* use
Benutzungsanalyse *f.* usage analysis, use analysis
Benutzungsanweisung *f.* manual
Benutzungsbedingung *f.* usage condition
Benutzungserlaubnis *f.* **für Leser** admissiom of readers
Benutzungsfrequenz *f.* usage frequency

Benutzungsgebühren *pl.* user fees

Benutzungshäufigkeitsrangliste *f.* density of use ranking

Benutzungsstudie *f.* use study

Benutzungsverhältnis *n.* usage contract

Benutzungszeit *f.* billable time, meter time

Beobachtung *f.* observation

Beobachtungswert *m.* observed value

beraten *vrb.* advise/to

beratendes Gremium *n.* advisory panel

Berater *m.* consultant

Beratung *f.* advisory service, advice, conference

Beratungsausschuß *m.* advisory board

Beratungsstelle *f.* information center, advisory center

Beratungstätigkeit *f.* advisory work

berechnen *vrb.* calculate/to

Berechnung *f.* calculation, computation

berechtigen *vrb.* authorize/to

Berechtigung *f.* authority

Berechtigungscode *m.* authority code

Bereich *m.* area, array, range, scope

Bereich *m.* **einer Notation** area of notation

Bereichsadresse *f.* area address

Bereichsangabe *f.* inclusive notation

Bereichsbezeichnung *f.* area identification

Bereichsbibliothek *f.* regional library

Bereichsdefinition *f.* area definition

Bereichsgrenze *f.* area boundary

Bereichsinformationszentrum *n.* sectoral information center

Bereichskonzept *n.* area concept

Bereichsname *m.* area name

Bereichsprüfung *f.* range check

Bereichsüberschreitung *f.* overload

Bereichsvariable *f.* area variable

Bereichsvereinbarung *f.* array declaration

bereinigen *vrb.* bowdlerize/to, expurgate/to

bereinigte Ausgabe *f.* bowdlerized edition, expurgated edition

bereits erschienene Ausgaben back file, back issue, back numbers

Bereitschaft *f.* stand-by

Bereitschaftsanzeige *f.* ready indicator

Bereitschaftssystem *n.* stand-by system

bereitstellen *vrb.* provide/to, schedule/to

Bereitstellung *f.* allocation, supply, provision

Bergakademie *f.* mining academy

Bergbau *m.* mining industry

Bergbauhochschulbibliothek *f.* mining school library

Bericht *m.* listing, report, statement

Bericht *m.* **zum Stand der**

Technik state of the art report

Berichterstattung *f.* coverage

Berichterstellung *f.* report preparation

berichtigen *vrb.* amend/to, correct/to

Berichtigung *f.* amendment

Berichtsjahr *n.* year under review

Berichtszeile *f.* report line

Berner Urheberrechtsabkommen *n.* Berne convention

Berner Urheberrechtsvereinigung *f.* Berne copyright union

Berücksichtigung *f.* consideration

Beruf *m.* profession, occupation

Berufsaussicht *f.* professional prospect

Berufsbild *n.* job description

Berufsbildungszentrum *n.* professional training center

Berufserfahrung *f.* professional experience

Berufsethos *m.* professional ethics

Berufsgliederung *f.* occupational classification

Berufsinformationszentrum *n.* professional information center

Berufsschulbibliothek *f.* vocational school library, occupational school library

Berufsschule *f.* vocational school

Berufsverband *m.* professional association

Berufsverbandspublikation *f.* professional association publication

Berührungspunkt *m.* point of contact

berührungssensitiver Bildschirm *m.* touch-screen terminal

beschädigter Buchstabe *m.* bad letter, damaged letter

Beschaffung *f.* procurement, acquisition

Beschaffungspolitik *f.* procurement policy

Beschäftigung *f.* occupation, job, employment

Bescheinigung *f.* certificate

Beschleuniger *m.* accelerator

Beschleunigungsbegrenzer *m.* acceleration limiter

Beschleunigungszeit *f.* acceleration time

Beschluß *m.* resolution, decision

beschneiden *vrb.* trim/to

beschränkte Variable *f.* bounded variable

beschränkter Zugang *m.* restricted access

Beschränkung *f.* limitation

beschreibbar *adj.* writeable

beschreiben *vrb.* specify/to, write/to

beschreibende Statistik *f.* descriptive statistics

beschreibender Ausdruck *m.* aspect

Beschreibung *f.* description

Beschreibungsblatt *n.* specification sheet

beschriften *vrb.* inscribe/to

beschrifteter Anhänger *m.* labelled tag

Beschriftung *f.* lettering

Beschriftungsroutine *f.* an-

notation routine
Beschriftungsstelle *f.* imprint
position
Besetztzeichen *n.* busy signal
Besetzungsniveau *n.* staffing
level
besondere Anhängezahlen *pl.*
analytical subdivision
Besonderheit *f.* particularity,
peculiarity
Besprechung *f.* critical review
Bestand *m.* collection, holding,
population
Bestandsabdeckung *f.* collection coverage
Bestandsaktualität *f.* collection currency
Bestandsanalyse *f.* holding
analysis, collection analysis
Bestandsaufbau *m.* collection
development
Bestandsaufnahme *f.* making
an inventory
Bestandsbewertung *f.* collection evaluation
Bestandsdatei *f.* inventory file
Bestandsdatenbank *f.* inventory data base
Bestandsentwicklung *f.* collection development
Bestandsergänzung *f.* collection improvement
Bestandserschließung *f.* indexing
Bestandsfunktion *f.* survival
function
Bestandsgröße *f.* collection
size
Bestandskatalog *m.* collection
catalog
Bestandskontrolle *f.* stock
control

Bestandsliste *f.* holding list
Bestandsnachweis *m.* item
identification
Bestandsnummer *f.* collection
number
Bestandsnutzung *f.* collection
utilization
Bestandspflege *f.* collection
maintenance
Bestandspolitik *f.* selection
policy
Bestandsprofil *n.* collection
profile
Bestandsprüfung *f.* checking
Bestandsrelation *f.* whole-part relation
Bestandsrevision *f.* weeding,
stock revision
Bestandsschwerpunkt *m.* collection emphasis
Bestandstyp *m.* collection type
Bestandsüberschneidung *f.*
collection overlap
Bestandsumfang *m.* collection
size
Bestandsvermehrung *f.*
growth of stock
Bestandsverwaltung *f.* collection management
Bestandsverzeichnis *f.* collection guide, inventory
Bestandsvollständigkeit *f.* collection completeness
Bestandswachstum *n.* collection growth
Bestandswissenschaft *f.* collection science
Bestandszuwachs *m.* growth
of stock, increase of stock
Bestandteil *m.* component,
constituent
Bestandteil *m.* **einer Bezeich-**

nung component of a term, constituent term
bestätigte Ausgabe *f.* responded output
Bestätigung *f.* acknowledgement, approval
Bestellbestand *m.* quantity on order
Bestellbuch *n.* order book
Bestelldatei *f.* on-order file, orders-outstanding file
bestellen *vrb.* order/to
Bestellformular *n.* order form
Bestelliste *f.* on-order list
Bestellkarte *f.* order card
Bestellkatalog *m.* order catalog
Bestellkatalogisierung *f.* order cataloging
Bestellnachweis *m.* order record
Bestellpunkt *m.* order point
Bestellschein *m.* call card, call slip, card slip, reader´s slip
bestellte Menge *f.* quantity ordered
bestelltes Material *n.* material on order
Bestellung *f.* order
Bestellvordruck *m.* call card, order form
Bestellvorgang *m.* order procedures
Bestellwunsch *m.* order request, purchase suggestion
Bestellzeit *f.* ordering time
Bestellzettel *m.* call slip
bestimmt *adj.* assigned
Bestimmung *f.* statement
Bestseller *m.* bestseller
Bestzeitcodierung *f.* minimum delay coding

Bestzeitprogrammierung *f.* minimum access programming, minimum delay coding
Besuch *m.* attendance
Besucherkarte *f.* calling card
betätigen *vrb.* press/to
Beteiligung *f.* participation
betitelt. *adj.* entitled
betonen *vrb.* underline/to
betrachten *vrb.* view/to
Betrachtungseinheit *f.* item
Betrag *m.* amount
Betreff *m.* subject
betreiben *vrb.* operate/to
betreuen *vrb.* serve/to, attend/to
Betrieb *m.* plant
Betriebsarchiv *n.* company archive
Betriebsart *f.* mode of operation, mode, operating mode
Betriebsartenfeld *n.* mode field, mode level field
Betriebsartenregister *n.* mode register
Betriebsartenwähler *m.* mode selector
betriebsbereit *adj.* ready
Betriebsdaten *pl.* production data
betriebsintern *adj.* in-house
Betriebskosten *pl.* operating cost, operationals
Betriebsmittel *pl.* resource, facilities
Betriebsoptimum *n.* ideal capacity
Betriebsschloß *n.* key log
Betriebssprache *f.* operating language
Betriebsstatus *m.* operating state

Betriebssystem *n.* operating system

Betriebsweise *f.* mode of operation

Betriebswirtschaft *f.* business administration

betriebswirtschaftliche Hochschulbibliothek *f.* management school library

Betriebszeit *f.* attended time, operating time, operation time, uptime

Betriebszustandsanzeige *f.* mode indicator

Betriebszuverlässigkeit *f.* operational reliability

betrügerischer Zugang *m.* fraudulent access

Beurteilung *f.* judgement

Beutelbuch *n.* bag binding, binding with yapp edges

bevorrechtigter Befehl *m.* privileged command, privileged instruction

bewahren *vrb.* keep/to

bewegliche Aufstellung *f.* movable location

Beweglichkeit *f.* mobility

Bewegung *f.* transaction

Bewegungsdaten *pl.* transaction data

Bewegungsdatum *n.* transaction date

Bewegungshäufigkeit *f.* activity rate

Bewegungssatz *m.* transaction record

Bewerber *m.* applicant

Bewerbungsformular *n.* application blank, application form

bewerten *vrb.* evaluate/to, rate/to, score/to, validate/to

Bewertung *f.* appraisal, evaluation, rating

Bewertungsfaktor *m.* evaluation factor

Bewertungskennziffer *f.* evaluation measure

Bewertungsuntersuchung *f.* evaluation study

bezeichnen *vrb.* label/to, signify/to

Bezeichnung *f.* designation, identifier, label, term

Bezeichnung *f.* **einer Begriffsgruppe** group term

Bezeichnung *f.* **einer Einheit** identifying a unit

Bezeichnung *f.* **mit gleichem Begriffsinhalt** co-extensive term

Bezeichnungsweise *f.* notation

Beziehung *f.* link, relationship, relation

Beziehung *f.* **des Enthaltenseins** intrinsic relation

Beziehung *f.* **zwischen Klassen** class relation

Beziehungsanalyse *f.* relational analysis

Beziehungsindexierung *f.* relational indexing

Beziehungsindikator *m.* relation indicator

Beziehungsmerkmale *pl.* extrinsic characteristics

Beziehungsverbindung *f.* particle of relation

Beziehungszeichen *n.* relation character

beziffern *vrb.* allocate/to numbers

Bezirksarchiv *n.* county archive

Bezirksbibliothek *f.* county library, district library
Bezirksbücherei *f.* district library
Bezirksrechtsbibliothek *f.* county law library
bezogen auf based on
Bezugnahme *f.* reference
Bezugsadresse *f.* base address, reference address
Bezugsangabe *f.* refer option
Bezugsfeld *n.* reference field
Bezugskante *f.* guide edge
Bezugsmaß *n.* absolute dimension
Bezugsquellennachweis *m.* product directory
Bezugsschlüssel *m.* key of reference
Bezugszahl *f.* indicator
Bibliograph *m.* bibliographer
Bibliographie *f.* bibliography, enumerative bibliography
Bibliographie *f.* **der Bibliographien** bibliography of bibliographies
Bibliographieren *n.* bibliographic checking, bibliographic verification
bibliographisch *adj.* bibliographic
bibliographisch getreue Aufnahme *f.* full cataloging
bibliographisch getreue Titelaufnahme *f.* bibliographical cataloging
bibliographische Abfrage *f.* bibliographical inquiry
bibliographische Angaben *pl.* bibliographic citation
bibliographische Anleitung *f.* bibliographic instruction

bibliographische Annotation *f.* bibliographic note
bibliographische Auskunft *f.* bibliographical information
bibliographische Beschreibung *f.* bibliographic description, bibliographical description
bibliographische Datenbank *f.* bibliographic database
bibliographische Einheit *f.* bibliographic unit, bibliographical unit
bibliographische Ermittlung *f.* bibliographic verification
bibliographische Kontrolle *f.* bibliographic control
bibliographische Kopplung *f.* bibliographic coupling
bibliographische Quelle *f.* bibliographical resource
bibliographische Suchanfrage *f.* bibliographical inquiry
bibliographische Suche *f.* bibliographical inquiry
bibliographischer Dienst *m.* bibliographic service
bibliographischer Eintrag *m.* bibliographic entry
bibliographischer Führer *f.* bibliographical guide
bibliographischer Nachweis *m.* bibliographic reference
bibliographisches Element *n.* bibliographic element
bibliographisches Retrieval *n.* bibliographic retrieval
bibliographisches Verzeichnis *n.* bibliographical index
bibliographisches Zentrum *n.* bibliographical center
Bibliometrie *f.* bibliometrics
bibliometrische Verteilung *f.*

bibliometric distribution
Bibliophile *m.* bibliophile
Bibliothek *f.* library
Bibliothek *f.* **auf Rädern** mobile library
Bibliothek *f.* **der Akademie der Wissenschaften.** academy of sciences library
Bibliothek *f.* **der Aluminiumindustrie** aluminium industry library
Bibliothek *f.* **der Evangelisch-Lutherischen Kirche** Evangelical Lutheran Church library
Bibliothek *f.* **der juristischen Fakultät** law school library
Bibliothek *f.* **der Lutherischen Kirche** Lutheran Church Library
Bibliothek *f.* **der Methodistischen Kirche** Methodist Church Library
Bibliothek *f.* **der Mormonenkirche** Mormon Church Library
Bibliothek *f.* **der römisch-katholischen Kirche.** Roman Catholic Church Library
Bibliothek *f.* **der Streitkräfte** armed forces library
Bibliothek *f.* **des British Council** British Council Library
Bibliothek *f.* **des Heeres** army library
Bibliothek *f.* **des Königs** King's library
Bibliothek *f.* **einer Besserungsanstalt** correctional institution library
Bibliothek *f.* **einer Bildungseinrichtung** educational institution library
Bibliothek *f.* **einer gemeinnützigen Einrichtung** nonprofit organization library
Bibliothek *f.* **einer Glaubensgemeinschaft** religious body library
Bibliothek *f.* **einer Militärakademie** military academy library
Bibliothek *f.* **einer Pädagogischen Hochschule** teacher college library
Bibliothek *f.* **einer Realschule** middle school library
Bibliothek *f.* **einer Technischen Hochschule** polytechnic library
Bibliothek *f.* **einer theologischen Fakultät** theological school library
Bibliothek *f.* **eines botanischen Gartens** botanical garden library
Bibliothek *f.* **eines Jesuitenkollegs** Jesuit college library
Bibliothek *f.* **eines Junior-College** junior college library
Bibliothek *f.* **fremdsprachlicher Verlage** foreign language publisher's library
Bibliothek *f.* **mittlerer Größe** medium-sized library
Bibliothekar *m.* librarian
bibliothekarische Einkaufszentrale *f.* library supply agency
bibliothekarische Fachkenntnis *f.* library skill
bibliothekarische Fachzeitschrift *f.* library periodical
bibliothekarische Klassifikation *f.* library classification

Bibliothekarsverband *m.* librarian association
Bibliotheksangestellter *m.* library clerk
Bibliotheksarbeit *f.* library work
Bibliotheksassistent *m.* assistant librarian
Bibliotheksaufgaben *pl.* function of the library
Bibliotheksausbildung *f.* library education
Bibliotheksausschuß *m.* library board, library committee
Bibliotheksausstattung *f.* library equipment
Bibliotheksautomatisierung *f.* automation of library, library automation
Bibliotheksbau *m.* library building
Bibliotheksbeleuchtung *f.* lighting of the library
Bibliotheksbenutzer *m.* library user
Bibliotheksbenutzung *f.* library use
Bibliotheksberater *m.* library consultant
Bibliotheksbestand *f.* library collection, library stock
Bibliotheksbewertung *f.* library evaluation
Bibliotheksdienst *m.* library service
Bibliotheksdirektor *m.* chief librarian, director of library, head librarian
Bibliothekseinführung *f.* library orientation
Bibliothekseinrichtung *f.* library equipment

Bibliotheksetat *m.* library budget
Bibliotheksforschung *f.* library research
Bibliotheksführung *f.* library tour
Bibliotheksfunktion *f.* library function
Bibliotheksgebäude *n.* library building
Bibliotheksgebühr *f.* library charge, library fee
Bibliotheksgehilfe *m.* attendant
Bibliotheksgeschichte *f.* library history
Bibliotheksgesetz *n.* library act
Bibliotheksinformation *f.* library information
Bibliotheksinformationssystem *n.* library information system
Bibliotheksinstitut *n.* library institute
Bibliothekskatalog *m.* catalog
Bibliotheksklassifikation *f.* bibliographical classification, book classification, library classification
Bibliothekskommission *f.* library commission
Bibliothekskonferenz *f.* library conference
Bibliothekskongreß *m.* library congress
Bibliotheksleiter *m.* chief librarian
Bibliotheksmanager *m.* library manager
Bibliotheksmaterial *n.* library material
Bibliotheksmitarbeiter *pl.* library staff

Bibliotheksname *m.* library name

Bibliotheksnetz *n.* library network

Bibliotheksnetzwerk *n.* library network

Bibliotheksnorm *f.* library standard

Bibliotheksoption *f.* library option

Bibliotheksordnung *f.* library regulation, library rules

Bibliotheksorganisation *f.* library organization

Bibliothekspersonal *n.* library personnel

Bibliotheksplanung *f.* library planning

Bibliothekspolitik *f.* library policy

Bibliotheksprogramm *n.* library subroutine

Bibliotheksrat *m.* library council

Bibliotheksrechenzentrum *n.* library computer center

Bibliotheksrecht *n.* library legislation

Bibliotheksschule *f.* library school

Bibliotheksschule *f.* **für Graduierte** graduate library school

Bibliotheksstandard *m.* library standard

Bibliotheksstatistik *f.* library statistics

Bibliothekssystem *n.* library system

Bibliothekstechnik *f.* library technology

Bibliothekstechniker *m.* library technician

Bibliothekstypen *pl.* kinds of libraries

Bibliotheksumfrage *f.* library survey

Bibliotheksverband *m.* library association

Bibliotheksverbund *m.* library network

Bibliotheksvergleich *m.* interlibrary comparison

Bibliotheksverwaltung *f.* library administration, library management

Bibliotheksverwaltungsrat *m.* library trustees

Bibliotheksverzeichnis *n.* library directory

Bibliothekswahl *f.* choice of library

Bibliothekswartung *f.* library maintenance

Bibliothekswerbung *f.* library publicity

Bibliothekswesen *n.* librarianship

Bibliothekswirtschaft *f.* library economy

Bibliothekswissenschaft *f.* library science

Bibliothekszweigstelle *f.* branch library

Bibliotherapie *f.* bibliotherapy

bidirektionaler Drucker *m.* reverse printer

bieten *vrb.* bid/to

Bild *n.* image, picture

Bild *n.* **abwärts** roll down

Bild *n.* **aufwärts** roll up

Bildabfragesprache *f.* pictorial query language

Bildagentur *f.* picture agency

Bildarchiv *n.* photo archive,

iconographic archive, picture archive, picture library, video archiv
Bildarchivierung f. picture archiving
Bildaufzeichnung f. video recording
Bildausgabe f. video display
Bildbereich m. image area
Bildbeschreibung f. iconography
Bildbestand m. picture collection
Bilddatenbank f. image database, pictorial database
Bilddokument n. iconic document
Bilddurchlauf m. rolling
Bildelement n. picture element
bilden vrb. build/to
Bilderbuch n. picture book, easy book
Bildergeschichten pl. comic strips
Bilderschrift f. pictography
Bildfeld n. image area
Bildgenerator m. video generator
Bildindex m. picture index
Bildinhalt m. image content
Bildkommunikation f. image communication
Bildleser m. video scanner
Bildmarke f. blip
Bildmodus m. image mode
Bildplatte f. optical disk, optical videodisk, videodisk
Bildpunkt m. pixel
Bildsammlung f. picture collection
Bildschirm m. CRT terminal, cathode-ray tube, display

screen, monitor, screen, video display unit, video display, video screen, video terminal
Bildschirmarbeitsplatz m. video work-station
Bildschirmart f. monitor type
Bildschirmauflösung f. screen resolution
Bildschirmaufteilung f. screen layout
Bildschirmausgabe f. soft copy
Bildschirmdiagonale f. screen diagonal
Bildschirmeinheit f. display, graphic device
Bildschirmentwurf m. screen design
Bildschirmfeld n. screen field
Bildschirmfenster n. screen window
Bildschirmformat n. display format, map, screen image
Bildschirmhandhabung f. screen handling
bildschirmorientiert adj. screen-based
Bildschirmraster n. screen pattern
Bildschirmsatz m. screen record
Bildschirmtext m. viewdata
Bildspeicher m. image storage, view storage
Bildtaste f. roll key
Bildtelephon n. video telephone
Bildübertragung f. image transmission
Bildung f. education
Bildungsfernsehen n. educational broadcasting, educational television

Bildungsforschung f. educational research
Bildungspolitik f. educational policy
Bildungsstätte f. educational institution
Bildungstheorie f. educational theory
Bildungswesen n. education system
Bildungszentrum f. education center
Bildunterschrift f. caption, legend
Bildverarbeitung f. image processing
Bildwörterbuch n. illustrated dictionary
Bildzeichen n. graphical symbol
Bildzerleger m. image dissector
Bildzerlegung f. image dissection
Billett n. billet
billig abgeben vrb. remainder/to
binär adj. binary
binär klassifizieren vrb. dichotomize/to
Binäranzeige f. binary display
Binärausgabeeinheit f. binary output unit
Binärcode m. binary code
binärcodierte Darstellung f. binary-coded notation
binärcodierte Dezimalziffern-darstellung f. binary-coded decimal code
binäre Deskriptorgewichtung f. binary term weighting
Binäreingabeeinheit f. binary input unit
Binärelement n. binary element
Binärelementenkette f. binary element string
binärer Überlauf m. binary overflow
binäres Zeitintervall n. binary time interval
Binärfeld n. binary item
Binärindexierung f. binary indexing
Binärinstruktion f. binary instruction
Binärklassifikation f. dichotomized classification
Binärkomma n. binary point
Binärnull f. binary zero
Binäroperation f. binary operation
Binäroperator m. binary operator
Binärschreibweise f. binary notation, binary recording mode
Binärsignal n. binary signal
Binärsteuerung f. binary control
Binärsuche f. binary search
Binärsystem n. binary notation, binary scale, binary system
Binärzahl f. binary number, binary numeral
Binärzähler m. binary counter
Binärzeichen n. binary character, binary element
Binärziffer f. binary digit, bit
Binden n. binding
Bindeprogramm n. link editor
Binder m. linker
Bindestrich m. hyphen

Binnenhandel *m.* home trade, domestic trade
Binnenmarkt *m.* home market
Binomialverteilung *f.* binomial distribution
bio-bibliographischer Katalog *m.* bio-bibliographical catalog
Biobibliographie *f.* author bibliography, bio-bibliography
Biochemie *f.* biochemistry
Biograph *m.* biographer
Biographie *f.* biography
Biographierte *m.* biographee
biographisch *adj.* biographical, biographic
biographische Daten *pl.* biographical data
biographisches Archiv *n.* biography file
biographisches Lexikon *n.* biographic lexicon
Biologie *f.* biology
Biomedizin *f.* biomedicine
Biophysik *f.* biophysics
Biotechnik *f.* biotechnology
bischöfliche Bibliothek *f.* episcopal library
Bit *n.* binary digit, bit
Bitdichte *f.* bit density
Bitfolgensuche *f.* bit string searching
Bitkombination *f.* bit combination
bitparallel *adj.* parallel by bit
Bitposition *f.* bit position
Bitstelle *f.* bit position
Bitstrom *m.* bit stream
Bitverarbeitung *f.* bit manipulation
Bitzuordnung *f.* bit assignment
Black Box *f.* black box

Blankopapier *n.* blank paper
Blatt *n.* leaf, sheet
blätterfähig *adj.* scrollable
blättern *vrb.* browse/to, page/to, scroll/to
Blattformular *n.* paper form
Blattmagazin *n.* paper cassette
Blattnumerierung *f.* foliation
Blattspender *m.* paper dispenser
Blattzahl *f.* foliation, leaf number
Blaupause *f.* blue print
Bleisatz *m.* hot type, lead typesetting, letterpress composition
Bleistift *m.* pencil
Blickkontrolle *f.* peek-a-boo
Blindband *m.* blank dummy
Blindenbibliothek *f.* library for the blind
Blindenbücherei *f.* braille library
Blindenhörbücherei *f.* sound library for the blind
Blindenschrift *f.* braille
Blindfeld *n.* dummy field
Blindmaterial *n.* leading
Blindpressung *f.* blind blocking
Blindstrom *m.* idle current
blinken *vrb.* blink/to
Blinkfeld *n.* blink field
Block *m.* block, pad
Blockadresse *f.* block address
Blockanzahl *f.* block count
Blockdiagramm *n.* block diagram
blocken *vrb.* block/to
Blockgröße *f.* block size
Blockheftung. *f.* flat stiching
Blockindexierung *f.* block indexing

Blocklänge *f.* block length
Blockmultiplexverarbeitung *f.*
block multiplexing
Blockprozessor *m.* block
processor
Blockprüfung *f.* block check
Blockprüfzeichen *n.* block
check character
Blockschrift *f.* block letters,
handprinting
Blocksicherungsverfahren *n.*
block securing
Blockübertragung *f.* block
transfer
Blockung *f.* blocking
Blockungsfaktor *m.* blocking
factor
blockweise *adj.* block by block
Blockzeichen *n.* block
character
Blockzeitbegrenzung *f.* block
time out
Boden *m.* bottom
Bogen *m.* gathering
Bogenformat *n.* folio
Bogensatz *m.* gathering
Bogenzählung *f.* numbering of
sections
Boolesch *adj.* Boolean, logical
Boolesche Algebra *f.* Boolean
algebra
Boolesche Disjunktion *f.* logi-
cal disjunct
Boolesche Funktion *f.* Boolean
function
Boolesche Komplementierung
f. Boolean complementation
Boolesche Logik *f.* Boolean
logic
Boolesche Operation *f.*
Boolean operation
Boolescher Ausdruck *m.*

Boolean expression, logical
expression
Boolescher Faktor *m.* Boolean
factor, logical factor
Boolescher Operand *m.* logical
operand
Boolescher Operator *m.*
Boolean operator, logical
operator
Boolescher Wert *m.* logical
value
Boolesches Datenfeld *n.*
Boolean data item
Boolesches Retrieval *n.*
Boolean retrieval
Boolesches Zeichen *n.* Boolean
character
Bottom-up Suche *f.* bottom-up
search
Boulevardpresse *f.* yellow
press
Boulevardzeitschrift *f.* yellow
journal
Bradfords Gesetz *n.* **der**
Streuung Bradford´s law of
scatter
Branchenschlüssel *m.* industry
code
Brandschutz *m.* fire
prevention
Brandschutztechnik *f.* fire pre-
vention technology
Brauchbarkeit *f.* usefulness
Breitband *n.* wide band
Breitbandkommunikation *f.*
broadband communication
Breite *f.* width
Breitformat *n.* oblong format
Brief *m.* letter
Briefkasten *m.* mailbox
Briefkastenleerung *f.* post
collection

Briefkopf *m.* letterhead
Briefträger *m.* mailman
Briefwechsel *m.* correspondence
Brillouin'sche Verteilung *f.* Brillouin distribution
broschieren *vrb.* bind/to in paper covers
broschiert *adj.* bound in paper covers
Broschur *f.* binding in paper covers, paperback
Broschur *f.* **mit Umschlagdeckel** Chinese style
Broschüre *f.* pamphlet, brochure
Broschürenbehälter *m.* pamphlet box
Brownesches System *n.* Browne system
Bruch *m.* fraction
Brücke *f.* jumper
Buch *n.* book
Buch bestellen *vrb.* ask/to for a book
Buch entleihen *vrb.* borrow/to a book
Buch *n.* **im Überformat** oversized book
Buch *n.* **in Kurzfassung** condensed book
Buch *n.* **in Rohbogen** book in sheets
Buch reservieren *vrb.* bespeak/to a book
Bucharchiv *n.* book archive
Buchaufstellung *f.* book shelving
Buchauktion *f.* book auction
Buchausgabe *f.* lending department
Buchausgabesystem *n.* book issue system

Buchauslage *f.* book display
Buchausleihe verbuchen *vrb.* charge/to a book
Buchausstellung *f.* book exhibition
Buchbesprechung *f.* book review, review, review article
Buchbesprechungswesen *n.* book reviewing
Buchbestand *m.* book collection
Buchbindehammer *m.* backing hammer
Buchbindekunst *f.* bibliopegy, binding art
Buchbindemeister *m.* master bookbinder
Buchbinden *n.* binding
Buchbinder *m.* bibliopegist, binder, bookbinder
Buchbinderei *f.* bindery
Buchbindereimaschine *f.* binding machine
Buchbindergeselle *m.* binding workman
Buchbinderjournal *n.* binding book, binding record, binding register
Buchbinderleim *m.* binder's glue
Buchbinderleinwand *f.* binder's cloth
Buchbindermesser *n.* binder's knife
Buchbinderpresse *f.* binding press
Buchbinderschnur *f.* binding cord
Buchbindertitel *m.* binder's title
Buchbestand *m.* book stock
Buchdruck *m.* relief printing, letterpress, letterpress printing
Buchdruckspezifikation *f.* body of the entry
Bucheinband *m.* cover

Buchempfehlungsliste *f.* list of recommended books
Bücheraufzug *m.* book elevator, book hoist, book lift
Bücherausgabestelle *f.* delivery room
Bücherausgabetheke *f.* charging desk, circulation desk, delivery desk, discharging desk, issue desk, loan desk
Bücherausstellung *f.* book exposition
Bücherauswahl *f.* book choice
Bücherbestand *m.* stock of books
Bücherboot *n.* book boat
Bücherbrett *n.* bookshelf
Bücherbrett *n.* mit Schiebeeinrichtung book-slide
Bücherbus *m.* book automobile, book mobile library, book wagon, bookmobile, book car
Bücherdieb *m.* biblioklept
Bücherei *f.* library
Büchereibenutzer *m.* library user
Büchereiverwaltung *f.* library administration
Bücherfreund *m.* bibliophile
Büchergeschoß *n.* deck
Büchergestell *n.* bookrack, bookstack
Büchergutschein *m.* book coupon, book tally, book token
Bücherhalle *f.* reading room
Bücherkiste *f.* book chest
Bücherkleptomane *m.* bibliokleptomaniac
Bücherliste *f.* booklist
Büchermagazin *n.* bookstacks
Büchermarkt *m.* book market
Büchermuseum *n.* book museum

Büchernachweisliste *f.* handlist
Büchernarr *m.* bibliomaniac
Büchersammler *m.* book collector
Bücherschrank *m.* bookcase
Bücherstand *m.* bookstall
Bücherstütze *f.* book brace, book end, book support
Bücherverkauf *m.* bookselling
Büchervernichter *m.* biblioclast
Büchervernichtung *f.* biblioclas▸
Bücherwagen *m.* book trolly
Bücherwurm *m.* book worm
Buchförderanlage *f.* book carrier
Buchformat *n.* book format
Buchgeschichte *f.* book history, historical bibliography
Buchgestaltung *f.* book design
Buchgewerbe *n.* book craft
Buchgröße *f.* book size
Buchgroßhandel *m.* book jobbing
Buchgroßhändler *m.* book jobber, book wholesaler
Buchhandel *m.* book trade
Buchhandelsbibliographie *f.* book trade bibliography
Buchhändler *m.* bookseller, dealer, jobber, retail bookseller
Buchhändlerzeitschrift *f.* book trade journal
Buchhandlung *f.* bookshop, bookstore
Buchherstellung *f.* book manufacture
Buchhülle *f.* forel
Buchillustration *f.* book illustration

Buchillustrator *m.* book illustrator
Buchindexierung *f.* book indexing
Buchinhalt *m.* body of book
Buchkarte *f.* book card, book slip, charging slip
Buchkartensystem *n.* card charging system
Buchkassette *f.* talking book
Buchkauf *m.* book buying
Buchklub *m.* book club
Buchkritik *f.* book review
Buchkunde *f.* bibliography
Buchkundiger *m.* bibliognost
Buchkunst *f.* book art
Büchlein *n.* booklet
Buchmesse *f.* book exchange, book fair, book trade fair
Buchpflege *f.* book maintenance
Buchproduktion *f.* book production
Buchrestaurierung *f.* book restoration
Buchrücken *m.* back of a book, backbone, back
Buchrückenbeschriftung *f.* spine labelling
Buchrückenpresse *f.* back liner
Buchrückenrunden *n.* back rounding
Buchrückenschild *n.* book tag
Buchrückgabe *f.* handing back a book, handing in a book
Buchschneidemaschine *f.* book cutting machine
Buchschrift *f.* book face, book hand
Buchse *f.* hub, jack
Buchsicherung *f.* book guard
Buchstabe *m.* alphabetic char-

acter, letter
Buchstabenbild *n.* face
Buchstabenfolge *f.* letter string
Buchstabenglaube *m.* literalism
Buchstabentaste *f.* alphabet key, letter key
Buchstabentastenreihe *f.* letter key row
Buchstabentyp *m.* letter type
Buchstabenumschalttaste *f.* alpha shift
Buchstabenumschaltung *f.* letter shift
buchstabenweise *adj.* letter-by-letter
buchstabenweise Sortierung *f.* letter-by-letter arrangement
buchstabieren *vrb.* spell/to
Buchtasche *f.* book pocket, satchel
Buchtext *m.* body of book
Buchung *f.* posting
Buchung austragen *vrb.* cancel/to, discharge/to books
Buchung löschen *vrb.* discharge/to books, cancel/to a loan
Buchungsdatum *n.* posting date
Buchungskarte *f.* posting card
Buchungsschlüssel *m.* posting key
Buchungstext *m.* entry description
Buchungsunterlage *f.* voucher
Buchvergoldung *f.* book gilding
Buchversand *m.* books-by-mail service
Buchwerbung *f.* blurb, book promotion, book publicity

Buchwissenschaftler *m.* bibliographer
Buchwünsche *pl.* book requests
Buchzeichen *n.* book number
Budget *n.* fund
Bulletin *n.* bulletin
Bundesarchiv *n.* federal archive
Bundesbibliothek *f.* federal library
Bundesland *n.* state
Bundesministerium *n.* federal ministry
Bundesregierung *f.* federal government
Bundesverwaltung *f.* federal administration
Bundsteg *m.* back margin, center margin, inner margin
Buntstift *m.* colored pencil
Bürge *m.* guarantor
Bürgerbücherei *f.* public library
Bürgerinformation *f.* community information
Bürgerinformationsdienst *m.* community information service
Bürgschaft *f.* guarantee
Büro *n.* office

Büroarbeiten *f.* clerical operations
Büroautomation *f.* office automation
Bürobedarf *m.* stationery
Bürocomputer *m.* office computer
Büroklammer *f.* clip, paper clip
Bürokommunikation *f.* office communication
Bürokommunikationssystem *n.* office communication system
Bürokraft *f.* clerical assistant
Büroorganisation *f.* office organization
büroorientiert *adj.* office-oriented
Büropersonal *n.* clerical staff
Bürosystem *n.* office automation system
Bürotechnik *f.* office technology
Bus *m.* bus
Büttenpapier *n.* hand-made paper
Büttenrand *m.* deckle edge
Byte *n.* byte
Bytegrenze *f.* byte boundary
Byteindex *m.* byte index

C

Carnegiebibliothek *f.*
Carnegie library
CD-ROM-Laufwerk *n.* CD-
ROM drive
Chapin-Diagramm *n.* Chapin
Charts
Charakterisikum *n.* character-
istic
charakteristische Eigenschaft *f.*
characteristic
Chefredakteur *m.* chief editor
Chemie *f.* chemistry
Chemieinformation *f.* chemi-
cal information
Chemiewirtschaft *f.* chemical
industry
chemische Formel *f.* chemical
formula
Chemotechnik *f.* technochemistry
chiffriert *adj.* in cipher, in code
Chip *m.* chip
Chiquadrattest *m.* chi-square
test
Chiropraktikerschulbibliothek
f. chiropractic school library
Chronik *f.* chronicle
Chronist *m.* chronicler
Chronologie *f.* chronology
**chronologisch geordnete Do-
kumentliste** *f.* calendar
chronologische Einteilung *f.*
division by date
chronologische Ordnung *f.*
chronological order
chronologische Ordnung *f.* von
Dokumenten chronological
filing system
chronologische Unterteilung *f.*
chronological division, chronological subdivision
chronologischer Deskriptor *m.*
chronological descriptor
Clearinghaus *n.* clearing
house
Cluster *n.* cluster
Clusteranalyse *f.* cluster analysis
Clusterbildung *f.* clustering
Clustersuche *f.* cluster search
Code *m.* code, identifier tag
Codebuch *n.* codebook
Codeelement *n.* code element,
code representation, code
value
Codetabelle *f.* coded character
set
Codetaste *f.* alternate coding
key
Codeumschaltung *n.* escape
character
Codeumsetzer *m.* code converter, encoder
codeunabhängig *adj.* transparent
Codieranleitung *f.* access
guide
codieren *vrb.* code/to, en-

code/to
Codierschlüssel *m.* coding scheme
codierte bibliographische Daten *pl.* coded bibliographical reference
codierter Zeichenvorrat *m.* coded character set
codiertes Referat *n.* coded abstract, encoded abstract
Codierung *f.* coding, encoding
Compiler *m.* compiler
Compilerprogramm *n.* compiling program
Computer *m.* computer
Computerausdruck *m.* computer printout
Computerdienste *pl.* computer services
computergestützt *adj.* computer-aided
computergestützte Bildverarbeitung *f.* computer vision
computergestützte Indexierung *f.* computer-aided indexing
computergestützte Übersetzung *f.* computer-aided translation
computergestützte Verbundkatalogisierung *f.* computer-aided union cataloging
computergestütztes Ausleihsystem *n.* computer-based circulation system
Computergraphik *f.* computer graphics
Computerkenntnisse *pl.* computer literacy
Computerkriminalität *f.* computer criminality
Computerlinguistik *f.* computational linguistics
Computernetzwerk *n.* computer network
Computerprogramm *n.* computer program
Computersatz *m.* computer-aided composition, computerized typesetting
Computersprache *f.* computer language
Computertechnik *f.* computer technology
Computertechnologie *f.* computer technology
computerunterstützt *adj.* computer-aided
computerunterstützter Unterricht *m.* computer-aided instruction
computerunterstütztes Lernen *n.* computer-aided learning
Computerverbund *m.* computer network
Computerwörterbuch *n.* machine dictionary, mechanical dictionary
Computerzentrum *n.* computer center
Covarianzanalyse *f.* analysis of covariance
Cross-Compiler *m.* cross compiler
Cursor *m.* cursor
Cutter-Klassifikation *f.* cutter classification
Cutter-Notation *f.* cutter number
Cutter-Tafel *f.* cutter table

D

Dachthesaurus *m.* macrothesaurus
Dämpfung *f.* loss
Danksagung *f.* acknowledgement
darstellen *vrb.* represent/to
Darstellung *f.* presentation, representation
Darstellungsfläche *f.* operating space
Darstellungsformat *n.* image
Datei *f.* data set, file
Datei *f.* **auf mehreren Einheiten** multi-unit file
Datei *f.* **in Schlüsselfolge** key-sequenced data set, key-sequenced file
Datei *f.* **ohne Kennsätze** unlabelled file
Dateiabschlußanweisung *f.* close statement
Dateiänderung *f.* file change
Dateianfangskennsatz *m.* beginning file label, file header label
Dateianfangspunkt *m.* initial point
Dateianordnung *f.* file layout
Dateiattribut *n.* file attribute
Dateiaufbau *m.* file setup
Dateiausdruck *m.* file expression
Dateibeschreibung *f.* file description

Dateibeschreibungsdokument *n.* file descriptor document
Dateiende *n.* end of file
Dateiendekennsatz *m.* end of file label
Dateieröffnungsanweisung *f.* OPEN statement
Dateierstellung *f.* file creation
Dateigeneration *f.* generation data set
Dateigenerierung *f.* generation data set
Dateigröße *f.* file size
Dateihandhabung *f.* file handling
Dateikennsatz *m.* field label, file label
Dateikennung *f.* file identifier
Dateikennungszahl *f.* generation number
Dateikennzeichen *n.* data set identifier, file mark
Dateikonstante *f.* file constant
Dateimenge *f.* file set
Dateiorganisation *f.* file architecture, file organization
Dateipflege *f.* file maintenance, file updating
Dateireorganisation *f.* file reorganization
Dateischutz *m.* file protection
Dateistruktur *f.* file structure
Dateitrennzeichen *n.* file separator

Dateiumsetzung *f.* file conversion

Dateiverarbeitung *f.* file processing

Dateiverbindung *f.* file connection

Dateiverfallsdatum *n.* file expiration date

Dateiverwaltung *f.* file management

Dateizugriff *m.* file access

Daten *pl.* data

Daten *pl.* mit festem Format fixed-format data

Datenabfrage *f.* data inquiry

Datenabrufsignal *n.* polling signal

Datenabrufverfahren *n.* polling technique

Datenanalyse *f.* data analysis

Datenanzeige *f.* data display

Datenaufbereitung *f.* data editing

Datenausgabe *f.* data output

Datenausschluß *m.* data cutoff

Datenaustausch *m.* data communication

Datenbank *f.* data bank, database

Datenbank *f.* bekannter Fehler known problems database

Datenbank *f.* für Dialogverarbeitung immediate database

Datenbankanbieter *m.* database vendor, online vendor

Datenbankaufbau *m.* database design

Datenbankauswahl *f.* database selection

Datenbankbeschreibung *f.* database description

Datenbankbetreiber *m.* host

Datenbankcomputer *m.* information retrieval machine

Datenbankentwurf *m.* database design

Datenbankintegrität *f.* database integrity

Datenbankmanagementsystem *n.* database management system

Datenbankmaschine *f.* database computer, database machine

Datenbankmodell *n.* database model

Datenbanknetzwerk *n.* database network

Datenbankproduzent *m.* database producer

Datenbankrecherche *f.* database inquiry

Datenbankrechner *m.* host computer

Datenbankschema *n.* scheme

Datenbanksprache *f.* database language

Datenbanksystem *n.* database system

datenbankübergreifende Recherche *f.* cross-file searching

Datenbankverzeichnis *n.* database directory

Datenbankwiederherstellung *f.* database recovery

Datenbankzugriff *m.* database access

Datenbasis *f.* database

Datenbeschreibungskatalog *m.* data dictionary

Datenbeschreibungssprache *f.* data description language

Datenbestand *m.* data file

Datenbewertung f. data evaluation
Datenblockung f. blocking of data
Datenbus m. data bus
Datencode m. data code
Datendateien pl. data files
Datendefinitionssprache f. data definition language
Datendokumentation f. data documentation
Dateneigentumsrechte pl. data ownership
Dateneingabe f. data entry, data input
Dateneinheit f. data unit, item
Dateneintrag m. data entry
Datenelement n. data element
Datenendeinrichtung f. data terminal
Datenerfassung f. data entry, data acquisition, data capture, data collection, data gathering
Datenerfassungsblatt n. data input sheet
Datenerfassungsgerät n. data capture terminal
Datenerhebung f. survey
Datenfeld n. basic field, data field, information field, item
Datenfeldbeschreibung f. basic field description
Datenfernübertragung f. remote data transmission
Datenfernverarbeitung f. remote processing, teleprocessing
Datenfernzugriff m. remote access
Datenfluß m. data flow
Datenflußplan m. data flow-

chart, data flowdiagram
Datenformat n. data format
Datengruppe f. group item
Datenhierarchie f. data hierarchy
Datenintegrität f. data integrity, integrity
Datenkanal m. information channel
Datenkommunikation f. data communication
Datenkonversion f. data conversion
Datenkonvertierung f. conversion of information
Datenmanipulationssprache f. data manipulation language
Datenmodelle pl. data models
Datenmultiplexer m. data multiplexer
Datennetz n. data network
Datennorm f. data standard
Datenobjekt n. data object
Datenorganisation f. data organization
Datenpaket n. packet
Datenqualität f. data quality
Datenquelle f. data source
Datenrepräsentation f. data representation
Datenretrieval n. data retrieval
Datensammelsystem n. data collection system
Datensatz m. data record, record
Datensatzauswahl f. record selection
Datensatzbereich m. record area
Datensatzbeschreibung f. record description

Datensatzsortierfeld *n.* intra-record sequence field
Datensatzverkettung *f.* chaining of records
Datenschutz *m.* protection of data privacy, data protection, privacy protection, protection of data
Datensenke *f.* data sink
Datensicherheit *f.* data integrity, security, data security
Datensicherung *f.* backup
Datensicherungsprozedur *f.* backup procedure
Datensicherungsverfahren *n.* backup processing
Datensichtgerät *n.* display screen, display
Datenspeicher *m.* data storage
Datenspeicher- und Retrieval-system *n.* data storage and retrieval system
Datenspeichereinheit *f.* data storage unit
Datensperre *f.* lock
Datenspur *f.* data track
Datenstation *f.* data station, data terminal, station, terminal installation, terminal
Datenstationsmodus *m.* terminal mode
Datenstationspuffer *m.* work station buffer
Datenstationssteuerung *f.* work station controller
Datenstationstabelle *f.* terminal list table
Datenstrom *m.* data stream, stream
Datenstromdatei *f.* stream file
Datenstruktur *f.* data

structure
Datensuchen *n.* file scan
Datentabelle *f.* data table
Datenträger *m.* data carrier, data medium, recording medium, volume
Datenträgereintrag *m.* volume entry
Datenträgergruppe *f.* pool of volumes
Datenträgerinhaltsverzeichnis *n.* volume table of contents
Datenträgerlöschen *n.* volume clean-up
Datenträgerschutz *m.* volume security
Datentyp *m.* type
Datenübertragung *f.* data communication, data transfer, data transmission
Datenübertragungsblock *m.* data transmission block
Datenübertragungseinheit *f.* unit of data transfer
Datenübertragungsumschalt-zeichen *n.* data link escape character
Datenübetragungsrate *f.* data transfer rate
Datenumsetzer *m.* data converter
Datenumsetzung *f.* conversion, data conversion, data transformation
Datenunabhängigkeit *f.* data independence, independence
Datenverarbeitung *f.* data processing, information processing
Datenverarbeitungsanlage *f.* data processing equipment, data processing machine

Datenverarbeitungsnetz *n.* data processing network
Datenverarbeitungssystem *n.* data processing system
Datenverdichtung *f.* data compression, data reduction
Datenverkehr *m.* data traffic
Datenverlust *m.* data overrun
Datenverschlüsselung *f.* data encryption
Datenverwaltungssystem *n.* data management system
Datenverzeichnis *n.* data dictionary
Datenvollständigkeit *f.* integrity of data
Datenvorbereitung *f.* data preparation
Datenwarteschlange *f.* data queue
Datenzelle *f.* data cell
Datenzentrum *n.* data center
Datenzusammenstellung *f.* data compilation
Datierung *f.* dating
Datum *n.* **des Urheberrechts** copyright date
Datum *n.* **in Buchstaben** alpha date, alphabetic date
Datumsfeld *n.* date field
Datumsstempel *m.* date stamp
Dauer *f.* time
Dauerauftrag *m.* blanked order
Dauerfunktion *f.* repeat function
Dauerleihe *f.* permanent loan
Dauerleihgabe *f.* deposit loan, deposit
Dauertaste *f.* repeat key
Deckel *pl.* boards
Deckelinnenseite *f.* inside

cover
Decoder *m.* decoder
Decodierer *m.* code translator, decoder
Decodierung *f.* decoding
Deduktion *f.* deduction
deduktive Textanalyse *f.* deductive text analysis
defekt *adj.* defective, incomplete
defektes Exemplar *n.* defective copy, imperfect copy
Definition *f.* definition
Definition *f.* **des Hilfebereiches** help area definition
Definitionsbeziehung *f.* definitive relation
Definitionswörterbuch *n.* explanatory dictionary
Deklination *f.* declination
Demographie *f.* demography
den Buchrücken abpressen *vrb.* back/to a book
Denkmal *f.* memorial
Denkschrift *f.* memorandum
denotative Bedeutung *f.* denotative meaning
Dependenzgrammatik *f.* dependency grammar
Depotbibliothek *f.* deposit library, depository library
Depotsammlung *f.* deposit collection
Desiderate *pl.* desiderata
Desiderienbuch *n.* desiderata book
Desiderienliste *f.* desiderata list
deskriptive Bibliographie *f.* descriptive bibliography
deskriptives Referat *n.* descriptive abstract

Deskriptor *m.* descriptor, descriptor term
Deskriptor *m.* **mit Rollenindikator** docuterm
Deskriptoreintrag *m.* item entry
Deskriptorenassoziationsliste *f.* descriptor association list
Deskriptorengruppe *f.* **für Referate** abstract descriptor group
Deskriptorennetzwerk *n.* descriptor network
Deskriptorensprache *f.* descriptor language
Deskriptorkandidat *m.* candidate descriptor
Desktop Publishing *n.* desktop publishing
detaillierte Klassifikation *f.* minute classification
detaillierter Entwurf *m.* detailed design
Determinante *f.* determinant
deterministisch *adj.* deterministic
Dewey-Dezimalklassifikation *f.* Dewey decimal classification
Dezentralisierung *f.* decentralization
Dezimalbruchnotation *f.* decimal fraction notation
dezimale Numerierung *f.* decimal numeration
dezimales Numeral *n.* decimal numeral
Dezimalklassifikation *f.* decimal classification
Dezimalkomma *n.* decimal point
Dezimalnotation *f.* decimal notation
Dezimalpunkt *m.* decimal point
Dezimalstellenformat *n.* fraction format
Dezimalunterteilung *f.* decimal division
Dezimalzahl *f.* decimal number
Dezimalziffer *f.* decimal digit
Diagnoseprogramm *n.* diagnostic program
Diagramm *n.* chart, diagram, plot, graph
Diagramm anzeigen *vrb.* show /to graph
diakritische Zeichen *pl.* diacritical marks, diacritical points
Dialekt *m.* dialect
Dialog *m.* dialog
Dialogbetrieb *m.* interactive mode
Dialogdatenerfassung *f.* interactive front end
Dialogdatenverarbeitung *f.* interactive data processing
Dialogerfassung *f.* interactive data entry
Dialogfähigkeit *f.* interactive facility
dialoggestützt *adj.* interactive
Dialogmodus *m.* dialog mode
Dialogrecherche *f.* interactive inquiry
Dialogsprache *f.* conversational language, dialog language
Dialogsystem *n.* dialog system
Dialogteilnehmerdienst *m.* timesharing service
Dialogverarbeitung *f.* interactive processing

Diapositiv *n.* slide
Diazokopie *f.* dye-line copy
Diazomikrofiche *m.* diazo
microform
Dichotomie *f.* dichotomy
dichotomische Einteilung *f.*
dichotomous division
dichotomische Klassifikation *f.*
bifurcate classification, classi-
fication by dichotomy
Dichte *f.* density
Dichtung *f.* fiction
Dicke *f.* width
Didaktik *f.* didactics
Dienst *m.* attendance, service
Dienstanweisung *f.* procedure
manual
Dienstkatalog *m.* official cat-
alog
Dienstleistung *f.* service
Dienstleistungsauftrag *m.*
service order
Dienstleistungsbetrieb *m.*
services enterprise
Dienstleistungsgewerbe *n.*
service industries
Dienstplan *m.* roster, time-
table
Dienstprogramm *n.* service
program, service routine,
utility program, utility
routine, utility
Dienststelle *f.* office
Dienststunden *pl.* office hours
Dienstzeit *f.* office hours
Diethelm-Klassifikation *f.*
Diethelm classification
diffundieren *vrb.* diffuse/to
Diffusionsverfahren *n.* diffu-
sion transfer process
digital *adj.* digital
Digital-Differentialanalysator

m. digital differential
analyser
Digitalausgabesteuerung *f.* digital output control
Digitaldaten *pl.* digital data
digitale Aufnahme *f.* digital
recording
digitale Darstellung *f.* digital
representation
digitale Daten *pl.* discrete
data
digitale Datenübermittlung *f.*
digital data transmission
digitaler Suchbaum *m.* digital
search tree
digitales Datenverarbeitungssystem *n.* digital data processing system
digitales Netzwerk *n.* digital
network
digitales Signal *n.* digital signal, discrete signal
digitalisieren *vrb.* digitize/to
Digitalrechner *m.* digital computer
Dimension *f.* dimension
Dimensionalität *f.* dimensionality
Dimensionsrelation *f.* dimensional relation
Diorama *n.* diorama
Diözesanarchiv *n.* diocesan
archive
Diözesanbibliothek *f.* diocesan
library
Diplom *n.* diploma, certification
Diplom *n.* eines Bibliothekars
certification of librarian
Diplomarbeit *f.* thesis
Diplombibliothekar *m.* graduated librarian

Diplomexamen *n.* diploma examination
diplomierter Bibliothekar *m.* chartered librarian
Diplomprüfung *f.* diploma examination
Diptychon *n.* diptych
Direktanschluß *m.* integrated file adapter
Direktanschluß *m.* **der Tastatur** keyboard attachment
Direktanschluß *m.* **für Datenfernverarbeitung** integrated communications adapter
Direktaufnahme *f.* direct recording
Direktausleihe *f.* direct lending
Direktbefehl *m.* immediate instruction
Direktbestellung *f.* direct application
Direktdaten *pl.* immediate data
direkte Adresse *f.* direct address, one-level address
direkte Adressierung *f.* direct address
direkte Datei *f.* direct file
direkte Dateiorganisation *f.* direct file organization
direkte Dokumentation *f.* direct documentation
direkte Kommunikation *f.* direct communication, face-to-face communication
direkte Verteilung *f.* primary distribution
Direkteingabe *f.* direct input
Direktoperand *m.* immediate operand
Direktoperation *f.* immediate

operation
Direktpositiv *n.* direct positive
Direktschlüssel *m.* direct code
Direktspeicherformat *n.* immediate-to-storage format
Direktzugriff *m.* arbitrary access, direct access
Direktzugriff *m.* **mit Adresse** addressed direct access
Direktzugriff *m.* **mit Schlüssel** keyed direct access
Direktzugriffsspeicher *m.* direct access storage, random access memory, random access storage
Disambiguierung *f.* disambiguation
Disjunktion *f.* disjunction, logical add, logical sum, OR operation
Diskette *f.* diskette, flexible disk, floppy disk
Diskettenänderungsprogramm *n.* diskette patch
Diskettenaustauschbarkeit *f.* diskette interchangeability
Diskettenlaufwerk *n.* diskette drive
Diskettenleser *m.* diskette input device
Diskettenschublade *f.* diskette drawer
Diskettenschutzhülle *f.* diskette envelope
diskret *adj.* discrete
diskrete Darstellung *f.* discrete representation
Diskriminante *f.* discriminant
Diskriminanzanalyse *f.* discriminant analysis
Diskriminanzfunktion *f.* discriminant function

Diskriminanzfunktion *f.* nach
Fisher Fisher´s discriminant
function
Diskriminanzwert *m.* dis-
crimination value
Diskussion *f.* discussion
Diskussionsbeitrag *m.* con-
tribution to a discussion
Diskussionsgrundlage *f.* basis
for discussion
Diskussionsleiter *m.* chairman
Diskussionsredner *m.* speaker
Diskussionsteilnehmer *m.*
panel member, discussion
participant
diskutabel *adj.* discussible
Disposition *f.* scheduling
Dissertation *f.* academic dis-
sertation, dissertation, doc-
toral dissertation
Distanzadresse *f.* bias address
Distanzprüfung *f.* bias test
Disziplin *f.* discipline
Doktorarbeit *f.* academic dis-
sertation, dissertation, doc-
toral dissertation
Dokument *n.* document
Dokument abrufen *vrb.* ob-
tain/to document
Dokument *n.* **mit verwandten**
Sujets aggregate
Dokumentablage *f.* document
filing
Dokumentanalyse *f.* document
analysis
Dokumentar *m.* documentalist
Dokumentaraufnahme *f.* doc-
umentary photograph
Dokumentardatei *f.* history
data set
Dokumentarfilm *m.* documen-
tary film

dokumentarisch *adj.* documentary
dokumentarische Bezugsein-
heit *f.* documentary unit
dokumentarische Klassifika-
tion *f.* documentary classification
Dokumentarstück *n.* documentary play
Dokumentart *f.* document type
Dokumentartag *m.* documentalists conference
Dokumentation *f.* documentation
Dokumentationsassistent *m.*
assistant documentalist
Dokumentationsbereich *m.*
coverage
Dokumentationsdatei *f.* documentation file
Dokumentationseinheit *f.*
documentary unit
Dokumentationseinrichtung *f.*
documentation department
Dokumentationsmethodik *f.*
documentation methodology
Dokumentationsprozeß *m.*
process of documentation
Dokumentationssprache *f.*
documentary language, documentation language, index
vocabulary, indexing lan-
guage, information language
Dokumentationsstelle *f.* clear-
inghouse, document center,
documentation center
Dokumentationssystem *n.*
documentation system
Dokumentationsverfahren *n.*
documentation technique
Dokumentationswesen *n.*
documentation

dokumentationswürdig *adj.*
relevant in documentation
Dokumentationswürdigkeit *f.*
documentation relevancy
Dokumentationszentrum *n.*
documentation center
Dokumentausgabe *f.* document output
Dokumentauslieferung *f.* delivery of documents
Dokumentaustausch *m.* document exchange
Dokumentauswahl *f.* selection of documents
Dokumentbeschreibung *f.* document description
Dokumentbesitzer *m.* document owner
Dokumentbestand *m.* document collection
Dokumentcluster *n.* document cluster
Dokumentdatum *n.* document date
Dokumenteintrag *m.* document entry, item entry
Dokumentenanalyse *f.* document analysis
Dokumentenklassifizierung *f.* classification of documents
Dokumentensammlung *f.* archive, collection
Dokumentenspeicher *m.* document storage
Dokumentenverarbeitungssystem *n.* document handling system
Dokumentenverzeichnis *n.* document directory, document index
Dokumenterfassung *f.* data entry of documents

Dokumentfehler *m.* document error
Dokumentfluß *f.* document flow
Dokumenthäufigkeit *f.* document frequency
dokumentieren *vrb.* document/to
Dokumentklassierung *f.* document classification
Dokumentlieferung *f.* document delivery
Dokumentmodifizierung *f.* document modification
Dokumentnachweise *m.* document identification
Dokumentnachweisretrieval *n.* reference retrieval
Dokumentnachweissystem *n.* reference retrieval system
Dokumentname *m.* document name
Dokumentnummer *f.* document number
Dokumentprofil *n.* document profile
Dokumentprüfung *f.* document examination
Dokumentrangreihung *f.* document ranking
Dokumentraum *m.* document space
Dokumentretrieval *n.* document retrieval
Dokumentsammlung *f.* collection
Dokumentspeicherdatei *f.* document storage file
Dokumenturheber *m.* document originator
Dokumentverarbeitung *f.* document processing

Dokumentverteilung *f.* document distribution
Dokumentverzeichnis *n.* document index
Dokumentvorschub *m.* increment document
Dombibliothek *f.* church library
Doppel *n.* duplicate
Doppelbuchstabe *m.* ligature
Doppeleintrag *m.* double entry, duplicate entry
Doppelname *m.* compound name
Doppelpunkt *m.* colon
doppeltes Merkband *n.* double register
Doppeltitel *m.* duplicate title
Dorfbibliothek *f.* rural library
dosieren *vrb.* pace/to
Dosierung *f.* pacing
Downloading *n.* downloading
Dozentur *f.* lectureship, lectorate
Draht *m.* wire
drahtgebundene Kommunikation *f.* wire communication
Drahtheftung *f.* wire stitching
drahtlos *adj.* wireless
drahtlose Übertragung *f.* wireless transmission
drahtloses Telephon *n.* wireless telephone station
Drahtquerschnitt *m.* wire size
drehen *vrb.* turn/to
Driver-Mock-Modell *n.* Driver-Mock model
Druck *m.* imprint, pressure, push
Druck *m.* **nach Bedarf** printing on demand
Druckaufbereitung *f.* editing

Druckausgabe *f.* print output
druckbares Zeichen *n.* printer graphic, keyboard graphic
Druckbild *n.* typography
Druckblock *m.* block of print
Druckbreite *f.* print span
Druckdatei *f.* print file
Druckdatensatz *m.* print data set
Druckeinheit *f.* print unit
drucken *vrb.* press/to, print/to
Drucken *n.* printing
Drucken *n.* **großer Mengen** bulk print
drücken *vrb.* press/to, push/to
Drucker *m.* printer, hard copy printer
Drucker *m.* **mit fliegendem Abdruck** hit on the fly printer
Druckerei *f.* print house, printing office
Druckerhalt *m.* hold print
Druckerschwärze *f.* black ink
Druckerwarteschlange *f.* print queue
druckfähig *adj.* printable
druckfähiges Datenfeld *n.* printable item
Druckfarbe *f.* ink
Druckfehler *m.* misprint, print error
Druckfehlerberichtigungen *pl.* corrigenda, errata
Druckfeld *n.* list field
druckfertig *adj.* pass for press, ready for press
druckfertig machen *vrb.* postedit/to
Druckformat *n.* print format
Druckformatierer *m.* print formatter
Druckgeschwindigkeit *f.* print

speed, printing rate
Druckindustrie *f.* printing industry
Druckjahr *n.* date of printing
Druckjob *m.* print job
Druckkette *f.* print chain
Druckkosten *pl.* type charge
Druckmaschine *f.* printing machine
Druckmodus *m.* print mode
Druckpuffer *m.* print buffer
Drucksache *f.* printed matter, publishing
Druckschriftenabteilung *f.* department of printed books
Druckspeicher *m.* print storage
Drucksperrimpuls *m.* non print
Drucksteuerzeichen *n.* print control character
Druckstock *m.* plate, printing block
Drucktaste *f.* print key, push button
Drucktechnik *f.* printing technology
Drucküberlauf *m.* printer overrun
Druckverfahren *n.* printing method
Druckvermerk *m.* imprint
Druckvorlage *f.* copy
Druckzeile *f.* print line
Druckzeilenbestimmung *f.* line control specification
Druckzone *f.* printing area
Druckzyklus *m.* printing cycle
dual *adj.* binary
duale Nutzung *f.* dual use
Dualzahl *f.* binary number
Dublette *f.* duplicate, duplicate

record
Dublettenbereinigung *f.* deduping
Dublettenkontrolle *f.* duplicate checking
Dublettenliste *f.* duplicate list
dummes Terminal *n.* dumb terminal
Dünndruck *m.* lightface
Dünnschichtspeicher *m.* thin-film memory
Duplexbetrieb *m.* both-way operation
Duplexmethode *f.* duplex method
Duplikat *n.* added copy, identical copy, multiple copy
duplizieren *vrb.* duplicate/to
Duplizität *f.* duplicity
durchblättern *vrb.* collate/to, interpolate/to, page through /to
Durchdruck *m.* stencil printing
Durchführbarkeit *f.* practicability
durchführen *vrb.* administer/to, implement/to, perform/to
Durchführung *f.* implementation, prosecution
durchgehend *adj.* non-stop
Durchlaßbereich *m.* pass-band
Durchlaßverzögerungszeit *f.* forward recovery time
Durchlauf *m.* pass, run through
DURCHLAUF-Befehl *m.* PERFORM statement
Durchlaufbetrieb *m.* free running
durchlaufen *vrb.* pass/to
durchlaufende Numerierung *f.*

continuous pagination
Durchlaufkamera *f.* flow camera
Durchlaufzeit *f.* lead time, throughput time, turnaround time
Durchnumerierung *f.* serialization
Durchsatz *m.* throughput
Durchschalten *n.* through switching
Durchschnitt *m.* average, mean
durchschnittlich *adj.* average, mean, medium
durchschnittliche Zugriffszeit *f.* average access time
durchschossen *adj.* leaded
Durchschreibeformular *n.* multipart form
Durchschreibepapier *n.* NCR paper

Durchschuß *m.* interleaf, leading
Durchschüsse *pl.* leads
Durchschußwähler *m.* leading dial
durchstreichen *vrb.* cancel/to, cross out/to
durchsuchen *vrb.* browse/to
durchziehen *vrb.* pull through /to
Dynamik *f.* dynamics
dynamische Zuordnung *f.* dynamic allocation
dynamischer Dokumentraum *m.* dynamic document space
dynamischer Speicher *m.* dynamic storage
dynamisches System *n.* dynamic system
dynamisches Unterprogramm *n.* dynamic subroutine

E

E-Maß *n.* e-measure
eben *adj.* plane
Ebene *f.* level, plane
ebene Koordinaten *pl.* plane coordinates
Ebenenaufbau *m.* level structure
Ebenennummer *f.* level number
Ebenenumschaltung *f.* level

switching
echt *adj.* authentic, true
Echtheit *f.* originality
Echtheitsbescheinigung *f.* authentication
Echtzeit *f.* real time
Echtzeitausgabe *f.* real time output
Echtzeitbetrieb *m.* real time operation

Echtzeitcomputersystem *n.*
real time computer system
Echtzeiteingabe *f.* real time
input
Echtzeitverarbeitung *f.* real
time processing
eckige Klammer *f.* square
bracket
edieren *vrb.* edit/to
EDV *f.* ADP
Effektivität *f.* effectivity
Effizienz *f.* efficiency
Effizienzkontrolle *f.* efficiency
control
Ehemaligenverband *m.* alumni
association
Eigenindexierung *f.* in-source
Eigenleitung *f.* intrinsic con-
duction
Eigenmerkmal *n.* intrinsic
characteristic
Eigenname *m.* proper name
Eigenschaft *f.* property
Eigenzitat *n.* self-citation
Eignungstest *m.* aptitude test
Eilauftrag *m.* rush-order
Eiljob *m.* hot job
Eilnachricht *f.* prompting mes-
sage
Ein-/ Ausgabe *f.* input/ output
Ein-/ Ausgabeanweisung *f.* in-
put/ output statement
Ein-/ Ausgabedatei *f.* input/
output file
Ein-/ Ausgabeeinheit *f.* input/
output device, input/ output
unit
Ein-/ Ausgabekanal *m.* input/
output channel
Ein-/ Ausgabemodell *m.* input/
ouput model
Ein-/ Ausgabeprozessor *m.* in-

put/ output processor
Ein-/ Ausgabeprozeß *m.* in-
put/ output process
Ein-/ Ausgaberegister *n.* in-
put/ output register
Ein-/ Ausgabesteuereinheit *f.*
peripheral control unit
Einarbeitung *f.* familiarizing
Einband *m.* binding
Einband *m.* **mit hohlem Rücken**
hollow-back binding
Einbanddecke *f.* binding case
Einbandgestaltung *f.* binding
design
Einbandmuster *n.* binding
pattern, binding sample, binding specimen
Einbandtitel *m.* binding title
einbaubar *adj.* mountable
einbinden *vrb.* bind/to
Einblattdruck *m.* broadsheet,
broadside
eindeutig *adj.* monosemantic,
unique
eindeutig definiert *adj.*
uniquely defined
eindeutige Benennung *f.*
monovalent term
Eindeutigkeit *f.* equivocality
eindimensional *adj.* unidimensional
eindimensionale Klassifikation
f. monodimensional classification, unidimensional classification
Eindruckvorrichtung *f.* imprinter
einfach *adj.* simple
einfache Genauigkeit *f.* single
precision
einfacher Ausdruck *m.* primitive expression

einfacher Begriff *m.* simple term
Einfachheit *f.* simplicity
Einfassung *f.* border
Einfluß *m.* **von Zeitschriften** journal influence
Einflußbeziehung *f.* influence relation
Einflußgröße *f.* influence quality
Einfügemodus *m.* include mode, insert mode
Einfügen *n.* inserting
einfügen *vrb.* file/to, insert/to, intercalate/to, patch/to
Einfügen *n.* **eines neuen Schlagwortes** intercalation
einfügen *vrb.* **nach** insert/to after
Einfügezeichen *n.* insert character, insertion character
Einfügung *f.* insertion, insert
Einfügung *f.* **eines neuen Schlagwortes** insertion of a new heading
Einfügungsanweisung *f.* include statement
Einfügungszeile *f.* include line
einführen *vrb.* implement/to, import/to
Einfuhrsteuer *f.* import tax
Einführung *f.* implementation, introduction
Einführungskurs *m.* introductory course
Eingabe *f.* input process, input
Eingabe *f.* **negativer Zahlen** negative entry
Eingabe *f.* **über die Tastatur** manual keyboard entry
Eingabe- und Fehlerprotokoll *n.* input and error listing

Eingabeabfragezeichen *n.* input prompting character
Eingabeaufforderung *f.* prompt
Eingabebefehl *m.* input command
Eingabedatei *f.* input data set, input file
Eingabedaten *pl.* inbound data, input data
Eingabeeinheit *f.* input unit
Eingabefeld *n.* input field
Eingabefolgenummer *f.* input sequence number
Eingabeformat *n.* format entry
Eingabeformateinheit *f.* format entry unit
Eingabeformatname *m.* format entry name
Eingabegerät *n.* input device
Eingabegeschwindigkeit *f.* input rate
Eingabekapazität *f.* input capacity
Eingabekarte *f.* input card
Eingabekennsatz *m.* input label
Eingabeliste *f.* option list
Eingabemedium *n.* input medium
Eingabemodus *m.* input state
Eingabeoperation *f.* alter operation, input operation
Eingabeprogramm *n.* input program, input routine
Eingabepuffer *m.* input buffer, read buffer
Eingaberate *f.* input transfer rate
Eingabespeicher *m.* input storage
Eingabespezifikation *f.* input

specification
Eingabesprache *f.* input language
Eingabesteuereinheit *f.* input control unit
Eingabesystem *n.* origin system
Eingabetabelle *f.* target table
Eingabewarteschlange *f.* input job queue, input queue
Eingabezeit *f.* input time interval, type-in time
Eingang *m.* gateway, inlet
Eingangsausdruck *m.* entry expression
Eingangsdatum *n.* date of entry, date of receipt
Eingangsgruppe *f.* incoming group
Eingangskanal *m.* input channel
Eingangskonfiguration *f.* input configuration
Eingangsnummer *f.* accession number
Eingangsvermerk *m.* admission record
eingebaut *adj.* integrated
eingebaute Prozeduren *pl.* built-in procedures
eingeben *vrb.* enter/to, input/to, key in/to
eingehend *adj.* incoming
eingelassen *adj.* recessed
eingerückt *adj.* indented
eingeschaltet *adj.* ON status
eingeschossene Bogen *pl.* interleaves
eingestellte Reihe *f.* ceased publications
eingetragen *adj.* registered
eingetragener Benutzer *m.*

registered borrower
eingetragenes Warenzeichen *n.* registered trade-mark
eingezogen *adj.* indented
eingrenzen *vrb.* localize/to
Eingrenzung *f.* localization
Eingriff *m.* intervention, mesh
Eingriff *m.* **erforderlich** intervention required
Eingruppierung *f.* group, classifying
Einheftkante *f.* binding edge
einheimisch *adj.* native
Einheit *f.* item, unit
Einheitenauswahl *f.* unit selection
Einheitennummer *f.* unit number
Einheitenprüfung *f.* unit check
Einheitenschlüssel *m.* unit control word
einheitlich *adj.* uniform
einheitliche Maschinensprache *f.* common machine language
einheitliche Numerierung *f.* uniform numbering
einheitliche Wortordnung *f.* all through
einheitliches Ablagesystem *n.* uniform filing system
Einheitskarte *f.* unit card
Einheitsklassifikation *f.* standard classification
Einheitssachtitel *m.* uniform title
Einkaufszentrale *f.* library supply center
einklammern *vrb.* bracket/to
Einkommen *n.* income
Einlage *f.* middle
einlagern *vrb.* swap in/to
einlegen *vrb.* file/to, pack

feed/to
einleiten *vrb.* initialize/to
einleitende Adreßselektion *f.*
initial selection
Einleitung *f.* introduction,
preliminary
Einleitungsmodus *m.* initial
mode
einlesen *vrb.* write in/to
Einnahme *f.* income
einordnen *vrb.* file/to, inter-
file/to
einordnen *vrb.* **durch Mischen**
order/to by merging
Einordnung *f.* **der Titelaufnahme** incorporation of
entries in a catalog
Einordnungsstelle *f.* access
point
einrastbare Taste *f.* latch-
down key
einreihen *vrb.* file/to,
order/to, queue/to
Einrichtung *f.* feature
einrücken *vrb.* indent/to
Einrücksteuerung *f.* level
control
Einrückung *f.* indentation,
indention
Einrückungsregel *f.* indentation convention
Einrückungsrichtlinie *f.*
indentation guideline
Eins-zu-Eins Beziehung *f.*
one-to-one relationship
Einsatz *m.* insert
einsatzbereit *adj.* stand-by
Einsatzgebiet *n.* field of
applications
Einsatzmöglichkeit *f.* range of
applications
Einsatzziel *n.* target

Einschaltblatt *n.* inserted leaf
Einschalten *n.* initial setup, insetting
Einschaltkarte *f.* inserted card
einschieben *vrb.* insert/to,
intercalate/to
Einschiebung *f.* insertion
Einschiebungsfolge *f.* insertion
sequence
einschiessen *vrb.* interleave/to
einschleusen *vrb.* let in/to
einschließen *vrb.* include/to
Einschluß *m.* inclusion
Einschlußbeziehung *f.*
inclusive relation
Einschränkung *f.* constraint,
limitation
Einschreibgebühr *f.* registration fee
Einschub *m.* rack adapter
Einschubrahmen *m.* line rag
einsehen *vrb.* view/to
einseitig *adj.* single-sided
einspaltig *adj.* in one column,
single column
Einspannen *n.* load
Einsparung *f.* saving
einspeichern *vrb.* bind/to, roll
in/to
einsprachig *adj.* monolingual
einstampfen *vrb.* pulp/to
einstecken *vrb.* insert/to,
push-in/to
einstellbar *adj.* adjustable
einstellbare Ausdehnung *f.*
adjustable extent
Einstellen *n.* presetting, setting
einstellen *vrb.* adjust/to, set/to
Einsteller *m.* adjuster
Einstellgenauigkeit *f.* setting
accuracy
einstellig *adj.* monadic

Einstellung *f.* adjustment, attitude, setting

Einstellungsänderung *f.* attitude change

einstufig *adj.* single-level, single-stage

einstufige Datei *f.* single-level file

einstufige Titelaufnahme *f.* one-level description

Einstufung *f.* classification

Eintagsmaterialien *pl.* ephemera

Eintastbereich *m.* key entry area

Eintasten *n.* keying

Eintrag *m.* entry, item

einen neuen Eintrag einfügen *vrb.* insert/to an extra entry

Eintrag *m.* **unter dem ersten Titelwort** first word entry

Eintrag *m.* **unter dem Vornamen** by-name entry, forename entry, given name entry

eintragen *vrb.* post/to, register/to

Eintragung *f.* enrollment, entering

Eintragung *f.* **einer Entleihung** charge

Eintragung *f.* **ins Zugangsverzeichnis** accessioning

einwerfen *vrb.* insert/to

Einzahlungsbeleg *m.* deposit slip

einzeilig *adj.* single-line, single-space

Einzelanschlag *m.* single key stroke

Einzelautor *m.* individual author

Einzelband *m.* odd part, odd volume

Einzelbeleg *m.* single document

Einzelblattzuführung *f.* sheet feeder

Einzeldatei *f.* unique file

Einzelelement *n.* identity element

Einzelexemplar *n.* odd copy

Einzelfehler *m.* single error

Einzelgerät *n.* single device

Einzelkatalog *m.* divided catalog

Einzelklasse *f.* isolate

Einzelkosten *pl.* direct cost

Einzelkostenanalyse *f.* direct cost analysis

einzeln *adj.* odd

Einzelrechner *m.* uniprocessor

Einzelschrittbetrieb *m.* step-by-step operation

Einzelstation *f.* single station, single terminal, stand-alone device

Einzelsteuerung *f.* individual control

Einzeltaste *f.* momentary key

einziehen *vrb.* indent/to

einzigartig *adj.* unique

einzige Ausgabe *f.* only edition

einziges Exemplar *n.* unique copy

Einzug *m.* hanging indention, indentation, indention

Eisenbahnbibliothek *f.* railway library

Elektronik *f.* electronics

elektronisch gespeicherte Information *f.* computer-based information

elektronische Datenverarbeitung *f.* electronic data pro-

cessing
elektronische Dokumentspei-cherung f. electronic document storage
elektronische Enzyklopädie f. automated encyclopaedia
elektronische Post f. electronic mail
elektronische Veröffentlichun-gen pl. electronic publications
elektronischer Dokumentver-sand m. electronic document delivery
elektronischer Schalter m. latch
elektronischer Thesaurus m. computerized thesaurus
elektronisches Arbeitsblatt n. electronic spreadsheet
elektronisches Lesegerät n. electronic reading machine
elektronisches Publizieren n. electronic publishing
elektronisches "Schwarzes Brett" n. electronic bulletin board
elektronisches Textbuch n. eletronic textbook
elektronisches Wörterbuch n. automatic dictionary
Elektrotechnik f. electrical engineering
Element n. element, item, member
elementare Fähigkeit f. basic competency
Elementarfunktion f. primitive function
Elementarprozeß m. unit process
Eliminierungsfaktor m. elimination factor

elliptisch adj. elliptical
elliptischer Titel m. elliptical title
Eltern-Kind-Relation f. parent-child relation
Emblembuch n. emblem book
Empfang m. receipt, receiving, reception
empfangen vrb. receive/to
Empfänger m. recipient, receiver
Empfängernummer f. recipient number
Empfangsaufrufzeichen n. addressing character
Empfangsbereitschaft f. ready for receiving, ready to receive
Empfangsbestätigung f. receipt confirmation
Empfangsbevollmächtigter m. authorized receiver
Empfangsdaten pl. received data
Empfangsdatenkennzeichnung f. received data present
Empfangsdiskette f. receive diskette
Empfangsfeld n. receiving field
Empfangsmodus m. receive mode, slave mode
Empfangspuffer m. receive buffer
Empfangsstation f. receiving terminal
Empfangsüberwachung f. receive timer
Empfangsunterbrechung f. read interrupt, receive interrupt
Empfangszähler m. receive count

Empfehlung *f.* recommendation
empfindlich *adj.* sensitive
Empfindlichkeit *f.* sensitivity
empirisch *adj.* empirical
empirische Untersuchung *f.* empirical study
Emulation *f.* emulation
Emulator *m.* emulator
emulieren *vrb.* emulate/to
Endbenutzer *m.* user
Endblatt *n.* free endpaper, inner endpaper
Endbuchstabe *m.* final letter
Endemarke *f.* end marker
Endfassung *f.* final form
Endfeld *n.* local link
Endgerät *n.* unit
endgültige Ausgabe *f.* definitive edition
endgültiger Maschinenbefehl *m.* absolute instruction
endlicher Automat *m.* finite state automaton
Endlosformular *n.* continuous form
Endlospapier *n.* web
Endnutzerrecherche *f.* user inquiry
Endprüfung *f.* final inspection
Endstelle *f.* terminating point
Endsumme *f.* final total, total
Endungswörterbuch *n.* ending dictionary
Energie *f.* energy
Energiefacette *f.* energy facet
englische Broschur *f.* case binding, cased, casing
Engpaß *m.* bottleneck
entfernen *vrb.* remove/to
entfernt *adj.* remote
entfernt stehende Datensta-

tion *f.* remote station, remote terminal, remote workstation
entgegengesetzt *adj.* reverse
enthalten *vrb.* include/to
Entität *f.* entity
entkatalogisieren *vrb.* uncatalog/to
entkoppeln *vrb.* isolate/to
Entladen *n.* unloading
Entladung *f.* discharge
entlehnter Begriff *m.* borrowed concept
entleihbare Objekte *pl.* loanable items
Entleihdaten *pl.* borrowing data
Entleihdatum *n.* date of issue
entleihen *vrb.* borrow/to
Entleiher *m.* borrower
Entleihinformation *f.* borrowing information
Entleihkontrolle *f.* circulation control
Entleihsystem *n.* circulation system
Entleihverbuchung *f.* borrowing data recording
entliehen *adj.* borrowed
entliehene Objckte *pl.* items on loan
entliehenes Buch *n.* book on-loan
Entnahme *f.* withdrawal
entnehmen *vrb.* withdraw/to
entpacken *vrb.* unpack/to
entriegeln *vrb.* unlatch/to
Entriegelung *f.* non-locking
Entropie *f.* entropy
Entschädigung *f.* indemnity
Entscheidung *f.* decision
Entscheidungsanalyse *f.* decision analysis

Entscheidungsbäume *pl.* decision trees
Entscheidungshilfe *f.* decision support
Entscheidungsorgan *n.* board
Entscheidungsprozeß *m.* decision making
Entscheidungstabelle *f.* decision table
entscheidungsunterstützendes System *n.* decision support system
entschlüsseln *vrb.* decode/to
Entschlüsselung *f.* decoding
Entschlüßler *m.* decoder
entsperren *vrb.* unlock/to
Entstehung *f.* beginning
entwerfen *vrb.* draft/to
Entwickler *m.* **einer Klassifikation** classificationist
Entwicklung *f.* development, processing
Entwicklungsabteilung *f.* development department
Entwicklungsplan *m.* development program
Entwicklungsstand *m.* state of development
Entwicklungssystem *n.* development system
Entwicklungstendenz *f.* trend
Entwurf *m.* design, draft, layout, proof copy
Entwurfsblatt *n.* spacing chart
Entzerrer *m.* repeater
Entzerrung *f.* equalization
enumerative Klassifikation *f.* enumerative classification
Enzyklopädie *f.* encyclopaedia, cyclopedia
Ephemera *pl.* ephemera
Epigraph *n.* epigraph

Eponym *m.* eponym
Ereignis *n.* event
Ereignisprüfpunktsatz *m.* incident record
Erfahrung *f.* practice, experience
Erfahrungsaustausch *m.* exchange of experience
Erfahrungsbericht *m.* report on experiences
Erfahrungswert *m.* pragmatical value
erfassen *vrb.* record/to, register/to
Erfassung *f.* registration
Erfassungsblatt *n.* record sheet
Erfassungsgerät *n.* input device
Erfassungsstelle *f.* key station
Erfassungszeitraum *m.* recorded time
Erfinder *m.* originator
erfinderisch *adj.* originative
Erfindung *f.* origination, invention
Erfindungsbeschreibung *f.* description of invention
erfolglos *adj.* ineffective
erfolglose Anwahl *f.* abandon call
Erfolgsrate *f.* yield
erforderliches Programm *n.* required program
erfordern *vrb.* require/to
Erfordernis *n.* requirement
Erfüllungsrate *f.* achievement rate
Ergänzung *f.* instruction modifier
Ergänzungsangabe *f.* option
Ergänzungsfeld *n.* sub-

sequence field
Ergänzungsmaschine *f.* hook-up machine
Ergebnis *n.* result
Erhaltungszustand *m.* condition
Erhebung *f.* survey, inquiry
erhöhte Helligkeit *f.* high light
Erhöhung *f.* increase
Erholzeit *f.* recovery time
erkennen *vrb.* identify/to
Erkenntnistheorie *f.* epistemology
Erkennung *f.* recognition
Erkennungssteuerblock *m.* recognition control block
erklärende Beschreibung *f.* narrative description
erklärt *adj.* elucidated, explained
Erklärung *f.* declaration, legend
Erlaß *m.* decree
Erlaubnis *f.* allowance
erläutert *adj.* elucidated, explained
Erläuterung *f.* commentary, scope note
Ermittlung *f.* investigation
Ernährungswissenschaft *f.* nutrition science
Erneuerung *f.* renewal
Eröffnungsprozedur *f.* sign-on procedure
Erotikum *n.* erotic publication
Erprobungsphase *f.* test
errechnete Adresse *f.* generated address
erregen *vrb.* impulse/to
Ersatzdatei *f.* alternate file
Ersatzexemplar *n.* replacement copy

Ersatzkanal *m.* alternative channel
Ersatzrechner *m.* backup computer
Ersatzregister *n.* deletion record
Ersatzteil *n.* spare part
Ersatzzeichen *n.* substitution character
Ersatzzettel *m.* removal slip
erscheint demnächst appears shortly
erscheint in Kürze about to be published
Erscheinungsbild *f.* appearance
Erscheinungsdatum *n.* publication date
Erscheinungsland *n.* country of publication
Erscheinungsort *m.* place of publication
Erscheinungsvermerk *m.* imprint
Erscheinungsweise *f.* frequency of publication
Erschließung *f.* indexing
Erschließungsprozeß *m.* indexing process
Erschließungsregeln *pl.* indexing rules
ersetzen *vrb.* replace/to, substitute/to
Ersetzung *f.* replacement
Ersetzungszeichen *n.* replacement character
Erstausgabe *f.* editio princeps, first edition, original document
Erstdruck *m.* first edition
erste Einrückung *f.* first indention

erste Normalform *f.* first normal form
erstellen *vrb.* establish/to, load/to
Erstellen *n.* von Referaten abstracting
Erstellung *f.* construction
Erstellungsnummer *f.* generation number
Erstexemplar *n.* first copy
Erstkarte *f.* primary card, primary
Erstkartendatei *f.* primary file
Erstkatalogisierung *f.* original cataloging
erstklassig *adj.* classic
Erstkorrektur *f.* first correction, house corrections
erstmalig erstellt initially created
Erwachsenenbildung *f.* adult education
Erwachsenenbildung *f.* durch Veranstaltungen in der Bibliothek extension library service
erweiterbare Tastatur *f.* modifiable keyboard
erweitern *vrb.* upgrade/to
erweiterte Ausgabe *f.* augmented edition, enlarged edition
erweiterte Boolesche Suchstrategie *f.* extended Boolean strategy
erweiterte Klasse *f.* amplified class
erweiterte Zugriffstechnik *f.* queued access method
erweiterter KWIC-Index *m.* augmented KWIC index
erweiterter KWOC-Index *m.* augmented KWOC index

erweitertes alphabetisches Sachregister *n.* enriched alphabetical subject index, augmented alphabetical subject index
erweitertes Übergangsnetzwerk *n.* augmented transition network
Erweiterung *f.* expander
Erweiterung *f.* von Abkürzungen abbreviation expansion
Erweiterungsanweisung *f.* option instruction
Erweiterungsfähigkeit *f.* flexibility, hospitality
Erweiterungsfähigkeit *f.* der Notation hospitality of notation
Erweiterungsfähigkeit *f.* einer Kette flexibility of a chain
Erwerb-Ausleih-Quote *f.* circulation/acquisitions ratio
erwerben *vrb.* acquire/to
Erwerbung *f.* acquisition
Erwerbungsabteilung *f.* accession department, acquisition department, order department
Erwerbungsetat *m.* acquisition budget, book budget, book funds
Erwerbungskommission *f.* acquisition committee
Erwerbungspolitik *f.* acquisition policy, book collecting policy, collecting policy
Erwerbungsrichtlinien *pl.* acquisition policy statement
Erwerbungsschlüssel *m.* purchasing key
erzeugende Funktion *f.* generating function

Erziehungswissenschaft *f.*
paedagogy
ESC-Folge *f.* escape sequence
Eselsohr *n.* dog's ear
Esoterik *f.* esotericism
Essay *m.* essay
Etat *m.* budget
Etikett *n.* tag, label
Etikettendrucker *m.* label
printer
Etikettenhalter *m.* label holder
Etikettieren *n.* labelling
etymologisches Wörterbuch *n.*
etymological dictionary
exakte Begriffsbestimmung *f.*
explicatum
exakte Definition *f.* explicatum
Exemplar *n.* copy
Exemplarnummer *f.* document
number
Exemplarsignatur *f.* copy letter
exklusive Referenz *f.* exclusive
reference
Exklusivität *f.* exclusiveness

Exlibris *n.* bookplate
Expansivklassifikation *f.* cutter classification, expansive
classification
Experiment *n.* experiment
Experimentaluntersuchung *f.*
experimental study
experimenteller Retrievalbestand *m.* experimental retrieval collection
Expertenbegutachtung *f.* peer
review
Expertendatei *f.* expert file
Expertensystem *n.* expert system
explizit *adj.* explicite
Export *m.* export
Exportfähigkeit *f.* exportability
externe Datei *f.* external data
set, external file
extra *adj.* spare
exzerpieren *vrb.* excerpt/to,
extract/to
Exzerpt *m.* excerpt

F

Fabel *f.* fable
Fabrik *f.* plant
fabrikneu *adj.* virgin
Facette *f.* facet
Facettenanalyse *f.* facet analysis
Facettenfolge *f.* citation order of facets, citation order, facet order
Facettenformel *f.* combination order of facets, facet formula
Facettenindikator *m.* facet indicator
Facettenklassifikation *f.* colon classification, facetted classification, multifacetted classification
Facettenordnung *f.* facet order
Fach *n.* class, rack
Facharbeiterprüfung *f.* professional skill test
Facharchiv *n.* special archive
Fachausbildung *f.* professional education
Fachausdruck *m.* technical term
Fachbegriff *m.* technical term
Fachbereich *m.* department
Fachbereichsbibliothek *f.* department library
Fachbereichsschrift *f.* faculty paper
Fachbericht *m.* technical report

Fachbibliographie *f.* bibliographical monograph, special bibliography, subject bibliography, technical bibliography
Fachbibliothek *f.* special library, technical library
Fachbibliotheksnetz *n.* special library network
Fachblatt *n.* technical journal
Fachbuch *n.* professional book, technical book
Fachdokumentar *m.* information specialist, information specialist
Fachfrage *f.* technical question
Fachgebiet *n.* field of knowledge, subject
Fachgebietsabdeckung *f.* subject coverage
Fachgebietsbezeichnung *f.* subject name
fachgebietsorientiert *adj.* subject-oriented
Fachgespräch *n.* technical discussion
Fachgruppe *f.* team of specialists, subject section
Fachhochschulausbildung *f.* vocational college education
Fachhochschulbibliothek *f.* vocational college library
Fachhochschule *f.* vocational college

Fachhochschulgesetz *n.* vocational college act
Fachidiot *m.* one-track specialist
Fachinformation *f.* scientific and technical information
Fachinformationspolitik *f.* scientific and technical information policy
Fachinformationsprogramm *n.* scientific and technical information program
Fachinformationssystem *n.* scientific and technical information system
Fachinformationszentrum *n.* scientific and technical information center
Fachkatalog *m.* special catalog
Fachklassifikation *f.* specialized classification
Fachkommmission *f.* expert commission
Fachkommunikation *f.* technical communication
Fachkonferenz *f.* scientific meeting
fachlich *adj.* vocational, technical, professional
Fachliteratur *f.* technical literature
Fachnormenausschuß *m.* engineering standards committee
Fachordnung *f.* subject classification scheme
Fachreferat *n.* technical lecture, departmental section
Fachreferent *m.* subject specialist
Fachrichtung *f.* branch of study
Fachschulabschluß *m.* professional school certificate
Fachschulbibliothek *f.* professional school library
Fachschulbibliothekswesen *n.* professional school librarianship
Fachschule *f.* professional school
Fachschulprüfung *f.* professional school examination
Fachsprache *f.* technical language, terminology, common technical language
Fachsprachenforschung *f.* terminology research
Fachstelle *f.* library counseling center
Fachstellenbibliothekar *f.* library adviser
Fachstudium *n.* major study
Fachtagung *f.* professional meeting
Fachtext *m.* technical text
Fachthesaurus *m.* mission-oriented thesaurus, subject-oriented thesaurus
fachübergreifend *adj.* interdisciplinary
Fachübersetzer *m.* technical translator
Fachverlag *m.* special publishing house
Fachwissen *n.* knowledge in a specialized field
Fachwort *n.* technical term
Fachwörterbuch *n.* special dictionary, subject dictionary, technical dictionary
Fachzeitschrift *f.* technical journal

Fachzentralkatalog *f.* specialized union catalog
Fähigkeit *f.* skill
Fahrbibliothek *f.* mobile library
Fahrplan *m.* timetable
Faksimile *n.* facsimile
Faksimileausgabe *f.* facsimile edition
Faksimilekatalog *m.* facsimile catalog
Fakten *pl.* facts
Faktendatenbank *f.* source database, factual database
Faktendokumentation *f.* source documentation
Faktenretrieval *n.* fact retrieval
Faktorenanalyse *f.* factor analysis
Faktorisierung *f.* factoring
Fakultätsbibliothek *f.* faculty library
Fakultätsschrift *f.* faculty paper
Fall *m.* event
fällig *adj.* due back, due for return, receivable
Fälligkeitsdatum *n.* due date
Fallsammlung *f.* casebook
Fallstudien *pl.* case studies
falsch *adj.* wrong
falsch adressieren *vrb.* misdirect/to
falsch auswerten *vrb.* misinterpret/to
falsch berechnen *vrb.* miscalculate/to
falsch datieren *vrb.* misdate/to
falsch handhaben *vrb.* mishandle/to
falsch informieren *vrb.* mis-

inform/to
falsch schreiben *vrb.* miswrite/to
Falschausrichtung *f.* misalignment
Falschauswertung *f.* misinterpretation
falsche Anwendung *f.* misapplication
falsche Daten *pl.* false data
falsche Diskette *f.* wrong disk
falsche Kombination *f.* false combination, false sorts
falsche Länge *f.* incorrect length
falsche Regalordnung *f.* misshelving
falsche Satzlänge *f.* incorrect length, wrong length record
Falscheingabe *f.* misentry
Falschklassifikation *f.* misclassification
Falschschreibung *f.* incorrect spelling
Fälschung *f.* fake, forgery
Faltblatt *n.* folded leaflet, leaflet
Faltbroschur *f.* folder
falten *vrb.* fold/to
Faltprospekt *m.* folded leaflet, folder
Falttabelle *f.* folded table
Faltung *f.* folding
Falz *m.* fold, groove, hinge, joint
Fälzeln *n.* guarding
Falzung *f.* folding
Familienbibliothek *f.* family library
Familienbuch *n.* family record book
Familienname *m.* family name

Farbband *n.* ink ribbon, ribbon
Farbbildschirm *m.* color monitor
Farbdruck *m.* color printing
Farbfilm *m.* color film
Farbkopie *f.* color photocopy
Farbmikrofiche *m.* color microfiche
Farbmikrofilm *m.* color microfilm
Faschismus *m.* fascism
Faschist *m.* fascist
Feder *f.* pen
Fehlanzeige *f.* nil return
Fehldruck *m.* waste sheet
fehlend *adj.* missing, omitted
fehlende Ausgabe *f.* missing issue
fehlende Nummer *f.* missing number
Fehler *f.* fault, error, mistake
Fehler akzeptieren *vrb.* accept /to with error
Fehler beseitigen *vrb.* debug/to
Fehler suchen *vrb.* troubleshoot/to
Fehlerbehebung *f.* recovery
Fehlerbereich *m.* range of error
Fehlerbeseitigung *f.* debugging, recovery management
Fehlererkennungscode *m.* error-detecting code
fehlerfrei *adj.* correct
Fehlerfreiheit *f.* accuracy
fehlerhaft *adj.* faulty
fehlerhafte Daten *pl.* dirty data
fehlerhafte Funktion *f.* failure, malfunction
fehlerhafte Operation *f.* invalid operation
fehlerhafte Verweisung *f.* wild branch
fehlerhafter Informationsnachweis *m.* false retrieval
fehlerhafter Rand *m.* faulty margin, unequal margin
Fehlerhäufigkeit *f.* error rate
Fehlerkennzeichen *n.* error flag
Fehlerkorrektur *f.* error correction, error recovery
Fehlerkorrektur *f.* **über Tastatur** keyboard correction
Fehlerprotokollierung *f.* logging of faults
Fehlerprüfcode *m.* error-checking code
Fehlersammelbereich *m.* error bucket
Fehlersuche *f.* error debugging, troubleshooting
Fehlerüberwachung *f.* error control
Fehlerverriegelung *f.* error lock
Fehlinformation *f.* misinformation
Fehlordnung *f.* imperfection
Fehlquote *f.* miss ratio
Fehlseitenbedingung *f.* page fault
Fehlseitenunterbrechung *f.* missing page interrupt, page fault interrupt
Fehlselektion *f.* false drop
Fehlverweisung *f.* blind cross-reference
Fehlzeit *f.* off time, time off
Feinklassifikation *f.* close classification, exact classification

Feld *n.* array, field, item
Feld lesen *vrb.* get/to field
Feldabhängigkeit *f.* field
dependence
Feldadressierung *f.* field ad-
dressing
Feldanfangscode *m.* begin
field code
Feldanfangszeichen *n.* field
definition character
Feldanzeige *f.* field display
Feldarbeit *f.* field work
Feldbestimmung *f.* field de-
finition
Feldbezugszahl *f.* field
indicator
Feldcharakteristik *f.* body line
Felddefinitionsanweisung *f.*
field definition specification
Feldgruppendatei *f.* array file
Feldgruppenindex *m.* array
index
Feldgruppenindexfehler *m.*
array index error
Feldinhalt *m.* field content
feldinterne Prüfung *f.* intra-
field check
Feldlänge *f.* field length, field
size
Feldmarke *f.* field mark, field
tag
Feldnamenerklärung *f.* data
dictionary
Feldnummer *f.* field number
Feldprüfung *f.* field validation
Feldschlüssel *m.* field code
Feldtrennzeichen *n.* field sepa-
rator
Feldunabhängigkeit *f.* field
independence
Fenster *n.* window
Fenstergröße *f.* window size

fern *adj.* remote
Fernanzeige *f.* remote display,
remote indication
Fernbestellung *f.* teleordering
Ferndatenkanal *m.* line data
channel
Ferndiagnose *f.* remote
diagnosis, telediagnosis
ferngesteuert *adj.* remote-
controlled
Fernkennung *f.* remote identification
Fernkopierer *m.* remote copier
Fernleihbestellung *f.* inter-li-
brary loan
Fernleihe *f.* inter-library lend-
ing, inter-library loan
Fernmeldeanlage *f.* telecom-
munication equipment
Fernmeldewesen *n.* telecom-
munications
Fernschreiben *n.* teleprint
fernschreiben *vrb.* tele-
script/to, teletype/to
Fernschreiber *m.* teleprinter,
teletypewriter
Fernschreibschlüssel *m.* tele-
code
Fernschreibsystem *n.* telex
system
Fernsehen *n.* television
Fernsehjournalist *m.* tele-
vision journalist
Fernsehproduktion *f.* tele-
vision production
Fernsprechdienst *m.* telephone
service
Fernsprechgebühr *f.* toll
Fernsprechleitung *f.* telephone
line
Fernsprechnetz *n.* toll network
Fernsprechteilnehmer *m.* tele-

phone subscriber
Fernsprechverzeichnis *n.* telephone directory
Fernsteuerung *f.* remote control, telecontrol
Fernstudium *n.* tele-education, distance education, correspondence course
Ferntransaktion *f.* remote transaction
Fernüberwachung *f.* remote supervision
Fernunterricht *m.* teaching by mail
Fernverarbeitung *f.* line loop operation, remote computing
Fernverwaltung *f.* remote administration
Fernwartung *f.* remote maintenance
Fernzugriff *m.* remote access
Fertigkeit *f.* talent, skill, facility
Fertigstellung *f.* completion
Fertigung *f.* production
Fertigungslinie *f.* pilot line
fest *adj.* non-varying
Festbestellung *f.* firm order
Festbild *n.* still picture
feste Aufstellung *f.* absolute location
feste Stelle *f.* permanent post
fester Arbeitszyklus *m.* fixed cycle operation
festes Feld *n.* fixed field
Festfeldcodierung *f.* fixed field coding
Festhaltefunktion *f.* hold function
Festival *n.* festival
Festkommaarithmetik *f.* fixed point arithmetic

Festkommadarstellung *f.* fixed point representation
Festkörperforschung *f.* solid-state research
festlegen *vrb.* state/to
Festplatte *f.* hard disk
Festschrift *f.* festschrift, commemorative volume, festive book, memorial volume
Festspeicher *m.* fixed storage, hardware buffer, non-erasable storage, permanent storage, read-only memory, read-only storage
Festspeicherbefehl *m.* read-only instruction
Feststellennumerierung *f.* fixed numbering
Feststeller *m.* shift lock
Festtermin *m.* mandatory date
festverdrahtete Steuerung *f.* hardwired controller
fett *adj.* bold
Fettdruck *m.* heavy print
fette Linie *f.* faced rule, full-face rule
fette Schrift *f.* bold type
fetter Buchstabe *m.* fat-face type, full-face type
Fettschrift *f.* black face
Feuchtigkeit *f.* damp, humidity
Filialbibliothek *f.* branch library
Film *m.* motion-picture, cinefilm, film
Filmarchiv *n.* film archive
Filmdatenbank *m.* motion-picture database
Filmlochkarte *f.* aperture card, aperture punched card
Filmothek *f.* film library
Filmstreifen *m.* film strip

Filmtitel *m.* motion-picture title
Filmverzeichnis *n.* index of films
Filmwissenschaft *f.* motion-picture studies
Finanzamt *m.* internal revenue office
Finanzanalyse *f.* financial analysis
Finanzen *pl.* finance
finanzieren *vrb.* fund/to
Finanzierung *f.* funding
Finanzierungsproblem *n.* budget problem
Finanzjahr *n.* fiscal year
Finanzwesen *n.* finance
Findbuch *n.* finding list
finden *vrb.* find/to
Firma *f.* company
Firmenadreßbuch *n.* company directory, trade directory
Firmenarchiv *n.* business archives
Firmenbibliothek *f.* firm library, company library, industrial library, industrial library
Firmeninformation *f.* business information
Firmenschrift *f.* company publication
Firmenverzeichnis *n.* trade directory
Firmenzeichen *n.* trademark
Firmenzeitschrift *f.* corporate periodical
fixe Kosten *pl.* fixed cost
Fixierung *f.* fixing
Fixierungsloch *n.* guide hole
Fixpunkt *m.* benchmark
Flachbettgerät *n.* flat-bed equipment
Flachdruck *m.* flat-bed printing
Fläche *f.* area
Flachkartei *f.* flat visible index
Flattermarke *f.* back mark, collating mark
Flattersatz *m.* flush paragraph, ragged-right setting, unjustified setting
Flattersatz *m.* **links ausgeschlossen** flush left
Flattersatz *m.* **rechts ausgeschlossen** flush right
Flexibilität *f.* flexibility, hospitality
flexible Heftung *f.* flexible fastening, flexible sewing
flexible Notation *f.* flexible notation
Flexionsendung *f.* ending
Flexionssymbole *pl.* flexional symbols
fliegendes Blatt *n.* fly-leaf
Fließband *n.* conveyer, assembly line
Fließtext *m.* continuous text
flüchtig *adj.* volatile
flüchtiger Speicher *m.* volatile memory
Flugblatt *n.* flier, leaflet
Flügel *m.* aisle
Flugschrift *f.* pamphlet
Flußdiagramm *n.* flow chart, flow diagram, process chart
Flußdiagrammsymbol *n.* flow chart symbol
Flußlinie *f.* flow line
Flußrichtung *f.* flow direction
Fokus *m.* focus
Folge *f.* series, string
Folge *f.* **von Bindebefehlen**

linking sequence

Folgeausfall *m.* secondary failure

Folgebedingung *f.* IF-THEN element

folgegebundene Information *f.* sequenced information

Folgegruppe *f.* sequence set

Folgekartenbeschriftung *f.* repetitive printing

Folgekontrolle *f.* sequence checking

Folgen *pl.* continuations

Folgenummer *f.* post number, sequence number

Folgeprüfung *f.* sequence checking

folgernd *adj.* illative

Folgesatzangabe *f.* next-sentence phrase

Folgesatzsuchfeld *n.* next-record field

Folgeschaltung *f.* IF-THEN gate

Folgestufe *f.* sequence set

Folgetitel *m.* successor title

Foliant *m.* folio

Folie *f.* foil

Förderband *n,* conveyer belt

Förderung *f.* promotion

formale Beziehung *f.* formal relation

formale Ordnung *f.* canonical order, mathematical order

formale Unterteilung *f.* form subdivision

Formaleintrag *m.* form entry

Formalkatalog *m.* descriptive catalog

Formalkatalogisierung *f.* descriptive cataloging

Formalparameter *m.* formal parameter

Format *n.* format, panel, size

Formatangabe *f.* format item, format specification

Formataufbau *m.* layout format

Formatauswahl *f.* format selection

Formatbeschreibung *f.* format description, panel description

Formatbreite *f.* length of form

Formatdatei *f.* format file

Formatdatenbank *f.* format database

Formatentwurf *m.* layout format

Formatfehler *m.* format error

formatfreie Daten *pl.* free format data

formatfreie Schreibanweisung *f.* unformatted write statement

formatfreie Zeichenfolge *f.* unformatted character string

formatfreier Datensatz *m.* unformatted record

formatfreier Datentransfer *m.* unformatted data transfer

formatfreier Modus *m.* unformatted mode

formatgebundener Datensatz *m.* formatted record

Formatgestaltung *f.* formatting, panel formatting

Formatgruppe *f.* format set

Formatidentifikationsfeld *n.* format identification field

Formatiermodus *m.* adjust mode

Formatiersprache *f.* format language

formatierte Anzeige *f.* format-

ted display
formatierte Diskette *f.*
formatted diskette
formatierter Datentransfer *m.*
formatted data transfer
Formatierung *f.* formatting
Formatierungsprogramm *n.*
formatter
Formatinstruktion *f.* format
instruction
Formatkennzeichen *n.* format
identifier
Formatkontrolle *f.* format
control
Formatmanagement *n.* panel
management
Formatsekundärausdruck *m.*
format secondary
Formatspeicherung *f.* format
feature
Formatsteuerung *f.* format
control
Formatsteuerzeichen *n.*
format effector, layout
character
Formatumwandler *m.* format
compiler
Formatvereinbarung *f.* image
statement
Formatwähler *m.* format
selector
Formatwechsel *m.* format
change
Formatzeichenfolge *f.* format
string
Formatzeile *f.* format line
Formblatt *n.* form
Formel *f.* formula
Formelzähler *m.* formula
counter
formen *vrb.* shape/to
Formgebung *f.* conformation

Formular *n.* form
Formulareingabe *f.* forms
entry
Formularführung *f.* forms
guide, paper guide
Formulargröße *f.* paper size
Formularlängensteuerung *f.*
page length control feature
Formularvorschub *m.* form
feed, form skip
Forscher *m.* researcher
Forschung *f.* **und Entwicklung**
f. research and development
Forschungsabteilung *f.* re-
search department
Forschungsarbeit *f.* research
work
Forschungsaufgabe *f.* research
problem
Forschungsbeirat *m.* research
commission
Forschungsbericht *m.* research
report, technical report, re-
search paper
Forschungsbibliothek *f.*
learned library, research li-
brary
Forschungsdokumentation *f.*
project documentation
Forschungsergebnis *m.* re-
search result
Forschungsinstitut *n.* research
institute
Forschungsprojekt *n.* research
project
Forschungsstipendium *n.* fellowship
Forschungszentrum *n.* research center
Forst *m.* forest
Forstwesen *n.* forestry
Forstwirtschaft *f.* forestry

Fortbildung *f.* postgraduate education

Fortbildungsveranstaltung *f.* postgraduate course

fortgeschrittene Technologie *f.* advanced technology

fortlaufend *adj.* serial

fortlaufende Bestellung *f.* continuation order

fortschreiben *vrb.* keep up-to-date/to, update/to

Fortschreibung *f.* updating

Fortschreibungsanweisung *f.* update command statement

fortschreitend *adj.* progressing, progressive

Fortschritt *m.* progress

fortschrittliches Computerkonzept *n.* advanced computer concept

Fortschrittsbericht *m.* advances, progress report

Fortschrittsfeld *n.* progress field

fortsetzen *vrb.* proceed/to

Fortsetzung *f.* continuation, proceeding

Fortsetzungsband *m.* continuation volume

Fortsetzungsformular *n.* window form

Fortsetzungskarte *f.* continuation card, extension card

Fortsetzungskartei *f.* continuation record

Fortsetzungsliste *f.* continuation list

Fortsetzungswerk *n.* part work, works in progress

Foto *n.* photo

Fotoarchiv *n.* photographic archives, photographic library

fotoelektrischer Leser *m.* photoelectric reader

fotoelektrisches Skannen *n.* photoelectric scanning

Fotographie *f.* photograph

Fotokopie *f.* photocopy

Fotokopierdienst *m.* photocopying service

Fotokopiergerät *n.* photocopying machine

Fotokopiersystem *n.* photocopying system

Fotolithographie *f.* photolithography

Fotomaske *f.* photomask

fotomechanisch *adj.* photomechanical

Fotomontage *f.* photomontage

Fotosatz *m.* photosetting

Fotosatzanlage *f.* photosetting equipment

Fotostelle *f.* photographic department

Fotozelle *f.* photo document sensor

Frage *f.* query, question

Frage-Antwort-Retrievalsystem *n.* question-answering retrieval system

Frage-Antwort-System *n.* question-answering system

Fragebogen *m.* questionnaire

Fragebogenentwurf *m.* questionnaire design

Fragedatei *f.* question file

fragen *vrb.* query/to, question /to

Fragezeichen *n.* interrogation mark, question mark

Fragment *n.* fragment

Frankiermaschine *f.* mailer
Frauenberuf *m.* women's
profession
frei *adj.* free, spare
freiberufliche redaktionelle Arbeit *f.* freelance editing
freiberufliches Indexieren *n.*
freelance indexing
freie Eingabe *f.* input allowed
freie Indexierung *f.* free indexing
freie Kapazität *f.* spare capacity
freie Seite *f.* unused page
freie Suchmöglichkeit *f.*
browsability
freier Aufbau *m.* unused setup
freier Datenträger *m.* public
volume
freier Mitarbeiter *m.* freelancer
freier Zugang *m.* open access
freies Element *n.* free element
freies Format *n.* free format
freies Schlagwort *n.* identifier
Freiexemplar *n.* complimentary copy, deposite copy, free
copy
Freigabe *f.* release
Freigabe *f.* **der Steuertasten**
allowing command keys
Freigabeversion *f.* release
freigeben *vrb.* declassify/to,
free/to, release/to
Freihaltezeit *f.* hold-off interval
Freihandaufstellung *f.* open
stack
Freihandausleihe *f.* openstack borrowing
Freihandbereich *m.* open-access area

Freihandbestand *m.* openstack collection
Freihandbibliothek *f.* open-access library
Freihandmagazin *n.* open
stack
Freihandsystematik *f.* openstack classification
freistehendes Bücherregal *n.*
double-faced shelf
Freitext *m.* free text
Freitextrecherche *f.* free-text
search
Freitextsuche *f.* free-text
search
Freizeit *f.* spare time
Freizustand *m.* idle condition
Fremddatenübernahme *f.* copy
cataloging
Fremdkatalogisierung *f.*
bought-in cataloging, copy
cataloging, derived cataloging
Fremdsprache *f.* foreign
language
Fremdsprachenausgleicher *m.*
multilingual package
Fremdsprachenunterricht *m.*
foreign language teaching
Fremdwörterbuch *n.* dictionary of foreign terms
Fremsprachenausbildung *f.*
foreign language education
Frequenz *f.* frequency
Freunde *pl.* **der Bibliothek**
friends of the library
Frist *f.* deadline
Fristkartei *f.* date file, date
record
Friststreifen *m.* date label,
date slip
Fristzettel *m.* date label, date

slip
Frühdrucke *pl.* early imprints
Frühgeschichte *f.* early history
Frühjahrstreffen *n.* spring
meeting
Fuchsschwanz *m.* binding saw
fühlen *vrb.* sense/to
führen *vrb.* guide/to
führende Null *f.* left-hand
zero, high order zero
führende Zeichen *pl.* leading
graphics
Führer *m.* guide book
Führung *f.* guide
Führungsanzeige *f.* guidance
indicator
Führungsgremium *n.* control-
ling body
Führungskante *f.* leading edge
Führungskraft *f.* executive
Führungsloch *n.* guide hole
Führungsrand *m.* guide edge
Führungsregler *m.* master
controller
Führungszeichen *n.* guidance
character, leading sign
Füllbyte *n.* padding byte
Füllzeichen *n.* fill character,
filler, gap character
Fundamentalkategorie *f.* fun-
damental category
Fundortregister *n.* location in-
dex
Fundstelle *f.* information
source
Fundstellenangabe *f.* locator
Funkhaus *n.* radio station
Funktion *f.* function
funktionale Abhängigkeit *f.*
functional dependency
funktionelle Berichtswege *f.*
functional guidance

Funktionsanforderung *f.* function request
Funktionsaufruf *m.* function
reference
Funktionsbeschreibung *f.* functional characteristic
Funktionsbezeichner *m.* func-
tion designator
Funktionsbezeichnung *f.* de-
signation of function
Funktionscode *m.* function
code
Funktionsdatei *f.* function file
Funktionsdefinition *f.* function
definition
Funktionsdiagramm *n.* action
chart
Funktionseinheit *f.* functional
unit
funktionsfähig *adj.* operational
Funktionsgruppe *f.* operation
group
Funktionslinie *f.* action line
Funktionsprüfung *f.* operation
checkout
Funktionstaste *f.* function key
Funktionsteilung *f.* task sharing
Funktionstest *m.* self-check
Funktionsübersicht *f.* function
chart
funktionsunfähig *adj.* inoperative
Funktionszeichen *n.* functional
character
Funktionszeit *f.* action period
Fußnote *f.* bottom note, foot
note
Fußsteg *m.* bottom of the
page, foot of the page, foot,
tail margin

Fußzeile *f.* bottom line, foot line, page footing
Fußzeilentext *m.* bottom margin text
Futteral *n.* book case
Futurologie *f.* futurology

G

Gang *m.* aisle
Ganze *n.* ensemble
ganzseitige Tafel *f.* full page plate
Ganzzahl *f.* integer number, integer
Ganzzahlaufbereitung *f.* integer editing
ganzzahlig *adj.* integer
ganzzahlige Konstante *f.* integer constant
ganzzahlige Lösung *f.* integer solution
ganzzahliger Teil *m.* integer part, integral part
ganzzahliges Attribut *n.* integer attribute
Garantie *f.* assurance, warranty
Garderobe *f.* cloakroom
Gärtnerschule *f.* gardening school
gastgebender Rechner *m.* host computer, host processor
Gastronomieschulbibliothek *f.* catering school library
Gatewayeinrichtung *f.* gateway facility
Gattungsname *m.* generic name, generic term
geänderte Daten *pl.* modified data
Gebietskörperschaft *f.* territorial authority
gebildet *adj.* educated
geblockte Daten *pl.* blocked data
geblockter Satz *m.* blocked record
Gebrauchsanweisung *f.* instruction for use, direction for use
Gebrauchsdefinition *f.* contextual definition, definition by context
Gebrauchsmuster *n.* registered design
gebrauchte Maschine *f.* used equipment
gebräulich *adj.* usual
gebrochener Exponent *m.* fractional exponent
Gebühr *f.* fee
Gebührenerhöhung *f.* increase of charges
Gebührenermäßigung *f.* reduction of charges
gebührenfrei *adj.* non-charge-

able, free of charge, without charge

gebührenfreie Bibliothek *f.* free library

Gebührenfreiheit *f.* exemption from charges, exemption from fees

Gebührenordnung *f.* scale of charges, fee schedule

gebührenpflichtig *adj.* subject to charges

gebührenpflichtige Leihbücherei *f.* commercial library

gebündelte Übertragung *f.* burst transmission

gebunden *adj.* bound

gebundener Band *m.* bound volume

gebundenes Buch *n.* bound book, bound volume

Gedächtnisstütze *f.* reminder

Gedankenstrich *m.* dash

gedeckt *adj.* lined

Gedenkbibliothek *f.* memorial library

Gedenkrede *f.* commemorative sermon

Gedenkschrift *f.* commemorative volume, memorial volume

Gedenkstätte *f.* memorial place

Gedicht *n.* poem

Gedichtform *f.* poetic form

Gedichtsammlung *f.* collection of poems

gedruckt *adj.* printed

gedruckter Katalog *m.* printed catalog

geeignete Technologie *f.* appropriate technology

Gefängnisbibliothek *f.* jail li-

brary, gaol library, prison library

gefütterter Einband *m.* padded binding

gegen Gebühr entliehenes Buch book on loan

Gegensatz *m.* antonym

Gegensatzbeziehung *f.* antonymic relation

Gegenstand *m.* matter

gegenüberliegende Seite *f.* opposite page

Gegenüberstellung *f.* comparison

Gehäuse *n.* rack enclosure

Geheimdienstbericht *m.* intelligence report

Geheimdokument *n.* secret document

Geheimhaltung *f.* secrecy

gehobener Dienst *m.* middlegrade staff

Geisteswissenschaften *pl.* humanities

geistige Freiheit *f.* intellectual freedom

geistiges Eigentum *n.* intellectual property

geistiges Niveau *n.* intellectual level

gekennzeichneter Datenname *m.* qualified data name

gekennzeichneter Name *m.* qualified name

gekennzeichnetes Schlagwort *n.* qualified heading

gelbe Seiten *pl.* yellow pages

Geldbedarf *m.* financial needs

Gelegenheitsnutzer *m.* occasional user

Gelehrsamkeit *f.* learning

gelehrt *adj.* scholarly, learned

Gelehrter *m.* scholar
Geleitwort *n.* preface, foreword
gelernt *adj.* trained, skilled
Gelernte *n.* knowledge
gelocht *adj.* perforated,
punched
Gemeinde *f.* community
Gemeindearchiv *n.* municipal
archive
Gemeindebibliothek *f.* community library
Gemeindebibliothekswesen *n.*
community librarianship
Gemeindeblatt *n.* parish bulletin
Gemeindebücherei *f.* municipal library, communal library
Gemeindehochschulbibliothek
f. community college library
Gemeindekrankenhausbibliothek *f.* community hospital library
Gemeinderegister *n.* parish
register
Gemeinkosten *pl.* overhead
Gemeinnützigkeit *f.* nonprofit
gemeinsam benutzen *vrb.*
share/to
gemeinsam benutzt *adj.* shared
gemeinsam benutzte Datei *f.*
shared file
gemeinsam benutzte Daten *pl.*
shared data
gemeinsame Erwerbung *f.* cooperative acquisition
gemeinsame Katalogisierung *f.*
cooperative cataloging,
shared cataloging
gemeinsame Nutzung *f.* der
Betriebsmittel resource shar-

ing
gemeinsamer Bereich *m.* same
area
Gemeinschaftsanschluß *m.*
shared line
Gemeinschaftsarbeit *f.* teamwork
Gemeinschaftsveröffentli-
chung *f.* co-publishing
gemeinsprachliche Bezeichnung *f.* general term
gemischte Dateien *pl.* mixed
data set
gemischte Datenaufzeichnung
f. miscellaneous data recorder
gemischte Eingabenzeile *f.*
mixed entry row
gemischte Funktion *f.* mixed
function
gemischte Notation *f.* mixed
notation
gemischte Systemauslegung *f.*
mixed environment
genau *adj.* minutely
Genauigkeit *f.* specificity, accuracy, minuteness
Genauigkeitsprüfung *f.* accuracy check
Genauigkeitsverlust *m.* lost
significance
Genehmigung *f.* approval
Generaldirektion *f.* headquarter
Generalstabskarte *f.* geographical survey map
Generalüberholung *f.* reconditioning
Generation *f.* generation
generative Grammatik *f.*
generative grammar
generative Transformations-

grammatik *f.* transformational generative grammar
Generator *m.* generator
generieren *vrb.* generate/to
Generierung *f.* generation
Generierung *f.* **der Produktionsdaten** manufacturing data generation
Generierungssprache *f.* generation language
generisch *adj.* generic
generische Aufnahme *f.* generic posting
generische Codierung *f.* generic coding
generische Kette *f.* generic chain
generische Relation *f.* generic relation, genus-species relation
generische Struktur *f.* generic structure
generischer Verweis *m.* general information reference
generisches Merkmal *n.* generic characteristic
generisches Schlagwort *n.* generic heading
Genossenschaft *f.* cooperative association
genossenschaftlich *adj.* cooperative
Genossenschaftsbibliothek *f.* cooperative movement library
Genus *m.* genus
Geochemie *f.* geochemistry
geöffnete Datei *f.* open data file
Geograph *m.* geographer
Geographie *f.* geography
geographisch *adj.* geographic

geographische Einteilung *f.* geographical division
geographische Gruppe *f.* geographical group
geographische Ordnung *f.* geographic arrangement, geographic filing method, geographical order
geographische Unterteilung *f.* local list, local subdivision
geographischer Katalog *m.* geographical catalog
Geologe *m.* geologist
Geologie *f.* geology
geologisch *adj.* geological
Geometrie *f.* geometry
Geophysik *f.* geophysics
geordnet *adj.* organized
geordnete Datenbank *f.* organized database
geordnete Datenmenge *f.* data set
gepaartes Segment *n.* paired segment
gepackt *adj.* packed
gepackte Form *f.* packed mode
gepackte Schlüssel *pl.* packed keys
gepackte Übertragung *f.* packed transmission
gepackter Druckbereich *m.* packed print zone
gepacktes Datenfeld *n.* packed data field
gepacktes Feld *n.* packed field
gepacktes Format *n.* packed format
geplante Aktualisierung *f.* update intent
geplante Wartung *f.* scheduled maintenance
geplanter Termin *m.* schedul-

ed date
geprüft *adj.* verified
geprüfte Datenbank *f.* verified database
gepufferte Nachrichtenverwaltung *f.* message buffering facility
gerade *adj.* even
Gerät *n.* equipment, unit, instrument
Gerät *n.* **mit Münzautomat** coin-operated equipment
Geräteausstattung *f.* hardware
Geräteschnittstelle *f.* terminal interface
Gerätesteuerzeichen *n.* device control character
Gerätezuweisung *f.* hardware assignment
geräuscharm *adj.* quiet
Gerichtsbibliothek *f.* court library
geringster Widerstand *m.* least effort
Germanistik *f.* Germanic languages and literature study
gerufene Station *f.* called station
gesammelte Werke *pl.* collected works, complete works
Gesamtantwortzeit *f.* total response time
Gesamtauflage *f.* whole edition
Gesamtausfall *m.* blackout
Gesamtausgabe *f.* complete edition
Gesamtbearbeitungszeit *f.* total processing time
Gesamtbegriff *m.* generic

term, comprehensive term
Gesamtkatalog *m.* central catalog, cumulative catalog, main catalog, union catalog
Gesamtkosten *pl.* overall costs
Gesamtlaufzeit *f.* total running time
Gesamtregister *n.* general index
Gesamtschulbibliothek *f.* comprehensive school library
Gesamtschule *f.* comprehensive school
Gesamtspeicher *m.* total memory
Gesamttitel *m.* common title
Gesamtverzeichnis *n.* union list
Gesamtwerk *n.* complete work
Gesamtzeit *f.* minutes total
Gesamtzeitschriftenverzeichnis *n.* union list of periodicals, union list of serials
geschachtelt *adj.* nested
geschachtelte Befehlsprozedur *f.* nested command procedure
geschachtelte Prozedur *f.* nested procedure
geschachtelte Struktur *f.* nested structure
Geschäftsgang *m.* book processing
Geschäftsjahr *n.* business year, financial year
Geschenk *n.* donation, gift
Geschenk- und Tauschstelle *f.* gift and exchange department
Geschenkausgabe *f.* gift edition
Geschichte *f.* story, history
Geschichtenbuch *n.* storybook

Geschichtenerzähler *m.* storyteller
Geschichtsbuch *n.* history book
Geschichtsforschung *f.* historical research
Geschichtskartographie *f.* historical cartography
Geschichtsschreibung *f.* historiography
Geschichtswissenschaft *f.* history
Geschlecht *n.* genus
geschlossen *adj.* closed
geschlossene Reihe *f.* closed
array
geschlossene Schleife *f.* closed
loop
geschlossener Laser *m.* laser
enclosure
geschlossenes System *n.* closed
system
geschlossenes Unterprogramm
n. closed subroutine
geschützt *adj.* safe, secure
geschützte Datei *f.* protected
file,secured file
geschützte Kopie *f.* protected
copy
geschützter Speicher *m.* protected storage
geschützter Speicherplatz *m.*
protected location, isolated
location
geschützter Warteschlangenbereich *m.* protected queue
area
geschützter Zugriff *m.* protected access
geschütztes Datenfeld *n.* protected data field
geschütztes Feld *n.* bypass
field

Geschwindigkeit *f.* velocity
Geschwindigkeitsumschalter
m. speed change control
geschwungene Klammer *f.*
brace, bow bracket
Gesellschaft *f.* society
Gesellschafts- und Vereinsbibliothek *f.* society and club library
Gesellschaftswissenschaften
pl. social sciences
gesellschaftswissenschaftlich
adj. sociological
Gesetz *n.* principle, law
Gesetzblatt *n.* law gazette
Gesetzbuch *n.* statute book
Gesetzessammlung *f.* legal file
Gesetzgeber *m.* legislator
gesetzlich *adj.* legal
gespeichert *adj.* stored
gespeichertes Programm *n.*
stored program
gesperrt *adj.* spaced
gesperrt gedruckt *adj.* spaced
out
gesperrte Datei *f.* unauthorized file
gesperrter Name *m.* locked
name
gesperrter Satz *m.* leaded
matter, locked record
Gespräch *n.* conversation
Gesprächsfluß *m.* conversational flow
Gesprächspartner *m.* participant
Gesprächsthema *n.* topic,
subject
Gestaltung *f.* conformation
Gestaltung *f.* von Veröffentlichungen layout
Gestell *n.* rack

gestörte Reihenfolge *f.* out of order
gestreut *adj.* diffuse
gestreute Datei *f.* direct file
gestreute Dateiorganisation *f.* direct file organization
gestreutes Lesen *n.* scattered read
Gesundheitswesen *n.* public health
geteilter Bildschirm *m.* split screen
gewerblich *adj.* commercial
gewerbliche Leihbibliothek *f.* rental collection, rental library
gewerbliche Literatur *f.* trade literature
Gewerkschaft *f.* labor union
Gewerkschaftsarchiv *n.* labor union archive
Gewerkschaftsbibliothek *f.* trade union library, labor union library
Gewicht *n.* weight
gewichtete Daten *pl.* weighted data
gewichtete Indexierung *f.* weighted indexing
gewichteter Durchschnitt *m.* weighted average
gewichtetes Retrieval *n.* weighted retrieval
Gewichtung *f.* weighting
Gewichtungsfaktor *m.* weighting factor
Gewichtungsfunktion *f.* weighting function
Gewinn *m.* profit
Gewinnmaximierung *f.* profit maximization
gewöhnliche Lesart *f.* ordinary

version
Giftinformationszentrum *n.* toxicological information center
Giftstoffe *pl.* toxicological substances
Gitternetz *n.* grid
Gitterstruktur *f.* lattice structure
Glasfaserkabel *n.* light-wave cable, optical fiber
Glasfaserübertragung *f.* optical fiber transmission
gleich *adj.* like
gleichgeordnete Klassen *pl.* coordinate classes
Gleichheit *f.* match
Gleichheitsattribut *n.* like attribute
Gleichheitszeichen *n.* equal mark, equal sign
gleichlautender Informationsgehalt *m.* equivocation
gleichnamig *adj.* by-name
gleichordnende Indexierung *f.* coordinate indexing
gleichordnendes Register *n.* coordinate index, concept-coordinate index
Gleichordnung *f.* coordination
Gleichordnung *f.* **von Begriffen** concept coordination
Gleichordnungsbeziehung *f.* coordinate relation
Gleichungsberechnung *f.* equation evaluation
gleichwertige Merkmale *pl.* equivalent characteristics
gleichzeitig *adj.* simultaneous
gleichzeitige Verarbeitung *f.* in-line processing
Gleichzeitigkeit *f.* simultaneity
Gleitblock *m.* backslide

gleitende Ersetzung *f.* floating replacement

gleitende Hauptspeicheradressierung *f.* floating storage address

Gleitkommaarithmetik *f.* floating-point arithmetic

Gleitkommabasis *f.* floating-point base

Gleitkommadarstellung *f.* floating-point representation

Gleitkommakonstante *f.* floating-point constant

Gleitkommaoperand *m.* floating-point operand

Gleitkommaprogramm *n.* floating-point routine

Gleitkommarechnung *f.* floating-point computation

Gleitkommaregister *n.* floating register

Gleitkommaunterprogramm *n.* floating-point subroutine

Gleitkommavergleich *m.* floating-point comparison

Gleitkommazahl *f.* floating-point number

Glied *n.* der Kette link in the chain

Gliederung *f.* breakdown, outline, structuring

global *adj.* global, non-local

globaler Hauptprozessor *m.* global processor

globaler Name *m.* global title

globaler Speicher *m.* global storage

Globalprüfung *f.* global checking

Globus *m.* globe

Glockenkurve *f.* bell-shaped curve

Glossar *n.* explanatory dictionary, glossary

Glosse *f.* gloss

Goffmans epidemische Theorie *f.* Goffman's epidemic theory

Goldschnitt *m.* gilt edge

gothische Schrift *f.* gothic

Grad *m.* grade

graduiert *adj.* graduated

Grammatik *f.* grammar

grammatikalisch analysieren *vrb.* parse/to

grammatikalische Analyse *f.* analysis of the grammatical form, grammatical analysis

grammatikalische Regeln *pl.* grammar rules

grammatikalischer Formalismus *m.* grammatical formalism

Grammatikmodelle *pl.* grammars

grammatische Modelle *pl.* grammatical models

Grammgewicht *n.* grammage

Graph *m.* graph

Graphem *n.* grapheme

Graphentheorie *f.* graph theory

Graphik *f.* chart

Graphikbildschirm *m.* graphic display

Graphikdrucker *m.* graphics printer

Graphikterminal *n.* graphics terminal

graphisch *adj.* graphic

graphische Ausgabe *f.* graphics output

graphische Darstellung *f.* graphics display, graph, graphic representation graphische Darstellung *f.* einer Klassifikation graphic representation of a classification

graphische Daten *pl.* graphic data

graphische Datenverarbeitung *f.* computer graphics

graphische Eingabe *f.* graphic input

graphische Information *f.* graphic information

graphische Zugriffsmethode *f.* graphics access method

graphischer Bildschirm *m.* graphics monitor

graphischer Datensatz *m.* graphic record

graphisches Gerät *n.* graphics device

graphisches Zeichen *n.* graphical symbol

Graphothek *f.* graphic art collection

graue Literatur *f.* grey literature, non-book trade publications

Grauwert *m.* half tone

Graveur *m.* engraver

Grenzabweichungen *pl.* limiting deviations

Grenze *f.* boundary, bound

Grenzfunktion *f.* boundary function

Grenzkosten *pl.* terminal cost

grenzüberschreitender Datenfluß *m.* transborder data flow

Grenzvorrang *m.* limit priority

Grenzwert *m.* limit value, limiting value, limit

Griffregister *n.* thumb index

grobe Schrift *f.* large face

grober Schnitt *m.* large face

Grobklassifikation *f.* broad classification

Grobrecherche *f.* area search

Grossist *m.* agent

Großbetrieb *m.* enterprise

Großbibliothek *f.* large library

Großbuchstabe *m.* capital letter, capital, full cap, upper case character, upper letter

Großdruck *m.* large print

Größe *f.* quantity, size

Großfolio *n.* large folio

Großformat *n.* large format

großformatig *adj.* large-sized

Großhandel *m.* wholesale

Großkernspeicher *m.* large-capacity storage

Großrechner *m.* mainframe

großschreiben *vrb.* capitalize/to

Großschreibung *f.* capitalization

Großsignal *n.* high level

Großstadtbibliothek *f.* city library

Großsystem *n.* large system

Grundausbildung *f.* basic training

Grundbedarf *m.* basic requirement

Grundbegriff *m.* basic concept

Grundbestandteil *m.* isolate

Grundbuch *n.* land register

Grundfehler *m.* intrinsic error

Grundfunktion *f.* basic function

Grundgebühr *f.* basic charge

Grundgesamtheit *f.* population

Grundgeschwindigkeit *f.* raw speed

Grundkatalog *m.* basic catalog
Grundklasse *f.* basic class
Grundlage *f.* foundation, basis
grundlegend *adj.* basic
Grundlinie *f.* base line, body line
Grundpreis *m.* basic price
Grundrecht *n.* basic right
Grundriß *m.* compendium
grundsätzliche Zuständigkeit *f.*
basic competency
Grundschreibfeld *n.* basic square
Grundschulbibliothek *f.*
primary school library,
elementary school library
Grundschulbücherei *f.* primary
school library
Grundschule *f.* primary
school, elementary school
Grundstellung *f.* home position, home row, home
Gründungsurkunde *f.* charter
Grundzahl *f.* base
Gruppe *f.* class, clump, group,
batch
Gruppe *f.* **von Dateigenerationen** generation data group
Gruppenadressierung *f.* group
addressing
Gruppenanzeige *f.* group indication
Gruppenarbeit *f.* teamwork
Gruppenbeziehung *f.* group
relation
Gruppenbildung *f.* clustering
Gruppendatei *f.* group data
set
Gruppendiskussion *f.* group
interview
Gruppenkennzeichnung *f.*
group indication
Gruppenkommunikation *f.*
group communication

Gruppenmarke *f.* group mark
Gruppenname *m.* group name
Gruppennotation *f.* group notation
Gruppennummer *f.* group
number
Gruppenschlagwort *n.* class
heading
Gruppenschlagwortkatalog *m.*
alphabetical-classed catalog
Gruppensteuersatz *m.* group
record
Gruppentrennzeichen *n.*
group separator, unit
separator
Gruppenverarbeitung *f.* group
processing
Gruppierung *f.* grouping
gültig *adj.* legal, valid
Gültigkeit *f.* validity
Gültigkeitsbereich *m.* scope
Gültigkeitsbit *n.* validity bit
Gültigkeitsfehler *m.* bus-out
check, validity error
Gültigkeitsprüfung *f.* validation, validity check
Gültigkeitsrecherche *f.* validity search
Gummi *m.* rubber
Gutachten *n.* estimate, expert
opinion, certificate
Gutachter *m.* expert, referee,
valuer, consultant
Gutachterausschuß *m.* rating
committee
Gutschein *m.* voucher, coupon
Gutschrift *f.* credit
Gymnasialbibliothek *f.* high
school library, grammmar
school library, gymnasium library
Gymnasium *n.* high school

H

Habilitation f. habilitation
Habilitationsschrift f. inaugural dissertation
haften vrb. adhere
Halbaddierer m. half-adder
halbautomatisch adj. semiautomatic
Halbband m. half binding, half-volume
Halbbildschaltung f. halfframe
Halbbyte n. half-byte
halbduplex adj. half duplex
Halbduplexbetrieb m. halfduplex operation
Halbduplexkanal m. halfduplex channel
Halbduplexleitung f. halfduplex communication line
Halbduplexübertragungsweg m. half-duplex facilities
halbe Geschwindigkeit f. halfspeed capability
halbfett adj. bold face, half-fat
halbgesteuerte Schaltung f. half controllable connection
Halbjahresschrift f. biannual, semiannual
halbjährlich adj. half-yearly, semiannual
Halbkanal m. half channel
Halbleiter m. semiconductor
halbmonatlich adj. halfmonthly, semimonthly

Halbmonatsschrift f. semimonthly
Halbpfad m. half-path
Halbschritt m. half cycle, half space
Halbschrittaste f. half-space key
Halbschritthebel m. half-backspace lever
Halbsubtrahierer m. half-subtractor
Halbton m. half tone
Halbwort n. halfword
Halbwortkonstante f. halfword constant
Halbwortoperand m. halfword operand
Halbwortparameter m. halfword parameter
Halbzeilenschaltung f. halfline spacing
Halt m. halt, pause
HALT-Befehl m. PAUSE statement
Haltanzeiger m. halt indicator
Haltbarkeit f. permanence
Haltbedingung f. stop condition
Haltbefehl m. pause instruction
Haltcode m. halt code
Halter m. fastener
Haltespeicher m. hold buffer
Haltestatus m. hold status

Haltezeit *f.* hold time
Haltinstruktion *f.* halt instruction
Haltkennzeichnung *f.* halt identifier
Hammer *m.* hammer
Hand *f.* hand
Handapparat *m.* handset
Handauswahl *f.* hand sorting, manual selection
Handbibliothek *f.* ready reference collection
Handbuch *n.* handbook, manual, reference manual
Handbuch *n.* **für allgemeine Informationen** general information manual
Handeinband *m.* extra
Handel *m.* trade, commerce
Handelsbericht *m.* trade report
Handelsbibliothek *f.* commercial library
Handelsblatt *n.* trade journal
Handelsbücher *pl.* commercial books
Handelshochschule *f.* school of commerce
Handelskammer *f.* chamber of commerce
Handelskammerbibliothek *f.* chamber of commerce library
Handelsliteratur *f.* trade literature
Handexemplar *n.* author's copy
handgeschrieben *adj.* handwritten
handgesetzt *adj.* hand set
handhaben *vrb.* handle/to
handkolorierte Handschrift *f.* illuminated manuscript

Händler *m.* retailer
Handlochkarte *f.* hand-operated punched card
Handprägung *f.* hand tooling
Handpresse *f.* hand-press
Handsatz *m.* hand set
Handschrift *f.* manuscript, autography, chirography, handwriting, hand
Handschriftenabteilung *f.* manuscript department
Handschriftenanalyse *f.* bibliothics
Handschriftenbestand *m.* manuscript collection
Handschriftenkatalog *m.* manuscript catalog
Handschriftenkatalogisierung *f.* manuscript cataloging
Handschriftenkonservierung *f.* manuscript preservation
Handschriftensammlung *f.* manuscript collection
handschriftlicher Zettel *m.* manuscript card
Handsteuerung *f.* manual control
Handwörterbuch *n.* concise dictionary
Handzettel *m.* dodger
Handzuführung *f.* hand-feed
Hängekartei *f.* vertical file
hängendes Attribut *n.* hanging attribute
Hardware *f.* hardware
Hardwarefehler *m.* hardware check
Hardwareinstruktionswiederholung *f.* hardware instruction retry
Hardwarepuffer *m.* hardware buffer

Harmonikafalz *m.* accordion fold, accordion pleat, concertina fold
harmonisierte Normen *pl.* harmonized standards
harter Maschinenfehler *m.* hard machine check
harter Stopp *m.* hard stop
hartsektoriert *adj.* hard-sectored
Hashcodierung *f.* hash coding
Hashfunktion *f.* hash function
Hashtabelle *f.* hash table
Häubchen *n.* headcap
Häufigkeit *f.* frequency
Häufigkeitsuntersuchung *f.* frequency analysis
Häufigkeitsverteilung *f.* frequency distribution
Häufigkeitswörterbuch *n.* frequency dictionary
häufigste Länge *f.* modal length
Hauptanschluß *m.* main line
Hauptanwendungsgebiet *n.* major application area
Hauptbedeutung *f.* primary meaning
Hauptbegriff *m.* generic term
Hauptbereich *m.* prime area
Hauptbibliothek *f.* main library
Hauptbuch *n.* ledger
Hauptbüro *n.* head office
Hauptdatei *f.* main file
Hauptdateischlüsselname *m.* master file key name
Hauptdatenbereich *m.* main data area, prime data area
Haupteintrag *m.* full description, heading, main entry
Haupteintragskarte *f.* main

entry card
Hauptfacettenunterteilung *f.* basic focus
Hauptfach *n.* major field of study
Hauptfeld *n.* major field
Hauptformular *n.* key form
Hauptindex *m.* master index
Hauptinformationsquelle *f.* chief source of information
Hauptkarte *f.* header card, main card
Hauptkatalog *m.* basic catalog, central catalog, general catalog, main catalog, master catalog
Hauptkennwort *n.* master password
Hauptklasse *f.* main class
Hauptknoten *m.* major node
Hauptkonsole *f.* master console
Hauptkontrollfeld *n.* major control field
Hauptmerkmal *n.* hightlight
Hauptprogramm *n.* main program, mainline program, master program
Hauptprozessor *m.* main processor
Hauptrechner *m.* host computer, host processor, host
Hauptrechnerunterbereich *m.* host subarea
hauptsächlich *adj.* major
Hauptsachtitel *m.* title proper
Hauptsatz *m.* master record, reference block
Hauptsatzzeichen *n.* alignment function character
Hauptschalter *m.* line switch
Hauptschema *n.* main

schedule
Hauptschlagwort *n.* main heading
Hauptschleife *f.* major cycle, major loop
Hauptschlüssel *m.* host master key, master key
Hauptschriftleiter *m.* chief editor
Hauptspeicher *m.* core memory, general storage, main memory, main storage, memory, processor storage
Hauptspeicheradressierung *f.* addressing main storage
Hauptspeicherauszug *m.* main storage dump
Hauptspeicherbenutzung *f.* processor storage utilization
Hauptspeicherbereich *m.* main storage region
Hauptspeicherdatenbank *f.* main storage database
Hauptspeichereinheit *f.* main storage unit
Hauptspeichererweiterung *f.* additional storage, memory expansion
Hauptspeichergröße *f.* main storage size
Hauptspeicherindex *m.* master track
Hauptspeicherlesebefehl *m.* memory read command
Hauptspeicherprozessor *m.* main storage processor
hauptspeicherresidentes Programm *n.* never-ending program
Hauptspeicherschreibbefehl *m.* memory write command
Hauptspeichersteuereinheit *f.*

main storage controller
Hauptspeicherzuordnung *f.* processor storage allocation
Hauptstation *f.* master station
Hauptstelle *f.* main station
Hauptsteuereinheit *f.* main control unit, main device scheduler
Hauptstruktur *f.* major structure
Haupttafel *f.* main schedule
Hauptteil *m.* body
Haupttitel *m.* full title, main title
Haupttitelblatt *n.* main title page
Hauptverfasser *m.* main author, principal author
Hauptverwaltung *f.* head-quarter
Hauptzeitscheibe *f.* major time slice
Hauptzyklus *m.* major cycle
Hausbinderei *f.* binding department, home binding
Hausdruckerei *f.* in-plant printer
Haushalt *m.* budget
Haushaltsführung *f.* budgeting
Haushaltsmittel *pl.* funds
Haushaltsordnung *f.* budget regulations
Haushaltstitel *m.* budget account
Haushaltsüberwachung *f.* budgetary control
hausinterne Zeitschrift *f.* in-house journal
hausinternes Material *n.* in-house material
hausinternes System *n.* in-

house system
Hauskorrektur *f.* reader´s proof
Haussatz *m.* home record
Hebel *m.* lever
heben *vrb.* lift/to
Hebeplattenkontrolle *f.* lift key
Heftdraht *m.* binding wire
Heftfaden *m.* binding thread
heftweise *adj.* in parts
Heimcomputer *m.* home computer
Heißsatz *m.* hot type
Helligkeit *f.* intensity
Helligkeitsstufe *f.* intensity level
herausgeben *vrb.* edit/to, publish/to
Herausgeber *m.* editor, public author
Herausgeberassistent *m.* assistant editor
Herausgebergremium *n.* editorial board
herausgegeben *adj.* edited
herausnehmen *vrb.* extract/to
heraussuchen *vrb.* pick/to, retrieve/to
herausziehen *vrb.* pull out/to
Herbstsitzung *f.* fall meeting
Herkunft *f.* source
Herkunftsmerkmal *n.* characteristic of origin
Hersteller *m.* authorized installer, implementor
Herstellung *f.* manufacturing
Herstellung *f.* **von Büchern** bibliogony
Herstellungsbeziehung *f.* productive relation
Herstellungskosten *pl.* production cost

Herunterladen *n.* downloading
hervorheben *vrb.* highlight/to
Heuristik *f.* heuristics
heuristisch *adj.* heuristic
heuristische Auswahl *f.* heuristic dispatching
heuristische Methode *f.* heuristic method
heuristische Näherung *f.* heuristic approach
hexadezimal *adj.* hexadecimal
hexadezimale Darstellung *f.* hexadecimal representation
hexadezimale Notation *f.* hexadecimal notation
Hexadezimalsystem *n.* hexadecimal numbering system
hierachisches Netz *n.* hierarchic network
Hierarchie *f.* hierarchy
Hierarchiespeicher *m.* hierarchy storage
hierarchisch *adj.* hierarchic
hierarchisch anordnen *vrb.* rank /to
hierarchisch direkte Zugriffsmethode *f.* hierarchical direct access method
hierarchisch indexsequentielle Zugriffsmethode *f.* hierarchical indexed-sequential access method
hierarchische Beziehung *f.* hierarchical relation
hierarchische Datei *f.* hierarchic file
hierarchische Klassifikation *f.* hierarchical classification
hierarchische Notation *f.* hierarchical notation
hierarchische Reihe *f.* hierar-

chical queue
hierarchische Struktur *f.* hierarchical structure
hierarchische Verbindung *f.* hierarchical linkage
hierarchischer Baum *m.* hierarchical tree
hierarchischer Pfad *m.* hierarchical path
hierarchischer Verweis *m.* hierarchical reference
hierarchisches Datenbankmodell *n.* hierarchical data base model
hierarchisches Klassieren *n.* hierarchical clustering
hierarchisches Zugriffsverfahren *n.* hierarchical sequential access method
Hilfe *f.* help
Hilfebereich *m.* help area
Hilfebereichsbestimmung *f.* help definition specification
Hilfeformat *n.* help format
Hilfetext *m.* help text
Hilfsdeskriptor *m.* auxiliary descriptor
Hilfseinrichtungen *pl.* auxiliary facilities
Hilfsgröße *f.* ancillary subject, dummy
Hilfskanal *m.* backward channel
Hilfskonjunktion *f.* auxiliary conjunction
Hilfsmaterial *n.* indirect material
Hilfsmittel *n.* resource, tools
Hilfsprogramm *n.* utility
Hilfsprogrammfunktion *f.* utility function
Hilfsprozessor *m.* auxiliary

processor
Hilfsschema *n.* auxiliary schedule
Hilfsspeicher *m.* auxiliary store, external storage
Hilfstafel *f.* auxiliary schedule, auxiliary table, categorial table
Hilfsthesaurus *m.* microthesaurus
Hilfsunterbefehl *m.* help subcommand
Hilfsvariable *f.* dummy variable
Hilfsverweise *pl.* auxiliary syndesis
Hilfszahl *f.* auxiliary number
hintere Anlegemarke *f.* collating marks
Hintergrund *m.* background
Hintergrundjob *m.* background job
Hintergrundleser *m.* background reader
Hintergrundmaterial *n.* background material
Hintergrundprogramm *n.* background program
Hintergrundspeicher *m.* auxiliary storage, backing storage
Hintergrundverarbeitung *f.* background processing
Hinterklebepapier *n.* back lining paper, back lining, book backing paper
Hinterlassenschaft *f.* bequest
hinterlegen *vrb.* deposite/to
Hinweis *m.* attention note, hint
Hinweisadresse *f.* pointer
Hinweisadresse *f.* **zum letzten Satz** last record pointer

Hinweisdatenbank f. reference database
Hinweise pl. reference data
hinweisen vrb. indicate/to, pinpoint/to, point out/to
Hinweisschild n. label
Hinweisspur f. library track
Hinweiszeichen n. attention identifier
hinzufügen vrb. add/to
Histogramm n. histogram
Historiographie f. historiography
historische Reihenfolge f. historical order
Hochdruck m. letterpress, letterpress printing
Hochformat n. lengthwise, upright format
Hochgeschwindigkeitsaddierzähler m. high-speed accumulating counter
Hochgeschwindigkeitspufferspeicher m. high-speed buffer
Hochgeschwindigkeitsübertragung f. high-speed data transfer
Hochglanzpapier n. glossy paper, high-glazed paper
Hochkommata pl. inverted commas
Hochleistungskanal m. high-speed channel
Hochschularchiv n. university archive, college archive
Hochschulausbildung f. university education, higher education
Hochschulbibliographie f. university bibliography
Hochschulbibliothek f. university library, college library

Hochschulbibliothekswesen n. higher education librarianship
Hochschulbuchhandlung f. college bookshop
Hochschule f. university, college
Hochschulinstitut n. university institute
Hochschullehrer m. professor
Hochschulschrift f. university publication, college publication
Hochschulstudent m. university student
Hochschulverzeichnis n. university directory
Hochschulwesen n. higher education system
höchste Stelle f. high-order position
Hochstellen n. half index up
hochstellen vrb. raising
Höchstkapazität f. maximum capacity
Höchstleistung f. maximum performance
Höchstleistungsgrenze f. peak capacity
Hofbibliothek f. court library
hohe Antwortgeschwindigkeit f. rapid response time
hohe Auflösung f. high resolution
höhere Programmiersprache f. high-level language
hohl adj. hollow
Holdatei f. get file
Hologramm n. hologram
Holographie f. holography
holographischer Speicher m. holographic memory

Holztafeldruck *m.* block book
homogen *adj.* homogeneous
Homogenität *f.* homogeneity
Homograph *n.* homograph
homolog *adj.* homologous
Homonym *n.* homonym
homonym *adj.* homonymous
Homonymie *f.* homonymy
homophon *adj.* homophonous
homotop *adj.* homotopic
Honorar *n.* royalty
Hörbarkeit *f.* audibility
Horizontalablenkung *f.* horizontal deflection
horizontale Feineinstellung *f.* horizontal fine adjustment
horizontale Steuerung *f.* horizontal drive
horizontale Tastatur *f.* horizontal keyboard
horizontaler Adreßzeiger *m.* horizontal pointer
horizontaler Rücklauf *m.* horizontal return
Horizontalsteuerung *f.* horizontal control
Horizontaltabulator *m.* horizontal tabulation
Horizontaltabulierung *f.* horizontal tabulating
Horizontalvorlauf *m.* horizontal transport
Host *m.* host
Hostcomputer *m.* host computer, host
Hostsystem *n.* host system
Hosttransaktionsverwalter *m.* host transaction manager
Hurenkind *n.* bad break
Hüttenwesen *n.* metallurgy
hybrid *adj.* hybrid
Hybrideingabeanschlußblock *m.* hybrid input terminal
Hybrideingabegruppe *f.* hybrid input matching point
Hybridrechner *m.* hybrid computer
Hydroelektrik *f.* hydroelectric
Hyperbel *f.* hyperbola
hyperbolisch *adj.* hyperbolic
Hypertext *m.* hypertext
Hypotaxe *f.* hypotaxis
Hypotenuse *f.* hypotenuse
Hypothese *f.* hypothesis

I

Identifikation f. identification
Identifikationscode f. identifying code
Identifikationsprüfung f. identification verification
Identifikationszeichen n. identification character
Identifikator m. key
identifizieren vrb. identify/to
Identifizierung f. identification
Identifizierungsnummer f. identification number
identische Gleichung f. identical equation
Identität f. identity
Identitätsbedingung f. identity gate
Identitätsglied n. identity gate
Identitätsvergleich m. logical comparison
Ideogramm n. ideogram
Ideographie f. ideography
ideographisches Schlagwort n. ideographic heading
Idiom n. dialect, idiom
Ikonographie f. iconography
illuminieren vrb. illuminate/to
illuminierte Handschrift f. illuminated manuscript
Illustration f. illustration
illustrativ adj. illustrative
Illustrator m. illustrator
illustrieren vrb. illustrate/to
illustriert adj. illustrated

Illustrierte f. little magazine
illustrierte Ausgabe f. illustrated edition
illustriertes Wörterbuch n. illustrated dictionary
im Dialogbetrieb interactive
im Hauptspeicher gehaltene Liste f. in-storage list
imaginär adj. imaginary
Imaginärteil m. imaginary part
Imaginärzahl f. imaginary number
implementieren vrb. implement/to
Implementierung f. implementation
Implementierungsphase f. implementation stage
Implikation f. implication, inclusion
implizit adj. implicit, implied
implizite Adresse f. implicit address, implied address
implizite Differentiation f. implicit differentiation
implizite Eröffnung f. implicit opening
implizite Funktion f. implicit function
implizite Länge f. implied length
implizite Typzuordnung f. implied association

implizite Vereinbarung f. implicit declaration
impliziter Dateiabschluß m. implicit close
implizites Attribut n. implied attribute
Importbuchhandlung f. import bookshop
Impressum n. imprint
Impuls m. impulse, pulse
in Bearbeitung in process
in Benutzung in use
in Buchform in book form
in Druck in press
in eckigen Klammern in square brackets
in eine Rangordnung f. **bringen** ranking
in Grundstellung bringen homing
in Klammer setzen vrb. parenthesize/to
in Klammern gesetzter Ausdruck m. parenthesized expression
in Rechnung stellen vrb. invoice /to
in runden Klammern in curves, in parenthesis, in round brackets
in spitzen Klammern in pointed brackets
In-Stream-Prozedur f. instream procedure
in streng alphabetischer Reihenfolge in strict alphabetical order
in Warteschlange eingereiht adj. queued
inaktiv adj. inactive
inaktive Datenstation f. inactive station

inaktive Leitung f. inactive line
inaktiver Rahmen m. inactive frame
inaktuell adj. not of immediate interest, not topical
Inbetriebnahme f. putting into service, start-up procedure
Index m. index, subscript
Indexanalysator m. index analyser
Indexdatei f. index file
Indexdatenbank f. index database
Indexeintrag m. index entry, index term, indexing term
Indexeintragung f. index control entry
Indexerkennung f. index detection
Indexerstellung f. index built
Indexfeld n. index data item, index field
Indexgruppe f. index set
indexieren vrb. enter/to into the index, index /to
Indexierer m. indexer
indexiert adj. indexed
indexierte Dateiorganisation f. indexed organization
Indexierung f. indexing
Indexierung f. **mit kontrolliertem Vokabular** controlled indexing
Indexierungsabteilung f. indexing department
Indexierungsbreite f. indexing density
Indexierungsdienst m. indexing service
Indexierungsgenauigkeit f. depth of indexing
Indexierungskonsistenz f. con-

sistency of indexing, indexing consistency

Indexierungskriterien *pl.* indexing criteria

Indexierungsnorm *f.* indexing standard

Indexierungsspezifizität *f.* indexing specificity

Indexierungssprache *f.* index vocabulary, indexing language

Indexierungssystem *n.* indexing system

Indexierungstiefe *f.* depth of indexing, exhaustivity of indexing, exhaustivity indexing exhaustivity

Indexierungsverfahren *n.* indexing technique

Indexkomponente *f.* index component, index level

Indexliste *f.* index list

Indexloch *n.* index access hole

Indexmarke *f.* index mark

Indexname *m.* index name

Indexpunkt *m.* index marker, index point

Indexregister *n.* indexing feature, modifier register

Indexsatz *m.* index record

Indexschlüssel *m.* index key

indexsequentielle Datei *f.* indexed file, indexed sequential data set, indexed sequential file

indexsequentielle Dateiorganisation *f.* index sequential organization

indexsequentieller Zugriff *m.* index sequential access

Indexstufe *f.* index level

Indexsuchverfahren *n.* index-

ed search

Indexterm *m.* indexing term

Indexverbindungseintrag *m.* index link entry

Indexwiederholung *f.* index replication

Indexwort *n.* index word

Indexzugriffsverfahren *n.* indexed access method

indikativ-informatives Referat *n.* indicative-informative abstract

indikative Beschreibung *f.* indicative entry

indikatives Referat *n.* indicative abstract

Indikator *m.* indicator

indirekt *adj.* indirect, multilevel

indirekte Adresse *f.* multilevel address

indirekte Benutzeruntersuchung *f.* indirect study

indirekte Datenadressliste *f.* indirect data address list

indirekte Dokumentation *f.* indirect documentation

indirekte Kommunikation *f.* indirect communication

indirekte Operation *f.* indirect operation

indirekte Retrievalmethode *f.* **nach Goffman** Goffman´s indirect retrieval method

indirekter Befehl *m.* indirect instruction

indirekter Zugriff *m.* indirect access

Individualbegriff *m.* individual concept

Individualsignatur *f.* unique call number

indizierte Daten *pl.* subscripted data
Induktion *f.* induction
Industrie *f.* industry
Industriebetrieb *m.* factory, industrial plant
Industriebibliothek *f.* industrial library
Industrieländer *pl.* industrialized countries
industrielle Datenverarbeitung *f.* industrial data processing
Infix *n.* infix
Informatik *f.* computer science, informatics
Informatiker *m.* computer scientist
Information *f.* information
Information Retrieval *n.* information retrieval
Information Retrievalsprache *f.* information retrieval language
Information Retrievalsystem *n.* information retrieval system, information selection system
Informationen *pl.* information
Informations- und Dokumentationsdienst *m.* information and documentation service
Informations- und Dokumentationswesen *n.* information and documentation
Informationsabteilung *f.* information department
Informationsanalyse *f.* information analysis
Informationsanalysezentrum *n.* information analysis center
Informationsanalytiker *m.* in-

formation analyst
Informationsanforderungen *pl.* information requirements
Informationsangebot *n.* information supply
Informationsausgabe *f.* information dispensing
Informationsaustausch *m.* information exchange
Informationsaustauschsystem *n.* information communicating system
Informationsbanken *pl.* information banks
Informationsbearbeitung *f.* information handling
Informationsbeauftragte *m.* information officer
Informationsbedarf *m.* information demand
Informationsbedürfnisse *pl.* information needs
Informationsbegriff *m.* information concept
Informationsberatung *f.* information consultation, information counseling
Informationsbeschaffung *f.* information collecting, information gathering
Informationsbeschaffungsmuster *n.* information gathering patterns
Informationsbewertung *f.* information evaluation
Informationsbrief *m.* news bulletin, newsletter
Informationsbroker *m.* information broker
Informationsdichte *f.* information density
Informationsdienst *m.* infor-

mation service
Informationseinheit *f.* information unit, item of information, item
Informationselemente *pl.* information elements
Informationsentropie *f.* information entropy
Informationsethik *f.* information ethics
Informationsexplosion *f.* information explosion
Informationsfachkraft *f.* information specialist
Informationsfachmann *m.* information professional
Informationsfeld *n.* information area
Informationsfluß *m.* flow of information, information flow
Informationsflußanalyse *f.* information flow analysis
Informationsflut *f.* information explosion
Informationsformat *n.* information format
Informationsfreiheit *f.* freedom of access to information, freedom of information
Informationsfunktion *f.* information function
Informationsgebrauch *m.* information use
Informationsgehalt *m.* information content, measure of information
Informationsgesellschaft *f.* information society
Informationsgewinn *m.* information gain
Informationshandel *m.* information trade
Informationsindustrie *f.* information industry
Informationsinteresse *n.* information interest
Informationskanal *m.* information channel
Informationskapazität *f.* information capacity
Informationslinguistik *f.* information linguistics
Informationsmanagement *n.* information management, information resource management
Informationsmarketing *n.* information marketing
Informationsmarkt *m.* information market
Informationsmaß *n.* measure of information
Informationsmedium *n.* information medium
Informationsnetz *n.* information network
Informationsnutzung *f.* information utilization
Informationsökonomie *f.* economics of information, information economy
Informationsplanung *f.* information planning
Informationspolitik *f.* information policy
Informationspräsentation *f.* information presentation
Informationsproblem *n.* information problem
Informationsprodukt *n.* information product
Informationsproduzent *m.* information producer

Informationsprozeß *m.* information process
Informationspsychologie *f.* information psychology
Informationsquelle *f.* information source
Informationsrahmen *m.* information frame
Informationsrecherchesprache *f.* information retrieval language
Informationsrecherchesystem *n.* information retrieval system
Informationsrecht *n.* information law
Informationsrückkopplungssystem *n.* information feedback system
Informationssammlung *f.* information gathering
Informationsschalter *m.* information desk
Informationsschranke *f.* information barrier
Informationsspeicher *m.* information store
Informationsspeicherung *f.* und -wiedergewinnung *f.* information storage and retrieval
Informationsspezialist *m.* information specialist
Informationsspur *f.* information track
Informationsstelle *f.* information center
Informationssuche *f.* information enquiry
Informationssuche *f.* durch Benutzer end user searching
Informationssuche *f.* im Dialog interactive retrieval
Informationssuchverhalten *n.* information seeking behavior
Informationssystem *n.* information system
Informationstätigkeit *f.* information work
Informationstechnik *f.* information technology
Informationstheorie *f.* information theory
Informationsträger *m.* information medium, information carrier
Informationstransfer *m.* information transfer
Informationstyp *m.* information type
Informationsüberlastung *f.* information overload
Informationsübertragungssystem *n.* information transmission system
Informationsverarbeitung *f.* information processing
Informationsverbreitung *f.* information dissemination
Informationsverbund *m.* information network
Informationsverfolgung *f.* tracking
Informationsverlust *m.* information loss
Informationsvermittler *m.* intermediar
Informationsvermittlung *f.* information brokerage
Informationsvermittlungsstelle *f.* referral center
Informationsversorgung *f.* information supply
Informationswert *m.* infor-

mation utility, value of information
Informationswiedergewinnung f. information retrieval
Informationswiedergewinnungssystem n. information retrieval system
Informationswissenschaft f. information science
Informationswissenschaftler m. information scientist
Informationszentrum n. information center, reference department
informativ adj. informatory
informatives Referat n. informative abstract
informelle Gruppe von Wissenschaftlern invisible college
Informetrie f. informetrics
Infrastruktur f. infrastructure
Ingenieurausbildung f. engineers education
Ingenieurhochschulbibliothek f. engineering college library
Ingenieurhochschule f. engineering college
Ingenieurwissenschaft f. engineering science
ingenieurwissenschaftliche Bibliothek f. engineering library
Inhalt m. contents, content
inhaltliche Abdeckung f. coverage
inhaltliche Erschließung f. subject analysis
Inhaltsanalyse f. content analysis
Inhaltsangabe f. argument, contents note, list of contents
inhaltsbeschreibender Titel m.

content title
Inhaltsdefinition f. definition by genus and difference, definition by genus and species, definition by intension, intensional definition
Inhaltserschließung f. indexing, subject analysis
Inhaltsfahne f. bibliographical strip
Inhaltsverzeichnis n. contents list, contents, table of contents
inhärentes Merkmal n. intrinsic characteristic
Initiale f. initial letter, initial
initialisieren vrb. initialize/to, prepare/to
Initialisierung f. initialization, initiation
Initialisierungsablauf m. initialization procedure
Initialisierungsanweisung f. initialize statement
Initialisierungsprogramm n. initializer
Initialisierungsschritt m. initialization step
Initiator m. initiator
Initiatorprozedur f. initiator procedure
Inkrement n. increment
inkrementale Darstellung f. incremental representation
Inkrementalrechner m. incremental computer
Inkrementgröße f. increment size
Inkunabel f. incunabulum, block book, early imprint
Inkunabelkatalogisierung f. incunabula cataloging
Inkunabelkatalog m. incu-

nabula catalog
Inkunabelsammlung *f.* incunabula collection
Innenkreis *m.* incircle
Innenstadtbibliothek *f.* inner city library
Innentitel *m.* inside title
Innenverbindung *f.* internal connection
innerbetrieblich *adj.* in-house, intracompany
innerbetriebliche Information *f.* in-house information
innerbetriebliches Computernetz *n.* in-house network
innerbetriebliches System *n.* in-house system
Innerborddatei *f.* inboard file
innere Form *f.* inner form
innerer Papierrand *m.* back margin, inner margin
Innovation *f.* innovation
Innovationsberatung *f.* innovation counseling
ins Regal stellen *vrb.* shelve/to
Inschrift *f.* inscription
Installation *f.* installation
Installationsvorgabe *f.* installation standard
installieren *vrb.* install/to, set up/to
installiertes Benutzerprogramm *n.* installed user program
Instandhaltung *f.* maintenance
Instandsetzungsdauer *f.* active repair time
Institut *n.* institute
Institution *f.* institution
Institutionendokumentation *f.* documentation of institutions
Instituts- und Gesellschafts-

bibliothek *f.* institute and society library
Institutsbibliothek *f.* department library, faculty library, institute library
Instruktion *f.* instruction, procedural statement
Instruktion *f.* **mit Indexadresse** indexed instruction
Instruktionsadreßregister *n.* instruction address register
Instruktionsphase *f.* instruction cycle
Instruktionsspeichermodul *n.* additional instruction storage
Instruktionszähler *m.* instruction counter
Instrument *n.* instrument
instrumentelle Beziehung *f.* instrumental relation
Integral *n.* integral
Integralregler *m.* integral action controller
Integralwert *m.* integral value
Integration *f.* integration
Integrationsgrad *m.* level of integration
Integrationsmodell *n.* integration model
Integrationspfad *m.* path of integration
Integrationspolitik *f.* integration policy
Integrationsprozeß *m.* integration process
integrierendes Netzwerk *n.* integrating network
integrierte Datenverarbeitung *f.* integrated data processing
integrierte Steuereinheit *f.* integrated control unit
integrierte Tastatur *f.* inte-

grated keyboard
integrierte Textverarbeitung *f.*
integrated word processing
integrierter Direktzugriffs-
speicher *m.* integrated direct
access storage
integrierter Schaltkreis *m.* integrated circuit
integriertes Verzeichnissystem
n. integrated directory sytem
integriertes Wörterbuchsystem
n. integrated dictionary system
Integrität *f.* integrity
Intelligenz *f.* intelligence
Intensivanzeige *f.* high-intensity display, intensified
display
Interaktion *f.* interaction, interactive operation
Interaktionszeit *f.* interaction
time
interaktiv *adj.* interactive
interaktive Suche *f.* interactive
searching
interaktiver Aufbau *m.* interactive format
interaktiver Testmonitor *m.*
interactive debug
interaktives Retrieval *n.* interactive retrieval
interdisziplinäre Sachgebiete
pl. interdisciplinary subjects
interdisziplinäres Informa-
tionszentrum *n.* interdisciplinary information center
interdisziplinäres Thema *n.*
interdisciplinary subject
Interessenliste *f.* interest profile, interests record
Interessenprofil *n.* interest
profile

Interindexiererkonsistenz *f.*
interindexer consistency
intern *adj.* internal
internationale Bibliographie *f.*
international bibliography
internationale Katalogkarte *f.*
international catalog card
internationale Norm *f.* international standard
internationale Standardbuch-
nummer *f.* international
standard book number
internationale Standardse-
riennummer *f.* international
standard serial number
internationaler Schriftenaus-
tausch *m.* international
exchange of publications
internationales Recht *n.* international law
Interndatei *f.* internal file
interne Datei *f.* intrapartition
data set
interner Leser *m.* internal
reader
interner Speicher *m.* internal
storage
interner Wartestatus *m.*
quiesce state
Interpolation *f.* interpolation
Interpolation *f.* **einer Reihe** interpolation in array
interpolieren *vrb.* interpo-
late/to
Interpretation *f.* interpreting
Interpreter *m.* interpreter
Interpretercode *m.* interpretive code
Interpreterfunktion *f.* interpreter function
Interpreterprogramm *n.* interpretive program

interpretieren *vrb.* interpret/to
Intersektionsdaten *pl.* intersection data
Intervallkennwort *n.* interval password
Intervallzeitgeber *m.* interval timer
Intervallzeitgeberunterbrechung *f.* interval timer interrupt
Interview *n.* interview
Intrafacettenkonnektor *m.* intrafacet connector
Intrafacettenrelationen *pl.* intrafacet relations
Intrapartition *f.* intrapartition
intrinsische Relation *f.* intrinsic relation
Inventar *n.* inventory
inventarisieren *vrb.* accession /to
Inventarisierung *f.* accessioning, making an inventory
Inventarnummer *f.* accession number
Inventur *f.* stocktaking
invers *adj.* inverse
inverse Dokumenthäufigkeit *f.* inverse document frequency
Inversion *f.* inversion
invertieren *vrb.* invert/to
invertierte Datei *f.* inverted file
invertierte Liste *f.* inverted file
invertierte Zahl *f.* inverted number
invertierter Eintrag *m.* indirect entry, inverted entry
invertierter Mehrwortbegriff *m.* inverted compound term
invertiertes gleichordnendes Indexieren *n.* inverted coordinate indexing
invertiertes Schlagwort *n.* inverted heading
irregulär *adj.* irregular
Irrelevanz *f.* irrelevance
Irrtum *m.* mistake
Isolat *n.* isolate
Isolierband *n.* rubber tape
isolieren *vrb.* extract/to
Istanalyse *f.* state of the art analysis
Iterationsindex *m.* iteration index
iterative Partitionierung *f.* iterative partitioning
iterative Suche *f.* iterative search
iterieren *vrb.* iterate/to
IuD Programm *n.* federal program on information and doc
IuD-Stelle *f.* information center

J

Jaccard-Koeffizient *m.* jaccard coefficient
Jahr *n.* year
Jahrbuch *n.* annual publication, annual, yearbook
Jahrbücher *pl.* annals
Jahresabonnement *n.* annual subscription
Jahresabschluß *m.* annual changeover
Jahresbericht *n.* annual report
Jahreserhebung *f.* annual survey
Jahreskonferenz *f.* annual conference
Jahreskongreß *m.* annual congress
Jahresrückblick *m.* annual review
Jahresversammlung *f.* annual meeting
Jahresverzeichnis *n.* annual index
Jahrgang *m.* year
jährlich *adj.* yearly
jährliche Veröffentlichung *f.* annual publication
Japanpapier *m.* japanese vellum
Job *m.* job
Jobabrechnung *f.* job accounting
Jobausgabegerät *n.* job output device

Jobauswahlschalter *m.* job select switch
Jobbeendigung *f.* job termination
Jobbezugszahl *f.* job indicator
Jobbibliothek *f.* job library
Jobdatei *f.* job file
Jobdefinition *f.* job definition
Jobeingabegerät *n.* job input device
Jobeinleitung *f.* job initiation
Jobfluß *m.* job flow
Jobidentifikation *f.* job identification
Jobkontrollanweisung *f.* job control statement
Jobkontrollsatz *m.* job control record
Jobkontrollsprache *f.* job control language
Jobname *m.* job name
Jobprofil *n.* job profil
Jobstapel *m.* job batch
Jobunterbrechung *f.* job interrupt
Jobverarbeitung *f.* job processing
Jobwarteschlangeneintrag *m.* job queue entry
Jobzyklus *m.* job cycle
Journal *n.* journal
Journalismus *m.* journalism
Journalist *m.* journalist
Jubiläumsausgabe *f.* annivers-

ary issue

Jugendabteilung *f.* children's department

Jugendausgabe *f.* young people's edition

Jugendbibliothek *f.* adolescent library, youth library

Jugendbuch *n.* children's book, juvenile book

Jugendbuchabteilung *f.* juvenile book department

Jugendbücherei *f.* children's library, youth library

Jugendbuchwoche *f.* juvenile

book week

Jugendliteratur *f.* juvenile literature

juristische Bibliothek *f.* law library

juristische Datenverarbeitung *f.* legal data processing

justieren *vrb.* adjust/to

Justierung *f.* adjustment, justification

Justiz *f.* justice

Justizbehörde *f.* legal authority

K

Kabel *n.* cable

Kabelfernsehen *n.* cable television

Kabelübertragung *f.* cable transmission

Kaffeehausbibliothek *f.* coffee house library

kaiserliche Bibliothek *f.* emperor's library

kaiserliche Hofbibliothek *f.* imperial court library

Kalender *m.* calendar

Kalkulationsbasis *f.* calculation basis

Kalligraph *m.* calligrapher, calligraphist, calligraph

Kalligraphie *f.* calligraphy

kalligraphisch *adj.* calligraphic

Kanal *m.* channel

Kanalaufteiler *m.* line splitter

kanonisch *adj.* canonical

kanonische Reihenfolge *f.* canonical sequence

kanonische Unterklasse *f.* **einer Hauptklasse** canonical class

Kantenabstand *m.* margin

Kantonalbibliothek *f.* canton library

Kapazität *f.* **einer Notation** capacity of a notation

Kapazitätsoptimum *n.* ideal capacity

Kapitalband *n.* headband

Kapitalismus *m.* capitalism

Kapitel *n.* chapter, section

Kapitelüberschrift *f.* caption

title, chapter heading, drop-down title, section header
karolingische Klosterbibliothek *f.* Carolingian monastic library
Karte *f.* chart, map
Kartei *f.* card file, card catalog, card index
Karteikarte *f.* card, file card, filing slip, index card, ledger card
Karteikartenabteilung *f.* card division, card service
Karteikarteneinordnung *f.* filing of cards
Karteikartenkasten *m.* card cabinet
Karteikartenschubfach *n.* card drawer, catalog tray
Karteikartenvorderseite *f.* card face
Karteikartenzuführung *f.* card feed
Karteikasten *m.* filing case
Karteikatalog *m.* card catalog
Kartenabteilung *f.* map department
Kartenarchiv *n.* map file
Kartenaufnahme *f.* mapping
Kartenbestand *m.* map stock
Kartenbibliographie *f.* cartobibliography
Kartenfeldbegrenzung *f.* neatline
Kartenkunde *f.* cartology
Kartenlesen *n.* map reading
Kartenleser *m.* map reading instrument
Kartenmagazin *n.* hopper, read hopper
Kartenmischer *m.* collator, interpolator

Kartenreiter *m.* flag
Kartensammlung *f.* map collection
Kartensockel *m.* housing shroud
Kartenständer *m.* map stand
Kartenstapel *m.* card deck, pack of cards
Kartenstau *m.* jam
Kartenwerk *n.* atlas
Kartenzeichner *m.* cartographer
kartesische Verknüpfungsoperation *f.* join operation
kartesisches Produkt *n.* Cartesian product
Kartograph *m.* cartographer
Kartographie *f.* cartography
kartographisches Material *n.* cartographic material
Karton *m.* board
kartonieren *vrb.* bind/to in boards
kartoniert *adj.* bound in boards, in boards
Kartonpapier *n.* cardboard
Kartothek *f.* map library
Kartuche *f.* cartridge
Kassette *f.* cassette
Kasten *m.* case
Kasusgrammatik *f.* case grammar
Katalog *m.* catalog
Katalog *m.* **in Buchform** catalog in book-form
Katalog *m.* **in Registerform** guard-book catalog, ledger catalog
Katalog *m.* **mit aufgeklebten Titelstreifen** catalog with pasted-in slips
Katalog *m.* **mit durch Verweise**

verbundenen Schlagwörtern
connective catalog
Katalogabteilung *f.* catalog
department
Katalogarten *pl.* kinds of catalogs
Katalogaufnahme *f.* description
Katalogbearbeiter *m.* cataloger
Katalogbenutzer *m.* catalog user
Katalogbenutzung *f.* catalog use
Katalogdaten *pl.* catalog data
Katalogdatenbank *f.* catalog database
Katalogeintrag *m.* catalog entry
Katalogerstellung *f.* catalog construction
Katalogform *f.* form of catalog
Katalogisieren *n.* cataloging
katalogisieren *vrb.* catalog/to
katalogisiertes Verfahren *n.* cataloged procedure
Katalogisierung *f.* cataloging
Katalogisierungsabteilung *f.* cataloging department
Katalogisierungsdatenbank *f.* cataloging database
Katalogisierungsraum *m.* cataloging room
Katalogisierungsregeln *pl.* catalog code, cataloging code
Katalogisierungsstelle *f.* cataloging agency
Katalogisierungssystem *n.* cataloging system
Katalogisierungstechnik *f.* cataloging technique

Katalogisierungsverbund *m.* cooperative cataloging
Katalogisierungsverbundsystem *n.* cooperative cataloging system
Katalogkarte *f.* catalog card
Katalogkartendienst *m.* catalog card service
Katalogkartenversand *m.* catalog card mailing service
Katalogkasten *m.* card tray
Katalogpflege *f.* catalog maintenance
Katalogprobleme *pl.* cataloging problems
Katalogrevision *f.* catalog revision, catalog editing
Katalogsachbearbeiter *m.* cataloger
Katalogschublade *f.* catalog drawer
Katalogwesen *n.* cataloging
kategoriale Beziehung *f.* categorial relation
Kategorie *f.* category
Kategorisierung *f.* categorization
Kathodenstrahlröhre *f.* cathode-ray tube
Kauf *m.* purchase
kaufen *vrb.* purchase/to
kaufmännische Bibliothek *f.* commercial library
Kausalbeziehung *f.* causation
Kaution *f.* deposit
kein Zugriff access inoperable
keine Antwort *f.* no response
keine Arbeit *f.* no assignment
keine gemeinsame Benutzung *f.* no sharing
keine Operation *f.* no operation

keine Übereinstimmung f. no match
Kellerspeicher m. nesting store, pushdown stack
Kennfeld n. addressing tag
Kennsatz m. header, identifying label, label record, label
Kennsatzbereich m. label area
Kennsatzfamilie f. label set
Kennsatzgruppe f. label group, label set
Kennsatzinformation f. label information
Kennsatzinformationsbereich m. label information area
Kennsatzkennzeichen n. label identifier
Kennsatzname m. label name
Kennsatznummer f. label number
Kennsatzroutine f. label handling routine
Kennsatzsektor m. label sector
Kennsatzspeicherbereich m. label storage area
Kennsatzspur f. label track
Kennsatzverarbeitung f. label processing
Kenntnis f. skill
Kennummer f. identification number
Kennungsgeber m. identifier
Kennungsspeicher m. identification storage
Kennwert m. characteristic value
Kennwort n. keyword, password
Kennwortanalyse f. fragmenting
Kennwortdateischutz m. password protection

Kennwortkontrolle f. password security
Kennwortschutz m. security feature
Kennwortsicherheit f. protect password security
Kennzahl f. ratio
Kennzahlweg m. final route
Kennzeichen n. attribute, flag, indication, mark, reference character, tag
Kennzeichenfeld n. identifier field
Kennzeichentaste f. delimiter key
kennzeichnen vrb. label/to
Kennzeichnerbindewort n. qualifying connective
Kennzeichnung f. labelling, label, qualification
Kennzeichnung f. **der Anschlußleitungen** line identification
Kennzeichnung f. **der Ursache** identification of cause
Kennzeichnungsfeld n. identification field
Kennzeichnungsmerkmal n. identification qualifier
Kennziffer f. characteristic
Kerbe f. notch
Kerblochkarte f. notched card
Kerbzange f. notching pliers
Kernbestand m. central collection, core collection
Kernbibliothek f. core library
Kerndokument n. core document
Kernenergietechnik f. nuclear energy technology
Kernproblem n. main problem
Kerntechnik f. nuclear tech-

nology

Kernveröffentlichung f. core publication

Kette f. chain, string

ketten vrb. append/to

Kettenindexierung f. chain indexing

Kettenklassifikation f. chain classification

Kettenmaß n. incremental coordinates, incremental dimension

Kettfeld n. link field

Kilobaud n. kilobaud

Kilobyte n. kilobyte

Kinder- und Jugendbibliothekswesen n. children´s and juvenile librarianship

Kinderabteilung f. children´s department

Kinderbibliothek f. junior library, children´s library

Kinderbibliotheksarbeit f. children´s library work

Kinderbuch n. children´s book

Kinderbücherei f. children´s library, junior library, youth library

Kinderkulturzentrum n. children´s cultural center

Kinderlektüre f. children´s literature

Kinderliteratur f. children´s literature

Kindertheater n. children´s theater

kinetische Beziehung f. kinetic relation

Kirchenarchiv n. church archive

Kirchenbibliothek f. church library, ecclesiastical library,

cathedral library

Klammer f. bracket

Klammer f. **auf** left parenthesis

Klappbilderbuch n. moveable picture book

Klappe f. flap

Klappenband m. binding with a folding flap

Klappentext m. flap blurb, jacket blurb

klar adj. distinct

Klarschrift f. normal text

Klarschriftcodierer m. character encoder

Klarschriftleser m. character reader, optical character reader

Klartext m. plaintext

Klasse f. class

Klasse-Objektbeziehung f. class-membership relation

Klassenbezeichnung f. class name, class term, class description

Klassenbildung f. clustering

Klassenmediothek f. class media center

Klassenmitglied n. class-mate

Klassennummer f. class mark, class number

Klassenzimmerbibliothek f. classroom library

klassieren vrb. class/to

Klassieren n. classing

Klassierung f. arrangement

Klassifikation f. classification

Klassifikationsforschung f. classification research

Klassifikationsnummer f. classification number

Klassifikationsproblem n.

classification problem
Klassifikationsregel *f.* classification code
Klassifikationsschema *n.* classification table, classification schedule, classification scheme
Klassifikationssystem *n.* classification system
Klassifikationstafel *f.* classification schedule, classification table
Klassifikationstheorie *f.* classification theory
Klassifikationsverfahren *n.* classification method
Klassifikator *m.* classifier
klassifikatorische Reihe *f.* array
klassifikatorische Struktur *f.* classificatory structure
klassifizierbar *adj.* classifiable
Klassifizieren *n.* classifying
klassifizieren *vrb.* classify/to, range/to
Klassifizierung *f.* classification
Klassiker *m.* classical author
klassisch *adj.* classic
klassische Ausgabe *f.* classical edition
Klausel *f.* clause
Klebeband *n.* adhesive tape
Klebebindung *f.* adhesive binding, perfect binding, lumbecking
kleben *vrb.* paste/to, splice/to, adhere/to
Klein- und Mittelbetriebe *pl.* small and medium-sized enterprises
Kleinbibliothek *f.* small library
Kleinbuchstabe *m.* lower case

character
Kleincomputer *m.* mini computer
Kleiner-als-Zeichen *n.* less than sign
kleines Deckblatt *n.* guard sheet
Kleinschreibung *f.* lower case
Kleinstadtbibliothek *f.* small town library
kleinste Untergruppe *f.* infima species
kleinste Unterteilung *f.* infima species, ultimate class
kleinstes Glied *n.* least term
Klimatisierung *f.* climatization
klinisch-medizinisches Bibliothekswesen *f.* clinical medical librarianship
Klischee *n.* printing block, block, cliche, plate
Klosterbibliothek *f.* monastery library, monastic library
Klosterbibliothekar *m.* armarian
Klumpenstichprobe *f.* cluster sample
Knappschaftsbibliothek *f.* miner´s institute library
Knoten *m.* node
Knoten-zu-Knoten Leitfunktion *f.* node-to-node routing function
Knotenbediener *m.* node operator
Knotenfehlerprogramm *n.* node error program
Knoteninitialisierungsblock *m.* node initialization block
Knotenname *m.* node name
Knotenteilung *f.* node splitting
Knotentyp *m.* node type

Koautor *m.* co-author, corporate author, joint author
Kochbuch *n.* cookery book
Kodex *m.* codex
Kodierung *f.* coding
Kognitionswissenschaft *f.* cognitive science
kognitiv *adj.* cognitive
kognitive Prozesse *pl.* cognitive processes
kognitive Strukturen *pl.* cognitive structures
Kolleg *n.* lecture
Kolloquium *n.* colloquium
Kolophon *m.* colophon
Kolumne *f.* column
Kolumnentitel *m.* running title
Kombination *f.* combination
kombinierte Datei *f.* combined file
kombinierte Randlochung *f.* combination coding
Komitee *n.* committee
Komma *n.* comma, virgule
Kommaeinstellung *f.* point setting
Kommando *n.* command
Kommandomodus *m.* command mode
Kommandosprache *f.* job control language
Kommaverschiebung *f.* point shifting
Kommentar *m.* commentary
Kommentarkarte *f.* explanatory guide card
Kommentator *m.* annotator
kommentieren *vrb.* annotate/to
kommentierte Ausgabe *f.* annotated edition
kommentierte Bibliographie *f.*

annotated bibliography
kommentierter Katalog *m.* annotated catalog
Kommentierung *f.* annotation, explanatory note
kommerziell *adj.* commercial
kommerzielle Leihbücherei *f.* rental library
kommerzieller Verlag *m.* commercial publisher
Kommission *f.* commision
Kommissionsbuchhändler *m.* wholesale bookseller
Kommunalarchiv *n.* municipal archive
Kommunalbehörde *f.* local authority
Kommunikation *f.* communication
Kommunikation *f.* **offener Systeme** open systems interconnection
Kommunikationsanalyse *f.* communication analysis
Kommunikationsforschung *f.* communication research
Kommunikationskanal *m.* line of communication
Kommunikationskultur *f.* communication culture
Kommunikationsmittel *n.* communication medium
Kommunikationsmuster *pl.* communication patterns
Kommunikationsnetzwerke *pl.* communication networks
Kommunikationspolitik *f.* communication policy
Kommunikationsprozeß *m.* communication process
Kommunikationssystem *n.* communication system

Kommunikationstechnik f. communication technique, communication technology
Kommunikationstheorie f. communication theory
Kommunikationswert m. communicative value
Kommunikationswissenschaft f. communication science
Kommunikationszentrum n. communication center
kommunikative Grammatik f. communicative grammar
Kommunikator m. communicator
Kompaktregal n. compact storage
Kompaktregalanlage f. compact shelving
Kompatibilität f. compatibility
Kompatibilitätsproblem n. compatibility problem
Kompendium n. compendium
komplex strukturierter Thesaurus m. complex-structured thesaurus
komplexes System n. complex system
Komplexität f. complexity
Komplexitätsniveau n. integrative level
Komponente f. component
Kompositum n. compound word, compound
Kompression f. compression
Konfektionierung f. packing
Konferenz f. conference
Konferenzbeitrag m. conference paper
konfessionelle öffentliche Bücherei f. denominational public library

Konfessionsmagazin n. confession magazine
Konfiguration f. configuration
Kongreß m. congress
Kongreßausschußbericht m. congress report, congressional committee report
Kongreßbericht m. proceedings
Kongreßbibliothek f. library of congress
königliche Bibliothek f. royal library
Konjunktion f. AND operation, conjunction, logical product
konjunktiv adj. conjunctive
Konkordanz f. concordance
konkreter Begriff m. concrete concept
Konkurrenz f. competition
konkurrenzlos adj. without competition
Konnektor m. connector
konnotative Bedeutung f. connotative meaning
Konservierung f. preservation
Konsistenz f. consistency
Konsistorialarchiv n. consistorial archive
Konsole f. control panel
konstant adj. non-varying
konstantes Textdokument n. shell document
Kontaktkopie f. contact copy
Kontaktstift m. pin
Kontext m. context
kontextfreie Grammatik f. context-free grammer
kontextfreier Begriff m. context-free term
Kontextoperator m. context

operator
Kontingenztabelle *f.* contingency table
kontinuierlich *adj.* continuous
Konto *n.* account
Kontrolle *f.* check
Kontrollfeld *n.* level field
Kontrollfunktion *f.* control
function, control operation
Kontrollgruppe *f.* control
group
kontrollieren *vrb.* verify/to
kontrollierte Ausleihe *f.* controlled circulation
kontrollierte Schlagwortliste *f.*
authority list, controlled term
list, subject heading list, controlled index term
kontrolliertes Vokabular *n.*
controlled vocabulary
Kontrolliste *f.* check list
Kontrollprogramm *n.* supervisory program, supervisory
routine
Kontrollpunkt *m.* checkpoint
Kontrollsatzdatei *f.* validate
file
Kontrollstempel *m.* process
stamp
Kontrollsumme *f.* hash total
Kontrollsummenfeld *n.* hash
total field
Kontrolltisch *m.* checking
counter
kontrovers *adj.* controversial
Konturschärfe *f.* acutance
Konvention *f.* convention
konventionalisierte Bedeutung
f. conventional meaning
konventionalisiertes Zeichen *n.*
conventional sign
konventionell *adj.* conven-

tional
**konventionelle Katalogisie-
rung** *f.* manual cataloging,
conventional cataloging
konventionelle Suche *f.* manual searching
konventioneller Katalog *m.*
manual catalog
Konventsbibliothek *f.* monastery library
Konvergenztheorie *f.* convergency theory
Konverter *m.* converter
konvertieren *vrb.* convert/to
Konvertierung *f.* conversion
Konvertierungsprogramm *n.*
conversion program
Konzentration *f.* concentration
Konzentrationsquote *f.* concentration ratio
Konzentrator *m.* concentrator
konzentriert *adj.* pooled
Konzept *n.* draft
Konzeption *f.* idea
Kooperation *f.* cooperation
Kooperationsvereinbarung *f.*
cooperation agreement
Koordinaten *pl.* coordinates
Koordinatenwandler *m.* re-
solver
koordinierte Indexierung *f.*
multi-aspect indexing
Koordinierung *f.* coordination
Kopf *m.* head, top
Kopf *m.* **einer Buchseite** head
of the page
Kopfabstand *m.* head gap
Kopfanweisung *f.* header
statement
Kopfauswahlzeit *f.* head selec-
tion time

Kopfformular *n.* header form
Kopfladebereich *m.* head loading zone
Kopflademagnet *m.* head load solenoid
Kopfpositionierungssystem *n.* head positioning system
Kopfprogramm *n.* header program
Kopfsteg *m.* head margin, top margin
Kopftabelle *f.* header table
Kopfträgereinheit *f.* head carriage assembly
Kopfzeile *f.* header line, page heading
Kopfzeilentext *m.* header margin text
Kopie *f.* copy, print
Kopierdienst *m.* copy service
kopieren *vrb.* copy/to, reproduce/to
Kopiergerät *n.* copier, copy machine
Kopierkarte *f.* copy card
Kopierprogramm *n.* image copy utility
Kopiertechnik *f.* copying technology
Kopierverfahren *n.* document copying
Kopist *m.* copyist
Koppler *m.* junctor
Kopplung *f.* assemblage, linking
Körperschaft *f.* corporate body
Körperschaftseintrag *m.* corporate entry, corporate heading
Korpus *m.* corpus
Korrektor *m.* copy reader, corrector, reviser

Korrektur *f.* patch, proof reader, revision
Korrektur *f.* **durch Abheben** lift-off correction
Korrektur lesen *vrb.* correct/to proofs
Korrekturabzug *m.* galley proof, proof pulling
Korrekturanweisung *f.* proof sheet
Korrekturband *n.* lift-off tape
Korrekturbereich *m.* patch area
Korrekturhilfe *f.* spelling check
Korrekturlesen *n.* proof reading
Korrekturlesen *n.* **ohne Vorleser** horsing
Korrekturzeichen *n.* proof mark
Korrelation *f.* correlation
Korrelationskoeffizient *m.* correlation coefficient
Korrelationstabelle *f.* correlation table
korrelativ *adj.* correlative
korrelative Indexierung *f.* correlative indexing
korrelatives Register *n.* correlative index
korrigieren *vrb.* patch/to
Kosinus *m.* cosine
Kosten *pl.* cost
Kosten-Leistungsanalyse *f.* cost-effectiveness analysis
Kosten-Nutzen-Analyse *f.* cost-benefit analysis
Kostenbewertung *f.* cost evaluation
Kostendeckung *f.* cost covering
Kostenerstattung *f.* refund

kostenfreie Erwerbung f. free acquisition
kostenlos adj. free of charge
kostenlose Materialien pl. free materials
Kostenrechnung f. accounting
Kostensensitivität f. cost sensitivity
Kostensensitivitätsanalyse f. cost sensitivity analysis
Kozitation f. cocitation
Krankenblatt n. clinical treatment report
Krankenhaus n. hospital
Krankenhausbibliothek f. hospital library
Krankenhausbücherei f. hospital library
Krankenhausinformationssystem n. hospital information system
Krankenpflegeschulbibliothek f. nursing school library
Krankenversicherungskarte f. health insurance identity card
Kreditwesen n. credit system
Kreisarchiv n. county archive
Kreisbibliothek f. metropolitan library, county library
Kreisdiagramm n. pie chart
Kreisergänzungsbücherei f. county supplement library
Kreisgericht n. county court
Kreiskrankenhaus n. county hospital
Kreistag m. county board
Kreisverwaltung f. district authority
Kreuzkatalog m. cross catalog, dictionary catalog, mixed alphabetical catalog
Kreuzworträtsel n. cross word

Kriegsarchiv n. military archive
Kriminalistik f. criminalistics
Kriterium n. criterion
Kritik f. criticism
Kritiker m. critic
kritische Bibliographie f. critical bibliography
kritische Indexierung f. critical indexing
kritisches Lesen n. critical reading
Kryptographie f. cryptography
Kühlprofil n. heat sink
Kulturabkommen n. cultural agreement
Kulturarbeit f. cultural work
Kulturform f. cultural pattern
Kulturgut n. cultural assets
Kulturpolitik f. cultural policy
Kulturzentrum n. cultural center
Kultusminister m. Minister of Culture
Kultusministerium n. Ministry of Culture
Kumulation f. cumulation
kumulative Bibliographie f. cumulative bibliography
kumulieren vrb. cumulate/to
kumulierend adj. cumulative
kumulierter Katalog m. cumulative catalog
kumuliertes Bücherverzeichnis n. cumulative book index, cumulative book list
kumuliertes Register n. consolidated index, cumulative index
Kunde m. client, customer
Kundendienst m. repair service

Kündigung *f.* notice
Kündigung *f.* **eines Abonnements** discontinue notice
Kündigungsfrist *f.* notice period
Kunst *f.* art
Kunstbibliographie *f.* art bibliography
Kunstbibliothek *f.* art library
Kunstdruck *m.* art print
Kunstgeschichte *f.* history of art
Kunsthochschulbibliothek *f.* art school library
künstlich *adj.* simulated
künstliche Einteilungsmerkmale *pl.* artificial characteristics of division
künstliche Intelligenz *f.* artificial intelligence, machineaided intelligence
künstliche Klassifikation *f.* artificial classification
künstliche Leitung *f.* artificial line
künstliches Schlagwort *n.* ideographic heading
Kunstsammlung *f.* art collection
Kunstsprache *f.* artificial language
Kunstwissenschaft *f.* science of fine arts
Kunstwort *n.* artificial word
Kupfertitel *m.* engraved title page
Kurs *m.* course
kursiv *adj.* italic
Kursivschrift *f.* italics, italic
Kurzadressierung *f.* abbreviated addressing
Kurzausgabe *f.* abridged edi-

tion, condensed edition
Kurzbenennung *f.* abbreviated term
Kurzbericht *m.* short report
kürzen *vrb.* abbreviate/to
Kurzfassung *f.* abridgment, compendium
Kurzfilm *m.* short film
kurzfristiger Finanzplan *m.* financial budget
Kurzgeschichte *f.* short story
kurzlebige Zeitschrift *f.* ephemera
Kurzleihbestand *m.* short loan collection
Kurzleihe *f.* short period loan
Kurzreferat *n.* indicative abstract
Kurzschlüssel *m.* abridged code
Kurzschrift *f.* shorthand
Kurztitel *m.* catchword title, lemma
Kurztitelaufnahme *f.* abbreviated entry, short-entry cataloging, minimal cataloging, limited cataloging
Kurztitelkatalog *m.* short-title catalog, abbreviated catalog
Kurztitelkatalogisierung *f.* brief cataloging
Kurztitelkatalogkarte *f.* abbreviated catalog card
Kurzübersetzung *f.* abridged translation
Kürzung *f.* reduction
Kurzwort *n.* abbreviated term, acronym
Kurzzeitdokumentation *f.* fugitive facts file
Kurzzeitinformationen *pl.* fugitive material

KWAC-Index *m.* keyword-
and-context index
KWIC-Index *m.* keyword-in-
context index
KWIT-Indexierung *f.*
keyword-in-title indexing

KWOC-Index *m.* keyword-
out-of-context index
KWOC-Indexierung *f.*
keyword-out-of-context
indexing
Kybernetik *f.* cybernetics

L

Label-Prozessorausgabe *f.* label processor output
Label-Prozessoreinheit *f.* label
processor input data set
**Label-Prozessorfehlernach-
richt** *f.* label processor error
message
labil *adj.* unstable
Laborschule *f.* experimental
school
ladbarer Kontrollspeicher *m.*
reloadable control storage
Ladeadresse *f.* load point
Ladeanzeiger *m.* load indicator
Ladebibliothek *f.* load module
library
Ladeeintragung *f.* load
member
Ladeformat *n.* load format
Lademodul *n.* load module
Laden *n.* load mode, loading
laden *vrb.* boot/to, load/to,
reload/to
Ladenpreis *m.* retail price,
publication price

Ladeprogramm *n.* bulk loader,
loader
Ladepunkt *m.* load point
Ladeverfahren *n.* load pro-
cedure
Ladezeit *f.* preexecution time
Lage *f.* gathering
Lagerbestand *m.* quantity on
hand
Lagerung *f.* storage
Ländernormdatei *f.* country
authority file
Länderreferent *m.* area biblio-
grapher
Landesarchiv *n.* state archive
Landesbehörde *f.* state
authority
Landesbibliothek *f.* state li-
brary
Landesgeschichte *f.* state
history
Landesinformationssystem *n.*
state information system
Landeskunde *f.* regional geo-
graphy
Landesmuseum *n.* state

museum
Landesparlament *n.* state parliament
Landesplanung *f.* country planning
Landesregierung *f.* state government
Landesveröffentlichung *f.* state government publication
Landesverwaltung *f.* state administration
Landkarten *pl.* cartographic material
Landkartenkunde *f.* cartographie
Landkartenzeichner *m.* cartographer
Landkreis *m.* district, county
Landtagsbibliothek *f.* state parliament library
Landwirtschaft *f.* farming, agriculture
Länge *f.* length
Längenangabe *f.* length specification
Längenfehler *m.* incorrect length
Längenfeld *n.* length field
Längenschlüssel *m.* length code, length modifier
langfristige Planung *f.* long-term planning
längsgerichtet *adj.* lengthwise
Langzeitabonnement *m.* long-term subscription
Laser *m.* laser
Laserbild *n.* laser vision
Laserdrucker *m.* laser printer
Laserplatte *f.* laser disk
Laserskanner *m.* laser scanner
Laserspeicher *m.* laser memory

Lastfaktor *m.* loading factor
Lauf *m.* run
Laufbereitschaft *f.* ready state
laufende Bestandskartei *f.* perpetual inventory file
laufende Bibliographie *f.* current bibliography
laufende Kosten *pl.* ongoing costs
laufende Nationalbibliographie *f.* current national bibliography
laufende Nummer *f.* current number, running number
laufende Zeitschrifteninhaltsübersicht *f.* contents list bulletin, current contents bulletin
laufendes Zugangsverzeichnis *n.* accessions list
Lauflänge *f.* run length
Laufrolle *f.* roller
Laufzeit *f.* propagation time, run duration, run time
Laufzeitspeicher *m.* delay line storage
Laufzeitverzögerung *f.* propagation delay
Laufzettel *m.* catalog card copy, cataloger´s slip, copy slip, guide slip, process slip
Lautschrift *f.* phonetic alphabet, phonetic writing
Lautsprecher *m.* loudspeaker
Layout *n.* layout
Layoutanweisung *f.* layout instruction
Layoutredakteur *m.* layout editor
Lebensabend *m.* last years
Lebensabriß *m.* biographical sketch
Lebensdauer *f.* life-span

Ledereinband *m.* leather binding

leer *adj.* vacuous, void

Leeradresse *f.* blank address

Leerantwort *f.* null response

Leeranweisung *f.* null statement

Leerausgabenachricht *f.* null output message

Leerbereichszuordnung *f.* space allocation

Leerblatt *n.* blank leaf, unprinted leaf

Leere *f.* vacuousness

leeren *vrb.* vacate/to

leerer Rahmen *m.* idle frame

Leerkarte *f.* blank card

leerlaufen *vrb.* idle/to

Leerlaufstatus *m.* idle state

Leerlaufzeit *f.* idle time

Leeroperation *f.* waste instruction

Leerseite *f.* blank page, blank, unused page

Leerspalte *f.* blank column

Leerspaltenprüfung *f.* space check

Leerstelle *f.* blank space, blank, vacancy

Leerstellenabschneidung *f.* blank truncation

Leersymbol *n.* empty symbol

Leertaste *f.* space bar, space key

Leerübertragung *f.* blank transfer

Leerzeichen *n.* blank character, blank space, blank, idle character, space character, space

Leerzeicheneinfügung *f.* idle insertion

Leerzeichenkette *f.* null character string, null string

Leerzeile *f.* blank line, null line, space line

Leerzeilennumerierung *f.* numbering of blank lines

Legende *f.* key to the signs used, legend

Legislativbibliothek *f.* legislature library

Lehrbeauftragter *m.* adjunct professor

Lehrbibliothekar *m.* teacher-librarian

Lehrbrief *m.* correspondence lesson

Lehrbuch *n.* textbook, undergraduate text

Lehrbuchsammlung *f.* undergraduate collection, undergraduate library

Lehrbuchversorgung *f.* textbook supply

Lehrer *m.* instructor

Lehrerbildung *f.* teacher training

Lehrfilm *m.* educational film

Lehrgang *m.* course

Lehrgebiet *n.* subject

Lehrkraft *f.* teacher

Lehrling *m.* trainee

Lehrmaterial *n.* instructional material, educational material

Lehrmethode *f.* instructional method

Lehrmittel *pl.* teaching aid, educational media

Lehrplan *m.* curriculum

Lehrstuhl *m.* professorship

Lehrveranstaltung *f.* lecture

Leihbestand *m.* loan collection

Leihbibliothek *f.* circulating library, lending library, subscription library
Leihbuch *n.* circulating book
Leihdaten *pl.* circulation data, lending data, loan data
Leihfrist *f.* borrowing period, loan period
Leihfrist verlängern *vrb.* extend/to a loan
Leihgabe *f.* loan
Leihgebühr *f.* loan fee
Leihkarte *f.* borrower´s identification card
Leihkasten *m.* issue tray
Leihordnung *f.* loan library rules
Leihschein *m.* borrower´s card, borrower´s ticket, call slip for a loan, charge card, charge slip, charging card, circulation card, issue slip, lending form
Leihstatistik *f.* loan statistic
Leihstelle *f.* circulation department, delivery room, home reading department, issuing department, lending department, loan department
Leihverkehr *m.* lending
Leihverkehrsordnung *f.* lending rules
Leihverkehrsregion *f.* lending area
Leihvermerk *m.* lending record
leihweise *adj.* as a loan, on loan
Leineneinband *m.* cloth bound
Leistung *f.* performance, wattage, effectiveness
Leistungsangabe *f.* performance specification

Leistungsbewertung *f.* performance evaluation
Leistungsbilanz *f.* balance of goods and services
Leistungsfähigkeit *f.* effectiveness
Leistungsfaktoren *pl.* performance factors
Leistungsgrad *m.* level of efficiency, performance efficiency, performance rate
Leistungsindikator *m.* effectiveness indicator
Leistungsmessung *f.* performance measurement
Leistungsniveau *n.* performance
Leistungsrate *f.* achievement rate
Leistungsstandard *m.* performance standard
Leistungssteigerung *f.* increase in efficiency
Leistungsstufe *f.* performance level
Leistungsvermögen *n.* capability
Leistungsziel *n.* performance objective
Leitartikel *m.* editorial
Leitartikelschreiber *m.* leader writer
Leitbildschirm *m.* master display station
Leitblatt *n.* master data sheet
Leitbuchstabe *m.* catch letter
leiten *vrb.* lead/to
Leiter *m.* **der Filialbibliothek** branch supervisor
Leiter *m.* **der Katalogabteilung** chief cataloger, head of catalog division

Leitfaden *m.* manual, guide
Leitkarte *f.* guide card, header card, history card, information card, issue guide, master card
Leitkarte *f.* **in der Fristkartei** date guide
Leitnachricht *f.* heading message
Leitrechner *m.* host computer, host processor, host
Leitsatzlänge *f.* header length
Leitselektor *m.* pilot selector
Leitstelle *f.* head office
Leitung *f.* line, physical line
Leitung abhängen *vrb.* line off /to
Leitung *f.* **unter Spannung** live wire
Leitungsabbruch *m.* line termination
Leitungsanschluß *m.* line adapter, line base adapter, line set
Leitungsart *f.* line type
Leitungsbelegung *f.* line occupancy
Leitungsdämpfung *f.* line loss
Leitungsdatenbereich *m.* line data area
Leitungseingang *m.* line entry
Leitungseinheit *f.* line unit
Leitungseinschaltung *f.* line-up
Leitungsfehler *m.* line error
Leitungsgebühr *f.* line charge
Leitungsgeräusch *n.* circuit noise
Leitungsgruppendatei *f.* line group data set
Leitungsnummer *f.* line number

Leitungsprotokoll *n.* line trace
Leitungsprozedur *f.* line control discipline
Leitungsprüfung *m.* line check
Leitungsstatistik *f.* line statistic
Leitungssteuerung *f.* line control
Leitungssteuerzeichen *n.* line control character, line control signal
Leitungsüberwachung *f.* line supervision
Leitungsumschaltung *f.* line transfer
Leitungsverkehr *m.* line traffic
Leitungsvermittlung *f.* line switching
Leitungszeitsperre *f.* line time out
Leitweg *m.* route
Leitwort *n.* guiding word
Lektor *m.* editor, reader
Lektorat *n.* lectorate, lectorship
Lemma *n.* lemma
Lemmatisierung *f.* lemmatization
Leporello *n.* moveable picture book
Leporellofalz *m.* accordion fold, accordion pleat, concertina fold
Lernelement *n.* answer set, question group
Lernhilfe *f.* hint
Lernmaterial *n.* tutorial
Lernumgebung *f.* learning environment
Lernziel *n.* objective
Lesart *f.* variant reading
lesbar *adj.* legible, readable

Lesbarkeit f. legibility, readability

Lese-/Schreibgeschwindigkeit f. read/write speed

Lese-/Schreibkopf m. read/write head

Lese-/Schreibspeicher m. read/write memory

LESE-Anweisung f. READ statement

Leseanforderung f. read request

Leseanweisung f. reading assignment

Lesebefehl m. read command

Lesebereich m. scannable area

lesebereit adj. ready to read

Leseclub m. reading club

Lesedatenfolge f. read data stream

Leseerziehung f. reading program

Lesefeld n. character sensing field

Lesefenster m. read window

Leseförderung f. reading promotion

Lesefreiheit f. freedom to read

Lesegerät n. scanner

Lesegesellschaft f. reading society

Lesegewohnheit f. reading custom

Lesehalle f. reading room

Lesehäufigkeit f. reading frequency

Lesehinweise pl. readers´ guide

Lesehülle f. book jacket

Leseimpulsgeber m. read emitter

Lesekarte f. library card

Lesekopf m. read head

Lesemodus m. read mode

Lesen n. reading

lesen vrb. fetch/to, pick up/to, read/to

Lesen n. **zur Entspannung** recreational reading

Lesepaßwort n. read password

Leseprozedur f. reader procedure

Leseprüfung f. read check

Lesepult n. book rest, reading desk

Leser m. client, reader

Leser pl. readership, clientele

Leserberatung f. readers´ advisory work, readers´ assistance, reader advisory

Leserkarte f. admission card

Leseroutine f. reader task

Leserschaft f. readership, reading clientele

Lesersteuerung f. reader adapter

Leserumfrage f. reading survey, readership survey

Lesesaal m. reading room

Lesesaalbestand m. reading room collection

Lesesperre f. fetch protection

Lesestift m. wand

Lesestift m. **für Magnetetiketten** magnetic wand reader

Lesestrahl m. beam

Lesestreifen m. character sensing strip

Leseverhalten n. reading behavior

Lesewarteschlange f. reader queue

Lesewiederholung f. rereading

Lesezeichen *n.* book-marker, book-mark
Lesezugriffszeit *f.* read access time
Lesezyklus *m.* read cycle
Lesezykluszeit *f.* read cycle time
Lesung *f.* reading
letzte Ausgabe *f.* last issue
letzte Indexstelle *f.* index end position
letzter Revisionsabzug *m.* final proof, final revise
letztes Zugriffsdatum *n.* last access date
Leuchtanzeige *f.* lighted message
Leuchtknopf *m.* lens
Lexem *n.* lexeme
lexikalisch *adj.* lexical
lexikalische Analyse *f.* lexical analysis
lexikalische Bedeutung *f.* lexical meaning
lexikalische Verzerrung *f.* lexical distortion
lexikalischer Inhalt *m.* lexical content
lexikalischer Prozeß *m.* lexical process
Lexikograph *m.* lexicographer
Lexikographie *f.* lexicography
lexikographisches Wort *n.* dictionary word
Lexikologie *f.* lexicology
Lexikon *n.* lexicon
Lichtemission *f.* light output
lichtempfindlich *adj.* light-sensitive, photosensitive
Lichtleiterübertragung *f.* fiber optic transmission
Lichtpause *f.* dye-line copy

Lichtsatz *m.* photocomposition, photosetting
Lichtsatzanlage *f.* phototype unit
Lichtsatzausgabe *f.* phototype output
Lichtsatztechnik *f.* phototype technology
Lichtstift *m.* light pen
Lichtstiftabruf *m.* light pen attention
Lichtstiftanschluß *m.* light pen attachment
Lichtstifteingang *m.* light pen input
Lichtstifterkennung *f.* light pen detection, light pen hit, light pen strike
Lichtstiftmodus *m.* light pen mode
Lichtstiftschalter *m.* light pen switching
Lichtstiftverfolgung *f.* light pen tracking
Lichtwellenleiter *m.* wave guide
Liebesbrief *m.* billet-doux
Liebhaberausgabe *f.* collector´s edition
Lieferant *m.* supplier, vendor
lieferbar *adj.* available, in print
Lieferbedingungen *pl.* terms of delivery
Lieferdatum *n.* delivery date
Lieferfrist *f.* term of delivery
liefern *vrb.* provide/to
Lieferschein *m.* packing slip
Lieferung *f.* delivery
Lieferungswerk *n.* suppliers´ plant
Liefervertrag *m.* delivery

contract
Lineal *n.* ruler
linear *adj.* linear
lineare Abtastung *f.* linear
scan
lineare Datei *f.* linear file
lineare Liste *f.* linear list
lineare Notation *f.* linear
notation, ordinal notation
lineare Optimierung *f.* linear
optimization
lineare Programmierung *f.* linear programming
lineares Modell *n.* linear
model
linearisieren *vrb.* linearize/to
Linearität *f.* linearity
Linearitätsfehler *m.* linearity
error
Linearklassifikation *f.* linear
classification
Linguistik *f.* linguistics
linguistisch *adj.* linguistic
linguistische Analyse *f.* linguistic analysis
linguistische Datenverarbeitung *f.* linguistic data processing
linguistische Mehrdeutigkeit *f.* linguistic ambiguity
linguistischer Prozessor *m.* linguistic processor
linguistischer Thesaurus *m.* linguistic thesaurus
linguistisches Verfahren *n.* linguistic method
Linie *f.* line
Liniennetz *n.* line communication network
Linientaste *f.* line key
Liniereinrichtung *f.* line ruler
linieren *vrb.* line/to

liniert *adj.* ruled
linke Randsteuerung *f.* left
margin control
linke Seite *f.* left part
linke Stelle *f.* left column number
linker Schreibrand *m.* left
margin
Linksausrichtung *f.* left justification
linksbündig *adj.* left adjusted,
left justified
Linse *f.* lens
Listdatei *f.* list file
Liste *f.* listing, list, report
Liste *f.* **der Abkürzungen** list of
abbreviations
Liste *f.* **der Neuerwerbungen**
accessions list
Liste *f.* **freier Schlagworte**
identifier list
Listenauswahl *f.* list selection
Listendatei *f.* report file
Listenelement *n.* list item
Listenformat *n.* report format
listengesteuert *adj.* list-directed
listengesteuerte Ein-/Ausgabe
f. list-directed input/output
listengesteuerte Übertragung
f. list-directed transmission
Listenkennung *f.* list identifier
Listenname *m.* list name
Listensteuerbefehl *m.* listing
control instruction
Listenverarbeitung *f.* list processing
Listenzeile *f.* report line
Listmodul *n.* reporting module
Listprogrammgenerator *f.* report program generator
Literal *n.* literal

Literalbereich *m.* literal pool
Literalkonstante *f.* literal constant
literarisch *adj.* literary, literate
literarisch Gebildeter *m.* literate
literarische Bildung *f.* literacy
literarische Renzension *f.* literary review
literarische Sprache *f.* literary language
literarische Tätigkeit *f.* literary activity
literarische Zeitschrift *f.* literary periodical
Literatur *f.* literature
literatur- und sprachwissenschaftliche Bibliothek *f.* literature and language library
Literaturanforderung *f.* book demand
Literaturangabe *f.* citation
Literaturangebot *n.* book supply
Literaturarchiv *n.* manuscripts archive
Literaturauswahl *f.* book selection
Literaturauswerter *m.* literature analyst
Literaturbericht *m.* analytical survey
Literaturbeschaffung *f.* book acquisition
Literaturbesprechung *f.* literature review
Literaturdatenbank *f.* bibliographic database
Literaturdienst *m.* bibliographic service
Literaturdokumentation *f.* bibliographic documentation, literature documentation
Literaturerschließung *f.* bibliographic indexing
Literaturführer *m.* literature guide, guide to the literature
Literaturgeschichte *f.* history of literature
Literaturinformationssystem *n.* bibliographic information system
Literaturkassette *f.* spoken book
Literaturkritik *f.* literary criticism
Literaturnachweis *m.* bibliographic reference
Literaturrecherche *f.* literature search
Literatursuche *f.* literature search
Literaturüberblick *m.* state of the art report
Literaturversorgung *f.* document supply, book supply
Literaturwissenschaft *f.* science of literature, literary studies
Literaturzuwachs *m.* literature growth
Lithographie *f.* lithography
Lizenz *f.* license
Lizenzabkommen *m.* license agreement
Lizenzerteilung *f.* licensing
Lizenzgeber *m.* licenser
Lizenzgebühr *f.* license, royalty
lizenzieren *vrb.* license/to
lizenziert *adj.* licensed
Lizenznehmer *m.* licensee
Lizenzprogramm *n.* license

program
Loch *n.* hole
lochen *vrb.* punch/to
Locher *m.* key punch, keyboard punch, keypunch, perforator, punch
Lochkarte *f.* body-punched card, punch card, punched card
Lochstelle *f.* code position
Lochstreifen *m.* paper tape, perforated tape, punched tape
Logarithmus *m.* logarithm
Logbuch *n.* log
Logbuchaufzeichnung *f.* log message
Logik *f.* logic
Logikanalysator *m.* logic analyser
Logikdiagramm *n.* logic diagram
logisch *adj.* logical
logische Adresse *f.* logical address
logische Dateiorganisation *f.* logical file organization
logische Datenbank *f.* logical database
logische Datenstrukturen *pl.* logical data structures
logische Differenz *f.* logical difference
logische Einheit *f.* logical unit
logische Einteilung *f.* logical analysis
logische Herkunftsadresse *f.* origination address field
logische Instruktion *f.* logical instruction
logische Konfiguration *f.* logical configuration

logische Operation *f.* logical operation
logische Ordnung *f.* logical sequence
logische Reihenfolge *f.* logical order
logische Relation *f.* logical relation
logische Schleife *f.* logical loop
logische Summe *f.* logical sum
logische Unterteilung *f.* differentiation
logische Variable *f.* logical variable
logische Verbindung *f.* logical link
logische Verknüpfung *f.* logical connective, logical relationship
logische Zeile *f.* logical line
logischer Anzeiger *m.* logical indicator
logischer Befehl *m.* logical instruction
logischer Dateianfang *m.* logical beginning
logischer Entwurf *m.* logical design
logischer Fehler *m.* logical error
logischer Operator *m.* logical operator
logischer Satz *m.* logical record
logischer Speicher *m.* logical storage
logisches Element *n.* logic element
logisches Flußdiagramm *n.* logical flowchart
logisches Produkt *n.* logical product

logisches Symbol *n.* logic element

Lohnausgleich *m.* wage adjustment

lokal *adj.* local, regional

Lokalbestandskatalog *m.* local catalog

Lokaldaten *pl.* local data

Lokaldatenkanal *m.* home-data channel

Lokaldatenregister *n.* home register

lokale Adresse *f.* local address

lokale Ausgabe *f.* local output

lokale Einheit *f.* local device

lokaler Befehl *m.* local command

lokaler Bestimmungsort *m.* local destination

lokaler Hauptprozessor *m.* local processor

lokaler Name *m.* local title

lokaler Schlüssel *m.* local key

lokaler Speicher *m.* local storage

lokales Clustern *n.* local clustering

lokales Netzwerk *n.* local area network

lokales System *n.* local system

lokalisieren *vrb.* locate/to

Lokalmodus *m.* home mode

Lokalverarbeitung *f.* home-loop operation

löschbarer Speicher *m.* erasable storage

Löschbefehl *m.* reset instruction

Löscheinrichtung *f.* eraser

löschen *vrb.* blank out/to, clear /to, delete/to, erase/to, expunge/to, obliterate/to, purge /to, reset/to

Löschen *n.* **nach Ausgabe** blank after

Löschen *n.* **nach dem Drucken** blank after print

löschendes Lesen *n.* destructive read

Löschkopf *m.* erase head

Löschmagnet *m.* bulk eraser

Löschtaste *f.* delete key

Löschung *f.* obliteration

Löschzeichen *n.* cancel character, del, delete character, deletion charcter

Loseblattbindung *f.* loose-leaf binding

Loseblattform *f.* loose-leaf format

Loseblattsammlung *f.* loose-leaf book

lösen *vrb.* unlock/to

Lösungsbuch *n.* answer book

Lösungsvorschlag *m.* approach

Lotkas Gesetz *n.* Lotka´s law

Lücke *f.* gap, lacuna, lag, vacancy

Luftbilder *pl.* cartographic material

Luftfeuchtigkeit *f.* humidity

Luftpost *f.* air mail

Lüftung *f.* ventilation

Luxuseinband *m.* luxury binding

Lyrik *f.* poetry

M

Machbarkeitsanalyse *f.* feasibility analysis
Machbarkeitsstudie *f.* feasibility study
Magazin *n.* closed shelves, closed stack, stacks
Magazinbestand *m.* stack collection
Magazinbibliothek *f.* closed-access library
Magazinebene *f.* deck
Magazingut *n.* closed-access material
magazinierter Bestand *m.* closed-access collection
Magazinierung *f.* stacking
Magazinsteuerung *f.* hopper control
Magnetband *n.* magnetic tape, tape
Magnetbanddienst *m.* tape service
Magnetbandeinheit *f.* magnetic tape unit
Magnetbandinformationsdienst *m.* magnetic tape information service
Magnetbandkassette *f.* magnetic tape cassette
Magnetbandlesegerät *n.* magnetic tape reader
Magnetbandschreibkopf *m.* magnetic tape writer
Magnetbandspeicher *m.* magnetic tape storage
Magnetblasenspeicher *m.* bubble memory
Magnetdraht *m.* magnetic wire
Magnetfilm *m.* magnetic film
Magnetfilmspeicher *m.* magnetic film storage
magnetisch *adj.* magnetic
magnetische Aufzeichnung *f.* magnetic recording
magnetische Codiereinrichtung *f.* magnetic encode station
magnetische Dünnschicht *f.* magnetic thin film
magnetische Prüfeinheit *f.* magnetic verification station
magnetische Zeichenerkennung *f.* magnetic ink character recognition
magnetischer Blasenspeicher *m.* magnetic bubble memory
magnetischer Dünnschichtspeicher *m.* magnetic thin film storage
magnetischer Speicher *m.* magnetic storage
Magnetkarte *f.* magnetic card
Magnetkarteneinheit *f.* magnetic card unit
Magnetkartenleser *m.* magnetic strip card reader
Magnetkartenspeicher *m.*

magnetic card storage
Magnetkopf *m.* head, magnetic head
Magnetkopf laden *vrb.* head load/to
Magnetplatte *f.* disk, hard disk, magnetic disk
Magnetplattenspeicher *m.* magnetic disk storage
Magnetplattenzuordnung *f.* disk allocation
Magnetschriftenleser *m.* magnetic character reader
Magnetspeicher *m.* magnetic core
Magnetspur *f.* magnetic track
Magnetstreifen *m.* magnetic strip
Magnetstreifenaufzeichnung *f.* magnetic strip recording
Magnetstreifenleser *m.* magnetic strip reader
Magnetstreifenspeicher *m.* magnetic strip storage
Magnettinte *f.* magnetic ink
Magnettrommel *f.* magnetic drum
Magnettrommelspeicher *m.* magnetic drum storage
Mahngebühr *f.* arrears letter fee, fine, overdue fine
Mahngebühren *pl.* late charges
Mahnung *f.* arrears letter, claim, overdue notice, reminder
Makro *n.* macro
Makroanalyse *f.* macro analysis
Makroauflösung *f.* macro expansion
Makroaufruf *m.* macro call

Makrobefehl *m.* macro instruction
Makrobibliothek *f.* macro library
Makrodefinition *f.* macro definition
Makrodokumente *pl.* macro documents
Makrogenerator *m.* macro generator
Makrogenerierung *f.* macro generation
Makrothesaurus *m.* macrothesaurus
Makroumwandler *m.* macro processor
Makrovorverarbeitung *f.* macro preprocessing
Makulatur *f.* discards
Management *n.* management
Managementinformationssystem *n.* management information system
Manager *m.* manager
Mangel *m.* lack
Manipulation *f.* manipulation
Manpower *f.* manpower
manuell *adj.* manual
manuelle Dateneingabe *f.* manual data input
manuelle Eingabe *f.* manual entry, manual input
manuelle Einzelblattzuführung *f.* rear document insertion
manuelle Funktion *f.* manual function
manuelle Indexierung *f.* manual indexing
manuelle Programmierung *f.* keyboard programming, manual programming
manuelle Selektion *f.* manual

selection

manueller Leitungsumschalter *m.* line transfer switch

manuelles Suchen *n.* manual scan

manuelles System *n.* manual system

Manuskript *n.* copy, manuscript, script

Mappe *f.* binder, folder, portfolio

Marke *f.* label

Markenkonstante *f.* label constant

Markenname *m.* trade mark name

Markenvariable *f.* label variable

Marketing *n.* marketing

markieren *vrb.* mark/to

Markierer *m.* marker

Markierung *f.* flag, marking, mark

Markierungsbeleg *m.* marked sheet

Markierungsbereich *m.* mark area

Markierungserkennung *f.* mark recognition

Marktanalyse *f.* market analysis

Marktbericht *m.* market report

Marktchancen *pl.* market opportunities

Marktforschung *f.* market research

Marktinformation *f.* market information

Marktsituation *f.* market situation

Marktübersicht *f.* market review

Maschine *f.* equipment

maschinell *adj.* automatic

maschinelle Datenverarbeitung *f.* automatic data processing

maschinelle Dokumentation *f.* mechanical documentation, mechanized documentation

maschinelle Indexierung *f.* machine indexing

maschinelle Katalogerstellung *f.* automatic cataloging

maschinelle Katalogisierung *f.* automatic cataloging

maschinelle Klassifizierung *f.* mechanized classification

maschinelle Literaturrecherche *f.* machine literature searching

maschinelle Recherche *f.* automatic searching

maschinelle Referateerstellung *f.* automatic abstracting

maschinelle Registererstellung *f.* automatic indexing

maschinelle Sortierung *f.* machine sorting

maschinelle Sprachverarbeitung *f.* automated language processing

maschinelle Übersetzung *f.* machine translation, mechanical translation, computerized translation

maschinelles Indexierungsverfahren *n.* automatic indexing technique

maschinelles Referat *n.* machine abstract

maschinelles Referieren *n.* machine abstracting

maschinelles Register *n.* mechanized index
maschinelles Retrievalsystem *n.* machine retrieval system
Maschinenausfall *m.* machine failure
Maschinenbau *m.* mechanical engineering
Maschinenbefehl *m.* computer instruction, machine instruction
Maschinenbefehlscode *m.* machine instruction code
Maschinencode *f.* machine code
Maschinencodeprogrammierung *f.* absolute programming
maschineneigener Zeichenvorrat *m.* native character set
Maschinenfehler *m.* hardware malfunction, machine error
maschinengebundene Darstellung *f.* hardware representation
maschinengeschriebene Veröffentlichung *f.* typescript
Maschinengeschwindigkeit *f.* machine speed
Maschinenlernen *n.* machine learning
maschinenlesbar *adj.* machine-readable
maschinenlesbare Datei *f.* machine-readable data file
maschinenlesbare Information *f.* machine-readable information
maschinenlesbarer Code *m.* machine-readable code
maschinenlesbarer Datenträger *m.* automated data medium
maschinenlesbarer Katalog *m.* machine-readable catalog
maschinenlesbares Wörterbuch *n.* machine-readable dictionary
Maschinenlesbarkeit *f.* machine readability
Maschinennummer *f.* machine serial number
maschinenorientierte Programmiersprache *f.* computer-oriented language, machine-oriented language
Maschinenprogramm *n.* machine program, object program, object
Maschinenschalter *m.* hardware switch
Maschinensprache *f.* machine language
Maschinenstandard *m.* machine standard
Maschinenstatus *m.* machine status
Maschinenstörung *f.* machine malfunction
Maschinenunterstützung *f.* hardware assistance
Maschinenwort *n.* computer word, machine word
Maschinenzeit *f.* machine time
maschineschreiben *vrb.* type /to
Maske *f.* mask, panel, picture
Maskenanweisung *f.* mask statement
Maskendatei *f.* panel data set
Maskenprüfung *f.* picture check
Maskenspezifikation *f.* picture specification

Maskentastatur *f.* matrix keyboard
Maskenzeichen *n.* picture character
Maskenzeichenfolge *f.* picture string
maskieren *vrb.* mask/to, truncate/to
maskiert *adj.* pictured, truncated
maskierter Suchbegriff *m.* truncated search key
Maskierung *f.* truncation
Maskierungszeichen *n.* universal match character
Massenauflage *f.* large edition
Massendaten *pl.* mass data
Massenkommunikation *f.* mass communication
Massenmedien *pl.* mass media
Massenproduktion *f.* mass production
Massenspeicher *m.* bulk storage, mass storage
Massenspeicherdatei *f.* mass storage file
Massenspeicherdatenträger *m.* mass storage volume
Massenspeichereinheit *f.* mass storage facility
Massenspeichersteuerung *f.* mass storage control
Massenspeichersystem *n.* mass storage system
Massenzugang *m.* mass sequential insertion
Maß *n.* measure
Maßeinheit *f.* scale unit
Maßnahme *f.* measure
Maßstab *m.* scale
maßstabsgerecht vergrößern *vrb.* scale up/to
maßstabsgerecht verkleinern

vrb. scale down/to
Material *n.* material
Materialbedarf *m.* material need, material requirement
Materialbudget *n.* material budget
Materialkontrolle *f.* material control
Materialkosten *pl.* material cost
Materialkostenermittlung *f.* material costing
Materialsatz *m.* material record
Materialschlüssel *m.* material code
Materialstatus *m.* material status
Materialstichtag *m.* material due date
Materialtransportzeit *f.* handling time
Materie *f.* matter
materiell *adj.* material
Mathematik *f.* mathematics
mathematisches Modell *n.* mathematical model
mathematisches Verfahren *n.* mathematical method
Matrix *f.* array, matrix
Matrixdrucker *m.* matrix printer, wire printer
Matrixname *m.* matrix name
Matrixspeicher *m.* matrix memory, matrix storage
Matrizenfolie *f.* stencil base paper
Matrizenschreibweise *f.* matrix notation
Matrizenzeile *f.* matrix row
Maus *f.* mouse
maximal *adj.* maximal

maximale Druckzeile *f.* maximum print line
maximale Länge *f.* maximum length
maximale Leerzeit *f.* maximum idle time
maximale Pufferzeit *f.* maximum float value
maximale Wortlänge *f.* maximal word size
Maximalwert *m.* maximum value
maximieren *vrb.* maximize/to
Maximum *n.* maximum
mechanische Tastatur *f.* mechanical keyboard
mechanische Verbindung *f.* mechanical linkage
mechanischer Drucker *m.* impact printer
mechanisches Buchungsverfahren *n.* mechanical charging
Mechanismus *m.* mechanism
Median *m.* median
Mediothek *f.* media center, media resource center
Medienzentrum *n.* resource center, media center
Medium *n.* medium
Medizin *f.* medicine
medizinische Bibliothek *f.* medical library
medizinische Hochschulbibliothek *f.* medical school library
Meeresbiologie *f.* oceanographic biology
Meeresforschung *f.* oceanographic research
Megabyte *n.* megabyte
Megahertz *n.* megacycle
mehr ist nicht erschienen all that has appeard, all that has been published
Mehradreßbefehl *m.* multiaddress instruction
Mehradreßrechner *m.* multiaddress computer
mehrbändige Veröffentlichung *f.* multivolume publication
mehrbändiges Werk *n.* muliple volume set, multivolume work
Mehrbenutzerrechner *m.* multi-user computer
Mehrdateienband *n.* multifile volume
Mehrdateienträger *m.* multifile volume
Mehrdateienverarbeitung *f.* multifile processing
Mehrdatenbanksuche *f.* multiple database search
Mehrdatenträgerdatei *f.* multivolume data set, multivolume file
mehrdeutige Bezugnahme *f.* ambiguous reference
mehrdeutiger Begriff *m.* obscure term
Mehrdeutigkeit *f.* ambiguity, polysemy
mehrdimensional *adj.* multidimensional
mehrdimensionale Kartographie *f.* multidimensional mapping
mehrdimensionale Klassifikation *f.* multidimensional classification
mehrdimensionale Skalierung *f.* multidimensional scaling
Mehrexemplar *n.* added copy
mehrfach *adj.* multiple, plural

mehrfach benutzbar *adj.* reusable

mehrfach benutzbare Datei *f.* reusable file

mehrfach benutzbares Programm *n.* reusable routine

mehrfach gekennzeichnet *adj.* multi-tagged

mehrfach strukturiert *adj.* multistructured

Mehrfachanzeige *f.* multiple display

Mehrfachauswahl *f.* multiple choice

Mehrfachautorenschaft *f.* multiple authorship, co-authorship

Mehrfachbenutzung *f.* multiple usage

Mehrfachdruck *m.* overprinting

mehrfache Zugriffswege *pl.* multiple index support

Mehrfacheinordnung *f.* einer Klasse cross classification

Mehrfacheintrag *m.* multiple entry

Mehrfachfunktionseinheit *f.* multifunction unit

mehrfachindexierte Datei *f.* multiple index file

Mehrfachkennzeichnung *f.* multi-tag

mehrfachstrukturierte Datei *f.* multistructured file

Mehrfachterminalzugriff *m.* multiple terminal access

Mehrfachzugriff *m.* multi-access, multiple access

Mehrfachzugriffsystem *n.* multiple access system

Mehrfunktionstaste *f.* multi-function key

Mehrheit *f.* majority

Mehrkanalanschluß *m.* parallel data adapter

Mehrkanalerweiterung *f.* parallel data extension

Mehrkanalzeitsperre *f.* parallel data timeout

Mehrleistung *f.* additional capacity

Mehrphasenprogramm *n.* multiphase program

Mehrplatzsystem *n.* multi-station system

Mehrprogrammbetrieb *m.* multiple programming, multiprogramming

Mehrprogrammsystem *n.* multiprogramming system

Mehrprozessorensystem *n.* multiprocessor system

Mehrpunktverbindung *f.* multipoint connection

Mehrrechnersystem *n.* multicomputer system, multiple computer system, multisystem

Mehrrechnersystemnetzwerk *n.* multisystem network

mehrreihige Kerblochmarkierung *f.* double-row coding

mehrsilbig *adj.* polysyllabic

Mehrspaltensucher *m.* multiple column control

mehrspaltige Datei *f.* multicolumn file

mehrsprachig *adj.* polyglot

mehrsprachig gedruckter Katalog *m.* multilingualprinted catalog

mehrsprachige Übersetzungshilfe *f.* multilingual translation aid

mehrsprachige Verschlagwortung *f.* multilingual subject indexing

mehrsprachiger Thesaurus *m.* multilingual thesaurus

mehrsprachiges Wörterbuch *n.* multilingual dictionary

Mehrspurband *n.* multi-track tape

Mehrspurkopf *m.* head stack

Mehrstück *n.* additional copy, extra copy, further copy

mehrstufig *adj.* multilevel

mehrstufige Programmunterbrechung *f.* multilevel interrupt

mehrwertig *adj.* polyvalent

Mehrwertigkeit *f.* polyvalence

Mehrwortbegriff *m.* compound term, complex term, term phrase

Mehrzeicheneingabe *f.* multicharacter input

Mehrzeilendruck *m.* multiline print

Mehrzeilenfeld *n.* multiline field

mehrzeilige Anzeige *f.* multiline display

mehrzeilige Funktion *f.* multiline function

Meinung *f.* opinion

Meinungsindex *m.* morale index

melden *vrb.* state/to

Meldung *f.* indication, message

Meldung *f.* **des Steuerprogramms** executor message

Memorandum *n.* memorandum

Menge *f.* bulk, quantity, set

Menge *f.* **der Codeelemente** code set

Mengenabweichung *f.* quantity variance

Mengenlehre *f.* set theory

Mengenrabatt *m.* quantity discount

Mengenschlüssel *m.* quantity key

Mengenvorgabe *f.* quantity standard

Mensch-Maschine-Dialog *m.* man-machine dialog

Mensch-Maschine-Kommunikation *f.* man-machine communication

Mensch-Maschine-Schnittstelle *f.* man-machine interface

menschlich orientierte Sprache *f.* human-oriented language

menschliche Informationsverarbeitung *f.* human information processing

Menü *n.* menu

Menüauswahl *f.* menu selection

menügesteuert *adj.* menudriven

Merkblatt *n.* instruction sheet

Merkmal *n.* attribute, characteristic, feature, label

Merkmalsdimension *f.* characteristic dimension

Messe *f.* fair

messen *vrb.* measure/to, scale/to

Messung *f.* measurement

Meßfühler *m.* sensor

Meßgerät *n.* measuring instrument

Meßniveau *n.* levels of mea-

surement
Metallurgie *f.* metallurgy
Metasprache *f.* metalanguage
Meteorologie *f.* meteorology
Methode *f.* approach, method
Methode *f.* **der graphischen
Darstellung** graphical
method
Methode *f.* **der Kettenindexie-
rung** chain procedure
Methode *f.* **der prozentualen
Verteilung** percentage
distribution method
Methode *f.* **der verzögerten
Suche** delayed search
technique
Methodik *f.* methodics
Mietleitung *f.* tie line
Mikrobild *n.* micro-image
Mikrobildspeicher *m.* micro-
form
Mikrocomputer *m.* microcom-
puter
Mikrodokumente *pl.* micro-
documents
Mikroelektronik *f.* microelec-
tronics
Mikrofiche *m.* fiche, micro-
fiche
Mikrofichelesegerät *n.* micro-
fiche reader
Mikrofilm *m.* microfilm
Mikrofilmarchiv *n.* microfilm
record-office
Mikrofilmgerät *n.* microfilm
equipment
Mikrofilmleser *m.* microfilm
reader
Mikrofilmlochkarte *f.* film sort
aperture card
Mikrofilmpublikation *f.*
micropublication

Mikrofilmsammlung *f.* micro-
film collection
Mikrofilmstreifen *m.* micro-
film strip
Mikrofilmtasche *f.* jacket
Mikrofilmtechnik *f.* microfilm
technology
Mikroform *f.* microform
Mikrographie *f.* micrography
Mikrokarte *f.* microcard
Mikrokartenleser *m.* micro-
card reader
Mikrokopie *f.* microcopy
Mikromodul *n.* micromodule
Mikrophon *n.* microphone
Mikroplanfilm *m.* microfiche
Mikroplanfilmtechnik *f.*
microfiche technology
Mikroprogramm *n.* micro-
code, microprogram
Mikroprogrammablauf *m.*
microprogram execution
**mikroprogrammierbarer Rech-
ner** *m.* microprogrammable
computer
Mikroprogrammierbarkeit *f.*
microprogrammability
Mikroprogrammierung *f.*
microprogramming
Mikroprogrammspeicher *m.*
microprogram memory
Mikroprozessor *m.* micro-
processor
Mikroprozessorsteuerung *f.*
microcontroller
Mikrosekunde *f.* microsecond
Mikrosynchronbetrieb *m.*
microsyncronization
Mikrothesaurus *m.* microthesaurus
Mikroverfilmung *f.* microfilming

Militärakten *pl.* military files
Militärarchiv *n.* military record-office
Militärbibliothek *f.* armed forces library
Militärjustiz *f.* military administration of justice
Militärwesen *n.* military affairs
Millisekunde *f.* millisecond
Mindestbearbeitungszeit *f.* minimum run time
Mineraloge *m.* mineralogist
Mineralogie *f.* mineralogy
Miniatur *f.* miniature
Miniaturisierung *f.* miniaturization
Minicomputer *m.* minicomputer
Minidiskette *f.* minifloppy disk
Minimum *n.* minimum
Miniplatte *f.* minidisk
Ministerium *n.* ministry
Ministerrat *m.* Council of Ministers
minus minus
Minuszeichen *n.* minus sign
Minute *f.* minute
Mischbetrieb *m.* asynchronous balanced mode
mischen *vrb.* collate/to, merge /to, mix/to
Mischlauf *m.* merge pass
Mischnotation *f.* mixed notation
Mission *f.* mission
Missionsarchiv *n.* missionary society archive
Missionsschulbibliothek *f.* missionary school library
Mißbrauch *m.* misapplication
Mißmanagement *n.* misman-

agement
mit Erweiterungsmöglichkeit *f.* open-ended
mit Nullen füllen *vrb.* zerofill /to, zeroize/to
mit Sternchen versehen *vrb.* asterisk/to
mit Vorzeichen *n.* signed
Mitarbeiter *m.* collaborator, contributor
Mitarbeiter *m.* der Erwerbungsabteilung accessioner
Mitarbeiter *pl.* personnel
Mitautor *m.* corporate author
mitgeschleppter Fehler *m.* inherited error
Mitglied *n.* member
Mitgliederversammlung *f.* general meeting
Mitgliedervollversammlung *f.* general plenary meeting
Mitgliedschaft *f.* membership, affiliation
Mitgliedsland *n.* member state
Mitherausgeber *m.* co-editor, joint editor
Mithörapparat *m.* listen-in set
Mithören *n.* monitoring
Mithörstelle *f.* listen-in extension
mitlaufender Fehler *m.* propagated error
Mitte *f.* middle
Mitteilung *f.* notice
mittelgroß *adj.* middle-sized
Mittelstufe *f.* intermediate grade
Mitteltransfer *m.* funds transfer
Mittelwert *m.* mean value, mean
Mittelzuweisung *f.* allocation

of funds
mittlere Auflösung f. medium resolution
mittlere Buchstabentastenreihe f. middle letter row
mittlere Datentechnik f. minicomputer
mittlere Häufigkeit f. mean frequency
mittlerer Ausfallabstand m. mean time between failures
mittlerer Fehler m. mean deviation
Mitverfasser m. co-author, joint author, secondary author
mitwirken vrb. participate/to
Mitwirkung f. participation
mnemotechnische Notation f. mnemonic notation
mnemotechnisches Zeichen n. mnemonic symbol
Möblierung f. furnishment
modaler Befehl m. modal command
Modell n. model
Modellanweisung f. model statement
Modellanwendung f. model application
Modellauswahl f. model select
Modellbibliothek f. model library
Modellbibliothekswettbewerb m. model library competition
Modellprofil n. model profile
Modellversuch m. pilot project
Modem n. modem
Modifikator m. modifier
modifizieren vrb. modify/to
Modul n. module
Modularität f. modularity

Modularprüfung f. modular check
Modulation f. modulation
Modulationsindex m. modulation index
Modulator m. modulator
Modus m. mode
möglich adj. potential
Möglichkeit f. possibility
Molekularbiologie f. molecular biology
Molekulardaten pl. molecular data
monadische Operation f. monadic operation
Monat m. month
monatlich adj. monthly
monatliche Veröffentlichung f. monthly publication
monatliche Zeitschrift f. monthly periodical
Monitor m. monitor
Monitormodus m. monitor mode
Monographie f. monograph, monographic issue
monohierarchische Klassifikation f. monohierarchical classification
monosem adj. monosemantic
Montage f. assembly, installation
Montanuniversität f. mining and steel university
montieren vrb. mount/to
Morgenzeitung f. morning paper
Morphem n. morpheme
Morphologie f. morphology
morphologische Analyse f. morphological analysis
morphologische Bestandteile

pl. morphological components
morphologisches Verfahren *n.*
morphological process
morphosyntaktische Analyse *f.*
morphosyntactic analysis
Mosaikdrucker *m.* mosaic printer
Moscheebibliothek *f.* mosque library
Motto *n.* epigraph
Multiadreßbefehl *m.* multiple address instruction
multihierarchische Indexierung *f.* multilevel indexing
Multikollinearität *f.* multicollinearity
multilingual *adj.* multilingual
Multimediamaterial *n.* multimedia material
Multimediazentrum *n.* multimedia center
multinationaler Zeichensatz *m.* multinational character set
Multioperation *f.* multi operation
multiple Regression *f.* multiple regression
multiplexen *vrb.* multiplex/to
Multiplexer *m.* multiplexer
Multiplexkanal *m.* multiplex channel
Multiplexmodus *m.* multiplex mode
Multiplikand *m.* multiplicand
Multiplikation *f.* multiplication
Multiplikator *m.* multiplier
multiplizieren *vrb.* multiply/to
Multiscan *n.* multiscan
Multitasking *n.* multitasking
Multitaskoperation *f.* multi-

task operation
multivariate Varianzanalyse *f.*
multivariate analysis of variance
Museum *n.* museum
Museumsbibliothek *f.* museum library
Museumsdokumentation *f.*
museum documentation
Musik- und Theaterhochschulbibliothek *f.* music and drama school library
Musikabteilung *f.* music department
Musikalien *pl.* printed music
Musikalienbestand *m.* printed music collection
musikalische Ausgabeform *m.*
music format
musikalische Notation *f.* musical notation
Musikarchiv *n.* music archive
Musikbibliothek *f.* music library
Musikbibliothekarsausbildung *f.* music librarian education
Musikbücherei *f.* music library
Musikdokumentationszentrum *n.* music documentation center
Musikhandschriften *pl.* written music
Musikhochschulbibliothek *f.*
conservatory library
Musikhochschule *f.* conservatory
Musikinformationszentrum *n.*
music information center
Musikkatalogisierung *f.* music cataloging
Musikschule *f.* music school
Musikvideo *n.* music video

Musikwissenschaft *f.* musicology
musikwissenschaftlicher Bibliothekar *m.* music librarian
Musikzeitschrift *f.* music magazine
Muster *n.* mapping, pattern
Musterband *m.* dummy volume, thickness copy
Musterdatei *f.* sample file

Mustererkennung *f.* pattern detection, pattern recognition
Mustervertrag *m.* standard contract
mutmaßlicher Verfasser *m.* attributed author, probable author
Mutterband *n.* master tape
Muttersprache *f.* native language

N

nach Ablauf *m.* on expiration
nach Bedarf *m.* **verteilter Bestand** demand-distributed collection
nach Manuskript setzen *vrb.* follow/to copy
Nachbarknoten *m.* adjacent node
Nachbarunterbereich *m.* adjacent subarea
Nachbearbeitung *f.* postprocessing
Nachbereitung *f.* post-editing
nachbestellen *vrb.* reorder/to
nachdatieren *vrb.* postdate/to
nachdatiert *adj.* postdated
Nachdruck *m.* reimpression, reprint
Nachdruck verboten all rights reserved
Nachfolgefunktion *f.* successor function

Nachfolger *m.* successor
nachgedruckt *adj.* faked
nachjustieren *vrb.* recalibrate /to
Nachlaß *m.* bequest
Nachlaßverzeichnis *n.* bequest inventory
Nachnormalisierung *f.* postnormalization
nachprüfen *vrb.* review/to
Nachredaktion *f.* postediting
nachredigieren *vrb.* postedit/to
Nachricht *f.* message, notice
Nachrichten *pl.* news
Nachrichtenagentur *f.* press agency
Nachrichtenanzeigeeinheit *f.* message display unit
Nachrichtenanzeiger *m.* message indicator
Nachrichtenaufbereitung *f.*

message editing
Nachrichtenausgabedeskriptor
m. message output descriptor
Nachrichtenblatt *n.* information paper
Nachrichtendatei *f.* message data set, message file
Nachrichtendienst *m.* news service
Nachrichteneingabedeskriptor *m.* message input descriptor
Nachrichteneinheit *f.* message unit
Nachrichtenelement *n.* basic information unit
Nachrichtenfehlersatz *m.* message error record
Nachrichtenfeld *n.* message field
Nachrichtenformat *n.* message format
Nachrichtenführer *m.* router
Nachrichtengruppe *f.* message set
Nachrichtenkanal *m.* message channel
Nachrichtenkennzeichnung *f.* message identifier
Nachrichtenkennzeichnungsnummer *f.* message identification code
Nachrichtenkopf *m.* message header
Nachrichtenlänge *f.* message length
Nachrichtenlöschoption *f.* message delete option
Nachrichtenmagazin *n.* news magazine
Nachrichtenmodus *m.* message mode
Nachrichtenpriorität *f.* message priority
Nachrichtenquelle *f.* information source, message source
Nachrichtensatellit *m.* communication satellite
Nachrichtensenke *f.* message sink
Nachrichtensteueranweisung *f.* message control statement
Nachrichtensteuerprogramm *n.* message control program
Nachrichtensteuerung *f.* message scheduling
Nachrichtenstruktur *f.* message structure
Nachrichtensystem *n.* message system
Nachrichtentechnik *f.* communication engineering
Nachrichtentext *m.* message text
Nachrichtenverarbeitung *f.* information processing, message processing
Nachrichtenvermittlung *f.* message routing
Nachrichtenverteilung *f.* message switching
Nachrichtenwarteschlange *f.* message queue
Nachrichtenwartezeit *f.* message waiting time
Nachrichtenzähler *m.* message count
Nachrichtenzeichen *n.* message character
Nachruf *m.* obituary
Nachrüstsatz *m.* kit
Nachsatz *m.* trailer
Nachschlagetafel *f.* quick reference chart
Nachschlagewerk *n.* quick re-

ference book, reference book, reference work

nachsehen *vrb.* peek/to

Nachsendesystem *n.* forwarding system

Nachspann *m.* final title strip

nächste auszuführende Anweisung *f.* next executable statement

Nachstellzeit *f.* reset time

nächster auszuführender Satz *m.* next executable sentence

nächster Datensatz *m.* next record

Nachtrag *m.* addendum, appendix

Nachtschaltung *f.* night service

Nachweis *m.* proof, referral

Nachweisdienst *m.* referral service

Nachweiskarte *f.* checking card

Nachweisquote *f.* retrieval ratio

Nachwort *n.* afterword

nachzählen *vrb.* recount/to

Nadel *f.* needle

Nadellochkarte *f.* needle-operated punch card

Nahbereichsbestand *m.* browsing collection

Näherung *f.* approximation

Name *m.* identifier, name, title

Namennormdatei *f.* name authority file

Namensfeld *n.* name field

Namensgeber *m.* eponym

Namenskatalog *m.* catalog of persons and places

Namenskonvention *f.* naming convention

Namensliste *f.* identifier list

Namensregister *n.* name index

Namensstempel *m.* name pallet

Namensverweisung *f.* name reference

Namensverzeichnis *n.* nomenclature

Nanosekunde *f.* nanosecond

Nationalbibliographie *f.* national bibliography

Nationalbibliothek *f.* national library

Nationalbiographie *f.* national biography

nationale Norm *f.* national standard

nationaler Austausch *m.* national exchange

nationales Informationssystem *n.* national information system

nationales Kennzeichnungssystem *n.* national certification system

Nationalliteratur *f.* national literature

Nationalmuseum *n.* national museum

Naturgesetz *n.* law of nature

natürlich *adj.* natural

natürliche Einheit *f.* natural unit

natürliche Klassifikation *f.* natural classification

natürliche Sprache *f.* natural language

natürliche Wortfolge *f.* natural word order

natürliche Zahl *f.* natural number

natürliches Merkmal *n.* natu-

ral characteristic of division
natürliches Zeichen *n.* arbitrary sign, natural sign
natürlichsprachige Suchanfragen *pl.* natural language queries
natürlichsprachige Suche *f.* natural language search
natürlichsprachige Verarbeitung *f.* natural language processing
natürlichsprachiger Zugriff *m.* natural language access
Naturschutz *m.* nature conservation, nature protection
Naturwissenschaft *f.* science
naturwissenschaftliche Bibliothek *f.* natural science library
Nebenanschluß *m.* extension
Nebenausgabe *f.* subsidiary edition
Nebenbedeutung *f.* connotation
Nebeneintrag *m.* added entry, secondary entry, subheading
Nebeneintragskarte *f.* added entry card
Nebeneintragsvermerk *m.* tracing
Nebenkarte *f.* inset map
Nebenknoten *m.* minor node
Nebenkosten *pl.* incidental charges
Nebenordnung *f.* parataxis
Nebenrechner *m.* subhost
Nebenschleife *f.* minor cycle, minor loop
Nebenstation *f.* slave station
Nebenstelle *f.* **einer Bücherei** deposite station
Nebentitel *m.* variant title
Nebenzeitscheibe *f.* minor time

slice
Nebenzyklus *m.* minor cycle
Negation *f.* negation
Negativ *n.* negative
negativ *adj.* negative
negative Antwort *f.* negative response
negative Rückkopplung *f.* negative feedback
negative Zahl *f.* negative number
negatives Empfangsanzeigezeichen *n.* negative acknowledge character
negieren *vrb.* negate/to
netto *adj.* net
Nettoladenpreis *f.* net published price
Netz *n.* network, net
netzabhängig *adj.* network-dependent
Netzarchitektur *f.* network architecture
Netzausfall *m.* power outage
Netzbedienungsprogramm *n.* network operation support program
Netzebene *f.* network level
Netzkabel *n.* lead
Netzknoten *m.* node, terminal node
Netzmodell *n.* network analog
Netznummer *f.* network number
netzorientiert *adj.* network-oriented
Netzplan *m.* network plan
Netzplandatei *f.* network file
Netzplanerstellung *f.* network preparation
Netzplangröße *f.* network size
Netzplantechnik *f.* network

analysis, network technique
Netzpriorität *f.* network priority
Netzspannung *f.* line voltage, mains voltage
Netzstrom *m.* line current
Netzstromversorgung *f.* mains supply
Netzstruktur *f.* network structure
Netzteil *n.* power
netzunabhängig *adj.* network-independent
Netzwerk *n.* lattice, network
Netzwerkadresse *f.* network address
Netzwerkanalysator *m.* network analyser, network calculator
Netzwerkarchitektur *f.* network topology
Netzwerkaufrufprogramm *n.* network solicitor
Netzwerkbeschreibung *f.* network description
Netzwerkbetrieb *m.* networking
Netzwerkdatenbankmodell *n.* network database model
Netzwerkdokumentverteilung *f.* network document distribution
Netzwerkeinheit *f.* network unit
Netzwerkelement *n.* network resource
Netzwerkentwurf *m.* network design
Netzwerkjobverarbeitung *f.* network job processing
Netzwerkkonfiguration *f.* network configuration
Netzwerkkoordinator *m.* network coordinator
Netzwerkmanagement *n.* network management
Netzwerkname *m.* network name
Netzwerkprotokoll *n.* network protocol
Netzwerkressourcenverzeichnis *n.* network resource dictionary
Netzwerksteuermodus *m.* network control mode
Netzwerksteuerprogramm *n.* network control program
Netzwerksteuerung *f.* network control
Netzwerktopologie *f.* network topology
Netzwerktransformationsregeln *pl.* network transformation rules
Netzwerkverwaltung *f.* network services
neu *adj.* new
neu adressieren *vrb.* revalue/to
neu gestartete Suche *f.* reopened search
neu zuordnen *vrb.* reassign/to
Neuaufbau *m.* reconstruction
Neuauflage *f.* remake
Neuausgabe *f.* added edition, new edition
Neubau *m.* new building
neubenennen *vrb.* rename/to
Neubewertung *f.* revaluation
neubinden *vrb.* recase/to
neudefinieren *vrb.* redefine/to
neudefiniertes Feld *n.* redefined field
Neudruck *m.* reprint

neue Reihe *f.* new series
neue Zeichenfolge *f.* new string
Neuentwurf *m.* redesign
neuer Absatz *m.* new paragraph
Neuerscheinungen *pl.* new books, new publications, new titles
Neuerscheinungsliste *f.* announcement bulletin, bulletin of new books
Neuerwerbung *f.* accession, intake
Neuerwerbungsauslage *f.* new book display
Neuerwerbungskatalog *m.* acquisition catalog
Neuerwerbungsliste *f.* acquisition list
neueste Vorausschätzung *f.* latest estimate
Neufassung *f.* revised form
neuformatieren *vrb.* reformat /to
Neugestaltung *f.* reformation
Neugründung *f.* new establishment
Neuheitsquote *f.* novelty ratio
Neuheitsrecherche *f.* novelty search
Neukatalogisierung *f.* recataloging
Neuklassifizierung *f.* reclassification
Neukonstruktion *f.* restructure
neunumerieren *vrb.* renumber /to
Neuorganisation *f.* reorganization
neupositionieren *vrb.* reposition /to

neuprogrammierbar *adj.* reprogrammable
neuprogrammierbare Steuerung *f.* reprogrammable controller
Neuprogrammierung *f.* reprogramming
Neuprüfung *f.* reverification
Neuregelung *f.* new regulation
Neusatz *m.* recomposition, resetting
neuschreiben *vrb.* retype/to
neutral *adj.* neutral
Neuverkabelung *f.* recabling
Neuzugang *m.* addition
nicht auf Lager *adj.* out of stock
nicht ausgerichtet *adj.* out of line
nicht auswechselbar *adj.* unchangeable
NICHT-Bedingung *f.* NOT condition, NOT
nicht berechenbar *adj.* noncomputational
Nicht-Buch-Material *n.* nonbook material
Nicht-Deskriptor *m.* non-descriptor
nicht erkennbar *adj.* unrecognizable
nicht festgeschrieben *adj.* uncommitted
nicht gekennzeichnet *adj.* untagged
nicht gemeinsam benutzbar non-sharable
nicht gemeinsam benutzter Kanal *m.* non-shared channel
nicht im Buchhandel private circulation

nicht markiert *adj.* unlabelled
nicht nutzbare Zeit *f.* inoperable time
NICHT-Operation *f.* NOT operation
NICHT-UND-Glied *n.* NOT-AND element
nicht unterstütztes Dokument *n.* unsupported document
nicht verfügbar *adj.* unavailable
nicht vorrätig *adj.* out of stock
nicht zu verkaufen not for sale
nicht zurückgegebenes Buch *n.* unreturned book
Nichtabfragemodus *m.* nonprompting mode
nichtadressierbarer Hilfsspeicher *m.* bump storage
nichtadressierbarer Speicher *m.* non-addressable storage
nichtanzeigbar *adj.* non-display
nichtausführbar *adj.* non-executable
nichtausführbare Anweisung *f.* non-executable statement
nichtauslagerbar *adj.* nonpageable
nichtauslagerbarer Speicherbereich *m.* non-swappable storage
nichtaustauschbares Zubehör *n.* non-interchangeable accessory
nichtautorisierte Ausgabe *f.* unauthorized edition
nichtautorisierte Übersetzung *f.* non-authorized translation
nichtbeeinflußbar *adj.* noncontrollable
nichtbehebbarer Fehler *m.* unrecoverable error, irrecoverable error
nichtbeschriftete Oberfläche *f.* clear area, clear band
nichtdruckbar *adj.* non-print
Nichtdrucktaste *f.* non-print key
nichtessentiell *adj.* non-essential
nichtfolgegebundene Information *f.* non-sequenced information
nichthierarchische Beziehung *f.* non-hierarchical relation
nichtindizierte Bezugnahme *f.* unsubscripted reference
nichtinitialisierter Datenträger *m.* virgin medium
nichtkommerziell *adj.* nonprofit
nichtkonventionelles Material *n.* non-conventional material
nichtlesbar *adj.* non-readable, non-scannable, non-linear
nichtlöschbar *adj.* nonerasable
nichtlöschendes Lesen *n.* nondestructive read
nichtmagnetisch *adj.* nonmagnetic
nichtnegative Zahl *f.* non-negative integer
nichtnormalisiert *adj.* unnormalized
nichtnumeriert *adj.* without pagination
nichtnumerisch *adj.* non-numeric
nichtnumerische Datenverarbeitung *f.* non-numeric data processing
nichtnumerisches Zeichen *n.* non-numerical character
nichtparametrische Statistik *f.*

non-parametric statistics
nichtprogrammierbar *adj.*
non-programmable
nichtqualifizierter Aufruf *m.*
unqualified call
nichtrelevant *adj.* non-relevant
nichtresident *adj.* non-resident
Nichts *n.* nought
nichtsegmentierter Satz *m.*
unspanned record
nichtsignifikant *adj.* non-significant
nichtstandardisiert *adj.* nonstandard
nichtstandardisiertes Vokabular *n.* uncontrolled vocabulary
Nichtstandardjob *m.* nonstandard job
Nichtstandardkennsatz *m.*
non-standard label
nichttemporäre Datei *f.* nontemporary data set
nichtübereinstimmend *adj.* inconsistent, unmatched
Nichtübereinstimmung *f.* mismatch
nichtverbunden *adj.* unconnected
nichtverbundene Datenstation *f.* unconnected terminal
nichtverstellbare Regalbretter *pl.* fixed shelves
nichtwiederherstellbare Transaktion *f.* unrecoverable transaction
nichtzugelassene Bezeichnung *f.* deprecated term
nichtzusammenhängender Speicher *m.* non-connected storage
niederwertigstes Bit *n.* least

significant bit
Nische *f.* bay
Niveau *n.* level
Niveauregler *m.* level regulator
noch nicht erschienen not out, not yet published
Nomenklatur *f.* nomenclature
Nominalkatalog *m.* name catalog
Nominalphrase *f.* noun phrase
nominell *adj.* nominal
Nomogramm *n.* nomogram
Norm *f.* standard
normal *adj.* normal
Normalbenutzer *m.* general user
Normalbetrieb *m.* normal operation
Normaldatenfluß *m.* normal flow
normale Ausführungsreihenfolge *f.* normal execution sequence
normale Bedingung *f.* normal condition
normale Fortsetzung *f.* normal sequence
normale Priorität *f.* normal priority
Normalform *f.* normal form
Normalformat *n.* standard size
normalisieren *vrb.* normalize/to
normalisiert *adj.* normalized
normalisierte Bewertungskennziffer *f.* normalized evaluation measure
normalisierte Form *f.* normalized form
normalisierte Präzision *f.* nor-

malized precision
normalisierter Recall *m.* normalized recall
Normalisierung *f.* normalization
Normalkapazität *f.* standard capacity
Normalverteilung *f.* normal distribution
Normblatt *n.* standard specification
Normdatei *f.* authority file
Normenausschuß *m.* standardization committee
Normierung *f.* scaling
Normung *f.* standardization
Notation *f.* notation
Notationsbasis *f.* base of notation, notational base
Notationskürzel *n.* brevity of notation
Notationssystem *n.* notational system
Note *f.* note
Notenpapier *n.* music paper
Notiz *f.* memorandum, note, notice
Notizblock *m.* scratchpad
Notizbuch *n.* notebook
Novelle *f.* novelette
Novellierung *f.* amendment
Nuklearforschung *f.* nuclear research
Null *f.* nil, nought, null, zero
Nulladresse *f.* zero address
Nullanzeiger *m.* zero indicator
Nullargument *n.* zero argument
Nullauslassung *f.* zero compression
Nulldivision *f.* zero division, zerodivide
Nulldivisionsbedingung *f.* ze-
rodivide condition
Nullebene *f.* zero level
Nulleichung *f.* zero adjust
Nulleinsteuerung *f.* zero fill, zero insertion, zero insert
Nulleintrag *m.* null entry
Nullelimination *f.* zero elimination
Nullknoten *m.* zero node
Nullkontrolle *f.* zero check, zero control
Nullnummer *f.* pilot issue
Nullprüfung *f.* zero test
Nullpunkt *m.* origin, zero point, zero
Nullpunktabweichung *f.* zero error
Nullpunkteinsteller *m.* zero adjuster
Nullpunktkorrektur *f.* zero correction
Nullpunktverschiebung *f.* zero displacement, zero offset, zero shift
Nullspanne *f.* zero float
nullstellig *adj.* niladic
Nullstellung *f.* zero position
Nullstellungsbefehl *m.* recalibrate command
Nullunterdrückung *f.* zero suppression
Nullwachstum *n.* zero growth
Nullwachstumspolitik *f.* zero growth policy, no growth policy
Nullzeichen *n.* null character, null token
Nullzustand *m.* nought state
Numeral *n.* numeral
Numerator *m.* numbering machine
numerieren *vrb.* allocate/to numbers, number/to

numeriert *adj.* numbered
numerierte Blätter *pl.* numbered leaves
numerierte Datei *f.* numbered data set
numeriertes Exemplar *n.* numbered copy
Numerierung *f.* numbering
numerisch *adj.* numerical, numeric
numerische Bandbreite *f.* numeric ranging
numerische Darstellung *f.* numeric representation
numerische Daten *pl.* numeric data, numerical data
numerische Datenbank *f.* numeric database
numerische Konstante *f.* numeric constant
numerische Notation *f.* numeric notation
numerische Position *f.* numeral position
numerische Steuerung *f.* numerical control
numerische Tastatur *f.* numeric keyboard
numerische Umschaltung *f.* numeric shift
numerische Zeichendaten *pl.* numeric character data
numerischer Bereich *m.* numeric area
numerischer Code *m.* numeric code
numerischer Datencode *m.* numeric data code
numerischer Modus *m.* numeric mode
numerischer Operator *m.* numeric operator

numerischer Zeichensatz *m.* numeric character set
numerisches Datenfeld *n.* numeric field
numerisches Eingabefeld *n.* numeric input field
numerisches Literal *n.* numeric literal
numerisches Wort *n.* numeric word
numerisches Zeichen *n.* numeric character
Nummer *f.* number
Nummernzeichen *n.* number sign
Nummerungstechnik *f.* numbering technique
nur zur Benutzung *f.* **in der Bibliothek** for reference only
Nut *f.* groove
nutzbar *adj.* usable
nutzbare Zeilenlänge *f.* usable line lenght
Nutzen *m.* benefit, consumer
Nutzen-Kosten-Analyse *f.* benefit-cost-analysis
Nutzenkennziffer *f.* utility measure
Nutzergemeinschaft *f.* user association
Nutzergruppe *f.* user group
Nutzerkennung *f.* customer number
Nutzerschulung *f.* consumer education
Nutzfläche *f.* usable area
Nutzung *f.* utilization
Nutzungsdauer *f.* service life, physical life
Nutzungsvertrag *m.* license agreement
Nutzzeit *f.* operable time

O

Oberbegriff *m.* broader term, generic term, genus
Oberbegriffs-/Unterbegriffs-beziehung *f.* genus-species relation, generic relation
Oberbegriffs-/Unterbegriffs-system *n.* genus-species system
obere *adj.* upper
obere Grenze *f.* upper bound
obere Seite *f.* top side
obere Zeile *f.* top row
oberer Falz *m.* upper fold
oberer Grenzwert *m.* upper limiting value
oberer Rand *m.* top margin
Oberfläche *f.* surface
Oberschicht *f.* upper class
Oberschule *f.* high school
Oberseite *f.* top, upper side
Oberteil *n.* top
Oberverwaltungsgericht *n.* Higher Administrative Court
Objekt *n.* item, object
objektbezogene Datei *f.* normal file
Objektbibliothek *f.* object library
Objektbibliotheksverzeichnis *n.* object library directory
Objektcode *m.* object code
Objektmodul *n.* object module
Objektname *m.* object name
Objektprogramm *n.* object program
Objektsprache *f.* object language, target language
obligatorisch *adj.* mandatory
Obmann *m.* chairman
Obsoleszenz *f.* obsolescence
ODER OR
ODER-Beziehung *f.* OR relationship
ODER-Glied *n.* OR element
ODER-Regel *f.* OR rule
ODER-Schaltung *f.* OR gate
ODER-Verbindungsoperator *m.* OR connector
ODER-Verknüpfung *f.* disjunction, OR operation
offene Frage *f.* open-end question
offene Schleife *f.* open loop
offenes System *n.* open system
offenes Unterprogramm *n.* open subroutine
öffentliche Bibliothek *f.* public library
öffentliche Dienstleistungen *pl.* public utilities
öffentliche Verwaltung *f.* public administration
öffentliche wissenschaftliche Bibliothek *f.* public research library
öffentlicher Dienst *m.* public services
öffentliches Bibliothekswesen

n. public librarianship
öffentliches Netz *n.* public network
öffentliches Recht *n.* public law
öffentliches Wählnetz *n.* public switched network
Öffentlichkeitsarbeit *f.* public relations
offline *adj.* offline
Offlinebetrieb *m.* offline operation
Offlinemodus *m.* offline mode
Offlinespeicher *m.* offline storage
Offlinesuche *f.* offline search
Offlinetest *m.* offline test
Offlineverarbeitung *f.* offline processing
öffnen *vrb.* open/to
öffnende Klammer *f.* left parenthesis
Öffnung *f.* aperture
Öffnungszeiten *pl.* hours of opening, opening hours
Offsetdruck *m.* offset
ohne Aufsicht *f.* unattended
ohne Einrückung *f.* without indention
ohne Jahresangabe *f.* no date, without date
ohne Namen *m.* anonymous
ohne Ortsangabe *f.* no place
ohne Prüfung non-verify
ohne Titel *m.* untitled
ohne Vorzeichen *n.* unsigned
oktal *adj.* octal
Oktalnotation *f.* octal notation
Oktalzahl *f.* octal number
Oktalziffer *f.* octal digit
Oktav *n.* octavo
online *adj.* online

Onlineabfragesystem *n.* online inquiry system, online query system
Onlineanschluß *m.* online connection
Onlineanwendung *f.* online application
Onlinebenutzergruppe *f.* online user group
Onlinebenutzerkatalog *m.* online public access catalog
Onlinebestellung *f.* online ordering
Onlinebetrieb *m.* online operation
Onlinebibliographie *f.* online bibliography
Onlinecomputersystem *n.* online computer system
Onlinedatenverarbeitung *f.* online data processing
Onlineerfassung *f.* online data entry
Onlinegesamtkatalog *m.* online union catalog
Onlineinformationsdienst *m.* online information service
Onlinekatalog *m.* online catalog
Onlinekatalogisierung *f.* online cataloging
Onlineliteraturbestellung *f.* online document ordering
Onlineproblemlösung *f.* online problem solving
Onlinerecherchedienst *m.* online search services
Onlineretrieval *n.* online information retrieval, online retrieval
Onlinespeicher *m.* online storage

Onlinesuche *f.* online searching
Onlinesystem *n.* online system
Onlinetest *m.* online test
Onlinetestsystem *n.* online test system
Onlineverarbeitung *f.* online processing
Onlinezugriff *m.* online access
Operand *m.* operand
Operandfeld *n.* operand field
Operation *f.* operation
operationaler Entwurf *m.* operational design
Operationsausnahmebedingung *f.* operation exception
Operationscode *m.* operation code
Operationsfeld *n.* operation field
Operationsregister *n.* operation register
Operationsstatus *m.* operation status
Operationssteuerung *f.* operation control
Operator *m.* operator
Operatoreingabetastatur *f.* operator keyboard console
Optik *f.* optics
Optimalbestand *m.* optimum inventory
optimale Größe *f.* optimal size
optimale Leistung *f.* optimal performance
Optimierer *m.* optimizer
Optimierung *f.* tuning
Optionsfeld *n.* option field
Optionstabelle *f.* option table
optisch lesbare Markierung *f.* photosensing mark
optisch lesbare Schrift *f.* optical font
optische Industrie *f.* optical industry
optische Speicherplatte *f.* digital optical disk
optische Übereinstimmung *f.* optical coincidence
optische Zeichenerkennung *f.* optical character recognition
optischer Belegleser *m.* optical character reader, optical reader, optical scanner
optischer Codeumsetzer *m.* optical encoder
optischer Markierungsleser *m.* mark scanning, optical mark reader
optischer Seitenleser *m.* optical page reader
optischer Speicher *m.* optical storage
optisches Lesegerät *n.* visual scanner
Ordinaldaten *pl.* ordinal data
Ordinalskala *f.* ordinal scale
Ordinate *f.* y-axis
Ordinatenwert *m.* y-coordinate
ordnen *vrb.* arrange/to, order /to, range/to
Ordnung *f.* level, order
Ordnung *f.* **vom Einfachen zum Komplexen** evolutionary order
Ordnungseinheit *f.* filing unit
Ordnungsfolge *f.* filing sequence
Ordnungsgesichtspunkt *m.* filing medium
Ordnungsgruppe *f.* filing section
Ordnungshilfe *f.* filing qualifier
Ordnungskriterium *n.* filing criterion

Ordnungsprinzip *n.* principle of order

Ordnungsregeln *pl.* filing rules

Ordnungszeichen *n.* filing character

Organigramm *n.* organization table, organizational chart

Organisation *f.* organization

Organisationsniveau *n.* level of organization

Organisator *m.* organizer

organische Struktur *f.* organic structure

organisieren *vrb.* organize/to

orientieren *vrb.* orient/to

Orientierungshilfe *f.* guideline assistance

original *adj.* original

Original *n.* original

Original *n.* eines Kunstwerkes art original

Originalanweisung *f.* original statement

Originalausgabe *f.* original edition

Originaldokument *n.* final form document, original document, source document

Originalfassung *f.* original version

Originalhandschrift *f.* autograph

Originalität *f.* originality

Originalplatte *f.* parent disk

Originalquellen *pl.* original sources

originalsprachlicher Titel *m.* original title

Ort *m.* place

orthographisch *adj.* orthographic

Ortsbezeichnung *f.* place name

Ortsbibliographie *f.* local bibliography

ortsfeste Aufstellung *f.* absolute location, fixed location

Ortsleihe *f.* local circulation, local lending, local loans

Ortslexikon *n.* gazetter

Ortsregister *n.* gazetter, index of places, place index, topographical index

Ortsschlüssel *m.* location number

Overheadprojektor *m.* overhead projector

Ozeanographie *f.* oceanography

P

Paar *n.* pair
Paarbildung *f.* pair generation, pair production
paarweises Klammern *n.*
paired parentheses
packen *vrb.* pack/to
Pädagogik *f.* pedagogics
paginieren *vrb.* number/to the
pages, paginate/to
Paginierung *f.* pagination,
paging
Paginiermaschine *f.* paginat-
ing machine
Paket *n.* packet
Paketübermittlung *f.* packet-
mode operation
Paketvermittlung *f.* packet
switching
Paketvermittlungsnetz *n.*
packet-switched network
Palette *f.* palette
Panel *n.* panel
Paperback *n.* paperback
Papier *n.* paper
Papier nachlegen *vrb.* add/to
paper
Papierablage *f.* paper stand
Papierauflage *f.* paper support
Papierbahn *f.* paper line
Papierbehälter *m.* paper tray
Papierbeschaffenheit *f.* grade
Papiereinlage *f.* paper insert
Papierfach *n.* paper drawer
Papierführung *f.* paper carrier

Papierhaltbarkeit *f.* paper
permanence
Papierhalter *m.* paper bail, pa-
per holder
Papierkopie *f.* hard copy
Papierlänge *f.* paper length
papierlos *adj.* paperless
**papierloses Informationssy-
stem** *n.* paperless informa-
tion system
Papierpfad *m.* paper path
Papierrestaurierung *f.* paper
restauration
Papierrichtung *f.* paper direc-
tion
Papierrolle *f.* web
Papierschildchen *n.* label
Papierschneidemaschine *f.*
guillotine
Papierschneider *m.* paper cut-
ter
Papierstapelbegrenzer *m.* pa-
per side guides
Papierstau *m.* jamming, jam,
paper jam
Papierstoff *m.* pulp
Papierstütze *f.* paper sheet
support
Papiertransport *m.* paper feed
Papiertrenner *m.* paper sep-
arator
Papiervorschub *m.* paper skip,
paper throw
Papierwaren *pl.* stationery,

paper goods
Papierzuführung *f.* paper feed, paper supply
Papyrus *m.* papyrus
Papyrussammlung *f.* papyrus collection
Paradigma *n.* paradigm
paradigmatische Beziehung *f.* paradigmatic relation
Paragraph *m.* paragraph, section
Paragraphenname *m.* paragraph name
parallel *adj.* parallel
parallel betreiben *vrb.* parallel /to
parallel-seriell *adj.* parallel-serial
Parallelbetrieb *m.* parallel mode, parallel operation
parallele Addition *f.* parallel addition
parallele Datenübertragung *f.* parallel data
parallele Schnittstelle *f.* parallel interface
Paralleleingabe *f.* parallel input
paralleler Unterbereich *m.* parallel section
paralleles Addierwerk *n.* parallel adder
paralleles Vorkommen *n.* co-occurrance
Parallelnummernsystem *n.* parallel numbering system
Parallelrechner *m.* simultaneous computer
Parallelregister *n.* parallel register
Parallelsachtitel *m.* parallel title

Parallelschaltung *f.* parallel connection
Parallelspeicher *m.* parallel storage
Parallelübertragung *f.* parallel transmission
Parallelübertragungssignal *n.* parallel transfer signal
Parallelverarbeitung *f.* parallel processing
Parallelverbindung *f.* parallel link
Parallelzugriff *m.* parallel access, simultaneous access
Parameter *m.* argument, parameter
Parameterbegrenzer *m.* parameter delimiter
Parameterbeschreiber *m.* parameter descriptor
Parameterkarte *f.* parameter card
Parameterliste *f.* parameter list
Parameterschätzung *f.* parameter estimation
Parameterübergabe *f.* parameter passing
Parameterzuordnung *f.* argument association
parametrische Statistik *f.* parametric statistics
parametrisieren *vrb.* parameterize/to
parametrisierte Prozedur *f.* parametric procedure
parametrisierter Befehl *m.* parametric instruction
parametrisiertes Programm *n.* parametric program
Paraphrase *f.* paraphrase
Parität *f.* parity

Paritätsbit *n.* parity bit
Paritätsfehler *m.* parity error
Paritätsprüfung *f.* odd-even
check, parity check
Parlament *n.* parliament
parlamentarisch *adj.* parliamentary
Parlamentsarchiv *n.* parliament archive
Parlamentsbibliothek *f.* parliamentary library
Parlamentsschrift *f.* parliamentary paper
Partei *f.* party
Parteiarchiv *n.* party archive
Parteitag *m.* party convention
partielle Abhängigkeit *f.* partial dependency
partielle Datenbankreorganisation *f.* partial database reorganization
partielle Integration *f.* integration by parts
partielle Klassenbildung *f.* partial clustering
partielle Korrelation *f.* partial correlation
partielle Übereinstimmung *f.* partial match
Partition *f.* partition
Partitionsaufteilung *f.* partition distribution
Partitionspriorität *f.* partition priority
Partitionszuordnung *f.* partition allocation
partitive Benennung *f.* partitive term
partitive Relation *f.* partitive relation
Partitur *f.* chorus score, full score

Partizipation *f.* participation
passend *adj.* suitable
passiver Fehler *m.* passive fault
Paßwort *n.* password
Patent *n.* patent
Patentabstract *n.* patent abstracts
Patentakten *pl.* patent records
Patentamt *n.* patent office
Patentanmeldung *f.* patent application
Patentanspruch *m.* patent claim
Patentanwalt *m.* patent attorney
Patentbibliothek *f.* patent library
Patentblatt *n.* patent bulletin
Patentbücherei *f.* patent library
Patentdatenbank *f.* patent database
Patentdokument *n.* patent document
Patentdokumentation *f.* patent documentation
Patentinformation *f.* patent information
Patentinformationsdienst *m.* patent information service
Patentinformationssystem *n.* patent information system
Patentinformationszentrum *n.* patent information center
Patentklassifikation *f.* patent classification
Patentliteratur *f.* patent literature
Patentrecherche *f.* patent search
Patentrecht *f.* patent law

Patentschrift *f.* patent specification

Patentschriftenauslegestelle *f.* patent depository

Patientenbibliothek *f.* patient library

Patrone *f.* cartridge

Pause *f.* pause

Perforation *f.* perforation

Perforiermaschine *f.* perforator

perforiert *adj.* perforated

Pergament *n.* parchment, vellum

Pergamenteinband *m.* bound in vellum

Periode *f.* period

Periodendefinition *f.* period definition

Periodikum *n.* periodical

periodische Auswertung *f.* periodic reporting

periodische Bibliographie *f.* periodical bibliography

periodische Funktion *f.* periodic function

periodische Veröffentlichung *f.* periodical publication

Periodizität *f.* frequency of publication, periodicity

periphere Einheit *f.* peripheral unit

periphere Übertragung *f.* peripheral transfer

peripherer Knoten *m.* peripheral node

peripherer Speicher *m.* peripheral storage

Peripherieausstattung *f.* peripheral equipment

Peripheriegeräte *pl.* peripherals

permanente Datei *f.* permanent file

permanente Eintragung *f.* permanent entry

permanenter Wartestatus *m.* hard wait state

permanentes Segment *n.* permanent segment

Permutation *f.* permutation

Permutationsverfahren *n.* permutation technique

permutieren *vrb.* permute/to

permutiertes Register *n.* permutation index, cyclic index, permuted index

permutiertes Titelregister *m.* permuted title index

Personal *n.* personnel, staff

Personal-Nutzer-Interaktion *f.* staff-user interaction

Personal-Nutzer-Quote *f.* staff-user ratio

Personalakte *f.* personal file

Personalaustausch *m.* staff exchange

Personalbedarf *m.* staff requirement

Personalbeschaffung *f.* recruitment

Personalbibliographie *f.* author bibliography, bio-bibliography, individual bibliography

Personalbibliothek *f.* staff library

Personalbudget *n.* manpower budget

Personalentwicklung *f.* staff development

Personalinformationssystem *n.* personnel information system

Personalkartei *f.* personnel file

Personalkennzeichen *n.* personal identifier
Personalkosten *pl.* personnel costs
Personalplanung *m.* manpower scheduling
Personalpolitik *f.* personnel policy
Personalverwaltung *f.* manpower management, personnel administration
personenbezogene Daten *pl.* personal data
Personenregister *n.* index of persons
Personenschlagwort *n.* personal heading
Personensuchen *n.* paging
persönlich *adj.* personal
Pertinenz *f.* pertinency
Petrochemie *f.* petrochemistry
petrochemische Bibliothek *f.* petrochemical library
Pfad *m.* path
Pfadanalyse *f.* path analysis
Pfadeintragung *f.* path entry
Pfadhauptknoten *m.* path major node
Pfadinformationseinheit *f.* path information unit
Pfadsteuerung *m.* path control
Pfadsteuerungsnetzwerk *n.* path control network
Pfadtabelle *f.* path table
Pfarrbücherei *f.* parish library
Pfarrkirchenbibliothek *f.* parish church library
Pflege *f.* **der Bücher** care of books
pflegen *vrb.* maintain/to
Pflichtablieferung *f.* legal deposit, compulsory deposit

Pflichtablieferungsbestimmungen *pl.* legal deposit regulations
Pflichtablieferungsmaterial *n.* legal deposit material
Pflichtenheft *n.* product requirements specification
Pflichtexemplar *n.* deposite copy, obligatory copy, statutory copy
Pflichtexemplarbibliothek *f.* copy right library, legal deposit library, depository library
Pflichtliteratur *f.* required reading
Pharmakologie *f.* pharmacology
pharmazeutisch *adj.* pharmaceutical
Pharmazie *f.* pharmacy
Phase *f.* phase, stage
Phasenbeziehung *f.* phase relation
Phasenlage *f.* phasing
Phasenmodulation *f.* phase modulation
Phasenname *m.* phase name
philanthropische Bibliothek *f.* philanthropic library
Philologie *f.* philology
Philosophie *f.* philosophy
Phonem *n.* phoneme
Phonetik *f.* phonetics
phonetisch *adj.* phonetic
phonetische Bestandteile *pl.* phonetic components
phonetische Umsetzung *f.* phonetic conversion
phonetische Verschlüsselung *f.* phonetic encoding
phonetischer Schlüssel *m.*

phonetic key
Phonothek *f.* gramophone records library, record library
Photokopie *f.* photocopy
Photoplatte *f.* plate
Photozelle *f.* light sensing device
Phrasenstrukturgrammatik *f.* phrase structure grammar
Physik *f.* physics
physikalische Größe *f.* physical quantity
physikalische Organisation *f.* physical organization
physikalische Übertragung *f.* physical transmission
physikalischer Zeiger *m.* physical pointer
physische Adresse *f.* physical address
physische Ausstattung *f.* physical make-up
physische Datei *f.* physical file
physische Datenbank *f.* physical database
physische Datenstation *f.* physical terminal
physische Datenstruktur *f.* physical data structure
physische Einheit *f.* physical unit
physische Seite *f.* physical page
physische Steuereinheit *f.* physical control unit
physische Verbindung *f.* physical connection, physical link
physische Zugriffsebene *f.* physical access level
physischer Aufbau *m.* physical structure
physischer Block *m.* physical block
physischer Datenbanksatz *m.* physical database record
physischer Satz *m.* physical record
physischer Seitenwechsel *m.* physical paging
physisches Modell *n.* physical model
physisches Segment *n.* physical segment
Piktogramm *n.* pictogram
Pilotanwendung *f.* pilot application
Pilotprojekt *n.* pilot project
Pilotstudie *f.* pilot study
Plakat *n.* poster
Plakatdruck *m.* broadsheet, broadside
Plakatsammlung *f.* poster collection
Plan *m.* plan, schedule
planen *vrb.* schedule/to
Planetarium *n.* planetarium
Plankostenanalyse *f.* planning cost analysis
planmäßig *adj.* scheduled
Planoformat *n.* atlas size, full size
Planquadrat *n.* grid square
Planstelle *f.* permanent post
Plantermin *m.* scheduled date
Planung *f.* planning
Planungsblatt *n.* planning worksheet
Planungshandbuch *n.* planning guide
Planungssystem *n.* planning system
Planungsunsicherheit *f.* planning exposure
Plastikfolie *f.* plastic sheet

Platine *f.* board
Platte *f.* disk
Plattenadresse *f.* disk address
Plattendatei *f.* disk file
Plattendateiname *m.* disk file name
Plattenfehler *m.* disk error
Plattenkasette *f.* disk cartridge
Plattenlaufwerk *n.* disk drive
Plattenprüfung *f.* disk checking
Plattensektor *m.* sector
Plattenspeicher *m.* disk file, disk storage
Plattenspieler *m.* audio player
Plattenstapel *m.* disk pack
Plattensteuereinheit *f.* disk controller
Platzhalter *m.* place holder
Platzhaltersatz *m.* place holder record
Plausibilität *f.* plausibility
Plausibilitätsprüfung *f.* plausibility check, reasonableness check
Plenarsitzung *f.* plenary session
Plural *m.* plural
plus plus
Pluszeichen *n.* plus sign
Pneumologie *f.* pneumology
Podium *n.* podium
Podiumsdiskussion *f.* panel discussion
Poissonverteilung *f.* poisson distribution
Polarforschung *f.* polar exploration
Politik *f.* policy, politics
Politologie *f.* political science
polydimensionale Klassifikation *f.* multi-aspect classification

Polyhierarchie *f.* polyhierarchy
polyhierarchische Klassifikation *f.* poly-hierarchical classification
Polynom *n.* polynominal
polynomial *adj.* polynomial
Polysemie *f.* polysemy
polytechnisch *adj.* polytechnical
Pool *m.* pool
Popmusik *f.* pop music
populärwissenschaftlich *adj.* popularized
pornographischer Bestand *m.* pornographic stock
Port *m.* port
portabel *adj.* portable
Portabilität *f.* portability
Portokosten *pl.* mailing costs
Porträt *n.* portrait
Position *f.* position
positionieren *vrb.* position/to, seek/to
Positionierungsfehler *m.* seek error
Positionierungszeit *f.* positioning time
Positionierzeit *f.* seek time
Positionsanzeige *f.* screen cursor
Positionsanzeiger *m.* position indicator, reposition indicator, position pointer
positiv *adj.* positive
positive Antwort *f.* positive response
positive Rückkopplung *f.* positive feedback
Post *f.* mail
Postamt *n.* post office
Postamtsleiter *m.* post master

Postanweisung *f.* post money
order
Postbeamter *m.* post clerk
Postbeutel *m.* mailbag
Postbote *m.* mailman
Posten *m.* item
Postfach *n.* post box
Postgebühr *f.* postage charge,
postage
Posthandwagen *m.* mailcard
posthume Ausgabe *f.* post-
humous edition
Postkarte *f.* post card
Postkoordination *f.* postcoor-
dination
postkoordinierte Indexierung
f. postcoordinate indexing
Postkutsche *f.* mail-coach
Postleitzahl *f.* zip code
Postsendung *f.* mail
Poststempel *m.* postmark
Postversand *m.* mail order
Postzug *m.* mail train
Potential *n.* potential
potentiell *adj.* potential
Prädikatenlogik *f.* predicate
calculus
Präferenzrelation *f.* preferen-
tial relation
Präfix *n.* prefix
Prägestempel *m.* binder´s
block, binder´s coin, binder´s
die, binder´s stamp, finishing
tool
Pragmatik *f.* pragmatics
Präkoordination *f.* precoordi-
nation
präkoordinierte Indexierung *f.*
precoordinate indexing
Praktiker *m.* practitioner
Praktikum *n.* hands-on training, practical training

Präliminarien *pl.* prelimi-
naries, prelims
Präposition *f.* preposition
Präsentation *f.* presentation
Präsenzbestand *m.* non-lend-
ing collection
Präsenzbibliothek *f.* reference
collection, reference library
Präsenzexemplar *n.* reference
book
Präsidentenbibliothek *f.* presi-
dential library
Praxis *f.* practice
praxisbezogen *adj.* practice-
related
Präzionsmaß *n.* precision ratio
Präzision *f.* precision
PRECIS preserved context in-
dex system
Preis *m.* price
Preisindex *m.* price index
Preispolitik *f.* price policy
Preissteigerung *f.* price increase
Presse *f.* press
Pressearchiv *n.* press archive
Pressearchivar *m.* press
archivist
Presseausschnittarchiv *n.* clip-
ping archive
Pressebibliothek *f.* press library
Pressedatenbank *f.* newspaper
database
Presseinformation *f.* news re-
lease, press release
Pressekonferenz *f.* press con-
ference
Pressestelle *f.* public informa-
tion office
Pressewesen *n.* press, journalisı
primär *adj.* primary
Primäranforderung *f.* primary
request

Primäranwendungsprogramm
n. primary application program
Primärbereich *m.* primary extent
Primärbibliographie *f.* primary bibliography
Primärdatenträger *m.* primary volume
Primärdokument *n.* primary document
primäre Systemsteuerungseinrichtung *f.* primary system control facility
Primäreingabe *f.* primary input
Primäreingangsstelle *f.* primary entry point
primärer Datensatzschlüssel *m.* prime record key
primäres Schlagwort *n.* primary keyword
Primärindex *m.* primary index, prime index
Primärinformationsquelle *f.* primary information source
Primärliteratur *f.* primary literature
Primärmaterial *n.* primary material
Primärquellen *pl.* primary sources
Primärschlüssel *m.* primary key, prime key
Primärspeicher *m.* primary storage
Primärspur *f.* primary track
Primärstation *f.* primary station
Primärsupervisor *m.* primary supervisor
Primärveröffentlichung *f.* primary publication
Primärzentraleinheit *f.* primary processing unit
Primärzugriff *m.* primary access
Priorität *f.* priority
Prioritätenzuordnung *f.* priority assignment
Prioritätsänderung *f.* priority change
Prioritätsanzeige *f.* priority indicator
Prioritätstabelle *f.* priority table
Prioritätswarteschlange *f.* priority queue
privat *adj.* private
Privatarchiv *n.* private archive
Privatbibliothek *f.* individual library, private library
privater Datenträger *m.* private volume
privater Speicher *m.* private storage
Privathaushalt *m.* household
Privatsammlung *f.* private collection
Privatsphäre *f.* privacy
Privatwirtschaft *f.* private sector
probabilistische Indexierung *f.* probabilistic indexing
probabilistisches Retrieval *n.* probabilistic retrieval
Probeabonnement *n.* trial subscription
Probeabzug *m.* flat proof, proof, pull
Probeausgabe *f.* sample issue
Probeband *m.* dummy volume
Probedruck *m.* specimen
Probeexemplar *n.* examina-

tion copy
Probeheft *n.* sample issue
Probelauf *m.* trial run
Problem *n.* problem, question
Problemaufzeichnung *f.* problem logging
Problembehebung *f.* problem recovery
Problembeschreibung *f.* problem description
Problembestimmung *f.* problem determination
Problemdaten *pl.* problem data
Problemfolgenummer *f.* problem sequence number
Problemlösung *f.* problem solution
problemorientierte Programmiersprache *f.* problem-oriented language
Problemstatus *m.* problem state
Problemstellung *f.* argument
Problemverfolgung *f.* problem tracking
Produkt *n.* product
Produktbeschreibung *f.* product description
Produktinformation *f.* product information
Produktion *f.* manufacturing, production
Produktionskapazität *f.* production capacity
Produktionskosten *pl.* production cost
Produktionsregeln *pl.* production rules
Produktionszeit *f.* manufacturing time, production time

Produktivität *f.* productivity
Produzent *m.* producer
produzieren *vrb.* produce/to
Professionalisierung *f.* professionalism
Profil *n.* profile
Profildienst *m.* selective dissemination of information
Prognose *f.* prediction
Programm *n.* handler, program, routine, software
Programm mit graphischer Anzeige *n.* graphic display program
Programmabbruch *m.* abnormal termination
programmabhängige Funktion *f.* program-dependent function
Programmablauf *m.* control sequence, program flow, program run
Programmablaufplan *m.* programming flowchart
Programmablaufschalter *m.* path switch
Programmabruf *m.* program fetch
Programmabruftaste *f.* program attention key
Programmabschnitt *m.* program section
Programmänderung *f.* program patch
Programmanzeiger *m.* program indicator
Programmaske *f.* program mask
Programmaufruf *m.* program request
Programmausführung *f.* program execution, run

Programmausgang *m.* program exit

Programmauswahl *f.* program selection

Programmbeschreibung *f.* program definition, program description

Programmbibliothek *f.* library of programs, library, program library

Programmcode *m.* program code

Programmdatei *f.* program data set, program file

Programmdateiname *m.* program file name

Programmdatum *n.* program date

Programmdiskette *f.* program diskette

Programmdokumentation *f.* program documentation

Programmebene *f.* program level

Programmeinheit *f.* program unit

Programmelement *n.* program item

Programmentwicklungsprozeß *m.* program development process

Programmentwicklungssystem *n.* program development system

Programmentwurf *m.* program design

Programmfehlersuche *f.* program debugging

Programmfeld *n.* program field

Programmfunktionstaste *f.* program function key

Programmgenerator *m.* program generator

Programmgenerierung *f.* program generation

Programmgenerierungssprache *f.* program generation language

programmgesteuerte Unterbrechung *f.* program-controlled interruption

Programmgrundstellung *f.* program reset

Programmheft *n.* Playbill

Programmieranleitung *f.* programmer's guide

Programmieraufwand *m.* programming effort

programmierbar *adj.* programmable

programmierbare Funktionstastatur *f.* program function keyboard

programmierbare Tastatur *f.* user-defined keyboard

programmierbarer Festspeicher *m.* programmable read-only memory

programmierbares Terminal *n.* programmable terminal

programmieren *vrb.* program /to

Programmierer *m.* programmer

Programmierfehler *m.* programming error

Programmiergrundunterstützung *f.* basic programming support

Programmierhandbuch *n.* programmer's manual

Programmierhilfe *f.* programming aid

Programmierhinweis *m.* programming note

Programmiersprache *f.* program language, programming language

Programmiersystem *n.* programming system

programmierte Prüfung *f.* programmed check

programmierter Halt *m.* programmed stop

programmierter Unterricht *m.* programmed instruction

Programmierung *f.* computer programming, program coding, programming

Programmierunterstützung *f.* programming support

Programminformationscode *m.* program information code

Programmkennzeichnung *f.* program identification

Programmkennzeichnungsnummer *f.* program identification number

Programmkorrektur *f.* debugging

Programmladen *n.* program load

Programmlader *m.* program loader

Programmlaufzeit *f.* object time, program production time

Programmnummer *f.* program number

Programmodus *m.* program mode

programmorientierte Routinen *pl.* program-oriented routines

Programmpaket *n.* package, software package

Programmpflege *f.* program maintenance

Programmphase *f.* program phase

Programmplatte *f.* program pack

Programmprüfung *f.* program check

Programmsatz *m.* sentence

Programmschleife *f.* loop, program loop

Programmschnittstelle *f.* program access facility, program interface

Programmschritt *m.* program step

Programmsegment *n.* program segment

Programmspeicher *m.* program memory, program storage

Programmspezifikation *f.* program specification

Programmstarttaste *f.* program start key

Programmsteuerung *f.* program control

Programmsteuerungsdaten *pl.* program control data

Programmstruktur *f.* program architecture

Programmsystemprüfung *f.* system verification

Programmteil *n.* program part

Programmtestzeit *f.* program test time

Programmtext *m.* program text

programmunabhängige Funktion *f.* program-independent function

Programmunterbrechung *f.* process interrupt, program interruption
Programmunterstützung *f.* program support
Programmverbindung *f.* link to program
Programmverbindungssymbol *n.* linkage symbol
Programmverwaltung *f.* program control program, program management
Programmverweilzeit *f.* program residence time
Programmwartung *f.* program maintenance
Programmwechsel *m.* program shift
Programmwiederanlauf *m.* program restart
Programmzeitsperre *f.* program time out
Programmzugriffscode *m.* program access code
Programmzyklus *m.* program cycle
Projekt *n.* project
Projektbericht *m.* advances, project report
Projektbibliothek *f.* project library
Projektdatenbank *f.* project database
Projektdokumentation *f.* project documentation
Projektendtermin *m.* project target date
Projektgruppe *f.* task force
Projektieren *n.* projecting
Projektierung *f.* project
Projektmanager *m.* project manager

Projektnummer *f.* project number
Projektor *m.* projector
Projektplanung *f.* project planning
Projektüberwachungsplan *m.* project control network
propagieren *vrb.* propagate/to, advertise/to
Proportionalschritt *m.* proportional step
Prorektor *m.* vice chancellor
Prosaliteratur *f.* fiction
Prospekt *m.* advertising leaflet
prospektive Bibliographie *f.* prospective bibliography
Protokoll *n.* history, log, minutes, protocol
Protokollausführung *f.* log utility
Protokolldatei *f.* history file, log data set, log file, logging file
Protokolliereinheit *f.* logging device
Protokolliereinrichtung *f.* logger
Protokollieren *n.* logging
protokollieren *vrb.* log/to, minute/to
Protokollüberlaufdatei *f.* history overflow file
Prototyp *m.* prototype
Provinzbibliothek *f.* provincial library
Provision *f.* commission
provisorisch *adj.* tentative
provisorische Katalogisierung *f.* temporary cataloging
Prozedur *f.* procedure
Prozeduranweisung *f.* procedure statement

Prozeduraufruf *m.* procedure reference, procedure start

Prozedurbefehl *m.* procedure command

Prozedurbibliothek *f.* procedure library

Prozedurebene *f.* procedure level

Prozedureintragung *f.* procedure member

Prozedurenbereich *m.* procedure area

Prozedurkopf *m.* procedure heading

Prozedurname *m.* procedure identifier, procedure name

Prozedurprozessor *m.* procedure processor

Prozedurschritt *m.* procedure step

Prozedursteuerbedingungen *pl.* procedure control expressions

Prozedurunterprogramm *n.* procedure subprogram

Prozenttaste *f.* percent key

Prozessor *m.* data processor, processor

Prozessoradreßbereich *m.* processor address space

Prozessoreinheit *f.* processor unit

Prozessorhauptspeicher *m.* processor main storage

Prozessormodul *n.* processor module

Prozessorprofil *n.* processor profile

Prozessorsteuereinheit *f.* processor controller

Prozeß *m.* process

Prozeßdaten *pl.* process data

Prozeßeintrag *m.* process entry

Prozeßidentifikation *f.* process identification

Prozeßmodell *n.* process model

Prozeßrechner *m.* sensor-based computer

Prozeßsimulation *f.* process simulation

Prozeßsteuerung *f.* process control

Prozeßvariable *f.* process variable

Prüfanweisung *f.* inspection instruction, test instruction

Prüfbedingung *f.* sense condition

Prüfbit *n.* parity bit

Prüfcode *m.* verification code, control code

Prüfdaten *pl.* sense data

Prüfen *n.* testing

prüfen *vrb.* check/to, sense/to, test/to, validate/to, verify/to

Prüfgerät *n.* verifier

Prüfkennzeichen *n.* test character

Prüfmerkmal *n.* inspection characteristic

Prüfmodus *m.* verify mode

Prüfnachricht *f.* verification message

Prüfoperation *f.* verify operation

Prüfprogramm *n.* test program, verifying program

Prüfroutine *f.* verification routine

Prüfspezifikation *f.* test specification

Prüfstand *m.* test bench

Prüfung *f.* check, sense, verification

Prüfung *f.* **auf Eingabefehler** input error checking

Prüfungsergebnis *n.* grade

Prüfungsordnung *f.* exams regulations

Prüfverfahren *n.* test method

Prüfwiederholung *f.* reverification

Prüfzeichen *n.* check character, testing character

Prüfziffer *f.* check digit, control number

Pseudodatei *f.* dummy data set

Pseudodateneintrag *m.* pseudodata entry

Pseudoklassifikation *f.* pseudoclassification

Pseudonym *n.* pen name, pseudonym

Pseudosatz *m.* pseudorecord

Psychiatrie *f.* psychiatry

Psychogramm *n.* psychogram

Psychologe *m.* psychologist

Psychologie *f.* psychology

Psychotherapie *f.* psychotherapy

Publikationsform *f.* publication type

Publikumskatalog *m.* public access catalog

publizieren *vrb.* publish/to

Publizistik *f.* journalism

Puffer *m.* buffer, pad, temporary store

Pufferadresse *f.* buffer address

Pufferbefehl *m.* buffer order

Pufferbegrenzung *f.* buffer limit

Pufferbereich *m.* queue space

Pufferdaten *pl.* buffer data

Puffereinheit *f.* buffer unit

Puffererweiterung *f.* buffer expansion

Pufferfreigabe *f.* buffer deallocation

Puffergröße *f.* buffer size

Pufferhauptspeicher *m.* buffer main storage

Pufferkettung *f.* buffer chaining

Pufferliste *f.* buffer list

puffern *vrb.* stack/to

Pufferprogramm *n.* buffer program

Pufferschleife *f.* buffer loop

Puffersegment *n.* buffer segment

Pufferspeicher *m.* buffer storage, buffer store

Pufferüberlauf *m.* buffer overrun

Pufferverlagerung *f.* buffer shift

Puffervorrat *m.* buffer pool

Pufferzeiger *m.* buffer pointer

Pufferzuordnung *f.* buffer allocation

Punkt *m.* full point, full stop, point

punktierte Linie *f.* dotted line, leaders

Punktzahl *f.* score

Q

Quadrat *n.* square
quadratisch *adj.* square
Quadratwurzel *f.* square root
Qualifikation *f.* skill, qualification
Qualifikator *m.* qualifier
qualifizieren *vrb.* qualify/to
qualifizierend *adj.* qualificatory
qualifizierender Zusatz *m.* qualifying element
qualifiziert *adj.* qualified
qualifizierter Name *m.* qualified name
qualifizierter Verbundschlüssel *m.* qualified compound key
qualifiziertes Buch *n.* qualified book
Qualität *f.* quality
qualitativ *adj.* qualitative
Qualitätsfähigkeit *f.* quality capability
Qualitätskontrolle *f.* quality control
Qualitätsmerkmal *n.* quality characteristic
Qualitätsnorm *f.* performance standard
Qualitätsprüfung *f.* quality test
Qualitätssicherung *f.* quality assurance
Qualitätsstandard *m.* quality standard

quantifizieren *vrb.* quantify/to, quantize/to
Quantifizierung *f.* quantification
Quantität *f.* quantity
quantitativ *adj.* quantitative
quantitative Daten *pl.* quantitative data
Quartband *m.* quarto
Quartformat *n.* quarto
Quasisynonym *n.* near-synonym, quasi-synonym
quasisynonym *adj.* near-synonymous
Quasisynonymie *f.* near-synonymity, quasi-synonymy
Quelle *f.* source
Quellenangabe *f.* background material
Quellendeskriptor *m.* source descriptor
Quellendokument *n.* source document
Quellendokumentation *f.* resources documentation
Quellenmaterial *n.* source material
Quellenschlüssel *m.* source key
Quellenthesaurus *m.* source thesaurus
Quellenverzeichnis *n.* references, bibliography
Quellenwerk *n.* source book
Quellprogramm *n.* program

source, source program
Quellprogrammdatei *f.* source
language file
Quellsprache *f.* source language
Querformat *n.* cabinet size,
oblong format
Querschnittsthesaurus *m.* the-
matical thesaurus
Quersummenkontrolle *f.*

parallel balance
Querverbindung *f.* tie line
Querweg *m.* high usage route
Quittung *f.* receipt
Quittungsbetrieb *m.* hand-
shaking
Quotenstichprobe *f.* quota
sample
Quotient *m.* quotient

R

Rabatt *m.* discount
Rad *n.* wheel
radiale Übertragung *f.* input/
output process
Radialübertragung *f.* radial
transfer
Radixschreibweise *f.* base no-
tation
Rahmen *m.* frame
Rahmenabkommen *n.* basic
agreement
Rahmenindex *m.* frame index
Rahmennummer *f.* frame
number
Rahmensatz *m.* frame record
Rahmenvertrag *m.* basic
contract
Rand *m.* margin, side
Rand einstellen *vrb.* margin
set/to
Rand lösen *vrb.* margin re-
lease/to
Randanzeiger *m.* margin indi-

cator
Randausgleich *m.* adjustment,
margin alignment
Randausgleichszone *f.* margin
adjust zone
Randbegrenzer *m.* margin stop
Randbemerkung *f.* marginal
note
Randeinsteller *m.* **links** margin
set left
Randeinstellung *f.* margin
position
Randerkennen *n.* edge detec-
tion
Randfeld *n.* surrounding area
Randlochkarte *f.* border-
punched card, edge-notched
card, edge-punched card
Randlöser *m.* margin release
key
Randnote *f.* marginal note
Randomisieren *n.* randomiz-
ing

Randomisierung *f.* randomization

Randsetzer *m.* margin reset key

Randsteuerung *f.* margin control

Randvergoldung *f.* edge gilding

Randzeiger *m.* margin stop indicator

Rang *m.* rank

Rangordnung *f.* rank order

Raster *n.* grid, raster

Rasterbildschirm *m.* raster display

Rastereinheit *f.* raster unit

Rasterfeinheit *f.* grid density

Rastern *n.* screening

rastern *vrb.* scan/to

Rasterpunkt *m.* grid point, grid position, screen dot

Rate *f.* rate

Ratenzahlung *f.* payment by installments

ratgebendes Zeichen *n.* advisory character

rationale Zahl *f.* rational number

Rationalisierung *f.* rationalization

Rationalskala *f.* ratio scale

Raubdruck *m.* book piracy

Raum *m.* room

Raumforschung *f.* space research

Raumgestaltung *f.* interior design

Raumnutzung *f.* space utilization

Raumplanung *f.* area planning

Rauschen *n.* noise

Rauschfaktor *m.* noise factor

Rauschkennziffer *f.* noise figure

Rauschsignal *n.* noise signal

Rauschstörung *f.* random disturbance

Reaktion *f.* reaction

Reaktionszeit *f.* reaction time

real *adj.* real

reale Adresse *f.* real address

reale Partition *f.* real partition

reale Speicheradresse *f.* real storage address

reale Zahl *f.* real number

realer Speicher *m.* real storage

realisieren *vrb.* realize/to

realisierter Gewinn *m.* realized profit

Realisierung *f.* realization

Realschule *f.* junior high school

Realspeicher *m.* real memory

Recall *m.* recall

Recallmaß *n.* recall measure

Rechenfehler *m.* miscalculation

Rechenfeld *n.* work area

Rechenmaschine *f.* calculator

Rechenregister *n.* arithmetic register

Rechenwerk *n.* arithmetic unit, operations unit

Rechenzentrum *n.* data processing center

Recherche *f.* search

Recherche *f.* **mit Booleschen Operatoren** conjunctive search

Recherche *f.* **zum Stand der Technik** art search

Rechercheergebnis *n.* search result

Recherchemittel *n.* search instrument

Recherchesprache *f.* retrieval language

Recherchestrategie *f.* search strategy

Rechercheur *m.* searcher

recherchieren *vrb.* search/to
Rechner *m.* calculator
Rechnerarchitektur *f.* computer architecture
Rechneridentifikation *f.* processor identification
rechnerisch *adj.* arithmetical
Rechnerkommunikation *f.* interprocessor communication
Rechnernetz *n.* computer network
Rechnerprüfung *f.* processor check
Rechnersystem *n.* host system
rechnerunterstützt *adj.* computer-aided
Rechnerverbundnetzwerk *n.* computer network
Rechnerverbundsystem *n.* computer network system
Rechnung *f.* bill, handbill, invoice
Rechnung ausstellen *vrb.* bill/to
Rechnungsdatei *f.* billing file
Rechnungsdatum *n.* billing data
Rechnungsjahr *n.* accounting year
Rechnungslegung *f.* billing
Rechnungsprüfer *m.* auditor
Rechnungsprüfung *f.* auditing
Rechnungsstelle *f.* accounting office
Rechnungswesen *n.* accounting
Recht *n.* law
rechte Seite *f.* odd page, odd-numbered page
Rechteck *n.* square
rechter Randsteller *m.* right margin set key
rechts *adj.* right

Rechtsberatungsbibliothek *f.* legal service library
rechtsbündig ausgerichtet *adj.* justified right-hand margin
Rechtschreibhilfe *f.* spell aid
Rechtschreibprüfung *f.* spell verify
Rechtschreibung *f.* correct spelling, orthography
Rechtsdatenbank *f.* legal database
Rechtsdokumentation *f.* legal documentation
Rechtsfragen *pl.* legal problems
Rechtsinformationssuche *f.* legal research
rechtskräftiges Dokument *n.* legal memorandum
Rechtsmaskierung *f.* right truncation
Rechtsstaat *m.* constitutional state
Rechtswissenschaft *f.* science of law, jurisprudence
Redaktion *f.* redaction
redaktionelle Bearbeitung *f.* editorial processing
Redaktionsschluß *m.* copy deadline
Rede *f.* speech
redigieren *vrb.* edit/to
redundant *adj.* redundant
Redundanz *f.* redundancy
Redundanzprüfung *f.* redundancy check
reduzierbar *adj.* reducible
reduzieren *vrb.* reduce/to
Referat *n.* abstract
Referatedienst *m.* abstract bulletin, abstracting service
Referatekarte *f.* abstract card

Referaterstellung *f.* abstracting

Referatezeitschrift *f.* abstract journal, abstract periodical

Referent *m.* abstractor

Referenzcode *m.* reference code

Referenzdatenbank *f.* reference database

Referenzsystem *n.* reference database system

Referieren *n.* abstracting

referieren *vrb.* abstract/to

Reflexion *f.* reflection

Reflexionsvermögen *n.* **des Papiers** background reflexion

Reflexkopie *f.* reflex copy

Regal *n.* shelf

Regalanordnung *f.* shelf arrangement

Regalaufstellung *f.* shelf arrangement, arrangement of the bookracks

Regalbrettanordnung *f.* arrangement of the bookshelves

Regalgang *m.* range aisle

Regalreihe *f.* range

Regalzubehör *n.* stack accessories

Regel *f.* rule

Regelausstattung *f.* basic configuration

Regelgerät *n.* automatic controller

regelmäßig *adj.* regular

Regeln *pl.* **für die formale Erfassung** descriptive cataloging rules

Regeln *pl.* **zur alphabetischen Katalogisierung** descriptive cataloging rules

Regeln *pl.* **zur Katalogisierung** cataloging rules

Regeln *pl.* **zur Referateerstellung** abstracting rules

Regelwerk *n.* code

regenerieren *vrb.* recycle/to, regenerate/to, reshape/to

Regierungsarchiv *n.* government archive

Regierungsstelle *f.* governmental agency

Regierungsstellenbibliothek *f.* government department library

Region *f.* region

regional *adj.* regional

Regional- und Stadtbücherei *f.* regional and city library

Regionalarchiv *n.* regional archive

Regionalausgabe *f.* regional edition

Regionalbibliographie *f.* regional bibliography

Regionalbibliothek *f.* regional library

regionale Aufbewahrung *f.* regional depository

regionaler Zentralkatalog *m.* regional union catalog

regionales Medienzentrum *n.* regional media center

Regionalia *pl.* area material

Regionalkatalog *m.* regional catalog

Register *n.* index, ledger, register

Register anlegen *vrb.* index/to

Register *n.* **auf Karteikarten** card index

Register *n.* **in Buchform** bookform index, index in bookform

Register *n.* **mit durch Verweise verbundenen Schlagwörtern** connective index
Register *n.* **mit kontrolliertem Vokabular** controlled indexes
Register *n.* **mit Mehrfachzugriff** multiport register
Register *n.* **ohne Verweisung** asyndetic index
Registerband *m.* index volume
Registerdatei *f.* index file
Registereintrag *m.* entry word, filing word, heading, index entry, index term, term entry
Registererstellung *f.* indexing
Registererweiterung *f.* additional control store
Registratur *f.* filing department
registrieren *vrb.* record/to, register/to
Registriergerät *n.* recording instrument
Registrierung *f.* registration
Regression *f.* regression
Regressionsanalyse *f.* regression analysis
Regressionskoeffizient *m.* regression coefficient
Reichhaltigkeit *f.* comprehensiveness
Reihe *f.* series, string, works in progress
Reihenfolge *f.* filing order, order, sequence
Reihenfolge *f.* **der Indexeinträge** indexing sequence
Reihenfolge *f.* **der Operationen** order of operation
Reihenwerke *pl.* continuations
rein *adj.* pure

reine Notation *f.* pure notation
reiner Binärcode *m.* natural binary code
reinigen *vrb.* edulcorate/to
Reinschrift *f.* fair copy
Reisebericht *m.* travelog
Reisebibliothek *f.* travelling library
Reiseführer *m.* guide book
reißen *vrb.* burst/to
Reißwolf *m.* paper shredder
Reißzwecke *f.* pushpin
Rekatalogisierung *f.* recataloging
rekonstruierbar *adj.* recoverable
Rektor *m.* chancellor
Rekursion *f.* recursion
rekursiv *adj.* recursive
rekursive Funktion *f.* recursive function
rekursive Prozedur *f.* recursive procedure
rekursives Unterprogramm *n.* recursive routine
Relation *f.* relation
relationale Datenbank *f.* relational database
relationales Datenbanksystem *n.* relational database system
relationales Datenmodell *n.* relational data model
relationales Indexierungssystem *n.* **nach Farradane** Farradane's relational indexing system
Relationenalgebra *f.* relational algebra
relative Adresse *f.* relative address
relative Adressierung *f.* rela-

tive addressing
relative Datei *f.* relative file
relative Häufigkeit *f.* relative
frequency
relativer Datensatz *m.* relative record
relativer Fehler *m.* relative
error
relativer Schlüssel *m.* relative
key
Relator *m.* relator
relevant *adj.* relevant
Relevanz *f.* pertinency, relevance
Relevanzbewertung *f.* relevance assessment
Relevanzfaktor *m.* pertinency
factor, relevance factor
Relevanzfeedback *n.* relevance
feedback
Relevanzgewicht *n.* relevance
weight
Relevanzmaß *n.* pertinency
ratio
Relevanzquote *f.* relevance
ratio
Relevanzrangliste *f.* relevance
ranking
Relevanzrückmeldung *f.* relevance feedback
Relevanzwahrscheinlichkeit *f.*
probability of relevance
Remittenden *pl.* returns
Reorganisation *f.* reassembling
reorganisieren *vrb.* reassemble/to, reorganize/to
reparieren *vrb.* repair/to
Report *m.* report
Reproduktion *f.* reproduction
reproduzieren *vrb.* duplicate/to

Reprographie *f.* reprography
Reserve *f.* stand-by
Reserveausrüstung *f.* stand-by
equipment
Reservedatenträger *m.* spill
volume
Reservekapazität *f.* reserve
capacity
Reserverechner *m.* stand-by
computer
Reservespeicher *m.* storage
cushion
reservieren *vrb.* acquire/to,
reserve/to
reservierter Name *m.* reserved identifier
reserviertes Wort *n.* reserved
word
Rest *m.* remainder
Restauflage *f.* remainders
Restaurator *m.* restorer
restaurieren *vrb.* restore/to
Restaurierung *f.* restoration
Restaurierungswerkstatt *f.*
restoration studio
restlich *adj.* remaining, residual
Resultat *n.* result
Resumee *n.* summary
Retrieval *n.* retrieval
Retrievalbewertung *f.* retrieval evaluation
Retrievaleffektivität *f.* retrieval effectiveness
Retrievaleffizienz *f.* retrieval
efficiency
Retrievalprozeß *m.* retrieval
process
Retrievalsprache *f.* retrieval
language
Retrievalstrategie *f.* retrieval
strategy

Retrievalsystem *n.* retrieval system
Retrievalverfahren *pl.* retrieval techniques
Retrospektive *f.* retrospective
retrospektive Recherche *f.* retrospective search
retrospektive Suche *f.* retrospective search
Revision *f.* review, check, appeal
Revolutionsarchiv *n.* revolution archive
Rezensent *m.* critic, reviewer
rezensieren *vrb.* review/to
Rezension *f.* book review, critical review, criticism, review
Rezensionsexemplar *n.* press copy, review copy
Rezensionszeitschrift *f.* review periodical
reziprok *adj.* inverse, reciprocal
richtig *adj.* right
Richtlinie *f.* guideline
Richtlinien *pl.* **der Programmverbindung** linkage convention
Richtungsänderung *f.* turnaround
Richtungsbeziehung *f.* bias relation
Richtungswechsel *m.* inversion
Richtwert *m.* standard value
Ringnetz *n.* loop network
Ringsystem *n.* loop system
Rinne *f.* groove
Rohdaten *pl.* raw data
Rohformat *n.* untrimmed size
Rohmaterial *n.* raw material
Rohstoff *m.* raw material
Rolle *f.* reel
rollen *vrb.* roll/to
Rollenindikator *m.* role indica-

tor
Rollenpapier *n.* roll paper
rollfähig *adj.* scrollable
Rollfilm *m.* roll microfilm
Roman *m.* novel
Romanistik *f.* Romance languages and literatures
Romanliteratur *f.* fiction
römische Ziffern *pl.* roman numeral
Rotationsregal *n.* compact storage
Rotationsregister *n.* rotated index
rotieren *vrb.* rotate/to
rotierter Eintrag *m.* rotated entry
rotiertes Register *n.* rotated index
Rückansicht *f.* rear panel
Rückbezugsname *m.* backward reference
rückbuchen *vrb.* back out/to
Rückendeckel *m.* back board, back cover
Rückenschild *n.* back label
Rückentitel *m.* back title
Rückerstattung *f.* refund
Rückforderung *f.* reclamation
Rückfrage *f.* interrogation
rückführbare Änderung *f.* restorable change
Rückführung *f.* return
Rückgabe *f.* refund
Rückgabedatum *n.* date of return
Rückgabetermin *m.* date due
Rückgabewert *m.* returned value
rückgekoppelte Steuerung *f.* feedback control
Rückhinweis *m.* backward reference

Rückkopplung f. feedback
rückläufig adj. regressive
rückläufige Notation f. retro active notation
Rücklauftaste f. return key
Rücklaufzeit f. fly back time
Rückmeldecode m. return code
Rückmeldeprozedur f. acknowledgement procedure
Rückmeldung f. response
Rückruf m. recall
Rückseite f. back of the page, rear, verso
rücksetzen vrb. backspace/to, reset/to
Rücksetzkode m. backspace code
Rücksetztaste f. backspace key, reset key
Rücksetzzeichen n. backspace character
Rücksprungadresse f. return address
Rücksprungregister n. return register
Rücksprungstelle f. reentry point
Rückspulen n. rewinding
rückspulen vrb. rewind/to
Rückspulsteuerung f. rewind control
Rückspultaste f. rewind key
Rückspulzeit f. rewind time
Rückstand m. backlog
Rückstände pl. arrearages
rückständig adj. underdeveloped, out-of-date, antiquated
Rückstandsschlüssel m. back-order code
Rückübertragung f. reverse extract
rückvergrößern vrb. reenlarge/to
Rückvergrößerung f. reen-largement
Rückvergrößerungsgerät n. reader-printer
Rückverweisung f. back-reference
rückverzweigen vrb. reenter/to
rückwärts adj. reverse, backward
rückwärtslesen vrb. read backward/to
rückwärtsschieben vrb. scroll backward/to
Rückwärtssteuerung f. backward supervision
Rückwärtsverarbeitung f. backward processing
Rückzug m. withdrawal
Rufnummer f. phone number
Ruhezeit f. unattended time
ruhig adj. quiet
Rundbrief m. newsletter
runde Klammer f. parenthesis
Runden n. truncation
runden vrb. round/to
Rundfunk m. radio, broadcasting
Rundfunkanstalt f. broadcasting corporation
Rundfunkarchiv n. broadcast corporation archive
Rundfunkbibliothek f. broadcasting library
Rundfunkgebühren pl. radio license fee
Rundlaufplan m. circulation record
Rundschreiben n. circular, multi-address service, multiple address message
Rundung f. rounding
Rundungsfehler m. rounding error, truncation error

S

Sachbereich *m.* subject area

Sachbibliographie *f.* topical bibliography

Sachbuch *n.* nonfiction

Sacherschließung *f.* subject indexing

Sacherschließungsmethode *f.* subject indexing method

Sacherschließungsmodell *n.* subject indexing model

Sacherschließungssystem *n.* subject indexing system

Sachgebiet *n.* class, subject area, subject field

Sachgebietsordnung *f.* arrangement of subjects, subject order

Sachgruppeneinteilung *f.* subject classification

Sachkatalog *m.* subject catalog

Sachkatalogisierung *f.* subject cataloging

Sachklassifikation *f.* subject classification

Sachmittel *pl.* material budget

sachorientiertes Information Retrieval *n.* information retrieval by subject

Sachrecherche *f.* subject search

Sachregister *n.* subject index, thematic index

Sachsuche *f.* subject inquiry

Sachtitel *m.* title

Sachtitelkatalog *m.* title catalog

Sachtitelzusatz *m.* other title information

Sachverhalt *m.* circumstances, fact

Sachverweisung *f.* subject cross reference

Saldierwerk *n.* accumulator

Sammelausgabe *f.* collected edition

Sammelband *m.* composite volume, omnibus volume, pamphlet volume

Sammelbezeichnung *f.* collective term

Sammelbibliographie *f.* retrospective bibliography

Sammelbiographie *f.* collective biography

Sammeleintrag *m.* collective entry

Sammelgang *m.* list off

Sammelgut *n.* collection items

Sammelkarte *f.* packed card

Sammelkatalogisierung *f.* collective cataloging

sammelndes Schreiben *n.* gathered write

Sammelobjekt *n.* collection items

Sammelreferat *n.* omnibus review

Sammelschwerpunkt *m.* collection emphasis, collection main field
Sammeltitel *m.* collective title, conventional title
Sammelverweis *m.* blanked reference
Sammelwerk *n.* collective work, composite book, composite work, serial
Sammler *m.* collector
Sammlung *f.* collection, compilation
Satellit *m.* satellite
Satellitenfernsehen *n.* satellite television
Satellitenrechner *m.* satellite computer, satellite processor
Satellitenübertragung *f.* satellite transmission
Satz *m.* block, composition, kit, sentence, record, set, typesetting
Satz *m.* **fester Länge** fixed-length record
Satz *m.* **variabler Länge** variable length record
Satzadreßdatei *f.* record address file
Satzadresse *f.* record address
Satzanalyse *f.* sentence analysis
Satzannullierungsfunktion *f.* record delete function
Satzanzahl *f.* record count
Satzart *f.* record type
Satzartbestimmung *f.* record code specification
Satzaufbau *m.* block format, record layout
Satzbegrenzung *f.* interchange record separator

Satzbeschreibungsfeld *n.* record definition field
Satzbild *n.* typographer design
Satzblock *m.* record block
Satzeinfügung *f.* record insert
Satzersetzung *f.* record replacement
Satzfolgenummer *f.* record sequence number
Satzformat *n.* record format
Satzformatbeschreiber *m.* record format descriptor
Satzgrenze *f.* record boundary
Satzgruppe *f.* order set, record set
Satzherstellung *f.* typesetting
Satzkennung *f.* record label
Satzkennzeichnung *f.* set identifier
Satzkennzeichnungsfeld *n.* record identification field
Satzkette *f.* record chain
Satzlänge *f.* length record, record length
Satzlücke *f.* interrecord gap
Satzmarke *f.* record mark
Satzmodus *m.* record mode
Satzname *m.* record name
Satznummer *f.* record number, sequence number, unique identification number
satzorientierte Datei *f.* record-oriented file
Satzparameter *m.* record specifier
Satzposition *f.* record position
Satzprogramm *n.* record program
Satzprüfung *f.* record checking
Satzrechner *m.* composition computer, typesetting computer

Satzschlüssel *m.* key in data set, record key
Satzsegment *n.* record segment
Satzspiegel *m.* print space, text field
Satzstopptaste *f.* sentence key
Satzstruktur *f.* sentence structure
Satzsuchlauf *m.* block search
Satzteil *m.* phrase
Satztrennzeichen *n.* interrecord separator, record separator
Satzüberlauf *m.* record overflow
Satzung *f.* statute
Satzvariable *f.* record variable
satzweise Übertragung *f.* record transmission
Satzzähler *m.* record counter
Satzzeichen *n.* punctuation mark
Satzzugriff *m.* batch retrieval
Satzzwischenraum *m.* interrecord gap, record gap
Säulendiagramm *n.* column chart
säumiger Bibliotheksbenutzer *m.* defaulter
Säumnisgebühr *f.* overdue fee
Schablone *f.* mask, template
Schadenersatzleistung *f.* indemnity
Schadenregulierung *f.* claims adjustment
Schale *f.* shell
Schallarchiv *n.* sound archive, audio library
Schallaufnahme *f.* phonorecord
Schallaufzeichnung *f.* sound recording
Schallplatte *f.* gramophone record, audiodisc
Schallplattenarchiv *n.* gramophone records library
Schallplattenverzeichnis *n.* discography
Schaltbild *n.* wiring diagram
Schalter *m.* closed loan counter, hatch, switch
Schalterausleihe *f.* closed counter lending, hatch system
Schaltfunktion *f.* logic function
Schaltsteg *m.* hook-on brackets
Schaltsymbol *n.* logic symbol
Schalttafel *f.* control panel, panel, patch panel
Schaltung *f.* wiring
Scharnier *n.* hinge
Schätzung *f.* estimate
Schaubild *n.* graph, diagram
Schauzeichen *n.* visible indicator
Scheck *m.* check
Scheibe *f.* wheel
Scheinglied *n.* fence
Scheinsatz *m.* pseudorecord
Scheitelpunkt *m.* peak point
Schema *n.* pattern, scheme
Schenker *m.* donor
Schenkung *f.* donation, gift
Schicht *f.* layer
Schieben *n.* shift
Schiffsbibliothek *f.* ship library
Schiffstagebuch *n.* logbook
Schilderhalter *m.* label holder
Schlagwort *n.* descriptor, filing word, heading, subject heading, subject word, topical heading, entry word
Schlagwort *n.* **für Sammeltitel**

conventional titles heading
Schlagworteintrag *m.* subject entry
Schlagwortindexierung *f.* subject indexing, verbal indexing
Schlagwortkatalog *m.* subject catalog
Schlagwortnormdatei *f.* descriptor authority file
schlagwortorientierte Karteikarteneinordnung *f.* filing of cards by subject
Schlagwortregister *n.* subject index
Schlagwortverweisung *f.* subject reference
Schlagwortverzeichnis *n.* subject index
Schlagzähigkeit *f.* impact resistance
Schlagzeile *f.* banner, headline
Schlauch *m.* hose
schlechtes Manuskript *n.* bad copy
Schleife *f.* loop
Schleifenbildung *f.* looping
Schleifendurchlauf *m.* loop cycle
Schleifenkennzeichen *n.* loop signalling
Schleifenprüfung *f.* wrap test
Schleifensteuerung *f.* loop control
schließen *vrb.* close/to
schließend *adj.* illative
Schließfach *n.* locker
Schließstange *f.* locking rod
Schlußbericht *m.* final report
Schlußbuchstabe *m.* final letter
Schlüssel *m.* key, code
Schlüsselangabe *f.* key option
Schlüsselbereich *m.* key range

Schlüsseldokument *n.* master document
Schlüsselfeld *n.* key area, key field
schlüsselfertig *adj.* turn-key
schlüsselfertiges System *n.* turn-key system
Schlüsselfolge *f.* key sequence
schlüsselgesteuerter Speicherschutz *m.* key-controlled protection
Schlüsselgrenze *f.* key limit
Schlüsselhinweisfeld *n.* key-pointer
Schlüsselindexzugriffsmethode *f.* key indexed access method
Schlüsselkennzeichnung *f.* key identification
Schlüssellage *f.* key location
Schlüssellänge *f.* key length
Schlüsselschalter *m.* key log
Schlüsselsortierung *f.* keysort
Schlüsseltitel *m.* key title
Schlüsselüberprüfung *f.* key verification
Schlüsselwerk *f.* key publication
Schlüsselwort *n.* keyword
Schlüsselwortoperand *m.* keyword operand
Schlüsselwortparameter *m.* keyword parameter
Schlüsselzahl *f.* key figure
Schlußfolgerung *f.* conclusion
Schlußkorrektur *f.* press proof
Schlußsatz *m.* final proposition
Schlußtitel *m.* colophon
Schlußzeichen *n.* final character
Schmutzblatt *n.* end sheet

Schmutztitel *m.* fly title, half title, mock title, bastard title

Schnellabschluß *m.* quick closedown

Schnelldienst *m.* alerting service, current awareness service

Schnelldrucker *m.* high-speed printer, hot writer

schneller Sprung *m.* high-speed skip

schneller Zugriff *m.* fixed head

Schnellesen *n.* speed reading, rapid reading

Schnellinformation *f.* alerting service

Schnellinformationsdienst *m.* current awareness bulletin, current awareness service, express information service

Schnellspeicher *m.* fast memory, high-speed store, quick-access storage, zero-access storage

Schnellstart *m.* hot start

Schnelltrennsatz *m.* unit sets

Schnellzugriff *m.* quick access

Schnellzugriffsspeicher *m.* rapid memory

Schnittdaten *pl.* intersection data

Schnitteil *n.* piece good

Schnittpunkt *m.* break point, intersection, point of intersection

Schnittstelle *f.* interface

Schnittstellenanpassung *f.* interface adaptor

Schnittstellendatei *f.* **für Stapelverarbeitung** batch interface file

Schnittstelleninformation *f.*

interface information

Schnittstellensteuerwort *n.* interface control word

Schnittverzierung *f.* edge decoration

Schönschrift *f.* calligraphic types

Schönschriftdruck *m.* letter-quality print

Schöpfer *m.* creator

schraffieren *vrb.* hatch/to

schräg *adj.* oblique

schräge Markierung *f.* slanted mark

Schrägschrift *f.* italic, italics

schrägstellen *vrb.* oblique/to

Schrägstrich *m.* diagonal slash, left oblique, oblique, oblique stroke, slash, stroke

Schranke *f.* barrier

Schraube *f.* screw

schraubenförmig *adj.* helical

Schreib- und Papierwaren *pl.* stationery

Schreib-/Lesezeit *f.* write-read cycle time

Schreibarbeiten *pl.* paperwork

Schreibart *f.* variant spelling

Schreibautomat *m.* word processor

Schreibbefehl *m.* write command

Schreibbefehlsteuerzeichen *n.* write control character

Schreibdatenfolge *f.* write data stream

Schreibdichte *f.* density, pitch

schreiben *vrb.* write/to

Schreibfehler *m.* misspelling, write error

Schreibfeld *n.* box, writing field

schreibgeschützte Platte *f.*
read-only disk
Schreibgeschwindigkeit *f.* typing speed
Schreibkopf *m.* recording head, write head
Schreibkraft *f.* typist
Schreiblinie *f.* writing line
Schreibmarke *f.* blob, cursor
Schreibmaschine *f.* typewriter
Schreibmodus *m.* write mode
Schreiboperation *f.* write operation
Schreibring *m.* write enable ring
Schreibschrift *f.* hand print
Schreibschutz *m.* write protection
Schreibschutzfehler *m.* write protect error
Schreibschutzfeld *n.* write protect field
Schreibsicherung *f.* proof feature
Schreibsperre *f.* write lockout
Schreibsperrenanzeige *f.* read-only flag
Schreibtaste *f.* type key
Schreibtinte *f.* ink
Schreibtisch *m.* desk
Schreibverbindung *f.* write-link
Schreibverfahren *n.* recording mode
Schreibweise *f.* spelling
Schreibwerk *n.* ohne Tastatur keyboardless printer
Schreibzeile *f.* recording line
Schreibzugriffszeit *f.* write access time
Schreibzyklus *m.* write cycle
Schrift *f.* handwriting

Schrift *f.* mit Begriffszeichen ideography
Schriftart *f.* font, kind of letter, kind of type, type style
Schriftartänderungszeichen *n.* font change character
Schriftbild *n.* written form
Schriftbreite *f.* typewidth
Schriftenaustausch *m.* publication exchange
Schriftenreihe *f.* monographic series, monographs in series, series
Schriftentausch *m* . exchange
Schriftgrad *m.* type size
Schriftgröße *f.* point size
Schriftgut *n.* documents
Schriftgutverwaltung *f.* paperwork management, records management
Schrifthöhe *f.* font size
Schriftkennung *f.* identification burst
schriftliche Befragung *f.* mail questionnaire, questionnaire survey
schriftliches Dokument *n.* hard copy document
Schriftlinie *f.* base line
Schriftsatz *m.* font
Schriftsetzer *m.* galley slave, compo, typesetter
Schriftstärke *f.* line weight
Schriftsteller *m.* author, writer
Schriftstück *n.* document
Schrifttum *n.* literature
Schrifttumsprüfer *m.* censor
Schriftzeichen *n.* letter, character, graphic character
Schriftzeile *f.* written line
Schritt *m.* increment, step

Schrittschaltung *f.* pitch escapement
Schrittsteuerung *f.* pacing
schrittweise *adj.* step-by-step
schrittweise Abtastung *f.* fractional scanning
Schrittzähler *m.* step counter
Schub *m.* batch, push
Schuber *m.* book case
Schulbibliothek *f.* school library
Schulbibliothekar *m.* school librarian
Schulbibliothekswesen *n.* school librarianship
Schulbuch *n.* textbook, school book, class book
Schulbücherei *f.* school library
Schulbuchsammlung *f.* textbook collection
Schule *f.* school
Schülerbücherei *f.* students' library
Schulfunk *m.* educational radio
Schulhaus *n.* school
Schulmediothek *f.* school media center
Schutz *m.* protection
Schutzbereich *m.* save area
Schutzdecke *f.* book jacket
Schutzfrist *f.* copyright duration
Schutzgebühr *f.* token fee
Schutzhülle *f.* book case
Schutzmaßnahme *f.* protection action
Schutzplatte *f.* protective disk
Schutzrecht *n.* trademark rights, patent rights
Schutzumschlag *m.* book jacket

Schutzziffer *f.* guard digit
schwach strukturiertes Datensystem *n.* less-structured data system
schwache Unterbrechung *f.* weak interrupt
Schwarzes Brett *n.* notice board
Schwelle *f.* threshold
Schwellpriorität *f.* limit priority
schwer zugängliche Literatur *f.* rare literature
Schwerpunkt *m.* main field
Schwerpunktthema *n.* main purpose
schwimmende Bibliothek *f.* book boat
Scientometrie *f.* scientometrics
Searcher *m.* searcher
Seefahrtsschulbibliothek *f.* nautical school library
Seekarte *f.* nautical chart
Seemannsbibliothek *f.* sailors' library
Segment *n.* segment
segmentiert *adj.* segmented
Segmentierung *f.* segmentation
Sehschwäche *f.* weak sight
Seite *f.* page, side
Seite *f.* **des Inhaltsverzeichnises** contents page, contents sheet
Seiten numerieren *vrb.* number /to the pages, foliate/to
Seitenadresse *f.* page address
Seitenanforderung *f.* paging demand
Seitenanzeige *f.* page display
Seitenauslagerung *f.* page-out operation

Seitenbegrenzung *f.* page limit
Seitenbeschreibung *f.* page description
Seitenbild *n.* page image
Seitendatei *f.* page data set, paging data set
Seitendaten *pl.* page data
Seitendrucker *m.* page printer, page-at-a-time printer
Seiteneinlagerung *f.* page-in operation
Seitenendanzeige *f.* page end indicator
Seitenentzug *m.* page stealing
Seitenersetzung *f.* page replacement
Seitenfach *n.* page slot
Seitenfixierung *f.* page fixing, page locking
Seitenfixierungseintrag *m.* page fix entry
Seitenformat *n.* page format
Seitenformatwechsel *m.* page format change
Seitengestaltung *f.* page layout
Seitenindex *m.* page index
Seitenkapazitätszähler *m.* page capacity count
Seitenkopf *m.* page heading
Seitenlänge *f.* page depth
Seitenlängenangabe *f.* page-size option
Seitenmigration *f.* page migration
Seitennummer *f.* page number
Seitennumerierschritt *m.* page number increment
Seitennumerierung *f.* page numbering, pagination, paging
Seitenrahmen *m.* page frame

Seitenrahmentabelle *f.* page frame table
Seitenreaktivierung *f.* page reclamation
Seitenrückforderung *f.* page reclamation
Seitenrumpf *m.* page body
Seitenspeicher *m.* page buffer storage, page buffer, page pool, page storage, paging area memory
Seitenspeichergerät *n.* paging device
Seitenstatus *m.* page state
Seitensteuerblock *m.* page control block
Seitensteuerung *m.* page control
Seitenstopptaste *f.* page key
Seitensupervisor *m.* page supervisor, paging supervisor
Seitentabelle *f.* page table
Seitenüberlauf *m.* page overflow, printer overflow
Seitenüberschrift *f.* page heading
Seitenübetragung *f.* page transfer
Seitenübertragungsfehler *m.* page-transition exception
Seitenumbruchdokument *n.* paginate document
seitenverkehrt *adj.* wrong-reading
Seitenverweis *m.* page reference
Seitenvorrat *m.* page pool
Seitenvorschubangabe *f.* page option
Seitenwartestatus *m.* page wait
Seitenwechsel *m.* page turning

Seitenwechseloperation *f.*
paging operation
Seitenwechselstatus *m.* paging status
seitenweise einlagern *vrb.*
page in/to
seitenweise überlagern *vrb.*
page/to
seitenweise Übertragung *f.*
page mode
seitenweises Lesen *n.* page read mode
seitenweises Schreiben *n.* page write mode
Seitenzahl *f.* folio, page number
Seitenzähler *m.* page counter
Seitenzugriffsfehler *m.* page-access exception
Sektion *f.* section, division
Sektor *m.* sector
Sektoradresse *f.* sector address
Sektorkennung *f.* sector identifier
sekundär *adj.* secondary
Sekundärbibliographie *f.* secondary bibliography
Sekundärdaten *pl.* secondary data
Sekundärdokument *n.* secondary document
Sekundäreingabe *f.* secondary input
Sekundärindex *m.* secondary index
Sekundärliteratur *f.* secondary literature
Sekundärnutzung *f.* secondary use
Sekundärprogramm *n.* secondary program

Sekundärpublikation *f.* secondary publication
Sekundärschlüsselwort *n.* secondary keyword
Sekundärspeicher *m.* secondary storage
Sekundärsystem *n.* upline subsystem
Sekundärtitel *m.* partial title
Sekundärverarbeitungsfolge *f.* secondary processing sequence
Sekundärveröffentlichung *f.* secondary publication
selbständig *adj.* stand-alone
selbständige Anhängezahl *f.* independent auxiliary
selbständige Textbearbeitung *f.* stand-alone text editing
selbständiger Rechner *m.* stand-alone computing system
selbständiges Hilfsprogramm *n.* stand-alone utility
selbständiges Programm *n.* stand-alone program
selbständiges Universum *n.* discrete universe
Selbstbedienung *f.* self-service
Selbstbiograph *m.* autobiographer
Selbstbiographie *f.* autobiography
selbstdefinierende Daten *pl.* self-defining data
Selbsthilfe *f.* self-help
selbstladend *adj.* self-loading
selbstprüfend *adj.* self-checking
selbsttätige Regelung *f.* automatic control
Selbstzensur *f.* self-censorship

Selbstzuordnungseigenschaft
f. generic assignment capability
selbstzurücksetzend *adj.* self-
resetting
Selbstzweck *m.* end in itself
Selektion *f.* selection
selektiv *adj.* selective
selektiver Speicherauszug *m.*
selective dump
Semantik *f.* semantics
semantische Analyse *f.* semantic analysis
semantische Begriffszerlegung
f. semantic factoring
semantische Beziehung *f.* semantic relation
semantische Notation *f.* expressive notation
semantischer Gehalt *m.* meaning
**semantischer Informationsge-
halt** *m.* semantic information
content
semantisches Modell *n.* semantic model
semantisches Netz *n.* semantic
network
Semester *n.* semester
Seminar *n.* workshop
Seminarbericht *m.* seminar
report
Seminarbibliothek *f.* seminary
library
Semiotik *f.* semiotics
Senatsbibliothek *f.* senate library
Sendeanforderung *f.* send request
Sendeaufruf *m.* polling
Sendeaufrufintervall *n.* polling interval

Sendeaufrufzeichen *n.* polling
character
Sendebereitschaft *f.* ready for
sending
Senden *n.* sending
senden *vrb.* transmit/to
Sender *m.* emitter, transmitter
Sendung *f.* delivery
Sensitivität *f.* sensitivity
Sensor *m.* sensor
Sensorbildschirm *m.* touch
screen
Sensortaste *f.* touch key
Separator *m.* separator
separierbare Programmierung
f. separable programming
sequentiell *adj.* sequential
sequentielle Adressierung *f.*
sequential addressing
sequentielle Datei *f.* extra partition data set, sequential file
sequentielle Suche *f.* sequential search
sequentielle Verarbeitung *f.*
sequential processing, stack
job processing
sequentieller Zugriff *m.* sequential access
sequentieller Zugriff *m.* **in
Schlüsselfolge** keyed sequential access
sequentieller Zugriff *m.* **mit
Adresse** addressed sequential
access
serialisieren *vrb.* serialize/to
Serialisierung *f.* serialization
Serie *f.* series publication,
series
seriell *adj.* serial
serielle Eingabe *f.* serial input
serielle Schnittstelle *f.* serial
interface

serielle Übertragung *f.* serial transfer
serieller Drucker *m.* serial printer
serieller Zugriff *m.* serial access
serielles Suchen *n.* serial search
Seriennummer *f.* serial number
Serientitel *m.* series title
Servicestelle *f.* service point
Set *m.* set
setzen *vrb.* compose/to, put/to, set/to, typeset/to
Setzer *m.* compositor, typesetter
Setzmaschine *f.* composing machine, typesetting machine
Setzverfahren *n.* type-setting technique
Sexualität *f.* sexuality
sich abmelden *vrb.* log out/to
sich anmelden *vrb.* log in/to
sich anpassendes System *n.* adaptive system
sich eignen *vrb.* qualify/to
sich wiederholen *vrb.* recur/to
sicher *adj.* safe, secure
Sicherheit *f.* guarantee, integrity, safety, security
Sicherheitscode *m.* security code
Sicherheitsdatei *f.* security file
Sicherheitsfilm *m.* safety film
Sicherheitsprüfung *f.* security check
sichern *vrb.* backup/to, save/to
sicherstellen *vrb.* put/to in custody, guarantee/to
Sicherung *f.* backing up, fuse, safeguard

Sicherungsanzeige *f.* save indicator
Sicherungsbereich *m.* recovery area, save area
Sicherungsbibliothek *f.* backup library
Sicherungsdatei *f.* backup file
Sicherungsdatenträger *m.* backup volume
Sicherungshäufigkeit *f.* backup frequency
Sicherungskopie *f.* backup copy
Sicherungssystem *n.* backup system
Sicht *f.* view
Sichtanzeige *f.* read out, visual display
sichtbar *adj.* sensitive, unblanked, visible, visual
Sichtgerät *n.* display device, visual display device
Sichtkartei *f.* flat visible index, visible file
Sichtkontrolle *f.* visual control
Sichtlochkarte *f.* aspect card, batten card, body-punched aspect card, body-punched feature card, coincidence hole card, peek-a-boo card, peephole card
Sichtlochkartensystem *n.* aspect card system, feature card system
Sichtprüfung *f.* peek-a-boo, sight check, visual test
Sieben *n.* screening
siehe-auch-Verweisung *m.* see also reference
siehe Seite see page
siehe-Verweisung *m.* see

reference
Signal *n.* signal
Signalausfall *m.* drop-out
Signalfolge *f.* line sequence,
signal sequence
Signalfrequenz *f.* signal tone
Signalisierung *f.* signalling
Signalumsetzer *m.* signal
transformation, signal shaping
Signatur *f.* book number, call
number, class mark, class
number, classification number, shelf mark, shelf number,
signature
Signaturbildung *f.* call number
formulation
Signaturen vergeben *vrb.* allot
/to the call number
signieren *vrb.* allot/to the call
number, allot/to the shelf-
mark, autograph/to
signiertes Exemplar *n.* autographed copy, inscribed copy
signifikant *adj.* significant
Signifikanz *f.* significance
Signifikanztest *m.* significance
test
Silbe *f.* syllable
Silbennotation *f.* syllabic notation
Silbentrennung *f.* hyphenation
Silbentrennzeichen *n.* syllable
hyphen
Simplexbetrieb *m.* simplex
mode
Simulation *f.* simulation
Simulator *m.* simulator
simulieren *vrb.* simulate/to
simuliert *adj.* simulated
simulierte Ladefunktion *f.* simulated load function

simultan *adj.* parallel, simultaneous
simultan benutzbar *adj.* re-
enterable
**simultan benutzbares Pro-
gramm** *n.* re-enterable pro-
gram, re-entrant program
Simultanbetrieb *m.* simultan-
eous mode, simultaneous
operation
Simultanverarbeitung *f.*
multiprocessing
Simultanverarbeitungssystem
n. multiprocessing system
Singularklasse *f.* isolate
Sinnspruch *m.* epigraph
Situation *f.* situation
Sitzplatz *m.* seat
Sitzung *f.* session
Skala *f.* scale
Skalieren *n.* scaling
Skalierung *f.* scale
Skanner *m.* scanner
Skizze *f.* draft
Skonto *n.* cash discount
Slawistik *f.* Slavic languages
and literature
soeben erschienen *adj.* just is-
sued, just published
**sofort ausführbare logische
Einheit** *f.* immediate logical
unit
sofortige Prüfpunktschreibung
f. immediate checkpoint
sofortiger Abbruch *m.* imme-
diate cancel
Sofortstopp *m.* high-speed
stop
Sofortverbindung *f.* non-dialled connection
Sofortvorschub *m.* immediate
skip

Software *f.* software
Softwaredokumentation *f.* software documentation
Softwareentwicklung *f.* software engineering
Softwarepaket *n.* software package
SOLANGE-Bedingung *f.* WHILE option
Soll *n.* debit
Sonderabteilung *f.* special department
Sonderdruck *m.* extracted article, offprint
Sonderheft *n.* special issue
Sondernummer *f.* special issue
Sonderregister *n.* special register
Sondersammelgebiet *n.* special subject collection
Sondersammelgebietsbibliothek *f.* special subject collection library
Sondersammelgebietsliteratur *f.* special subject literature
Sondersammlung *f.* special collection
Sonderschule *f.* special school
Sonderzeichen *n.* special character
Sonderzeichentaste *f.* special symbol key
sonstige Zeit *f.* incidental time, miscellaneous time
Sortierdatei *f.* sort file
sortieren *vrb.* sort/to
Sortierer *m.* sorter
Sortierfeld *n.* sort field
Sortierfolge *f.* collating sequence, marshalling sequence, sequence, sort order
Sortierlauf *m.* sort run

Sortiernadel *f.* needle
Sortierprogramm *n.* sort program, sorter, sorting program
sortiert *adj.* sorted
Sortierung *f.* sorting
Sortimentsbuchhandlung *f.* general bookstore
Sozialarbeit *f.* social work
Sozialismus *m.* socialism
Sozialpädagogik *f.* social pedagogy
Sozialprodukt *n.* national product
Sozialpsychologie *f.* social psychology
Sozialrecht *n.* social legislation
Sozialversicherung *f.* social security
Sozialversicherungsrecht *n.* social security legislation
Sozialwissenschaft *f.* social science
Soziologie *f.* sociology
soziologisch *adj.* sociological
Spalte *f.* column
Spalte löschen *vrb.* delete/to column
Spalte versetzen *vrb.* move/to column
Spaltenanordnung *f.* column arrangement
Spaltenbreite *f.* column width
Spaltlagenstreuung *f.* gap scatter
Spaltung *f.* splitting
Spannung *f.* voltage
spannungsführende Verbindung *f.* hot junction
Sparmaßnahme *f.* economy measure

späte Ausnahmeerkennung *f.*
late exception recognition
spätester Endtermin *m.* latest
end date
spätester Fertigstellungstermin *m.* latest finish date
spätester Starttermin *m.* latest
start date
Speicher *m.* memory device,
memory, storage device,
storage
Speicher *m.* mit indexsequentiellem Zugriff indexed sequential storage
Speicher *m.* mit indirektem Zugriff indirectly accessible
storage
Speicher *m.* mit schnellem Zugriff high-speed storage
Speicher *m.* mit sequentiellem
Zugriff sequential access
storage
Speicher *m.* mit seriellem Zugriff serial access memory
Speicher zuordnen *vrb.* allocate /to
Speicherabzug *m.* memory
map
Speicheradapter *m.* adapter
memory
Speicheradresse *f.* storage
location
Speicheradreßregister *n.*
memory address register
Speicheränderung *f.* memory
modification
Speicheranzeige *f.* memory
display
Speicherauszug *m.* dump,
memory dump, storage dump
Speicherauszugsdatei *f.* dump
file

Speicherbereich *m.* bank, storage area
Speicherbereichsname *m.*
block name
Speicherbereichsschutz *m.*
area protection feature
Speicherbibliothek *f.* repository library
Speicherblock *m.* storage block
Speicherdatei *f.* storage file
Speicherdatenregister *n.* storage data register
Speicherdichte *f.* storage
density
Speichereinheit *f.* memory device, storage unit
Speichereinheiten *pl.* units of
memory
Speicherelement *n.* memory
cell, memory element
Speichererweiterung *f.*
storage expansion, storage
extension
Speicherfläche *f.* magnetic
surface
Speicherfunktion *f.* memory
function
Speichergröße *f.* memory size,
storage size
Speicherkapazität *f.* storage
capacity
Speicherlesezyklus *m.* memory
read cycle
Speichermedium *n.* storage
medium
speichern *vrb.* poke/to,
save/to, stage/to, store/to
Speicherorganisation *f.*
storage organization
Speicherparitätsfehler *m.*
memory parity error
Speicherparitätsprüfung *f.*

memory parity check
Speicherproblematik *f.*
storage problem
speicherresident *adj.* resident
speicherresidente Datei *f.* resident file
speicherresidentes Programm *n.* resident program
Speicherschreibmaschine *f.* memory typewriter
Speicherschutz *m.* memory protect
Speicherstapel *m.* storage stack
Speicherstelle *f.* storage location
Speichersteuereinheit *f.* storage control unit
Speicherung *f.* storage
Speicherverwaltung *f.* storage management, memory management
Speicherwahltaste *f.* storage select key
Speicherzeit *f.* storage time
Speicherzelle *f.* location
Speicherzuweisung *f.* storage allocation
Speicherzykluszeit *f.* storage cycle time
Spendenverzeichnis *n.* donation book
Sperradresse *f.* no station address
Sperrangabe *f.* lock phrase
Sperrdruck *m.* letter spacing
Sperre *f.* barring
Sperreingang *m.* inhibit input
Sperreinrichtung *f.* barring feature
sperren *vrb.* latch/to, lock/to
Sperrmodus *m.* lock mode

Sperrsicherheit *f.* barring reliability
Sperrsignal *n.* blocking signal
Sperrtabelle *f.* barring table
Sperrtaste *f.* lock key
Sperrverwaltung *f.* lock manager
Sperrzustand *m.* off-state
Spezialausbildung *f.* special training
Spezialbestand *m.* special collection
Spezialbibliographie *f.* bibliographical monograph
Spezialbibliothek *f.* special library
Spezialbildung *f.* special education
Spezialgebiet *n.* speciality
Spezialklassifikation *f.* special classification
Spezialklassifikationsmodell *n.* special classification scheme
Spezialsammlung *f.* special collection
Spezialthesaurus *m.* subject-oriented thesaurus
Spezifikation *f.* specification
Spezifikationszeichen *n.* specifier
Spezifikator *m.* qualifier, specificator
spezifisch *adj.* specific
spezifisches Schlagwort *n.* specific heading
spezifizieren *vrb.* itemize/to, specify/to
Spezifizierung *f.* specification
Spielfilm *m.* movie
Spindelpresse *f.* bench press
Spiralbindung *f.* coil binding
Spitzenbelastung *f.* peak load

splitten *vrb.* split/to
Sport *m.* sport
Sportbericht *m.* sport report
Sportbibliothek *f.* sports library, gymnasium library
Sporthochschule *f.* college of physical education
sprach- und literaturwissenschaftliche Bibliothek *f.* language and literature library
Sprachanalyse *f.* speech analysis
Sprachanweisung *f.* language statement
Sprachatlas *m.* language atlas
Sprachaufzeichnungsgerät *n.* voice recording set
Sprachausgabe *f.* voice output
Sprachausgabeeinheit *f.* audio response unit
Sprachbarriere *f.* language barrier
Sprachdatenverarbeitung *f.* language data processing
Sprache *f.* language
Spracheingabe *f.* voice entry
Sprachentwicklung *f.* language development
Spracherkennung *f.* speech pattern recognition, voice recognition
Spracherkennungsgerät *n.* voice recognition unit
Sprachführer *m.* phrase book
Sprachgenerator *m.* voice synthesizer
Sprachgenerierung *f.* language generation
Sprachkassette *f.* language tape
Sprachkurs *m.* language course

Sprachlabor *n.* language laboratory
sprachliche Unterteilung *f.* language subdivision
Sprachmuster *n.* language pattern
Sprachprozessor *m.* language processor
Sprachprüfung *f.* language test
Sprachschulbibliothek *f.* language school library
Sprachschule *f.* language school
Sprachtheorie *f.* language theory
Sprachverarbeitung *f.* language processing, voice processing
Sprachverbindung *f.* interlanguage facility
Sprachverdichtung *f.* language comprehension
sprachverstehendes System *n.* language understanding system
Sprachwissenschaft *f.* linguistics, philology
Sprechweise *f.* speech
springen *vrb.* skip/to, wrap/to
Sprung *m.* jump, skip
Sprungbefehl *m.* control transfer instruction, GO TO statment, jump instruction, skip instruction
Sprungfeld *n.* skip field
Sprungtaste *f.* jumps partition key, skip key
Spulbetrieb *m.* spooling, spool
Spule *f.* reel
Spur *f.* track
Spuradresse *f.* home address

Spurkennzeichnung *f.* track i-
dentifier
staatlich *adj.* governmental
Staatsanzeiger *m.* gazette
Staatsarchiv *n.* state archive,
national archive
Staatsbibliothek *f.* state li-
brary, government library
Staatsrecht *n.* public law
stabil *adj.* stable
stabiler Zustand *m.* homo-
stasis
Stabilisieren *n.* stabilizing
Stabilisierung *f.* stabilization
Stabilität *f.* stability
Stadtarchiv *n.* town archive
Stadtbezirk *m.* district
Stadtbezirksbibliothek *f.*
district library
Stadtbibliographie *f.* munici-
pal bibliography
Stadtbibliothek *f.* city library,
municipal library, town li-
brary, urban library
Stadtbücherei *f.* municipal li-
brary, urban library
Stadtgeschichte *f.* urban histo-
ry
Stamm *m.* stem
Stammdatei *f.* master file
Stammdaten *pl.* master data
Stammesinformationszentrum
n. tribal information center
Stammkarte *f.* basic entry
card, master card, unit card
Stammsatz *m.* master record
Stammwort *n.* morpheme-
word, root-word
Stammwörterbuch *n.* stem
dictionary
Standard *m.* standard
Standardaufbereitung *f.* basic

edit
Standardausgabe *f.* classical
edition
Standardbefehlsvorrat *m.*
basic instruction set
Standardbuchnummernkenn-
zeichnung *f.* standard book
numbering
Standarddatei *f.* standard file
Standarddatenformat *n.*
standard data format
Standardeingabesatz *m.*
standard input record
Standardformat *n.* default
format, master format
Standardfunktion *f.* basic
function
Standardisierung *f.* standard-
ization
Standardprofil *n.* standard
profile
Standardprofildienst *m.* se-
lective dissemination of information
Standardregister *m.* principal
register
Standardschlagwortliste *f.* de-
scriptor authority list
Standardseriennummern-
kennzeichnung *f.* standard
serial numbering
Standardsoftware *f.* standard
software
Standleitung *f.* dedicated line
Standort *m.* location
Standort bezeichnen *vrb.* allot
/to the shelf-mark
Standort *m.* eines Buches loca-
tion of a book
Standortbezeichnung *f.* mark-
ing
Standortcode *m.* location code

Standortdaten *pl.* location data

Standortkatalog *m.* shelf catalog, shelf list

Standortkennung *f.* location identification

Standortnummer *f.* call mark, call number, shelf mark, shelf number, location mark

Standortregister *n.* location index

Standpunkt *m.* viewpoint

Stapel *m.* batch, deck, pack, stack

Stapelbetrieb *m.* batch mode

Stapelbetriebseingabe *f.* batch input

Stapeldatenaustausch *m.* batch data exchange

Stapeldatenübertragung *f.* batch data transfer

Stapeldruckfunktion *f.* batch print function

Stapelfernverarbeitung *f.* remote batch processing

Stapelfunktion *f.* batch function

Stapelinitiierung *f.* batch initiation

Stapeljob *m.* batch job

stapeln *vrb.* stack/to

Stapelnachricht *f.* batch message

Stapelnumerierung *f.* batch numbering

Stapelnummer *f.* batch number

Stapelspeicher *m.* nesting store

Stapelübertragung *f.* batch communication, batch transmission

Stapelumgebung *f.* batch environment

Stapelverarbeitung *f.* batch mode data processing, batch processing, batching

Stapelverarbeitungsdatei *f.* batch file

Stapelverarbeitungsprogramm *n.* batch processing program, batch program

Stapelverarbeitungssystem *n.* batch system

Stapelzuführstation *f.* hopper input station

Stapelzuführung *f.* pack feed slot, stack feeder

Start *m.* begin, start

Startband *n.* leader strip, leader

starten *vrb.* begin/to, boot/to, start/to

Startklammer *f.* begin bracket

Startknopf *m.* activate button

Startmenü *n.* initial display, sign-on menu

Starttaste *f.* start key

Startzeichen *n.* start character, starting character

Startzeile *f.* initial line

Statik *f.* statics

stationär *adj.* stationary

statisch *adj.* static

statische Aufladung *f.* static charge

statische Datei *f.* static file

statische Eingabe *f.* static input

statische Pufferzuordnung *f.* static buffer allocation

statische Verschiebung *f.* static relocation

statischer Speicher *m.* static

memory, static storage
statischer Speicherauszug *m.*
static dump
Statistik *f.* statistics
Statistikdatei *f.* history file
statistische Analyse *f.* statistical analysis
statistische Bibliographie *f.* statistical bibliography
statistische Daten *pl.* statistical data
statistische Erhebung *f.* census
statistische Stichprobenziehung *f.* statistical sampling
statistische Untersuchung *f.* statistical survey
statistisches Verfahren *n.* statistical technique
Status *m.* status
Statusanzeige *f.* state indicator, status indication
Statusanzeiger *m.* status indicator
Statusinformation *f.* status information
Statusveränderung *f.* status modification
Statut *n.* statute
Stecker *m.* jack
steckerkompatibel *adj.* pin-compatible
Steckkarte *f.* board, jack panel
Steckkontakt *m.* wrap connection
Stecktafel *f.* pinboard
steigende Funktion *f.* increasing function
steigende Nachfrage *f.* growing demand
Stelle *f.* position
stellen *vrb.* put/to
Stellenbeschreibung *f.* job description

scription
Stellenschreibweise *f.* positional representation
Stellenwert *m.* place value, significance, weight
Stellgeschwindigkeit *f.* floating speed
Stellglied *n.* final control element
Stellung *f.* position
Stellungnahme *f.* comment
Stellungsgeber *m.* position encoder
stellvertretend *adj.* subsidiary
stellvertretender Bibliothekar *m.* deputy librarian
stellvertretender Bibliotheksdirektor *m.* associate librarian
Stempel *m.* impress
Stempelkarte *f.* attendance card
Stempeluhr *f.* attendance recorder
Sternadresse *f.* asterisk address
Sternchen *n.* asterisk
Sternnetz *n.* umbrella network
Steuer *f.* tax
Steuerbefehlsregister *n.* control register
Steuereinheit *f.* control unit
Steuerinformation *f.* format record
Steuerkarte *f.* pilot card
Steuerknüppel *m.* joystick
Steuerprogramm *n.* application customizer, machine program, scheduler
Steuerrecht *n.* fiscal law
Steuerrechtsdokumentation *f.* fiscal law documentation
Steuersystem *n.* control sys-

tem
Steuerung *f.* control
Steuerzeichen *n.* control character, control symbol
Stichprobe *f.* sample
Stichprobenbildung *f.* sampling
Stichprobenerhebung *f.* sample survey
Stichprobenfehler *m.* sampling error
Stichprobengröße *f.* sample size
Stichprobenprüfung *f.* batch test
Stichprobenverfahren *n.* sampling method
Stichtag *m.* year-to-date
Stichwort *n.* catchword, cue word, keyword
Stichwortbildung *f.* extraction of terms
Stichworteintrag *m.* catchword entry
Stichwörter *pl.* **mit Farbzeichen** color coding
Stichwortindexierung *f.* catchword indexing, keyword indexing
Stichwortkatalog *m.* catchword catalog, keyword catalog
Stichwortliste *f.* keyword list
Stichwortregister *n.* catchword index
Stichworttitel *m.* catchword title
Stichwortvergleich *m.* code comparison
Stifter *m.* donor
Stiftung *f.* foundation
Stiftungsbibliothek *f.* endowed library

stillegen *vrb.* quiesce/to
Stillegung *f.* shutdown
Stillstand *m.* **im Funktionsablauf** deadlock
Stillstandskosten *pl.* idle plant expenses
Stimmanalyse *f.* voice analysis
Stimme *f.* voice
Stipendium *n.* scholarship
Stoff *m.* matter
Stopp *m.* halt, stop
Stoppbefehl *m.* stop instruction
Stoppcode *m.* stop
Stopproutine *f.* stop sequence
Stoppsignal *n.* stop element
Stoppstatus *m.* stop status
Stopptaste *f.* stop control, stop key
Stoppverzeichnis *n.* halt procedure
Störfestigkeit *f.* noise immunity
Störgröße *f.* influence quality
Stornotaste *f.* void key
Störsignal *n.* drop-in, noise, unwanted signal
Störspannung *f.* interfering signals
Störstelle *f.* imperfection
Störung *f.* buzz, interference
Störung *f.* **in der Zuführung** improper feeding
Störungsanzeiger *m.* malfunction indicator
Störungsbericht *m.* problem reporting
Störungsdauer *f.* malfunction time
störungsfrei *adj.* noisefree, noiseless

Stoßbetrieb *m.* burst mode
stoßfrei *adj.* hitchless
Strafrecht *n.* criminal law
Straßenkarte *f.* road map
Straßenverkehr *m.* traffic
Strategie *f.* strategy
Streckensteuerung *f.* line motion control system
streichen *vrb.* cancel/to, delete /to
Streifen *m.* strip
Streifenvorspann *m.* magnetic tape leader
streuen *vrb.* scatter/to
Streuung *f.* scattering
Streuungsbild *f.* scatter diagram
Strich *m.* vinculum
Strichcode *m.* bar code
Strichcodeetikett *n.* bar code lable
Strichcodeleser *m.* bar code reader, bar code scanner
Strichcodierung *f.* bar coding
Strom *m.* power
Stromausfall *m.* power failure
stromlose Zeit *f.* idle interval
Stromnetz *n.* mains
Stromquelle *f.* power source
Stromverbrauch *m.* power consumption, wattage
Stromversorgung *f.* power supply
Struktogramm *n.* structure chart
Struktur *f.* structure
Struktur *f.* **eines Graphen** graph structure
strukturelle Bauteile *pl.* structural components
Strukturformel *f.* structural formula

Strukturglied *n.* structure member
strukturierte Daten *pl.* structured data
strukturierte Notation *f.* expressive notation, structured notation
strukturierte Programmierung *f.* structured programming
Strukturierung *f.* structuring
Strukturprinzip *n.* structural principle
Strukturreferat *n.* structural abstract
Strukturvariable *f.* structure variable
Strukturwandel *m.* structural change
Stückkosten *pl.* unit cost
Stücktitel *m.* entry for a single item of a series
Stücktitelaufnahme *f.* analytical entry
Student *m.* student
Studentenbücherei *f.* students´ library
Studie *f.* report, study
Studienbibliothek *f.* learned library
Studienfahrt *f.* field trip
Studienjahr *n.* academic year
Studienplan *m.* curriculum
Studienreise *f.* educational trip
Studienzeit *f.* study time
studieren *vrb.* study/to
Studium *n.* studies
Stufe *f.* level, stage
Stufenbezeichnung *f.* level indicator
Stufenkennung *f.* level identifier

stufenweise *adj* . gradual
Stundensatz *m.* hourly charge, hourly rate
Stützpunktbücherei *f.* deposit station
Subjekt *n.* subject
Subjektassoziation *f.* allocation
subskribieren *vrb.* subscribe/to
subskribiert *adj.* subscripted
Subskribierung *f.* subscripting
Subskription *f.* subscription
Substantiv *n.* noun
Substitution *f.* substitution
Subsystem *n.* subsystem
Subsystemname *m.* location name
subtrahieren *vrb.* subtract/to
subventionieren *vrb.* subsidize /to
Suchadresse *f.* seek address
Suchanfrage *f.* information request, inquiry, query, search request, search, enquiry
Suchanfragen-Dokument-Ähnlichkeit *f.* query document similarity
Suchanfragenanalyse *f.* query analysis
Suchanfragenbildung *f.* query formulation
Suchanfragenerweiterung *f.* query expansion
Suchanfragenformular *n.* search request form
Suchanfragenklassifizierung *f.* query classification
Suchanfragenmodifizierung *f.* query modification
Suchanfragenoptimierung *f.* query optimization
Suchanfragenreformulierung
f. query reformulation
Suchanfragenrepräsentation *f.* query representation
Suchanfragenspezifikation *f.* query specification
Suchanfragenteilung *f.* query splitting
Suchanfragenvektor *m.* query vector
Suchargument *n.* search argument
Suchauftrag *m.* search order
Suchbaum *m.* search tree
Suchbefehl *m.* seek command
Suchbegriff *m.* query term, search key, search term
Suchbegriffsgewichtung *f.* query term weights
Suchbereich *m.* area of search
Suchbericht *m.* search report
Suche *f.* search, inquiry
Suche *f.* **mit Folgeadressen** chaining search
Sucheinstieg *m.* access point
Suchen *n.* browsing
suchen *vrb.* scan/to, search/to, seek/to, browse/to
Suchergebnisbereich *m.* hold area
Suchfeld *n.* search field
Suchfrage *f.* search query
Suchgebiet *n.* area
Suchhilfe *f.* search aid
Suchkriterien *pl.* search criteria
Suchlauf *m.* browsing, retrieval run
Suchliste *f.* finding list, scan list
Suchlogik *f.* search logic
Suchmodus *m.* search mode
Suchprofil *n.* search profile

Suchreihenfolge *f.* search
order
Suchschleife *f.* search cycle
Suchsteuerwort *n.* search control word
Suchstrategie *f.* search strategy
Suchverfahren *n.* search procedure
Suchvorgang *m.* search process
Suchwort *n.* approach term, search word
Suchzeichen *n.* scan character
Suchzeit *f.* access motion time, search time, seek time
Suffix *n.* postfix, suffix
Summand *m.* addend
Summandenregister *n.* addend register
Summationsoperator *m.* adding operator
Summenfeld *n.* accumulator
Summenliste *f.* non-detailed list
Summenspeicher *m.* accumulator
Summenzeile *f.* total line
Summer *m.* signal buzzer
summieren *vrb.* accumulate/to
Summierer *m.* summer
Supervisor *m.* executive program, supervisor
suspendieren *vrb.* suspend/to
Suspendierungszeit *f.* suspend time
Symbol *n.* symbol
Symbol *n.* **mit Sinnvariationen** amalgamate
Symbolalphabet *n.* alphabet of symbols
Symbolenalphabet *n.* base of

symbolism
symbolische Adresse *f.* name, symbolic address
symbolische Codierung *f.* symbolic coding
symbolische Datei *f.* symbolic file
symbolische Programmiersprache *f.* symbolic language
symbolischer Befehl *m.* symbolic instruction
symbolisches Programm *n.* symbolic program
Symboltaste *f.* symbol key
Symbolverteilung *f.* apportionment of notation
Symbolverzeichnis *n.* symbol dictionary
symmetrisch *adj.* symmetric
Symposium *n.* symposium
Synchronzähler *m.* parallel counter
syndetisch *adj.* syndetic
syndetischer Katalog *m.* connective catalog
syndetisches Register *n.* connective index
Synonym *n.* synonym
Syntaktik *f.* syntactics
syntaktische Analyse *f.* syntactic analysis
syntaktische Indexierung *f.* syntactic indexing
syntaktisches Netz *n.* syntactic network
Syntax *f.* syntax
Syntaxanalysator *m.* parser
Syntaxanalyse *f.* parsing
Syntaxfehler *m.* syntax error
Synthese *f.* synthesis
synthetische Klassifikation *f.* composite classification, syn-

thetic classification
synthetische Relationen *pl.*
synthetic relations
synthetisches Objekt *n.* composite subject
System *n.* system
System *n.* **mittlerer Größe**
medium system
System-Nutzer-Schnittstelle *f.*
system-user interface
systemabhängig *adj.* online
systemabhängige Erfassung *f.*
online data entry
systemabhängige Feldsumme
f. online field total
Systemablaufplan *m.* system
flowchart
Systemanalyse *f.* system analysis, systems analysis
Systemanwendung *f.* system
application
Systematik *f.* systematics
systematisch *adj.* methodical
systematisch geordnet *adj.* in
classified order, in subject order
systematische Anordnung *f.*
von Dokumenten classified
filing system
systematische Aufstellung *f.*
classified arrangement
systematische Begriffsliste *f.*
classified list of concepts
systematische Bibliographie *f.*
systematic bibliography
systematische Ordnung *f.* classified order, systematic arrangement
systematische Reihenfolge *f.*
classified sequence
systematischer Ausfall *m.* systematic failure

systematischer Fehler *m.* bias
systematischer Katalog *m.*
class catalog, classed catalog,
classified catalog, systematic
catalog
systematischer Sachkatalog *m.*
classified subject catalog
systematischer Stichproben-
fehler *m.* sample bias
systematischer Thesaurus *m.*
systematic thesaurus
systematisches Archiv *n.* classified file
systematisches Register *n.*
classified index
Systemaufruf *m.* system call
Systemaufwand *m.* system effort
Systemausfall *m.* system failure
Systemausgabeeinheit *f.* system output unit
Systembefehl *m.* system command
Systemberater *m.* systems engineer
Systembeschreibung *f.* system
description
Systembewertung *f.* system evaluation
Systembibliothek *f.* system library
Systemdatei *f.* hard copy log,
system data set
Systemdatenanalysator *m.*
system data analyzer
Systemdefinition *f.* system definition
Systemdienstprogramm *n.*
system utility program
Systemdokumentation *f.* system documentation

Systemeffektivität *f.* system effectiveness
Systemeinführung *f.* system introduction
Systemeingabeeinheit *f.* system input unit
Systementwurf *m.* system design, systems design
Systemfehler *m.* system error
Systemfunktion *f.* system function
Systemgenerierung *f.* system generation
Systemgestaltung *f.* system design
Systemgrundstellung *f.* system reset
Systemidentifikation *f.* system identification
Systeminitialisierung *f.* system initialization
systemintern *adj.* intrasystem
Systemkonsole *f.* basic console, master console
Systemleistungsdaten *pl.* system performance data
Systemnachricht *f.* prompt
Systemplanung *f.* system design
Systemprogrammierfehler *m.* system programming error
Systemprotokoll *n.* system log
Systemrelevanz *f.* system relevance
Systemsicherheit *f.* system security
Systemsicherung *f.* system backup
Systemsimulator *m.* system simulator
Systemsperre *f.* system lock
Systemsteuerprogramm *n.* system control program, system support program
Systemsteuersprache *f.* operation control language
Systemsteuerung *f.* systems management
Systemtest *m.* system testing
Systemtestzeit *f.* system test time
Systemumgebung *f.* system environment
Systemumstellung *f.* migration
systemunabhängig *adj.* offline
systemunabhängige Ausgabe *f.* offline output
systemunabhängige Erfassung *f.* offline data entry
systemunabhängige Feldsumme *f.* offline field total
Systemvariable *f.* system variable
Systemverbund *m.* systems interconnection
Systemverwaltung *f.* system administration
Systemwiederanlauf *m.* system restart
Systemzeit *f.* system production time
Systemzugriffskonsole *f.* system access panel

T

t-Test *m.* t-test
tabellarische Abfragesprache *f.* tabular query language
Tabelle *f.* schedule, table
Tabellenänderung *f.* table modification
Tabellenbegrenzer *m.* table delimiter
Tabelleneintrag *m.* table entry, table item
Tabellenfunktion *f.* table function
Tabellenkalkulationsprogramm *n.* calculation program
Tabellensuche *f.* table search
Tabellenüberschrift *f.* caption
tabellieren *vrb.* tabulate/to
Tabulator *m.* tab
Tabulatorrücktaste *f.* back tab key
Tabulatortaste *f.* skip key, tab key
Tabuliertaste *f.* tabulate key
Tag *m.* **des Bibliothekars** librarian´s day
Tagebuch *n.* journal, day book, diary
Tageslichtprojektor *m.* overhead projector
Tagesordnung *f.* agenda
Tageszeit *f.* time of day
Tageszeitung *f.* daily newspaper, daily paper, journal, newspaper
täglich *adj.* daily
tägliche Eintragung *f.* daily entering-up
Tagung *f.* conference, congress, meeting
Tagungsbeitrag *m.* conference paper
Tagungsbericht *m.* conference proceedings, proceedings
Tagungsliteratur *f.* proceedings
Tagungsort *m.* meeting place
Taktgeber *m.* clock
Taschenatlas *m.* hand atlas
Taschenbuch *n.* pocket book
Taschenrechner *m.* hand calculator, pocket calculator
Taschenwörterbuch *n.* pocket dictionary
Tastatur *f.* keyboard modul, keyboard, keypad
Tastaturabfrage *f.* keyboard inquiry
Tastaturänderung *f.* keyboard substitution
Tastaturbereich *m.* keypad area
Tastaturblockierung *f.* keyboard lock-up
Tastaturdatei *f.* keyboard file
tastaturgesteuert *adj.* keyboard-controlled
Tastaturunterschied *m.* key-

board difference
Tastaturwechsel *m.* keyboard change
Taste *f.* key
Taste-Druck-System *n.* key-to-type system
Taste *f.* **mit wechselnder Funktion** alternate function key
Tastenanordnung *f.* keyboard arrangement
Tastenanschlag *m.* key stroke, key touch, keyboard stroke
Tastenauswahl *f.* keyboard scanning
Tastenbeschreibung *f.* key description
Tastenbetätigung *f.* key operating
Tastenbetätigungsdauer *f.* key operating time
tastengesteuert *adj.* key-controlled, keyboard-controlled
Tastenknopf *m.* key-button, keytop
Tastenreihe *f.* key row
Tastensteuerung *f.* key control
Tastensymbol *n.* key symbol
Tastenwirkdauer *f.* key contact time
Tätigkeit *f.* activity, occupation
Tätigkeitsbereich *m.* field of work
Tätigkeitsbericht *m.* work report, progress report
Tatsache *f.* fact
tatsächliche Adresse *f.* actual address
Taubstummenalphabet *n.* finger alphabet, hand alphabet, manual alphabet
Tausch *m.* exchange

Tauschdatei *f.* swap data set
Tauschliste *f.* exchange list
Tauschstelle *f.* exchange center, exchange department
Tauschvereinbarung *f.* exchange arrangement
Taxonomie *f.* taxonomy
Technik *f.* technology
Techniker *m.* technician
technische Abteilung *f.* processing department, technical services
technische Änderung *f.* altering
technische Angabe *f.* operating characteristic
technische Beschreibung *f.* physical description
technische Nutzungsdauer *f.* physical life
technische Spezifikation *f.* technical specification
technische Unterstützung *f.* technical support
technische Veralterung *f.* obsolescence
technischer Arbeitsbericht *m.* incident report
technischer Berater *m.* technical consultant
technisches Handbuch *n.* technical reference manual
Technologie *f.* technology
Technologiefolgenabschätzung *f.* technology assessment
Technologiepolitik *f.* technology policy
Technologietransfer *m.* technology transfer
technologische Grenzen *pl.* technology limitations
Teil *n.* part

Teil-Ganze-Relation *f.* part-whole relation, partitive relation, whole-part relation

Teilantwortkontrolle *f.* partial answer processing

Teilausfall *m.* partial failure

Teilband *m.* part of a volume

Teilbegriff *m.* part term

Teilbereich *m.* subarea

Teilbetriebszeit *f.* partial operating time

Teilenummer *f.* part number

Teilfeld *n.* subfield

Teilkanal *m.* partial channel

Teilmenge *f.* eines Zeichenvorrats character subset

Teilnahme *f.* participation

teilnehmen *vrb.* participate/to

teilnehmende Beobachtung *f.* participant observation

Teilnehmer *m.* subscriber, participant

Teilschlüssel *m.* partial key

Teilseite *f.* partial page

Teilsystem *n.* subsystem

Teilsystemsimulator *m.* partial system simulator

Teilübertragung *f.* partial carry

Teilung *f.* pitch, splitting

Teilungsgruppe *f.* pitch group

teilweise *adj.* partial

teilweise freigeben *vrb.* downgrade/to

teilweise spezifizierter Name *m.* partially qualified name

Teilzeitarbeit *f.* part-time employment

Telearbeit *f.* telework

Telebestellung *f.* teleordering

Telebrief *m.* mailgram

Telefax-Übermittlung *f.* tele-facsimile transmission

Telefaxdienst *m.* telefax service

Telefon *n.* telephone

Telefonapparat *m.* telephone set

Telefonbefragung *f.* phone survey

Telefonbuch *n.* telephone directory

telefonischer Zugang *m.* dial access

Telefonnummer *f.* telephone number

Telefonstecker *m.* jackplug

Telekommunikation *f.* telecommunication

Telekommunikationsnetzwerk *n.* telecommunication network

Telekommunikationssystem *n.* telecommunication system

Telekonferenz *f.* teleconference

Telekopie *f.* telecopy, telefax

Telekopierer *m.* facsimile transmitter, telecopier

Telekopierverfahren *n.* telefax technique

Teletext *m.* teletex

Teletextdienst *m.* teletex service

Telex *n.* telex

Telexdienst *m.* telex service

Temperatur *f.* temperature

temperaturempfindlich *adj.* temperature-sensitive

temporär *adj.* temporary

Temporärbibliothek *f.* temporary library

temporäre Datei *f.* temporary file

temporäre Platte *f.* temporary disk
Tendenz *f.* tendency, trend
Termin *m.* appointment, deadline
Terminal *n.* terminal
Terminaldrucker *m.* keyboard printer
Terminierungsschlüssel *m.* date key
Terminologe *m.* terminologist
Terminologie *f.* terminology
Terminologiearbeit *f.* terminology work
Terminologiedatenbank *f.* terminology database
Terminologieforschung *f.* terminology research
terminologische Kontrolle *f.* terminological control, vocabulary control
terminologischer Abgleich *m.* vocabulary matching
Terminplan *m.* date schedule
Terminplanung *f.* time-scheduling
terrestrisch *adj.* terrestrial
tertiäre Datenbank *f.* tertiary database
Test *m.* **unter Einsatzbedingungen** live test
Testabfragetaste *f.* test request key
Testbefehl *m.* test command
Testbetrieb *m.* test mode
testen *vrb.* test/to
Testergebnis *n.* score
Testlauf *m.* debugging run, pilot run, test run
Testlauftaste *f.* test button
Testschleife *f.* loop test
Testvorlage *f.* test chart

Text *m.* text
Text anpassen *vrb.* arrange/to a text
Text versetzen *vrb.* move/to text
Textanalyse *f.* text analysis
Textanordnung *f.* page layout
Textbaustein *m.* specific text component, standard paragraph, text module
Textbearbeitung *f.* text editing
Textdatei *f.* text file
Textdatenbank *f.* text database, textual database
Texteinfügung *f.* insertion in a text
Textformatierung *f.* text formatting
Textgliederung *f.* formatting
Textkorrektur *f.* improved revision
Textretrievalsystem *n.* text retrieval system
Textsammlung *f.* corpus
Textspeicherung *f.* text storage
Textsuche *f.* text searching
Textvariante *f.* alternative version
Textverarbeitsprogramm *n.* text processing program
Textverarbeitung *f.* text processing, word processing
Textverarbeitungssystem *n.* word processing equipment, word processor
Textverdichtung *f.* text compression
Textvergleich *m.* collation
Textzeile *f.* body line
Textzugriff *m.* text access
Theater *n.* theater

Theater- und Musikschulbibliothek f. drama and music school library

Theaterarchiv n. theater archive

Theaterkritik f. play review

Theatermuseum n. theater museum

Theaterwissenschaft f. studies of dramaturgy

Theaterzettelsammlung f. playbill collection

Thema n. subject

Thematik f. topic

Theologie f. theology

Theorie f. theory

Theorie f. **der Bibliographie** bibliology

Theorie f. **der unscharfen Menge** fuzzy set theory

Thermographie f. thermography

thermographischer Drucker m. thermographic printer

Thesaurus m. dictionary of descriptors, thesaurus

thesaurusartig adj. thesauruslike

Thesaurusbewertung f. thesaurus evaluation

Thesauruserstellung f. thesaurus construction

Thesaurusformat n. thesaurus format

Thesaurusforschung f. thesaurus research

Thesaurusinhalt m. thesaurus content

Thesaurusklasse f. thesaurus class

Thesauruskonstruktion f. thesaurus construction

Thesauruspflege f. thesaurus updating

Thesaurusregister n. thesaurus index

Thesaurusstruktur f. thesaurus structure

Tiefenindexierung f. exhaustive indexing, in-depth indexing

Tiefeninterview n. depth interview

Tiefenstruktur f. deep structure

Tiefenunterteilung f. exhaustive division

tiefes Indexieren n. deep indexing

tiefstehende Ziffer f. descending figure, hanging figures, inferior character, inferior figure

tiefstehender Buchstabe m. inferior letter

Tiefstellen n. half index down

Tiefstellung f. lowering

Tiermedizin f. veterinary medicine

Tilde f. tilde

Tilgungszeichen n. deletion mark

Tintenschreiber m. pen recording instrument

Tintenstrahldrucker m. ink jet printer, jet printer

tippen vrb. type/to

Tippfehler m. keying mistake, typing error, misspelling

Tisch m. table

Tischcomputer m. personal computer

Titel m. title

Titel-Autor-Katalog m. title

and author catalog
Titeländerung *f.* title change
Titelaufdruck *m.* **bei Einbänden**
binder's title
Titelaufnahme *f.* bibliographic
record, catalog entry, description, descriptive entry, record
Titelaufnahmeregeln *pl.* descriptive cataloging rules
Titelausgabe *f.* title edition
Titelbild *n.* frontispiece, title
frame
Titelblatt *n.* title-leaf
Titeldrucken *n.* lettering
Titeleintrag *m.* title entry
Titelfeld *n.* title area, title
space
Titelinversion *f.* inversion of
titles, inverted title
Titelkatalog *m.* title catalog
Titelleiste *f.* masthead
titellos *adj.* untitled
titelloser Umschlag *m.* blank
cover
Titelschutz *m.* copyright of a
title
Titelseite *f.* title page
Titelsichtleiste *f.* title strip
Titelübersicht *f.* information
card
Titelvorlage *f.* title card
Titelzeile *f.* headline
Todesanzeige *f.* obituary
Token-Passing-Verfahren *n.*
token passing
Toleranz *f.* tolerance
Ton-Bild-Schau *f.* audio-
visual presentation
Tonaufnahme *f.* sound record
Tonaufnahme *f.* **auf Magnet-
band** magnetic tape sound
record

Tonaufzeichnung *f.* audio
recording, phonogram
Tonband *n.* audio tape
Tonbandgerät *n.* audio
recorder
Tonbandkassette *f.* audio-cartridge
Toner *m.* toner
Tonkassette *f.* audio cassette
Tonträger *m.* recording
medium
Tonträgerarchiv *n.* audio
archive
toter Buchstabe *m.* dead letter
Tottaste *f.* dead key, non-escaping key
Totzeit *f.* unavailability
Tourismus *m.* tourism
Toxikologie *f.* toxicology
Tradition *f.* tradition
tragbarer Computer *m.* portable, portable computer, lapsize computer
tragbares Lesegerät *n.*
portable reader
Tragbarkeit *f.* mobility, portability
Trägerinstitution *f.* parent institution
Tragweite *f.* range, importance
Transaktion *f.* transaction
Transaktionsfehler *m.* transaction error
Transaktionsidentifikation *f.*
transaction identification
Transaktionsmanagement *n.*
transaction management
Transaktionsprotokoll *n.* journal of transactions
Transaktionstabelle *f.* program control table

Transferliste *f.* transfer list
Transformationsgrammatik *f.*
transformational grammar
Transformator *m.* transformer
Transistor *m.* transistor
transkribieren *vrb.* transcribe
/to, transliterate/to
Transkription *f.* transcription
Transliteration *f.* metagraphy,
transliteration
transparent *adj.* transparent
Transparentpapier *n.* vellum
Transport *m.* feed, transport
Transportfehler *m.* misfeed
Transportlöcher *pl.* feed holes
Transportweg *m.* haul
Transportwesen *n.* transportation system
Transportzeit *f.* transport time
Treffer *m.* hit
Trefferquote *f.* hit rate, hit ratio, recall factor, recall ratio
Treffpunkt *m.* meeting point
Treffsicherheit *f.* accuracy
Trend *m.* trend
Trenneinrichtung *f.* burster
trennen *vrb.* burst/to

Trennlinie *f.* separator line
Trennsymbol *n.* separate
clause
Trennung *f.* separation
Trennungszeichen *n.* hyphen
Trennzeichen *n.* break character, delimiter, information
separator, marker, separating character, separator
Tresor *m.* safe
Trigger *m.* trigger
Triggerprogramm *n.* trigger
program
Trivialliteratur *f.* light fiction
Trommelspeicher *m.* drum
Türschild *n.* door label
Typ *m.* type
Typenrad *n.* print wheel, type
wheel
Typenraddrucker *m.* daisy-wheel printer, type wheel
printer, wheel printer
typisch *adj.* normal
Typisierung *f.* classification
Typograph *m.* typographer
Typographie *f.* typography
Typologie *f.* typology
Typoskript *n.* typescript

U

üben *vrb.* practice/to
überarbeiten *vrb.* revise/to
überarbeitete Auflage *f.* revised edition
Überblick *m.* digest, summary
übereinstimmend *adj.* matched
übereinstimmende Meinung *f.* consensus
übereinstimmende Sätze *pl.* matching records
Übereinstimmung *f.* coincidence, match
überfällig *adj.* past due
überfälliges Material *n.* overdue material
Übergabe *f.* delivery
Übergabestelle *f.* interchange point
Übergang *m.* change-over, gateway, junction, migrating, transit
Übergangspfad *m.* migration path
Übergangsregelung *f.* transitional regulations
Übergangsspeicher *m.* intrapartition destination
Übergangszeit *f.* inter-operation time, transition time
Übergehangabe *f.* ignore option
Übergehen *n.* skip
übergehen *vrb.* bypass/to, ignore/to

übergeordnete Klasse *f.* parent class
übergeordnete Körperschaft *f.* parent body
Überhang *m.* kern
überhängender Buchstabe *m.* kerned letter
überholen *vrb.* recondition/to, refit/to
überlagern *vrb.* swap/to
Überlagerung *f.* interference, overlay
Überlagerungsprogramm *n.* overlay program
überlappen *vrb.* interleave/to, overlap/to
Überlappung *f.* overlap
Überlastfaktor *m.* overload capacity
Überlastung *f.* overloading
Überlauf *m.* overflow, overrun
Überlaufanzeige *f.* overflow indicator
Überlaufbedingung *f.* overflow condition
Überlaufdatei *f.* spill file
überlaufen *vrb.* spill/to
Überlauffeld *n.* overflow field
Überlaufsatz *m.* non-home record, overflow record
Überlaufseite *f.* overflow page
Überlaufspur *f.* overflow track
Überlaufzeile *f.* overflow line

Überlaufzeit *f.* overrun time
Überleitung *f.* transition
Überlieferung *f.* tradition
Übermittlung *f.* transmission
Übermittlung *f.* per Fax
facsimile transmission
Übermittlungsvorschrift *f.* link
protocol
Übernahme *f.* assumption
Übernahme *f.* des Benutzerprofils adopting user profil
Übernahmepolitik *f.* takeover
policy
überregionales Netz *n.* wide
area network
überschneiden *vrb.* overlap/to
Überschneidung *f.* overlap
Überschneidungskennziffer *f.*
overlap measure
überschreiben *vrb.* over-
write/to
überschreiten *vrb.* override/to
Überschrift *f.* heading, head
Überschrift *f.* für Schlüsselfeld
key heading
übersetzen *vrb.* translate/to
Übersetzer *m.* compiler, language processor, language
translator, translator
Übersetzung *f.* language
translation, translation
Übersetzungsdienst *m.* translation service
Übersetzungsprogramm *n.*
translating program
Übersetzungswissenschaft *f.*
translation science
Übersicht *f.* schedule
übersichtlich aufstellen *vrb.* e-
numerate/to
Übersichtsbericht *m.* analytical
survey

Übersichtsblatt *n.* general
chart
Übersichtskarte *f.* index map,
key to sectional map
Übersichtszettel *m.* contents
card
Übersiedlung *f.* emigration
übertragbare Datei *f.* portable
file
Übertragbarkeit *f.* transferability, applicability
übertragen *vrb.* move/to,
transfer/to, transmit/to
übertragene Bedeutung *f.*
transferred meaning
übertragene Bezeichnung *f.*
transferred term
übertragene Daten *pl.* transmitted data
Übertragung *f.* transcription,
line circuit, transmission
Übertragungsart *f.* mode of
transmission
Übertragungsbereich *m.* transient area
Übertragungsbereitschaft *f.*
ready for data
Übertragungsdaten *pl.* transient data
Übertragungseinheit *f.* remote
communications unit
Übertragungsendezeichen *n.*
end of transmission character
Übertragungsfehler *m.* line
transmission error, transaction error, transmission error
Übertragungsfolge *f.* transmission sequence
Übertragungsgeschwindigkeit
f. bit capacity, bit rate, data
signaling rate, line speed,
transmission speed

Übertragungsgeschwindig-keitswahl *f.* line speed options

Übertragungskanal *m.* channel, communication channel

Übertragungskontrolle *f.* transfer check

Übertragungskosten *pl.* communication cost

Übertragungsleitung *f.* telecommunication line, transmission line

Übertragungsmodus *m.* move mode

Übertragungsnummer *m.* transient number

Übertragungspriorität *f.* transmission priority

Übertragungsrate *f.* transfer rate, transmission rate

Übertragungssatz *m.* transmittal record

Übertragungssteuerung *f.* line control, transmission control

Übertragungssteuerzeichen *n.* communication control character

Übertragungstaste *f.* transfer key

Übertragungsweg *m.* bus

Übertragungszeichenfolge *f.* information message

Übertragungszeit *f.* transfer time

Übertragunsgsignal *n.* transfer signal

überwachen *vrb.* attend/to, monitor/to

Überwachung *f.* monitoring

Überwachung *f.* **der laufenden Veröffentlichungen** current publication survey

Überwachungseinrichtung *f.* monitoring feature

Überwachungsprogramm *n.* monitor program

Überwachungsprozedur *f.* monitoring procedure

Überweisung *f.* remittance

üblich *adj.* usual

Übung *f.* tutorial

übungsintensiv *adj.* practice-intensive

Übungsprüfung *f.* pretest

Uhrzeit *f.* time of day

Ultraschall *m.* ultrasound

umarbeiten *vrb.* arrange/to

Umarbeitung *f.* adaptation

Umbau *m.* remodeling

umbenennen *vrb.* rename/to

umbrechen *vrb.* wrap around/to

Umbruch *m.* page make-up

Umbruchkorrektur *f.* page proof

Umdrehung *f.* rotation

Umfang *m.* size

Umfangsdefinition *f.* definition by extension, extensional definition

Umfassungsrelation *f.* comprehensive relation

Umfeld *n.* environment

Umformer *m.* transformer

Umfrage *f.* survey

Umgangssprache *f.* colloquial language, common language, every day language

Umgebung *f.* environment

umgekehrt *adj.* inverse

Umgestaltung *f.* reconfiguration

umkehrbar *adj.* reversible

umkehren *vrb.* invert/to

Umkehrfunktion *f.* reversal function
Umkehrung *f.* **der natürlichen Wortfolge** inversion of heading
Umlage *f.* apportionment
Umland *n.* metropolitan
Umlaufdatei *f.* wraparound file
Umläufe *pl.* routings
umordnen *vrb.* rearrange/to, reorder/to
Umpositionierung *f.* repositioning
Umrahmung *f.* border
umrandete Überschrift *f.* boxheading, boxhead
Umsatz *m.* income, turnover
Umsatzsteuer *f.* sales tax
Umschaltcode *m.* switch code
umschalten *vrb.* shift/to, switch /to
Umschalter *m.* alteration switch
Umschaltfeststeller *m.* shift interlock
Umschalthöhe *f.* shift motion
Umschalttaste *f.* shift key, upper shift key
Umschaltung *f.* shift, turnaround
Umschaltung lösen *vrb.* shift unlock/to
Umschlag *m.* cover, jacket, reversal, turnover
Umschlagbild *n.* cover picture
Umschlagtitel *m.* cover title
umschlüsseln *vrb.* recode/to
umschreiben *vrb.* transcribe/to, transliterate/to
Umschreibung *f.* paraphrase
Umschrift *f.* metagraphy, transcription
Umschulung *f.* retraining
umsetzen *vrb.* transform/to
Umsetzer *m.* converter
Umsetzung *f.* transformation
Umsetzung *f.* **der Eingabedaten** input data translation
umsignieren *vrb.* change/to class mark
umspeichern *vrb.* restore/to
Umstellung *f.* relocation, readjustment
Umstellung *f.* **des Altbestandes** retrospective conversion
umstrittenes Material *n.* controversial material
Umwälzung *f.* radical change
umwandeln *vrb.* assemble/to, transform/to
Umwandlung *f.* displacement, modification, transformation
Umwandlungsphase *f.* generation phase
Umwandlungszeit *f.* assembly time
Umweg *m.* detour
Umweltforschung *f.* environmental research
Umweltinformationssystem *n.* environmental information system
Umweltplanung *f.* environmental planning
Umweltschutz *m.* environmental protection
Umweltverschmutzung *f.* environmental pollution
Umzug *m.* removal
unabhängige Datenübermittlung *f.* independent data communication
unabhängige Forschungsbi-

bliothek *f.* independent research library
unabhängige Schulbibliothek *f.* independent school library
unabhängige Zugriffsmethode *f.* independent access method
unabhängiges Dienstprogramm *n.* independent utility program
unauffindbar *adj.* unrecognizable
unaufgefordert *adj.* unsolicited
unausgerichtet *adj.* unaligned
unbedingt *adj.* unconditional
unbedingte Anweisung *f.* imperative statement, unconditional statement
unbedingter Programmsatz *m.* imperative sentence
unbedingter Sprungbefehl *m.* unconditional jump
unbedruckte Bogen *pl.* blank sheets
unbegrenzt *adj.* unlimited
unbehebbar *adj.* non-recoverable
unbehebbarer Fehler *m.* nonrecovery
unbekannte Bezeichnung *f.* unknown term
unbekannte Größe *f.* unknown quantity
unbenannte Steuersektion *f.* unnamed control section
unbeschnittenes Exemplar *n.* untrimmed copy
unbesetzt *adj.* vacant
unbestätigt *adj.* unverified
unbestimmt *adj.* indefinite, uncertain, undefined
unbestimmter Ausdruck *m.* indeterminate
unbestimmter Koeffizient *m.*

undetermined coefficient
unbetitelt *adj.* untitled
unbewertet *adj.* unweighted
uncodiert *adj.* uncoded
UND AND
UND-Beziehung *f.* AND relationship
UND-Glied *n.* AND element
UND-Regel *f.* AND rule
UND-Symbol *n.* AND symbol
UND-Verbindungsoperator *m.* AND connector
UND-Verknüpfung *f.* AND operation
undatiert *adj.* undated
undefiniert *adj.* undefined
undefinierter Begriff *m.* explicandum
undefinierter Satz *m.* undefined record
undefiniertes Symbol *adj.* undefined symbol
unendliche Menge *f.* infinite set
unentgeltlich *adj.* free of charge
unerwartete Nachricht *f.* unsolicited message
unerwartetes Stichwort *n.* unsought heading
unfertig *adj.* premature
unformatierte Anzeige *f.* unformatted display
ungeblockt *adj.* unblocked
ungeblockter Satz *m.* unblocked record
ungebunden *adj.* in sheets, unbound
ungedruckt *adj.* hitherto unpublished
ungekürzt *adj.* unabridged
ungenannter Verfasser *m.* anonymous author

ungenutzte Kapazität *f.* idle capacity

ungeordnet *adj.* unclassified

ungeordnete Dokumentsammlung *f.* coacervate

ungepuffert *adj.* unbuffered

ungerade *adj.* odd

ungerade Parität *f.* odd parity

ungerade Seitenzahl *f.* odd page, odd-numbered page

ungerade Zahlen *pl.* odd numbers

ungesteuert *adj.* uncontrolled

ungeteiltes System *n.* nonshared system

ungetrennter Blocksatz *m.* hyphenless justification

ungewöhnlicher Wissensstand *m.* anomalous state of knowledge

ungleich *adj.* unequal

Ungleichung *f.* inequality

Ungleichwertigkeit *f.* nonequivalence

ungültig *adj.* invalid, nonvalid

ungültige Adresse *f.* invalid address

ungültige Auswahl *f.* invalid choice

ungültige Eingabe *f.* invalid entry

ungültige Operation *f.* invalid operation

ungültige Programmdiskette *f.* invalid program diskette

ungültige Taste *f.* invalid key

ungültige Zeichenkombination *f.* invalid combination of character

ungültiger Empfang *m.* invalid reception

ungültiger Fehlerstatus *m.* invalid error status

ungültiger Name *m.* invalid name

ungültiger Zugriff *m.* invalid access action

ungültiges Feld *n.* invalid field

Ungültigkeitserklärung *f.* cassation

Ungültigkeitszeichen *n.* cancel character, ignore character

Unikat *n.* unicum, unique copy

Uniterm *m.* uniterm

Unitermindexierung *f.* uniterm indexing

Unitermsystem *n.* uniterm system

Universalbibliographie *f.* universal bibliography, world bibliography

Universalbibliothek *f.* general library, universal library

Universaldezimalklassifikation *f.* universal decimal classification

Universaleingang *m.* universal element

Universalklassifikation *f.* universal classification

Universalklassifikationsschema *n.* general classification scheme

Universalprogramm *n.* general-purpose program

Universalrechner *m.* general-purpose computer

universelle Dezimalklassifikation *f.* Brussels system

universeller Befehlssatz *m.* universal instruction set

universeller Zeichensatz *m.* universal character set

Universität *f.* university
Universitätsbibliothek *f.* university library
Universitätsverlag *m.* university press
unkontrollierbar *adj.* uncontrollable
unkontrolliert *adj.* unchecked, uncontrolled
unkontrollierte Ausleihe *f.* circular routing
unlesbar *adj.* unreadable, unscannable
unmittelbar untergeordnet *adj.* immediate subordinate
unmittelbare Adressierung *f.* immediate addressing
unmittelbarer Sprechweg *m.* inter-operator connection
unmittelbarer Status *m.* immediate state
unmittelbarer Zugriff *m.* immediate access
unmodifizierter Befehl *m.* presumptive instruction
unnumeriert *adj.* unnumbered
unpaginiert *adj.* unpaged
unqualifiziert *adj.* unqualified
unqualifiziertes Buch *n.* nonqualified book
unreduzierbar *adj.* irreducible
Unreduzierbarkeit *f.* irreducibility
unregelmäßig *adj.* irregular
unscharfe Menge *f.* fuzzy set
unselbständige Ergänzungszahl *f.* dependent auxiliary
unselbständiges Schlagwort *n.* bound term
Unsicherheitsreduktion *f.* emmorphosis
unsortiert *adj.* unsorted

unspezifische Lokalisation *f.* implicit location
Unstimmigkeit *f.* inconsistency
unsymmetrisch *adj.* unbalanced
unsystematisch *adj.* non-systematic
unter Aufsicht attended
unter Spannung stehend *adj.* hot
Unterbefehl *m.* subcommand
Unterbegriff *m.* minor, narrower term, species, subordinate concept, narrow catchword
unterbrechbare Instruktion *f.* interruptable instruction
unterbrechen *vrb.* abort/to, break/to, interrupt/to, suspend/to
Unterbrechung *f.* abnormal end, abnormal ending, attention, interruption, interrupt, recess
Unterbrechungsaktion *f.* interruption action
Unterbrechungsanforderung *f.* interrupt request
Unterbrechungsbedingung *f.* interruption condition
Unterbrechungscode *m.* break scan code, interruption code
unterbrechungsfrei *adj.* uninterruptable
Unterbrechungsmodus *m.* interrupt mode
Unterbrechungsnetzwerk *n.* interruption network
Unterbrechungspriorität *f.* interrupt priority
Unterbrechungspunkt *m.* point of interruption

Unterbrechungssignal *n.* interrupt signal

Unterbrechungssteuerprogramm *n.* interrupt service routine

Unterbrechungssteuerung *f.* interrupt controller

Unterbrechungstaste *f.* attention key

Unterbrechungsüberwachung *f.* interruption supervision

Unterbrechungszeit *f.* break time

unterbringen *vrb.* station/to

unterbrochen *adj.* halted

unterbrochene Funktion *f.* halted function

unterdrückbare Bedingung *f.* repressible condition

untere Grenze *f.* lower bound

untere Zeile *f.* bottom row

unterer Seitenrand *m.* bottom margin, foot margin

Unterfeld *n.* minor field, subfield

untergeordnet *adj.* subordinate, subsidiary

untergeordnetes Feld *n.* subordinate field

untergliederte Datei *f.* partitioned data set, partitioned file

untergliederter Index *m.* partitioned index

untergliederter Schlüssel *m.* partitioned key

Untergliederung *f.* segmentation

Untergliederungsgesichtspunkt *m.* basis of division, characteristic of division, difference

Untergruppe *f.* minor, subgroup

Untergruppenkontrolle *f.* minor control

Untergruppenkontrollfeld *n.* minor control field

Untergruppentrennung *f.* minor control change

Unterkette *f.* substring

Unterklasse *f.* subclass

Unterlauf *m.* underflow

Unternehmen *n.* firm, enterprise, company

Unternehmensforschung *f.* operations analysis, operations research

Unternehmensführung *f.* management

Unterordnung *f.* hypotaxis

Unterprogramm *n.* subprogram, subroutine

Unterprogrammprozedur *f.* subroutine procedure

Unterprozedur *f.* subprocedure

Unterricht *m.* teaching, lessons, instruction

Unterrichtsmaterial *n.* instructional material

Unterrichtsmethode *f.* teaching method

Unterrichtsraum *m.* classroom

Unterscheidungsfacette *f.* differential facet

Unterschied *m.* difference

Unterschlagwort *n.* subheading, topical subdivision

unterschreiben *vrb.* autograph /to, signature/to

Unterschrift *f.* autograph, signature

Untersektion *f.* sub-section

unterstreichen *vrb.* underline
/to, underscore/to
Unterstreichungszeichen *n.*
break character, underscore
character
Unterstruktur *f.* minor struc-
ture
Unterstufe *f.* lower grades
unterstützen *vrb.* support/to
Unterstützung *f.* support
Unterstützung *f.* mehrerer Bibliotheken multiple library
support
Unterstützungsprogramm *n.*
support program
Untersuchung *f.* inspection
Untersuchung *f.* von Kanäle
zur Informationsübertragung
channel study
Untersuchungsbericht *m.*
examination report
Untersuchungsergebnis *n.* test
result, findings
Untersuchungsmethode *f.*
examination method
Unterteil *n.* bottom
Unterteilung *f.* partition
Unterteilungsgesichtspunkt *m.*
basis of subdivision, difference
Untertitel *m.* alternative title,
caption, head, secondary title,
subtitle
unterzeichnen *vrb.* sign/to
unveränderlich *adj.* unchangeable
unveränderliche Zeilenschaltung *f.* index return
unveränderter Nachdruck *m.*
impression
unverkürzt *adj.* unabridged
unveröffentlicht *adj.* hitherto
unpublished, unpublished

unverriegelt *adj.* unlatched
unverträglich *adj.* in-
compatible
unverzögerter Konfigurationswiederanlauf *m.* immediate
configuration restart
unvollständig *adj.* defective,
incomplete
unvollständige Kartographie *f.*
incomplete mapping
unvollständige Reihe *f.* ceased
publications
unvollständiges Exemplar *n.*
defective copy
unwesentliche Eigenschaft *f.*
incidental characteristic
unwirksam *adj.* ineffective
Unwirksamkeit *f.* inefficiency
unwirtschaftlich *adj.* ineffective
Unwirtschaftlichkeit *f.* inefficiency
unzustellbarer Brief *m.* dead
letter
Urbeleg *m.* original document
Urheber *m.* originator, public
author
Urheberrecht *n.* author´s
right, copy right
Urheberrechtsverletzung *f.*
infringement of copyright
Urkunde *f.* charta, document,
certificate
Urkundenbestand *m.*
document collection
Urkundenbuch *n.* cartulary,
chartulary
Urkundenlehre *f.* diplomatics
Urkundenregister *n.* cartulary,
chartulary
Urkundenrestaurierung *f.*
document restauration

Urkundensammlung *f.* archive
urkundlich *adj.* archival
Urlader *m.* bootstrap
Urschrift *f.* autograph
Ursprung *m.* origin, source
Ursprungsbeleg *m.* master
document
Ursprungsdaten *pl.* source
data
Ursprungskosten *pl.* original
costs
Urteil *n.* judgement
Urtext *m.* original text
utopischer Roman *m.* science
fiction

V

Vademecum *n.* vademecum
Vakuum *n.* vacuum
variabel *adj.* variable
Variable *f.* variable
variable Daten *pl.* variable
data
variable Kosten *pl.* variable
cost
variable Länge *f.* variable
length
variable Satzlänge *f.* variable
record length
variable Wortlänge *f.* variable
word length
variabler Eingabebereich *m.*
variable input area
variabler Name *m.* variable i-
dentifier
variabler Text *m.* variable text
variables Blockformat *n.* variable block format
variables Feld *n.* variable field
variables Format *n.* variable
format
variables Satzformat *n.* variable record format
variables Zeichen *n.* variable
symbol
Varianz *f.* variance
Varianzanalyse *f.* analysis of
variance, variance analysis
Variation *f.* variation
variierbar *adj.* varying
**variierbare Leseempfindlich-
keit** *f.* vary sensing
variieren *vrb.* vary/to
Vektor *m.* vector
Vektoranalysis *f.* vector
analysis
Vektorgenerator *m.* line generator, vector generator
Vektorgraphik *f.* vector graphics
vektoriell *adj.* vectorial
vektorielle Ähnlichkeit *f.*
vector similarity
Vektorkonstante *f.* vector constant

Vektorrechner *m.* array processor, parallel processors, pipeline processor, vector processor

Venn-Diagramm *n.* venn diagram

Verallgemeinerung *f.* abstraction, generalization

Veralten *n.* obsolescence

veraltet *adj.* out of date

veralteter Begriff *m.* archaic term, obsolete term

veraltetes Material *n.* obsolete material

veränderbar *adj.* varying

veränderbare Dimension *f.* adjustable dimension

veränderliche Information *f.* volatile information

verändern *vrb.* replace/to

Verändern *n.* einer Größe variable adjustment

Veränderung *f.* substitution

Veränderungsanzeiger *m.* modified data indicator

Veränderungsoperator *m.* update operator

veranschlagen *vrb.* assess/to

Veranstaltung *f.* event

verantwortlich *adj.* liable

Verantwortung *f.* responsibility

Verarbeitbarkeit *f.* processibility

verarbeiten *vrb.* process/to

Verarbeitung *f.* processing

Verarbeitung *f.* gesprochener Sprache voice processing

Verarbeitung *f.* von ankommenden Anforderungen inbound request processing

Verarbeitungsanforderung *f.* processing request

Verarbeitungsdatei *f.* holding file

Verarbeitungshinweis *m.* processing information

Verarbeitungskosten *pl.* processing cost

Verarbeitungslimit *n.* processing limit

Verarbeitungsoption *f.* processing option

Verarbeitungsparameter *m.* processing parameter

Verarbeitungsprogramm *n.* processing program

Verarbeitungsservice *m.* processing service

Verarbeitungsstufe *f.* processing level

Verarbeitungssystem *n.* processing system

Verarbeitungstiefe *f.* processing depth

Verarbeitungsüberlappung *f.* processing overlap

Verarbeitungswarteschlange *f.* process queue

Verarbeitungszeit *f.* processing time

Verb *n.* verb

verbal *adj.* verbal

Verband *m.* union, society, federation, association

verbessern *vrb.* amend/to, correct/to

verbesserte Antwortzeit *f.* improved response time

verbesserte Auflage *f.* improved edition

verbesserte Ausgabe *f.* improved edition

verbesserte Patentbeschreibung *f.* amended specification

Verbesserung *f.* amendment,

improvement
Verbesserungsvorschlag *m.*
improvement proposal
verbinden *vrb.* interface/to,
join/to, link edit/to, splice/to
verbindliche Namensliste *f.*
name authority file
verbindliche Schlagwortliste *f.*
subject authority file
Verbindung *f.* joint, junction,
link connection, linkage
Verbindung *f.* **von Anwendun-**
gen application combination
Verbindungsabbruch *m.* disconnection
Verbindungsarbeit *f.* liaison
work
Verbindungsaufbau *m.* teleconnection
Verbindungsbibliothekar *m.*
contact librarian
Verbindungselement *n.* link
Verbindungsindikator *m.* link
indicator
Verbindungskabel *f.* interconnecting cable
Verbindungsleitung *f.* link
circuit
Verbindungsprotokoll *n.* link
protocol
Verbindungsstation *f.* link station
Verbindungstest *m.* link test
Verbindungsvorsatz *m.* link
header
Verbindungszeichen *n.* connecting symbol
Verbindungszeit *f.* connect
time
verborgene Klassifikation *f.*
concealed classification
verborgene Linie *f.* hidden line

verborgene Variable *f.* hidden
variable
Verbraucher *m.* consumer
Verbreitung *f.* **einer Innovation**
diffusion of innovation
verbuchen *vrb.* book/to
Verbund *m.* union
Verbundbibliotheken *pl.* associated libraries
verbundene Datei *f.* associated
file
verbundenes Unterprogramm
n. linked subroutine
Verbundkarte *f.* combination
card, dual card
Verbundkatalog *m.* union
catalog
Verbundkatalogisierung *f.*
union cataloging
Verbundrechner *m.* subhost
verbürgt *adj.* authentic
verdeckte Funktion *f.* locked
function
Verdichtung *f.* compression,
condensation
Verdichtungsfaktor *m.* packing
factor
Verdopplung *f.* **der inhaltlichen**
Abdeckung duplication of
coverage
verdrahtet *adj.* wired
Verdrahtung *f.* wiring
Verein *m.* club
Vereinbarung *f.* agreement,
concord, declaration
Vereindeutigung *f.* disambiguation
vereinfachen *vrb.* simplify/to
vereinfachte Titelaufnahme *f.*
simplified cataloging
Vereinheitlichung *f.* unification, standardization

Vereinigung f. association, federation
Vereinsbibliothek f. club library
Verfahren n. approach, procedure
verfahrensorientierte Programmierspache f. procedure-oriented language, procedural language
Verfahrenstechnik f. process engineering
Verfallsdatum n. expiration date
Verfasser m. author
Verfasser m. **des Vorworts** author of the preface
Verfasser- und Sachkatalog m. author-title catalog
Verfasser- und Sachnebeneintrag m. author-title added entry
Verfasser- und Sachregister n. author-title index
Verfasserangabe f. author statement
Verfassereintrag m. author entry, author heading, name entry
Verfasserkarte f. author card
Verfasserkatalog m. author catalog, name catalog
Verfassernamensnormdatei f. author authority file
Verfassernamensverzeichnis n. author list
Verfassersignatur f. author mark, author notation, author number
Verfasserverzeichnis n. author index
Verfassung f. constitution
Verfassungsrecht n. constitutional law
verfehlen vrb. miss/to
verfeinern vrb. refine/to
Verfeinerung f. refinement
verfilmen vrb. film/to
Verfilmung f. film
Verfilmungsrechte pl. film rights
verfolgen vrb. pursue/to, trace/to
Verfolgung f. prosecution
verfügbar adj. available
Verfügbarkeit f. availability
Verfügbarkeitsfeld n. accessibility field
Verfügbarkeitstabelle f. availability table
Vergangenheit f. past
Vergangenheitsdaten pl. historical data
vergessen adj. lost
vergilben vrb. yellow/to
vergilbt adj. yellowed
Vergleich m. comparison, matching, relation
Vergleichbarkeit f. comparability
vergleichen vrb. compare/to, match/to
vergleichend adj. comparative
vergleichende Bibliothekswissenschaft f. comparative librarianship
Vergleichsanzeiger m. matching record indicator
Vergleichsbeziehung f. comparative relation
Vergleichsebene f. match level
Vergleichseinrichtung f. comparator
Vergleichsfeld n. match field
Vergleichsoperator m. rela-

tional operator
Vergleichsregister *n.* comparand register
Vergleichsschlüssel *m.* match code
vergriffen *adj.* out of print
vergriffene Ausgabe *f.* exhausted edition, out of print edition
vergrößern *vrb.* magnify/to
Vergrößerung *f.* enlargement
Vergütung *f.* compensation
Verhalten *n.* behavior
Verhältnis *n.* ratio
Verhandlung *f.* negotiation
verhindern *vrb.* preempt/to, prevent/to
verifizieren *vrb.* verify/to
Verkauf *m.* sale
verkaufen *vrb.* sell/to
Verkaufsauftrag *m.* sales order
Verkaufsbedingungen *pl.* sales terms
Verkaufskatalog *m.* sales catalog
Verkaufsleiter *m.* sales manager
Verkaufspreis *m.* selling price
Verkehrsleistung *f.* traffic capacity
Verkehrsmuseum *n.* traffic museum
Verkehrstechnik *f.* transportation technology
Verkehrswesen *n.* traffic system, transportation
Verketten *n.* **von Bibliotheken** library chaining
Verkettung *f.* linkage
Verkettungsadresse *f.* link address
verkleinern *vrb.* reduce/to

Verkleinerung *f.* reduction
Verkleinerungsfaktor *m.* reduction factor, reduction ratio
verknoten *vrb.* interconnect/to
Verknüpfung *f.* relationship
Verknüpfungsdaten *pl.* relationship data
Verknüpfungssteuerung *f.* logic control
verkürzte Ausgabe *f.* abridged edition
verkürzte Katalogisierung *f.* minimal cataloging
verkürzte Leihfrist *f.* reduced loan period
verkürzter Eintrag *f.* abbreviated entry
verkürztes Dokument *n.* abridged document
Verlag *m.* publishing house
Verlagsbuchhandlung *f.* publishing bookshop
Verlagshaus *n.* publishing house
Verlagslektor *m.* publisher´s editor
Verlagsort *m.* place of publication
Verlagsrecht *n.* right of publication
Verlagsvertrag *m.* publishing contract
Verlagswesen *n.* publishing
Verlängerung *f.* renewal
Verläßlichkeit *f.* reliability
verlegen *vrb.* publish/to
Verleger *m.* publisher
Verleih *m.* loan service
Verleihdienst *m.* lending service
verliehen *adj.* issued, lent, on loan, out

verloren *adj.* lost
Verlust *m.* loss
Verlustrate *f.* loss parameter
Verlustzeit *f.* interference
time, lost time
Vermächtnis *n.* bequest
Vermaschung *f.* intermeshing
vermitteln *vrb.* inter-
mediate/to, switch/to
Vermittlung *f.* exchange
Vermittlungsdienst *m.* exchange service
Vermittlungsplatz *m.* operator
desk
vermutete Ausgabe *f.* ghost
edition
verneint *adj.* negated
Verneinung *f.* negation
vernetzt *adj.* networked
Vernetzung *f.* networking
veröffentlichte Dokumente *pl.*
published documents
Veröffentlichung *f.* announcement, publication
Veröffentlichung *f.* **auf Anfrage**
on-demand-publishing
Veröffentlichung *f.* **der Ehemaligen** alumni publication
Veröffentlichungsdatum *n.*
date of publication, publication date
Veröffentlichungssprache *f.*
publication language
Verordnung *f.* decree
Verpackungstechnik *f.* packing
technology
verpassen *vrb.* miss/to
verramschen *vrb.* remain-
der/to
verriegeln *vrb.* lock/to
Verriegelung *f.* interlock, locking, lock

Verriegelungsknopf *m.* lock
bar knob
Verriegelungsmechanismus *m.*
locking mechanism
Verriegelungsmodus *m.* lock
mode
verringern *vrb.* lessen/to
Versal *m.* capital letter, capital
Versammlung *f.* assembly
Versand *m.* mail service, delivery
Versandhaus *n.* mail order firm
Versandliste *f.* mailing list
Versandrolle *f.* mailing tube
verschachteln *vrb.* nest/to
Verschachtelung *f.* nesting
verschiebbar *adj.* relocatable
verschiebbare Adresse *f.* relocatable address
verschiebbares Format *n.* relocatable format
Verschiebbarkeit *f.* relocatability
verschieben *vrb.* move/to, re-
locate/to, reschedule/to,
scroll /to
Verschiebung *f.* displacement,
relocation, shifting
Verschiebungsverzeichnis *n.*
relocation dictionary
verschiedene Lesarten *pl.*
alternative version
verschiedenes *adj.* miscellaneous
verschlagworten *vrb.* enter/to
under the subject
Verschleiß *m.* wearout failure,
wear
verschlüsseln *vrb.* code/to,
scramble/to
verschlüsselte Daten *pl.* enciphered data

verschlüsselte Suchanfrage *f.*
encoded question
Verschlüsselung *f.* encoding,
encryption
Verschlüsselungsvorschrift *f.*
access guide
Verschluß *m.* fastener, inter-
lock
Verschlußsache *f.* classified
document
Verschmelzung *f.* conflation
verschwinden *vrb.* vanish/to
versenden *vrb.* send/to, ship/to
Versetzen *n.* shift
Versetzung *f.* dislocation
Versicherung *f.* insurance
Versicherungspolice *f.* insurance policy
Versicherungsvertrag *m.* insurance contract
Versicherungswesen *n.* insurance business
Version *f.* version
Versorgung *f.* supply
Verständigung *f.* notification
Verständlichkeit *f.* audibility
Verstärker *m.* repeater
verstärkt *adj.* reinforced
versteckte Bibliographie *f.* hidden bibliography
Versteigerer *m.* auctioneer
versteigern *vrb.* auction/to
Versteigerung *f.* auction
verstellbare Regalbretter *pl.*
adjustable shelves
verstellbarer Randanschlag *m.*
adjustable margin feature
verstellen *vrb.* misplace/to
verstreut *adj.* diffuse
Versuch-Irrtum-Verfahren *n.*
trial-and-error method
vertagen *vrb.* adjourn/to

Verteidiger *m.* defendant
Verteildienst *m.* dissemination
service
Verteilerstelle *f.* clearing house
verteilte Datenbank *f.* distributed database
verteilte Datenverarbeitung *f.*
distributed data processing
verteiltes System *n.*
distributed system
Verteilung *f.* distribution
Verteilung *f.* nach Mandelbrot,
Zipf und Bradford Mandel-
brot-Zipf-Bradford distribution
Verteilung *f.* von Information
dissemination of information
Verteilungskurve *f.* distribution curve
vertikal Tabulieren *n.* vertical
tabulating
vertikale Ausrichtung *f.* vertical alignment
vertikale Formatsteuerung *f.*
vertical format control
vertikale Redundanzprüfung *f.*
vertical redundancy check
vertikale Tastatur *f.* vertical
keyboard
vertikale Zuführung *f.* vertical
feed
vertikaler Adreßzeiger *m.* vertical pointer
vertikaler Druckzonenabstand
m. line separation
vertikales Tabulierzeichen *n.*
vertical tabulation character
Vertikalsteuerung *f.* vertical
control
Vertikaltabulator *m.* vertical
tabulation
Vertikaltabulatorentabelle *f.*

vertical tab table
Vertikaltabuliertaste *f.* vertical
tabulator key
Vertrag *m.* contract
Verträglichkeit *f.* compatibility
Vertragsrecht *n.* law of
contract
vertrauliche Dokumente *pl.*
confidential documents, confidential file
Vertraulichkeit *f.* privacy
Vertreter *m.* dummy, repre-
sentative
Vertrieb *m.* marketing
Vertriebsleiter *m.* marketing
manager
Vertriebspolitik *f.* marketing
policy
verursachen *vrb.* originate/to
Vervielfachungsfaktor *m.*
multiplication factor
vervielfältigen *vrb.* reproduce
/to
Vervielfältiger *m.* letter press
Vervielfältigung *f.* duplication
Vervielfältigungsgerät *n.* duplicating machine
Vervielfältigungsmatrize *f.*
stencil
Verwaltung *f.* administration
Verwaltungsarchiv *n.* record
office
Verwaltungseinheit *f.* administrative unit
Verwaltungsfunktion *f.* management service
Verwaltungsrecht *n.* admini-
strative law
Verwaltungsvorschrift *f.* administrative regulation
Verwaltungszentrum *n.* ad-
ministrative center

verwandter Begriff *m.* related
term
Verwandtschaft *f.* **von Benen-
nungen** association of terms
Verwandtschaft *f.* **von Doku-
menten** association of docu-
ments
Verwandtschaftshinweis *m.*
association trials
Verweildauer *f.* residence time
Verweilzeit *f.* residence time,
turnaround time
Verweis *m.* reference, cross-
reference
Verweis *m.* **mit Erklärung** explanatory reference
verweisen *vrb.* refer/to
Verweiskarte *f.* reference card
Verweiszeichen *n.* reference
character
Verwendbarkeit *f.* usability
Verwendung *f.* application,
usage, utilization
Verwendungscode *m.* usage
code
Verwerfung *f.* warpage
Verwirklichung *f.* realization
verzahnen *vrb.* interleave/to
verzeichnen *vrb.* calendar/to,
enter/to in the index, index/to
Verzeichnis *n.* directory, memorandum, register
Verzeichnis *n.* **der Abbildungen**
list of illustrations
Verzeichnis *n.* **der Fortsetzungswerke** continuation
record, continuation register
Verzeichnis *n.* **der Reihenwerke** continuations check-
list
Verzeichnis *n.* **lieferbarer Bücher** catalog of books in print

Verzeichnisdatei *f.* directory file
Verzeichniseintrag *m.* directory entry
Verzettelung *f.* dissipation
Verzögerung *f.* lag
Veterinärmedizin *f.* veterinary medicine
Videoband *n.* video tape
Videoclip *m.* video clip
Videokamera *f.* video camera
Videokassette *f.* video cassette
Videokatalog *m.* video catalog
Videokommunikation *f.* video communication
Videokonferenz *f.* video conference
Videorecorder *m.* video recorder
Videotechnik *f.* video technology
Videotext *m.* teletext, videocast, videotext
Videotext *m.* **einer Sendeanstalt** broadcast videotex
Videotextseite *f.* videotext page
Viehzuchtschulbibliothek *f.* animal husbandry school library
Vielfachheit *f.* multiplicity
Vielfachleitung *f.* highway
Vielfachregister *n.* **zum Speicher** multiple register to storage
Vielfachschaltung *f.* multiple connection
Vielfalt *f.* variety
Vierteljahreschrift *f.* quarterly
vierzehntägige Zeitschrift *f.* fortnightly periodical
Vignette *f.* vignette

virtuell *adj.* virtual
virtuelle Adresse *f.* virtual address
virtuelle Adressierung *f.* virtual addressing
virtuelle Einheit *f.* virtual device, virtual unit
virtuelle Einheitenadresse *f.* virtual unit address
virtuelle Instruktion *f.* virtual instruction
virtuelle Leitung *f.* virtual line
virtuelle logische Einheit *f.* virtual logical unit
virtuelle Partition *f.* virtual partition
virtuelle Platte *f.* virtual disk
virtuelle Speichergröße *f.* virtual storage size
virtuelle Speicherzugriffsmethode *f.* virtual storage access method
virtuelle Übertragungsadresse *f.* virtual transfer address
virtuelle Wartezeit *f.* virtual wait time
virtueller Adreßraum *m.* virtual address area
virtueller Datenträger *m.* virtual volume
virtueller Modus *m.* virtual mode
virtueller Rechner *m.* virtual computer, virtual machine
virtueller Speicher *m.* apparent storage, virtual memory, virtual storage
virtueller Zeitgeber *m.* virtual timer
virtuelles Betriebssystem *n.* virtual operating system
virtuelles Laufwerk *n.* virtual

drive
Visitenkarte *f.* calling card
visuelle Eingabekontrolle *f.*
visual input control
Vitrine *f.* show-case
Vokabular *n.* vocabulary
Vokabularliste *f.* term list
Völkerkunde *f.* ethnology
Volksbibliothek *f.* public library
Volksbücherei *f.* popular library
Volkshochschule *f.* evening
school, adult evening classes
Volkswirtschaftlehre *f.*
economics
Vollerhebung *f.* total survey
vollgekennzeichneter Name *m.*
fully qualified name
vollständige Ausgabe *f.* complete edition
vollständige Bibliographie *f.*
complete bibliography, comprehensive bibliography
vollständige Kette *f.* complete
chain
vollständige Reihe *f.* complete
series
vollständiger Verfassername
m. author fullness
Vollständigkeit *f.* completeness
Volltext *m.* full text
Volltextdatenbank *f.* full text
database
Volltextrecherche *f.* full text
searching
Volltextretrieval *n.* full text
retrieval
Volltextspeicherung *f.* full text
storage
Volltextsuche *f.* full text
searching

Volltextverarbeitung *f.* full
text processing
Vollversammlung *f.* plenary
meeting
Vollzeitarbeit *f.* full time
employment
vom Benutzer benannt user-
named
Vorabdruck *m.* preprint
Vorabkatalogisierung *f.* prepublication cataloging
Vorankündigungsliste *f.* advance list
Voranschlag *m.* estimate
Voranzeige *f.* preliminary announcement, preliminary
notice
Vorauflage *f.* advance copy
vorausdatieren *vrb.* ante-
date/to
Vorausexemplar *n.* advance
copy
vorausgehender Datensatz *m.*
preceding record
Vorausindexierung *f.* in-source
indexing
Vorauskatalogisierung *f.* cataloging in publication, precataloging, in-source cataloging,
cataloging in publication,
cataloging in source
Voraussage *f.* prediction
Voraussetzung *f.* prerequisite
Vorauszahlung *f.* advance
payment, prepayment
Vorbearbeitung *f.* preparation
vorbereiten *vrb.* initialize/to
Vorbereitung *f.* preparation
Vorbereitungszeit *f.* make
ready time, preparation time
Vorbericht *m.* preliminary
report

Vorbestellung *f.* advance order, prepublication order
vorbeugen *vrb.* preapply/to
vordatieren *vrb.* antedate/to
vordefinierter Ausdruck *m.* predefined phrase
vordefinierter Vorgang *m.* predefined process
Vordruck *m.* printed form
Vordruckbenennung *f.* form title
Vordruckmaskenname *m.* overlay name
voreingestellt *adj.* preset
voreingestellte Zeichen *pl.* leading graphics
Voreinsteller *m.* preset key
Vorentwicklung *f.* advance development
Vorentwurf *m.* preliminary draft
vorformatieren *vrb.* preformat /to
Vorführung *f.* demonstration
Vorgabezeit *f.* standard time
Vorgang *m.* operation, process, transaction
Vorgangsdatei *f.* exception log
Vorgangsdaten *pl.* transaction data
Vorgangsdokumentation *f.* transaction documentation
vorgenerieren *vrb.* pregenerate /to
vorgesetzte Unterteilung *f.* anterior subdivision
Vorgesetzter *m.* supervisor
Vorgriff *m.* look ahead
Vorgriffsfeld *n.* look-ahead field
Vorgriffssatz *m.* look-ahead record

Vorhaben *n.* project
vorherig *adj.* previous
vorherrschend *adj.* prepotent
vorkalkuliert *adj.* predetermined
vorkonfigurieren *vrb.* preconfigure/to
vorkonfigurierte Systemdefinition *f.* preconfigured system definition
vorladen *vrb.* precharge/to
Vorlage *f.* master, original
Vorlaufbestimmung *f.* header specification
vorläufig *adj.* preliminary, temporary
vorläufige Ausgabe *f.* preliminary edition, provisional edition
vorläufiger Bericht *m.* interim report
vorläufiges Katalogisieren *n.* preliminary cataloging
vorläufiges Programm *n.* preliminary program
Vorlaufkarte *f.* header record
Vorlesung *f.* lecture
Vormerkdatei *f.* possible purchase file
Vormerkliste *f.* waiting list
Vorrang *m.* precedence
vorrangig *adj.* major
Vorrangssteuerung *f.* priority control
Vorrangsunterbrechungsebene *f.* interruption priority level
Vorrangsverarbeitung *f.* priority processing
vorrätig *adj.* in stock
Vorrechner *m.* front-end processor
Vorredaktion *f.* pre-editing

vorredigieren *vrb.* pre-edit/to
Vorsatz *m.* header entry,
header portion, header,
leader record
Vorsatzblatt *n.* fly-leaf, inner
end paper
Vorsatzinformation *f.* header
information
Vorsatzpuffer *m.* headed buf-
fer
Vorsatzsegment *n.* header
segment
Vorschau *f.* preview
Vorschlag *m.* suggestion
Vorschrift *f.* regulation
vorschriftsmäßig *adj.* regular
Vorschub *m.* feed, increment-
ing, skip
Vorschublinie *f.* line of access
Vorschubzeichen *n.* alignment
mark
Vorschule *f.* preschool
vorsetzen *vrb.* forward space
/to
Vorsetzzeichen *n.* anterioriz-
ing symbol
Vorsilbe *f.* prefix
vorsortiert *adj.* presequenced
Vorspannstreifen *m.* leader
vorspeichern *vrb.* prestore/to
Vorstand *m.* exectutive board
Vorstellung *f.* notion, concep-
tion
Vorstudie *f.* pilot study
Vortitel *m.* fly title, half title,

mock title
Vortrag *m.* conference paper,
lecture
Vortragsreihe *f.* series of
lectures
**vorübergehende Unterbre-
chung** *f.* temporary stop
Voruntersuchung *f.* pretest
Vorverarbeitung *f.* preprocessing
Vorveröffentlichung *f.* prepublication
Vorwähler *m.* preselector
vorwärts forward
vorwärtsblättern *vrb.* page
down/to
Vorwärtsrichtung *f.* forward
direction
vorwärtsschieben *vrb.* scroll
forward/to
Vorwärtssteuerung *f.* forward
supervising
Vorwärtszugriffsoperation *f.*
access forward operation
**vorwegnehmende Postkoordi-
nation** *f.* anticipatory post-
coordination
Vorwort *n.* foreword, preface
Vorzeichen *n.* leading sign
vorzeichenlose Zahl *f.* unsigned number
vorzeitig *adj.* premature
Vorzugsbenennung *f.* preferred term

W

Wachstum *n.* growth
Wachstumsbegrenzung *f.* limitation of growth, growth limitation
Wachstumsbeschränkung *f.* restriction of growth
Wachstumsmuster *n.* growth pattern
Wagenrücklaufzeichen *n.* carriage return character
Wahldatei *f.* optional file
wählen *vrb.* dial-up/to
Wähler *m.* selector
wahlfreie Adressierung *f.* random addressing
wahlfreie Verarbeitung *f.* random processing
wahlfreier Dateizugriff *m.* random file
wahlfreier Zugriff *m.* arbitrary access, random access, random seek
Wählleitung *f.* dial-up line
Wahlpflichtfach *n.* elective core course
wahlweise *adj.* optional
wahlweise *adj.* **nach Schlüssel** random by key
Wahlwort *n.* optional word
wahr *adj.* true
Wahrheit *f.* truth
Wahrheitstabelle *f.* truth table
Wahrheitswert *m.* truth value
wahrscheinlicher Fehler *m.*

probable deviation
Wahrscheinlichkeit *f.* probability
Wahrscheinlichkeitskurve *f.* probability curve
Wahrscheinlichkeitsrechnung *f.* probability calculus
Währung *f.* currency
Wanderbuch *n.* hiking guide
Wandkatalog *m.* wall catalog
Wandregal *n.* perimeter shelves
Wandtafel *f.* blackboard
Wappenbuch *n.* armorial
Ware *f.* product, goods
Warenbeschreibung *f.* product description
Warenzeichen *n.* trade mark
Warenzeichenrecht *n.* trademark law
Wärmeabgabe *f.* heat output
Warmstart *m.* warm restart, warm start
Warnanzeige *f.* warning indicator
Warnmeldung *f.* warning message
Warnstreifen *m.* warning mark
Wartbarkeit *f.* maintainability
Warteanzeiger *m.* wait indicator
Warteaufruf *m.* wait call
Wartebedingung *f.* wait condi-

tion

warten *vrb.* maintain/to, wait /to

Warteschlange *f.* queue, wait list, waiting line

Warteschlange *f.* **aktiver Seiten** active page queue

Warteschlange bilden *vrb.* queue/to

Warteschlange *f.* **für Programme mit hoher Priorität** high priority record queue

Warteschlange *f.* **reservierter Seiten** hold page queue

Warteschlange *f.* **verfügbarer Einheiten** available unit queue

Warteschlangenbildung *f.* queuing

Warteschlangenelement *n.* queue element

Warteschlangenname *m.* queue name

Warteschlangensteuerblock *m.* queue control block

Warteschlangentheorie *f.* queuing theory

Warteschleife *f.* wait loop

Wartestatus *m.* wait state, waiting state

Wartesteuerung *f.* wait control

Wartezeit *f.* latency, queue time, stand-by time, wait time, waiting time

Wartung *f.* maintenance, service

Wartungsdienst *m.* maintenance service

Wartungskosten *pl.* maintenance charges

Wartungszeit *f.* maintenance time

Waschzettel *m.* blurb

wasserfest *adj.* water-resistant

Wasserflecken *pl.* damp stains

wasserfleckig *adj.* damp-spotted

Wasserzeichen *n.* water mark

Watt *n.* watt

Wechsel *m.* interchange

Wechselbetrieb *m.* half-duplex transmission

Wechselbeziehung *f.* inter-relation

Wechselfeld *n.* alternating field

wechselnde Kopfzeile *f.* alternating header

wechselnde Sortierfolge *f.* alternate collating sequence

Wechselplatte *f.* moving head disk, removable disk

wechselseitig *adj.* both way

Wechselwirkung *f.* interactive operation, interaction

WEDER-NOCH-Bedingung *f.* NOR

Weglassen *n.* truncation

Wegsuche *f.* path finding

weite Verbreitung *f.* active dissemination

Weiterbildung *f.* continuing education

Weiterentwicklung *f.* progress

Weiterführung *f.* continuation

weitergereichte Datei *f.* passed data set

Weiterleitung *f.* routing

Weiterschaltung *f.* rerouting

Weltbibliographie *f.* world bibliography

Weltraumforschung *f.* space research

WENN-Anweisung *f.* IF-

statement
WENN-Bedingung *f.* IF-
clause, WHEN option
Werbeausgabe *f.* publicity edi-
tion
Werbemittel *pl.* advertising
budget
Werbung *f.* publicity, advertis-
ing
Werdegang *m.* career
Werk *n.* plant
Werke *pl.* works
Werkstattbericht *m.* workshop
report
Werkstoff *m.* material
Werkstoffdaten *pl.* material
data
Werkstoffdatenbank *f.* mate-
rial database
Werkstofforschung *f.* material
research
Werkzeuge *pl.* tools
Wert *m.* value
Wertattribut *n.* value attribute
Wertberichtigung *f.* allowance
Wertbestimmung *f.* **einer Infor-
mation** evaluation of inform-
ation
Wertigkeit *f.* valence
Werttrennsymbol *n.* value se-
parator
Wertzuwachs *m.* increment
Wertzuweisung *f.* value as-
signment
**wesentliches Unterteilungs-
merkmal** *n.* essential
character of division
Wettbewerb *m.* competition
wichtiges Ereignis *n.* highlight
Widerdruck *m.* backing up
widerrufen *vrb.* revoke/to
widerspiegeln *vrb.* reflect/to

Widmung *f.* dedication
Widmungsexemplar *n.* dedication copy
Wiederanlauf *m.* crash recovery
Wiederanlaufbedingung *f.* restart condition
Wiederanlaufbefehl *m.* restart
instruction
Wiederanlaufdatei *f.* restart
data set
wiederanlaufen *vrb.* re-
cover/to, restart/to
Wiederanlaufverfahren *n.* restart procedure
Wiederanschluß *m.* reattachment
Wiederaufbau *m.* rebuilding
Wiederaufbereitung *f.* reprocessing
Wiederauffinden *n.* retrieval
wiederaufnehmen *vrb.* resume
/to
Wiedergabe *f.* image, play
back, reproduction
wiedergewinnen *vrb.* retrieve
/to
wiederherstellbar *adj.* refreshable
**wiederherstellbare Transak-
tion** *f.* recoverable transaction
wiederherstellbarer Fehler *m.*
recoverable error
wiederherstellbarer Katalog
m. recoverable catalog
wiederherstellen *vrb.* recover
/to, recreate/to
Wiederherstellung *f.* recovery,
recreation
Wiederherstellungsverfahren
n. recovery procedure

Wiederholangabe *f.* repeat option, replicator
wiederholen *vrb.* iterate/to, repeat/to, replicate/to
Wiederholspeicher *m.* refresh memory
wiederholte Mahnung *f.* follow-up notice
Wiederholung *f.* repetition, replication, retry
Wiederholungsadressierung *f.* repetitive addressing
Wiederholungsaufforderung *f.* request for repeat
Wiederholungslauf *m.* rerun
Wiederholungsspezifikation *f.* repetitive specification
Wiederholungsstück *n.* additional copy, extra copy, further copy
Wiederholungszeit *f.* rerun time
wiederladbar *adj.* reloadable
Wiedervereinigung *f.* reunification
Wiederveröffentlichung *f.* republication
wiederverwendbar *adj.* reenterable
Wiedervorlage *f.* hold-file
Wiegendruck *m.* incunabulum
wirklichkeitstreue Wiedergabe *f.* literalism
wirksam *adj.* active
Wirkung *f.* action
Wirkungsbeziehung *f.* effect relation
Wirkungsgrad *m.* efficiency
wirkungslos *adj.* ineffective
Wirkungsmessung *f.* impact measurement
Wirtschaft *f.* economy
Wirtschaftlichkeit *f.* economic efficiency
Wirtschaftlichkeitsanalyse *f.* economic analysis
Wirtschaftsarchiv *n.* commercial archive
Wirtschaftsdatenbank *f.* business database
Wirtschaftsdokumentation *f.* commercial documentation
Wirtschaftsfaktor *m.* economic factor
Wirtschaftsinformation *f.* commercial information
Wirtschaftspresse *f.* financial press
Wirtschaftsrecht *n.* business law
Wirtschaftswissenschaften *pl.* economics
wirtschaftswissenschaftliche Bibliothek *f.* commerce library, economics library
Wirtsrechner *m.* host computer, host processor
Wirtssprache *f.* host language
Wissen *n.* knowledge, learning
Wissensbank *f.* knowledge database
wissensbasiertes System *n.* knowledge based system
Wissensbasis *f.* knowledge base
Wissenschaft *f.* science
Wissenschaftler *m.* scientist
wissenschaftliche Bibliothek *f.* research library, academic library
wissenschaftliche Fachqualifikation *f.* academic expertise
wissenschaftliche Information *f.* scientific information
wissenschaftliche Kommunikation *f.* scientific communication

wissenschaftliche Mitarbeiter
pl. academic staff
wissenschaftliche Spezialbibliothek *f.* scholarly library, special library
wissenschaftliche Systematisierung *f.* scientific systematization
wissenschaftliche Veröffentlichung *f.* academic publication, scholarly publication, learned publication
wissenschaftlicher Bibliothekar *m.* science librarian, academic librarian
wissenschaftliches Bibliothekswesen *n.* academic librarianship
Wissenschaftsfreiheit *f.* freedom of science
Wissenschaftsrat *m.* scientific council
Wissensdarstellung *f.* knowledge presentation
Wissenserwerb *m.* knowledge acquisition
Wissensgebiet *n.* field of knowledge, knowledge field
Wissensingenieurwesen *n.* knowledge engineering
Wissensniveau *n.* level of knowledge
Wissensrepräsentation *f.* knowledge representation
Wissenstransfer *m.* knowledge transfer
Wissensvermittlung *f.* dissemination of knowledge
Wissenszuwachs *m.* growth of knowledge
Woche *f.* week
Woche *f.* **der Bibliothek** library week

Wochenschrift *f.* weekly paper
wöchentlich *adj.* weekly
Wohngebiet *n.* residential area
Wohnheim *n.* lodging house
Wort *n.* word
Wort für Wort literally
Wort trennen *vrb.* divide/to a word, hyphenate/to
Wortanfangszeichen *n.* leading string character
Wortbegrenzer *m.* word separator
Wortbegrenzungszeichen *n.* word separator character
Wortelement *n.* morpheme, ultimate constituent, word element
Wörterbuch *n.* dictionary
Wörterbuchdatenbank *f.* dictionary database
Wörterbuchverzeichnis *n.* dictionary index
Wörterverzeichnis *n.* glossary, vocabulary
Wortfamilie *f.* word family
Wortfolge *f.* word order
wortgetreue Übersetzung *f.* literal translation, metaphrase
Wortgruppe *f.* phrase, word group
Wortgut *n.* vocabulary
Worthäufigkeit *f.* word frequency
Worthäufigkeitsanalyse *f.* word frequency analysis
Wortkombination *f.* word combination
Wortkonstante *f.* word constant
Wortlänge *f.* word length,

word size
wörtlich *adj.* verbatim, word by word, literal
wörtlich wiedergeben *vrb.* literalize/to
wörtliche Bedeutung *f.* literality
Wortmarke *f.* word mark
Wortpuffer *m.* word buffer
Wortregister *n.* word index
Wortschatz *m.* thesaurus
Wortschrift *f.* lexigraphy
Wortstamm *m.* stem
Wortstammwörterbuch *n.* root dictionary

Wortunterstreichung *f.* word underline, word underscore
Wortverbindung *f.* combination of morphemes, word combination
wortweise *adj.* on a word basis, word by word
Wortzeit *f.* word time
Wortzwischenraum *m.* word spacing
Wunschliste *f.* want file, want list
Wurzel *f.* radix, root
Wurzelzeichen *n.* radical sign

X, Y

x-Achse *f.* x-axis
x-Sprung *m.* x-skip
x-y-Schreiber *m.* x-y-plotter
Xerographie *f.* xerography

xerographischer Drucker *m.* xerographic printer
y-Achse *f.* y-axis
Yard *n.* yard

Z

Zahl *f.* digit number, number
zählen *vrb.* number/to
Zahlenbereich *m.* numerical capacity
Zahlendarstellung *f.* number representation, numeration
Zahlenformat *n.* number format
Zahlensystem *n.* numbering system
Zähler *m.* accumulator, meter, tally
Zahlungsbedingungen *pl.* terms of payment
zahnmedizinische Bibliothek *f.* dental library
Zeichen *n.* character, sign, token
Zeichenabgleich *m.* character comparison
Zeichenabstand *m.* character distance
Zeichenabtastung *f.* scanning
Zeichenanordnung *f.* **der Tastatur** keyboard arrangement
Zeichenaustausch *m.* signalling exchange
Zeichenaustauschsystem *n.* signalling system
Zeichenbegrenzung *f.* character boundary
Zeichenbreite *f.* character width
Zeichencodierung *f.* character coding
Zeichendichte *f.* character density, horizontal spacing, packing density
Zeichenerkennung *f.* character recognition
Zeichenerkennungstabelle *f.* recognition table
Zeichenerkennungstabellenfehler *m.* recognition table error
Zeichenerklärung *f.* key to the signs used
Zeichenfehler *m.* digit error
Zeichenfehlstelle *f.* void
Zeichenfeld *n.* character area
Zeichenfläche *f.* plotting size
Zeichenfolge *f.* string data, token
Zeichenformat *n.* alpha format
Zeichengenerator *m.* character generator, pattern generator
Zeichengerät *n.* plotter
Zeichengültigkeitskontrolle *f.* character validity check
Zeichenhöhe *f.* character height
Zeichenkette *f.* character string
Zeichenkettensuche *f.* string search
Zeichenkontrolle *f.* character check
Zeichenleser *m.* character

reader
Zeichenmittenabstand *m.* character spacing
zeichenparallel *adj.* parallel by character
Zeichenprüfung *f.* graphic check
Zeichenregister *n.* character register
Zeichensatz *m.* character set
Zeichensetzung *f.* punctuation
Zeichenspeicher *m.* raster pattern storage
Zeichenstelle *f.* character position
Zeichenteilfolge *f.* substring
Zeichentrickfilm *m.* cartoon
Zeichenumsetzung *f.* folding
Zeichenvorrat *m.* character set, code set
Zeichenzulässigkeitsprüfung *f.* alphameric block checking
zeichnen *vrb.* draw/to, plot/to
Zeichnung *f.* drawing
zeigen *vrb.* point/to
Zeiger *m.* locator, pointer
zeigerbezogen *adj.* based
zeigerbezogene Variable *f.* based variable
zeigerbezogener Speicher *m.* based storage
zeigergesteuert *adj.* vectored
Zeigerkennzeichnung *f.* locator qualification, pointer qualification
Zeigerstruktur *f.* pointer structure
Zeigervariable *f.* locator variable, pointer variable
Zeile *f.* line, row
Zeilenabstand *m.* interlinear spacing, line pitch, line space,
line spacing
Zeilenabstandeinsteller *m.* line space selector, line space set key
Zeilenabstandhebel *m.* line space lever
Zeilenabstandsvoreinsteller *m.* line space preset key
Zeilenabtaster *m.* line scanner
Zeilenabtastung *f.* raster scan
Zeilenadressierung *f.* line addressing
Zeilenanfang *m.* line beginning, line start
Zeilenanzeiger *m.* line position indicator
Zeilenausrichtung *f.* alignment consideration
Zeilenbreite *f.* printing width
Zeilendrucker *m.* line printer
Zeileneinstellung *f.* line posting
Zeilenendsignal *n.* line end signal
Zeilenerweiterung *f.* line expand
Zeilenformat *n.* line format, row format
Zeilenformatwechsel *m.* line format change
Zeilenfortsetzung *f.* line continuation
Zeilenhöhe *f.* line height
Zeilenkennzeichnung *f.* line mark
Zeilenlänge *f.* line length, line limit
Zeilenlöschzeichen *n.* line cancel character
Zeilenmarkierung *f.* line finder mark
Zeilennummer *f.* line number,

record number

Zeilennumerierung *f.* margin line number

Zeilenschalter *m.* line spacer

Zeilenschalttaste *f.* line space key

Zeilenschaltung *f.* line feed, line spacing

Zeilenschritt *m.* line transport

Zeilensprung *m.* horizontal skip, line skip, step-over

Zeilentransport *m.* line spacing

Zeilentrennsymbol *n.* line separator

Zeilenverlängerung *f.* line expand

Zeilenvorschub *m.* line feed, line skipping, new line, vertical spacing

Zeilenvorschubtaste *f.* new line key

Zeilenvorschubzeichen *n.* line feed character, new line character

zeilenweise *adj.* line-by-line

Zeilenwiederholung *f.* line return

Zeilenzähler *m.* marginal figure

Zeit *f.* time

zeitabhängig *adj.* time-dependent

Zeitabhängigkeit *f.* time dependency

Zeitalter *n.* era, age

Zeitanalyse *f.* time analysis

Zeitberechnung *f.* timing

Zeiteinheit *f.* unit of time

Zeitfaktor *m.* time value

Zeitgeber *m.* interval timer, timer

Zeitgeschichte *f.* contemporary history

Zeitintervall *n.* time interval

Zeitintervallkontrollprogramm *n.* interval control program

zeitlich bestimmen *vrb.* time/to

zeitliche Unterteilungen *pl.* historical subdivisions

Zeitlimitüberschreitung *f.* time-out

Zeitmessgerät *n.* horologe

Zeitmessung *f.* horology

Zeitmultiplexleitung *f.* highway

Zeitmultiplexverfahren *n.* time division

Zeitplan *m.* schedule

Zeitplanregelung *f.* time program control

Zeitplanung *f.* scheduling

Zeitpunkt *m.* moment

Zeitraum *m.* period

Zeitscheibenverarbeitung *f.* time sharing

Zeitscheibenverfahren *n.* time slicing

Zeitschlüssel *m.* period subdivision

Zeitschrift *f.* journal, magazine, periodical

Zeitschrift *f.* **mit kontrollierter Auflage** controlled circulation journal

Zeitschriftenabteilung *f.* periodicals department

Zeitschriftenaufsatz *m.* periodical article

Zeitschriftenauswertung *f.* periodicals indexing

Zeitschriftenbestand *m.* periodical holdings, periodicals

collection, serial holdings
Zeitschriftenbestellung *f.* journal subscription
Zeitschriftendatenbank *f.* periodical database
Zeitschriftenerwerbung *f.* journal acquisition
Zeitschriftenerwerbungsetat *m.* periodical fund
Zeitschriftenetat *m.* periodical fund
Zeitschriftenfach *n.* magazine case
Zeitschrifteninhaltsbibliographie *f.* periodical index
Zeitschrifteninhaltsdienst *m.* current contents service
Zeitschriftenkatalog *m.* catalog of periodicals, catalog of serial works, serial catalog
Zeitschriftenkatalogisierung *f.* periodical cataloging, serial cataloging
Zeitschriftenkontrollsystem *n.* cardex
Zeitschriftenkopf *m.* masthead
Zeitschriftenlesesaal *m.* magazine room, periodical room
Zeitschriftenliste *f.* periodical holding list
Zeitschriftenregal *n.* periodical display shelves, periodical rack
Zeitschriftenregister *n.* index of periodicals
Zeitschriftenschachtel *f.* magazine box
Zeitschriftenstelle *f.* serials department
Zeitschriftenumlauf *m.* routing of periodicals
Zeitschriftenverleger *m.* periodical publisher
Zeitschriftenverwaltungsystem *n.* periodical holding system
Zeitschriftenverzeichnis *n.* periodicals checklist, periodicals directory
Zeitschriftenzentralkatalog *m.* union catalog of periodicals
Zeitschriftenzirkulation *f.* periodical circulation
Zeitschriftenzugangsnachweis *m.* periodical accession record, periodical receipt record
Zeitschriftenzuwachs *m.* growth of periodicals
Zeitsschriftenbibliographie *f.* periodical bibliography
Zeitstudie *f.* time study
zeitunabhängig *adj.* time-independent
Zeitung *f.* newspaper
Zeitungsartikel *m.* newspaper article, journal article
Zeitungsartikeltitel *m.* journal article title
Zeitungsausschnitt *m.* press clipping, newspaper cutting, clipping, cutting, press cutting
Zeitungsausschnittbüro *n.* clipping bureau
Zeitungsausschnittdienst *m.* clipping service
Zeitungsausschnittsammlung *f.* clipping file
Zeitungsbestand *m.* newspaper collection
Zeitungsdokumentation *f.* newspaper documentation
Zeitungserschließung *f.* newspaper indexing
Zeitungshalter *m.* newspaper stick, newspaper holder

Zeitungskiosk *m.* news stand, newspaper kiosk

Zeitungskorrespondent *m.* correspondent

Zeitungsleseraum *m.* newspaper room

Zeitungspapier *n.* newsprint

Zeitungsregal *n.* newspaper stand

Zeitungssammlung *f.* newspaper collection

Zeitungsstand *m.* press stand

Zeitungsstil *m.* journalese

Zeitungsverlagsbibliothek *f.* newspaper publishers´ library

Zeitunterteilung *f.* period division

Zeitverzögerung *f.* time-lag

Zeitwert *m.* present worth

zensieren *vrb.* censor/to

Zensor *m.* censor

Zensur *f.* censorship

Zensus *m.* census

Zentralarchiv *n.* central archive

Zentralbibliothek *f.* central library, main library

Zentralbücherei *f.* central library

Zentrale *f.* headquarter

zentrale Fachbibliothek *f.* central special library

zentrale Leihbücherei *f.* central lending library

zentrale Online-Ausleihkontrolle *f.* centralized on-line circulation control

zentrale Standortliste *f.* central shelflist

zentrale Zugriffsmethode *f.* host access method

Zentraleinheit *f.* central processing unit, central processor, processing unit, system unit

zentraler Datenverkehr *m.* host conversational

zentraler Knoten *m.* host node

zentrales System *n.* host system

zentralisierte Aufbewahrung *f.* centralized depository

zentralisierter Leihverkehr *m.* centralized interloan

zentralisiertes System *n.* centralized system

Zentralisierung *f.* centralization

Zentralkatalog *m.* central catalog, joint catalog, main shelf list, master catalog, union catalog

Zentralkatalog *m.* **auf Karten** card union catalog

Zentralkatalogisierung *f.* centralized cataloging

Zentralrechner *m.* host processor

Zentralspeicher *m.* central memory, internal storage

Zentralstelle *f.* head office, central office

Zentralvermittlung *f.* head exchange

zentriertes Hauptschlagwort *n.* centred heading

Zentrum *n.* center

zerfallen *vrb.* decay/to

zerknittert *adj.* crumpled

zerknüllt *adj.* crumpled

Zerlegung *f.* factoring

zerlesen *adj.* worn

zerstreuen *vrb.* diffuse

Zerstückelung *f.* fragmentation

Zertifikat *n.* certificate
Zettelkatalog *m.* card catalog, card index
Zettelmanuskript *n.* card manuscript
Zettelstütze *f.* backslide
Zeugnis *n.* certificate
Zickzackfalz *m.* accordion fold, accordion pleat, concertina fold
ziehen *vrb.* pull/to
Ziel *n.* goal, target
Ziel *n.* **eines Dokuments** intent of a document
Zielbezugnahme *f.* target reference
Zieldeskriptor *m.* target descriptor
Zielfunktion *f.* objective function, performance function
Zielort *m.* final destination
Zielprogramm *n.* target program
Zielsetzung *f.* objective
Zielsprache *f.* object language, target language
Zielvorgaben *pl.* objectives
Ziffer *f.* digit, figure
ziffermäßige Notation *f.* **für chemische Verbindungen** chemical cipher
Ziffernanzahl *f.* number of digits
Ziffernnotation *f.* digital notation, numeric notation
Ziffernstelle *f.* digit place, number position, units position
Zifferntaste *f.* digit key, numeric key
Zifferntastenreihe *f.* numeral row

Zifferrnteil *n.* part of number
Ziffernzeichen *n.* digit character
Zipfsches Gesetz *n.* Zipf's law
Zirkular *n.* circular
Zirkusbibliothek *f.* circus library
Zitat *n.* citation, quotation
Zitatanalyse *f.* citation analysis
Zitatensuche *f.* citation search
zitieren *vrb.* cite/to, quote/to
Zitierhäufigkeit *f.* citation frequency
Zitierindex *m.* citation index
Zitierindexierung *n.* citation indexing
Zitiermuster *n.* citation pattern
Zitiernetzwerk *n.* citation network
Zitierrate *f.* **von Zeitschriften** journal citation
Zitierregister *m.* citation index
Zitierung *f.* allusion
Zivilgesetzbuch *n.* civil code
Zone *f.* area, zone
Zoobibliothek *f.* zoo library
zu ermäßigtem Preis *m.* at a reduced price
Zubehör *n.* accessory, constituent, supplies
Zufall *m.* contingency
zufällig *adj.* contingent
Zufälligkeit *f.* contingency
Zufallsauswahl *f.* random failure
Zufallsfehler *m.* random error
Zufallsfolge *f.* random sequence
Zufallsstichprobe *f.* random sample

Zufallsvariable *f.* variate
Zufallszahl *f.* random number
Zuführeinrichtung *f.* feeder
Zuführung *f.* feed
Zuführungsfehler *m.* misfeed
Zugang *m.* accession, access
zugängliche Register *pl.* accessible registers
Zugangsabteilung *f.* accession department, acquisition department
Zugangsberechtigung *f.* clearance
Zugangsdatei *f.* accession file
Zugangsdatum *n.* accession date
Zugangserlaubnis *f.* clearance
Zugangsfolge *f.* entry sequence
Zugangskatalog *m.* accessions catalog
Zugangskontrolle *f.* physical access control
Zugangsnachweis *m.* acquisition record
Zugangsnummer *f.* accession number
Zugangsordnung *f.* accession order
Zugangsstelle *f.* acquisition unit
Zugangsverzeichnis *n.* accession book, accession register
Zugbibliothek *f.* train library
Zugehörigkeit *f.* appurtenance
Zugehörigkeitsbegriff *m.* appurtenance term
Zugehörigkeitsbeziehung *f.* appurtenance relation
zugelassene Benennung *f.* permitted term, tolerated term
zugeordnete Datei *f.* associated data set

zugeordnete Variable *f.* allocated variable
zugeordneter Speicher *m.* allocated storage
zugreifen *vrb.* access/to
Zugriff *m.* access
Zugriffsausnahme *f.* access exception
zugriffsberechtigte Datei *f.* authorized file
Zugriffsberechtigter *m.* accessor
Zugriffsberechtigung *f.* access authority, authorization
Zugriffsberechtigungsdatei *f.* authority file
Zugriffscode *m.* access code
Zugriffsebene *f.* access level
Zugriffsfehler *m.* picker failure
Zugriffsgebühr *f.* access charge, access fee
Zugriffsgruppe *f.* access group
Zugriffskontrollfeld *n.* access control field
Zugriffslänge *f.* access length
Zugriffsmechanismus *m.* access mechanism, accessor
Zugriffsmethode *f.* access method
Zugriffsmodus *m.* access mode
Zugriffsmöglichkeit *f.* accessibility
Zugriffspfad *m.* access path, path
Zugriffspriorität *f.* priority of access
Zugriffspunkt *m.* access point
Zugriffsrecht *n.* access right
Zugriffsroutine *f.* fetch routine
Zugriffsschlüssel *m.* access key, program access key
Zugriffssicherheit *f.* access

safety
Zugriffssteuerung *f.* access control, accessor control
Zugriffsumgebung *f.* access environment
Zugriffswartezeit *f.* latency time
Zugriffszeit *f.* access time
Zugriffszustand *m.* access state
Zugriffszyklus *m.* access cycle
Zukunft *f.* future
Zukunftsforschung *f.* futurology
zukunftsorientiert *adj.* progressive
Zukunftsperspektive *f.* outlook
Zukunftsroman *m.* science fiction
zulässig *adj.* receivable, valid
Zulässigkeit *f.* admissibility
Zulassung *f.* admission
Zulassung *f.* **von Lesern** admission of readers
Zulassungsvoraussetzung *f.* admission requirement
zum Drucken aufbereiten *vrb.* edit/to
Zunahme *f.* increase
zunehmend *adj.* progressive
zunehmende konkrete Beschaffenheit *f.* increasing concreteness
zuordnen *vrb.* allocate/to, allot/to, assign/to, bind/to, collate/to, interpolate/to
Zuordnung *f.* allocation, allotment, association
Zuordnung *f.* **durch Äquivalenz** equivalence association
Zuordnung *f.* **von Dateien** allocation of data sets

Zuordnungseinheit *f.* allocation unit
Zuordnungsklasse *f.* allocation class
Zuordnungsname *m.* assignment name
Zuordnungsprogramm *n.* allocation program
Zuordnungsstatus *m.* assignment status
Zuordnungszeichen *n.* assignment symbol
zur Ansicht *f.* for review, on approbation, on approval
zur Zeit der Programmausführung at object time
zurückblättern *vrb.* page back/to, page up/to
zurückfordern *vrb.* recall/to
zurückführbar *adj.* reducible
Zurückholen *n.* recalling
zurückkehren *vrb.* return/to
zurückladen *vrb.* import/to
zurücknehmen *vrb.* reclaim/to, withdraw/to
zurückrufen *vrb.* recall/to
zurücksetzen *vrb.* back out/to
zurückspringen *vrb.* return/to
zurückstellen *vrb.* reshelve/to
zurückweisen *vrb.* reject/to
Zurückweisung *f.* rejection
Zusammenarbeit *f.* cooperation
zusammenfassen *vrb.* abridge /to, abstract/to, epitomize/to, recap/to, sum up/to, summarize/to
zusammenfassende Operationen *pl.* aggregate operations
Zusammenfassung *f.* conclusion, epitome, summary
Zusammenfassung *f.* **des Ver-**

fassers author's summary
zusammengefaßt *adj.* pooled
zusammengefaßte Bibliothek *f.*
pooled library
zusammengefaßte Information
f. consolidated information
zusammengehend *adj.* concomitant
zusammengesetzte Notation *f.*
analet
zusammengesetzte Stichworte
pl. compound catchwords,
hyphenated catchwords
zusammengesetzte Zahl *f.* combined number, compound number
**zusammengesetztes Schlag-
wort** *n.* composite heading,
compound heading, compound
subject heading, compound
subject name
Zusammenhang *m.* connection
Zusammenschluß *m.* merger,
pooling
zusammenstellen *vrb.* compile/to
Zusammenstellung *f.* collocation, compilation
Zusammenstellung *f.* **von Buch-
und Leserkarte** card charging
zusammentragen *vrb.* assemble
/to, gather/to
Zusammentragetisch *m.* collating table
Zusammentragmaschine *f.* collating machine, gathering
machine
zusammenwirkend *adj.* synergistic
Zusatz *m.* addendum, option
Zusatzausbildung *f.* complementary education
Zusatzeinrichtung *f.* addition-

al device, special feature
Zusatzfeld *n.* option field
Zusatzgerät *n.* attachment
zusätzlich *adj.* auxiliary
zusätzliche Titelseite *f.* added
title page
zusätzlicher Speicher *m.* ad-
ditional storage feature
Zusatznutzen *m.* value added
Zusatzprüfung *f.* additional
examination
Zusatzregister *n.* adjunct register
Zusatzregistersatz *m.* adjunct
register set
Zusatzstudium *n.* complemen-
tary studies
Zusatzüberschrift *f.* special
heading
Zusatzwort *n.* additional
vocabulary word
Zuschauer *m.* viewer
Zuschuß *m.* allowance, contribu-
tion, grant
Zusendung *f.* distribution
Zusicherung *f.* assurance
Zustand *m.* state, status
Zuständigkeit *f.* responsibility
Zuständigkeitsbereich *m.* purview
Zustelldienst *m.* delivery service
Zustellgebühr *f.* delivery fee
Zustellraum *m.* **im Magazin**
allowance for expansion of
stock
Zustellung *f.* delivery
zuteilen *vrb.* apportion/to
Zuteilung *f.* apportionment
zutreffend *adj.* true
zuverlässig *adj.* reliable
Zuverlässigkeit *f.* reliability
Zuverlässigkeitsangabe *f.* reli-
ability data
Zuwachs *m.* accession, increment

Zuwachsrate *f.* growth rate
Zuwachssicherung *f.* incremental backup
Zuwachsspielraum *m.* allowance for expansion of stock
zuweisen *vrb.* assign/to
Zuweisung *f.* assignment
Zweck *m.* **eines Dokuments** intent of a document
Zweckbau *m.* functional building
Zweckbestimmung *f.* appropriation
zweifelhafte Autorenschaft *f.* doubtful authorship
zweifelhaftes Eigentum *n.* doubtful ownership
Zweig *m.* path
Zweigbibliothek *f.* branch library
zweigleisig *adj.* double-tracked
Zweigstelle *f.* branch
Zweijahreshaushalt *m.* biennial budget
Zweijahresschrift *f.* biennial
zweimonatlich *adj.* bimonthly
Zweimonatsschrift *f.* bimonthly
Zweirichtungsübertragung *f.* bidirectional transfer
zweischichtig *adj.* double-layered, bilaminated
zweispaltig *adj.* two-columned
zweisprachig *adj.* bilingual
zweisprachiges Wörterbuch *n.* bilingual dictionary
zweite Mahnung *f.* follow-up notice
zweiteiliger Graph *m.* bipartite graph
Zweitexemplar *n.* duplicate
Zweiwochenschrift *f.* biweekly
zwingend *adj.* mandatory

zwischen den Zeilen interlinear
Zwischenarchiv *n.* interim archive
Zwischenbericht *m.* interim report, status report
Zwischenbilanz *f.* interim results
Zwischenblatt *n.* interleaf
Zwischenblockzeitbegrenzung *f.* inter-block time cut
Zwischendatei *f.* intermediate file
Zwischenergebnis *n.* intermediate data
Zwischeninformation *f.* intermediate information
Zwischenkopie *f.* intermediate copy
Zwischenoriginal *n.* intermediate master
Zwischenraum *m.* bay, blank volume, gap, lacuna, space
Zwischenspeicher *m.* buffer storage, buffer, hold area, intermediate storage, temporary storage
Zwischenspeicherbibliothek *f.* staging library
Zwischenspeichereinheit *f.* stage device
Zwischenspeicherfehler *m.* staging error
zwischenspeichern *vrb.* buffer /to, stage/to
Zwischenspeicherung *f.* spooling
Zwischensummenzähler *m.* batch accumulator
Zwischentext *m.* intermediate text
Zwischenüberschrift *f.* cross head
Zykluszeit *f.* cycle time